Large-Scale C++ Software Design

Addison-Wesley Professional Computing Series

Brian W. Kernighan, Consulting Editor

Ken Arnold/John Peyton, *A C User's Guide to ANSI C*

Tom Cargill, *C++ Programming Style*

William R. Cheswick/Steven M. Bellovin, *Firewalls and Internet Security: Repelling the Wily Hacker*

David A. Curry, *UNIX® System Security: A Guide for Users and System Administrators*

Erich Gamma/Richard Helm/Ralph Johnson/John Vlissides, *Design Patterns: Elements of Reusable Object-Oriented Software*

David R. Hanson, *C Interfaces and Implementations*

John Lakos, *Large-Scale C++ Software Design*

Scott Meyers, *Effective C++: 50 Specific Ways to Improve Your Programs and Designs*

Scott Meyers, *More Effective C++: 35 New Ways to Improve Your Programs and Designs*

Robert B. Murray, *C++ Strategies and Tactics*

David R. Musser/Atul Saini, *STL Tutorial and Reference Guide: C++ Programming with the Standard Template Library*

John K. Ousterhout, *Tcl and the Tk Toolkit*

Craig Partridge, *Gigabit Networking*

J. Stephen Pendergrast Jr., *Desktop KornShell Graphical Programming*

Radia Perlman, *Interconnections: Bridges and Routers*

David M. Piscitello/A. Lyman Chapin, *Open Systems Networking: TCP/IP and OSI*

Stephen A. Rago, *UNIX® System V Network Programming*

Curt Schimmel, *UNIX® Systems for Modern Architectures: Symmetric Multiprocessing and Caching for Kernel Programmers*

W. Richard Stevens, *Advanced Programming in the UNIX® Environment*

W. Richard Stevens, *TCP/IP Illustrated, Volume 1: The Protocols*

W. Richard Stevens, *TCP/IP Illustrated, Volume 3: TCP for Transactions, HTTP, NNTP, and the UNIX® Domain Protocols*

Gary R. Wright/W. Richard Stevens, *TCP/IP Illustrated, Volume 2: The Implementation*

Large-Scale C++ Software Design

John Lakos

ADDISON-WESLEY PUBLISHING COMPANY
Reading, Massachusetts Menlo Park, California New York
Don Mills, Ontario Wokingham, England Amsterdam Bonn
Sydney Singapore Tokyo Madrid San Juan
Seoul Milan Mexico City Taipei

Many of the designations used by manufacturers and sellers to distinguish their products are claimed as trademarks. Where those designations appear in this book and Addison-Wesley was aware of a trademark claim, the designations have been printed with initial capital letters.

The authors and publishers have taken care in the preparation of this book, but make no expressed or implied warranty of any kind and assume no responsibility for errors or omissions. No liability is assumed for incidental or consequential damages in connection with or arising out of the use of the information of programs contained herein.

The publisher offers discounts on this book when ordered in quantity for special sales. For more information please contact:

Corporate & Professional Publishing Group
Addison-Wesley Publishing Company
One Jacob Way
Reading, Massachusetts 01867

Library of Congress Cataloging-in-Publication Data

Lakos, John, 1959–
Large-scale C++ software design / John Lakos.
p. cm. -- (Addison-Wesley professional computing series)
Includes bibliographical references and index.
ISBN 0-201-63362-0 (pbk. : alk. paper)
1. C++ (Computer program language) 2. Computer software–
–Development. I. Title. II. Series.
QA76.73.C153L342 1996
005.13'3--dc20 95-52106
CIP

DEDICATION

To my parents, Marci and Gene, who prepared and encouraged me.
To my wife, Cathy, who suffered through it with me.
To my daughter, Sarah, who was born in the middle of it all.

Copyright © 1996 by Addison-Wesley Publishing Company, Inc.

All rights reserved. No part of this publication may be reproduced, stored in a retrieval system, or transmitted, in any form, or by any means, electronic, mechanical, photocopying, recording, or otherwise, without the prior consent of the publisher. Printed in the United States of America. Published simultaneously in Canada.

ISBN 0-201-63362-0

Text printed on recycled and acid-free paper
1 2 3 4 5 6 7 8 9 10 CRW 99989796
First Printing, June 1996

Contents

PART II: PHYSICAL DESIGN CONCEPTS 97

PART III: LOGICAL DESIGN ISSUES 551

Chapter 8: Architecting a Component 553

Chapter 9: Designing a Function 583

Chapter 10: Implementing an Object 661

Figure List

Preface

As a member of the IC Division at Mentor Graphics Corporation, I am fortunate to have worked with many bright, talented software engineers, developing very large systems.

Back in 1985, Mentor Graphics became one of the first companies to attempt a truly large project in C++. Back then no one knew how to do that, and no one could have anticipated the cost overruns, slipped schedules, huge executables, poor performance, and incredibly expensive build times that a naive approach would inevitably produce.

Many valuable lessons were learned along the way—knowledge obtained through bitter experience. There were no books to help guide the design process; object-oriented designs on this scale had never before been attempted.

Ten years later, with a wealth of valuable experience under its belt, Mentor Graphics has produced several large software systems written in C++, and in doing so has paved the way for others to do the same without having to pay such a high price for the privilege.

During my 13 years as a C (turned C++) Computer-Aided Design (CAD) software developer, I have seen over and over again that planning ahead invariably produces a higher-quality, more maintainable product. My emphasis at Mentor Graphics has been on helping to ensure that quality is an integral part of the design process from the very start.

In 1990 I developed the graduate course "Object-Oriented Design and Programming" at Columbia University. As the instructor of this course since 1991, I have had the opportunity to share many of the insights that we at Mentor Graphics gained during our industrial-strength software development efforts. Questions and feedback from literally hundreds of graduate students and professional programmers have helped me to crystallize many important concepts. This book is a direct result of that experience. To my knowledge, this is the first text that identifies development and quality issues that arise only in large C++ projects. I hope that this information will be as useful in your work as it is in mine.

Audience

Large-Scale C++ Software Design was written explicitly for experienced C++ software developers, system architects, and proactive quality-assurance professionals. This book is particularly appropriate for those involved in large development efforts such as databases, operating systems, compilers, and frameworks.

Developing a large-scale software system in C++ requires more than just a sound understanding of the logical design issues covered in most books on C++ programming. Effective design also requires a grasp of physical design concepts that, although closely tied to the technical aspects of development, include a dimension with which even expert professional software developers may have little or no experience.

Yet most of the advice presented in this book also applies to small projects. It is typical for a person to start with a small project and then begin to take on larger and more challenging enterprises. Often the scope of a particular project will expand, and what starts out as a small project becomes a major undertaking. The immediate consequences of disregarding good practice in a large project, however, are far more severe than they are for disregarding good practice in a smaller project.

This book unites high-level design concepts with specific C++ programming details to satisfy two needs:

1. An object-oriented design book geared specifically to practical aspects of the C++ programming language.

2. A C++ programming book describing how to use the C++ programming language to develop very large systems.

Make no mistake, this is an advanced text. This is not the book from which to learn C++ syntax for the first time, nor is it likely to expose you to the dark corners of the language. Instead, this book will show you how to use the full power of the C++ language in ways that scale well to very large systems.

In short, if you feel that you know C++ well, but would like to understand more about how to use the language effectively on large projects, this book is for you.

Examples in this Text

Most people learn by example. In general, I have supplied examples that illustrate real-world designs. I have avoided examples that illustrate one point but have blatant errors in other aspects of the design. I have also tried to avoid examples that illustrate a detail of the language but serve no other useful purpose.

Except where otherwise indicated, all examples in this text are intended to represent "good design." Examples presented in earlier chapters are therefore consistent with all practices recommended throughout the book. A disadvantage of this approach is that you may see code that is written differently from the code you are used to seeing, without yet knowing exactly why. I feel that being able to use all of the examples in the book for reference compensates for this drawback.

There are two notable exceptions to this practice: comments and package prefixes. Comments for many of the examples in this text have simply been omitted for lack of space. Where they are presented, they are at best minimal. Unfortunately, this is one place where the reader is asked to "do as I say, not as I do"—at least in this book. Let the reader be assured that in practice I am scrupulous about commenting all interfaces *as* I write them (not after).

The second exception is the inconsistent use of package prefixes in the early examples of the book. In a large project environment package prefixes are required, but they are awkward at first and take some getting used to. I have elected to omit the consistent use of registered package prefixes until after they are formally presented in Chapter 7, so as not to detract from the presentation of other important fundamental material.

Many texts note that inline functions are used in examples for textual brevity when illustrating intended functionality. Since much of this book is directly related to organizational issues such as when to inline, my tendency will be to avoid inline functions in examples. If a function is declared `inline`, there is a justification for it beyond notational convenience.

Developing large systems in C++ is a constant series of engineering trade-offs. There are almost no absolutes. It is tempting to make statements using words such as *never* and *always*. Such statements allow for a simplified presentation of the material. For the level of C++ programmers whom I expect will read this book, such sweeping statements would be challenged—and rightly so. To avoid getting side-tracked in such situations, I will state what is (almost) always true, and then provide a footnote or a pointer to the exceptional case.

There are a variety of popular file name extensions used to distinguish C++ header files and C++ implementation files. For example:

Header File Extensions:	`.h`	`.hxx`	`.H`	`.h++`	`.hh`	`.hpp`
Implementation File Extensions:	`.c`	`.cxx`	`.C`	`.c++`	`.cc`	`.cpp`

Throughout the examples we consistently use the `.h` extension to identify C++ header files and the `.c` extension to identify C++ implementation files. In the text, we will frequently refer to *header files* as *`.h` files* and to *implementation files* as *`.c` files*. Finally, all of the examples in this text have been compiled and are syntactically correct using SUN's version of CFRONT 3.0 running on SUN SPARC stations, as well as on HP700 series machines running their native C++ compiler. Of course, any errors are the sole responsibility of the author.

A Road Map

There is a lot of material to cover in this book. Not all readers will have the same background. I have therefore provided some basic (but essential) material in Chapter 1 to help level the field. Expert C++ programmers may choose to skim this section or simply refer to it if needed. Chapter 2 contains a modest collection of software design rules that I would hope every experienced developer will quickly ratify.

Chapter 0: Introduction.

An overview of what lies in wait for the large-scale C++ software developer.

PART I: BASICS

Chapter 1: Preliminaries.
A review of basic language information, common design patterns, and style conventions used in this book.

Chapter 2: Ground Rules.
Important design practices that should be followed in any C++ project.

The remainder of the text is divided into two main sections. The first, entitled "Physical Design Concepts," presents a sequence of important topics related to the physical structure of large systems. The material in these chapters (3 through 7) focuses on aspects of programming that will be entirely new to many readers, and cuts right to the bone of large program design. This section is presented "bottom up," with each chapter drawing on information developed in previous chapters.

PART II: PHYSICAL DESIGN CONCEPTS

Chapter 3: Components.
The fundamental physical building blocks of a system.

Chapter 4: Physical Hierarchy.
The importance of creating a hierarchy of components with acyclic physical dependencies for testing, maintainability, and reuse.

Chapter 5: Levelization.
Specific techniques for reducing link-time dependencies.

Chapter 6: Insulation.
Specific techniques for reducing compile-time dependencies.

Chapter 7: Packages.
Extending the above techniques to yet larger systems.

The final section, entitled "Logical Design Issues," addresses the conventional discipline of logical design in conjunction with physical design. These chapters (8 through 10) address the design of a component as a whole, summarize the myriad issues surrounding sensible interface design, and address implementation issues in the context of a large-project environment.

PART III: LOGICAL DESIGN ISSUES

Chapter 8: Architecting a Component.
An overview of considerations important to the overall design of components.

Chapter 9: Designing a Function.
A detailed survey of the issues involved in creating a component's functional interface.

Chapter 10: Implementing an Object.
Several organizational issues specific to the implementation of objects in a large-project environment.

Topics found in the appendixes are referenced throughout the text.

Acknowledgments

This book would not have been possible without the diligence of my many colleagues at Mentor Graphics who have contributed to the company's landmark architectural and development efforts.

First and foremost, I would like to recognize the contributions of my friend, colleague, and former college classmate Franklin Klein, who reviewed virtually every page of the manuscript in its raw form. Franklin provided a sounding board for presenting many concepts that will be new to most software developers. The depth of Franklin's wisdom, intelligence, knowledge, diplomacy, and grasp of the nuances of effective communication is unprecedented in my experience. His detailed comments are responsible for countless revisions in the content, flow, and demeanor of the presentation.

Several dedicated and gifted software professionals reviewed all or most of the material in this book during its formative stages. I consider myself fortunate that they agreed to invest their valuable time reviewing this book. I would like to thank Brad Appleton, Rick Cohen, Mindy Garber, Matt Greenwood, Amy Katriel, Tom

O'Rourke, Ann Sera, Charles Thayer, and Chris Van Wyk for the enormous energy they spent helping to make this book as valuable as it could be. In particular, I would like to thank Rick Eesley for many fertile discussions and practical recommendations—especially his plea for a summary at the end of each chapter.

Several expert software developers and quality assurance engineers reviewed individual chapters. I would like to thank Samir Agarwal, Jim Anderson, Dave Arnone, Robert Brazile, Tom Cargill, Joe Cicchiello, Brad Cox, Brian Dalio, Shawn Edwards, Gad Gruenstein, William Hopkins, Curt Horkey, Ajay Kamdar, Reid Madsen, Jason Ng, Pete Papamichael, Mahesh Ragavan, Vojislav Stojkovic, Clovis Tondo, Glenn Wikle, Steve Unger, and John Vlissides for their technical contributions. I would also like to thank Lisa Cavaliere-Kaytes and Tom Matheson of Mentor Graphics for their suggestions regarding some of the figures in this text. In addition I would like to acknowledge the contributions of Eugene Lakos and Laura Mengel.

This book might never have been written were it not for a promotional letter I received at Columbia University offering me a complimentary review copy of Rob Murray's book. Since I teach only during the Spring semester, I returned the enclosed form, but requested that the book be sent to Mentor Graphics instead of Columbia. Soon after that, I received a call from Pradeepa Siva (of Addison-Wesley's Corporate & Professional Publishing Group) determined to get to the bottom of this unusual request. After convincing her of its legitimacy (and some perhaps gratuitous self aggrandizement) she remarked, "I think my boss would like to talk with you." A few days after that, I met with her boss—the publisher. I had always revered the excellence of the Professional Computing Series produced by this group, and it is that reputation that ultimately compelled me to commit to writing this book for that series.

I owe a great deal to the members of the Corporate & Professional Publishing Group at Addison-Wesley. John Wait, its publisher, has patiently provided me with insights into people and communication that I will forever cherish. From relentlessly reading books and reviews, to direct discussions with individual software professionals, to standing in bookstores and discretely observing the buying habits of potential readers, John Wait has his fingers on the pulse of the industry.

The production staff headed by Marty Rabinowitz is dedicated to excellence in all its respects. Despite apprehension expressed to me by authors in academia (associated with other publishers), I was delighted with the tremendous importance placed by

Marty on delivering a technically accurate, readily usable, and aesthetically appealing rendering of the author's ideas. I especially want to thank Frances Scanlon for her tireless and seemingly endless efforts in typesetting this entire book.

Brian Kernighan, the technical editor of this series, provided valuable contributions on both style and substance, as well as finding many typographical errors and inconsistencies that no one else caught. The depth and breadth of his knowledge coupled with his concise writing style has in no small way contributed to the success of this series.

Finally, I would like to thank the other authors in this series for documenting fundamental logical concepts and design practices that this book takes for granted.

0

Introduction

Developing good C++ programs is not easy. Developing highly reliable and maintainable software in C++ becomes even more difficult and introduces many new concepts as projects become larger. Just as experience gained from building single-family homes does not qualify a carpenter to erect a skyscraper, many techniques and practices learned through experiences with smaller C++ projects simply do not scale well to larger development efforts.

This book is about how to design very large, high-quality software systems. It is intended for experienced C++ software developers who strive to create highly maintainable, highly testable software architectures. This book is not a theoretical approach to programming; it is a thorough, practical guide to success, drawing from years of experience of expert C++ programmers developing huge, multi-site systems. We will demonstrate how to design systems that involve hundreds of programmers, thousands of classes, and potentially millions of lines of C++ source code.

This introduction considers some of the kinds of problems encountered when developing large projects in C++, and provides a context for the groundwork we must do in the early chapters. In this introduction several terms are used without definition. Most of these terms should be understandable from context. In the chapters that follow, these terms are defined more precisely. The real payoff will come in Chapter 5, where we begin to apply specific techniques to reduce the coupling (i.e., the degree of interdependency) within our C++ systems.

0.1 From C to C++

The potential advantages of the object-oriented paradigm in managing the complexity of large systems are widely assumed. As of the writing of this book, the number of C++ programmers has been doubling every seven to nine months.[1] In the hands of experienced C++ programmers, C++ is a powerful amplifier of human skill and engineering talent. It is completely wrong, however, to think that just using C++ will ensure success in a large project.

C++ is not just an extension of C: it supports an entirely new paradigm. The object-oriented paradigm is notorious for demanding more design effort and savvy than its procedural counterpart. C++ is more difficult to master than C, and there are innumerable ways to shoot yourself in the foot. Often you won't realize a serious error until it is much too late to fix it and still meet your schedule. Even relatively small indiscretions, such as the indiscriminate use of virtual functions or the passing of user-defined types by value, can result in perfectly correct C++ programs that run ten times slower than they would have had you written them in C.

During the initial exposure to C++, there is invariably a period during which productivity will grind to a halt as the seemingly limitless design alternatives are explored. During this period, conventional procedural programmers will be filled with an uneasiness as they try to get their arms around the concept referred to as *object oriented*.

Although the size and complexity of the C++ language can at first be somewhat overwhelming for even the most experienced professional C programmers, it does not take too long for a competent C programmer to get a small, nontrivial C++ program up and running. Unfortunately, the undisciplined techniques used to create small programs in C++ are totally inadequate for tackling larger projects. That is to say, a naive application of C++ technology does not scale well to larger projects. The consequences for the uninitiated are many.

0.2 Using C++ to Develop Large Projects

Just like a program in C, a poorly written C++ program can be very hard to understand and maintain. If interfaces are not fully encapsulating, it will be difficult to tune

[1] **stroustrup94**, Section 7.1, pp. 163–164.

or to enhance implementations. Poor encapsulation will hinder reuse, and any advantage in testability will be eliminated.

Contrary to popular belief, object-oriented programs *in their most general form* are fundamentally more difficult to test and verify than their procedural counterparts.[2] The ability to alter internal behavior via virtual functions can invalidate class invariants essential to correct performance. Further, the potential number of control flow paths through an object-oriented system can be explosively large.

Fortunately, it is not necessary to write such arbitrarily general (and untestable) object-oriented programs. Reliability can be achieved by restricting our use of the paradigm to a more testable subset.

As programs get larger, forces of a different nature come into play. The following subsections illustrate specific instances of some of the kinds of problems that we are likely to encounter.

0.2.1 Cyclic Dependencies

As a software professional, you have probably been in a situation where you were looking at a software system for the first time and you could not seem to find a reasonable starting point or a piece of the system that made sense on its own. Not being able to understand or use any part of a system independently is a symptom of a cyclically dependent design. C++ objects have a phenomenal tendency to get tangled up in each other. This insidious form of tight physical coupling is illustrated in Figure 0-1. A circuit is a collection of elements and wires. Consequently, class `Circuit` knows about the definitions of both `Element` and `Wire`. An element knows the circuit to which it belongs, and can tell whether or not it is connected to a specified wire. Hence class `Element` also knows about both `Circuit` and `Wire`. Finally, a wire can be connected to a terminal of either an element or a circuit. In order to do its job, class `Wire` must access the definitions of both `Element` and `Circuit`.

The definitions for each of these three object types reside in separate physical components (translation units) in order to improve modularity. Even though the implementations of these individual types are fully encapsulated by their interfaces, however, the `.c` files for each component are forced to include the header files of the other two.

---

[2] **perry**, pp. 13-19.

The resulting dependency graph for these three components is cyclic. That is, no one component can be used or even tested without the other two.

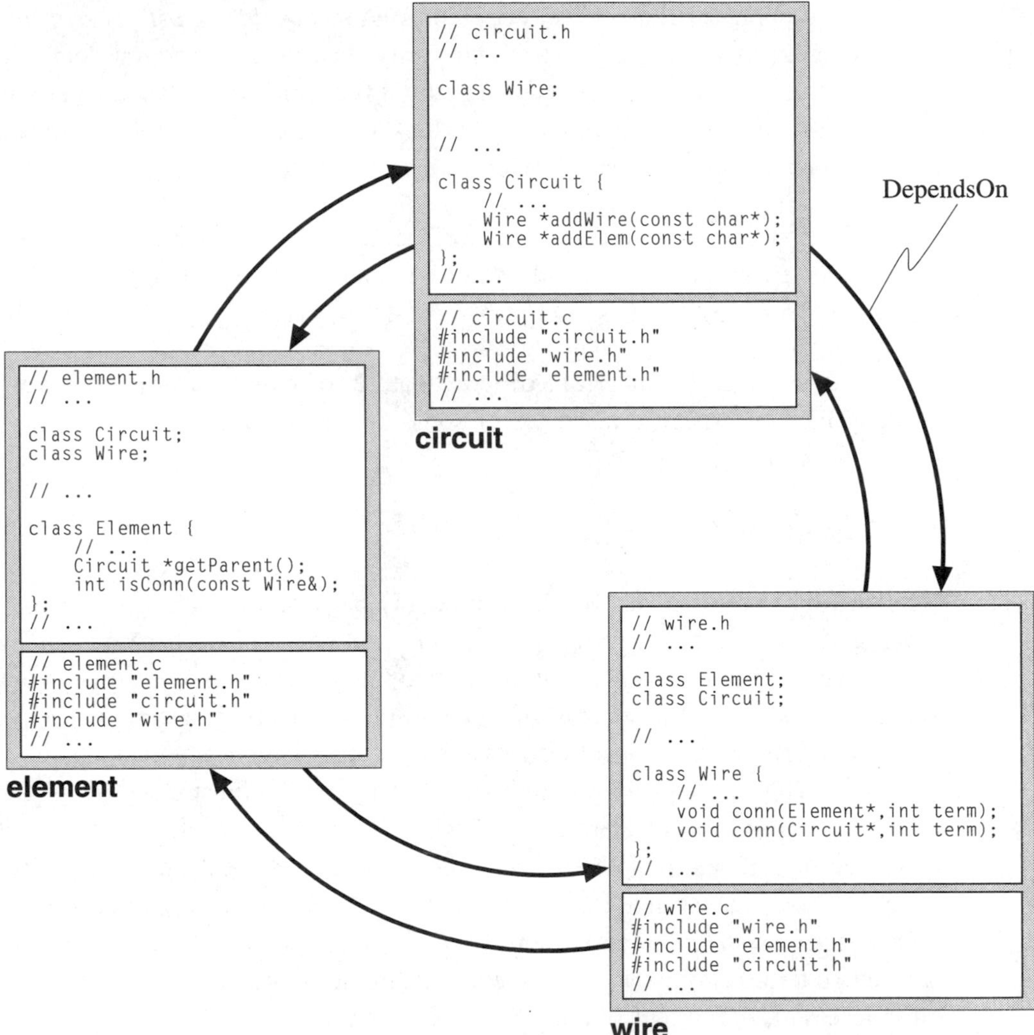

Figure 0-1: Cyclically Dependent Components

Large systems that are naively architected tend to become tightly coupled by cyclic dependencies and fiercely resist decomposition. Supporting such systems can be a nightmare, and effective modular testing is often impossible.

A case in point is an early version of an electronic-design database. At the time, its authors did not realize the need for avoiding cyclic dependencies in the physical design. The result was an interdependent collection of files containing hundreds of classes with thousands of functions, and no way to use or even test it except as a single module. This system had very poor reliability, proved impractical to extend or maintain, and ultimately had to be thrown out and rewritten from scratch.

By contrast, hierarchical physical designs (i.e., without cyclic interdependencies) are relatively easy to understand, test, and reuse incrementally.

0.2.2 Excessive Link-Time Dependencies

If you have attempted to link to a small amount of functionality in a library and found that your time to link has increased disproportionately to the benefit you are deriving, then you may have been trying to reuse heavy-weight rather than light-weight components.

One of the nice things about objects is that it is easy to add missing functionality as the need presents itself. This almost seductive feature of the paradigm has tempted many conscientious developers to turn lean, well-thought-out classes into huge dinosaurs that embody a tremendous amount of code—most of which is unused by the vast majority of its clients. Figure 0-2 illustrates what can happen when the functionality in a simple `String` class is allowed to grow to fill the needs of all clients. Each time a new feature is added for one client, it potentially costs all of the rest of the clients in terms of increased instance size, code size, runtime, and physical dependencies.

C++ programs are often larger than necessary. If care is not taken, the executable size for a C++ program could be much larger than it would be if the equivalent program were written in C. By ignoring external dependencies, overly ambitious class developers have created sophisticated classes that directly or indirectly depend on enormous amounts of code. A "Hello World" program employing one particularly elaborate `String` class produced an executable size of 1.2 megabytes!

```
// str.h
#ifndef INCLUDED_STR
#define INCLUDED_STR

class String {
    char *d_string_p;
    int d_length;
    int d_size;
    int d_count;
    // ...
    double d_creationTime;

  public:
    String();
    String(const String& s);
    String(const char *cp);
    String(const char c);
    // ...
    ~String();
    String &operator=(const String& s);
    String &operator+=(const String& s);
    // ...
    // (27 pages omitted!)
    // ...
    int isPalindrome() const;
    int isNameOfFamousActor() const;
};

// ...

#endif
```

```
// str.c
#include "str.h"
#include "sun.h"
#include "moon.h"
#include "stars.h"
// ...
// (lots of dependencies omitted)
// ...
#include "everyone.h"
#include "theirbrother.h"
String::String()
: d_string_p(0)
, d_length(0)
, d_size(0)
, d_count(0)
// ...
// ...
// ...
```

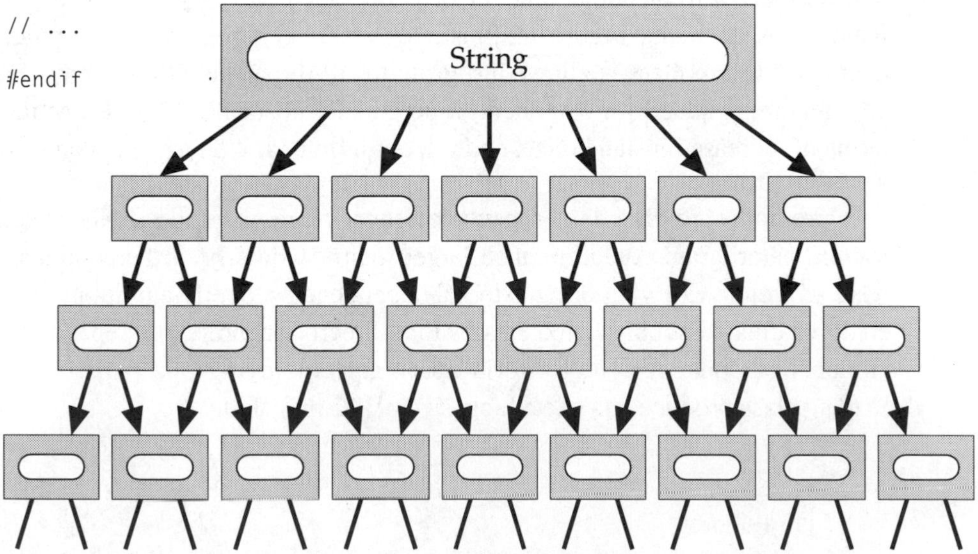

Figure 0-2: Oversized, Heavy-Weight, Non-Reusable `String` Class

Overweight types such as this `String` class not only increase executable size but can make the linking process unduly slow and painful. If the time necessary to link in `String` (along with all of its implementation dependencies) is large relative to the time it would otherwise take to link your subsystem, it becomes less likely that you would bother to reuse `String`.

Fortunately, techniques exist for avoiding these and other forms of unwanted link-time dependencies.

0.2.3 Excessive Compile-Time Dependencies

If you have ever tried to develop a multi-file program in C++, then you know that changing a header file can potentially cause several translation units to recompile. At the very early stages of system development, making a change that forces the entire system to recompile presents no significant burden. As you continue to develop your system, however, the idea of changing to a low-level header file becomes increasingly distasteful. Not only is the time necessary to recompile the entire system increasing, but so is the time to compile even individual translation units. Sooner or later, there comes a point where you simply refuse to modify a low-level class because of the cost of recompiling. If this sounds familiar, then you may have experienced excessive compile-time dependencies.

Excessive compile-time coupling, which is virtually irrelevant for small projects, can grow to dominate the development time for larger projects. Figure 0-3 shows a common example of what appears to be a good idea at first but turns bad as the size of a system grows. The `myerror` component defines a `struct`, `MyError`, that contains an enumeration of all possible error codes. Each new component that is added to the system naturally includes this header file. Unfortunately, each new component may have its own error codes that have not already been identified in the master list.

```
// myerror.h
#ifndef INCLUDED_MYERROR
#define INCLUDED_MYERROR

struct MyError {
    enum Codes {
        SUCCESS = 0,
        WARNING,
        ERROR,
        IO_ERROR,
        // ...
        READ_ERROR,
        WRITE_ERROR,
        // ...
        // ...
        BAD_STRING,
        BAD_FILENAME,
        // ...
        // ...
        CANNOT_CONNECT_TO_WORK_PHONE,
        CANNOT_CONNECT_TO_HOME_PHONE,
        // ...
        // ...
        MARTIANS_HAVE_LANDED,
        // ...
    };
};

#endif
```

Figure 0-3: An Insidious Source of Compile-Time Coupling

As the number of components gets larger, our desire to add to this list will wane. We will be tempted to reuse existing error codes that are, perhaps, only roughly appropriate just to avoid changing `myerror.h`. Eventually, we will abandon any thought of adding a new error code, and simply return `ERROR` or `WARNING` rather than change `myerror.h`. By the time we reach this point, the design is unmaintainable and practically useless.

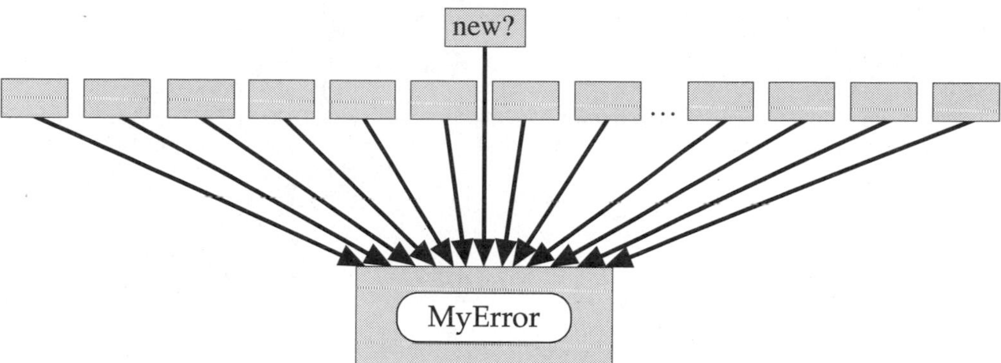

There are many other causes of unwanted compile-time dependencies. A large C++ program tends to have many more header files than an equivalent C program. The unnecessary inclusion of one header file by another is a common source of excessive coupling in C++. In Figure 0-4, for example, it is not necessary to include the definition of objects in the simulator header file *just* because a client of class `Simulator` may find these definitions useful. Doing so forces the client to depend at compile-time on all such components whether or not they are actually used. Excessive include directives not only increase the cost of compiling the client, but increase the likelihood that the client will need to be recompiled as a result of a low-level change to the system.

By ignoring compile-time dependencies, it is possible to cause each translation unit in the system to include nearly every header file in the system, reducing compilation speed to a crawl. One of the first truly large C++ projects (literally thousands of staff years) was a CAD framework product developed at Mentor Graphics. The developers initially had no idea how much compile-time dependencies would impede their efforts. Even using our large network of workstations, recompiling the entire system was taking on the order of a week!

The problem was due to organizational details illustrated in part by the simulator component shown in Figure 0-4. Cosmetic techniques were developed to mitigate this problem, but the real solution came when the unnecessary compile-time dependencies were eliminated.

```
// simulator.h
#ifndef INCLUDED_SIMULATOR
#define INCLUDED_SIMULATOR
#include "cadtool.h"                    // required by "IsA" relationship
#include "myerror.h"                    // bad idea (see Section 6.9)
#include "circuitregistry.h"            // unnecessary compile-time dependency
#include "inputtable.h"                 // unnecessary compile-time dependency
#include "circuit.h"                    // required by "HasA" relationship
#include "rectangle.h"                  // unnecessary compile-time dependency
// ...
#include <iostream.h>                   // unnecessary compile-time dependency

class Simulator : public CadTool {      // mandatory compile-time dependency
    CircuitRegistry *d_circuitRegistry_p;
    InputTable& d_inputTable;
    Circuit d_currentCircuit;           // mandatory compile-time dependency
    // ...
  private:
    Simulator(const Simulator &);
    Simulator& operator=(const Simulator&);
  public:
    Simulator();
    ~Simulator();
    // ...
    MyError::Code readInput(istream& in, const char *name);
    MyError::Code writeOutput(ostream& out, const char *name);
    MyError::Code addCircuit(const Circuit& circuit);
    MyError::Code simulate(const char *outputName,
                           const char *inputName,
                           const char *circuitName);
    Rectangle window(const char *circuitName) const;
    // ...
};

#endif
```

Figure 0-4: Unnecessary Compile-Time Dependencies

As with link-time dependencies, there are several specific techniques available for eliminating compile-time dependencies.

0.2.4 The Global Name Space

If you have ever worked on a multi-person C++ project, then you know that software integration is a common forum for unwanted surprises. In particular, the proliferation of global identifiers can become problematic. One obvious danger is that these names can collide. The consequence is that the individually developed parts of the system cannot be integrated without modification. For larger projects with hundreds of header files, it can be difficult even to find the declarations of a global name.

For example, I have used object libraries that have consisted of literally thousands of header files. I recall trying to find the definition of a type `TargetId` at file scope that looked like a class (but wasn't):

```
TargetId id;
```

I remember trying to "grep"[3] through all of the thousands of header files looking for the definition, only to receive a message to the effect that there were too many files. I wound up having to nest the grep command in a shell script that split up the header files based on the first letter in order to pare down the problem into 26 problems of manageable size. I eventually discovered that the "class" I was looking for was not a `class` at all. Nor was it a `struct` or a `union`! As illustrated in Figure 0.5, the type `TargetId`, it turned out, was actually a `typedef` declaration at file scope for an `int`!

```
// upd_system.h
#ifndef INCLUDED_UPD_SYSTEM
#define INCLUDED_UPD_SYSTEM

typedef int TargetId;          // bad idea!
class upd_System {
    // ...
  public:
    // ...
};

#endif
```

Figure 0-5: Unnecessary Global Name Space Pollution

The `typedef` had introduced a new type name into the global name space. There was no indication that type was an `int`, nor was there any hint of where I might find its definition.

---

[3] "grep" is a Unix search utility program.

```
// upd_system.h
#ifndef INCLUDED_UPD_SYSTEM
#define INCLUDED_UPD_SYSTEM

class upd_System {
    // ...
  public:
    typedef int TargetId;         // much better!
    // ...
};

#endif
```

Figure 0-6: Typedefs in Class Scope Are Easy to Find

Had the `typedef` declaration been nested within a class (as suggested in Figure 0-6), the reference would have been qualified with that class name (or the declaration would have been inherited), making it straightforward to track down:

```
upd_System::TargetId id;
```

Following simple practices like the one suggested above can minimize the likelihood of collisions and at the same time make logical entities easier to find in large systems.

0.2.5 Logical vs. Physical Design

Most books on C++ address only logical design. Logical design is that which pertains to language constructs such as classes, operators, functions, and so on. For example, whether a particular class should or should not have a copy constructor is a logical design issue. Deciding whether a particular operator (e.g., `operator==`) should be a class member or a free (i.e., nonmember) function is also a logical issue. Even selecting the types of the internal data members of a class would fall under the umbrella of logical design.

C++ supports an overwhelmingly rich set of logical design alternatives. For example, *inheritance* is an essential ingredient of the object-oriented paradigm. Another, called *layering*, involves composing types from more primitive objects, often embedded directly in the class definition. Unfortunately there are many who would try to use inheritance where layering is indicated: A `Telephone` is not a kind of `Receiver`, `Dial`, or `Cord`; rather, it is composed of (or "layered on") those primitive parts.

Misdiagnosing a situation in this way can lead to inefficiencies in both time and space, and can obscure the semantics of the architecture to a point where the entire system becomes difficult to maintain. Knowing when (and when not) to use a particular language construct is part of what makes the *experienced* C++ developer so valuable.

Logical design does not address issues such as where to place a class definition. From a purely logical perspective, all definitions at file scope exist at the same level in a single space without boundaries. Where a class is defined relative to its member definitions and supporting free operators is not relevant to logical design. All that is important is that these logical entities somehow come together to form a working program, and that, because the entire program is thought of as a single unit, there is no notion of individual *physical* dependencies. The program as a whole depends on itself.

There are several good books on logical design (see the bibliography). Unfortunately, there are also many problems, which arise only as programs get larger, that these books do not address. This is because much of the material relevant to successful large-system design falls under a different category, referred to in this book as *physical design*.

Physical design addresses the issues surrounding the physical entities of a system (e.g., files, directories, and libraries) as well as organizational issues such as compile-time or link-time dependencies between physical entities. For example, making a member `ring()` of class `Telephone` an `inline` function forces any client of `Telephone` to have seen not only the declaration of `ring()` but also its definition in order to compile. The logical behavior of `ring()` is the same whether or not `ring()` is declared `inline`. What is affected is the degree and character of the physical coupling between `Telephone` and its clients, and therefore the cost of maintaining any program using `Telephone`.

Good physical design, however, involves more than passively deciding how to partition the existing logical entities of a system. Physical design implications will often dictate the outcome of logical design decisions. For example, relationships between classes in the logical domain, such as IsA, HasA, and Uses, collapse into a single relationship, DependsOn, between components in the physical domain. Furthermore, the dependencies of a sound physical design will form a graph that has no cycles. Therefore we avoid logical design choices that would imply cyclic physical dependencies among components.

Simultaneously satisfying the constraints of both logical and physical design may, at times, prove challenging. In fact, some logical designs may have to be reworked or even replaced in order to meet the physical design quality criteria. In my experience, however, there have always been solutions that adequately address both domains, although it may (at first) take some time to discover them.

For small projects that fit easily into a single directory, physical design may warrant little concern. However, for larger projects the importance of a sound physical design grows rapidly. For very large projects, physical design will be a critical factor in determining the success of the project.

0.3 Reuse

Object-oriented design touts reuse as an incentive, yet like many other benefits of the paradigm, it is not without cost. Reuse implies coupling, and coupling in itself is undesirable. If several programmers are attempting to use the same standard component without demanding functional changes, the reuse is probably reasonable and justified.

Consider, however, the scenario where there are several clients working on different programs, and each is attempting to "reuse" a common component to achieve somewhat different purposes. If those otherwise independent clients are actively seeking enhancement support, they could find themselves at odds with one another as a result of the reuse: an enhancement for one client could disrupt the others. Worse, we could wind up with an overweight class (like the `String` class of Figure 0-2) that serves the needs of no one.

Reuse is often the right answer. But in order for a component or subsystem to be reused successfully, it must *not* be tied to a large block of unnecessary code. That is, it must be possible to reuse the part of the system that is needed without having to link in the rest of the system.

Not all code can be reusable. Attempting to implement excessive functionality or robust error checking for implementation objects can add unnecessarily to the development and maintenance cost as well as to the size of the executable.

Large projects stand to benefit from their implementors' knowing both when to reuse code and when to make code reusable.

0.4 Quality

Quality has many dimensions. *Reliability* addresses the traditional definition of quality (i.e., "Is it buggy?"). A product that is easy to use and does the right thing most of the time is often considered adequate. For some applications, however—in areas such as aerospace, medical, and financial, for example—errors can be extremely costly. In general, software cannot be made reliable through testing alone; by the time you are able to test it, the software's intrinsic quality has already been established. Not all software can be tested effectively. For software to be tested effectively, it must be designed from the start with that goal in mind.

Design for testability, although rarely the first concern of smaller projects, is of paramount importance when successfully architecting large and very large C++ systems. Testability, like quality itself, cannot be an afterthought: it must be considered from the start—before the first line of code is ever written.

There are many other aspects to quality besides reliability. *Functionality*, for example, addresses whether a product does what the customer expects. Sometimes a product will fail to gain acceptance because it does not have enough of the features that customers have come to expect. Worse, a product can miss its mark altogether: if a customer expects to buy a screwdriver, the best hammer in the world will fail a functionality test. Having a clear functional specification that meets marketing requirements *before* development is underway is an important first step toward ensuring appropriate functionality. In this book, however, we consider techniques that address how to design and build large systems, and not what large systems to design.

Usability is yet another measure of quality. Some software products can be very powerful in the right hands. However, it is not enough that the developer be able to use the product effectively. If the product is too complex, difficult, awkward, or painful for the typical intended customer to pick up and use, it will not be used. Often when we say *user*, we think of the *end user* of the system. In a large, hierarchically designed system, however, the clients of your component are probably just other components. Early feedback from customers (including other developers) is essential for ensuring usability.

Maintainability measures the relative cost to support a working system. Support includes such things as tracking down bugs, porting to new platforms, and extending the features of the product to meet the anticipated (or even unanticipated) future needs of customers. A poorly designed system written in C++ (or any other language, for that matter) can be expensive to maintain and even more expensive to extend. Large, maintainable designs don't just happen; they are engineered by following a discipline that ensures maintainability.

Performance addresses how fast and small the product is. Although object-oriented design is known to have valuable advantages in the areas of extensibility and reuse, there are aspects of the paradigm that, if applied naively, can cause programs to run more slowly and require more memory than is necessary. If our code runs too slowly, or if it requires much more memory than a competitor's product, we cannot sell it. For example, modeling every character in a text editor as an object, although perhaps theoretically appealing, could be an inappropriate design decision if we are interested in optimal space/time performance.[4] Attempting to replace a heavily used fundamental type (such as `int`) with a user-defined version (such as a `BigInt` class) will inevitably degrade performance. If we fail to address our performance goals in the beginning, we may adopt architectures or coding practices that will preclude our ever achieving these goals, short of rewriting the entire system. Knowing where to accept some inelegance and knowing how to contain the effects of performance trade-offs distinguishes software engineers from mere programmers.

Each of these dimensions of quality is important to the overall success of a product. However, achieving each of them has one thing in common: we must consider each aspect of quality from the very start of a project. There is simply no way to add the quality once the design is complete.

0.4.1 Quality Assurance

Quality assurance (QA) is typically an organization within a company responsible for "assuring" that a certain measure of quality has been attained. A significant obstacle to achieving high-quality software is that QA often does not get involved until late in the development process, after the damage is already done. QA often does not influence the design of a software product. QA is rarely involved in low-level engineering design decisions. Typically, the testing that QA performs is at the end-user level, and it relies on the developers themselves for any low-level regression testing.

---

[4] See the Flyweight pattern in **gamma**, Chapter 4, pp. 195–206 for a clever solution to this particular kind of performance problem.

In this all-too-common process model, it is engineering's job to produce raw software that it then "throws over the wall" to QA. The software is often poorly documented, hard to understand, difficult to test, and unreliable. QA is now, somehow, expected to instill quality into the software. But how? Over and over, this model for assuring quality has demonstrated its ineffectiveness at achieving high-quality software in large projects. We now suggest a different model.

0.4.2 Quality Ensurance

QA must become an integral part of development. In this process model, developers have the responsibility for *ensuring* quality. That is, the quality must already be there in order for test engineers to find it.

In this process model, the distinction of QA and development is blurred; the technical qualifications for either position are essentially the same. One day, an engineer could write an interface and have another engineer review it for consistency, clarity, and usability. The next day the roles could be reversed. To be truly effective, the culture must be one of teamwork—each member helping the other to ensure high-quality software *as it is being developed.*

Providing a complete process model is a huge task and well beyond the scope of this book. However if high-quality software is to be achieved, system architects and software developers must take the lead by designing in the quality all along the way.

0.5 Software Development Tools

Large projects can benefit from many kinds of tools, including browsers, incremental linkers, and code generators. Even simple tools can be very useful. A detailed description of a simple dependency analyzer that I have found invaluable in my own work is provided in Appendix C.

Some tools can help to mitigate the symptoms of a poor design. Class browsers can help to analyze convoluted designs and find definitions for logical entities that would otherwise be hidden—buried within a large project. Sophisticated programming environments with incremental linkers and program databases can help to push the envelope of what can be accomplished even with a poor physical design. But none of these tools address the underlying problem: a lack of inherent design quality.

Unfortunately there is no single quick and easy way to achieve quality. Tools alone cannot solve fundamental problems resulting from a poor physical design. Although tools can postpone the onset of some of these symptoms, no tool will design in the quality for you, nor will it ensure that your design complies with its specification. Ultimately, it is experience, intelligence, and discipline that yield a quality product.

0.6 Summary

C++ is a whole lot more than just an extension of C. Cyclic link-time dependencies among translation units can undermine understanding, testing, and reuse. Unnecessary or excessive compile-time dependencies can increase compilation cost and destroy maintainability. A disorganized, undisciplined, or naive approach to C++ development will virtually guarantee that these problems occur as projects become larger.

Most C++ design books address only logical issues (such as classes, functions, and inheritance) and ignore physical issues (such as files, directories, and dependencies). In larger systems, however, physical design quality will dictate the correct outcome of many logical design decisions.

Reuse is not without cost. Reuse implies coupling, and coupling can be undesirable. Unwarranted reuse is to be avoided.

Quality has many dimensions: reliability, functionality, usability, maintainability, and performance. Each of these dimensions contributes to the success or failure of large projects.

Achieving quality is an engineering responsibility: it must be actively sought from the start. Quality is not something that can be added after a project is largely complete. For a QA organization to be effective, it must be an integral part of the entire design process.

Finally, good tools are an important part of the development process. But tools cannot make up for a lack of inherent design quality in large C++ systems. This book is about how to design in that quality.

PART I: BASICS

This book covers quite a bit of material relating to object-oriented design and C++ programming. Not all readers will have the same background. In Part I of this text, we address the fundamentals in an effort to reach a common starting point from which to launch further discussions.

Chapter 1 is a review of several key properties of the C++ language, basic object-oriented design principles and notation, and standard coding and documentation conventions used throughout this text. The purpose of this chapter is to help level the field. It is expected that much of this material will be familiar to many readers. Nothing presented here is new. Expert C++ programmers may choose to skim this chapter or simply refer to it as needed.

Chapter 2 describes a modest collection of commonsense design practices that most experienced software developers have already discovered. Adherence to the fundamental rules presented here is an integral part of successful software design. These rules also serve to frame the more advanced and subtle principles and guidelines presented throughout the book.

1

Preliminaries

This chapter reviews some important aspects of the C++ programming language and object-oriented analysis that are fundamental to large-system design. Nothing revolutionary is presented; some material, however, may be unfamiliar. We start by examining multi-file programs, declaration versus definition, and internal versus external linkage in the contexts of both header (`.h`) and implementation (`.c`) files. Next we explore the use of typedef declarations and assert statements. After considering a few matters of style regarding naming conventions and class member layout, we explore one of the most common object-oriented design patterns: *iterator*. We conclude with a thorough discussion of the logical design notation used throughout this book, a brief discussion of *inheritance* versus *layering*, and, finally, a recommendation for minimality in our interfaces.

1.1 Multi-File C++ Programs

For all but the tiniest programs, it is neither wise nor practical to place an entire program in a single file. For one thing, each time you made a change to any part of the program, you would be forced to recompile the program in its entirety. You also would not be able to reuse any part of your program in another program without copying the source code to another file. Such duplication can quickly become a maintenance headache.

Placing the source code for cohesive parts of a program in separate files enables the program to be compiled more efficiently, while enabling its parts to be reused in other programs.

In this section, we review some basic properties of the structure of the C++ language with regard to programs that are created from several source files. These concepts will be used frequently throughout this book.

1.1.1 Declaration versus Definition

A declaration is a definition unless:[1]

- it declares a function without specifying its body,
- it contains an `extern` specifier and no initializer or function body,
- it is the declaration of a static class data member within a class definition,
- it is a class name declaration, or
- it is a typedef declaration.

A definition is a declaration unless:

- it defines a static class data member or
- it defines a non-inline member function.

> **DEFINITION: A *declaration* introduces a name into a program; a *definition* provides a unique description of an entity (e.g., type, instance, function) within a program.**

A declaration introduces a name into a scope. A declaration differs from a definition in that it is legal in C++ to repeat a declaration within a given scope. By contrast, there must be exactly one definition of each entity (e.g., class, object, enumerator, or function) used in the program. For example,

```
int f(int,int);
int f(int,int);
class IntSetIter;
class IntSetIter;
typedef int Int;
typedef int Int;
friend IntSetIter;
friend IntSetIter;
extern int globalVariable;  // bad idea (global variable declaration)
extern int globalVariable;  // (see Section 2.3.1)
```

[1] **ellis**, Section 3.1, p. 14.

are all declarations, and can be repeated any number of times within a single scope. On the other hand, the following declarations at file scope are also definitions, and therefore cannot be seen more than once in a given scope without triggering a compile-time error:

```
int x;                                // bad idea (global variable)
char *p;                              // bad idea (global variable)
extern int globalVariable = 1;        // bad idea (global variable)
static int s_instanceCount;
static int f(int, int) { /* ... */ }
inline int h(int, int) { /* ... */ }
enum Color { RED, GREEN, BLUE };
enum DummyType {};
enum { SIZE = 100 };
enum {} silly;
const double DEFAULT_TOLERANCE = 1.0e-6;
class Stack { /* ... */ };
struct Util { /* ... */ };
union Rep { /* ... */ };
template<class T> void sort(const T** array, int size) { /* ... */ }
```

We should note that function and static data member declarations are exceptions that, although not definitions, may not be repeated within the definition of a class:

```
class NoGood {
    static int i;       // declaration
    static int i;       // illegal in C++
  public:
    int f();            // declaration
    int f();            // illegal in C++
};
```

1.1.2 Internal versus External Linkage

When a `.c` file is compiled, the header files are first included (recursively) by the C preprocessor (cpp) to form a single source file containing all the necessary information. This intermediate file (called a *translation unit*) is then compiled to produce a `.o` file (object file) with the same root name. Linkage connects the symbols produced within the various translation units to form an executable program. There are two distinct kinds of linkage: *internal* and *external*. The kind of linkage used will directly influence how we incorporate a given logical construct in our physical design.

> **<u>DEFINITION</u>: A name has *internal linkage* if it is local to its translation unit and cannot collide with an identical name defined in another translation unit at link time.**

Internal linkage means that access to the definition is limited to the current translation unit. That is, a definition with internal linkage is not "visible" to any other translation unit and therefore cannot be used to resolve undefined symbols during the linking process. For example,

```
static int x;
```

is defined at file scope, but the keyword `static` forces the linkage to be internal. Another example of internal linkage is an enumeration:

```
enum Boolean { NO, YES };
```

Enumerations are definitions (not just declarations), but never themselves introduce symbols into the `.o` file. In order for definitions with internal linkage to affect other parts of a program, they must be placed in the header file, not the `.c` file.

An important example of a definition with internal linkage is that of a class. The description of class `Point` (shown in Figure 1-1) is a definition, not a declaration; hence, it cannot be repeated in a translation unit in the same scope. For classes to be used outside of a single translation unit, they must be defined in a header file. An inline function definition (such as the one shown for `operator==` at the bottom of Figure 1-1) is another example of a definition with internal linkage.

```
class Point {
    int d_x;
    int d_y;

  public:
    Point (int x, int y) : d_x(x), d_y(y) {}          // internal linkage
    int x() const { return d_x; }                     // internal linkage
    int y() const { return d_y; }                     // internal linkage
    // ...
};                                                    // internal linkage

inline int operator==(const Point& left, const Point& right)
{
    return left.x() == right.x() && left.y() == right.y();
}                                                     // internal linkage
```

Figure 1-1: Some Definitions with Internal Linkage

> **<u>DEFINITION</u>: A name has *external linkage* if, in a multi-file program, that name can interact with other translation units at link time.**

External linkage means that the definition is not limited to a single translation unit. Definitions with external linkage produce external symbols in the `.o` file that are accessible by all other translation units for resolving their undefined symbols. Such external symbols must be unique throughout the program or the program will not link.

Non-inline member functions (including static members) have external linkage, as do non-inline, non-static free (i.e., nonmember) functions. Examples of functions with external linkage are shown in Figure 1-2.

```
// non-inline member function:
Point& Point::operator+=(const Point& right)
{
    d_x += right.d_x;
    d_y += right.d_y;
    return *this;
}                                           // external linkage

// non-inline free function:
Point operator+(const Point& left, const Point& right)
{
    return Point(left.x() + right.x(), left.y() + right.y());
}                                           // external linkage
```

Figure 1-2: Some Function Definitions with External Linkage

Note that we will consistently refer to a nonmember function as a *<u>free</u> function* and never as a *friend function*. A free function need not be a friend of any class; whether or not it is should be an implementation detail (see Section 3.6).

Where possible, the C++ compiler substitutes the body of an inline function directly in place of the function call and introduces no symbols into the `.o` file. Sometimes the compiler will elect (for various reasons, such as recursion or dynamic binding) to lay down a static copy of an inline function. This static copy introduces only a local symbol into the current `.o` file, which cannot interact with external symbols.

Because a declaration is solely for the benefit of the current translation unit, declarations themselves introduce nothing at all into a `.o` file. Consider the following declarations:

```
/* 1 */        int f();          // bad idea (see Section 2.3.2)
/* 2 */        extern int i;     // bad idea (see Section 2.3.1)
               struct S {
/* 3 */            int g();      // fine
               };
```

None of these declarations themselves affects the contents of the resulting `.o` file. Instead, each of these declarations merely names an external symbol, enabling the current translation unit to gain access to the corresponding global definition if needed. It is actually the *use* of the symbol name (e.g., calling a function) and not the declaration itself that causes an undefined symbol to be introduced into the `.o` file. It is precisely this fact that allows early prototyping: as long as the missing functionality is not needed, partially implemented objects can be used in running programs.

In the previous example, each of the three declarations enabled access to an externally defined function or object. We might be sloppy and say that these "declarations" have external linkage. But there are other kinds of declarations that do not serve to enable access to external definitions. We will often refer to these kinds of declarations as having "internal" linkage. For example,

```
typedef int Int;                      // internal linkage
```

is a typedef declaration. It does not introduce any symbols into the `.o` file, nor does it enable access to a global object with external linkage: its linkage is internal. An important kind of declaration that happens to have internal linkage is that of a class.

```
class Point;                          // internal linkage
struct Point;                         // internal linkage
union Point;                          // internal linkage
```

All of the above have the identical effect of introducing the name `Point` as some kind of user-defined type; the particular declaration type (e.g., `class`) need not match the actual definition type (e.g., `union`):

```
class Rep;
// ...
union Rep {
    // ...
};
```

The definitions to which these declarations potentially refer also have internal linkage; this property distinguishes class declarations from the external declarations in previous examples. Both class declarations and class definitions contribute nothing to the `.o` file and are solely for the benefit of the current translation unit.

On the other hand, static class data members (declared within the class definition) have external linkage:

```
class Point {
    static int s_numPoints;  // declaration of external object
    // ...
};
```

The static class data member `s_numPoints` (shown above) is only a declaration, but its definition in the `.c` file has "external" linkage:

```
// point.c
int Point::s_numPoints;        // definition of external object
                               // (initialized to 0 by default)
```

Note that, according to the language specification, every static class data member *must* be defined exactly once somewhere in the final program.[2]

Finally, the C++ language treats enumerations and classes differently:

```
enum Point;                    // error
```

It is not possible in C++ to declare an enumeration without defining it. As we will see, class declarations are quite often used in place of preprocessor `include` directives to declare a class without defining it.

1.1.3 Header (`.h`) Files

In C++ it is almost always a programming error to place a definition with external linkage in a `.h` file. If you do, and you include that header in more than one translation unit, linking them together will fail with a message such as

```
MULTIPLY DEFINED SYMBOL.
```

---

[2] **ellis**, Section 9.4, p. 179; Section 18.3, p. 405.

It is legal in C++ to place definitions with internal linkage, such as static functions or static data, at file scope within a header file, but it is undesirable. Not only do these file-scope definitions pollute the global name space but, in the case of static data and functions, they consume data space in every translation unit that includes the header. Even data declared `const` at file scope can cause this same problem, especially if the address of the constant is ever taken. Compare a file-scope constant (with internal linkage) with a static constant class member (which has external linkage): there will be only a single copy of the class-scoped constant in the entire program. Some examples of what does and doesn't belong in a header file are provided in Figure 1.3.

```
// radio.h
#ifndef INCLUDED_RADIO
#define INCLUDED_RADIO

int z;                                // illegal: external data definition
extern int LENGTH = 10;               // illegal: external data definition
const int WIDTH = 5;                  // avoid: constant data definition
static int y;                         // avoid: static data definition
static void func() {/*...*/}          // avoid: static function definition

class Radio {
    static int s_count;               // fine: static member declaration
    static const double S_PI;         // fine: static const member dec.
    int d_size;                       // fine: member data definition
    // ...
  public:
    int size() const;                 // fine: member function declaration
    // ...
};                                    // fine: class definition

inline int Radio::size() const
{
    return d_size;
}                                     // fine: inline function definition

int Radio::s_count;                   // illegal: static member definition

double Radio::S_PI = 3.14159265358;  // illegal: static const member def.

int Radio::size() const { /*...*/ }  // illegal: member function definition

#endif
```

Figure 1-3: What Does and Does Not Belong in a Header File

The redundancy of duplicated nonmember data definitions affects not only program size but also runtime performance by defeating the caching mechanism of the host computer.

Occasionally, however, there are valid reasons for placing a static instance of a user-defined object in a header file at file scope. In particular, the constructor of such an object can be used to ensure that a particular global facility (such as `iostream`) has been initialized before it is used.[3] Although this solution may be elegant for small and medium-sized systems, it is problematic for very large systems. We will return to this issue in Section 7.8.1.3.

1.1.4 Implementation (`.c`) Files

We will sometimes elect to define functions and data for use in our own implementation that we do not want exposed outside of our translation unit. Definitions with internal but not external linkage can appear at file scope in a `.c` file without affecting the global (symbol) name space. The definitions to be avoided at file scope in `.c` files are data and functions that have *not* been declared static. For example,

```
// file1.c

int i;                                                // external linkage
int max(int a, int b) { return a > b ? a : b }        // external linkage
```

The above definitions have external linkage and could potentially collide with other similar names in the global name space. Because inline and static free functions have internal linkage, these kinds of functions can be defined at file scope in a `.c` file and not pollute the global name space. For example,

```
// file2.c

inline int min(int a, int b) { return a < b ? a : b }               // internal

static int fact(int n) { return n <= 1 ? 1 : n * fact(n - 1); } // internal
```

Enumeration definitions, nonmember objects declared `static`, and (by default) `const` data definitions also have internal linkage. It is safe to define all of these entities at file scope in the `.c` file. For example,

---

[3] **ellis**, Section 3.4, pp. 21–22.

```
// file3.c
#include <math.h>
class Link;                                                    // internal

enum { START_SIZE = 1, GROW_FACTOR = 2 };                      // internal

const double PI_SQ = M_PI * M_PI;                              // internal

static const char *names[] = { "Ntran", "Ptran", "NPN", "PNP" }; // internal

static Link *s_root_p;                                         // internal
Link *const s_first_p = s_root_p;                              // internal
```

Other constructs such as typedef declarations and preprocessor macros do not introduce exported symbols into the `.o` file. They too may appear in `.c` files at file scope without affecting the global name space. For example,

```
typedef int (PointerToFunctionOfVoidReturningInt *)();

#define CASE(X) case X: cout << "X" << endl; // Classic C preprocessor

#define CASE(X) case X: cout << #X << endl;  // ANSI C preprocessor
```

Typedefs and macros have limited usefulness in C++, and they can be harmful if abused. We will explore the perils of typedefs in Sections 1.2 and 2.3.3, and those of macros in Section 2.3.4.

1.2 `typedef` Declarations

A `typedef` declaration creates an alias for an existing type, not a new type. A `typedef`, therefore, gives only the illusion of type safety. Consequently, typedefs in the interface can easily do more harm than good.

Consider class `Person` shown in Figure 1-4. We have decided to nest `typedef` declarations within the `Person` class to avoid affecting the global name space and to make them easier to find. The `setWeight` member function is defined to take a weight argument in "Pounds," while the `getHeight` method returns height in "Inches."

```
// person.h
#ifndef INCLUDED_PERSON
#define INCLUDED_PERSON

class Person {
    // ...
  public:
    typedef double Inches;
    typedef double Pounds;
    //...
    void setWeight(Pounds weight);
    Inches getHeight() const;
    //...
};

#endif
```

Figure 1-4: Typedefs Are Not Type-Safe

Unfortunately, a nested `typedef` offers no more type safety than one declared at file scope:

```
void f (const Person& person)
{
    Person::Inches height = person.height();
    person.setWeight(height);                          // ok ??
};
```

The two type names `Inches` and `Pounds` are structurally equal and therefore completely interchangeable. These typedefs afford absolutely no compile-time type safety, yet make it difficult to know the actual type.

Typedefs do, however, have their place when it comes to defining complex function arguments. For example,

```
typedef int (PCPMFDI::*Person)(double) const;
```

declares `PCPMFDI` to be of type: pointer to a `const Person` member function taking a `double` argument and returning an `int`. Typedefs are also useful in defining data members that must maintain a constant size across different compilers and computer hardware (see Section 10.1.3).

1.3 Assert Statements

The standard C library provides a macro called `assert` (see `assert.h`) for guaranteeing that a given expression evaluates to a non-zero value; otherwise an error message is printed and program execution is terminated.[4] Assertions are convenient to use and are a powerful implementation-level documentation tool for developers. Assert statements are like active comments—they not only make assumptions clear and precise, but if these assumptions are violated, they actually do something about it.

The use of assert statements can be an effective way to catch program logic errors at runtime, and yet they are easily filtered out of production code. Once development is complete, the runtime cost of these redundant tests for coding errors can be eliminated simply by defining the preprocessor symbol `NDEBUG` during compilation. Be sure, however, to remember that code placed in the assert itself will be omitted in the production version. Consider the following partial definition of a `String` class:

```
class String {
    enum { DEFAULT_SIZE = 8 };
    char *d_array_p;
    int d_size;
    int d_length;

  public:
    String();
    // ...
};
```

If (as with the code below) the expression argument to the `assert` macro affects the state of the software, then the production version will exhibit disparate behavior.

```
String::String()
: d_size (DEFAULT_SIZE)
, d_length(0)
{
    assert(d_array_p = new char[d_size]);    // error
}
```

We can avoid this problem by making sure that the asserted code is completely independent of the normal operation of the object:

---

[4] **plauger**, Chapter 1, pp. 17–24.

```
String::String()
: d_size (DEFAULT_SIZE)
, d_length(0)
{
    d_array_p = new char[d_size]);
    assert(d_array_p);                          // fine
}
```

A generalization of this technique that addresses fault tolerance is to `throw` an exception such as `CodingError`.[5] This way it will be up to the software at higher levels to `catch` and address this problem. In the absence of a handler for programming errors, the default behavior reduces to that of an assert.[6]

1.4 A Few Matters of Style

When programmers get together to start a project, they often discuss what coding standards to adopt. Few of these standards contribute to the quality of the product. Often they are concerned with questions such as

> Should we indent 2, 4, or 8 spaces?
>
> Should we put a space between the right parenthesis of an `if` statement and the following left bracket like this
>
> ```
> if (exp) {
> ```
>
> Or should we not put a space like this
>
> ```
> if (exp){
> ```

At the beginning of one big project, we spent weeks arguing about standards. We concluded that although there is an advantage to standardization, the list of standards should be as small as possible, and each should be driven by clear engineering principles. Both of the examples above fail these criteria.

Another thing we learned is that when it comes to enforcing standards, there are two domains: the interface and the implementation. A good interface is much more important than a good implementation. Interfaces have a direct impact on clients and they

---

[5] **murray**, Section 9.2.1, pp. 208–210.

[6] For more on the intended use of exceptions, see **ellis**, Section 15.1, p. 355.

also have global implications. Implementations should affect only the authors and maintainers of code.

There are clear reasons to impose strict standards on interfaces, particularly in large projects. Interfaces are generally much more difficult and costly to repair than implementation. It is usually not too difficult to throw out a poor implementation and replace it with a better one, provided the interface is a good encapsulating one.

1.4.1 Identifier Names

The following coding conventions have been debated ad infinitum and have survived the ordeal. Most of the recommendations proposed here focus on aspects that affect interfaces, where their benefit will be most strongly felt. Then again, much of this is a matter of personal taste. If there is one rule, it is to *be consistent*.

1.4.1.1 Type Names

C++ syntax is complex. Subtle clues about the nature of its constructs are always welcome. A fairly standard and widely accepted practice is to treat type names with special consideration. In this text we consistently make the first character of a type name an uppercase letter; non-type names begin with a lowercase letter.

For our purposes, types are those entities that are neither data nor functions:

- Classes
- Structures
- Unions
- Typedefs
- Enumerations
- Templates

Here are some declarations that illustrate this programming style:

```
class Point;
struct Date;
union Value;
enum Temperature { COLD, WARM, HOT, VERY_HOT } temp;7
typedef Temp Temperature;
template class Stack<int>;
int Point::getX() const;
void Point::setX(int xCoord);
```

Lexicographically distinguishing type names from other names is an objectively verifiable standard that improves readability for both clients and implementors alike. If used consistently, this practice can make interfaces easier to understand and code easier to maintain.

1.4.1.2 Multi-Word Identifier Names

There are two kinds of people when it comes to naming identifiers—those who advocate the use of the underscore character ('_') to delimit words, and those who advocate capitalizing the second and subsequent words:

```
this_is_a_very_long_identifier   vs.   thisIsAVeryLongIdentifier
```

There are arguments for both sides. I was originally in the underscore camp but was forced to make the change by consensus. Now I realize that it makes no difference: it is just a matter of what you are used to. Perhaps the capitals are a bit better because the names are shorter; they become easier to read once you are used to them. Using capitals also leaves open the use of underscore for other purposes (see Sections 6.4.2 and 7.2.1). The important thing is that there be consistency throughout the product line.

It appears unprofessional and can be annoying for one set of classes to use one naming convention while other classes in the same product use the other, especially if outside paying customers will (or some day could) have direct access to the underlying C++ classes. Some programmers, however, may dismiss these inconsistencies as simply a matter of style.

---

[7] In this text the names of enumerators and (static) constants are all uppercase and make use of underscores to delimit words.

In this book I have adopted the `uppercaseStandard`. Whatever you adopt, however, I strongly recommend that you `be_consistent`, particularly in the interface.

1.4.1.3 Data Member Names

Readability and maintainability are greatly served if people remember to add a consistent prefix (such as `d_`) to the data members of their classes. Consider the following `Shoe` class:

```
class Shoe {
    double d_temperature;
    int d_size;
    // ...
  public:
    // ...
    void expand(double calories);
    // ...
    void setSize(int size);
    // ...
};
```

Values held in local (automatic) variables within member functions are only temporary; they do not exist after the member function returns. On the other hand, class member data defines the state of the object, which exists between member function calls:

```
void Shoe::expand(double calories)
{
    const double FACTOR = 42.57;         // Always initialized to same value
    // ...                               // (probably belongs at file scope).

    double factor = calories * FACTOR; // short lived automatic variables

    d_temperature += FACTOR / d_size;  // use of "state" variables
}
```

The primary purpose of the `d_` is to highlight class data members in a context-independent, mechanical way. Because of the very different purposes for these two types of data, lexicographically distinguishing class data member names from those of local variables helps to make object implementations easier to understand.

It is common to see member functions that set an instance variable (e.g., `d_size`) to contain a single assignment expression:

```
inline
void Shoe::setSize(int size)
{
    d_size = size;
}
```

Putting the d_ in front of data members also obviates dreaming up weird names (e.g., sz) for the manipulator function's argument:

```
void Shoe::setSize(int sz)
{
    size = sz;
}
```

The choice of a d_ prefix is quite arbitrary. We do not use only an underscore (_) as a prefix because identifiers beginning with an underscore are reserved for use by C compilers.[8] Some prefer to use a trailing underscore for this purpose:

```
void Shoe::setSize(int size)
{
    size_ = size;
}
```

I find it useful to leave the suffix open for other purposes (such as _p to identify a pointer data member).[9] You may also want to use a different prefix (such as s_ to identify static class data). Whether in a class or at file scope, non-const static data potentially contains instance-independent state information. As discussed in Section 6.3.5, static class data members may be moved to file scope in a .c file to help avoid compile-time coupling. Because of the very similar properties and interchangeability of these two types of data, it makes sense to identify state variables in the .c file with an s_ as well. Consistently following this naming convention makes it easy to search for all instance-independent state variables in a component.

It is worth noting that static class or file scope constant data is stateless. We can identify the nature and lifetime of this data simply by making its name all uppercase. For constant data in class scope, a name such as S_DEFAULT_VALUE or simply DEFAULT_VALUE could work equally well. In this book we prefer S_DEFAULT_VALUE for class-scoped constant static data to remind us of the need to keep it private (see Section 2.2).

---

[8] **ellis**, Section 2.4, p. 7.

[9] See Section 6.4.2 for another use of an identifier suffix.

By contrast, a non-static constant data member has a more limited lifetime and its value need not always be the same in each incarnation of the object. Consequently, its name would appear in lowercase and begin with a `d_` prefix:

```
class Set { /* ... */ }
class SetIter {
    Set *const d_set_p;         // d_set_p is a const pointer to a Set.
    const double D_PI;          // bad idea (should be static)
    // ...
};
```

The `d_` convention was adopted, without complaint, by our entire company.

1.4.2 Class Member Layout

When using an unfamiliar object, figuring out where to find things can be difficult. Although member function ordering within a class is clearly a matter of style, from a client's point of view it helps to be consistent. A fundamental way to classify member functionality is by whether or not it potentially affects the state of the object.

An organization useful for both a developer and a client is illustrated in Figure 1-5. This organization has the advantage of grouping by categories of functionality that are present in nearly every C++ class. This organization is also independent of the particular abstraction being implemented.

```
class Car {
    // ...
  public:
    // CREATORS
    Car(int cost = 0);
    Car(const Car& car);
    ~Car();

    // MANIPULATORS
    Car& operator=(const Car& car);
    void addFuel(double numberOfGallons);
    void drive(double deltaGasPedal);
    void turn(double angleInDegrees);
    // ...

    // ACCESSORS
    double getFuel() const;
    double getRPMs() const;
    double getSpeed() const;
    // ...
};
```

Figure 1-5: Creator/Manipulator/Accessor Member Organization

CREATORS bring objects into and out of existence. Notice that operator= is not a *creator*, but rather (by convention) the first *manipulator*. MANIPULATORS are simply non-const member functions; ACCESSORS are const member functions. This purely objective grouping makes it easy to verify at a glance that all of the accessors and none of the manipulators are declared as const members of the class. But the principal benefit is to provide a common starting point for dissecting the fundamental functionality of an unfamiliar class. For larger classes, it can be helpful to sort members within each section alphabetically. For very large classes such as wrappers (discussed in Sections 5.10 and 6.4.3), other organizations may be more appropriate.

Sometimes people will try to group member functions as get/set pairs as illustrated in Figure 1-6. For some users, this style is a result of the misguided belief that an object is little more than a public data structure that has data members, each of which must have both a "get" (accessor) function and a "set" (manipulator) function. This style itself could, for some, impede the creation of truly encapsulated interfaces in which the data members are not necessarily transparently reflected in the behavior of the object.

```
class Car {
    double d_fuel;
    double d_speed;
    double d_rpms;

  public:
    Car(int cost = 0);
    Car(const Car& car);
    Car& operator=(const Car& car);
    ~Car();

    double getFuel() const;
    void setFuel(double numberOfGallons);

    double getRPMs() const;
    void setRPMs(double rpms);

    double getSpeed() const;
    void setSpeed(double speedInMPH);

    // ...
};
```

Figure 1-6: Get/Set Member Organization

Finally, there is the question of where to place the data members. Properly encapsulated classes do not have public data. From a logical point of view, data members are merely implementation details of the class. Consequently, many people prefer to place the implementation details of a class, including the data members, at the end of the class definition, as illustrated in Figure 1-7.

```
class Car {
  public:
    Car(int cost = 0);
    Car(const Car& car);

    // ...

  private:
    double d_fuel;
    double d_speed;
    double d_rpms;
};
```

Figure 1-7: Trailing Data Member Organization

Although this organization may be more readable to naive clients, the attempt to hide the implementation details at the end of the class definition belies the fact that they are not hidden. The presence of implementation details in the header file imposes a degree of compile-time coupling that does not evaporate simply by relocating these details within the class definition.

Since this book addresses physical and organizational design issues, we consistently place implementation details in the header file *ahead* of the public interface (partly to emphasize their presence). In Chapter 6, we discuss how such implementation-level clutter can be removed from a header file entirely, and thus truly hidden from the client.

1.5 Iterators

Perhaps the most common pattern in object-oriented design is that of an iterator.[10, 11] An iterator is an object that is intimately coupled to and supplied with a primary object of some kind; its purpose is to allow clients to sequence through the parts, attributes, or subobjects of the primary object.

Often objects will represent a collection of other objects. Such objects are commonly referred to as *containers*. Sets, lists, stacks, heaps, queues, hash tables, and so on are

---

[10] **gamma**, *Iterator*, Chapter 5, pp. 257–271.

[11] **stroustrup**, Sections 5.3.2, p. 160; 7.8, p. 243; and 8.3.4, p. 267.

typical container objects. Note that where relevant, we often identify the source file for a body of code with a leading comment. For example,

```
// stack.h
#ifndef INCLUDED_STACK
// ...
```

```
// stack.c
#include "stack.h"
// ...
```

Consider, for example, the simple class implementing a set of integers shown in Figure 1-8. As we can see from its header file, `IntSet` is implemented using `IntSetLink` objects, but that fact is an encapsulated implementation detail of the class. In this minimal implementation, we have elected to prevent users from constructing a copy of an `IntSet` or assigning to one by making these otherwise automatically generated functions private. (The comment NOT IMPLEMENTED indicates that the functionality does not exist even privately.) Users of `IntSet` are allowed only to create an empty set, add integers to it, check for membership, and destroy it.

```
// intset.h
#ifndef INCLUDED_INTSET
#define INCLUDED_INTSET

class IntSetLink;
class IntSetIter;
class ostream;

class IntSet {
    // DATA
    IntSetLink *d_root_p;  // root of a linked list of integers

    // FRIENDS
    friend IntSetIter;

  private:
    // NOT IMPLEMENTED
    IntSet(const IntSet&);
    IntSet& operator=(const IntSet&);

  public:
    // CREATORS
    IntSet();
        // Create an empty set of integers.
    ~IntSet();
        // Destroy this set.
```

```
    // MANIPULATORS
    void add(int i);
        // Add an integer to this set.  If the given integer is
        // already present, this operation has no effect.

    // ACCESSORS
    int isMember(int i) const;
        // returns 1 if integer i is a member of the set,
        // and 0 otherwise.
};

#endif
```

Figure 1-8: A Simple Integer Set Class

A tiny test driver that exercises this limited functionality is shown in Figure 1-9. Note that driver programs in this book are indicated by using the file name suffix `.t.c`.

```
// intset.t.c
#include "intset.h"
#include <iostream.h>

main()
{
    IntSet a;

    a.add(1); a.add(2); a.add(3); a.add(2); a.add(4); a.add(6);

    for (int i = 0; i < 10; ++i) {
        cout << ' ' << i << '-' << (a.isMember(i) ? "yes" : "no");
    }

    cout << endl;
}

// Output:
//      john@john: a.out
//       0-no 1-yes 2-yes 3-yes 4-yes 5-no 6-yes 7-no 8-no 9-no
//      john@john:
```

Figure 1-9: Trivial Driver Exercising `IntSet` Functionality

Suppose we would like to find out what members exist in the set in order to print them. Theoretically, we could write the output function ourselves as shown in Figure 1-10, but the performance of that implementation would be somewhat lacking.

```
#include <limits.h>     // defines INT_MIN and INT_MAX
ostream& operator<<(ostream& o, const IntSet& intSet)
{
    o << "{ ";
    for (int i = INT_MIN; i <= INT_MAX; ++i) {
        if (intSet.isMember(i)) {
            o << i << ' ';
        }
    }
    return o << '}';
}
```

Figure 1-10: Infeasible Implementation of `IntSet` Output Operator

An obvious solution is to make the `operator<<` function a friend of class `IntSet` in order to take advantage of its internal representation. We could do that, but what if a client is not happy with the format supplied by this operator's implementation? What happens if later we find we need to access the internal members, say, to compare two `IntSet` objects?

```
class IntSet {
    // ...
  public:
    // ...

void reset();
    // Reset to beginning of sequence of integers.  The Current
    // integer will be invalid only if the set is empty.

void advance();
    // Advance to the next integer in the set.  If the current
    // integer was the last in the set, the current integer
    // will be invalid after advance returns.  Note that the
    // behavior is undefined if the current integer is already
    // not valid.

int current() const;
    // Return the current integer in the sequence.  Note that the
    // behavior is undefined if the current integer is not valid.

int isCurrentValid() const;
    // Return 1 if the current integer is valid, and 0 otherwise.
    // Note that the current integer is valid if the set is not
    // empty and we have not advanced beyond the last integer
    // in the set.
}
```

Figure 1-11: Attempting to Add Iteration Capability to the Container Itself

We could keep adding new members and friends, but each time we do, we put both our clients and ourselves at risk by increasing the complexity of the class. Repeatedly revisiting and extending the functionality of an object is a well-recognized way of introducing bugs into software. Also, unless you plan to support multiple versions, other clients that do not care about this new functionality will have it forced upon them.

Instead of dealing with these deficiencies one at a time, we can address most of them at once by providing a general and efficient way to access the individual members of the set. Suppose we decided to add this capability directly to the `IntSet` class itself, as depicted in Figure 1-11. It is now possible for a client to iterate through an instance of class `IntSet` and print out the contents of that object in any format that is desired. Figure 1-12 illustrates some of the power of iteration. Regardless of how the implementation of the set may change, the client's code will not be affected.

```
ostream& operator<<(ostream& o, const IntSet& intSet)
{
    o << "{ ";
    for (intSet.reset(); intSet.isCurrentValid(); intSet.advance()) {
        o << intSet.current() << ' ';
    }
    return o << '}';
}
```

Figure 1-12: Another Implementation of the `IntSet` Output Operator

Unfortunately, there are still problems with the design shown in Figure 1-12. For a given object, there can be at most one iteration going on at any one time. Suppose we are trying to implement a comparison function for our `IntSet` and decide, for debugging purposes, to print out the contents of the sets midway through the comparison iteration. The print routine would have the unwanted side effect of corrupting the iteration state for the comparison. The problem is that `IntSet` allocates enough space to hold state information for exactly one iteration. That space remains allocated whether or not an iteration is active. If for some reason we want to have a pair of nested `for` loops that iterate over the elements in the same set, we would have to duplicate the entire set.

This problem could be addressed by having the client hold on to the internal state or retain some other form of place holder. If the client allocates the state dynamically, the client must remember to delete the state to avoid a memory leak.

If the place holder is in the form of an integer index, there could be some additional practical constraints on the underlying implementation of the set. For example, if the set is implemented as a linked list (instead of an array), there is the potential for quadratic—i.e., O(N^2)—behavior during iteration because each iteration of the `for` loop would result in having to traverse the list.

The standard approach is to supply an iterator class along with each container class (in the same header file). The iterator is declared a `friend` of the container and therefore has access to its internal organization. The iterator class is defined in the same header file as the container class to avoid the problems associated with "long-distance" friendship (discussed in Section 3.6). Iterators for concrete containers such as `IntSet` are typically created on the program stack; thus their state is destroyed automatically when the iterator goes out of scope. Iterator objects can be more space efficient because the space for each iteration need exist only during the iteration process itself. Also, any number of iterators can be independently active on a given container at any time without interfering with one another.

As a practical matter, it is common for iterators to assume that the objects on which they operate are not modified or destroyed during the course of iteration. It is also common for the order in which objects are presented during iteration to be implementation dependent and subject to change without notice. Ideally, iterator developers would explicitly state whether or not the order of iteration is defined. To be safe, clients of iterators should not assume an order unless one is specified.

Figure 1-13 illustrates the design of the standard iterator pattern used throughout this book. This iterator object is intended for use with `for` loops. The syntax of this iterator is quite terse. The use of the operators is by no means obvious, especially if you have never seen them used this way before. One could easily argue that this style is an abuse of operator overloading because readability is reduced. There is more to this story, however.

```
class IntSetIter {
    // DATA
    IntSetLink *d_link_p;      // root of linked list of integers

  private:
    // NOT IMPLEMENTED
    IntSetIter(const IntSetIter&);
    IntSetIter& operator=(const IntSetIter&);
```

```
  public:
    // CREATORS
    IntSetIter(const IntSet& IntSet);
        // Create an iterator for the specified integer set.

    ~IntSetIter();
        // Destroy this iterator (an unnecessary comment).

    // MANIPULATORS
    void operator++();
        // Advance the state of the iteration to next integer in set.

    // ACCESSORS
    int operator()() const;
        // Return the value of the current integer.

    operator const void *() const;
        // Return non-zero value if iteration is valid, otherwise 0.
};
```

Figure 1-13: A Standard Iterator for the `IntSet` Container

Because of the frequency with which iterators can and do occur in large designs, the most important consideration for developers must be consistency. If we avoid operator overloading and use functions instead, it is important to use the same function names every time; otherwise we will find ourselves unwittingly misnaming these functions and forever having to revert to header files for the syntactic details. A representative few of the many possible equivalent function names are shown in Figure 1-14.

```
it       it.more()    it.isMore()    it.valid()     it.notDone()
++it     it.next()    it.getNext()   it.advance()   it.getMore()
it()     it.item()    it.getItem()   it.element()   it.value()
```

Figure 1-14: Which Names Should We Use?

Our experience has shown that adopting the operators indicated in the left column of Figure 1-14 for each of these standard iteration methods produces a consistent, easy-to-use, and soon familiar and easily recognized idiom for iteration over concrete types. Whatever you decide to use, be sure to be consistent throughout your product line. The final implementation of the `IntSet` output operator is shown in Figure 1-15; the terse iterator notation affords a succinct implementation.

```
ostream& operator<<(ostream& o, const IntSet& intSet)
{
    o << "{ ";
    for (IntSetIter it(intSet); it; ++it) {
        o << it() << ' ';
    }
    return o << '}';
}
```

Figure 1-15: `IntSet` **Output Operator Using Succinct Iterator Implementation**

The choice of pre-increment (`++it`) over the post-increment (`it++`) in Figure 1-15 is deliberate; the post-increment version requires a second dummy argument and is not universally available.[12] Furthermore, the semantics of increment for an iterator more closely pattern those for pre-increment when applied to the fundamental types (see Section 9.1.1).

1.6 Logical Design Notation

Object-oriented design lends itself to a rich set of notations.[13] Most of these notations denote relationships between the logical entities of a design.

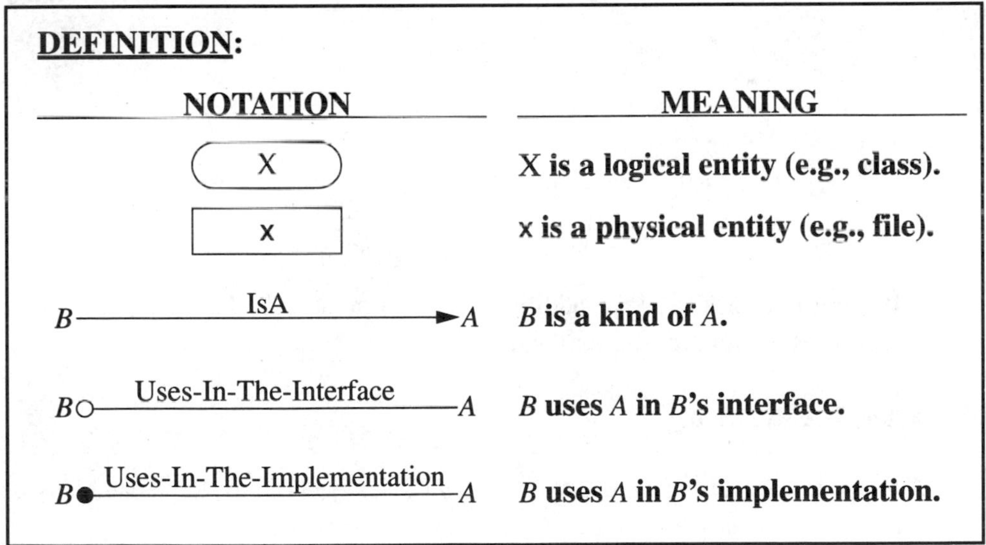
DEFINITION:
NOTATION
MEANING
X
X is a logical entity (e.g., class).
x
x is a physical entity (e.g., file).
B
IsA
A
B is a kind of A.
B
Uses-In-The-Interface
A
B uses A in B's interface.
B
Uses-In-The-Implementation
A
B uses A in B's implementation.

[12] See **ellis**, Section 13.4.7, pp. 338–339.

[13] **booch**, Chapter 5, pp. 171–228.

Throughout this text, we consistently identify logical entities (e.g., classes, structures, and unions) with an ellipse-like bubble:

Car

```
class Car {
    // ...
};
```

as opposed to a rectangle for physical entities:

car.c

```
// car.c
#include "car.h"
// ...
```

For our purposes, three logical notations will suffice:

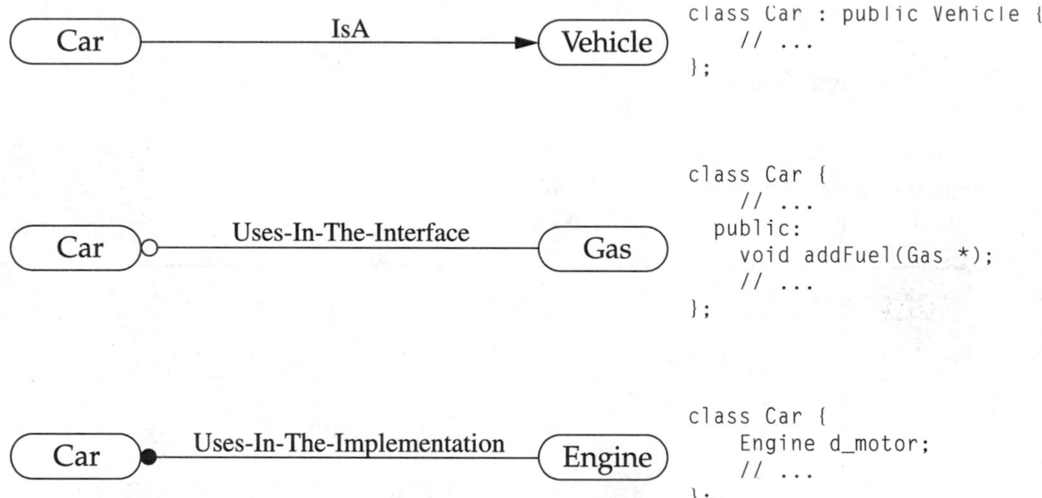

If there is ever a need for additional logical notation, a labeled arrow that explicitly identifies the relationship will suffice.

1.6.1 The IsA Relation

Suppose a `Word` is a kind of `String`. That is, an object of type `Word` can be used wherever a `String` object is required.

```
class String {
    // ...
  public:
    // ...
};

class Word : public String {
    // ...
  public:
    // ...
};
```

(a) Elided Class Definitions

String
Word

(b) Notational Representation

Figure 1-16: The IsA Relation

As we can see from the definitions of Figure 1-16a, class `Word` inherits from class `String`, and an arrow is used to denote this relationship in Figure 1-16b:

D —IsA→ *B*

That is, *D*——→*B* means that "*D* is a kind of *B*" and that "*D* inherits from *B*."

The direction of the arrow is significant; it points in the direction of implied dependency. Class `D` depends on `B` because `D` is derived from `B`. `B` must come first in order for `D` to name `B` as a base class:

```
class B { /* ... */ };
class D : public B { /* ... */ };
```

Often you will see the arrow pointed in the opposite direction, which can be misleading. An arrow shows an asymmetric relationship between two entities denoted by its label (in this case "IsA"). To draw the arrow the other way, we would logically have to call the relation something else, such as "Derives" or "Is-A-Base-Class-Of":

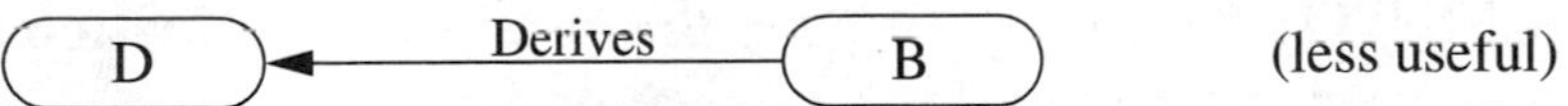

This alternative notation is less desirable because the arrow points in the direction opposite to that of implied dependency.

Because analyzing physical dependencies is essential to good design, we adopt the notation assuming the IsA label and point our arrows in the direction of implied dependency. Figure 1-17 provides one last illustration of inheritance notation using the classic shape example.

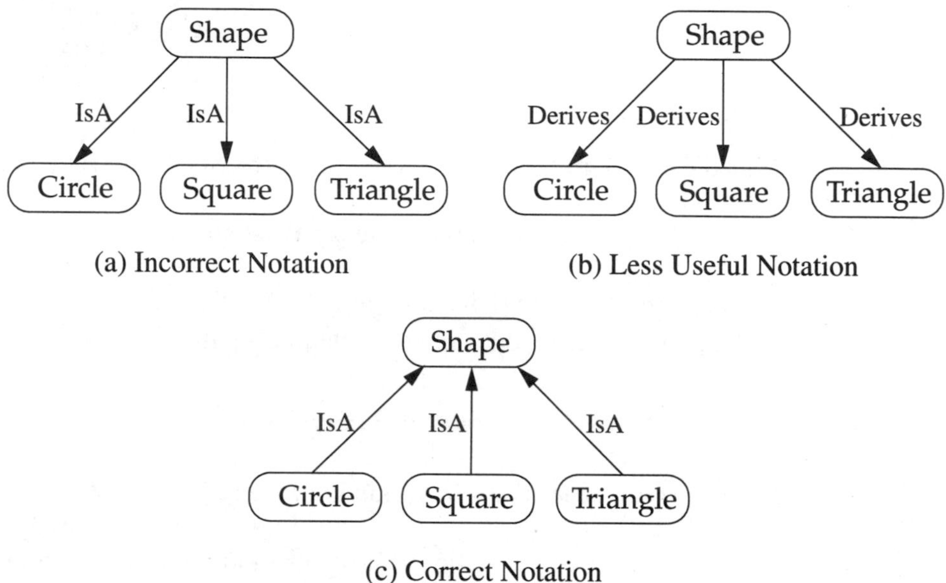

Figure 1-17: Notations Used to Indicate Derivation

1.6.2 The Uses-In-The-Interface Relation

Whenever a function names a type in its parameter list or names a type as a return value, that function is said to use that type in its interface. That is, a type is used in the interface of a function if the type name is part of the function's return type or signature.[14]

> **<u>DEFINITION</u>: A type is *used in the interface* of a function if the type is referred to when declaring that function.**

[14] Exclude the possible use of typedefs, which are just synonyms.

For example, the free function

```
int operator==(const IntSet&, const IntSet&);
```

clearly makes use of class `IntSet` in its interface. This function happens to return an `int`, so `int` also would be considered part of this function's interface. However, fundamental types are ubiquitous and omitted from such consideration in practice.

DEFINITION: A type is *used in the (public) interface* of a class if the type is used in the interface of the (public) member function of that class.

There are three levels of logical access for classes in C++: `public`, `protected`, and `private`. The *public interface* of a class is defined as the union of the interfaces of the public *member* functions of that class. The protected interface of a class is defined similarly. In other words, when a (`public`) member function of class `B` uses class `A` in its interface, we say that class `B` uses class `A` in `B`'s (`public`) interface.[15] For example, the constructor for class `IntSetIter`, `IntSetIter(const IntSet&)` uses class `IntSet` in its interface; therefore `IntSet` is used in the interface of `IntSetIter`.

The Uses-In-The-Interface relation is one of the most common and is denoted by

○ Uses-In-The-Interface

That is, *B*○——— *A* means "*B* uses *A* in *B*'s interface." We will sometimes be sloppy and say "*B* uses *A* in its interface," but we will always mean that *B* uses *A* in *B*'s interface, and never that *B* uses *A* in *A*'s interface.

You can think of the ○——— symbol as an arrow with its tail at the bubble and the head missing (or as a conductor's baton pointing at a member of the orchestra). The direction of the implied arrow is important—it points in the direction of *implied dependency*. That is, if *B* uses *A*, then *B* depends on *A* and not vice versa. (We will talk more about implied dependency in Section 3.4.)

---

[15] The interaction between friendship and the Uses-In-The-Interface relation is discussed in Section 3.6.1.

Figure 1-18 shows the logical view of the `intset` component, including the Uses-In-The-Interface relation among the logical entities (classes and free operator functions) defined there. The figure reflects that `IntSetIter` and both free operators use `IntSet` in their respective interfaces.

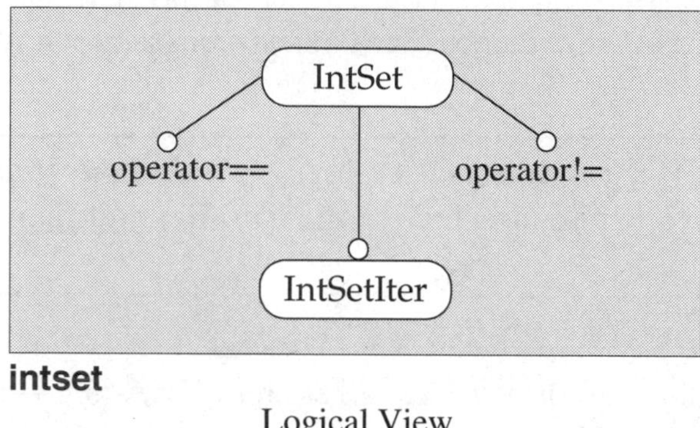

Logical View

Figure 1-18: The Uses-In-The-Interface Relation within the `intset` Component

The Uses-In-The-Interface relation is a valuable tool for both logical and physical design. This notation is most useful when confined to logical entities (classes and free operators) at file scope. Free operators are frequently omitted from logical diagrams in order to reduce notational clutter.

The actual logical interface for a class can be quite large and complex. Often the property we are most interested in exhibiting is one of intrinsic dependency rather than detailed usage. The set of types used in the interface of a class is more stable (i.e., less likely to change during development and maintenance) than the set of types used by any particular member function. The more abstract usage characteristics of the class taken as a whole are, therefore, more resilient to small changes in the logical interface than are the usage characteristics of its individual member functions.

1.6.3 The Uses-In-The-Implementation Relation

The Uses-In-The-Implementation relation augments a designer's ability to express logical dependencies abstractly. The notation that one logical entity will make use of another in its implementation (even though it is not used in its interface) can be very helpful in analyzing the underlying structure of a design. Like its counterpart, Uses-In-The-Implementation suggests a physical dependency between two logical entities.

Architects can make good use of this information as they refine high-level designs and cast them into discrete physical components.

> **<u>DEFINITION</u>: A type is *used in the implementation* of a function if the type is referred to in the definition of that function.**

Consider the following implementation of the free function `operator==`, which *assumes* that the members of equivalent `IntSet` objects are always returned by the iterator in the *same order*:

```
int operator==(const IntSet& left, const IntSet& right)
{
    IntSetIter lit(left);
    IntSetIter rit(right);
    for (; lit && rit; ++lit, ++rit) {
        if (lit() != rit()) {
            return 0;
        }
    }
    // At least one of lit and rit now evaluates to 0.
    return lit == rit;
}
```

In the above implementation, two iterators are created: one for each `IntSet` argument. The body of the `for` loop is entered only while both iterators refer to valid set elements. With each iteration through the loop, integers at corresponding positions in the sets are compared. If any such comparison fails, then the sets are immediately recognized as being not equal. On exit from the `for` loop, both of the following conditions must be true:

1. At least one of the iterators has reached the end of its set and is now invalid.

2. No corresponding entries of the set have been found to be unequal.

The two `IntSet` objects are equal if and only if both iterators are now invalid.

Note that `operator==(const IntSet&, const IntSet&)` is not a `friend` of class `IntSet`. Therefore any efficient implementation of this operator must take advantage of class `IntSetIter`. The Uses relationship between the implementation of `operator==` and class `IntSetIter` produces an implied dependency of `operator==` on class `IntSetIter`. Because IntSetIter is used in the implementation of this operator but not in its logical interface, we employ a slightly different symbol to denote the relationship:

●——— Uses-In-The-Implementation ———

That is, *B* ●——— *A* means that *A* is used in the implementation of *B*.

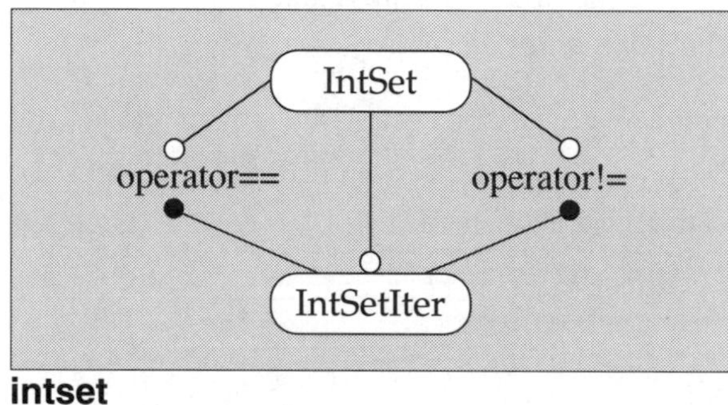

Logical View

Figure 1-19: Both Kinds of Uses Relations Within the `intset` Component

Figure 1-19 again shows us the logical view of the `intset` component along with both kinds of uses relationships. In particular we see that

```
int operator==(const IntSet&, const IntSet&)
```

uses class `IntSet` in its interface and class `IntSetIter` in its implementation. Although `operator!=` is shown implemented symmetrically to `operator==`, `operator!=` would probably be implemented in terms of `operator==` in practice.

If an object is used in the interface of a function, it is automatically considered to be used in the implementation of that function. We can therefore conclude from seeing the ●——— symbol that the indicated usage is *not* in the interface. For example, we can infer directly from Figure 1-19 that `operator!=` does *not* use `IntSetIter` in its interface.

<u>DEFINITION</u>: A type is *used in the implementation* of a class if that type (1) is used in a member function of the class, (2) is referred to in the declaration of a data member of the class, or (3) is a private base class of the class.

A class can use another type in its implementation in several ways. As we will see in Section 3.4, the particular way in which our class uses a type will affect not only how our class depends on that type but also to what extent clients of our class will be forced to depend on that type. For the time being, we simply exhibit the ways in which a class can use a type in its implementation:

<u>DEFINITION</u>:

Specific kinds of the Uses-In-The-Implementation Relationship:

Name	Meaning
Uses	**The class has a member function that names the type.**
HasA	**The class embeds an instance of the type.**
HoldsA	**The class embeds a pointer (or reference) to the type.**
WasA	**The class privately inherits from the type.**

1.6.3.1 Uses

If any member function of a class (including a private member) names a type in either its interface or its implementation, that type is considered to be used in the logical implementation of the class.

```
class Crook {
  private:
    void bribe();
    // ...
};

class Judge;

void Crook::bribe() {
    Judge *bad = 0;
    // ...
};
```

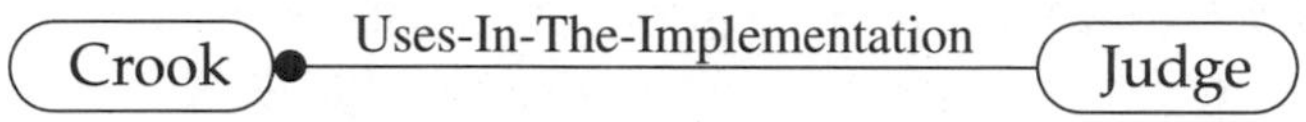

Figure 1-20: `Crook` **Uses** `Judge`

Figure 1-20 illustrates that since type `Judge` is named in the body of a member function (`bribe`) of class `Crook`, `Judge` is used in the implementation of `Crook`. In other words, class `Crook` ***uses*** `Judge`.

1.6.3.2 HasA and HoldsA

Another form of usage occurs when a class, `X`, embeds a (private) data member of type `T`. This kind of internal usage is commonly referred to as *HasA*. Even if class `X` contains a data member whose type is merely derived (in the C-language sense) from `T` (e.g., `T*` or `T&`), `T` is still considered to be used in the logical implementation of `X`. We will occasionally refer to this kind of internal usage as *HoldsA*.

```
class Tower { /* ... */ };
class Cannon;                     // declaration only

class BattleShip {
    Tower d_controlTower;
    Cannon *d_replaceableForwardBattery_p;
    Cannon& d_fixedAftBattery;
    // ...
};
```

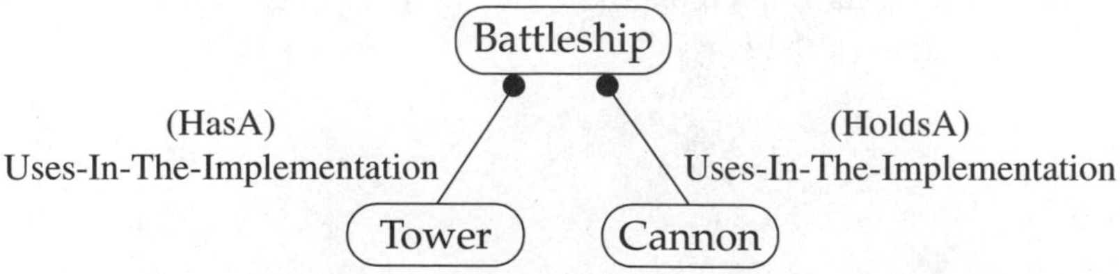

Figure 1-21: `Battleship` **HasA** `Tower` **and HoldsA** `Cannon`

Figure 1-21 shows a class definition for `Tower` and a class declaration for `Cannon`. Both of these types are used in the implementation of class `Battleship`. In particular, `Battleship` HasA `Tower` and `Battleship` HoldsA `Cannon`. We make no distinction in the symbolic notation we use: both HasA and HoldsA are indicated with the usual ●——— notation.

1.6.3.3 WasA

Inheriting privately from a type is yet another way to use that type in the logical implementation of a class. *Private inheritance* is an implementation detail of the derived class. From a logical point of view, a private base class (like a private data member) is invisible to clients. Private inheritance is a technique that can be used to propagate only a subset of the attributes of its base class. This seldom-used relation has been affectionately termed WasA, and is illustrated in Figure 1-22.

```
class Battleship { /* ... */ };
class Shop { /* ... */ };
class Exhibit;                        // declaration only

class ArizonaMemorial : private Battleship {
    Shop d_giftShop;
    Exhibit *d_current_p;
    Exhibit& d_default;
    // ...
};
```

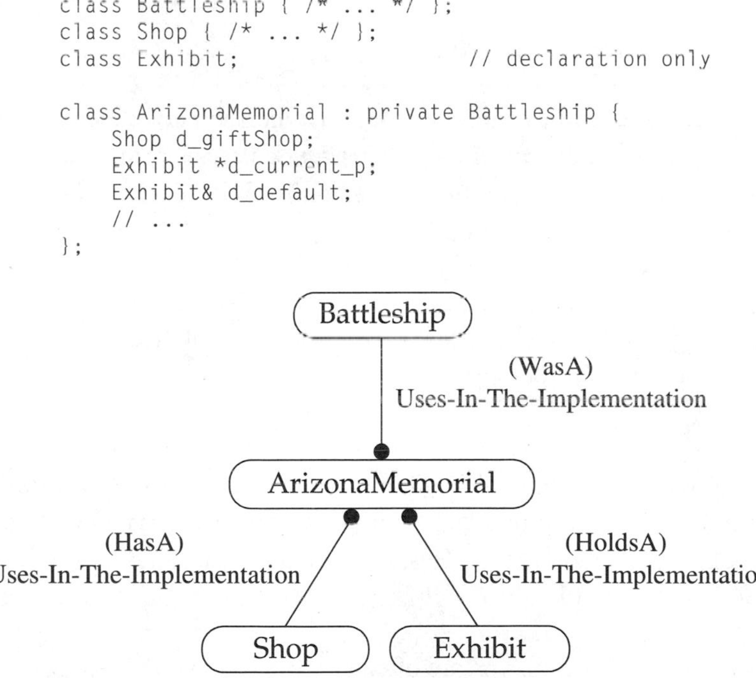

Figure 1-22: `ArizonaMemorial` **WasA** `Battleship`

Figure 1-22 shows a class definition for `Battleship` that acts as a private base class for `ArizonaMemorial`. Once in active service, the battleship *Arizona* was one of the casualties of the 1941 bombings of Pearl Harbor. The *Arizona* is now a museum with a gift shop and exhibits.

Although private inheritance is an implementation detail, public and protected inheritance are not. Inheritance increases the set of types that are compatible with the base type. Nonprivate inheritance therefore introduces information that is programmatically accessible by clients. The unique properties of public and protected inheritance make them worthy of their own notation, as presented in Section 1.6.1.

We have now reviewed all of the logical notation we need to get down to the serious business of physical design. The logical and physical aspects of design are tightly coupled. Each of the logical relations—IsA, Uses-In-The-Interface, and Uses-In-The-Implementation—implies a physical dependency between logical entities. As we will see in Chapter 3, it is ultimately these logical relations that dictate the physical interdependencies within our system.

1.7 Inheritance versus Layering

In the context of object-oriented design, when someone mentions the word *hierarchy*, many people think *inheritance*. *Inheritance* is one form of logical hierarchy—*layering* is another. By far, the more common form of logical hierarchy in object-oriented design results from layering.

DEFINITION: A class is *layered* on a type if the class uses that type substantively in its implementation.

Layering is the process of building on smaller, simpler, or more primitive types to form larger, more complex, or more sophisticated types. Often layering occurs through composition (e.g., HasA or HoldsA), but any form of substantive use (i.e., any use that would induce a physical dependency) qualifies as layering.

Instances of a layered type are often not programmatically accessible to clients via the interface of the higher-level object. The connotation is that the primitive type is at a lower level of abstraction. For example, a person has a heart, a brain, a liver, and so on, yet these layered organ objects are not part of the public interface of most healthy people. An object as simple as a list is often implemented as a collection of links, yet the `Link` class itself is not used in the interface of most well-written `List` classes.

Inheritance, along with dynamic binding, distinguishes object-oriented languages (such as C++) from object-based languages (such as Ada) that support user-defined types and layering but not inheritance.[16] The semantics of inheritance are quite different from those of layering. For example, the public functionality of both base and derived classes is accessible by clients.[17] With inheritance, the more specialized or concrete class depends on the more general or abstract class(es). With layering, the class at a higher level of abstraction depends on the class(es) at a lower level of abstraction.

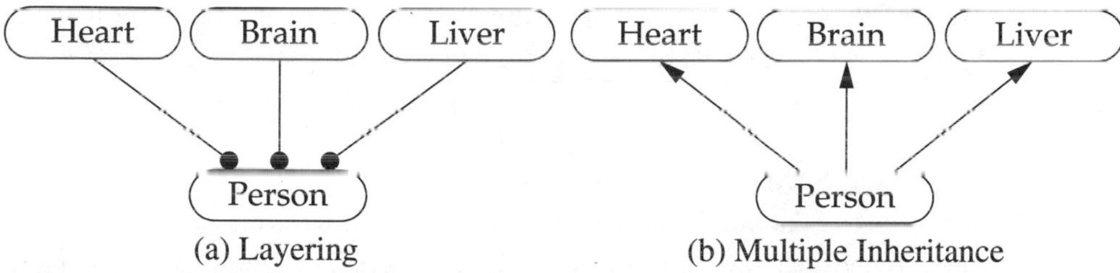

Figure 1-23: Layering versus Multiple Inheritance

Layering is an important and often underdeployed weapon in the arsenal of the object-oriented designer. It is not uncommon for novice programmers to attempt to use inheritance where layering is indicated. Figure 1-23 shows two examples of logical hierarchy. In both cases, `Person` implicitly depends on `Heart`, `Brain`, and `Liver` in order to do its job. Layering is clearly the correct approach here because a `Person` is not a `Heart`, a `Brain`, or a `Liver`. Instead, a `Person` *has* a `Heart`, a `Brain`, and a `Liver`. Furthermore, these organs must not be exposed in the interface of a `Person`. With layering, a client need not be subjected to the interfaces of these internal details.

1.8 Minimality

Some class authors want their classes to be all things to all people. Such classes have been referred to, affectionately, as Winnebago classes. This very common and seemingly noble desire is cause for concern. As developers, we must remember that

[16] See **booch**, Chapter 2, p. 39.

[17] Note: private inheritance is a form of layering.

just because a client asks for an enhancement doesn't mean that it is appropriate for our class. Suppose you are the author of a class and each of 10 clients asks you for a different enhancement. If you agree, two things will happen:

1. You will have to implement, test, and document 10 new features that you did not originally consider part of the abstraction that you were trying to implement (which in itself is a symptom of a problem).

2. Each of your 10 clients will be given 9 new features that they did not ask for and probably don't need or want.

Every time you add a feature to please one person, you disrupt and potentially annoy the rest of your client base. It has happened that classes that were originally lightweight and very useful have, over time, become so bloated that instead of being good for everything, they have become, quite literally, good for nothing.

Notice that in Section 1.5 we chose to disallow explicitly the possibility of initialization or assignment for instances of both `IntSet` and `IntSetIter` by declaring the respective member functions private. Making a copy of a collection can result in nontrivial development effort, and such functionality for iterators is rarely needed in practice. We can defer the implementation and testing of superfluous functionality unless or until a need for that functionality presents itself. Deferring implementation is also one way to keep our options open. Not only does it require less work to implement, test, document, and maintain software, but by deliberately not supplying functionality prematurely, we commit to neither its behavior nor its implementation. In fact, not implementing functionality can improve usability. For example, making the copy constructor private prevents inadvertently passing an object by value—a technique used in the iostream package.[18]

This minimalist approach of making components sufficient but not necessarily complete applies to large projects under development where the users of the component are "in-house" or in a position to request and receive additional functionality quickly should it turn out to be needed. The most extreme case occurs where the component is highly specialized and the author is the only intended user. In that case, implementing any unneeded functionality is probably unwarranted. Of course, omitting the imple-

---

[18] Passing user-defined types by value is a common cause of unnecessary performance degradation (see Section 9.1.11).

mentation of functionality intrinsic to an abstraction would not make sense for, say, a commercial component library where the users are paying customers and will expect robust and fully functional objects. This issue is not black and white; between the two extremes lies a spectrum that corresponds to how widely a component will be used. In evaluating the trade-offs, remember to consider that functionality is invariably easier to add than to remove.

1.9 Summary

Large C++ programs reside in more than a single source file. Partitioning programs into separate translation units makes recompilation more efficient and reuse possible.

Although most C++ *declarations* can be repeated in a given scope, there must be exactly one *definition* of every object, function, or class used in a C++ program.

Definitions with internal linkage are confined to a single translation unit and cannot affect other translation units unless placed in a header file. Such definitions can exist at file scope in `.c` files without affecting the global (symbol) name space.

Definitions with external linkage can be used to resolve undefined symbols in other translation units at link time. Placing such definitions in header files is almost certainly a programming error.

Typedef declarations are only aliases for types and provide no additional compile-time type safety.

Assert statements can be used effectively to detect coding errors during development without affecting program size or runtime performance in the production version of a product.

In this book we adopt the following style conventions:

- Type identifier names begin with an uppercase letter.
- Functions and data begin with a lowercase letter.
- Multi-word identifier names capitalize the first letter of the second and subsequent words.

- Constants and macros are all uppercase (with words separated by a single underscore).

- Class data members are prefixed by `d_` (or `s_` for static members).

- Class member function will be organized according to creator, manipulator, and accessor categories.

- Private details will precede the public interface in class definitions (primarily to emphasize their presence in the header file).

The iterator design pattern is used to sequence over the parts, attributes, or sub-objects of some primary object. An iterator is declared to be a `friend` of the primary object, and its definition should reside in the same header file as that object. The iterator notation used in this book tersely conforms to a `for`-loop model.

Object-oriented design lends itself to a rich set of logical notations. In this text, however, we will limit ourselves to three:

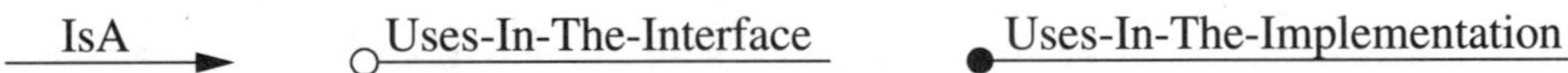

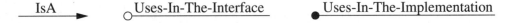

The orientation of each symbol (shown here from left to right) should be consistent with its label and point in the direction of implied dependency. There are a few special names for some particular kinds of Uses-In-The-Implementation (Uses, HasA, HoldsA, and WasA); however, the notation used to represent each of these variations is the same.

Inheritance and layering are two forms of logical hierarchy. Layering is by far the more common, often involving an implementation-only dependency. Layering, specifically composition, is preferable to derivation when the class in question cannot sensibly be thought of as a kind of the proposed base class(es). Finally, extending the functionality of a single class in response to several clients often results in a class that is overweight and undesirable. For classes that are not widely used, implementing excessively complete functionality can unnecessarily increase development time, maintenance cost, and code size. Deferring the implementation of functionality that is not yet needed reduces development time while keeping options open. On the other hand, commercial component libraries are expected to be fully functional and robust.

2

Ground Rules

This chapter describes a modest collection of fundamental design rules that have proved useful in practice and that serve as framework for discussing the material surrounding more advanced rules presented later in this book. These fundamental rules address basic practices such as restricting member data access and reducing the number of identifiers in the global name space. In particular, we examine what types of constructs can safely be placed at file scope in a header file. The need for both internal and redundant external include guards will be established. This chapter concludes with a discussion of what constitutes adequate documentation (such as explicitly identifying behavior that is undefined), followed by a short list of identifier-naming conventions.

2.1 Overview

The beauty of any fine art comes not only from creativity but also from discipline. So it is with programming. C++ is a large language, and there is ample room to be creative with it. However, the design space is so big that without discipline—that is, without some modest constraints on the design structure—large projects can easily become intractable and unmaintainable. These constraints are presented in the form of design rules, guidelines, and principles.

Design Rules: Experience tells us that certain coding practices that are perfectly legal in C++ simply should never be used in a large-project environment. Recommendations that flatly proscribe or require a given practice without exception are referred to in this book as *design rules*. Verifying adherence to these rules cannot be a subjective process. Design rules must be sufficiently precise, specific, and well defined so that complying with these rules can be verified objectively. To be effective, design rules must lend themselves to impersonal, mechanical verification via automated tools.

Guidelines: Experience also tells us that certain other practices should be avoided wherever possible. Suggested practices of a more abstract nature for which exceptions are sometimes legitimately made are called *guidelines*. Guidelines are like rules of thumb to be followed unless other, more compelling, engineering reasons dictate otherwise.

Principles: There are certain observations and truths that have often proved useful during the design process but must be evaluated in the context of a specific design. These are referred to as *principles*.

Gaining consensus on software coding standards among independent programmers can be quite challenging. Every programmer has his or her own extended set of conventions. I impose many more rules on myself than I could possibly share with you, but they mostly involve style, not substance. If we can agree on the 10 percent of the rules that buy us 90 percent of the real benefit, we will be doing very well indeed.

This book contains many recommendations. In this chapter I present a set of very basic design rules that I call *ground rules*, explaining and (I hope) justifying each rule as I go. You may not agree with all of them at first, but over time they have proved both workable and effective for very large projects.

I have subdivided design rules into two distinct categories: *major* and *minor. Major design rules* refer to practices that must always be followed. Deviating from a major design rule is likely to affect the quality not only of the offending component, but also of other components within the system. Even infrequent violations could undermine the success of a large project. Throughout this book, I have assumed that major design rules are never violated. As always, *never* never means *NEVER*. If extraordinary circumstances and common sense dictate that one or more major design rules be violated, it is incumbent upon developers to fully understand and appreciate the implications and possible consequences of their actions. *Minor design rules* refer to practices that are strongly recommended but not necessarily critical to a project's overall success—for example, issues involving constructs that are used only in the implementation, are unlikely to affect other developers, and are otherwise relatively contained and easy to fix in isolated instances. Draconian adherence to minor design rules is not critical because (unlike adherence to major rules) the cost of a project increases only *incrementally* with each minor rule violation.

Because it is not expected that there will ever be an engineering reason to violate any design rule (major or minor), any design rule that proscribes one approach must offer a suitable alternative that will work in all cases.

2.2 Member Data Access

Encapsulation is a term used to describe the concept of hiding implementation details behind a procedural interface. Comparable terms include *information hiding* or *data hiding*. Directly accessing a data member of a class violates encapsulation.

Major Design Rule

Keep class data members private.

Consider the definition of class `Rectangle` in Figure 2-1. This `Rectangle` is defined by providing two `Point` objects (see Figure 1-1) that identify its lower-left and upper-right corners. Since this particular implementation of `Rectangle` stores these `Point` values internally, we might be tempted to make the data members public to avoid supplying manipulator (i.e., `set`) and accessor (i.e., `get`) functions for each.

```
// rectangle.h
#ifndef INCLUDED_RECTANGLE
#define INCLUDED_RECTANGLE

class Rectangle {
  public:
    Point d_lowerLeft;     // bad idea (public data)
    Point d_upperRight;    // bad idea (public data)

  public:
    // CREATORS
    Rectangle(const Point& lowerLeft, const Point& upperRight);
    Rectangle(const Rectangle& rect);
    ~Rectangle();

    // MANIPULATORS
    Rectangle& operator=(const Rectangle& rect);
    void moveBy(const Point& delta);
    // ...
```

```
    // ACCESSORS
    int area() const;
    // ...
};

// ...

inline
void Rectangle::moveBy(const Point& delta)
{
    d_lowerLeft += delta;
    d_upperRight += delta;
}

// ...

#endif
```

Figure 2-1: Poor (Unencapsulating) `Rectangle` Class Interface

Now consider the impact on clients when we discover that `Rectangle` objects are frequently moved. To improve performance, we might try changing the representation of `Rectangle` objects. For example, instead of storing the absolute location of the upper-right corner, we might represent that value implicitly by storing its position relative to the lower-left corner:

```
class Rectangle {
  public:
    Point d_lowerLeft;                    // same purpose as in Figure 2-1
    Point d_upperRightOffset              // new "relative" representation
```

With this new representation, the `moveBy` member function can be implemented in one line instead of two because the relative position of the upper-right corner with respect to the lower-left is not affected by the move:

```
inline
Rectangle::moveBy(const Point& delta)
{
    d_lowerLeft += delta;
}
```

The location of the upper-right corner is no longer stored in the `Rectangle` object and therefore must be calculated when needed:

```
void client(const Rectangle& rect)
{
    Point upperRight = rect.d_lowerLeft + rect.d_upperRightOffset;
    // ...
}
```

Any clients who previously accessed the `d_upperRight` data member directly will now be forced to rework their code. Component reuse compounds this problem. If a class defining public data is shared among executables, then changing the data representation of a single class could necessitate modifying the source code for any number of separate programs.

DEFINITION: A contained implementation detail (type, data, or function) that is not accessible or detectable programmatically through the logical interface of a class is said to be *encapsulated* by that class.

Encapsulation is an important tool of object-oriented design.[1] By encapsulation we mean that a collection of low-level information is brought together, potentially to interact in a tightly coupled, intimate way. Information hiding is then applied to limit the external world from interacting with details that are not germane to the abstraction the class is supposed to help implement.

Keeping all data members private and providing the appropriate accessor and manipulator functions, as shown in Figure 2-2, leaves us free to change the internal representation without forcing our clients to rework their code. The implementation of `getUpperRight()` could have been modified to compute that value on demand without changing its logical interface.

Besides maintainability, there are reasons not to have public data members. For example, the values of data members in a class are rarely independent. Direct (writable) access to data (such as `d_area` in Figure 2-2) could easily leave an object in an inconsistent state. Providing only a functional interface grants class authors the level of control necessary to ensure the integrity of their objects. Providing manipulator and accessor functions also affords developers the opportunity to insert temporary code (e.g., print statements for debugging, reference counts for performance tuning, and assert statements for reliability).[2]

---

[1] **booch**, Chapter 2, pp. 49–54.

[2] For a further discussion of why to avoid public data, see **meyers**, Item 20, pp. 71–72.

```
// rectangle.h
#ifndef INCLUDED_RECTANGLE
#define INCLUDED_RECTANGLE

class Rectangle {
    Point d_lowerLeft;     // Yet another representation!
    int d_width;           // Fortunately, these data members are private.
    int d_height;
    int d_area;            // Store this redundantly to improve performance.

  public:
    // CREATORS
    Rectangle(const Point& lowerLeft, const Point& upperRight);
    Rectangle(const Rectangle& rect);
    ~Rectangle();

    // MANIPULATORS
    Rectangle& operator=(const Rectangle& rect);
    void moveBy(const Point& delta);
    // ...

    // ACCESSORS
    int area() const;
    Point getLowerLeft() const;
    Point getUpperRight() const;
};

// ...

inline
void Rectangle::moveBy(const Point& delta)
{
    d_lowerLeft += delta;
}

// ...

inline
Point Rectangle::getUpperRight(const Point& delta) const
{
    return d_lowerLeft + Point(d_width, d_height);
}

// ...
```

Figure 2-2: Better (Encapsulating) `Rectangle` **Class Interface**

Note that public access to data members of a `struct` (or class) that itself is entirely hidden (either privately within another class or locally within a `.c` file) is a separate matter not covered by the above rule (see Sections 6.4.2 and 8.4). When data members are not private, it is preferable to denote the deliberate lack of encapsulation by using the keyword `struct` instead of `class`.

Some people advocate the use of protected data to facilitate arbitrary access from a derived class. But from a maintainability perspective, `protected` access is like `public` access because anyone who wants to get at protected data can do so with only the modest additional effort of deriving a class. Unlike friendship, which explicitly denotes who has access to private details, making class data protected results in an unbounded breach of encapsulation.

The same arguments that applied to the public interface also apply to the protected interface. Base-class authors can preserve maintainability by treating their protected and public interfaces as separate but equally important. Keeping all member data private and supplying the appropriate protected functions will enable the base-class implementation to change independently of any derived classes.

2.3 The Global Name Space

For projects of even moderate size involving more than a single developer, there is a danger of name collisions when independently developed parts are integrated into a single program. The severity of the problem grows exponentially with system size, and is exacerbated when the collisions result from integrating software provided by third-party vendors.

There are various ways to pollute the global name space, some more onerous than others. All of them are counterproductive in a large system environment. We now address several of these issues independently and conclude this section with a design rule that describes what kinds of declarations and definitions may exist safely at file scope in C++ header files.

2.3.1 Global Data

It has been said that global variables are like a cancer: you can't live with them, but once established, they are often impossible to cut out. We can always get away without using external global variables in a new C++ project. Exceptions to this rule might involve access in a baroque program (such as Lex or YACC) that communicates via global variables or perhaps within embedded systems.

Major Design Rule

Avoid data with external linkage at file scope.

File scope data with external linkage risks collision with global names in other translation units (whose authors were egocentric enough to believe that they, too, owned the global scope). But name pollution is only one of the many ways in which global variables damage a program. Global variables tie objects and code together in ways that make it virtually impossible to reuse translation units selectively in other programs. Debugging, testing, and even understanding systems that make liberal use of global variables can become overwhelmingly costly in large projects.

Provided that you are not forced to use a system that already requires using global variables in its interface, there are a couple of simple transformations that can unglobalize these variables:

1. Put all global variables in a structure.

2. Then make them private and add static access functions.

Suppose you had the following global variables:

```
int size;
double scale;
const char *system;
```

These variables can be removed from the global name space by enclosing them in a `struct` and making them `static` members of that structure:[3]

```
struct Global {
    static int s_size;               // bad idea (public data)
    static double s_scale;           // bad idea (public data)
    static const char *s_system;     // bad idea (public data)
};
```

[3] **meyers**, Item 28, pp. 93–95.

Remember, of course, to define these static data members in the corresponding `.c` file. Now, instead of accessing the global variables using

`size`, `scale`, or `system`

you would use

`Global::s_size`, `Global::s_scale`, or `Global::s_system`

respectively. The probability of collisions is now reduced to the probability of colliding with a single class name (and it is easy to address even that possibility using the techniques discussed in Section 7.2).

Although we have solved the global name space problem, we have not done all that we should. Experience shows that just as with non-static (i.e., instance-specific) member data, directly accessing static (i.e., class-specific) member data makes large systems profoundly more expensive to maintain. If we were to change the exported data type of a member (e.g., `s_size`) from `int` to `double`, that would be an interface change; all clients would be affected regardless of what we do. But we may decide to change the implementation of `s_size` to a computed value based on other, more primitive values (such as `s_width` and `s_height`). Providing static function members to access (and manipulate) static data members allows us to make such local changes without perturbing clients of the global scope.

The next step is to eliminate the public data by making `Global` a class and providing static manipulator and accessor methods, as illustrated in Figure 2-3. Class `Global` now acts as a logical module accessible from anywhere in the program. Because all the interface functions are static, there is no need to instantiate an object in order to use this class. Declaring the default constructor private and leaving it unimplemented enforces this usage model.

To achieve a flexible design, we should be careful not to overuse global state information. The mere fact that we expect to have only a single instance of an object is not sufficient reason to make it a module instead of an instantiatable class. Globally accessible modules make sense when they correspond to inherently unique entities (such as a system console) or for system-wide constants (such as those found in `limits.h`) that are not dictated by a particular application (see Section 6.2.9). Global modules are best avoided when other, more localized (e.g., object-based) implementation will suffice.[4]

```
class Global {
    static int s_size;
    static double s_scale;
    static const char *s_system;

  private:
    // NOT IMPLEMENTED
    Global(); // prevent inadvertent instantiation

  public:
    // MANIPULATORS
    static void setSize(int size) { s_size = size; }
    static void setScale(double scale) { s_scale = scale; }
    static void setSystem(const char *system) { s_system = system; }

    // ACCESSORS
    static int getSize() { return s_size; }
    static double getScale() { return s_scale; }
    static const char *getSystem() { return s_system; }
};
```

Figure 2-3: Logical Module Containing Global State Information

2.3.2 Free Functions

Free functions, too, can be a threat to the global name space, especially when they do not involve any user-defined type in their argument signature. If a free function is defined with internal linkage in a `.h` file or with external linkage in a `.c` file, it may collide with another function definition with the same name (and signature) during program integration. Operator functions are an exception.

Major Design Rule

Avoid free functions (except operator functions) at file scope in `.h` files; avoid free functions with external linkage (including operator functions) in `.c` files.

---

[4] See the Singleton design pattern in **gamma**, Chapter 3, , pp. 127–134.

Fortunately, free functions can always be grouped into a utility class (`struct`) containing only static functions. The resulting cohesion is not necessarily optimal, but it does reduce the likelihood of global name collisions. Here's an example:

```
int getMonitorResolution();                                   // bad idea
void setSystemScale(double scaleFactor);                      // bad idea
int isPasswordCorrect(const char *usr, const char *psw);      // bad idea
```

The above free functions could always be replaced by the following static methods:

```
struct SysUtil {
    static int getMonitorResolution();
    static void setSystemScale(double scaleFactor);
    static int isPasswordCorrect(const char *usr, const char *psw);
};
```

The only symbol at risk would be the class name `SysUtil`.

Unfortunately, free operator functions cannot be nested inside classes. This is not a serious problem because free operators require at least one of their arguments to be a user-defined type. Hence the likelihood of free operators colliding is remote, and such collisions are typically not a problem in practice.

2.3.3 Enumerations, Typedefs, and Constant Data

Enumerations, typedefs, and (by default) file scope const data all have internal linkage. People often declare constants, enumerations, or typedefs at file scope in header files. This is a mistake.

Major Design Rule

Avoid enumerations, typedefs, and constants at file scope in `.h` files.

Because C++ fully supports nested types, enumerations can be defined (and typedefs declared) within the scope of a class without conflicting with other names in the global name space. By choosing a more limited scope in which to define an enumeration, you ensure that all enumerators of that enumeration become similarly scoped and thus will not conflict with other names defined outside that scope.

Consider the following enumerations:

```
// paint.h
enum Color { RED, GREEN, BLUE, ORANGE, YELLOW };      // bad idea

// juice.h
enum Fruit { APPLE, ORANGE, GRAPE, CRANBERRY };       // bad idea
```

These two enumerations were probably not written by the same developer, yet it is quite possible that they could someday be included in the same file, resulting in an ambiguity, `ORANGE`, that cannot be resolved!

```
// picture.c
#include "picture.h"
#include "paint.h"
#include "juice.h"
```

If these two enumerations are instead defined within separate classes, one can easily use scope resolution to resolve the ambiguity: `Paint::Orange` or `Juice::Orange`.

For similar reasons, typedefs and constant data should also be placed within class scope in header files. Most constant data is integral, and nested enumerations work well to provide integral constants within the scope of a class. Other constant types (e.g., `double`, `String`) must be made static members of the class and initialized within the `.c` file:

```
// array.h
#ifndef INCLUDED_ARRAY
#define INCLUDED_ARRAY

class String;

class Array {
    enum { DEFAULT_SIZE = 100 };
    static const double DEFAULT_VALUE;
    static const String DEFAULT_NAME;

    // ...
};

#endif
```

```
// array.c
#include "array.h"


#include "str.h" // class String



double Array::DEFAULT_VALUE = 0.0;
String Array::DEFAULT_NAME = "";

// ...
```

In large projects, aside from the global name collisions, there is a very real problem with even finding enumerations, typedefs, and constants at file scope. Nesting a typedef within a class forces the name to be fully qualified (or the declaration to be inherited), making it relatively easy to find. The same reasoning applies to enumerations, but even stronger arguments for nesting enumerations within classes have already been presented.

2.3.4 Preprocessor Macros

There is almost no need for macros in C++. They are useful for include guards (see Section 2.4), and in a very few cases their benefits outweigh their problems in a `.c` file (most notably, when used to achieve conditional compilation for portability or debugging). But in general, preprocessor macros are inappropriate for production software.

Major Design Rule

Avoid using preprocessor macros in header files except as include guards.

The preprocessor is not part of the C++ language; its basis is completely textual, making macros painfully hard to debug. Although macros can make code easier to write, their free form often makes code much harder to read and understand. Consider the following code fragment:

```
#define glue(X,Y) X/**/Y
glue(pri,ntf) ("Hello World");
```

How would you tell your debugger, browser, or other automated tool to deal with the above at the source level?

As bad as macros are in `.c` files, there are even stronger software engineering reasons for keeping macros out of header files. Take the case of defining a preprocessor constant using `#define` in a header file. Since macros are not part of C++, they cannot be placed inside the scope of a class. Any file that includes a header file with a `#define` will take on that definition.

Suppose `theircode.h` defines a constant value `GOOD` as a preprocessor constant:

```
// theircode.h
#ifndef INCLUDED_THEIRCODE
#define INCLUDED_THEIRCODE

// ...

#define GOOD 0   // bad idea

// ...

#endif
```

```
// ourcode.c
#include "ourcode.h"
#include "theircode.h"

// ...

int OurClass::aFunction()
{
    enum { BAD = -1, GOOD = 0 } status = GOOD;

    // ...

    return status;
};

 // ...
```

When file `ourcode.c` is compiled, the compiler first calls the preprocessor. Even though `GOOD` is defined within the protective scope of a function, it is not safe from the preprocessor, which mercilessly replaces the enumerator `GOOD` with the literal integer `0`:

```
// ...

int OurClass::aFunction
{
    enum { BAD = -1, 0 = 0 } status = 0;

    // ...

    return status;
};
```

When the compiler encounters the enumeration, it spits out `Syntax Error`, but you won't know why until you have spent an eternity "grepping" through `.h` files looking to see who has `#define`'d one of your enumerators. Notice that this problem would not have occurred if the preprocessor symbol had instead been either a `const` or an `enum` at file scope (which, by the way, are also design-rule violations according to Section 2.3.3):

```
// theircode.h
#ifndef INCLUDED_THEIRCODE
#define INCLUDED_THEIRCODE

// ...

const int GOOD = 100;    // bad idea
    // file-scope constant data

// ...

#endif
```

```
// theircode.h
#ifndef INCLUDED_THEIRCODE
#define INCLUDED_THEIRCODE

// ...

enum { GOOD = 100 };   // bad idea
    // file-scope enumerated value

// ...

#endif
```

Preprocessor macros can also be used to implement templates in cases where that C++ language feature is missing or inadequately implemented. If macros are used for this purpose, then macro functions will appear in header files. There are ways to approach this problem, other than resorting to macros, that may be better suited for large projects. In any event, template-related issues should be addressed early in the development process.

2.3.5 Names in Header Files

A name declared at file scope in a header file has the potential to collide with any file-scope name in any file in the entire system. Even names with internal linkage declared at file scope in a `.c` file are not safe from file-scope names in a `.h` file.

Major Design Rule

Only classes, structures, unions, and free operator functions should be *declared* at file scope in a `.h` file; only classes, structures, unions, and inline (member or free operator) functions should be *defined* at file scope in a `.h` file.

The only things we expect to find at file scope in a header file are class declarations, class definitions, free operator declarations, and inline function definitions. Nesting all other constructs within class scope eliminates most of the trouble associated with name collisions.

To help illustrate this rule, an otherwise meaningless header file containing several constructs is provided with commentary in Figure 2-4. Note that a static instance of user-defined type is a special case, which is discussed in Section 7.8.1.3. For now, avoidance of these static user-defined objects in `.h` files may be treated as a guideline and not a rule.

```
// driver.h                                 // fine: comment
#ifndef INCLUDED_DRIVER                     // fine: internal include guard
#define INCLUDED_DRIVER                     // fine: (see Section 2.4)

#ifndef INCLUDED_NIFTY                      // fine: redundant include guard
#include "nifty.h"                          // fine: CPP include directive
#endif                                      // fine: (see Section 2.5)

#define PI 3.14159265358                    // AVOID: macro constant
#define MIN(X) ((X)<(Y)?(X):(Y))            // AVOID: macro function

class ostream;                              // fine: class declaration
struct DriverInit;                          // fine: class declaration
union Uaw;                                  // fine: class declaration

extern int globalVariable;                  // AVOID: external data declaration
static int fileScopeVariable;               // AVOID: internal data definition
const int BUFFER_SIZE = 256;                // AVOID: const data definition
enum Boolean { ZERO, ONE };                 // AVOID: enumeration at file scope
typedef long BigInt;                        // AVOID: typedef at file scope

class Driver {
    enum Color { RED, GREEN };              // fine: enumeration in class scope
    typedef int (Driver::*PMF)();           // fine: typedef in class scope
    static int s_count;                     // fine: static member declaration
    int d_size;                             // fine: member data definition

  private:
    struct Pnt {
        short int d_x, d_y;
        Pnt(int x, int y)
        : d_x(x), d_y(y) {}
    };                                      // fine: private struct definition
    friend DriverInit;                      // fine: friend declaration
```

```
  public:
    int static round(double d);          // fine: static member
                                          //       function declaration
    void setSize(int size);              // fine: member function declaration
    int cmp(const Driver&) const;        // fine: const member
                                          //       function declaration
};                                        // fine: class definition

static class DriverInit {
    // ...
} driverInit;                             // special case (see Section 7.8.1.3)

int min(int x, int y);                    // AVOID: free function declaration

inline
int max(int x, int y)
{
    return x > y ? x : y;
}                                         // AVOID: free inline
                                          //        function definition

inline
void Driver::setSize(int size)
{
    d_size = size;
}                                         // fine: inline member
                                          //       function definition


ostream& operator<<(ostream& o,
                    const Driver& d);     // fine: free operator
                                          //       function declaration


inline
int operator==(const Driver& lhs,
               const Driver& rhs)
{
    return compare(lhs, rhs) == 0;
}                                         // fine: free inline operator
                                          //       function definition

inline
int Driver::round(double d)
{
    return d < 0 ? -int(0.5 - d)
                 : int(0.5 + d);
}                                         // fine: inline static member
                                          //       member function definition

#endif                                    // fine: end of internal include guard
```

Figure 2-4: Various Constructs at File Scope in a Header File

2.4 Include Guards

If we follow the above recommendation that only class, struct, union, and inline function definitions appear at file scope in header files, we will still have a problem if the same header file gets included twice in a single translation unit. This problem could occur with the simple include graph shown in Figure 2-5.

When component `c.`'s .c file is compiled, the preprocessor first includes the corresponding header file, `c.h`, which in turn includes the contents of `a.h`. Next `c.h` includes file `b.h`, triggering a second inclusion of `a.h`. If `a.h` has any definitions at all (and in C++ it almost surely does) the compiler will complain about multiple definitions.

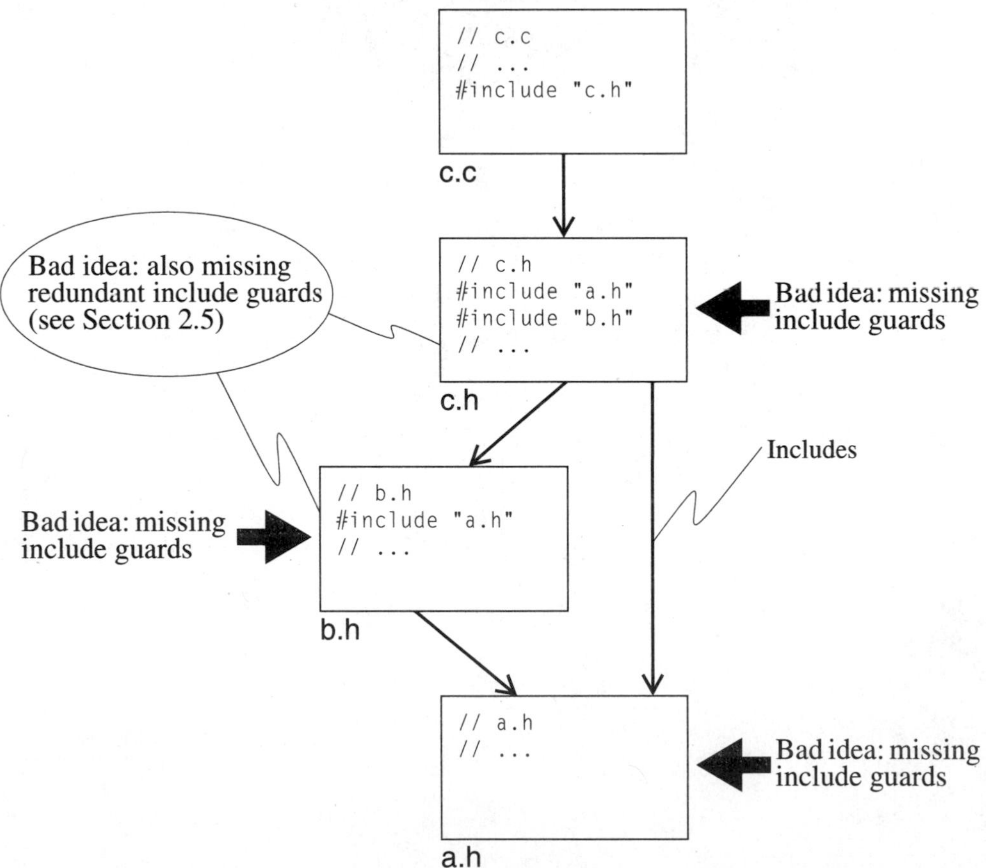

Figure 2-5: Reconvergent Include Graph Causing Compile-Time Error

Major Design Rule

Place a unique and predictable (internal) include guard around the contents of each header file.

The time-honored, traditional way of solving this problem is to require an internal protective wrapper around the contents of each header file. This wrapper ensures that class and inline function definitions are seen only once in a given translation unit regardless of the include graph. Note that we are not trying to stop cyclic inclusion (which is probably a design error); we are trying to stop any repeated inclusion that might come from reconvergence in an *acyclic* include graph. A solution to the compiling problem in the previous example is shown in Figure 2-6. Note that we are still missing redundant (external) include guards (discussed in Section 2.5).

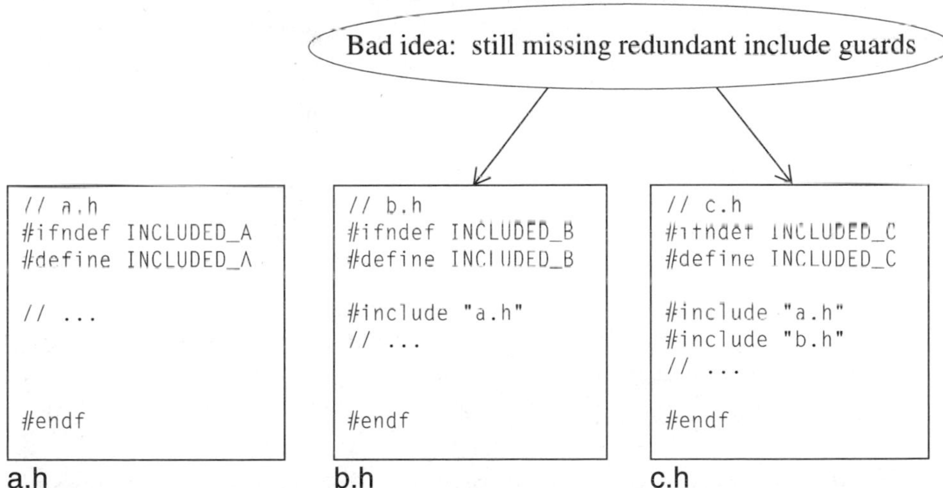

Figure 2-6: Accommodating Repeated Inclusion Using Include Guards

For example, when `a.h` is included in a translation unit, the preprocessor will first check to see if the preprocessor symbol `INCLUDED_A` is defined. If not, the guard symbol `INCLUDED_A` will be defined once and for all (for this translation unit), and then preprocessing will proceed by reading the definitions contained within the rest of the header file. The second (and any subsequent) time this header file is included, the contents inside the preprocessor `#ifndef` conditional (i.e., the rest of the file) will be ignored.

The actual symbol used for the include guard is not important so long as it does not match any other symbol in the entire system. Since the include guard is tied to a given header file, and that header file name must be unique in the system, incorporating that name in the guard symbol can ensure that no two guard symbols are the same.

The preprocessor knows nothing of C++ scoping rules. We must therefore ensure that the include guard symbols do not match any other symbols at all—even those within functions defined in a `.c` file.

Adopting a standard naming convention of prefixing the root name of the header file in upper case (e.g., `STACK`) with a globally reserved prefix (e.g., `INCLUDED_`) ensures unique and predictable guard names:

```
// stack.h
#ifndef INCLUDED_STACK
#define INCLUDED_STACK
// ...
#endif
```

```
// iccad_transistor.h
#ifndef INCLUDED_ICCAD_TRANSISTOR
#define INCLUDED_ICCAD_TRANSISTOR
// ...
#endif
```

The need for predictability will be made clear in Section 2.5.

2.5 Redundant Include Guards

Practical isn't always pretty, and this is one of those cases. Theoretically, unique internal include guards are sufficient. With large projects, however, it can be very costly not to consider a bit further.

A well-designed system consists of layers of abstractions. Where possible, it is desirable to create a small number of primitive object types and then compose them to form objects at higher levels of abstraction. A scientific application might model the various different kinds of atoms as classes. There are 100 some odd kinds of atoms in the periodic table. Instances of these relatively few primitive types are composed (via layering) in various ways and proportions to create all the different types of molecules in the universe.

Another example of this type of layered design might be an object-oriented window system. Suppose we have a collection of *N* primitive widgets (such as buttons, dials, slide switches, displays, etc.). We'll name these primitive widget classes W1, W2, . . . , W*n* for short. Each widget, `Wi`, exists in its own separate translation unit, `wi.c`, with its corresponding header file `wi.h`. New screen types are created by composing the various types of widget objects. We'll call these *M* screen classes S1, S2, . . . , S*m*, and each `Si` lives in its own translation unit with header file `si.h`.

Typically, each screen uses a substantial number of the available widgets. For the purposes of this discussion, assume each screen type uses all (or most) of these primitive types in a substantive way that prompts the implementors to include all of `w1.h`, `w2.h`, . . . , `wn.h` files in each `si.h` file. The header file for a typical screen, `S13`, is shown in Figure 2-7.

```
// s13.h
#ifndef INCLUDED_S13
#define INCLUDED_S13
#include "w1.h"
#include "w2.h"
#include "w3.h"
// ...
#include "wn.h"
#include <math.h>

class S13 {
    W1 d_w1a;
    W1 d_w1b;
    W2 d_w2;
    W3 d_w3;
    // ...
    Wn d_wn;
};

#endif
```

Figure 2-7: Typical Screen Composed of Many Widgets

Do you see a potential problem? Let's continue. Suppose you have developed a good number of screens, and in some translation unit of your system, `ck.c`, you need to include all of the screen headers (say to create them). The include graph for a window application with $N = 5$ widgets and $M = 5$ screens is shown in Figure 2-8.

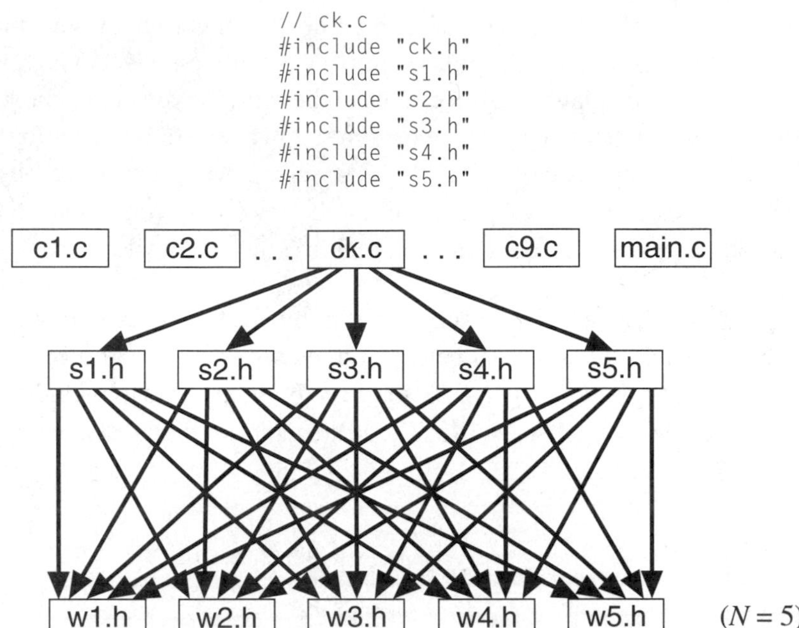

Figure 2-8: Include Graph for One Component in Window System of Size *N* = 5

When the preprocessor sees that `ck.c` has included `s1.h`, it also includes `w1.h` through `w5.h`. Upon encountering `s2.h`, each of the widget header files must still be reopened and reprocessed line by line in its entirety searching for the trailing `#endif` (only to find that there is nothing else to be done). This redundant preprocessing occurs with `s3.h`, `s4.h`, and again with `s5.h`. Although this program will compile and work properly, we had to wait for 25 widget header files to be processed when 5 would have done the job!

Unless care is taken to ensure otherwise, C++ tends to have large, dense include graphs (much more than C). Although inheritance and layering contribute to this problem, the underlying cause is often the misguided belief on the part of C++ developers that they are somehow doing their clients a favor by including in their header file every other header that a client might need.

Avoiding dense include graphs is part of the topic of Insulation, covered in Chapter 6. What follows is a practice that will minimize the impact of such reconvergent inclusion, even in a poor design. Note that some development environments are smart enough to keep track of previously included header files, but many common environments are not. If portability is an issue, it is better safe than sorry.

Minor Design Rule

Place a redundant (external) include guard around each preprocessor include directive in every header file.

Place a redundant (external) include guard around each include directive that occurs in a header file. This technique, applied to a typical screen header file, is shown in Figure 2-9. Processing file `s13.h` for the first time will still cause files `w1.h`, `w2.h`, `...`, `wn.h` to be included. Including another screen, however, will not lead to any redundant parsing of widget headers.

Notice that the redundant include guard for the math standard library header is different from the rest. Although `math.h` does have its own internal include guard, it probably doesn't follow our standard. The runtime libraries supplied with different compilers are likely to have different naming conventions for the include guards they use, and these guard names may not always be consistent. Components supplied by third-party vendors may use yet another convention. For all components that are not guaranteed to follow our include-guard naming convention, it will be necessary to add a line that defines the appropriate include guard symbol *after* the corresponding include directive (as was done for `math.h`).

Using redundant include guards is admittedly unpleasant. It now takes not one but at least three lines to include a header in a header file—four lines if the included header came from outside our sphere of influence. Redundant include guards not only make headers take longer to write, they make headers harder to read. Using redundant include guards also requires following a consistent and predictable naming convention. Is it worth it?

Experience with truly large projects that have dense include graphs shows that the answer is a resounding YES! Initial builds of projects consisting of several million lines of C++ source code were taking on the order of a week to compile using a large network of work stations. Inserting redundant include guards reduced compile time significantly, with no substantive change to the code.

```
// s13.h
#ifndef INCLUDED_S13
#define INCLUDED_S13

#ifndef INCLUDED_W1
#include "w1.h"
#endif

#ifndef INCLUDED_W2
#include "w2.h"
#endif

#ifndef INCLUDED_W3
#include "w3.h"
#endif

// ...

#ifndef INCLUDED_WN
#include "wn.h"
#endif

#ifndef INCLUDED_MATH
#include <math.h>
#define INCLUDED_MATH              // extra line
#endif

class S13 {
    W1 d_w1a;
    W1 d_w1b;
    W2 d_w2;
    W3 d_w3;
    // ...
    Wn d_wn;
};

#endif
```

Figure 2-9: Typical Screen Component with Redundant Include Guards

What we have just discussed is typically not an issue for a small or even a medium-size system. But what would happen if we were dealing with systems that contained the equivalent of hundreds of primitive widgets with hundreds of primitive screens? To provide quantitative information demonstrating the benefits of using redundant include guards, I tried the following experiment.

I let *N* be number of widgets as well as the number of screens. I then generated subsystems and measured the compile time (which is dominated by the C preprocessor time) for a single translation unit, including all of the screen header files with and without redundant include guards. I tried the experiment with header files having 10 lines each and again with header files of 100 lines each. I defined the *speedup factor* to be the compilation time without redundant include guards divided by the corresponding compilation time with redundant include guards added. The results are shown in Figure 2-10.

	10 lines/header			100 lines/header		
	CPU seconds		Speedup	CPU seconds		Speedup
N	Without	With	Factor	Without	With	Factor
1	0.2	0.2	1.00	0.2	0.2	1.00
2	0.2	0.2	1.00	0.2	0.2	1.00
4	0.3	0.3	1.00	0.4	0.3	1.33
8	0.5	0.3	1.67	0.7	0.4	1.75
16	0.7	0.4	1.75	1.7	0.5	3.40
32	1.5	0.5	3.00	5.8	0.9	6.44
64	5.8	1.1	5.27	22.1	2.0	11.05
128	25.9	3.5	7.40	89.5	5.2	17.21
256	126.5	13.6	9.30	376.5	17.1	22.02
512	702.3	61.6	11.40	1697.4	68.6	24.74
1024	4378.5	306.6	14.28	8303.8	330.6	25.12

Figure 2-10: Preprocessor Times with/without Redundant Include Guards

For systems with fewer than eight widgets and eight screens, the speed-up is either non-existent or minimal, but given that the total compile time was less than 1 CPU second, it hardly matters.

Header files in C++ are seldom only 10 lines long; 100 lines is still small but more typical. For systems with 32 widgets, the time spent in the C preprocessor compiling each client component on my machine can be reduced by a factor of more than 6 (from 5.8 to 0.9 CPU seconds). For systems with 64 widgets, the speedup is a factor of over 11! Redundant include guards are ugly, but do no real harm. Not using redundant guards runs the risk of quadratic (i.e., $O(N^2)$) behavior at compile time.

Note that redundant guards are not necessary in `.c` files. Short of deliberately duplicating `#include` directives in the `.c` file, the (pathological) worst-case behavior, $2N$ remains linear (i.e., $O(N)$) with respect to the number of distinct `.h` files, N.

The data in this section reflects CFRONT running on Unix-based workstations. Other development environments may have somewhat different characteristics. In Chapter 6 we will see that nesting `#include` directives in header files is not only undesirable but often unnecessary. The ugliness of the redundant include guards, if nothing else, reminds us that we want to avoid placing `#include` directives in header files whenever it makes sense to do so.

2.6 Documentation

The examples in this book do not set a good example for what are sufficient comments for production code (otherwise this would be three books, not one). But comments, especially in the interface, are an essential part of the development process.

Guideline

Document the interfaces so that they are usable by others; have at least one other developer review each interface.

To see why it is valuable to have another developer review your interface, try to put yourself in the position of a client or a test engineer trying to understand your class. You know very well how to use your interface—after all, you designed it! The terse names you supplied as member functions are "obvious" and "self-explanatory." But unless you have taken the time to have someone else review your interface and documentation, chances are that there is significant room for improvement—particularly in its usability.

A big part of usability is being able to pick up an unfamiliar header and just start using it. In practice, header file comments are often the only documentation (or at least the only up-to-date documentation) that exists for an interface. If clients are forced to peek at the implementation in order to figure out how to use your component, then it is not documented properly.

Guideline

Explicitly state conditions under which behavior is undefined.

Another important aspect of documentation is explicitly identifying conditions under which behavior is not defined. Consider the following declaration:

```
struct MathUtil {
    // ...
    static int fact(int n);
        // Returns the product of consecutive integers between 1 and n.
};
```

What do you think about the comment for function fact? We might guess that `fact` is supposed to be the common mathematical function *factorial* (*n*!), and that `fact(0)` is actually 1 and not 1 • 0 = 0 or undefined. However, that is not what the comment says. What the comment fails to say is what is supposed to happen when *n* is non-positive!

A factorial is not defined for negative integral values. It may be that our particular implementation returns 0 in these cases. What `fact(n)` returns when the value of `n` is negative is an artifice of the implementation and not part of the specification; clients should be told explicitly not to rely on this behavior. Another implementation replacing this one could easily provide different behavior for negative values of *n* (including causing your program to crash).

Unless explicitly stated in our comments, clients and test engineers will, in general, have no way to distinguish between what is intended or required behavior and what is simply coincidental behavior resulting from the particular implementation choice. A better, more usable interface is presented below:

```
struct MathUtil {
    // ...
    static int factorial(int n);
        // Returns the product of consecutive integers between 1 and n
        // for positive n.  If n is 0, 1 is returned.
        // Note that the behavior is not defined for negative values
        // of n nor for results that are too large to fit in an int.
};
```

Failing to specify explicitly the conditions under which behavior is undefined inadvertently commits the software to support irrelevant behavior that could affect performance or limit implementation choice. If a test engineer is not on the ball, you may find irrelevant behavior produced by your implementation choice inexorably cast in stone by a suite of regression tests that explicitly test for that behavior. Even worse, clients, through improper (unintended) use, may come to depend on this coincidental behavior.

Principle

The use of `assert` statements can help to document the assumptions you make when implementing your code.

Error checking throughout every level of a system in order to detect logic errors can become expensive, especially for large systems. Good documentation can be a viable alternative to writing excessive code. For example, some software developers feel that it is necessary to handle every pointer that comes into a function, even if that pointer is null. If this function is part of a widely used interface, favoring robustness might well prove to be a good decision. Alternatively, it can be sufficient to make it clear to clients that passing a null pointer will result in undefined behavior, backing that up with an assert statement at the beginning of the function implementation:

```
// stdio.c
#include <stdio.h>
#include <assert.h>
/* ... */
int printf(const char *format ...)
{
    assert(format);
    /* ...
    */
}
```

The effective use of both documentation and assert statements can lead to lighter-weight code that is still quite usable. If someone misuses the function, it is their own fault—and they'll find out about it soon enough!

It would be laudable if every developer always made it clear when, for example, a pointer argument to functions cannot be null. Responsible clients, however, should not assume that a pointer argument can be null unless the resulting behavior is explicitly stated.

2.7 Identifier-Naming Conventions

Distinguishing data member, type, and constant names from other identifier names in a *consistent* and *objectively verifiable* way can be a significant advantage when maintaining a large system. Section 1.4.1 presented a collection of naming conventions that we tersely punctuate here with three design rules and two guidelines.

The practice of lexigraphically identifying class data members can be stated concisely, and its value transcends issues of mere style. This practice is therefore presented as a design rule.

Minor Design Rule

Use a consistent method (such as a `d_` prefix) to highlight class data members.

You may also elect to use `s_` to distinguish static from instance data. The above practice is a minor design rule because clients will never have to deal with this issue (since, according to Section 2.2, data members should always be private).

Minor Design Rule

Use a consistent method (such as an uppercase first letter) to distinguish type names.

The above practice is presented as a rule and not a guideline because it is a widely accepted and objectively verified standard that improves readability in general, making interfaces easier to understand and code easier to maintain. It is a minor rule because an isolated lapse is not the end of the world.

Minor Design Rule

Use a consistent method (such as all uppercase with underscore) to identify immutable values such as enumerators, `const` data, and preprocessor constants.

The above practice helps to distinguish constant (and therefore "stateless") variables from both local variables and member (state) variables. It is presented as a design rule and not a guideline because it helps to improve maintainability, it is objectively verifiable, and it requires no exceptions.

Guideline

Be consistent about identifier names; use either uppercase or underscore but not both to delimit words in identifiers.

The above practice is also objectively verifiable, but not everyone can be convinced of its virtue, and it is largely a matter of style. Its utility is in making identifier names somewhat easier to remember and in exhibiting a more professional image to most customers. It is presented here as a guideline (particularly for the interface), but tolerates some degree of individuality in the implementation. (In this book we have adopted the uppercase standard.)

Guideline

Be consistent about names used in the same way; in particular adopt consistent method names and operators for recurring design patterns such as iteration.

Attaining consistency across the interface of a large system can enhance usability and can also be surprisingly difficult to accomplish. Empowering a group of top-notch developers to act as "Interface Engineers" has proven effective in achieving consistency across development groups in large projects. Container classes, along with their iterators, also lend themselves to template implementations (see Section 10.4) that can be effective at enforcing consistency across otherwise unrelated objects.

2.8 Summary

C++ is a large language, giving way to an even larger design space. In this chapter we have described a modest set of fundamental design rules and guidelines that have proven themselves to be useful in practice.

Major design rules are presumed never to be violated. Even infrequent violations could compromise the integrity of a large system. Throughout this text, we will assume that all major design rules have been followed consistently.

Minor design rules are also presumed to be followed but perhaps not with draconian adherence. Deviating from a minor rule in isolated instances is unlikely to have a severe global impact.

Guidelines are presented as rules of thumb, and should be followed unless there is a compelling engineering reason to do otherwise.

Exposing the member data of a class to its clients violates encapsulation. Providing non-private access to member data implies that local changes in representation may force clients to rework their code. Furthermore, by allowing writable access to data members, there is no way to prevent accidental misuse from leaving data in an inconsistent state. Protected member data is like public member data in that there is no limit to the number of clients that might be affected by a change to that data.

Global variables pollute the global name space and warp the physical structure of a design in ways that can make independent testing and selective reuse virtually impossible. There is no need to use global variables in new C++ projects. We can systematically eliminate global variables by placing them in class scope as private static members, and then provide public static function members to access them. Excessive dependency on such modules, however, is a symptom of a poor design.

Free functions, particularly those that do not operate on any user-defined type, are likely candidates for collision with other functions during integrations. Nesting such functions in class scope as static members all but eliminates the danger of collision.

Enumerations, typedefs, and constant data also threaten the global name space. By nesting enumerations within class scope, any ambiguity can be resolved via scope resolution. A typedef at file scope can look suspiciously like a class, and be surprisingly difficult to find in a large project. By nesting typedefs in class scope, they become relatively easy to track down. An integral constant defined in a header file is often best expressed by an enumerator in class scope. Other types of constants can be scoped by making them static const members of some class.

Preprocessor macros are difficult to understand for both human beings and machines. Since macros are not part of the C++ language, they are irreverent of scope, and, if placed in a header file, they can collide with any identifier in any file in the system. Consequently macros should not appear in header files except as include guards.

All things considered, we will avoid introducing anything into file scope in a header file other than classes, structures, unions, and free operators. We will, of course, allow inline member function definitions in headers.

Including a definition twice results in a compile-time error. Since most C++ header files contain definitions, it is essential that we protect against the possibility of a reconvergent include graph. Wrapping the definitions inside a header with internal include guards ensures that the contents of each header will be incorporated at most once in any translation unit.

Redundant (external) include guards, although not strictly necessary, ensure that we avoid potentially quadratic behavior at compile time. By wrapping include directives in header files with redundant guards, we ensure having to open a header file at most twice per translation unit.

Good documentation is an essential part of development. A lack of documentation degrades usability. An important part of documentation involves stating what is *undefined*; otherwise clients may come to depend on coincidental behavior resulting solely from the particular implementation choice.

Not all code must be robust. Redundant, runtime program-error checking at every level of the system can have an unacceptable impact on performance. A combination of documentation and assertions can serve the same purpose, but with superior runtime performance in the final product.

Finally, providing a consistent set of naming conventions to distinguish data members, types, and constants can improve readability across development groups. We suggested using a `d_` prefix for data members (`s_` if static); using an uppercase first letter to denote a type and a lowercase one to denote a variable or function; using all uppercase (including underscore) to denote enumerators, `const` data, and preprocessor constants; and using an uppercase first letter to delimit words in multi-word identifiers. We also recommended using consistent names for recurring design patterns such as iterators.

PART II: PHYSICAL DESIGN CONCEPTS

Developing a large-scale software system in C++ requires more than just a sound understanding of logical design issues. Logical entities, such as classes and functions, are like the flesh and skin of a system. The logical entities that make up large C++ systems are distributed across many physical entities, such as files and directories. The physical architecture is the skeleton of the system—if it is malformed, there is no cosmetic remedy for alleviating its unpleasant symptoms.

The quality of the physical design of a large system will dictate the cost of its maintenance and the potential it has for the independent reuse of its subsystems. Effective design requires a thorough grasp of physical design concepts that although closely tied to many logical design issues include a dimension with which even expert professional software developers may have little or no experience. Part II of this book presents a thorough introduction to the fundamental concepts of good physical design.

Chapter 3 introduces the component as the fundamental unit of design. Several physical design rules are presented to ensure that all our designs have certain important desirable properties. The many logical design relationships (e.g., IsA, HasA, Uses) collapse into a single physical relationship: DependsOn. We see how our logical design decisions can potentially affect physical dependency. We also see how to extract physical dependencies efficiently from a collection of existing components.

Chapter 4 describes the importance of physical hierarchy (i.e., layering) with respect to development, maintenance, and testing. In this chapter we explore how to characterize individual components, subsystems, and entire systems in terms of their physical dependencies. We see how to exploit the hierarchical structure of sound physical designs to achieve higher reliability at lower cost through isolation, incremental, and hierarchical testing. We also measure how the physical dependencies in a system contribute to the cost of maintenance and regression testing in terms of link time and disk space.

Chapter 5 explores many common causes of excessive link-time dependencies. This chapter catalogs several techniques and transformations for reducing the link-time dependencies within a system—a process referred to in this book as *levelization*. We use many examples taken from various applications to illustrate these techniques.

Chapter 6 addresses the maintenance cost associated with excessive compile-time coupling. Several common language constructs that force clients to depend on encapsulated implementation details are identified. Techniques for mitigating or eliminating compile-time dependencies on individual details as well as wholesale techniques for distancing clients from the implementation are presented—a process referred to in this book as *insulation*. Finally, the runtime cost associated with insulation is characterized to identify situations under which insulation is *not* appropriate.

Chapter 7 extends the concept of levelization to very large systems. Additional physical structure beyond that of individual components is needed to support the complex functionality of such systems. Packages represent a physically cohesive collection of cooperating components and provide a higher level of physical abstraction than can be achieved with components alone. In this chapter we revisit the concepts of levelization and insulation in the context of packages as a whole. We also touch on issues pertaining to the process of developing and releasing stable snapshots of a very large system. Finally, we discuss the role of `main()` in object-oriented systems and the relative advantages of various strategies for initialization.

3

Components

This chapter introduces the notion of physical design in contrast to the more popular topic of logical design. The component is presented as the fundamental unit of design. Next we explore a small collection of physical rules that ensure important desirable properties in large designs. We then discuss the DependsOn relation among components and see how to infer this relation from abstract logical relationships at design time. We also see how to track physical dependencies efficiently by examining the `#include` graph among components. Finally, we explore the subtle physical implications of granting friendship both inside and outside components.

3.1 Components versus Classes

Logical design emphasizes the interaction of the classes and functions defined within a system. From a purely logical point of view, a design can be thought of as a sea of classes and functions where no physical partitions exist—every class and free function resides in a single seamless space. Interactive object-oriented languages such as Smalltalk and CLOS with their rich, runtime environments geared toward a single developer have no doubt helped to foster this monolithic perspective.

Logical design, however, looks at only one side of the design process. Logical design does not take into account physical entities such as files and libraries. Compile-time coupling, link-time dependency, and independent reuse are simply not addressed by logical design. For example, whether or not a function is declared `inline` does not affect what it does, but can greatly affect readily measurable characteristics such as runtime, compile time, link time, and executable size. Without considering the physical view of a design, it is not possible to consider the organizational issues that become important when developing very large systems.

Principle

Logical design addresses only *architectural* issues; physical design addresses *organizational* issues.

Physical design focuses on the physical entities in the system and how they are interrelated. In most conventional C++ programming environments, the source code for every logical entity in the system must reside in a physical entity, commonly referred to as a *file*. Ultimately, the physical structure of every C++ program can be described as a collection of files. Some of these files will be header (`.h`) files and some of them will be implementation files (`.c`) files. For small programs, this description is sufficient. For larger programs, we need to impose additional structure in order to create maintainable, testable, and reusable subsystems.

DEFINITION: A *component* is the smallest unit of physical design.

A component is not a class and vice versa.[1] Conceptually, a component embodies a subset of the logical design that makes sense to exist as an independent, cohesive unit. Classes, functions, enumerations, and so on are the logical entities that make up these components. In particular, every class definition resides in exactly one component.

Structurally, a component is an indivisible, physical unit, none of whose parts can be used independently of the others. The physical form of a component is standard and independent of its content. A component consists of exactly one header (`.h`) file and one implementation (`.c`) file.[2]

---

[1] The notion of a component is presented in **stroustrup**, Section 12.3, pp. 422–425. In this chapter, we expand on that discussion by introducing physical design concepts that make the definition of a component in C++ concrete.

[2] We will ignore extraordinary circumstances that might justify a component having more than a single `.h` or `.c` file.

A component will typically define one or more closely related classes and any free operators deemed appropriate for the abstraction it supports. Basic types such as `Point`, `String`, and `BigInt` will each be implemented in a component containing a single class (Figure 3-1a). Container classes such as `IntSet`, `Stack`, and `List` will typically be implemented in a component containing (at least) the principle class and its iterator (Figure 3-1b). More complex abstractions involving multiple types such as `Graph` can embody several classes in a single component (see Figure 3-1c). Finally, classes that provide a wrapper for an entire subsystem (see Section 5.10) may form a thin encapsulating layer consisting of one or more principle classes and many iterators (Figure 3.1d).

Each of the components in Figure 3-1 (like every other component) has a physical as well as a logical view. The physical view consists of the `.h` file and the `.c` file, with the `.h` file included as the first substantive line of the `.c` file. The physical implementation of a component *always* depends on its interface at compile time. This internal physical coupling contributes to the need to treat these two files as a single physical entity.

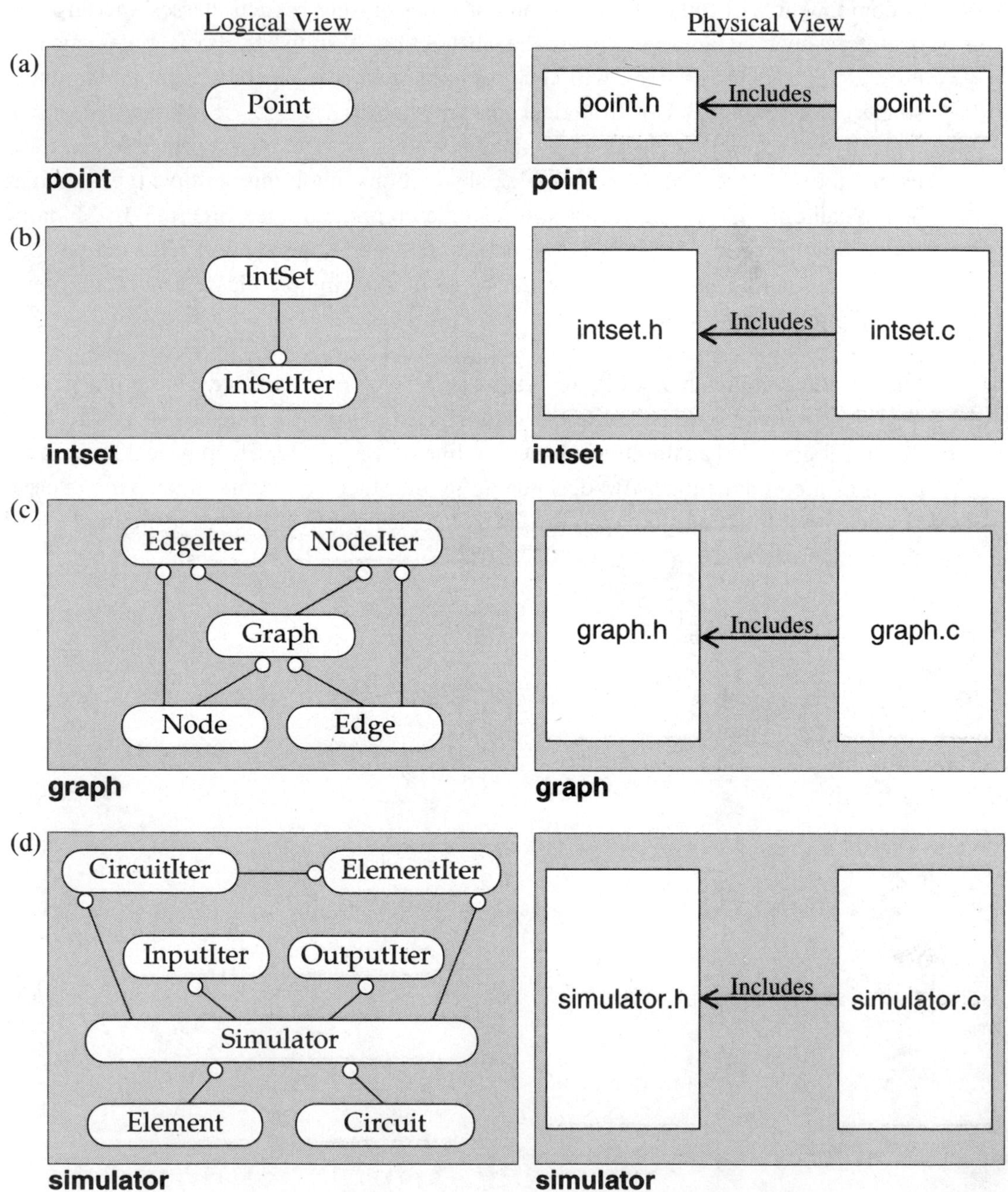

Figure 3-1: Logical versus Physical View of Several Components

Principle

A component is the appropriate fundamental unit of design.

A component (and not a class) is the appropriate fundamental unit of both logical and physical design for at least three reasons:

1. A component bundles a manageable amount of cohesive functionality that often spans several logical entities (e.g., classes and free operators) into a single physical unit.

2. Not only does a component capture an entire abstraction as a single entity, but it also allows for consideration of physical issues not addressed by class-level design.

3. An appropriately designed component (being a physical entity unlike a class) can be lifted as a single unit from one system and reused effectively in another system without having to rewrite any code. Throughout this book, the need to consider physical as well as logical design issues will become increasingly evident.

As a concrete example, Figure 3-2 shows the header file for a `stack` component containing two classes defined at file scope, namely, `Stack` and `StackIter`. We can also see that there are two free (i.e., not member) operator functions implementing == and `!=` between two `Stack` objects. Peeking at the implementation, we would discover that `operator==` uses `StackIter`, and that `operator!=` is implemented in terms of `operator==`. The complete set of logical entities at file scope in component `stack` is pictured in Figure 3-3a. The physical entitles (`stack.h` and `stack.c`) along with their canonical physical relationship are depicted in Figure 3-3b.

```
// stack.h
#ifndef INCLUDED_STACK
#define INCLUDED_STACK

class StackIter;

class Stack {
    int *d_stack_p;                           // pointer to array of int
    int d_sp;                                 // stack pointer (index)
    int d_size;                               // size of current array of int
    friend StackIter;                         // (no comment needed)

  public:
    // CREATORS
    Stack();                                  // create an empty Stack
    Stack(const Stack& stack);                // (no comment needed)
    ~Stack();                                 // (no comment needed)

    // MANIPULATORS
    Stack& operator=(const Stack& stack);     // copy Stack from Stack
    void push(int value);                     // push integer onto this Stack
    int pop();                                // pop integer off this Stack
                                              // undefined if Stack empty
    // ACCESSORS
    int isEmpty() const;                      // 1 if empty else 0
    int top() const;                          // integer on top of this Stack
};                                            // undefined if Stack empty

int operator==(const Stack& lhs, const Stack& rhs);
    // 1 if two stacks contain identical values else 0

int operator!=(const Stack& lhs, const Stack& rhs);
    // 1 if two stacks do not contain identical values else 0

class StackIter {                             // iter order: top to bottom
    int *d_stack_p;                           // points to orig. stack array
    int d_sp;                                 // local stack pointer (index)
    StackIter(const StackIter&);              // not implemented
    StackIter& operator=(const StackIter&); // not implemented

  public:
    // CREATORS
    StackIter(const Stack& stack);            // initialize to top of Stack
    ~StackIter();                             // (no comment needed)

    // MANIPULATORS
    void operator++();                        // advance state of iteration
                                              // undefined if done
    // ACCESSORS
    operator const void *() const;            // non-zero if not done else 0
    int operator()() const;                   // value of current integer
};                                            // undefined if done

#endif
```

Figure 3-2: Header File `stack.h` for a `stack` Component

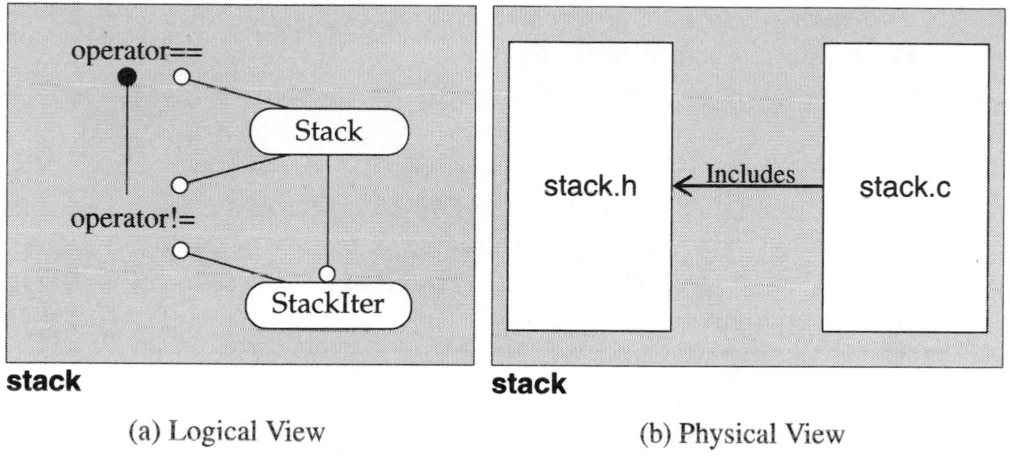

(a) Logical View (b) Physical View

Figure 3-3: Two Views of a `stack` Component

We have chosen a simple stack to ensure that the application functionality does not obscure the points we want to illustrate. In this example, almost every member is commented (which is a bare minimum for production code). A stack is a kind of container. Access to other than the top element of a stack is not normally thought of as part of a stack abstraction. We have provided the iterator to make the functionality defined in this `stack` component more generally extensible by clients, while preserving encapsulation (see Section 1.5). We make no mention of a maximum stack size because a stack abstraction has no maximum size. Providing functionality such as `isFull` or a return status that exposes artificial limitations imposed by a substandard implementation not only violates the abstraction but also complicates its use. Such unexpected, implementation-based limitations are better treated as exceptions. Sometimes, however, we will allow a client to "help" an object to anticipate future events, potentially improving performance. In order to avoid exposing a particular implementation choice, such "help"—like `register` in C or `inline` in C++—should be only a hint and have no programmatically detectable effect (see Section 10.3.1).

DEFINITION: The *logical interface* of a component is that which is programmatically accessible or detectable by a client.

The logical interface of a component is the set of types and functionality defined in the header file that are programmatically accessible by clients of that component. Private implementation details that for organizational reasons reside in the `.h` file are encapsulated and not considered part of the logical interface.

> **DEFINITION: A type is *Used-In-The-Interface* of a component if the type is used in the public (or protected) interface of any class defined, or any free (operator) function declared at file scope in the `.h` file for that component.**

In the same sense that the public interface of a class consists of the union of the interfaces of the public members of that class (Section 1.6.2), the "public" interface of a component consists of the collection of *all* public member functions, typedefs, enumerations, and free (operator) functions declared in the component's `.h` file.

For example, the public member functions of both `Stack` and `StackIter` contribute to the logical interface of component `stack`. The free operator function

```
operator==(const Stack&, const Stack&)
```

is not a member of `Stack` and therefore is not considered as part of the logical interface of class `Stack`. Nonetheless, this operator does extend the set of programmatically accessible functions defined in *component* `stack` and therefore does extend the component's logical interface. The somewhat subtle issues surrounding friendship are discussed in Section 3.6.

Figure 3-4 shows a tiny driver program, `stack.t.c`, that creates a `Stack` object, pushes a few integers onto it, and then prints out its contents in order, from top to bottom. The driver can access the logical interface of the `stack` component, but not its organizational structure. However, there is more information present in the `stack` component's `.h` file than is programmatically accessible.

```
// stack.t.c
#include "stack.h"
#include <iostream.h>

main()
{
    Stack stack;
    stack.push(111);
    stack.push(222);
    stack.push(333);

    for (StackIter it(stack); it; ++it) {
        cout << it() << endl;
    }
};

// Output:
//      333
//      222
//      111
```

Figure 3-4: Driver `stack.t.c` **for Component** `stack`

> **DEFINITION: The *physical interface* of a component is *everything* in its header file.**

The *physical interface* of a component consists of all of the information available in the `.h` file (regardless of access privilege). The more information contained within its `.h` file, the more likely that changes to a component's implementation will affect its clients and cause them to recompile.

Any programmer can tell merely by looking at `stack.h` that this is an array-based stack (it is not implemented, for example, as a linked list). For a compiler to do its job, it must look at `stack.h` in its entirety. The compiler must consider even private information (e.g., `d_stack_p`) that, from a logical point of view, is strictly an implementation detail. A consequence of this physical exposure is that an implementation change that leaves the logical view of the `stack` component's interface untouched can still make it mandatory for all clients that include `stack.h` to recompile.

As programmers, we observe that none of the functions in `stack.h` have been declared `inline`. Modifying the bodies of any of the functions in this component therefore will not alter the physical interface, thus forcing clients to recompile. The downside is that for a lightweight object such as `Stack`, removing inline functions could result in an order-of-magnitude loss in runtime performance (see Section 6.6.1).

DEFINITION: A type is *Used-In-The-Implementation* of a component if that type is referred to by name anywhere in the component.

From a logical point of view, what is and is not used in the implementation of a component is an encapsulated detail and unimportant. From a physical point of view, such usage can imply physical dependencies on other components. It is these physical dependencies that will affect maintainability and reusability in large systems.

Good design requires that the developer understand the issues involved in both logical and physical design. Logical design is the natural place to start. We must consider what logical entities either naturally belong together or are sufficiently interdependent that they cannot reasonably be separated. We must also consider how much of the implementation detail we want to expose in the physical interface. Furthermore, we need to decide on what other components our component will depend, and what impact changes in these components will have on both our own component and its clients. A component has not been designed properly until all of these issues have been addressed.

3.2 Physical Design Rules

This section considers the fundamental rules of physical design. These rules are necessary if our other practices and techniques are to be effective. It is virtually impossible to correct a large design that has not followed these practices in essence from the start.

Major Design Rule

Logical entities declared within a component should not be defined outside that component.

It may seem obvious, but this rule should be stated clearly once. For a component to be reusable it must be reasonably self-contained. A component may have dependencies on other components. However, any logical constructs (apart from class declarations) that a component declares within its own header file—if defined at all—should be defined entirely within that component.

Figure 3-5 is an example of how *not* to partition logical entities into physical units. Class `Stack` has been defined in component `stack`, but its implementation is not confined to the `stack` component. `Stack::push` is defined in `set.c`, and `Stack::pop` is defined in `main.c`!

```
// intset.h
#ifndef INCLUDED_INTSET
#define INCLUDED_INTSET
class IntSet {
    // ...
  public:
    // ...
    // ...
    // ...
};
#endif
```

intset.h

```
// stack.h
#ifndef INCLUDED_STACK
#define INCLUDED_STACK
class Stack {
    // ...
  public:
    // ...
    void push(int i);
    int pop();
};
#endif
```

stack.h

```
// intset.c
#include "intset.h"
// ...
Stack::push(int i)
{
    // ...
}

// ...
```

intset.c

```
// stack.c
#include "stack.h"
// ...
// ...
// ...
// ...
// ...

// ...
```

stack.c

```
// main.c
#include "intset.h"
#include "stack.h"
int Stack::pop()
{
    // ...
}

// ...
```

main.c

Figure 3-5: Illegal Physical Partitioning of Logical Entities

In addition to causing a maintenance nightmare, failing to adhere strictly to the above design rule can result in the loss of many desirable physical properties of a design (in particular, the ability to pick up and reuse translation units in other programs). Following this rule meticulously will improve both the modularity and maintainability of a project of any size.

Minor Design Rule

The root names of the `.c` file and the `.h` file that comprise a component should match exactly.

It is important for maintainability that the root names of a component's files match exactly. Knowing, for example, that `stack.c` and `stack.h` comprise a single component not only facilitates manual maintenance but also opens the door to simple object-oriented design automation tools (see Appendix C).

Unfortunately, some existing object code archivers place relatively low character limits (e.g., 13) on object file names. Hence it is not always possible to have the name of the component's `.c` file mirror the name of its principal class. Worse, some operating systems limit file names to only eight characters (plus a three-character suffix), which can be a significant burden when developing very large systems.

Major Design Rule

The `.c` file of every component should include its own `.h` file as the first substantive line of code.

We must include the `.h` file of a component in its `.c` file because the compiler must see the declaration of a class member before it can compile its definition. This practice is required by the language and also by many common dependency-analysis tools. The reason for placing this `#include` directive at the top of the file is somewhat subtle.

Principle

Latent usage errors can be avoided by ensuring that the `.h` file of a component parses by itself—without externally-provided declarations or definitions.

Including the `.h` file as the very first line of the `.c` file ensures that no critical piece of information intrinsic to the physical interface of the component is missing from the `.h` file (or, if there is, that you will find out about it as soon as you try to compile the `.c` file).

Consider the following header file for component `wildthing`:

```
// wildthing.h
#ifndef INCLUDED_WILDTHING
#define INCLUDED_WILDTHING

class WildThing {
    // ...
  public:
    WildThing();
    // ...
};

ostream& operator<<(const ostream& o, const WildThing& thing);
    // Note: uses class ostream in the interface

#endif
```

Notice that we have overloaded the left-shift operator (<<) in the way that is normal and customary for stream output. Next consider the implementation:

```
// wildthing.c
#include <iostream.h>
#include "wildthing.h"
// ...

ostream& operator<<(const ostream& o, const WildThing& thing)
{
    // ...
}
```

We try to compile the implementation, and it compiles just fine. Next we create a test file for `wildthing`:

```
// wildthing.t.c
#include <iostream.h>
#include "wildthing.h"

int main()
{
    WildThing wild;

    // ...
    // ...

    cout << wild << endl;

    return 0;
}
```

File `wildthing.t.c` compiles and links. The program runs perfectly, and we go tell all our friends that we are done. But there is a bug and a physical bug at that! The following program will not compile. Why?

```
// product.c
#include "wildthing.h"
#include <iostream.h>

int main()
{
    WildThing wild;

    // ...
    // ...

    cout << wild << endl;

    return 0;
}
```

The problem is that we did not declare class `ostream` before we tried to use it in the interface of `operator<<` that is declared in `wildthing.h`. The order of the `#include` directives was reversed in the client code, and now the header itself doesn't parse because the `ostream` identifier is not yet declared. How do we fix the problem?

When you figure out the bug, the fix is simple: add the declaration "`class ostream;`"[3] to `wildthing.h` at file scope before the first use of ostream:

```
// wildthing.h
#ifndef INCLUDED_WILDTHING
#define INCLUDED_WILDTHING

class ostream;           // was missing before, oops!

class WildThing {
    // ...
  public:
    WildThing();
    // ...
};

ostream& operator<<(const ostream& o, const WildThing& thing);

#endif
```

The more important question is How do we *prevent* the problem? The answer is equally simple. Always make the `.c` file of each component include the `.h` file for that component before including or declaring anything else. In this way each component ensures that its own header file is self-sufficient with respect to compilation.

Guideline

Clients should include header files providing required type definitions directly; except for non-private inheritance, avoid relying on one header file to include another.

Whether or not one header file should include another is a physical, not a logical, issue. In cases where the header file itself needs a definition in another header file in order to compile (see Section 6.3.7), it is correct to place the appropriate `#include` directive in that header file (surrounded, of course, by redundant external include guards as described in Section 2.5).

---

[3] And not the preprocessor directive `#include <iostream.h>` (as explained in Section 6.3.7).

Except for public and protected inheritance, however, the need to include a type's definition rather than forward declare it in the header file is almost always dictated by encapsulated logical implementation details.

For example, if class `MyType` uses class `Stack` in its implementation, it may be necessary to include `stack.h` in `mytype.h` to ensure that `mytype.h` compiles. If I decide to change the implementation of `MyType` to use `List` instead of `Stack`, I would no longer need the `#include "stack.h"` directive in `mytype.h`. Any client that depended on `mytype.h` to include `stack.h` would now have to be changed to include `stack.h` directly.

How we layer one type on another will affect the degree of compile-time coupling. Incrementally reducing compile-time coupling is the topic of Section 6.3. For example, whether `MyType` HasA (embeds) `Stack` or HoldsA (pointer to) `Stack` could determine whether `mytype.h` includes `stack.h` or simply forward-declares class `Stack` (see Section 6.3.2). If I alter the implementation of `MyType` so that it now HoldsA (instead of HasA) `Stack`, the `#include` directive may no longer be needed in `mytype.h`. If I remove that directive, then clients who depended on *how* `Stack` was used in the implementation of `MyType` would also be forced to change. Even if `Stack` were used in the logical interface of `MyType`, there might still be no need for `mytype.h` to include `stack.h` (see Section 6.3.7). It is up to each client that uses `Stack` substantively to include its definition directly.

Inheritance is an exception because it always implies a compile-time dependency and is also part of the logical interface of the derived class. Altering the inheritance hierarchy in any way that would permit component authors to remove `#include` directives from component header files would also change the logical interface, forcing clients to be revisited regardless of physical issues. It is therefore reasonable for clients to include only a derived class definition and rely on the derived class's header file to include the base class definition.

For similar reasons, it would be unwise for a client to rely on the header of some component to forward declare a class used only in that component's logical implementation.

Major Design Rule

Avoid definitions with external linkage in the `.c` file of a component that are not declared explicitly in the corresponding `.h` file.

For analysis, maintenance, and particularly testing, it is important that someone (or some tool) be able to look at only the physical interface of a component and understand the complete logical interface of that component. Requiring a component to declare its entire logical interface in its header file serves to improve

1. Usability—by making it possible to fully understand from the interface alone the entire abstraction a component supports.

2. Reusability—by ensuring that all supported functionality supplied by the component is equally accessible to all.

3. Maintainability—by avoiding unsupported "backdoor" interfaces that would violate the abstraction the component supports.

Suppose someone defined an external free function (or variable) in the `.c` file of component `foo` and failed to declare it as external function (or variable) in `foo.h`. Another component, `bar`, that happened to link with `foo` could obtain access to that function (or variable) by creating the appropriate external declaration locally. This unfortunate scenario is depicted in Figure 3-6. Note that this example illustrates a poor design (the kind of example I have tried to avoid presenting in this book).

As the figure shows, the `.c` file of `bar` is dependent on the definitions supplied by the physical implementation of `foo` but is independent of `foo`'s physical interface. There is a "backdoor" usage of `foo` and an implicit physical dependency of `bar` upon `foo` that cannot be detected easily. Automated dependency generators for makefiles (mkmf, gmake, etc.) that take into account only the `#include` graph would have no clue of this subtle dependency. Moreover, to the maintainers of this code there is no immediate evidence that these two components are coupled. Yet, when we go to reuse `bar`, the link phase will fail because the definition of function `f` (and global variable `size`) will be missing.

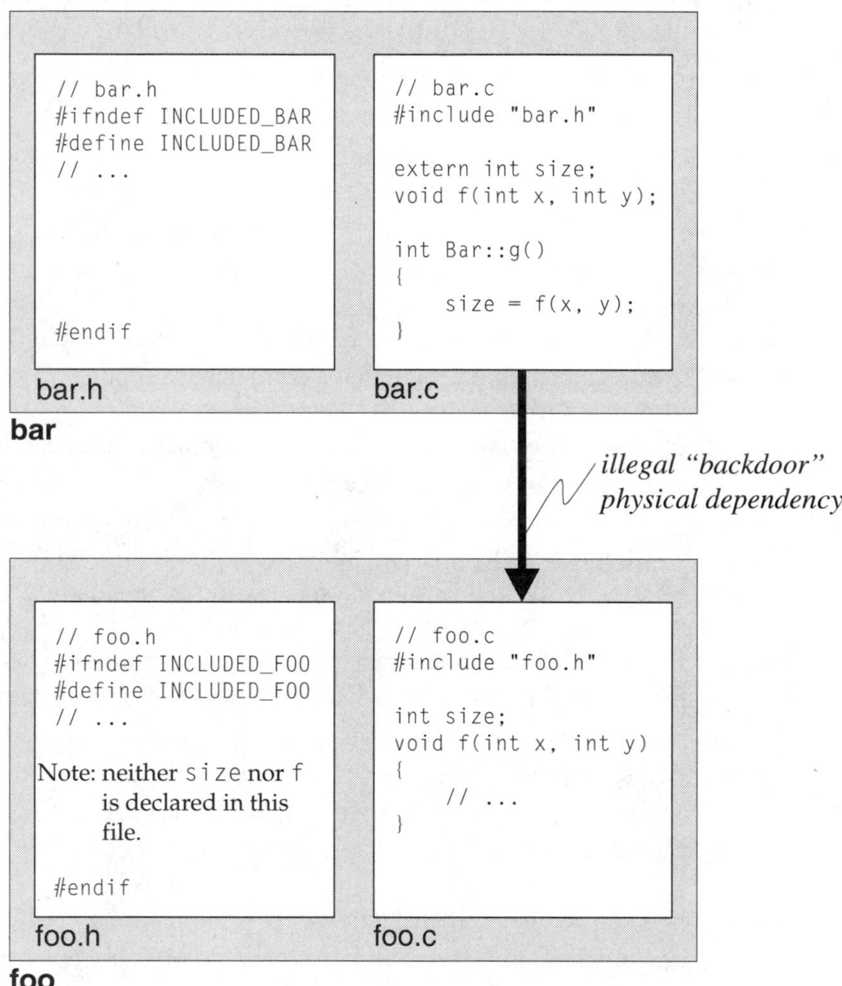

Figure 3-6: Poor Physical Design Where `bar.c` Depends on `foo.c` Directly

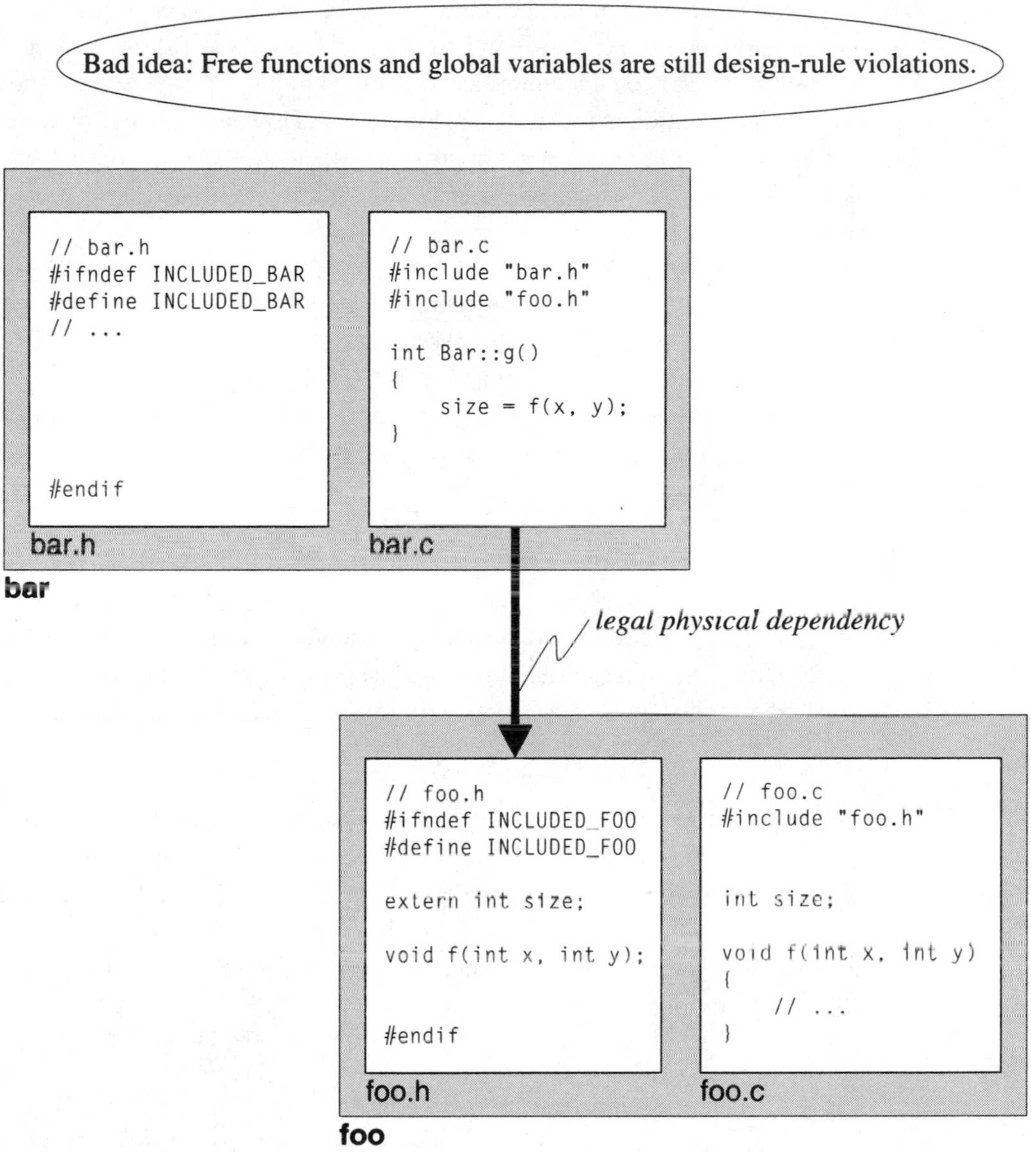

```
// bar.h
#ifndef INCLUDED_BAR
#define INCLUDED_BAR
// ...


#endif
```



```
// bar.c
#include "bar.h"
#include "foo.h"

int Bar::g()
{
    size = f(x, y);
}
```



```
// foo.h
#ifndef INCLUDED_FOO
#define INCLUDED_FOO

extern int size;

void f(int x, int y);


#endif
```



```
// foo.c
#include "foo.h"


int size;

void f(int x, int y)
{
    // ...
}
```


Figure 3-7: (Somewhat) Better Physical Design Where `bar.c` Depends on `foo.h`

Had the complete interface been specified in `foo.h`, the client component, `bar`, could simply have included the `foo.h` file in its own `.c` file, making the dependency of the implementation of `bar` on the interface of `foo` explicit. This new and somewhat improved implementation is illustrated in Figure 3-7. However, the use of an external global variable or an external free function is still a violation of the design rules presented in Section 2.3.1 and 2.3.2, respectively.

Classes defined at file scope entirely within the `.c` file of a component could easily violate this rule, since non-inline class member functions and static member data have external linkage. If we impose the same restrictions on classes defined entirely in a `.c` file that the C++ language itself imposes on local class definitions (i.e., classes defined entirely within a single function),[4] we can avoid creating external definitions and thereby avoid violating this rule.

Though technically a rule violation, defining a class entirely within a `.c` file is relatively harmless in practice because name mangling will tend to discourage one from trying to make direct use of the external symbols. The only real danger is that the external definition may collide with some other identical definition (which would still be the case if that class were defined in its own separate component). A more compelling reason to avoid defining classes entirely in a `.c` file might be that it cannot then be tested directly (see Section 8.4).

Avoiding backdoor usage is critical to good physical design and effective reuse. It is not enough to put the burden solely on the author of a component. To close all the loopholes, we must make a reciprocal requirement that no client attempt to make use of any construct with external linkage via local declarations. Instead, clients are required to include the `.h` file of a component in order to access any definitions that the component provides.

---

[4] **ellis**, Section 9.8, pp. 188–189.

Major Design Rule

Avoid accessing a definition with external linkage in another component via a local declaration; instead, include the `.h` file for that component.

Our reason for following this rule is primarily to make the dependency on external definitions in other components explicit.

Including the header as opposed to supplying a local function declaration has advantages for clients as well. Occasionally headers change. How will your local declarations change to reflect these header changes? An incorrectly declared function with C++ linkage can at least be caught at link time,[5] but incorrect local declarations of functions from the Standard C Library (with C linkage) could go undetected until runtime.

For example, the following will compile and link:

```
// foo.c
#include "foo.h"
extern "C" double pow(double, int); // bad idea: local extern declaration

double Foo::func(double x, double y)
{
    return pow(x, y) + pow(y, x);
}
```

However, we will get incorrect results at runtime because the local `extern` declaration does not match the actual definition of `pow`:[6]

```
extern "C" double pow(double, double)
{
    /* ... */
}
```

[5] See Type-Safe Linkage in **ellis**, Section 7.2c, pp. 121–126.
[6] **plauger**, Chapter 7, p. 138.

The mismatched declarations will cause the second argument of `pow` to become garbled. We can avoid such problems and make the dependency explicit by including the `.h` file instead:

```
// foo.c
#include "foo.h"
#include <math.h>      // pow()

double Foo::func(double x, double y)
{
    return pow(x, y) + pow(y, x);
}
```

By including the header files, inconsistencies with functions having either linkage characteristic will be caught at *compile time*, which is eminently preferable to either link time or runtime.

It is important to mention that class declarations of the form

```
class QueueLink;       // forward declaration of class QueueLink
```

are an entirely different matter because class definitions have *internal* linkage. Such declarations are not only common but desirable, especially where they can eliminate preprocessor `#include` directives in header files. This use of class declarations is discussed with respect to link-time dependencies in Section 5.10 and again with respect to compile-time dependencies in Section 6.4.3.

3.3 The DependsOn Relation

Physical dependencies among the components that make up a system will affect its development, maintenance, testing, and independent reuse. The logical relations among classes and free (operator) functions will imply physical dependencies among the components in which they reside. We can define implementation dependency for functions loosely by saying that a function depends on a component if that component is needed in order to compile and link the body of that function. We can define implementation dependency for classes in a similar way. More generally, we can define precisely a central and purely physical relation among components.

> **<u>DEFINITION</u>: A component** y ***DependsOn*** **a component** x **if** x **is needed in order to compile or link** y**.**

The DependsOn relation is quite different from the relations we have already seen. IsA and Uses are logical relations because they apply to logical entities, irrespective of the physical components in which those logical entities reside. DependsOn is a physical relation because it applies to components as a whole, which are themselves physical entities.

The notation used to represent the dependency of one physical unit on another is a (fat) arrow. For example,

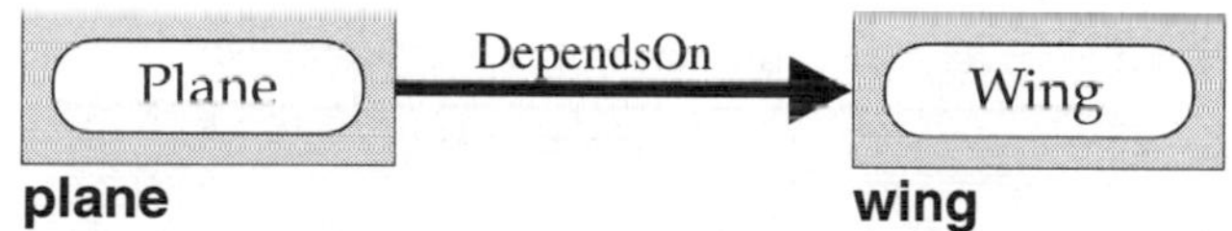

implies that component `plane` depends on component `wing`. That is, component `plane` cannot be used (i.e., it cannot be linked into a program or possibly even compiled) unless component `wing` is also available.

As has been our convention, logical entities are represented by ellipses, and physical entities are represented by rectangles. Notice that the arrow used to indicate physical dependency is drawn between components and not individual classes. The (fat) arrow notation used to denote physical dependency should never be confused with the arrow notation used to denote inheritance. An inheritance arrow always runs between two classes (which are logical entities); a DependsOn arrow connects physical entities (such as files, components, and packages).

To illustrate the DependsOn relation in action, consider the following skeleton header file for a string component. By the way, don't try to name your component "string"; it may not work well in the presence of the standard C library header `string.h`.

```
// str.h
#ifndef INCLUDED_STR
#define INCLUDED_STR

#ifndef INCLUDED_CHARARRAY
#include "chararray.h"
#endif

class String {
    CharArray d_array;  // HasA
    // ...
  public:
    // ...
};

// ...

#endif
```

There is just enough information visible for us to see that class `String` has a data member of type `CharArray`. We know from C that if a `struct` has an instance of a user-defined type as a data member, it will be necessary to know the size and layout of that data member even to parse the definition of the `struct`.

> **<u>DEFINITION</u>: A component `y` exhibits a *compile-time* dependency on component `x` if `x.h` is needed in order to compile `y.c`.**

More specifically, it is not possible to compile any file that needs the definition of `String` without first including `chararray.h`. For that reason we are justified in nesting `#include` "`chararray.h`" in the header file of component `str` along with the concomitant, redundant include guards.

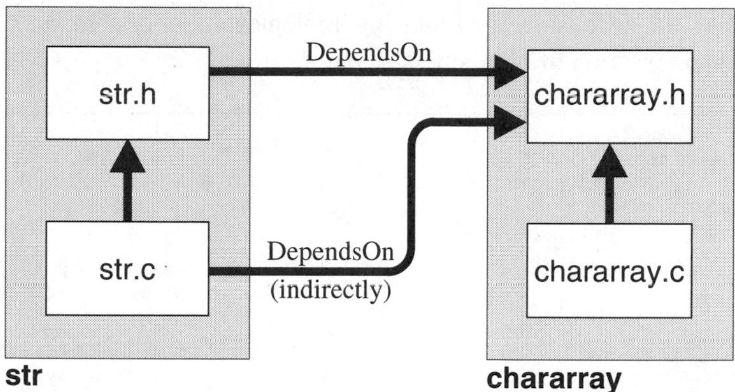

Figure 3-8: Indirect Compile-Time Dependency of `str.c` **on** `chararray.h`

Figure 3-8 illustrates the physical dependency of component `str` on component `chararray`. A component's `.c` file must always depend on its `.h` file at compile time. Since `str.c` will not compile without `str.h`, and `str.h` will not compile without `chararray.h`, `str.c` has an indirect compile-time dependency on `chararray.h`. Notice again that the arrow used to indicate the physical dependency is drawn between two physical entities (in this case, files). A more abstract representation of physical dependency at the component level is shown in Figure 3-9.

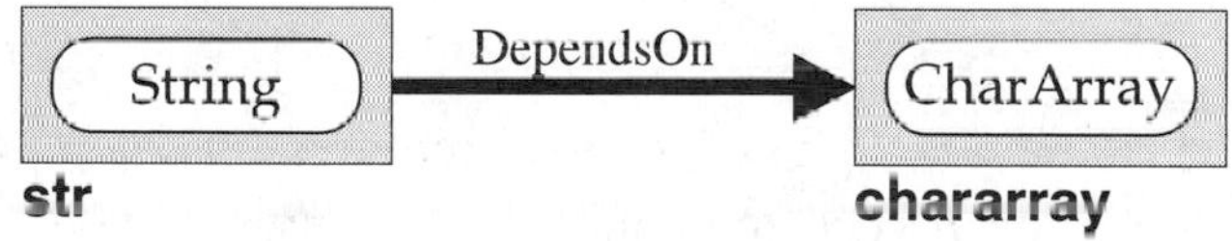

Figure 3-9: Abstract Representation of Component Dependency

A component need not be dependent on another at compile time to be dependent on it at link time. Consider the following implementation for component `word` and an *alternate* implementation of component `str`:

```
// word.h
#ifndef INCLUDED_WORD
#define INCLUDED_WORD

#ifndef INCLUDED_STR
#include "str.h"
#endif

class Word {
    String d_string;  // HasA
    // ...
  public:
    Word();
    // ...
};

#endif
```

```
// str.h
#ifndef INCLUDED_STR
#define INCLUDED_STR


class CharArray;


class String {
    CharArray *d_array_p;  // HoldsA
    // ...
  public:
    String();
    // ...
};

#endif
```

```
// word.c
#include "word.h"


// ...
```

```
// str.c
#include "str.h"
#include "chararray.h"

// ...
```

Compiling `chararray.c` of course requires `chararray.h`. Both `str.h` and `chararray.h` are needed to compile `str.c`. Finally, both `word.h` and `str.h` are needed to compile `word.c`. Notice that `chararray.h` is *not* needed in order to compile `word.c`. There is no compile-time dependency of component `word` on component `chararray`. However, `word` still exhibits a physical dependency on `chararray`, which will become obvious as soon as we try to link `word` to a test driver.

> **DEFINITION: A component `y` exhibits a *link-time* dependency on component `x` if the object file `y.o` (produced by compiling `y.c`) contains undefined symbols for which `x.o` may be called upon either directly or indirectly to help resolve at link time.**

Recall that, except for inline functions, all class member functions and static data members in C++ have external linkage. For all practical purposes we can say that if a component needs to include another component in order to compile, it is going to depend on that component at link time to resolve undefined symbols at the object-code level.

Principle

A compile-time dependency almost always implies a link-time dependency.

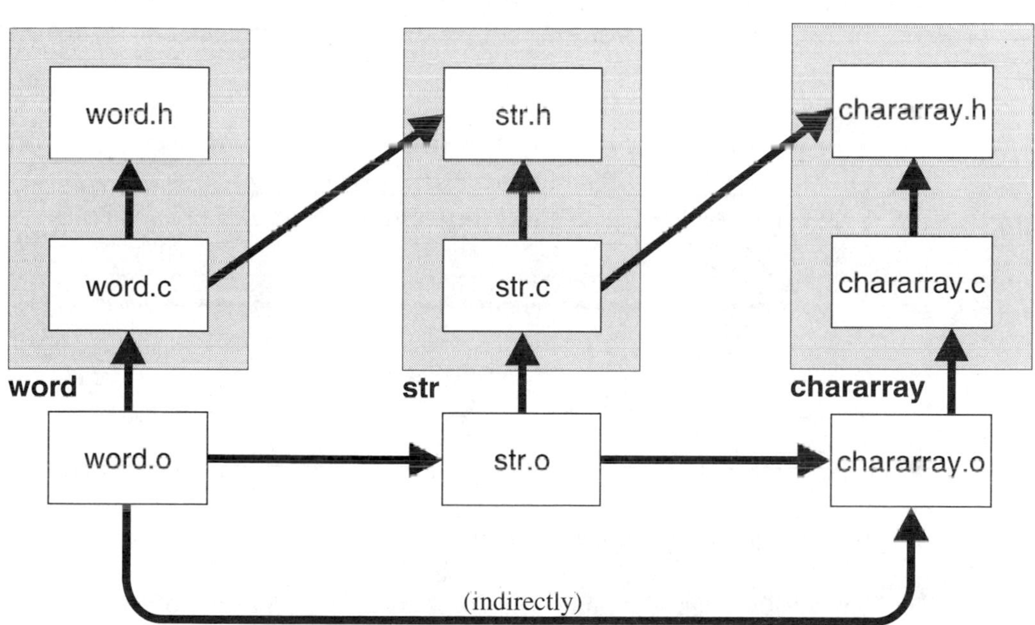

Figure 3-10: Link-Time Dependency of `word` **on** `chararray`

As Figure 3-10 shows, `word.o` depends on external names defined in `str.o`. Even if `word.o` does not directly use names defined in `chararray.o`, it does use names defined in `str.o`. The names used in `str.o` to resolve these undefined symbols will probably introduce new undefined symbols whose definitions must be supplied by `chararray.o`. Given the above, we come to an interesting and important conclusion.

Principle

The DependsOn relation for components is transitive.

For example, assume `x`, `y`, and `z` are components. If `x` depends on `y`, and `y` depends on `z`, then `x` depends on `z`. The transitive property of dependency among components makes no mention of which file in one component is dependent on which file in the other. Any such file-level dependency is sufficient to produce an implementation dependency for the components as a whole.

The abstract, component-level dependency diagram for the previous example is shown in Figure 3-11. The compile-time dependencies of `word` on `str` and of `str` on `chararray` have produced the indirect (link-time) dependency of `word` on `chararray`.

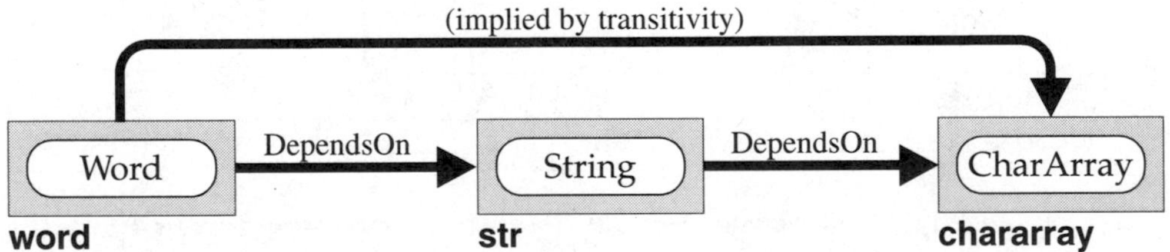

Figure 3-11: Abstract, Component-Level Dependency Diagram

The DependsOn relation is important to physical design because it indicates all the components required for the functionality supplied by a given component to be maintained, tested, and reused. We have just seen how to infer physical dependency from the source code itself. As we will see in Section 3.4, it is possible to infer physical dependency directly from abstract logical relationships such as IsA and Uses. Inferring physical dependencies at the design stage will help us to achieve a sound physical architecture early in the development process.

3.4 Implied Dependency

Logical designs imply certain physical characteristics. We would like to be able to take full advantage of known logical relationships in order to predict the physical implications of our logical design *before* it is implemented. Resulting undesirable physical characteristics will often force us to alter or even entirely rework our logical designs. In this section we focus on the implications of logical design on physical dependency, beginning with the Uses relation.

Principle

A component defining a function will *usually* have a physical dependency on any component defining a type used by that function.

Unless otherwise stated, we will assume that if a function uses a user defined type, it does so in a substantive way. To explain what we mean by *substantive*, let us assume for the moment that if a function uses a type in its interface, it will be necessary for the component defining that function to include the `.h` file for the component defining that type.

```
// two.c
#include "two.h"
#include "one.h"
// ...
int Two::getInfo(const One& one)
{
    return one.info();
}
// ...
```

```
// one.h
#ifndef INCLUDED_ONE
#define INCLUDED_ONE
// ...
class One {
    // ...
    int info() const;
    // ...
};
// ...
#endif
```

Figure 3-12: The Uses Relation Often Implies a Compile-Time Dependency

Figure 3-12 illustrates our assumption that if function `Two::getInfo` uses class `One` in its interface, then it likely does something with `One` in its implementation that would require having seen `One`'s definition. In this example, `Two::getInfo` invokes the const member function info of class One, which requires the compiler to see the definition of One in order to compile two.c.

The assumption that the Uses relation implies a compile-time dependency is too strong. However, this assumption predicts physical implementation dependencies fairly accurately. It is not necessary for the Uses relation to cause a compile-time dependency in order to induce an indirect physical dependency. To see how an indirect link-time dependency can occur, consider adding another component, three, and two more files, two.h and three.c, to those of the previous example.

```
// three.c
#include "three.h"
#include "two.h"
// ...
int Three::x2info(const One& one)
{
    return 2 * Two::getInfo(one);
}
// ...
```

```
// two.h
#ifndef INCLUDED_TWO
#define INCLUDED_TWO
class One;
// ...
class Two {
    // ...
  public:
    static int getInfo(const One& one);
    // ...
};
// ...
#endif
```

Figure 3-13: Uses Relation Almost Always Implies a Link-Time Dependency

As shown in Figure 3-13, three.c defines a member function, x2info, which uses class One in its interface. However, the argument to x2info is passed by reference and x2info makes no substantive use of One's definition before passing its argument off to Two's static member function getInfo, which also accepts a One object by reference. The x2info function in component three treats class One opaquely and does not know anything about One other than that it is a class, struct, or union.

Suppose that no other function in class Three uses One (substantively), and also that there is no other compile-time dependency of component three on component one. That is, three.h and two.h alone are sufficient to compile three.c, even though One is used in the interface of three. But function x2info does depend on One indirectly. If we try to test three, we will not be able to link until we have written and compiled two.c. To do that, two.c will have to include one.h.

As Figure 3-14 illustrates, implementation dependency brought on by using an object is transitive. That is, if `Three` uses `Two` and `Two` uses `One`, then the component that defines `Three` (almost always) DependsOn the component that defines `One`. In this case, function `x2info` in component `three` used `One` (trivially) but also used function `getInfo` defined in component `two`. Function `getInfo` also uses `One` in its interface, but this time `getInfo` uses `One` substantively in its implementation.

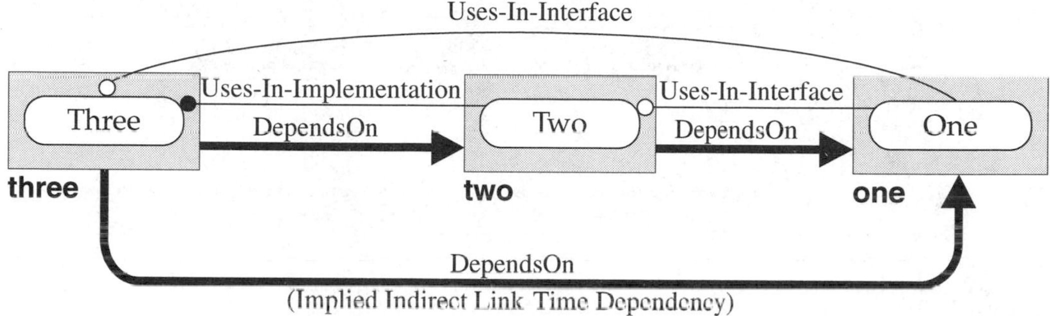

Figure 3-14: Logical Uses Relation Implying Component Dependency

It is possible to use another object without inducing either a compile-time or link-time dependency on that object. In practice, such limited usage sometimes occurs by design, but almost never by chance. We will explore this design technique in Section 5.4.

Principle

A component defining a class that IsA or HasA user-defined type *always* has a compile-time dependency on the component defining that type.

Certain logical relationships have strong physical implications. For example, deriving from a type (IsA) or embedding an instance of a type (HasA) always implies that a class will depend on that type at compile time. In fact, these logical relations imply a compile-time dependency not only for the class itself, but also for any client of the class.

Figure 3-15 illustrates the physical implications of IsA and HasA for the example in Figure 3-11. This time `Word` is a kind of `String`, and `String` has a `CharArray` data member. The definitions for both `String` and `CharArray` must be available in order for `word.c` to compile. Moreover, every client of `Word` will also require the definitions both `String` and `CharArray` in order to compile. These same strong physical implications hold for private derivation and for inline functions that make substantive use of a type. In all of these cases we are justified in nesting the required `#include` directives in the component's `.h file`.

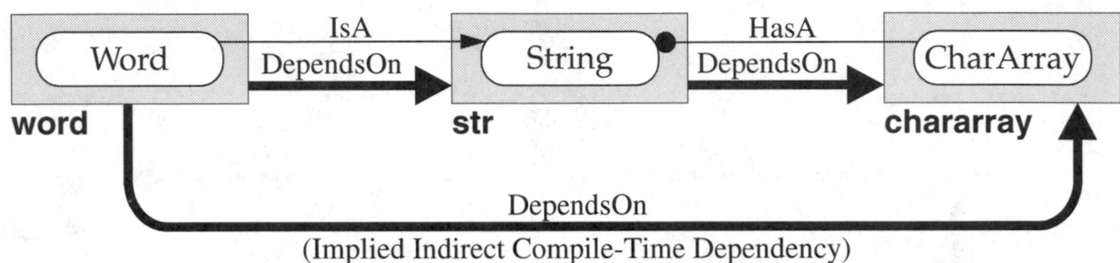

Figure 3-15: Logical IsA and HasA Relations Implying Component Dependency

Such strong physical coupling is not necessarily implied if a class HoldsA type (that is, if it has a pointer or reference to that type as a data member), nor is it implied if the type is used substantively in the body of a non-inline function. Such usage does *not* justify forcing clients of the component to depend at compile time on its implementation types as would result from nesting the `#include` directive in the component's header. These subtle but important distinctions will be exploited to reduce compile-time coupling in Chapter 6.

So far we have dealt with only two or three classes at a time. Now we will infer, from a given abstract logical representation, the physical dependencies among a somewhat larger collection of components. The diagram in Figure 3-16 depicts a small subsystem used to support an online glossary.

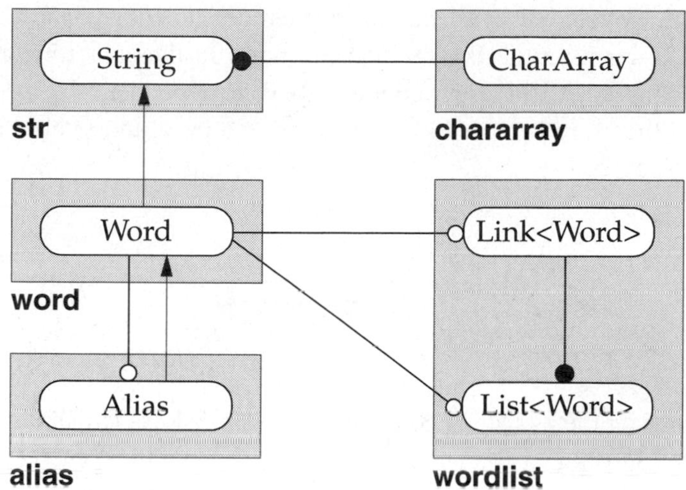

Figure 3-16: Intercomponent Logical Relationships

At the upper right of Figure 3-16, we see class `CharArray` in its own separate component. The `String` class (to its left) uses `CharArray` in its implementation, so we infer a likely physical dependency of component `str` on component `chararray`:

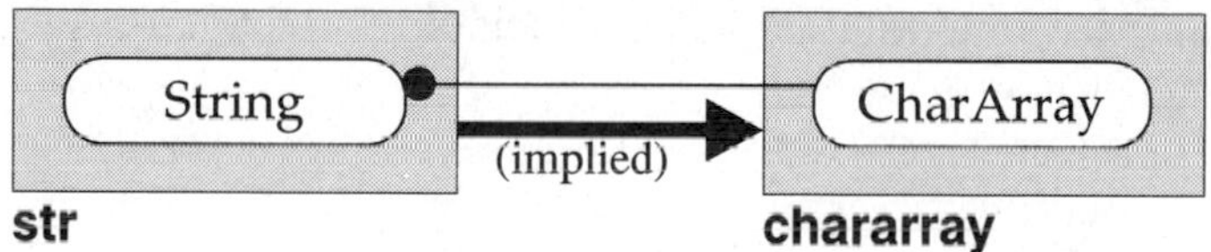

As we saw previously, a `Word` is a kind of `String`. An arrow from class `Word` to class `String` is used to denote this relationship. We also know that the IsA relationship always implies a compile-time physical dependency between the defining components (in the same direction as the inheritance arrow). Hence `word` definitely depends on `str`.

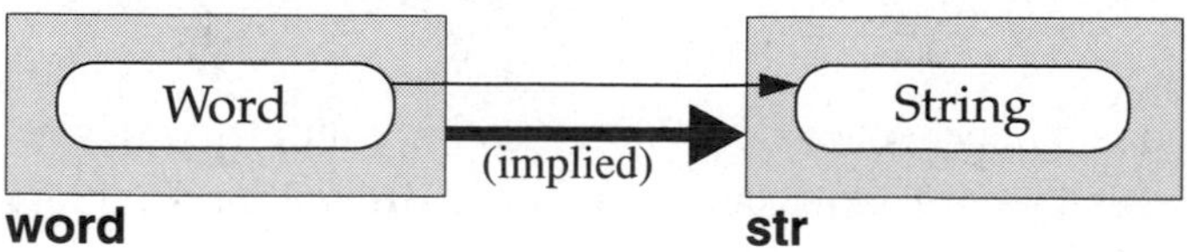

As we can see from Figure 3-16, Alias not only IsA Word but also Uses Word in its interface. Notice, however, that the implied dependency of the Uses relationship and the arrow denoting the IsA relationship point in the same direction (from Alias to Word). Consequently, there is no implied cyclic dependency between Word and Alias. It would therefore be possible to use word in a program without including or linking to alias.

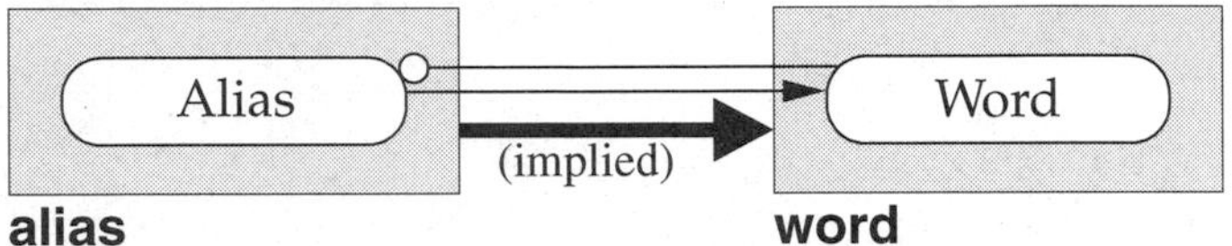

Now consider the wordlist component of Figure 3-16, which defines two presumably template classes Link<Word> and List<Word>. Within component wordlist we see that there is a logical Uses-In-The-Implementation relationship between List<Word> and Link<Word>. Since these classes are already defined within the same component, logical relationships between them cannot affect physical dependencies.

Both Link<Word> and List<Word> use Word in their respective interfaces. Either one of these logical relationships alone would be sufficient for us to infer a likely physical dependency of the entire wordlist component on word. Notice again that component word can exist in a program without including or linking to wordlist, but not vice versa.

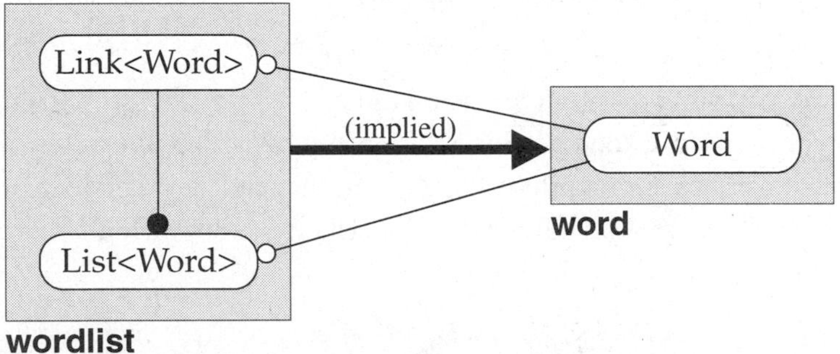

A component dependency diagram produced by inferring physical dependencies from the abstract logical relationships of Figure 3-16 is shown in Figure 3-17. Actually, this diagram does not show a complete component dependency graph. For example, it does not explicitly show the indirect dependency of word on chararray, or of `wordlist` on `str`. The complete dependency diagram is obtained if we draw each *indirect* dependency as if it were a direct dependency. Such a graph is called a *transitive closure*.

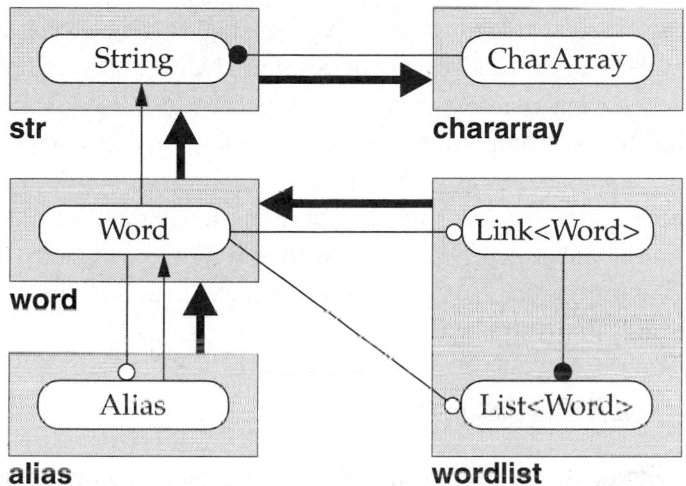

Figure 3-17: Component Diagram Showing Only Direct Dependencies

The transitive closure of the dependency graph in Figure 3-17 is shown in Figure 3-18a. All of the edges in this graph labeled with a *t* are called *transitive edges* because their existence is implied by other edges that represent "direct" dependencies. Removing these redundant transitive edges does not lose essential information, but it does reduce clutter and make the graph easier to understand.

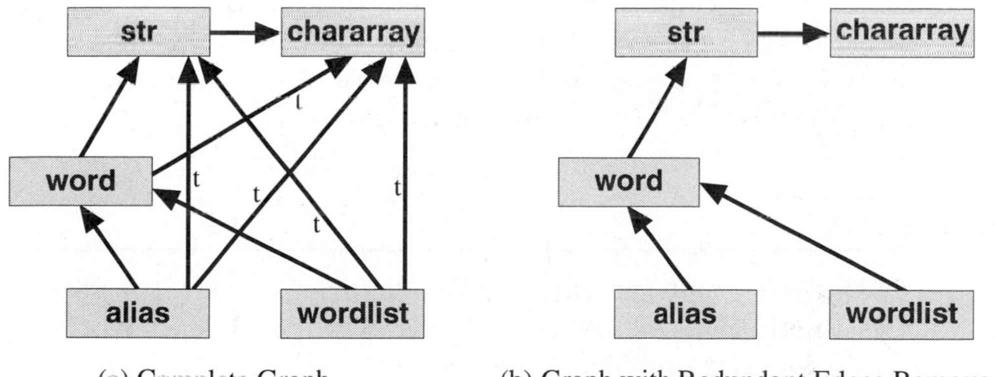

(a) Complete Graph (b) Graph with Redundant Edges Removed

Figure 3-18: Transitive Closure of Direct Dependency Graph

It is easy to tell from Figure 3-18b that `word` depends indirectly on `chararray` and that `wordlist` depends indirectly on `word`. In general, a component `x` DependsOn component `y` if and only if there is path in the dependency graph from `x` to `y`.

To recap: logical relationships imply physical dependencies. Relationships such as IsA and HasA between logical entities will always imply compile-time dependencies when implemented across component boundaries. Relationships such as HoldsA and Uses are likely to imply link-time dependencies across components. By considering implied dependencies at design time, we can evaluate the physical quality of our architecture long before any code is written. In Chapter 4 we discuss the characteristics of component dependencies that both improve testability and promote reuse. In the following section, we see how to extract the actual physical dependencies from source code more efficiently.

3.5 Extracting Actual Dependencies

Suppose now that we are designing a large project, guided by implied dependencies. After the design stage is largely complete and development is under way, we would like to have a tool that could extract the actual physical dependencies among our components. We could then track the actual component dependencies and compare them with our initial design expectations.

Although it is possible to parse the source for an entire C++ program to determine the exact component dependency graph, doing so is both difficult and relatively slow. However, provided the design rules presented in Section 3.2 have been followed, it is possible to extract the component dependency graph directly from the components' source files by parsing only the C++ preprocessor `#include` directives. Such processing is relatively fast as and is done by a number of standard, public-domain dependency analysis tools (such as gmake, mkmf, and cdep).

Principle

The include graph generated by C++ preprocessor `#include` directives should alone be sufficient to infer all physical dependencies within a system provided the system compiles.

To see why this claim is true, consider the following line of reasoning. If component x makes direct substantive use of component y, then in order to compile x, the compiler will have to see the definition supplied in y.h. The only way this can happen is for component x to directly or indirectly include y.h. As a result of the design rules in Section 3.2, any such direct substantive use is synonymous with a compile-time dependency.

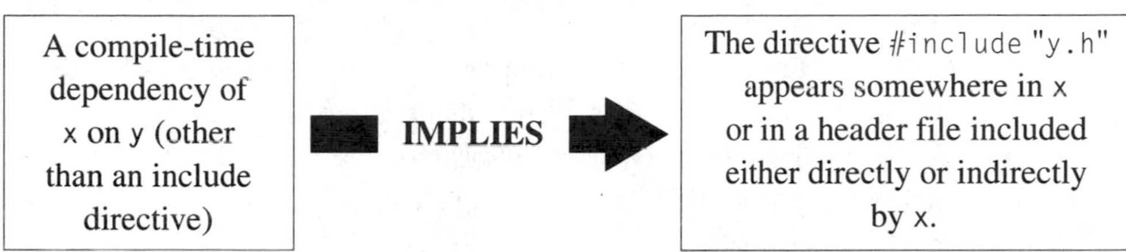

The contrapositive (that if x does *not* include y.h, then x does *not* have a compile-time dependency on y) is certainly true, provided x compiles.

Going the other way, the only reason component x would legitimately include the header file of component y is if component x did in fact make direct substantive use of component y. Otherwise the inclusion itself would be superfluous and introduce unwanted compile-time coupling.

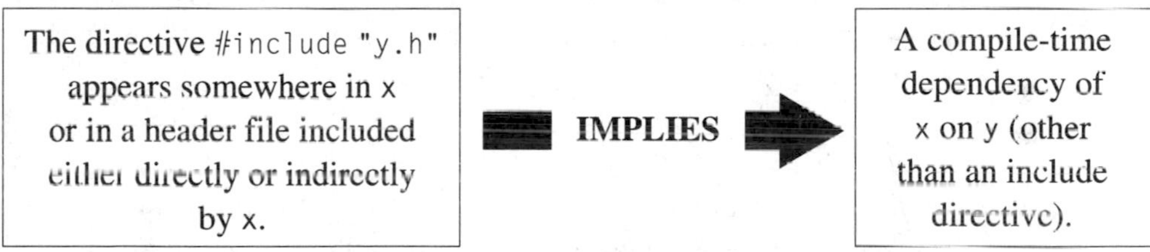

The contrapositive (that if x does *not* have an intrinsic compile-time dependency on y, then x does *not* include y.h) should always be true—but occasionally, through human oversight, it is not.

Guideline

A component x should include y.h only if x makes direct substantive use of a class or free operator function defined in y.

The very fact that one component includes the header of another forces a compile-time dependency whether or not one previously existed. If we assume that all `#include` directives in a component are necessary, then it is likely that the compile-time dependency will be accompanied by a link-time dependency (which we already know is transitive). In other words, "substantive use" *should* equate to "header file inclusion," and that substantive use almost always implies a kind of physical dependency that is transitive.

The `#include` graph for a set of components is just another relation that happens to reflect the dependency among components quite accurately. If we interpret "`x` Includes `y.h` (either directly or indirectly)" as "`x` DependsOn `y` directly," then the relation resulting from the `#include` graph accurately reflects compile-time physical component dependencies.

The design rule stating that all substantive use of a component must be flagged by including its header file (rather than via local `extern` declarations) *guarantees* that the transitive closure of the Includes relation indicates all actual physical dependencies among components.

These extracted dependencies occasionally err on the side of being too conservative. The dependency graph extracted in this manner may indicate additional, fictitious dependencies brought on by unnecessary `#include` directives (which should be removed). But, provided that all the major design rules are followed, the graph will never omit an actual component dependency.

The ability to extract actual physical dependencies from a potentially large collection of components quickly and accurately allows us to verify *throughout the development process* that these dependencies are consistent with our overall architectural plan. A physical dependency extractor/analyzer tool is described in Appendix C.

3.6 Friendship

We now digress to discuss the subtle issues regarding friendship and how granting friendship affects the logical interface of a class and of a component. The interaction between friendship and physical design is surprisingly strong. Although ostensibly a logical design issue, friendship *will* influence the way in which we collect logical constructs into components. The desire to avoid friendship across component boundaries can even induce us to restructure our logical design. We refer to the material presented in this section frequently throughout this book.

Guideline

Avoid granting (long-distance) friendship to a logical entity defined in another component.

According to the *Annotated C++ Reference Manual*, "A friend is as much a part of the interface of a class as a member is."[7] In making this claim, there is an implicit assumption that the friend is inseparably tied to an object granting it friendship.

From a purely logical point of view, if a class makes a declaration of friendship, then, according to the definition of Encapsulation (Section 2.2), that declaration is *not* an encapsulated detail of the class. Anyone who defines a function whose declaration exactly matches that of a `friend` declaration within a class can gain programmatic access to the private members of that class, provided no other function matching the `friend` declaration is defined in the same program. In that very precise sense, the `friend` declaration itself is part of the interface of the class—the actual function definition is not.

Principle

Friendship within a component is an implementation detail of that component.

By treating the component and not the class as the fundamental unit of design, we gain an entirely different perspective. As long as friendship is granted locally (i.e., as long as it is granted only to logical entities defined within the same component), the friends are, in fact, inseparably tied to the object granting friendship.

---

[7] **ellis**, Section 11.4, p. 248.

DEFINITION: A contained implementation detail (type, data, or function) that is not accessible or detectable programmatically through the logical interface of a component is said to be *encapsulated* by that component.

By definition, it must be possible to determine what is in the logical (public) interface programmatically. Consider the equality operator defined within component `stack`:

```
int operator==(const Stack&, const Stack&);
```

If this operator were suddenly declared a `friend` of class `Stack`, allegedly placing the operator itself in the (public) interface of `Stack`, then it should be possible to detect this change programmatically—right? But, provided that the operator is defined within the same component, granting the operator friend status has absolutely no effect on the logical interface of that component. In fact, from any client's point of view, whether `operator==` is or is not a friend of class `Stack` is an encapsulated implementation detail of this component!

To illustrate this point further, consider briefly a `String` class that defines (among other things) member `operator+=` to implement concatenation to itself.

```
String {
    //...
  public:
    //...
    String(const String& string);                   // copy constructor
    //...
    String& operator+=(const String& rhs);          // concatenate to me
};
```

We can now choose to implement nondestructive concatenation (+) in the same component, without making the operator a friend:

```
String operator+(const String& lhs, const String& rhs)
{
    return String(lhs) += rhs;
}
```

If after analysis we find it necessary to improve the performance of `operator+`, we can extend the encapsulation of class `String` by declaring `operator+` a friend of `String`:

```
String {
    //...
    friend String operator+(const String&, const String&);
  public:
    //...
    String(const String& string);                    // copy constructor
    //...
    String& operator+=(const String& rhs);           // concatenate to me
};
```

Declaring `operator+` to be a `friend` of `String` allows for a more efficient implementation and potentially increases the cost of maintenance, but does *not* affect the logical interface of the component:

```
String operator+(const String& lhs, const String& rhs)
{
    // clever, more efficient implementation using private members
}
```

There is simply no programmatic way for a client of a component to tell whether a given logical entity defined within the component is declared a `friend` of a class defined within that same component.[8]

Principle

Granting (local) friendship to classes defined within the same component does *not* violate encapsulation.

Granting local friendship does not threaten to expose the private details of an object to unauthorized users. Because classes that are declared friends are defined (locally) *within the header file* of the same component, anyone who tries to use the object granting friendship will have the valid definitions of all friend classes thrust upon

[8] The C++ language makes no distinction based on the location of the friend declaration within a class. However, placing the declaration in a private area of the class reflects the *component*'s semantics with respect to local friendship.

them. Any attempt to redefine these friend classes will be prevented by the compiler, which will promptly issue the error:

```
MULTIPALLY DEFINED CLASS.
```

Principle

Defining an iterator class along with a container class *in the same component* enables user extensibility, improves maintainability, and enhances reusability *while preserving encapsulation*.

Locally, within a single component, friendship should be granted where necessary to achieve proper encapsulation for the component as a whole. As with the Container/Iterator pattern, we would always like to keep logical entities with access to our implementation physically close to reflect the high degree of logical intimacy. Granting friendship to logical entities outside a component, referred to in this book as *long-distance friendship*, is an entirely different matter.

Principle

Granting (long-distance) friendship to a logical entity defined in a separate physical part of the system violates the encapsulation of the class granting that friendship.

Granting private access to another physical piece of the system leaves a hole in the encapsulation that could be abused by plugging in a counterfeit component to obtain access. For example, suppose the `StackIter` class from Section 3.1 were declared in component `stackiter`, separate from class `Stack`. Then there would be nothing to stop a user of the `stack` component from substituting his or her own component defining a customized `StackIter`, and thereby obtaining private access to the `Stack` class. Once this happens, the class granting the long-distance friendship has no protection against access to its private members—its encapsulation has been violated.

Beside being a violation of encapsulation, long-distance friendship is a symptom of a poorly structured design. Having physically separate logical entities intimately dependent on one another subtly degrades maintainability. Specifically, long-distance friendships reduce modularity by allowing local changes to private implementation details to affect physically remote parts of the system.

Excessive use of even local friendship affects maintainability. Granting friendship extends the "interface" of a class itself. The more functions that have access to the encapsulated details of an object's implementation, the more code that will have to be revisited (and possibly reworked) in the event of an implementation change. The fewer the lines of code that directly access private information, the easier it is to experiment with alternative implementations.

3.6.1 Long-Distance Friendship and Implied Dependency

Although discouraged, the possibility of granting friendship outside of a component leads us to establish whether functions matching a `friend` declaration of a class should themselves be considered when determining the Uses relation involving that class. The answer to this subtle question is important, but only when it comes to inferring physical dependency based on the Uses relation where friendship transcends a single component.

Principle

Friendship affects access privilege but not implied dependency.

A class is an indivisible logical unit. A free function is a distinct logical unit. Whether the free function is or is not a friend of a class never affects any implied physical dependency in the system.

Consider the free operator function

```
// barop.h
class Bar;
int operator==(const Bar&, const Bar&);
```

defined in its own component, `barop`. Figure 3-19 shows this operator along with class `Stack` and class `StackIter` (now shown in separate components as well). This free operator is neither a member nor a friend of `Stack`, and therefore it clearly does not extend the interface of class `Stack`. But what exactly changes when we declare this operator a `friend` of `Stack`?

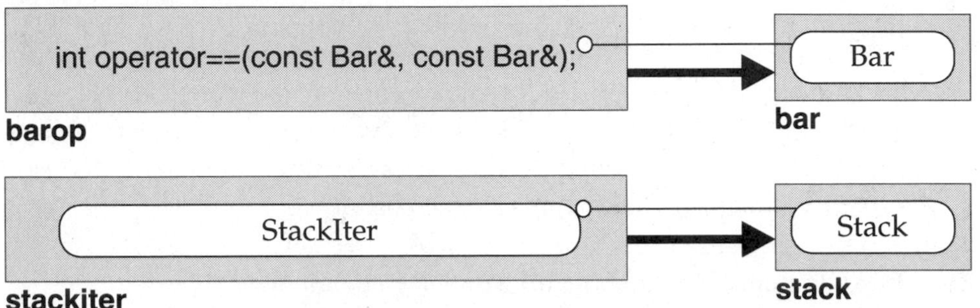

Figure 3-19: Related Logical Entities in Distinct Components

Would `operator==(const Bar&, const Bar&)` now be considered part of the interface of class `Stack`? If so, then `Stack` uses `Bar` in its interface, and there is an erroneous implied dependency of component `stack` on component `bar` as shown in Figure 3-20.

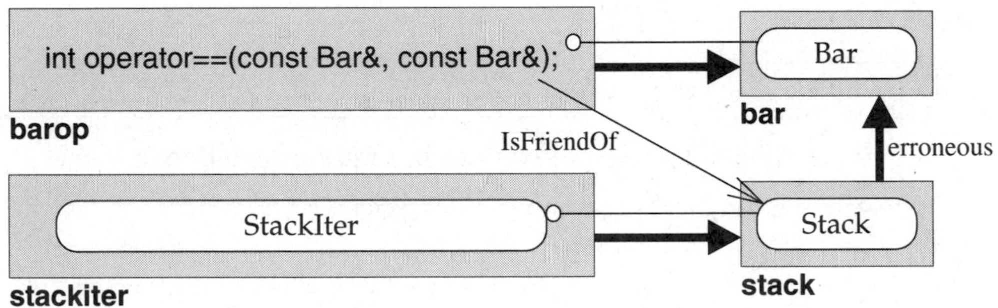

Figure 3-20: Erroneously Inferred Dependency of `stack` **on** `bar`

The physical dependencies of `Stack` do not suddenly assume those of `barop` just by granting the operator friendship. Using a type implies a dependency on *all* of its members but *not* necessarily on *any* of its friends. In particular, `operator==(const Bar&, const Bar&)` is a friend of `Stack`. `StackIter` Uses `Stack`, but this in no way implies that `StackIter` Uses `operator==(const Bar&, const Bar&)` either directly or indirectly.

Notice the direction of the arrow used to indicate the IsFriendOf relation in Figure 3-20. The arrow indicates that `operator==(const Bar&, const Bar&)` is now *permitted* to depend on `Stack` in a more intimate way than before, but it does not guarantee any actual dependency. There is no physical dependency whatsoever in the opposite direction—as would be implied by treating `operator==(const Bar&, const Bar&)` as if it were part of the `Stack`'s logical interface. To summarize, only access privilege and not physical dependency is altered by granting friendship.

The importance of this principle is illustrated by the following pair of free operators used to compare objects of type `Stack` and type `Foo` (symmetrically):

```
int operator==(const Stack&, const Foo&)
int operator==(const Foo&, const Stack&)
```

We do not need to look inside the header file for either `Stack` or `Foo` to know that these operators are not members and therefore are not part of the logical interface of either class. Since these operators are not part of either class, we could define them in an entirely separate component that could then be included by clients only when needed. Regardless of the access privilege, the Uses-In-The-Interface relation points in one direction, from operator to class, as shown in Figure 3-21.

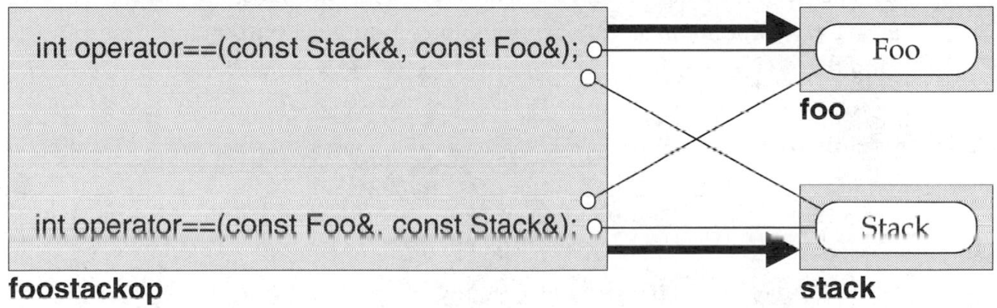

Figure 3-21: Acyclic Dependency of Free Operators on Classes

Now consider the highly questionable decision to add instead the following two `operator==` *member* functions:

```
int Stack::operator==(const Foo&   rhs) const;
int   Foo::operator==(const Stack& rhs) const;
```

As members, these operator functions are clearly part of the interfaces of their respective classes. Each member operator uses the other class in its interface. The presence of these operators introduces an undesirable, cyclic Uses-In-The-Interface relationship between `Foo` and `Stack` as shown in Figure 3-22. No such cyclic dependency was induced when the operators were free and defined in a separate component. Adding free (operator) functions never affects the logical interface of any class regardless of access because free operators, unlike members, are not an intrinsic part of any class. (Note that making `operator==` a member is a poor decision in terms of purely logical design considerations, as discussed in Section 9.1.2.)

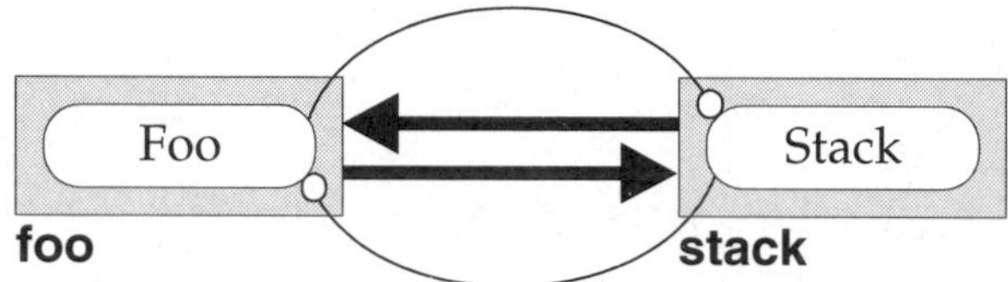

Figure 3-22: Cyclic Dependency of Member Operators on Classes

Although granting friendship in itself never directly affects implied dependencies, friendship can indirectly affect physical coupling. In trying to avoid the problems associated with long-distance friendships, we may find ourselves grouping several intimately dependent logical entities into a single component, thus physically coupling them (see Section 5.8).

3.6.2 Friendship and Fraud

Protecting one's implementation from unauthorized use is important for large projects, which may span several levels of management as well as several geographical locations. In such cases, just saying, "I'm leaving a hole, but please keep out!" doesn't work. People (particularly customers) who have access to your code at the source level will do what they need to do to get their programs working. If using one of your private data members will solve their problem, given half a chance they will probably use it. If users are able to access your implementation directly, you may meet with unwanted resistance should you try to improve it in the future.

An unscrupulous developer can gain access to private details simply by defining the friend class locally (at file scope). The developer can then exploit these details via inline functions, which do not have external linkage and hence will not collide with the legitimate function definitions, even if they are linked into the program. For the same reason, declaring an individual non-inline free (operator) function a `friend`—even locally—is not immune to fraud via inline replacement. People actually do this in production code. You have been warned!

Figure 3-23 illustrates the highly questionable practice of taking deliberate advantage of the hole in encapsulation left by employing long-distance friendships. Class `Jail` defines a private member `release()` and befriends a class *named* `JailKey`, defined outside the `jail` component. The authorized `JailKey` is defined within component `jailkey`, which is linked into the program. A malevolent `visitor` component declares a local version of class `JailKey` hidden entirely within the `visitor.c` file. Since this illicit version of `JailKey` has no members with external linkage, it is able to coexist silently in a program and still take advantage of the friendship afforded by `Jail`. The constructor for the `Visitor` object named "bugsy" defined in `main()` creates an instance of its own `JailKey`, which on construction calls the private `release()` method of Jail. Escape is inevitable.

Sadly, there are even easier and more heinous ways to violate encapsulation:

```
// felon.c
#define private public          // capital offense
#include "jail.h"

void Felon::breakOut(Jail *jail)
{
    jail->release();
}

// ...
```

However, writing headers such as

```
// jail.h
#if !defined(INCLUDED_JAIL) && !defined(protected) && !defined(private)
#define INCLUDED_JAIL

class Jail {                    // maximum security
// ...

#endif
```

is probably going too far.

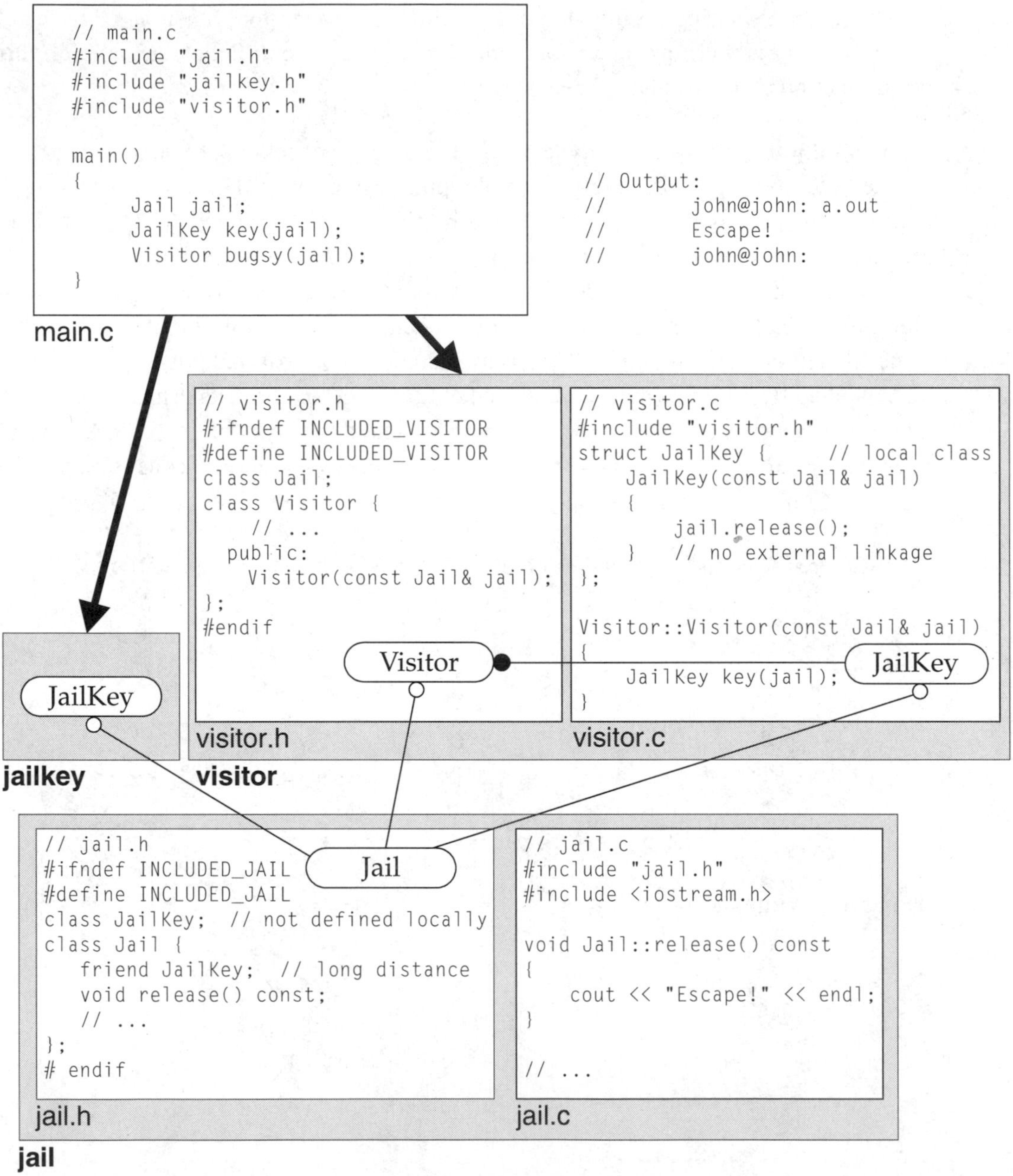

```
// main.c
#include "jail.h"
#include "jailkey.h"
#include "visitor.h"

main()
{
     Jail jail;
     JailKey key(jail);
     Visitor bugsy(jail);
}
```

main.c

```
// Output:
//        john@john: a.out
//        Escape!
//        john@john:
```

```
// visitor.h
#ifndef INCLUDED_VISITOR
#define INCLUDED_VISITOR
class Jail;
class Visitor {
    // ...
  public:
    Visitor(const Jail& jail);
};
#endif
```

visitor.h

```
// visitor.c
#include "visitor.h"
struct JailKey {      // local class
    JailKey(const Jail& jail)
    {
        jail.release();
    }   // no external linkage
};

Visitor::Visitor(const Jail& jail)
{
    JailKey key(jail);
}
```

visitor.c

visitor

JailKey

jailkey

```
// jail.h
#ifndef INCLUDED_JAIL
#define INCLUDED_JAIL
class JailKey;  // not defined locally
class Jail {
   friend JailKey;  // long distance
   void release() const;
   // ...
};
# endif
```

jail.h

```
// jail.c
#include "jail.h"
#include <iostream.h>

void Jail::release() const
{
    cout << "Escape!" << endl;
}

// ...
```

jail.c

jail

Figure 3-23: Example of Abusing Friendship

3.7 Summary

Developing maintainable, testable, and reusable software demands a thorough knowledge of physical as well as logical design. Physical design addresses organizational issues, beyond the scope of the logical domain, that affect readily measurable characteristics such as runtime, compile time, link time, and executable size.

A component is a physical entity consisting of a `.c` file and a `.h` file, which embodies the concrete realization of a logical abstraction. A component will typically contain one, two, or even several classes, along with appropriate free operators needed to support the overall abstraction. A component and not a class is the appropriate unit of both logical and physical design because it enables

1. several logical entities to represent a single abstraction as a cohesive unit,
2. consideration of both physical and organizational issues, and
3. selective reuse of translation units in other programs.

The logical interface of a component is limited to that which can be accessed programmatically by clients, while the physical interface involves its entire header file. Using a user-defined type, `T`, in the physical interface of a component, even if `T` is an encapsulated logical detail, can force clients of that component to depend on the definition of `T` at compile time.

Components are self-contained, cohesive, and potentially reusable units of design. Logical constructs declared within a component should not be defined outside that component. A component's `.c` file should immediately include its `.h` file to ensure that the `.h` file will parse on its own. Consistently including the header file for each required type definition, rather than depending on one header file to include another, avoids problems when an encapsulated change to a component allows a `#include` directive to be removed from its header file. To improve usability, reusability, and maintainability, we should avoid placing constructs with external linkage in a component's `.c` file that are not declared in its `.h` file. By the same reasoning, we should avoid employing local declarations to access definitions with external linkage.

The DependsOn relation identifies physical (compile-time or link-time) dependencies among components. A compile-time dependency almost always implies a link-time dependency, and the DependsOn relation among components is transitive.

We can infer a guaranteed compile-time dependency from a logical IsA or HasA relationship across component boundaries. The logical HoldsA and Uses relations suggest a likely link-time dependency in such cases. By taking advantage of abstract logical relationships to infer the physical ramifications of our design decisions, we can predict and correct physical design flaws before any code is written.

We would like to track actual physical dependencies throughout development to ensure consistency with our initial design. Parsing all of the source code in a large C++ system is time consuming. Provided that we have followed the major design rules in this book, however, it is possible to infer all physical dependencies among components from their include graph alone. A description of such a tool is provided in Appendix C.

Finally, friendship, although ostensibly a logical issue, influences physical design. Within a component, friendship (local) is an encapsulated implementation detail of that component. It is common for a container class to befriend an iterator within the same component in order to improve both usability and user extensibility, without violating encapsulation.

Across component boundaries, friendship (long-distance) becomes part of the interface of a component and results in a violation of that component's encapsulation. Long-distance friendships further affect maintainability by allowing intimate access to physically remote parts of a system.

Friendship directly affects access privilege but not implied dependency. Indirectly, however, our desire to avoid long-distance friendships will force us to package intimately related logical entities within a single component, thereby coupling them physically. Ignoring these physical considerations invites clients to exploit the breach of encapsulation caused by all long-distance friendships, and even by local friendships, to individual, non-inline free (operator) functions.

4

Physical Hierarchy

Physical hierarchy among components as defined by the DependsOn relation is analogous to the logical hierarchy implied by layering. Avoiding cyclic physical dependencies is central to effective comprehension, maintainability, testing, and reuse. Well-designed interfaces are small, easy to understand, and easy to use, yet these kinds of interfaces make user-level testing expensive.

In this chapter we explore how to exploit physical hierarchy to facilitate the effective testing of "good" interfaces. We introduce the notion of level numbers to help characterize components in terms of their physical dependencies. Using a complex example, we demonstrate the value of testing in isolation as well as testing hierarchically and incrementally. Finally, we derive an objective metric for quantifying the degree of physical coupling within an arbitrary subsystem. This metric will help us to evaluate the impact of various design alternatives by making the notion of physical design quality more objective and concrete.

4.1 A Metaphor for Software Testing

When a customer test-drives a car, he or she is looking to see how well the car performs as a unit—how well the car handles, corners, brakes, and so on. The customer is also interested in subjective usability—how "nifty" the car looks, how comfortable the seats are, how plush the interior is, and, in general, how satisfying the car would be to own. Typical customers do not test the air-bags, ball-joints, or engine mounts to see whether they will perform as expected in all circumstances. When buying a new car from a reputable manufacturer, the customer simply takes for granted this important low-level reliability.

For the car to function properly, it is important that each of the objects on which the car depends works properly as well. Customers do not test each part of the car individually—but somebody does. It is not the responsibility of the customer to "QA" the car. The customer is paying for a quality product, and part of that quality is the satisfaction of knowing that the car works properly.

In the real world, each part of a car has been designed with a well-defined interface and has been tested in isolation under extreme conditions to ensure that it meets its specified tolerances long before it is ever integrated into a car. In order to maintain a car, mechanics must be able to gain access to its various parts from time to time in order to diagnose and fix problems.

Complex software systems are like cars. All of the low-level parts are objects with well-defined interfaces. Each part or component can be stress tested in isolation. These parts can then be integrated, via layering, into a sequence of increasingly complex subsystems—each subsystem with a test suite to ensure that the incremental integration has occurred properly. This layered architecture enables test engineers to access the functionality implemented in the lower levels of abstraction without exposing clients of the product to these lower-level interfaces. The final product is also tested to ensure that it meets customer expectations.

To summarize: a well-designed car is built from layered parts that have been tested thoroughly by the manufacturer:

1. in isolation,
2. within a sequence of partially integrated subsystems, and
3. as a fully integrated product.

Once assembled, these parts are easily accessible by mechanics to facilitate proper testing and maintenance. In software, the concepts remain essentially the same.

4.2 A Complex Subsystem

As a concrete example of a software subsystem, consider a point-to-point wire router for a computer-aided electronic design application. This subsystem solves a fairly complex problem with a relatively simple description:

PROBLEM STATEMENT

Given:

1. An enclosing region (described as a simple closed polygon).
2. A set of obstructions or "holes" (each described as a simple closed polygon) within the enclosing region, which do not overlap (but may touch) each other or the perimeter of the enclosing region.
3. A starting point (represented as a point).
4. An ending point (also represented as a point).
5. A width (represented as an integer).

Determine whether a rectilinear path of the specified width exists between the specified starting and ending points, and (optionally) return the center line of any shortest rectilinear path (as an open polygon), if one exists.

Figure 4-1 illustrates an instance of the point-to-point routing problem.[1] The enclosing region contains three holes that a successful path may touch but not overlap. The starting point is indicated by *s* and the ending point is indicated by *e*. One of the many possible shortest rectilinear paths of specified width is defined by the center line, shown in the figure connecting *s* and *e*.

[1] We present this authentic example in all its detail. It is not necessary, however, to understand every aspect of this example in order to benefit from the discussions that follow. A cursory reading will be sufficient.

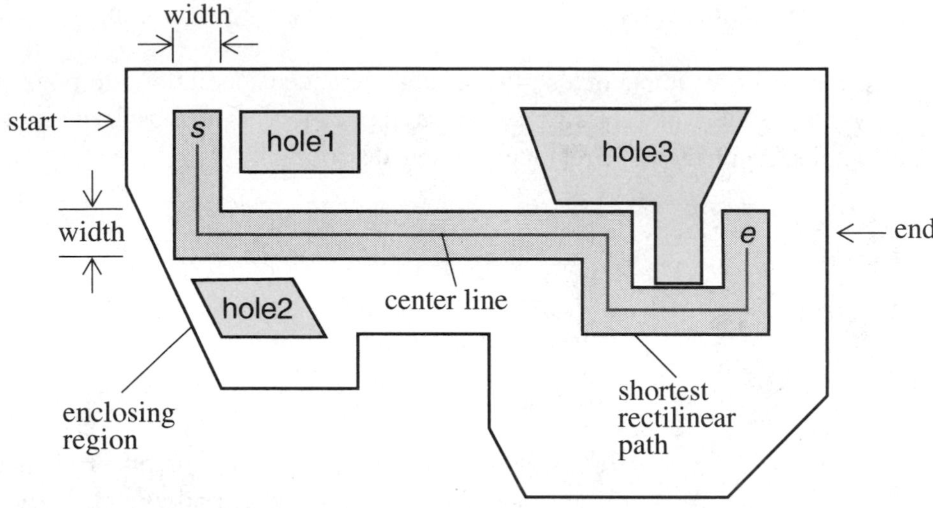

Figure 4-1: Example Problem for a Point-to-Point Router

The logical interface for a component solving this complex problem can be deceptively simple. The header file `p2p_router.h` describing the client's interface for the point-to-point router subsystem is shown in its entirety in Figure 4-2. The (registered) class prefix `p2p_` identifies this component as belonging to the `p2p` package as well as eliminating the possibility of identifier name collisions among classes belonging to distinct packages (see Section 7.2).

```
// p2p_router.h
#ifndef INCLUDED_P2P_ROUTER
#define INCLUDED_P2P_ROUTER

class geom_Point;
class geom_Polygon;
class p2p_RouterImp;

class p2p_Router {
    p2p_RouterImp *d_data_p;

    // NOT IMPLEMENTED
    p2p_Router(const p2p_Router&);
    p2p_Router& operator=(const p2p_Router&);

  public:
    // CREATORS
    p2p_Router(const geom_Polygon& enclosingRegion);
        // Create router for specified enclosing region.
        // The region must be a simple, closed polygon.
    ~p2p_Router();
```

```
    // MANIPULATORS
    int addObstruction(const geom_Polygon& hole);
        // Add obstruction; obstruction must be a simple, closed polygon.
        // If obstruction overlaps another obstruction or the perimeter
        // of the enclosing shape, return non-zero with no effect and 0
        // otherwise.  Note: Regions are allowed to touch but not overlap.

    // ACCESSORS
    int findPath(geom_Polygon *returnValue, const geom_Point& start,
            const geom_Point& end, int width) const;
        // Determine whether a rectilinear path of specified width exists
        // in the current obstructed region between specified start and
        // end points.  Return 1 if such a path exists and 0 otherwise.
        // If a path exists and returnValue is not 0, store the center
        // line of any shortest path in (*returnValue).
};

#endif
```

Figure 4-2: Complete Header File for `p2p_Router`

There are two user-defined types used in the logical interface of the point-to-point router subsystem. These types (`geom_Polygon` and `geom_Point`) are part of a public package (`geom`) of geometric types used widely throughout the entire system. For reference purposes, the respective interfaces of `geom_Point` and `geom_Polygon` are sketched in Figure 4-3.

```
class geom_Point {
    // ...
  public:
    geom_Point(int x, int y);
    geom_Point(const geom_Point& point);
    ~geom_Point() {};
    geom_Point& operator=(const geom_Point& point);
    void setX(int x);
    void setY(int y);
    int x() const;
    int y() const;
};
```

```
class geom_Polygon {
    // ...
  public:
    geom_Polygon();
    geom_Polygon(const geom_Polygon& pgn);
    ~geom_Polygon() {};
    geom_Polygon& operator=(const geom_Polygon& pgn);
    void appendVertex(const geom_Point& point);
    // ...
    int numVertices() const;
    const geom_Point& vertex(int vertexIndex) const;
    // ...
};
```

Figure 4-3: Sketch of `geom_Point` **and** `geom_Polygon` **Class Interfaces**

An actual implementation of this subsystem involves some 5,000 lines of C++ source code (not including comments), yet using the point-to-point router component is very easy. A straightforward driver that runs the example of Figure 4-1 is given for completeness in Figure 4-4. Note that the advantage of this long, linear style is its simplicity. It is typical of drivers actually used during development and testing.

```
// p2p_router.t.c
#include "p2p_router.h"
#include "geom_polygon.h"
#include "geom_point.h"
#include <iostream.h>

main()
{
    geom_Polygon enclosingRegion;
    enclosingRegion.appendVertex(geom_Point(0, 1000));
    enclosingRegion.appendVertex(geom_Point(0, 600));
    enclosingRegion.appendVertex(geom_Point(700, -100));
    enclosingRegion.appendVertex(geom_Point(2100, -100));
    enclosingRegion.appendVertex(geom_Point(2100, 100));
    enclosingRegion.appendVertex(geom_Point(3000, 100));
    enclosingRegion.appendVertex(geom_Point(3000, -200));
    enclosingRegion.appendVertex(geom_Point(3200, -400));
    enclosingRegion.appendVertex(geom_Point(4500, -400));
    enclosingRegion.appendVertex(geom_Point(5000, 100));
    enclosingRegion.appendVertex(geom_Point(5000, 1000));
    enclosingRegion.appendVertex(geom_Point(0, 1000));

    geom_Polygon hole1;
    hole1.appendVertex(geom_Point(800, 900));
    hole1.appendVertex(geom_Point(800, 700));
    hole1.appendVertex(geom_Point(1400, 700));
    hole1.appendVertex(geom_Point(1400, 900));
    hole1.appendVertex(geom_Point(800, 900));

    geom_Polygon hole2;
    hole2.appendVertex(geom_Point(600, 300));
    hole2.appendVertex(geom_Point(800, 100));
    hole2.appendVertex(geom_Point(1600, 100));
    hole2.appendVertex(geom_Point(1400, 300));
    hole2.appendVertex(geom_Point(600, 300));

    geom_Polygon hole3;
    hole3.appendVertex(geom_Point(2600, 900));
    hole3.appendVertex(geom_Point(2900, 600));
    hole3.appendVertex(geom_Point(3800, 600));
    hole3.appendVertex(geom_Point(3800, 300));
    hole3.appendVertex(geom_Point(4200, 300));
    hole3.appendVertex(geom_Point(4200, 600));
    hole3.appendVertex(geom_Point(4500, 900));
    hole3.appendVertex(geom_Point(2600, 900));
```

```
        p2p_Router router(enclosingRegion);
        router.addObstruction(hole1);
        router.addObstruction(hole2);
        router.addObstruction(hole3);

        geom_Polygon centerLine;
        geom_Point start(400, 800), end(4600, 500);
        int width = 400;

        if (router.findPath(&centerLine, start, end, width)) {
            cout << centerLine << endl;
        }
        else {
            cout << "Could not find path." << endl;
        }
    }

    // Output:
    // john@john a.out
    // { (400, 800) (400, 500) (3400, 500) (3400, 200) (4600, 200) (4600, 500) }
    // john@john
```

Figure 4-4: Straightforward Driver for Point-To-Point Routing Problem

3.8 The Difficulty in Testing "Good" Interfaces

A truly effective use of object-oriented technology is to hide tremendous complexity behind a small, well-defined, easy-to-understand, and easy-to-use interface. Yet it is precisely these kinds of interfaces that, if naively implemented, can lead to the development of subsystems that are exceedingly difficult to test.

For example, the `p2p_router` component (Figure 4-2) contains only four public functions:

1. a constructor that establishes the enclosing region,

2. a destructor,

3. a function to accumulate a collection of obstructions within the enclosing region, and

4. a function to determine the shortest rectilinear path of specified width between any two points inside the region (excluding the interior of the obstructions accumulated so far).

The output at the end of Figure 4-4 tells us that this component produced *an* answer. Now stop for a moment and imagine that you are a quality assurance test engineer assigned to this project. How would you go about thoroughly testing such an interface?

First consider that in general there will be many equally good solutions for an instance of this problem. Verifying that a solution is a rectilinear path of a given width that connects two points in a region with obstructions is not trivial, but it can be done without extraordinary effort. Verifying that a solution to this problem is optimal is, in general, as difficult as finding the solution in the first place.

You could verify the output by trying several test cases and inspecting them by hand. Although time consuming, manual inspection can be effective during development. Consider what happens when the development phase has ended and the subsystem moves into the maintenance/tuning phase. It would be impractical to think that you or the developers would be willing or even able to manually review the output of every subsystem on every release.

DEFINITION: *Regression testing* refers to the practice of comparing the results of running a program given a specific input with a fixed set of expected results, in order to verify that the program continues to behave *as expected* from one version to the next.

One approach commonly used to help automate regression testing involves running a large number of test cases through the system at the top level and capturing the results. These results are then inspected once by hand to verify their accuracy. Before each release, new results are obtained and compared with the original results. Presumably, if the new output matches the old output exactly, the subsystem is correct.

A significant drawback with regression tests for many complex problems, including this one, is that there may be multiple correct solutions. Although each of the components of the point-to-point router subsystem may have completely predictable behavior, there is room in the specification for the developer to alter `p2p_Router`'s implementation in ways that produce a different (but equally good) final result for a given input.

On a much smaller scale, consider the specification for a simple iterator on some collection. Typically there is no constraint on the order in which the elements must be presented. The requirement is that each element in the collection be presented exactly once. Verifying that an iterator is behaving properly in isolation is not difficult. But when the iterator is embedded in the implementation of a complex subsystem (such as that headed by the `p2p_router` component), the ability to test that iterator effectively may be lost.

Although the point-to-point router is guaranteed to produce an optimal result if one exists, many complex problems are too difficult to solve optimally in a reasonable amount of time. In such cases, heuristic methods are employed that produce a good (but not necessarily a best) solution. Heuristic techniques often take the form of an intelligent trial-and-error strategy and are, by their nature, unpredictable. Experimentation is used to determine which heuristic techniques tend to produce the best solutions. Software that depends on heuristic methods is resistant to high-level regression testing, since any improvement in the heuristics would invalidate the regression data.

Testing complex, heuristic-based software at a high-level interface is made even more difficult because failures in the more predictable underlying components may not cause the entire subsystem to fail outright. Instead, these insidious errors silently degrade the quality of the subsystem's output. Since it is not always possible to verify that the result is optimal, this degradation could easily go undetected.

Even worse than the pseudo-random behavior of heuristic-based systems is the completely unpredictable behavior[1] associated with systems that employ asynchronous communication. Such systems produce results that are generally not repeatable. In these cases, high-level regression testing could be virtually useless.

Minimizing the "surface area" in our designs (i.e., providing sufficient but minimal interfaces) is a cornerstone of good software engineering. Yet there is a cruel irony in knowing that the very interfaces we strive so hard to achieve can present a formidable barrier to conventional testing techniques. Fortunately there are techniques that we can use to overcome these testing problems. The proverb about an ounce of prevention being worth a pound of cure especially pertains here.

3.9 Design for Testability

A major component of designing in quality is design for testability (DFT). The importance of DFT is well recognized in the integrated circuit (IC) industry. In many cases

[1] For more on pseudo-random functionality, see `rand()` in **plauger**, Chapter 13, p. 337.

it is impractical to test IC chips, some with over a million transistors, from the outside pins alone.

When an IC chip is fabricated, it acts as a "black box" and can be tested only from the external inputs and outputs (pins). Figure 4-5a illustrates the process of trying to test a hardware subsystem `w` using only the interface provided to regular clients of the chip itself. In order to test `w`, it is necessary not only to figure out what would make a good test suite for `w`, but also how to propagate that test suite through the chip to reach the inputs of `w`. As if that weren't bad enough, each result that `w` produces must then be propagated from the output of `w` to some output of the chip itself in order to observe and verify that `w` has behaved correctly. Ensuring propagation of this information requires detailed knowledge about the entire chip—knowledge that has nothing to do with the correct functionality of `w`.

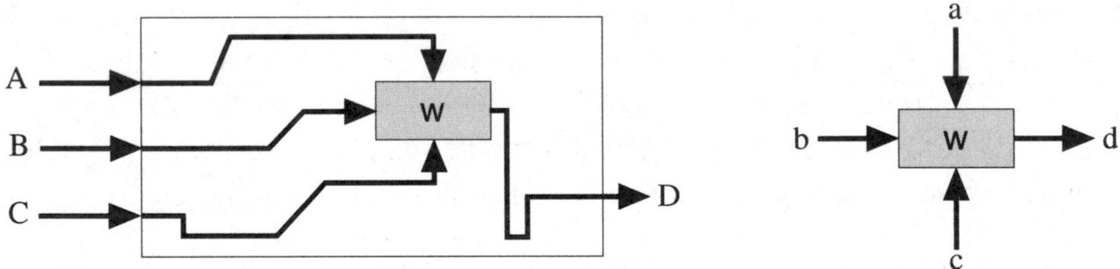

(a) Testing a Component from the System Level (b) Testing a Component Directly

Figure 4-5: Design for Testability in Integrated Circuits

One form of DFT for IC chips called SCAN is accomplished with extra pins and additional internal circuitry provided solely for testing purposes. Using these special features, test engineers are able to isolate the various subsystems within the chip. In so doing they are able to gain direct access to the inputs and outputs of internal subsystems and to exercise their functionality directly. In other words, this DFT approach attempts to grant the tester direct access to a subsystem, thereby eliminating the cost of propagating signals through the entire chip. In this way, the full functionality of the subsystem can be explored efficiently as illustrated in Figure 4-5b, without regard to the details of how the subsystem is used in the larger system.

When first employed, DFT was great for improving quality; however, IC designers did not appreciate having this additional design requirement. Not only was this an extra consideration, but it made their designs bigger and therefore much more expensive to produce. Many designers were frustrated, considering this disciplined approach to be an infringement on their creativity.

Today DFT is an IC industry standard. No competent hardware engineer would consider designing a complex chip without directly addressing the testability issue. By comparison, the functionality of large software systems can be orders of magnitude more complex than would be found in even the largest integrated circuit. Surprisingly, there is often no plan in place to ensure that the software is testable. Attempts to mandate software testability are frequently met with the same frustration felt in the IC industry over a decade ago. Often it is people rather than the technology itself who pose the greater challenge to solving an otherwise technical problem.

Principle

With respect to testing, a software *class* is analogous to a real-world *instance*.

Like IC design, object-oriented software involves the creation of a relatively small number of types, which are then instantiated repeatedly to form a working system. For example, a `String` class is a primitive type in many software systems. Many instances of this class may be created during a typical invocation of the system.

Both disciplines require that the functionality in these types be tested thoroughly to ensure correct behavior when instantiated. But, unlike IC design where each individual instance of a type must be tested for physical defects, software objects are immune to such defects. If a class is implemented correctly, then, by definition, all instances of that type are correctly implemented as well.

Principle

Distributing system testing throughout the design hierarchy can be much more effective per testing dollar than testing at only the highest-level interface.

From the point of view of testing, each software type is like a real-world instance. Testing the functionality of a `String` class is easiest and most effective if done directly, rather than by attempting to test it as part of a larger system. And, unlike IC testing, we automatically have direct access to the interface of the software subsystem—the `String` class.

Put another way, if we have only *X* dollars to spend on testing, we can achieve more thorough coverage if we distribute the testing effort throughout the system, thus testing individual component interfaces directly, than we can by testing from the end user's interface alone.

Consider again the `p2p_router` component of Figure 4-2. Even assuming entirely predictable behavior, it would be ineffective to attempt to test this component entirely from the highest level, especially given its tiny interface. In analogy to IC testing (see Figure 4-6), this would be like trying to test a one-million-transistor microprocessor chip with only two pins![2]

Software testing is inherently easier than hardware testing because instances of a class created *within* a system are *no different* from instances of the same class created independently, *outside* that system. If a complex software subsystem were truly analogous to an IC chip, the implementation would reside entirely within a single physical component. If the functionality declared in `p2p_router.h` were implemented entirely within `p2p_router.c`, we would probably be forced to violate encapsulation by providing extra functionality in the public interface—just to enable effective testing.

---

[2] Other kinds of IC testing strategies such as Build-In Self Test (BIST) place additional circuitry on the chip that can be enabled to verify that the chip is working properly without having to propagate specific information to the interface. BIST is somewhat analogous to the use of `assert` statements in software. Adding public functionality, such as `testMe()`, would be a more accurate analogy, but the physical hierarchy in our software architecture allows us to achieve the same result without adding any test-specific functionality to the interface of a component.

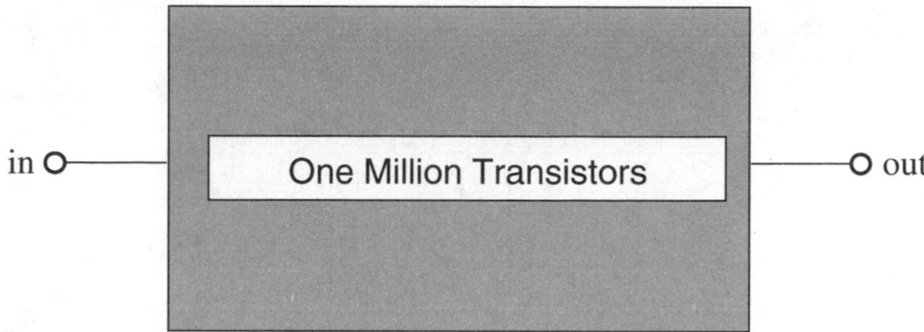

Figure 4-6: Fictitious Highly Test-Resistant IC Chip with Only Two Pins

Fortunately, the implementation of the point-to-point router does not live in a single component. Instead, this implementation is deliberately distributed throughout a physical hierarchy of components. Even though the client of a `p2p_Router` object has no programmatic access to the layered objects that make up the router, it is still possible for test engineers to identify subcomponents with predictable behaviors that can be tested and verified much more efficiently in isolation.

3.10 Testing in Isolation

In a well-designed modular subsystem, many components can be tested in isolation. Consider a very real situation involving the point-to-point router subsystem that will eventually support all-angle geometry. For the time being, the system is still in the prototype stage and handles only manhattan (90-degree) angles. The point-to-point router is object based, and so it is layered on many objects, most of which currently support all angles. Since some of the components have not yet been upgraded to all-angle, the `p2p_router` itself can accept only manhattan test cases.

Principle

Independent testing reduces part of the risk associated with software integration.

Consider the physical architecture for the `p2p_router` shown in Figure 4-7. By designing the `p2p_router` so that each of its subsystems can be developed and tested individually, we can ensure that each of their upgraded functionalities is in place even though they cannot be verified through the completed routers interface until some future date. If programming errors occur, they can be detected and fixed in parallel.

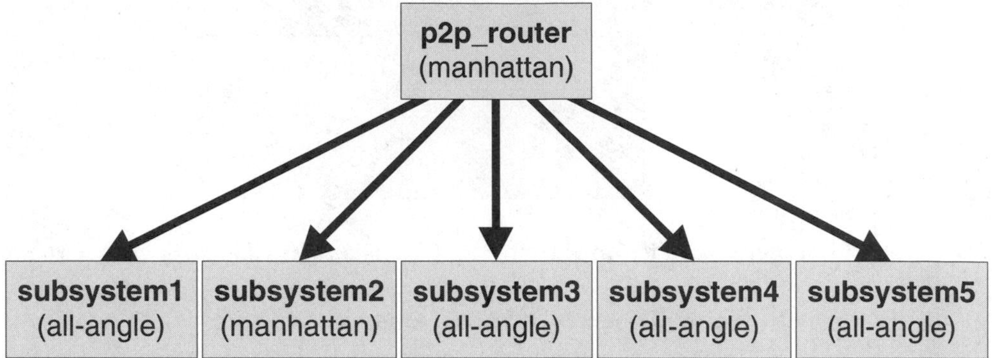

Figure 4-7: Physical Dependency for a `p2p_router` Implementation

An alternative, less disciplined but widely used "method" of integrating software is to wait until all the software is in place before trying it. This is commonly referred to as the *big bang* approach. The name is somewhat misleading: the anticipated "bang" is all too often a fizzle.

Integration is where most specification errors are detected. When the integrated system fails to perform as anticipated, the development team must scramble to diagnose the problems. Inevitably, they will find many coding bugs not intrinsically related to the integration itself. Independent testing could have at least allowed these coding errors to have been diagnosed and fixed much earlier in the development process.

DEFINITION: *Isolation testing* refers to the practice of testing an individual component or subsystem independently of the rest of the system.

Principle

Testing a component in isolation is an effective way to ensure reliability.

At the lowest levels of a complex system, components are often heavily optimized, increasing the likelihood of subtle errors and the need for detailed regression tests. For example, carefully designed, object-specific memory management can often double runtime performance. However, custom memory managers are quite error prone, and these errors are among the most difficult to detect and repair. Instrumenting global operators `new` and `delete` in an isolated component test driver can ensure that the memory-management scheme is functioning properly under a wide variety of conditions, including those encountered only infrequently in practice.

Not all programs use all functionality in reusable components. For example, if a program does not call the `pop()` member of a `Stack` class, there is no way that `pop()` can be tested just by testing that program. Even if a particular program calls every function, there may be states in which objects are supposed to behave properly, but which the surrounding software does not allow them to attain.

Consider a `String` class that is developed as part of an interpreter. The interpreter never sees a zero-length identifier, so it never tries to create an empty `String` to represent one. (This boundary condition would certainly be addressed by a thorough test designed specifically for the `string` component.) As our system evolves, we may at some later point reuse the `String` class in other parts of the same system, but in new ways (e.g., to hold `String` variables). At this point an instance of an empty String *can* occur within this system. The enhancement may have been made at a fairly high level in the system, but the potential bug exists at the lowest level—in the `String` class—which has been working "perfectly" for quite some time!

In a large project, the author of the `String` class is probably not the same individual as the one whose valid enhancement exposes the problem. Detecting and then repairing such bugs, not to mention the frustration that ensues, is far more expensive than simply avoiding them in the first place through early, component-level testing *in isolation*.

It would be redundant and unnecessarily costly for every system that uses a library facility such as `iostream` to have tests to verify that the needed `iostream` functionality is working properly. People have come to assume that `iostream` does work as intended. For large systems, there will probably be many application libraries developed in house. No single executable will make use of all of this functionality, yet all of it should be tested thoroughly *in isolation*.

We can avoid the redundancy by grouping the testing effort with the components themselves. In so doing, one extends the notion of object-oriented design to include, as a single unit, not only the component but also the supporting tests and documentation. Furthermore, well-written component-level tests can facilitate reuse by providing prospective users with a suite of small but comprehensive examples. The functionality supplied by each component can now be tested thoroughly in a single place; clients who depend on these components may reasonably assume they are reliable.

Isolation testing is ideal for identifying low-level problems that result from enhancements and is especially useful for porting a system to new platforms. These low-level tests ensure the preservation of basic functionality and make it easy to track down any discrepancies. Occasionally defects escape local detection and are caught by tests at higher levels. The low-level component test should be updated to expose the errant behavior *before* the defect is repaired. Doing this will both facilitate the repair and preserve modularity by making the testing of this component independent of any particular client.

There is a point of diminishing returns to testing in isolation. For example, placing the definition of a `Link` class for a simple `List` object in a distinct component so that it may be tested in isolation is absurd for two reasons:

1. The normal operation of a `List` object will thoroughly exercise the `Link`'s functionality.

2. The additional component will unnecessarily increase the physical complexity of the system, making it more difficult to understand and maintain.

Determining this point for component-level isolation testing should be done objectively, based on a cost/benefit analysis, not solely by how much a given developer loathes (or enjoys) testing.

3.11 Acyclic Physical Dependencies

For a design to be tested effectively, it must be possible to decompose the design into units of functionality whose complexity is manageable. A component is ideal for this purpose. Consider the header files for three components `c1`, `c2`, and `c3` depicted in Figure 4-8. Note that we have declared class `C1` in component headers `c2.h` and `c3.h` without providing its definition because it is not necessary to define a class that is returned by value in order to declare that function.

```
// c1.h
#ifndef INCLUDED_C1
#define INCLUDED_C1
class C1;

class C1 {
    // ...
  public:
    C1 f();
};

#endif
```
c1.h

```
// c2.h
#ifndef INCLUDED_C2
#define INCLUDED_C2
class C1;

class C2 {
    // ...
  public:
    C1 g();
};

#endif
```
c2.h

```
// c3.h
#ifndef INCLUDE_C3
#define INCLUDE_C3
class C2;

class C3 {
    // ...
  public:
    C1 h(const C2& arg);
};

#endif
```
c3.h

Figure 4-8: Components with Acyclic Implied Dependencies

We can observe (Section 3.4) that there are no implied dependencies of `c1` on any other component. Class `C2` uses class `C1` in its interface. Therefore it is likely that component `c2` depends on component `c1`, but, we hope, not on `c3`. Class `C3` uses both `C2` and `C1` in its interface, and so `c3` is likely to depend on both `c2` and `c1`. The implied dependencies in this system form a directed acyclic graph (DAG) as shown in Figure 4-9a.

Component dependency graphs that contain no cycles have very positive implications for testability, but not all component dependency graphs are acyclic. To see why, consider what would happen if we changed the return type of `C1::f` from a `C1` to a `C2` as follows:

```
class C1 {
    //...
  public:
    // C1 f();            // old
    C2 f();               // new
};
```

Now `C1` uses `C2` in its interface and (probably) depends on it. The implied component dependency graph for this modified system now has a *physical* cycle, and is shown in Figure 4-9b.

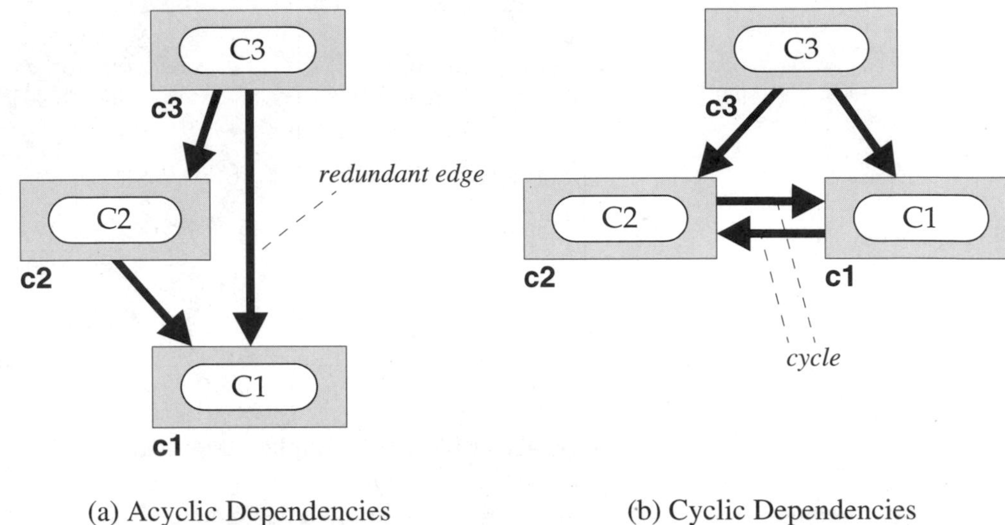

(a) Acyclic Dependencies (b) Cyclic Dependencies

Figure 4-9: Acyclic versus Cyclic Physical Dependencies

Systems with acyclic physical dependencies (such as the one shown in Figure 4-9a) are far easier to test effectively than those with cycles. Whenever the component dependencies in a system are acyclic, there is (at least) one reasonable order to go about testing the system. Since component `c1` depends on nothing else, tests to verify its functionality in isolation can be written first. Next we see that component `c2` depends only on component `c1`. Because we were able to write effective tests for `c1`, we may presume `c1` to be functioning properly. We can now write tests for the functional value added by `c2`. We need not retest the contribution of `c1` since that functionality is already covered. Then we look at `c3` which depends on both `c1` and `c2`. Because we presumably have already written tests to verify the functionality supplied by both `c1` and `c2`, we need address only the additional functionality implemented in `c3`.

3.12 Level Numbers

In this section we introduce a method for partitioning components based on their physical dependencies into equivalence classes called levels. Each level is associated with a non-negative integer index, referred to in this book as the *level number.* The next few paragraphs describe the origins of level numbers and how they were used in their original context. Then we apply these well-established concepts in a new context: software engineering.

3.12.1 The Origin of Level Numbers

The notion of level numbers is borrowed from the field of digital, gate-level, zero-delay circuit simulation.[3] Here, a *gate* implements a low-level block of Boolean functionality. Each gate has two or more connection points called *terminals*. A *circuit* consists of an interconnected collection of gates. Like a gate, a circuit has both input terminals and output terminals. *Primary inputs* are inputs to the circuit itself. These inputs are connected to the inputs of some of the gates within the circuit by pair-wise terminal connectors called *wires*. The outputs of these gates are connected by wires to the inputs of still other gates, and so on. A simple circuit with four primary inputs (a, b, c, and d) is illustrated in Figure 4-10a.

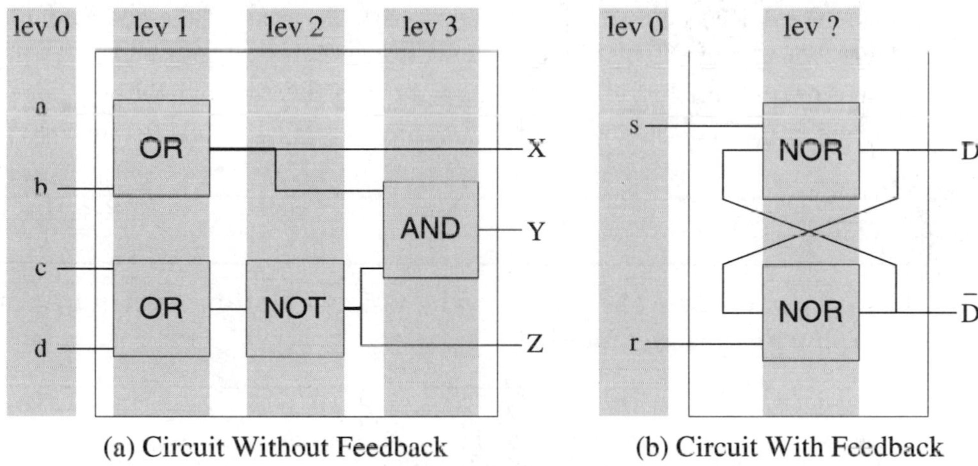

(a) Circuit Without Feedback (b) Circuit With Feedback

Figure 4-10: Logic Circuits Without and With Feedback

Simulating a circuit involves setting its primary inputs with logical values and then evaluating each of the (layered) gates in turn. But before any particular gate can be evaluated, we must make sure that its inputs are valid by ensuring that all gates that feed this particular gate have already been evaluated.

A circuit is a kind of graph. Here, *gates* and *primary inputs* are treated as vertices of a graph, and *wires* are treated as (directed) edges.[4] The level number in this context

---

[3] The zero-delay approximation is used primarily in a special kind of circuit simulator known as a *fault simulator*. The discovery of this analogy between hardware and software arose, in part, from the author's Ph.D. research at Columbia University with Professor Stephen H. Unger.

[4] The gates themselves impose the edge direction, which reflects the dependency of the gate on its input source (e.g., either a primary input or the output of another gate in the circuit).

indicates the longest path from a particular gate to a primary input. Primary inputs are defined to have a level of 0. By evaluating these gates in order of increasing levels, we can guarantee that every gate's inputs will be valid.

Primary input values are assumed, and do not require evaluation. During simulation, level-1 gates are fed only by primary inputs. These gates are evaluated first, in arbitrary order. Next to be evaluated are all level-2 gates. Since level-2 gates are fed only by one or more level-1 gate (and possibly also by primary inputs), we are assured at this point that all inputs for level-2 gates have been evaluated. Since a gate at level *N* depends only on levels [0 . . . *N*–1] for its inputs, evaluating gates in levelized order guarantees a successful simulation.

In Figure 4-12a, a level-1 `OR`-gate feeds the only input of the `NOT`-gate, making it a level-2 gate. The `AND`-gate is fed both by a level-1 `OR`-gate and a level-2 `NOT`-gate. The longest path from the `AND`-gate to a primary input is 3 (through the `NOT`-gate to primary input `c` or `d`). The `AND`-gate belongs to the highest level, 3, and is evaluated last.

Principle

Every directed acyclic graph can be assigned unique level numbers; a graph with cycles cannot.

Notice that, with the pair of cross-coupled `NOR`-gates in Figure 4-10b, the longest path from either gate to either primary input (*r* or *s*) is unbounded. This circuit cannot be levelized—that is, it cannot be assigned unique level numbers. The property that makes a circuit levelizable is that it has no feedback. This lack of feedback makes the circuit qualitatively easier to understand, develop, analyze, and test. For these reasons, feedback is used in large systems only under very restricted circumstances. For completely analogous reasons, a "lack of feedback" is exactly the property we would like our software designs to possess.

<u>DEFINITION</u>: A physical dependency graph that can be assigned unique level numbers is said to be *levelizable*.

3.12.2 Using Level Numbers in Software

Turning back to software engineering, if the component dependencies in a software system happen to form a DAG, we can define the *level* of each component.

> **DEFINITION:**
>
> *Level 0*: **A component that is external to our package.**
>
> *Level 1*: **A component that has no local physical dependencies.**
>
> *Level N*: **A component that depends physically on a component at level *N*–1, but not higher.**

In this definition, we assume that all components outside our current package[5] (e.g., `iostream`) have already been tested and are known to function properly. These components are treated as "primary inputs" and have a "level" of 0. A component with no local physical dependencies is defined to have a level of 1. Otherwise, a component is defined to have a level one more than the maximum level of the components upon which it depends.

Figure 4-11 shows the component dependency diagram from Figure 3-17 of Section 3.4, which happens not to have any cycles, and hence is levelizable. The level number is shown in the upper right corner of each component. Component `chararray` does not depend on any other components locally but does depend on the standard library components (which are all assumed to be at level 0), so `chararray` has a level of 1. A level-1 component (such as `chararray`) that depends only on compiler-supplied libraries is called a *leaf* component. Leaf components are always testable in isolation.

---

[5] Assume for now that *package* means the current project directory.

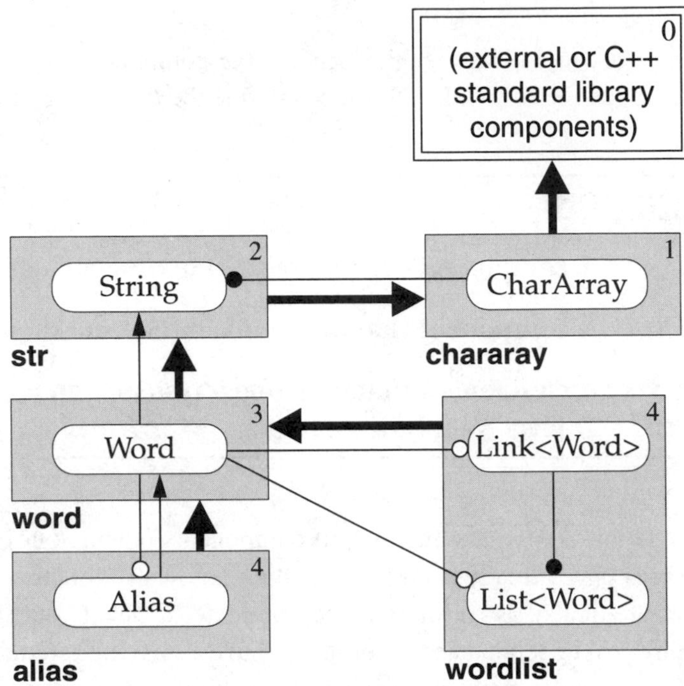

Figure 4-11: Levelized Component Dependency Diagram

Component `str` depends only on `chararray`. The level of `str` is 2, one more than that of `chararray`. Component `word` depends on `str` (and indirectly on `chararray`). Since `str` has a level of 2, `word` has a level of 3. Since `word` is at level 3, and the only component on which `alias` depends directly is `word`, `alias` is at level 4. The `wordlist` component also depends directly on `word` but does not depend on `alias`, so `wordlist` is also at level 4.

> **DEFINITION: The *level* of a component is the length of the longest path from that component through the (local) component dependency graph to the (possibly empty) set of external or compiler-supplied library components.**

With a levelized diagram it is easy to tell what components in this system are testable in isolation. In the example of Figure 4-12 there is only one independently testable component: `chararray`. By starting at the lowest level (i.e., 1) and testing all components on the current level before moving to the next higher level, we are assured that all the components on which the current component depends have already been tested. In the example of Figure 4-11, we can test either `wordlist` or `alias` last, but the rest of the testing order is implied by the level numbers.

Principle

In most real-world situations, large designs must be levelizable if they are to be tested effectively.

Notice that the term *levelizable* applies to *physical*, not logical, entities. Although an acyclic logical dependency graph might imply that a testable physical partition exists, the level numbers of (physical) components, along with our design rules, imply a viable order for effective testing. Moreover, Figure 4-11 identifies what subsystems can be reused independently. Figure 4-12 indicates the other components that must accompany the reuse of any of these components.

To test or reuse	You also need
$\texttt{chararray}_1$:	
$\texttt{string}_2$:	$\texttt{chararray}_1$
$\texttt{word}_3$:	$\texttt{string}_2$ $\texttt{chararray}_1$
$\texttt{alias}_4$:	$\texttt{word}_3$ $\texttt{string}_2$ $\texttt{chararray}_1$
$\texttt{wordlist}_4$:	$\texttt{word}_3$ $\texttt{string}_2$ $\texttt{chararray}_1$

Figure 4-12: Independently Reusable Subsystems

Another significant advantage to levelizable designs is that they are more easily comprehended incrementally. The process of understanding a levelizable design can proceed in an orderly manner (either top down or bottom up). Not all subsystems formed by hierarchical designs are reusable. But, to be maintainable, each component must have a well-defined interface that can be readily understood, regardless of how general its applicability.

Of course, not all designs are levelizable. Sometimes whether or not a design is levelizable is not immediately obvious from a logical diagram. Consider the diagram of

Figure 4-13. Can you tell from this diagram whether or not the components in this design are levelizable?

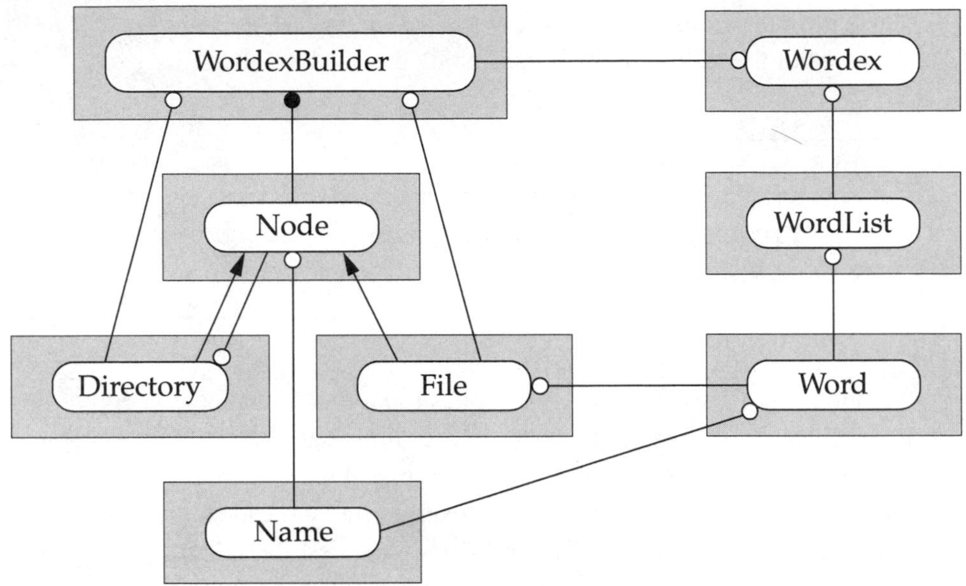

Figure 4-13: Is This Design Levelizable?

The indicated logical relationships in this design do *not* imply cyclic physical dependencies among any of the components. In fact, our design rules ensure that there can be no hidden physical dependencies (e.g., on external global variables). Figure 4-14 shows the implied component dependencies and the resulting component level numbers for this design.

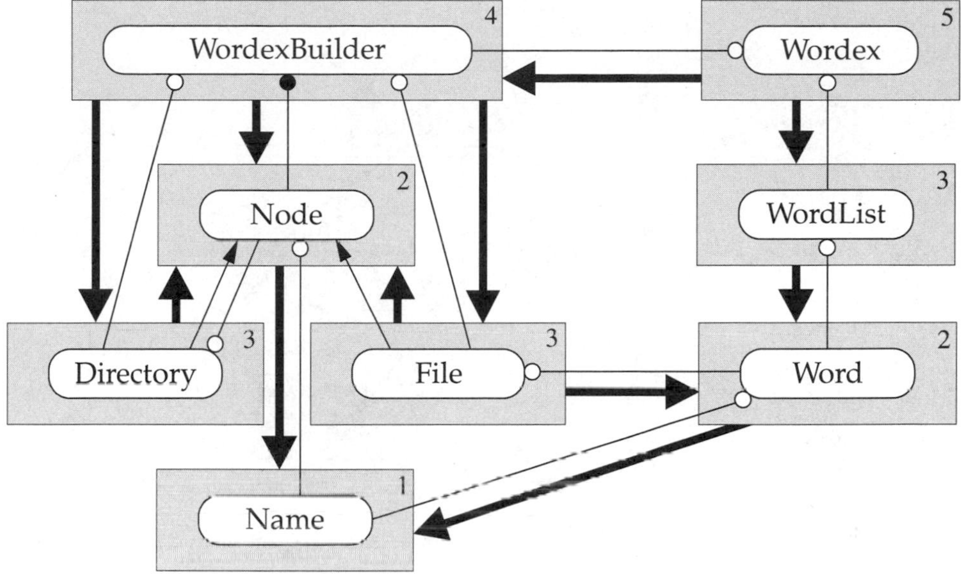

Figure 4-14: Component/Class Diagram

The component/class diagram is cluttered and contains more information than needed to understand the physical structure of the system. If we rearrange the placement of the components and eliminate the logical detail, we obtain the strikingly lucid component dependency diagram of Figure 4-15.

There is one redundant edge in the diagram of Figure 4-15. Component `wordexbuilder` depends directly on components `directory`, `file`, and `node`. As we know from Section 3.3, the DependsOn relationship is transitive. Since `directory` (and `file` also) depends on `node`, the dependency of `wordexbuilder` on `node` is implied and can be removed without affecting level numbers. The diagram in Figure 4-15 is clearly acyclic and typical of those for subsystems that address a specific application. At this level of abstraction, the design appears to be sound.

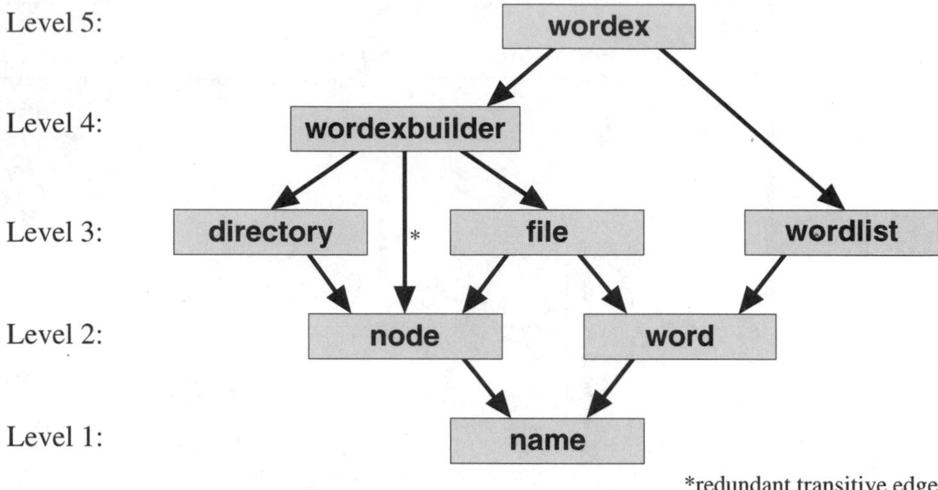

Figure 4-15: Component (Direct) Dependency Diagram

One of the great values of this analysis is that, after untangling the component dependency diagram, we were able to make a substantive, qualitative comment about the integrity of the physical design without even the tiniest discussion of the application domain. Simple tools to help automate this process are easy to write, and have proven to be invaluable for large projects. Appendix C describes a simple component-dependency analyzer.

3.13 Hierarchical and Incremental Testing

Components are the fundamental building blocks of a system. Every component is different. Each is an "instance" of the *physical design pattern*: "component." Outwardly, they all have the same basic physical structure—a physical interface (`.h` file) and a physical implementation (`.c` file).

In this sense, implementing and testing a software system is like building a house. After the overall architectural design is complete, the bricks (i.e., the *components*, not objects) are put in place one by one. The successful addition of each brick depends not only on its own integrity but also on the integrity of the mortar used to integrate the brick with the lower-level bricks on which this brick depends. It is easy enough to inspect each brick for defects along the way. But once complete, the house is often large and complex, presenting too many barriers to inspect each detail.

DEFINITION: *Hierarchical testing* refers to the practice of testing individual components at each level of the physical hierarchy.

In the house-building analogy, a brick represents a unique component (i.e., one or more classes), not individual instances. In practice, thorough testing requires testing the integrity of each component *before* putting it in place. Exercising a component before installation in no way precludes the possibility of more thorough testing in isolation later. Testing component interfaces at each level of the physical hierarchy is referred to in this book as *hierarchical testing*.

Principle

Hierarchical testing requires a separate test driver for every component.

In this approach, a separate test driver for each component is created by the developer concurrently with the component itself to exercise and verify functionality implemented in that component. Not only is this test driver used extensively during development, but it is later made available to quality assurance (QA) in order to help describe the intended behavior of the component that it verifies.

Each component can be tested using an individual test driver that exercises the functionality implemented in that particular component. Physical dependency governs the order in which tests are developed and run. Level numbers serve both to characterize the relative complexity of a component locally within a package and to provide an objective strategy for testing.

Individual drivers are necessary in order to ensure that physical design rules are followed—otherwise we will be unable to demonstrate that functionality declared within a component is available solely within the subset of components indicated by that component's dependency graph. To illustrate why this is so, consider the design-rule violation (shown in Figure 4-16), where component `a` defines a class `A` with member function `f()`, and a component `b` (layered on `a`), which illegally implements `A::f()`.

As illustrated in Figure 4-16a, a single test driver that links to both `a` and `b` is incapable of detecting this major design rule violation. As far as anyone can tell from the dependency graph, component `a` is independent of component `b` and therefore can be reused independently of `b`. If someone tries to reuse component `a` independently of `b` and calls `f()`, `A::f` will show up as an undefined symbol at link time.

In Figure 4-16b, distinct drivers are provided to exercise the functionality in each component. When linking the driver for component `a`, component `b` is deliberately excluded from the link process. If the driver for `a` is at all thorough (i.e., calls each function at least once), then if `A::f` is not defined, the error will be caught at link time —that is, without even having to run the driver. This same technique also serves to detect components that are not levelizable.

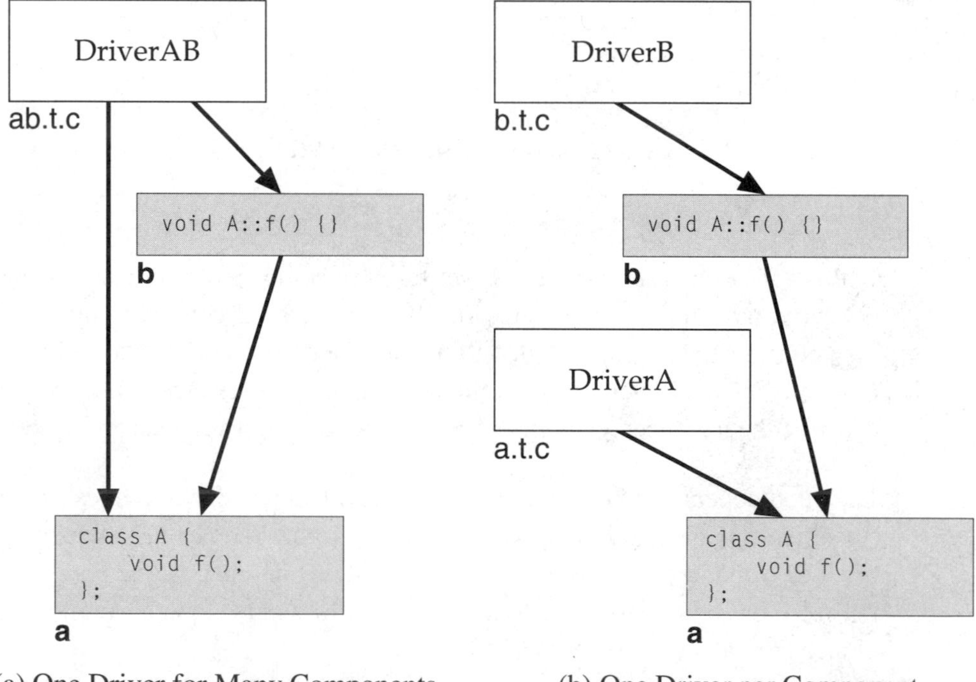

(a) One Driver for Many Components (b) One Driver per Component

Figure 4-16: The Need for Individual Component Drivers

Another compelling reason for insisting on individual drivers is that a single component typically provides ample functionality for a test driver to exercise thoroughly. Lumping tests for several components within a single driver would lead to excessively large (or, more likely, inadequate) tests.

Figure 4-17 illustrates the abstract physical structure of the hierarchical testing strategy. Each component at level 1 can depend on only external components (all of which are at level 0). Therefore each component at level 1 can be tested independently of all other (local) components.

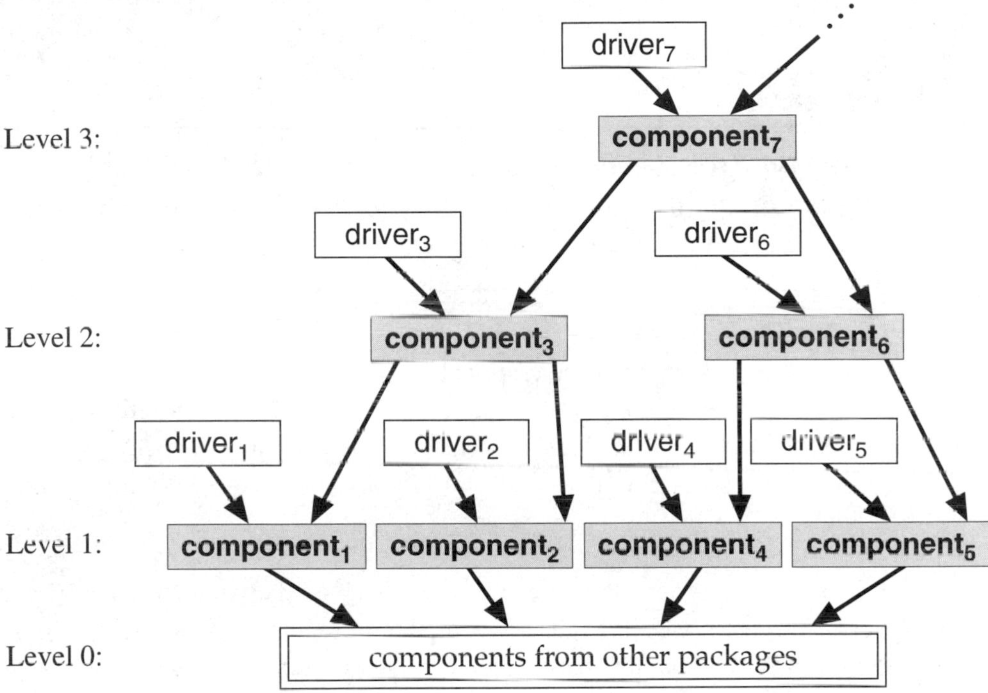

Figure 4-17: Hierarchical Testing Strategy

As we proceed to higher levels of the physical design hierarchy, the complexity of the subsystems will grow, often exponentially. This explosive growth implies that we will soon reach the point where tests designed to cover the complete behavior of a high-level interface will be too difficult to write or take too long to run.

DEFINITION: *Incremental testing* refers to the practice of deliberately testing only the functionality actually implemented within the component under test.

Our hierarchical approach makes it unnecessary to retest the internal behavior of lower-level components. If instead we attempt to test only the functional value added by a given component, the test complexity for each component is more likely to be kept to a manageable level. The practice of targeting only the new functionality added by a given component is referred to in this book as *incremental testing*.

Principle

Testing only the functionality *directly implemented* within a component enables the complexity of the test to be proportional to the complexity of the component.

Since we can assume that the components at lower levels are supplying objects that are working properly, the task of incremental testing is often reduced to testing the way in which these lower-level objects combine to form higher-level objects. Writing incremental tests is not always easy in practice, and requires intimate knowledge of the implementation of the component.

For example, suppose a user-defined type `X` is layered upon three other types, `A`, `B`, and `C`, each of which lives in a separate component. Figure 4-18a shows part of the definition for class `X`. From this partial header we can observe the logical uses relationships of Figure 4-18b. Now, given that each class resides in a separate component, we can infer the component dependencies shown in Figure 4-18c.

In this highly simplistic example, testing functions `f` and `g` of class `X` amounts to verifying that functions `X::f` and `X::g` are properly hooked up to the appropriate underlying functions `C::u` and `C::v`, respectively. Since component `c` is at a lower level than component `x`, we can assume that `c` has already been tested and is internally correct, making it unnecessary to retest `C::u` or `C::v` in the driver for component `x`. By contrast, the implementation of `X::h` is substantial, and therefore is where most of the testing effort for this component should be focused.

```
class X {
    A d_a;
    B d_b;
    C d_c;
  public:
    //...
    int f() { return d_c.u(d_a); }
    int g() { return d_c.v(d_a, d_b); }
    int h();
};
```

(a) Definition of Class `X`

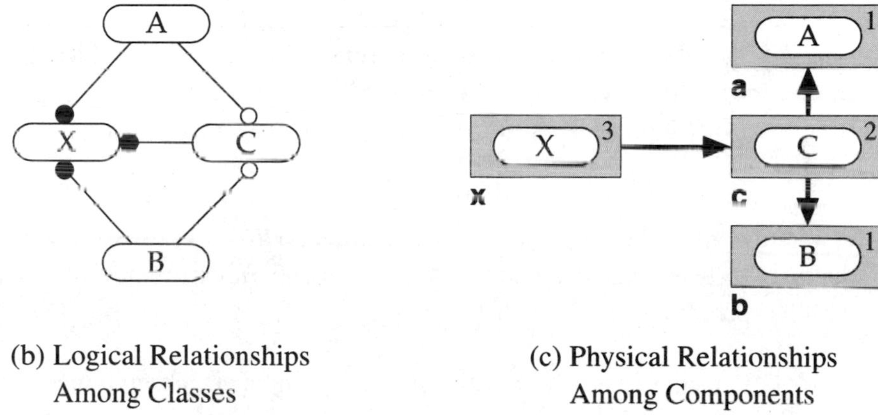

(b) Logical Relationships Among Classes

(c) Physical Relationships Among Components

Figure 4-18: Analyzing a Layered Object for Testing Purposes

> **<u>DEFINITION</u>: *White-box testing* refers to the practice of verifying the expected behavior of a component by exploiting knowledge of its underlying implementation.**

Exploiting knowledge of the implementation of the component is a genre of testing known as *white-box* testing. White-box testing allows the tester to approach nearly complete internal code coverage with a much smaller test driver by carefully choosing test cases that exercise all of an object's internal functionality.

White-box tests are effective at helping the developer flush out low-level programming errors such as simple coding errors, and often even basic algorithmic errors resulting in memory leaks and even forced program terminations. Since white-box tests are implementation dependent, a complete reimplementation of an underlying object may render such tests ineffective.

White-box testing and 100 percent code coverage are necessary but are not sufficient to ensure high-quality components. For example, if, as a developer analyzing a problem, I miss a special case that requires extra processing, it is not likely that the omission would be uncovered through white-box testing alone.

DEFINITION: *Black-box testing* refers to the practice of verifying the expected behavior of a component based solely on its specification (i.e., without knowledge of its underlying implementation).

Unlike the white-box test that verifies that the code works as the developer intended, the *black-box* test verifies that the component satisfies its requirements and complies with its specification.

Black-box testing is driven directly from the component's requirements and specification. Black-box testing is, for the most part, independent of implementation. Black-box testing is also appropriate for an independent tester, say from a QA department, who must understand the behavior and proper use of the component from its documentation alone.

As suggested by Figure 4-19, black-box and white-box testing are complementary techniques with some degree of overlap. Both are important, and each addresses separate aspects of quality. White-box testing tends to ensure that we have solved a problem correctly, and black-box testing helps to make sure that we have solved the correct problem.

Development will tend to emphasize white-box testing to ensure reliability. QA will probably use white-box testing to ensure coverage, but will also employ black-box testing to verify the accompanying specifications and documentation. Moreover, black-box tests may be given to clients as *acceptance tests* in order to demonstrate functionality, whereas white-box tests, being implementation dependent, would probably remain inhouse. Thorough tests of complex components will make effective use of both strategies.

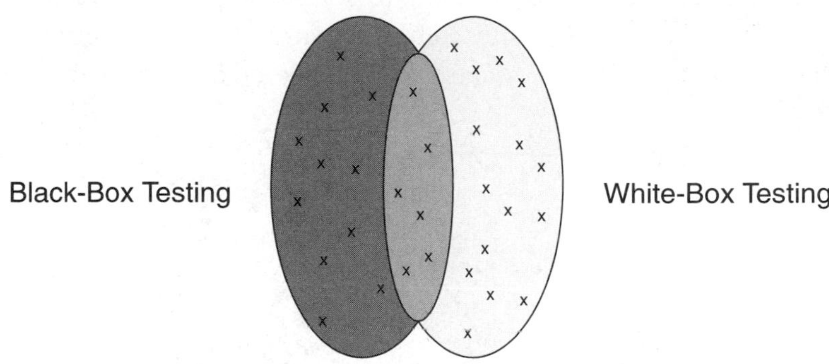

Figure 4-19: Defects Detectable Through Testing

One of the appealing properties of incremental testing is that the difficulty of testing any given component is roughly proportional to the functional value added by that component itself rather than to the combined complexity of the lower-level components on which that component depends. Regardless of how extensive the functionality in components a, b, and c might be, it may be possible to write a relatively short but thorough incremental test for component x because `X::f` and `X::g` merely propagate information to and from a working `C` subobject.

To summarize this section: we want the complexity of the test to correspond to the complexity of the component under test. We want to test all leaf components in isolation. All higher-level components are tested assuming the lower-level components on which they depend are internally correct. This incremental, hierarchical strategy allows us to focus our testing effort where it can do the most good, and to avoid the redundancy of retesting already tested software.

3.14 Testing a Complex Subsystem

Let us return once again to the point-to-point router example of Figure 4-2. As discussed earlier, the interface for `p2p_router` is difficult to test effectively. It is precisely for these kinds of interfaces that hierarchical testing is most needed to ensure quality.

An actual implementation of this example is distributed throughout the levelizable hierarchy shown in Figure 4-20. Some but not all of the components in this subsystem are reused by other components at higher levels. Both the `geom_point` and geom_polygon components belong to a separate package, geom, and are assumed by the p2p package implementor to be internally correct. These reusable library components account for a nontrivial portion of the router's implementation.

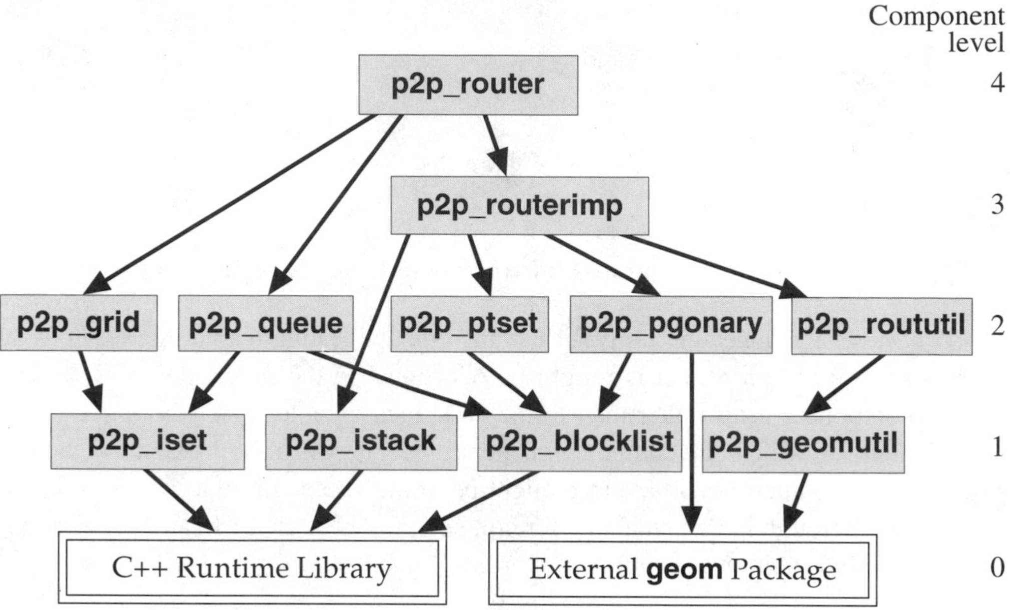

Figure 4-20: Component Dependency Diagram for Point-to-Point Router

Let us assume that in our p2p_router subsystem, each of the lowest-level components has predictable behavior and is eminently testable. The level-1 components are, as ever, testable in isolation—independently of any other p2p components. Each of the level-2 components in this subsystem depends on at most two level-1 components. Each of the level-2 components implements an appropriate amount of additional functionality that, in combination with the already-tested lower-level functionality, is not difficult to understand and verify.

The p2p_router component insulates its clients of the router from all details of its implementation, pushing much of its implementation down into the p2p_routerimp component. In turn, p2p_routerimp serves to expose to test engineers subfunctionality that would otherwise be inaccessibly defined within p2p_router.c.

In the actual implementation, p2p_router implements less than 10 percent of the solution; its job is primarily to coordinate the functionality implemented in the lower-level components of the `p2p` subsystem. We have improved maintainability by carefully distributing the implementation of the functionality of this complex component across a hierarchy of some 10 other local subcomponents, each with independent, well-defined interfaces, and each implementing a manageable amount of predictable functionality.

To summarize: we have designed in testability for a component that is potentially difficult to test by factoring its implementation into a levelizable hierarchy of independently testable (and perhaps reusable) components. Distributing the testing effort throughout the router subsystem will exponentially reduce the amount of regression testing that would be needed at the highest level to achieve the same degree of quality. Human validation is expensive and prone to error, and is frequently omitted due to lack of time and resources. However, the levelized hierarchy enables the predictable behavior of the subcomponents to be tested using more robust methods that do not require human intervention.

In short, hierarchical physical implementations of complex subsystems can be both more reliable and less costly to test than non-hierarchical alternatives.

3.15 Testability versus Testing

Testability and *testing* are not the same thing. In fact, they are largely independent aspects of quality. By *testable*, we mean that there is an effective test strategy that will allow us to verify that the functionality indicated by the interface (along with supporting documentation) is realized by the implementation. By *tested*, we are saying that the product has demonstrated that it now conforms to its specifications. *Testable* is something we strive to make our products from the moment we start our design. *Tested* is a state our product must attain before we release it to our customers. *Testing* is something we do all along the way.

Principle

Thorough regression testing is expensive but essential; the appropriate time to create thorough regression tests is tied to the stability of the subsystem to be tested.

Knowing when and how much to test is an engineering trade-off. The more thorough the developer is at testing the code as it is being implemented, the less likely it will be that unforeseen bugs will affect the development schedule down the road.

On the other hand, developing thorough tests is time consuming and can significantly increase the up-front cost of development. Often this extra effort is more than compensated by reduced time spent in maintenance, future enhancements, and even current development.

Unfortunately, it is inevitable that the interfaces of many components will change substantially during the early stages of the development process. Some components will split apart, others will merge together, and still others will disappear entirely. Consequently, developing thorough regression tests at the preliminary stages of a project may in some cases turn out *not* to be cost-effective.

As a project progresses, various components will become mature. The interfaces to these components will become more stable—they will change less frequently than, say, once a month. It is at this point that it may be appropriate for QA to make a second pass at writing thorough, systematic regression tests to validate these components and report any missing or ambiguous documentation.

As long as developers design their components to be testable and provide sufficient and appropriate documentation, it should be fairly straightforward for test engineers to write detailed systematic tests to verify the functionality supplied by each component.[6]

If developers do not consider testability when designing their systems, then the testing process may not be straightforward or effective. In order to facilitate efficient testing, the testability of a system must be in place long before its components are ever tested.

3.16 Cyclic Physical Dependencies

Often designs begin with acyclic dependencies and then, as they evolve, cyclic dependencies creep in during enhancements. For example, consider adding to class `C1` in Figure 4-8 of Section 4.6 the member `g()` returning a `C2` by value as follows:

---

[6] See **marick** for a thorough treatment of systematic testing.

```
class C1 {
    // ...
  public:
    C1 f();
    C2 g();     // new
};
```

Member `g()` introduces an additional dependency, resulting in the cycle of Figure 4-9b. With the addition of this function, components `c1` and `c2` must "know about" each other (i.e., their respective components must include each other's header files) and are therefore mutually dependent. It will no longer be possible to test or use either `C1` or `C2` without the other.

Principle

Cyclic physical dependencies among components inhibit understanding, testing, and reuse.

Having cyclic physical dependencies among components is undesirable, not only because it makes them hard to test and impossible to reuse independently, but also because it makes them much more difficult for people to understand and maintain. Once two components are mutually dependent, it is necessary to understand both in order to fully understand either.

Guideline

Avoid cyclic physical dependencies among components.

It is not uncommon for closely related classes to be mutually dependent; however, these classes will properly reside in a single component. If we find that two (or more) components `c1` and `c2` are mutually dependent, we have three alternatives:

1. Repackage `c1` and `c2` so they are no longer mutually dependent.
2. Physically combine `c1` and `c2` into a single component, `c12`.
3. Think of `c1` and `c2` as if they were a single component, `c12`.

The best solution is to correct cyclic dependencies before they happen; or, if they do creep in, to detect and correct them as soon as they occur. Chapter 5 addresses techniques for restructuring a cyclically dependent design to eliminate the cycles while preserving the intended behavior.

Merging components into a single component is the right solution when the objects in the combined abstraction are naturally tightly coupled and other issues do not override. If one class befriends another, this would further suggest that the classes belong in the same component (see Section 3.6.1). Merging tightly coupled, cohesive components also has the welcome benefit of reducing the number of components, and hence the physical complexity of the system, without further compromising testability or independent reuse.

Occasionally a single, tightly coupled abstraction will be deemed too large to fit in one component and will be split into mutually dependent components. Most of the time, however, the tightly coupled part of the abstraction can be isolated from the rest of the implementation and placed in a single component, which in turn depends on other independent components. These independent components can now be tested thoroughly in isolation (see Section 5.9).

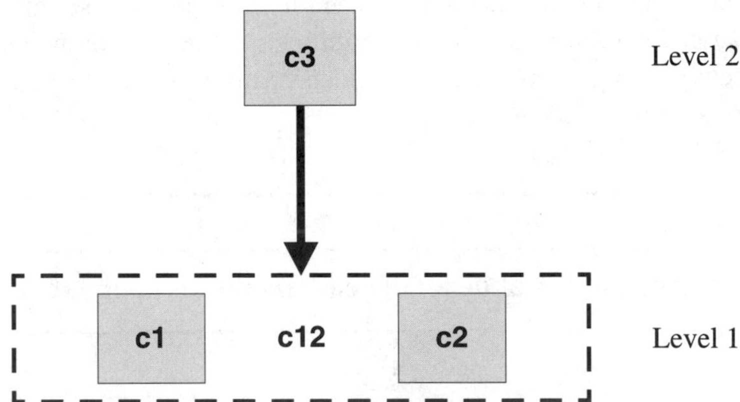

Figure 4-21: Two Mutually Dependent Components Treated as One

If no other solution is forthcoming, we can mentally treat mutually dependent components as if they were just one big component, as illustrated in Figure 4-21. This approach is easy in the short term but is the least desirable alternative for the long term. These physically separate yet tightly coupled components must artificially be treated as a single physical unit, which detracts from the uniformity of a maintainable design. Although such dependencies are undesirable, the overall testability of a system will not be lost so long as the number and size of such "blobs" are kept to a minimum.

3.17 Cumulative Component Dependency

We now formalize our discussion of designing in quality by providing a metric referred to in this book as the *cumulative component dependency* (*CCD*) of a subsystem that is closely tied to the link-time cost of incremental regression testing. More generally, the CCD provides a numerical value that indicates the relative costs associated with developing and maintaining a given subsystem.

> **DEFINITION:** ***Cumulative component dependency (CCD)*** **is the sum over all components C_i in a subsystem of the number of components needed in order to test each C_i incrementally.**

Linking large programs takes a long time. Typically, developers will need to link a single component many times in the process of creating both the component and its test driver. After that, the component will need to be linked to its driver whenever regression tests are run. For small projects, link times are comparable to the compile times of individual components. As projects get larger, the link time grows to be much larger than the time needed to compile even the largest of components.

Most of our development time is spent on low-level components, primarily because there are simply a lot more low-level components than high-level ones. These low-level pieces of the system can be intricate and are sometimes selected for performance tuning. It is to our advantage to streamline the process of developing, testing, and maintaining low-level components.

For the sake of this discussion, let's say that the dependencies in a design formed a perfect binary tree. Just over half of the components would be at level 1 and could be tested in complete isolation. Another quarter would each depend on two leaf components. If we let L represent the number of distinct levels in the tree, then only one of the 2^L-1 components would actually depend on all the rest. Although real designs are not nearly so regular, the advantage of testing a hierarchy of components with acyclic dependencies remains clear.

Consider the costs associated with developing a set of components. For the moment, let's assume that link time is proportional to the number of components being linked together.[7] For instance, if linking one component to a test driver takes 1 CPU second, then linking five components would take roughly 5 CPU seconds.

In the presence of cyclic dependencies, it may be necessary to link in most or all of the components in order to test any one of them. It is not necessary that every component depend directly on every other component for a design to be fully interdependent.[8] Suppose our system is very tightly coupled and each component is either directly or indirectly dependent on all the others. If we let N represent the number of components in our system, the cost of linking any one of these components to its test driver is proportional to N. The link cost alone of building all N test drivers for these components is then proportional to N^2. This fact explains why linking often dominates the cost of running thorough regression tests for large systems.

Principle

Let *N* be the number of components in the system.

$$\mathbf{CCD}_{\substack{\text{Cyclically}\\\text{Dependent}\\\text{Graph}}}(N) = \left(\begin{array}{c}\textbf{total number}\\\textbf{of components}\end{array}\right) \cdot \left(\begin{array}{c}\textbf{link-time cost}\\\textbf{of testing a}\\\textbf{component}\end{array}\right)$$

$$= N \cdot N$$

$$= N^2$$

[7] This assumption is of course only a crude approximation, since link cost will clearly be affected by variation in component sizes and by the structure of the function-call hierarchy.

[8] A fully interdependent design has a direct-dependency graph that is "strongly connected" but not necessarily "complete." See **aho**, Section 5.5, p. 189 and Section 10.3, p. 375 for formal definitions of these respective terms.

Now consider what would happen if our dependencies were acyclic and formed a binary tree. Now, not all components have equal link cost. Components at level 1 could be linked to their respective test drivers in unit time (e.g., 1 CPU second). Fully half of the link cost associated with component testing could be virtually eliminated. Each component at level 2 would depend on two components at level 1 and comprise a subsystem of size 3 (it would take 3 CPU seconds to link). That is, another quarter of the test cost associated with linking could be reduced dramatically (by a factor of *N*/3). Only one component in this hypothetical system, the root, would require the full *N* CPU seconds of link time previously required by each of the *N* components.

Mathematically we can show that the total link cost to incrementally test a system whose physical dependencies form a binary tree is proportional to $N \log(N)$ instead of N^2 (see Figure 4-22). For example, in the case with 15 components,

$$CCD_{\substack{\text{Balanced}\\\text{Binary}\\\text{Tree}}}(15) = (15 + 1) \cdot (\log_2(15 + 1) - 1) + 1 = 49$$

Principle

Acyclic physical dependencies can dramatically reduce link-time costs associated with developing, maintaining, and testing large systems.

The benefits of acyclic dependencies are enormous. The average time to link an individual test driver for an acyclic design with tree-like dependencies is proportional to the *log* of the number of components, rather than to the number of components itself, as is the case for cyclic designs.

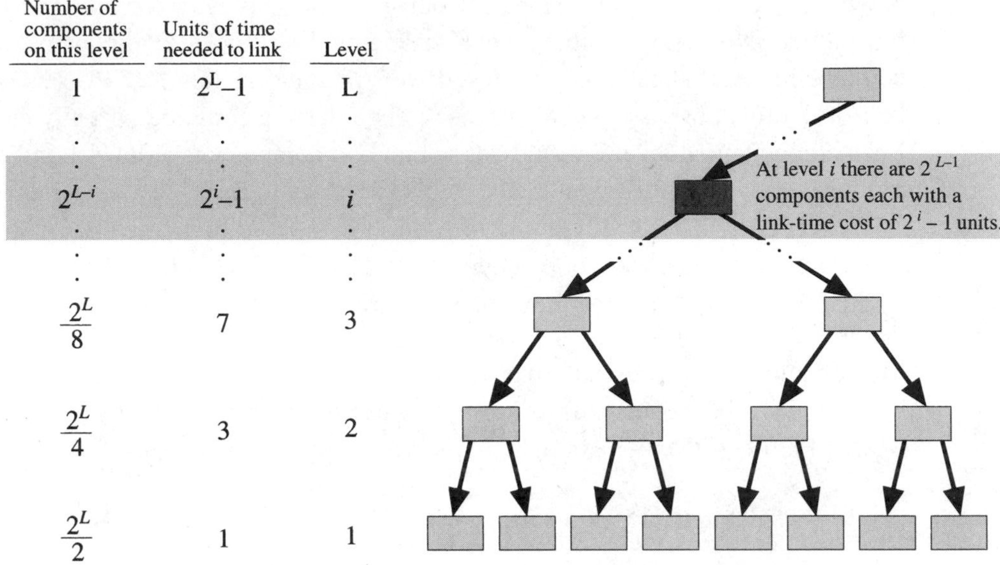

Number of components on this level
Units of time needed to link
Level
1
2L–1
L
2L–i
2i–1
i
2L/8
7
3
2L/4
3
2
2L/2
1
1
At level i there are 2 L–1 components each with a link-time cost of 2 i – 1 units.

Let L be the number of levels in the system (depth of the binary tree).
Let $N = 2^L - 1$ be the number of components in the system.

$$\mathrm{CCD}_{\substack{\text{Balanced}\\\text{Binary}\\\text{Tree}}}(N) = \sum_{i=1}^{L} \left(\begin{array}{c}\text{number of}\\\text{components}\\\text{on level } i\end{array}\right) \bullet \left(\begin{array}{c}\text{link-time cost of}\\\text{testing a component}\\\text{on level } i\end{array}\right)$$

$$= \sum_{i=1}^{L} 2^{L-i} \bullet (2^i - 1)$$

$$= \sum_{i=1}^{L} 2^L - \sum_{i=1}^{L} 2^{L-i}$$

$$= 2^L \bullet \sum_{i=1}^{L} 1 - \sum_{i=1}^{L} 2^{i-1}$$

$$= 2^L \bullet L - (2^L - 1)$$

$$= 2^L \bullet (L - 1) + 1$$

{ Useful for comparison with a binary dependency tree of integral height L.

$$= (N + 1) \bullet (\log_2(N + 1) - 1) + 1$$

$$= (N + 1) \bullet \log_2(N + 1) - N$$

{ Useful for comparison with theoretical binary tree of arbitrary positive size N.

$$= O(N \bullet \log(N))$$

{ Asymptotic link-time cost.

Figure 4-22: Computing Link-Time Cost for a Binary Tree of Dependencies

Figure 4-23 compares link-time costs associated with testing cyclic and hierarchical systems with $N = 1$, 3, 7, and 15 components. The number shown corresponding to each component position in the dependency graph indicates the link cost associated with incrementally testing that component. The CCD for each system is calculated and shown at the bottom of its dependency graph. The CCD for each tree-like system is calculated in two ways: once level by level and once using the equation derived in Figure 4-22

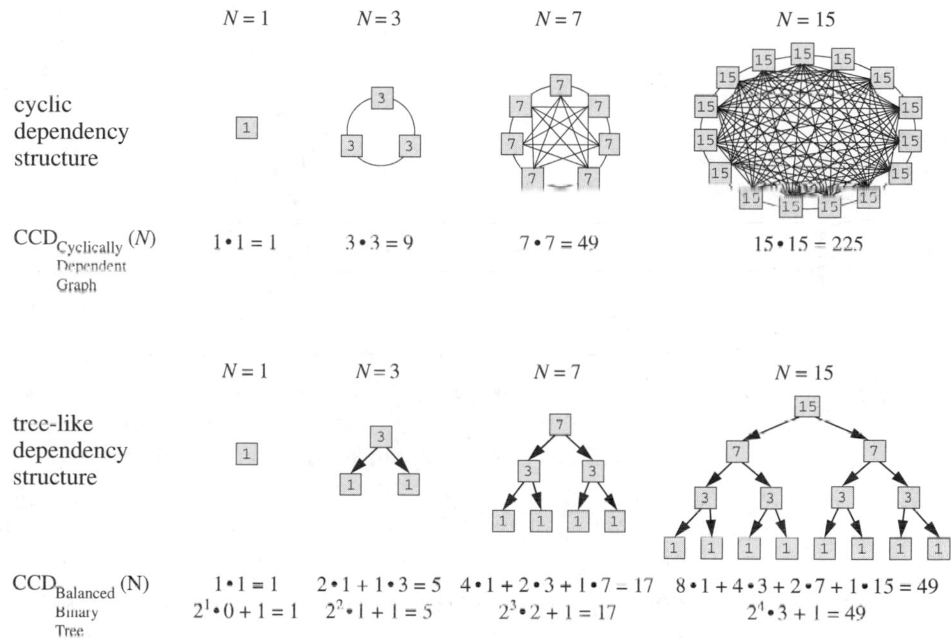

Figure 4-23: Relative Link Costs Associated with Incremental Testing

Suppose that you are developing a system that has 63 components, each with its own test driver. In a cyclic design, each component would take 63 seconds to relink in order to test. Compare this to a hierarchical design (analyzed in Figure 4-24), in which fully half of the components can be linked in 1 CPU second, a quarter in 3 CPU seconds, an eighth in 7 CPU seconds, and so on. Only one of the 63 components takes the full 63 CPU seconds to link in order to test it. The total cost of linking all 63 test drivers is calculated in two ways in Figure 4-24 to be 321 CPU seconds (5.35 CPU minutes). Compare this with the $63^2 = 3{,}969$ CPU seconds (1.1 CPU hours) it would take to link all 63 test drivers to a cyclically dependent system.

Level number	Number of components on this level		Cost to link a component on this level		Link cost for all components on this level
1	32	•	1	=	32
2	16	•	3	=	48
3	8	•	7	=	56
4	4	•	15	=	60
5	2	•	31	=	62
6	1	•	63	=	63
			Total	=	321

$$\begin{aligned} CCD_{\substack{\text{Balanced}\\\text{Binary}\\\text{Tree}}}(63) &= (63 + 1) \bullet (\log_2(63 + 1) - 1) + 1 \\ &= 64 \bullet 5 + 1 \\ &= 321 \end{aligned}$$

Figure 4-24: Link Cost for Balanced Binary Tree Hierarchy, $N = 63$

If the number of components were even larger, say 1,023 components, then the average cost of linking a component in a tree-like design would be two orders of magnitude less than for a cyclic design (9 versus 1,023 CPU seconds per component on average). We can use the equation derived in Figure 4-22 to predict the CCD of this system. The total link time alone for building component regression tests on a system with 1,023 components could range from 1,024 • 9 + 1 = 9,217 CPU seconds (just over 2.5 hours) for the hierarchically designed system to 1,023 •1,023 = 1,046,529 CPU seconds (over 12 days) for the cyclically dependent system.

It is unlikely that a single project would grow to 1,023 components without being further partitioned into what we call *packages*. The importance of ensuring acyclic dependencies among packages is even greater than that for individual components (see Section 7.3).

CCD is also a predictor of the cumulative disk space requirements for incremental regression testing. Disk space can become an important consideration when incrementally testing a large system concurrently. The size of each independent executable test programs on disk will be roughly proportional to the number of components to which the test driver must statically link. Consequently, cyclically interdependent systems can require significantly more disk space than do hierarchical designs.

To summarize: our goal is to be able to build a test driver for each component that links with the component to be tested and only the (few) components on which that component depends. CCD is a metric that quantifies the coupling of a system in terms of the total link-time cost associated with testing each component incrementally. Cyclically dependent components exhibit quadratic behavior in terms of the link time and disk space required in order to test them incrementally. In contrast, forming an acyclic (tree-like) hierarchy of component dependencies reduces the link cost of incremental component testing dramatically.

3.18 Physical Design Quality

In this section we characterize what makes a design maintainable in terms of its physical dependencies. We continue to discuss CCD and how it is used to indicate the overall maintainability of a subsystem. We also show how to use CCD to measure incremental improvements in physical design quality.

Imagine joining a company that is developing a very large system. You are handed a subsystem of about 150,000 lines of C++ code and you are asked to understand what it does and make suggestions as to how to improve it. Upon examination, you find that the components (for the most part) are consistent with the rules and guidelines set forth in Chapters 2 and 3. You then discover that most of the components in the system depend (either directly or indirectly) on most of the other components. What do you do? Unfortunately there is no happy ending to this story. The best anyone can do may be to try to fit the entire design into his or her head, and that may take months.

Had the same subsystem been designed with an eye toward minimizing CCD, most—if not all—cyclic dependencies would have been eliminated. It would be possible to study pieces of the subsystem in isolation, to test, verify, tune, and even replace them, without having to involve the entire subsystem either mentally or physically. In other words, actively reducing the intercomponent dependencies, as quantified by CCD, improves understandability and therefore maintainability.

Comprehension is one of several hard-to-quantify yet very real advantages of minimizing intercomponent dependencies; selective reuse is another. Consider the architecture of the subsystem illustrated in Figure 4-25. This system consists of seven components, each of which depends either directly or indirectly on every other component in the system. Each of the components can be tested directly, but none of them can be tested in isolation or reused independently of the rest. Because each independent test driver is forced to link with the entire system, the amount of disk space required just to store these independent drivers will be quadratic as well.

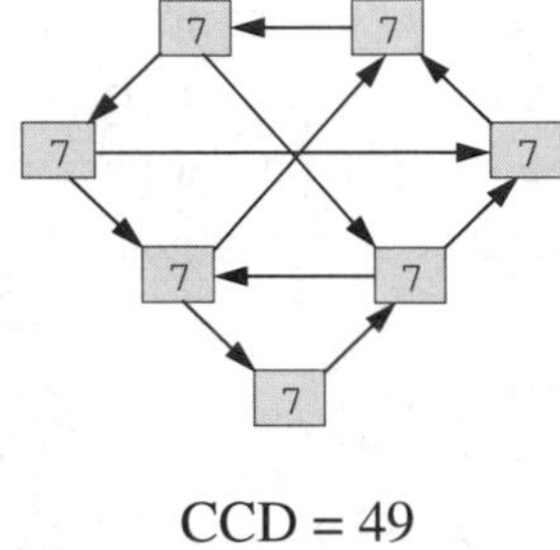

CCD = 49

Figure 4-25: Cyclically Dependent Subsystem Architecture of Size 7

Assume now that the cyclic dependencies in the design of Figure 4-25 are removed, making it levelizable. Although levelizability is highly desirable, some levelizable architectures are more maintainable and reusable than others. Consider the design hierarchies shown in Figure 4-26. Each hierarchy contains seven components, and each is levelizable. Figure 4-26a shows one extreme version of levelization. Designs of this nature are termed *vertical*. Each component in this system depends on all of the components at lower levels. Vertical subsystems exhibit a high degree of coupling, which inhibits independent reuse. Reusing a randomly chosen component in a vertical system of size N will on average result in having to link to $(N - 1)/2$ additional components. The average disk space required to hold incremental test driver programs will be correspondingly large.

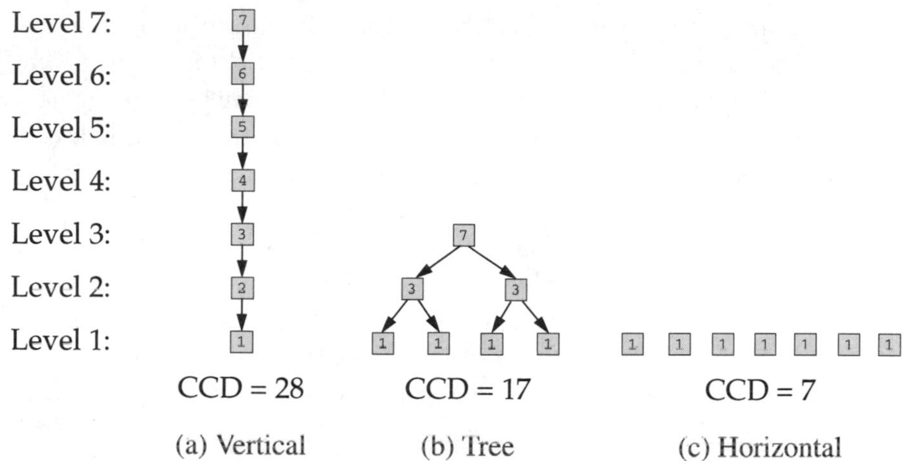

Figure 4-26: CCD for Various Component Hierarchies of Size 7

Vertical systems are highly inflexible with respect to both testing and reuse. There is only a single order in which to test purely vertical systems, and that order is entirely determined by its levelization. Developing a vertical subsystem is also relatively expensive in terms of link times. The total link cost (CCD) of 28 units for this system is more than half of the 49 units for the cyclically dependent subsystem shown in Figure 4-25. Furthermore, a vertical subsystem will be relatively difficult to partition into parallel development efforts, spread across multiple developers. A vertical subsystem is, however, acyclic and therefore qualitatively easier to maintain than if it were cyclic.

Figure 4-26b shows a design hierarchy in the form of a binary tree. As we know, over half of the components in this design contribute only a single unit each to the CCD. Designs will not be perfect binary trees, but the CCD of a binary tree serves as a good benchmark against which to compare many typical applications. Tree-like designs, with their lower degree of coupling, are much more flexible and suited to reuse than vertical designs. At each level there are typically several subsystems that can be tested and possibly reused independently of the rest of the system. The disk space requirement for holding most of the incremental test driver programs will be relatively low.

By making the dependency graph flatter rather than taller, we increase flexibility. The flatter the design, the greater the potential for independent reuse. Flattening the dependencies also helps to decrease the time needed for understanding and maintenance. The flatter the design, the more likely a bug can be tracked to a single, isolated component or a small independent subsystem, and therefore the less disk space will be required by the driver executable to exercise the defect.

Figure 4-26c shows the other end of the levelization spectrum. This type of design is characterized as *horizontal* because all of the components are entirely independent and decoupled from one another. Components belonging to purely horizontal subsystems may be tested in any order and reused in any combination desired. The disk space requirement for every incremental test driver program will be quite low. Such dependency characteristics are typical in reusable component libraries but atypical of subsystems in general.

We can make some objective, quantitative statements about the relative maintainability and reusability (but not necessarily the "goodness") of a design of a given size based on its CCD. Design dependencies form a continuum that ranges from cyclic to vertical to tree-like to horizontal. Even in the presence of cycles, every design can be assigned a CCD. All other things being equal, the lower the CCD, the less expensive (in terms of link time and disk space) the system will be to develop and maintain.

There is yet another reason to strive for a hierarchical system with a minimal CCD. Requirements are rarely cast in stone and may change during the development of a project. By distributing the implementation throughout a hierarchy of components, the design becomes more resilient to change. The more horizontal an architecture, the less it is likely that any changes in specification will affect the overall system. This expected cost due to changes in specification is directly related to the average component dependency (ACD) in the system.

DEFINITION: *Average component dependency (ACD)* is defined as the ratio of the CCD of a subsystem to the number of components *N* in the subsystem:

$$\text{ACD(subsystem)} = \frac{\text{CCD(subsystem)}}{N_{\text{subsystem}}}$$

For example, changing the specification of a single component in a fully horizontal subsystem causes only one component to change. For a tree-like architecture with N components, up to roughly $\log(N)$ components may need to change on average. For a vertical structure, we might expect to revisit as many as $(N + 1)/2$ components as a result of having to modify the interface to just one. Finally, for a fully cyclically dependent design, all N components could be affected by a single change.

Principle

The primary purpose of CCD is to quantify the change in overall coupling resulting from a minor perturbation to a given architecture.

As an illustration of reducing CCD, consider the two systems with similar dependency structure shown in Figure 4-27. Design A has a cyclic dependency between two of its components. Testing either one of these components requires linking to both of them, along with all of the components on which either one of them depends; this gives each of them an individual component dependency of 7. Notice also that at the right of Design A, a portion of the hierarchy is purely vertical.

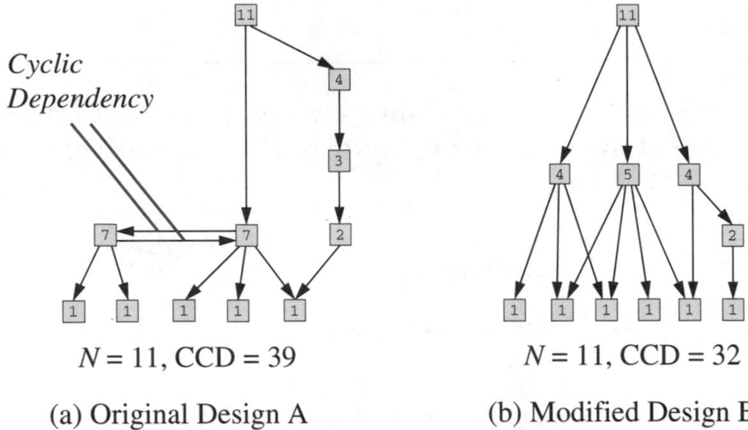

Figure 4-27: Dependency Graphs for Two Alternative Designs of a Subsystem

Several techniques for reducing link-time dependencies are presented in detail in Chapter 5. To improve this design we would first like to try to break the cyclic dependency and then examine the vertical section to see if it can be made less serial. In this case, it may be possible to break the cycle merely by escalating some code to a higher level and/or factoring out a shared resource. As for the vertical section, it may be that one or more components in the chain can be removed and made into leaf components, independent of the rest. The result of making these modifications is Design B, shown in Figure 4-27b. The CCD of 39 for our original Design A is much lower than the CCD of 121 for a fully interdependent design. Yet we were still able to reduce the CCD in this nearly hierarchical system from 39 to 32—an improvement of about 18 percent.

CCD is an objective metric that characterizes the physical coupling within a system. CCD can flag subsystems with unusually high incremental development and maintenance costs. For example, a vertical chain is the levelizable configuration with the highest CCD: $N(N + 1)/2$. Therefore a CCD of greater than $N(N + 1)/2$ implies that at least one cyclic dependency exists. However, CCD is *not* (by itself) a measure of the quality of a subsystem.

We can conveniently use the alternate equation derived in Figure 4-22 to determine the CCD for a (theoretical) binary-tree-like architecture of the same size as those shown in Figure 4-27. Figure 4-28 demonstrates that a binary-tree-like architecture with 11 components has a CCD of 32.02, which is comparable with that of Design B.

$$\mathrm{CCD}_{\substack{\text{Balanced}\\\text{Binary}\\\text{Tree}}}(N) = (N+1) \bullet \log_2(N+1) - N$$

$$\mathrm{CCD}_{\substack{\text{Balanced}\\\text{Binary}\\\text{Tree}}}(11) = (11+1) \bullet \log_2(11+1) - 11$$

$$= 12 \bullet \log_2(12) - 11$$

$$= 32.02$$

Figure 4-28: Computing the CCD of a Theoretical Balanced Tree of Size 11

DEFINITION: ***Normalized cumulative component dependency (NCCD)*** **is defined as the ratio of the CCD of a subsystem containing *N* components to the CCD of a tree-like system of the same size.**

$$\mathrm{NCCD(subsystem)} = \frac{\mathrm{CCD(subsystem)}}{\mathrm{CCD}_{\substack{\text{Balanced}\\\text{Binary}\\\text{Tree}}}(N_{\text{subsystem}})}$$

The NCCD of a system can be used to characterize the degree of physical coupling within the system relative to a theoretical binary-dependency tree of the same size. Referring back to Figure 4-27, the NCCD of Design B was 32/32.02 = 1.00 as compared with an NCCD of 39/32.02 = 1.21 for Design A (and 121/32.02 = 3.78 for the completely interdependent implementation).

An NCCD of less than 1.0 can be thought of as more "horizontal" or loosely coupled; such a system probably employs little reuse. An NCCD of greater than 1.0 can be thought of as more "vertical" and/or tightly coupled; such a system may be making extensive reuse of components. An NCCD substantially greater than 1.0 indicates that there may be significant cyclic physical coupling within the system.

The degree of maintainability in terms of the CCD that we are able to achieve depends on the nature of the subsystem. We will not always achieve perfect tree-like maintainability. For horizontal component libraries, we would expect a much lower

CCD. The CCD will be higher for highly interconnected topologies that employ reuse heavily, such as the window system shown in Figure 2-8 of Section 2.5.

NCCD is *not* a measure of the relative quality of a system. NCCD is simply a tool for characterizing the degree of coupling within a subsystem. Increasing the number of components in a system could artificially reduce the NCCD. One way to do this is to eliminate completely valid reuse; this would likely not be an improvement.

Figure 4-29 shows two designs with equivalent functionality. Design B is 50 percent larger than A with a 25 percent larger CCD. On the other hand Design A, through reuse, exhibits more physical coupling for its size than does Design B. Nonetheless, Design A may very well be the better engineered and more maintainable design.

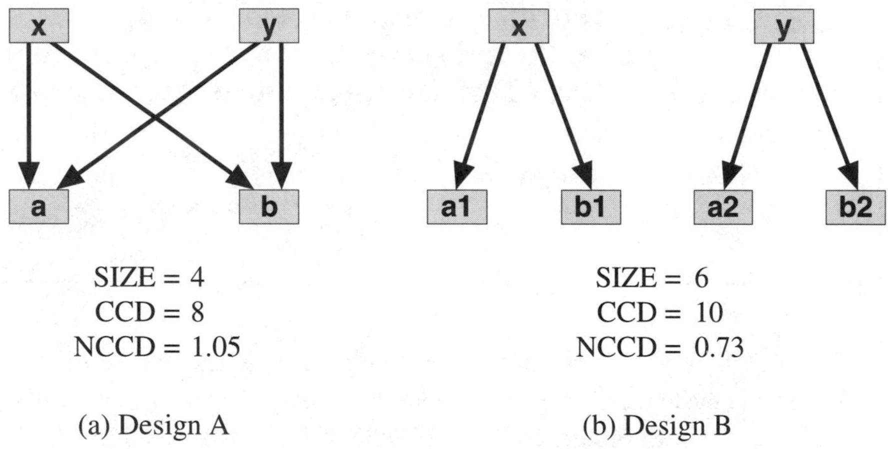

Figure 4-29: Illustrating the Effects of Redundancy

Principle

Minimizing CCD for a given set of components is a design goal.

Reducing the CCD in a system of a given size is almost always desirable. Reducing the size (number of components) of a system is also desirable but not at the cost of introducing cyclic dependencies, inappropriately merging components, or creating unmanageably large translation units. When increasing the number of components in a system actually reduces the CCD, chances are that the overall quality of the design has been improved.

In conclusion, the CCD metric has been introduced to identify explicitly the kind of dependencies we would like to minimize. NCCD gives us a quantitative way of characterizing the physical dependencies of a subsystem as horizontal, tree-like, vertical, or cyclic. The precise numerical value of the CCD (or the NCCD) for a given system is not important. What is important is actively designing systems to keep the CCD for each subsystem from becoming larger than necessary.

3.19 Summary

High-quality, complex subsystems are composed of many components layered on top of each other to form an acyclic physical hierarchy. Thorough testing at the system level is not just expensive, but highly infeasible—if not impossible—particularly for "good" interfaces.

A "good" interface encapsulates the complexity of the implementation behind a simple facade that is easy to use. At the same time, it makes our ability to test the implementation through this interface exceedingly difficult.

Much of the testing strategy in this chapter is motivated by the success of Design For Testability (DFT) over a decade ago. But, unlike real-world objects, instances of classes defined within a software system are no different from instances of the same classes defined outside that system. We can exploit this fact to verify portions of the design hierarchy in isolation, thereby reducing part of the risk of integration.

Isolation testing is a cost-effective way of ensuring reliability in complex, low-level components. By pushing the testing to the lowest possible level in the design hierarchy, we ensure that if the component or subsystem is enhanced, ported, or reused in another system, it will continue to adhere to its specified behavior independently of its clients.

Level numbers characterize components in terms of their physical dependencies on other components within a subsystem. Furthermore, level numbers provide an order in which systems with acyclic component dependency graphs can be tested effectively. Subsystems whose component dependencies form a directed acyclic graph (DAG) are said to be *levelizable*. A levelized component dependency diagram makes the physical structure of a system easier to understand, and consequently easier to maintain.

Hierarchical testing refers to testing components at each level of the physical hierarchy. Each lower-level component should provide a well-defined interface and implement predictable functionality that can be tested, verified, and reused independently of components at higher levels.

Incremental testing refers to having individual drivers test only the functionality actually implemented within the component under test; functionality implemented at lower levels of the physical hierarchy is presumed at this point to be internally correct. Consequently, incremental tests mirror the complexity of the implementation of the component under test and not that of the hierarchy of components upon which this component depends. Incremental testing is a form of white-box testing, which relies on knowing the implementation of the component in order to improve reliability. Black-box testing derives from requirements and specifications, and is independent of implementation. These two forms of testing are complementary, and both contribute to ensuring overall quality.

Testability is a design goal. Cyclic physical dependencies inhibit testing, understanding, and reuse. Cumulative component dependency (CCD) provides a crude numerical measure of the overall link-time cost associated with incrementally testing a given subsystem. More generally, CCD is an indicator of the relative maintainability of a given design.

Cyclically dependent designs are not levelizable. Such systems are known to be difficult to maintain and have a correspondingly high CCD. Among designs that are levelizable, the more horizontal the hierarchy, the lower the CCD. Flattening physical dependencies helps to decrease the time needed for understanding, development, and maintenance, while improving the flexibility, testability, and reusability of a system. NCCD (normalized CCD) helps to categorize the physical structure of arbitrary designs as *cyclic*, *vertical*, *tree-like*, or *horizontal*.

5

Levelization

Link-time dependencies within a system (as quantified by CCD) play a central role in establishing the overall physical quality of a system. More conventional aspects of quality, such as understandability, maintainability, testability, and reusability, are all closely tied to the quality of the physical design. If not carefully prevented, cyclic physical dependencies will rob a system of this quality, leaving it inflexible and difficult to manage.

Even revisable designs can be unnecessarily costly to maintain and enhance. Forced dependency on large, low-level subsystems can pose a significant development burden on higher-level subsystems. Minimizing the impact of such dependencies contributes to the physical quality of the system.

In this chapter, we explore several techniques for eliminating cyclic or otherwise excessive link-time dependencies. Escalation and demotion are related techniques that move a cyclicly dependent portion of the design to a different level in the physical hierarchy. Opaque pointers and dumb data are used to remove the physical implications of conceptual dependency. Redundancy and callbacks are yet two other techniques we discuss to prevent unwanted physical dependencies. Finally, a manager class is presented along with two general techniques (factoring and escalating encapsulation) to help create efficient, encapsulating hierarchies of testable and reusable components.

Throughout this chapter we use many examples taken from several application domains to illustrate these techniques in a variety of contexts. Occasionally we present a substantial body of source code to make the example concrete for reference purposes.

5.1 Some Causes of Cyclic Physical Dependencies

In this section we look at three ways in which cyclic physical dependencies can occur in practice. To demonstrate the breadth of this problem, we present and discuss each of these examples in a separate subsection without attempting to resolve them. These specific problems and many others will be solved as appropriate techniques are presented throughout the remainder of this chapter.

5.1.1 Enhancement

Initial designs are usually carefully planned and often levelizable. In time, the unanticipated needs of clients can evoke less-well-thought-out enhancements that induce unwanted cyclic dependencies. For example, we sometimes find we have similar objects that, for one reason or another (e.g., performance), coexist in a system but that contain essentially the same information.

Figure 5-1 shows a simple but illustrative example consisting of two classes, each representing a kind of box. A `Rectangle` is defined by two points that determine its lower-left and upper-right corners. A `Window` is defined by a center point, a width, and a height. These objects have distinct performance characteristics but contain the same logical information.

```
// rectangle.h
#ifndef INCLUDED_RECTANGLE
#define INCLUDED_RECTANGLE

class Rectangle {
    // ...
  public:
    Rectangle(int x1,
              int y1,
              int x2,
              int y2);

    // ...
    int lowerLeftX() const;
    // ...
};

#endif
```

```
// window.h
#ifndef INCLUDED_WINDOW
#define INCLUDED_WINDOW

class Window {
    // ...
  public:
    Window(int xCenter,
           int yCenter,
           int width,
           int height);

    // ...
    int width() const;
    // ...
};

#endif
```

Figure 5-1: Two Representations of a Box

Each of these objects will be used to facilitate the rendering of very large designs interactively on a graphics terminal; draw speed will be critical. For performance reasons, we do not even consider employing virtual functions, and most of the functions are declared `inline`.

Principle

Allowing two components to "know" about each other via `#include` directives implies cyclic physical dependency.

It turns out that clients will occasionally need to be able to convert between these two types of boxes, perhaps to obtain the performance characteristics of the other. This is one way in which good designs can sometimes start to deteriorate.

Consider the "solution" set forth in Figure 5-2. We have added to each class a constructor that takes as its only argument a `const` reference to the other class. We can now pass a `Window` object to a function requiring a `Rectangle` and vice versa, the conversion being performed implicitly. How does that sound to you?

If it sounded good to you, you are not alone. But it is not a good solution. For one thing, any speed benefit that might be realized could be lost by having to construct a temporary object of the other type on entry to a function. Since the conversion is implicit and automatic, your clients may not even realize that the extra temporary is being created (and will blame you for your "slow" class).

Much more importantly, we have introduced a cyclic physical dependency between the header files of two previously independent components. Each of these components now must "know" about the other. It is no longer possible to compile, link, test, or use either one of these components without the other. Most clients will not be concerned about the subtle differences in performance characteristics between these classes and would opt to use either one, but rarely both. This unlevelizable enhancement forces them to take both.

```
// rectangle.h
#ifndef INCLUDED_RECTANGLE
#define INCLUDED_RECTANGLE

#ifndef INCLUDED_WINDOW
#include "window.h"
#endif

class Rectangle {
    // ...
  public:
    // ...
    Rectangle(const Window& w);
    // ...
};

inline
Rectangle::Rectangle(const Window& w)
{
    // ...
}

// ...


#endif
```

```
// window.h
#ifndef INCLUDED_WINDOW
#define INCLUDED_WINDOW

#ifndef INCLUDED_RECTANGLE
#include "rectangle.h"
#endif

class Window
    // ...
  public:
    // ...
    Window(const Rectangle& r);
    // ...
};

// ...


inline
Window::Window(const Rectangle& w)
{
    // ...
}

#endif
```

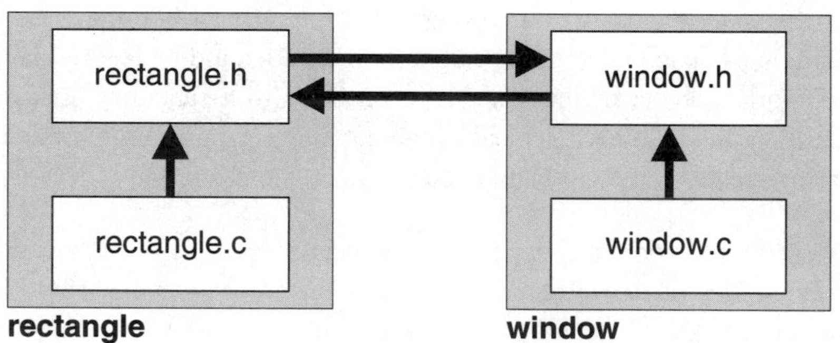

Figure 5-2: Two Mutually Dependent Components

We can move the preprocessor `#include` directives from the `.h` files to the `.c` files (as shown in Figure 5-3), but this does not eliminate the physical coupling. Both components still depend on each other at compile time, and each will potentially depend on the other at link time. We need to do something a bit more radical.

```
// rectangle.h
#ifndef INCLUDED_RECTANGLE
#define INCLUDED_RECTANGLE

class Window;

class Rectangle {
    // ...
  public:
    // ...
    Rectangle(const Window& w);
    // ...
};

#endif
```

```
// window.h
#ifndef INCLUDED_WINDOW
#define INCLUDED_WINDOW

class Rectangle;

class Window {
    // ...
  public:
    // ...
    Window(const Rectangle& r);
    // ...
};

#endif
```

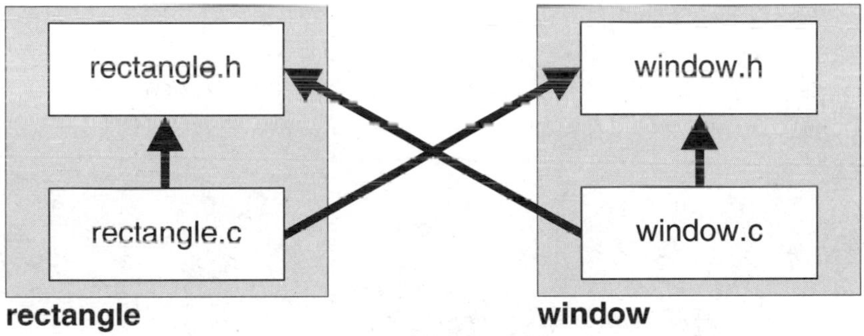

Figure 5-3: Two Components Still Mutually Dependent

> **DEFINITION: A subsystem is *levelizable* if it compiles and the graph implied by the include directives of the individual components (including the `.c` files) is acyclic.**

Suppose a subsystem consists of a collection of components that follow all of the major design rules set forth in Chapters 2 and 3. We can make use of the above alternative definition of *levelizable* to help us avoid enhancements that cause components to become physically coupled. Somehow we must find a way to allow a client to convert between rectangles and windows without requiring each component to include the other.

5.1.2 Convenience

Often, in an effort to make a system usable, developers are tempted to create designs that are not structurally sound. As a second, more involved example of this recurring theme, consider a graphical shape editor whose design is depicted abstractly in Figure 5-4. The `Shape` class is abstract and defines a protocol that all concrete shapes must implement. Every shape has a location that we will assume for now must be manipulated as quickly as possible (i.e., via inline functions). Since some of the functionality in the `Shape` class is already implemented, `Shape` serves not only to define a common interface, but also to factor the common part of the implementation.[1]

[1] Section 6.4.1 describes how we could reduce compile-time coupling between consumers and suppliers of the `Shape` interface if we relaxed the speed requirement for the `moveTo` function.

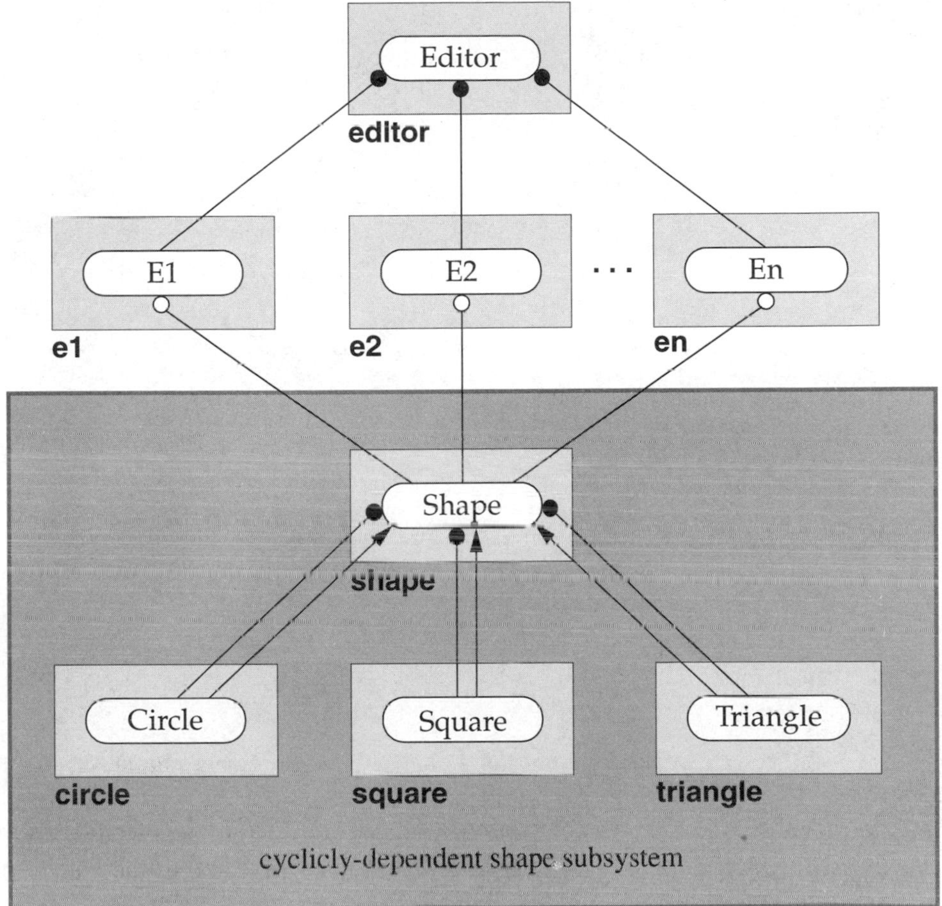

Figure 5-4: Unlevelizable Design of a Shape Editor

The Shape class could potentially define a large number of pure virtual functions. A sparse representation of the header file for the shape component is presented in Figure 5-5. Clients of the Shape class will need to be able to create actual shapes, but they will not need to interact with the derived class interfaces directly. In order to insulate clients of Shape from concrete classes derived from Shape, the ability to create specific kinds of Shape is incorporated directly into Shape's interface.

```
// shape.h
#ifndef INCLUDED_SHAPE
#define INCLUDED_SHAPE

class Screen;

class Shape {
    int d_xCoord;
    int d_yCoord;

  protected:
    Shape(int x, int y);
    Shape(const Shape& shape);
    Shape& operator=(const Shape& shape);

  public:
    static Shape *create(const char *typeName);
    virtual ~Shape();
    // ...
    void moveTo(int x, int y) { d_x = x; d_y = y; }
    // ...
    virtual Shape *clone() const = 0;
    virtual void draw(Screen *s) const = 0;
    // ...
};

#endif
```

Figure 5-5: Elided `.h` File for Component `shape`

To make it easy to add new shapes by name, the `Shape` class implements the static member function `create`. This method takes the type name of the `Shape` (as a `const char *`) and returns a pointer to a dynamically allocated, newly constructed `Shape` of the appropriate concrete type derived from `Shape`.[2] If no shape corresponding to that type name exists, the function returns `0`. The entire `.c` file for the `shape` component is presented in Figure 5-6.

---

[2] Returning a pointer to a dynamically allocated object is error prone because it leaves the responsibility of deallocation with the client. Failing to catch an exception can easily result in a memory leak. Handle classes (as discussed in Section 6.5.3) can be used to reduce the potential for memory leaks.

```
// shape.c
#include "shape.h"
#include "circle.h"
#include "square.h"
#include "triangle.h"
#include "screen.h"
#include "string.h"    // strcmp()

Shape::Shape(int x, int y)
: d_xCoord(x)
, d_yCoord(y)
{}

Shape::Shape(const Shape& s)
: d_xCoord(s.d_xCoord)
, d_yCoord(s.d_yCoord)
{}

Shape& Shape::operator=(const shape& s)
{
    d_xCoord = s.d_xCoord;
    d_yCoord = s.d_yCoord;
    return *this;
}

Shape::~Shape() {}

Shape *Shape::create(const char *s)
{
    if (0 == strcmp(s, "Circle")) {
        return new Circle(x, y, 1);                   // unit radius
    }
    else if (0 == strcmp(s, "Square")) {
        return new Square(x, y, 1);                   // unit side
    }
    else if (0 == strcmp(s, "Triangle")) {
        return new Triangle(x, y, 1, 1, 1);           // unit side
    }
    else {
        return 0;                                     // unknown shape
    }
}
```

Figure 5-6: Entire `.c` File for Component `shape`

The `Editor` class itself is layered upon a number of custom types (`E1, ..., En`) used solely in the implementation of `Editor`. Each of these types uses `Shape` in its interface in order to perform various abstract operations on shapes (e.g., `moveTo`, `scale`, `draw`, and so on). Only one of the implementation components, `e1`, which implements the add command, needs to be able to create a shape from a type name. The rest of these components can use `Shape`'s virtual functions to access a particular Shape's functionality, and do not need to depend on any concrete Shape directly. Does this sound reasonable?

Although this design may seem appealing from a usability standpoint, it has a design flaw that makes it quite a bit more expensive to maintain than it need be. The `create` member function of `Shape` uses a constructor of each of the classes derived from `Shape`, which forces a mutual dependency between `Shape` and all classes derived from `Shape`. It is therefore not possible to test a specific kind of Shape independently of all the rest, significantly increasing the link time and disk space required during incremental testing. The shape subsystem, which is otherwise horizontal and therefore highly reusable, is turned into an all-or-nothing proposition.

Adding a new kind of shape to this subsystem requires modifying the `Shape` base class, which could produce errors in functionality pertaining to the other independently derived classes. The high degree of coupling brought on by having a base class "know" about its derived classes implies a considerable increase in maintenance cost and a considerable loss of flexibility and reuse.

The maintenance disadvantage worsens when we consider that only component `e1` needs to create each of the `Editor`'s concrete shapes and therefore only `e1` needs to depend on all of the individual concrete shape components. Components `e2`, `e3`, `...`, `en` merely use these shapes via the virtual functions of the abstract base class `Shape`. If we can assume that the functionality of each shape is working properly, then we need test only that each editor subsystem component is interacting with the `Shape` protocol properly. There could be dozens or even hundreds of different kinds of shapes, and it is neither necessary nor practical to test each editor subsystem component with every type of shape all the time. Yet, because of the coupling in the shape subsystem, we are forced to link to all shapes whenever incrementally testing any one of the editor implementation components.

In order to improve the maintainability of this system, we need to find a way to repackage the shape subsystem so that it becomes acyclic and therefore levelizable.

5.1.3 Intrinsic Interdependency

Interconnected networks of objects present an engineering challenge for software system architects. The high degree of inherent coupling, particularly in the interface, makes achieving levelization less obvious and intuitive. In this final introductory example we examine the difficulty in implementing a graph, which is among the most basic of object networks.

Principle

Inherent coupling in the interface of related abstractions makes them more resistant to hierarchical decomposition.

Consider the graph shown in Figure 5-7. A graph consists of a collection of nodes and edges. The nodes within this graph are connected by directed edges. In general, the edges in the graph will form cycles.[3] Each node consists of some data and some information about how the node is incorporated into the graph. In this example the node's data is no more than a name. The connectivity is represented simply as a list of edges to or from that node.

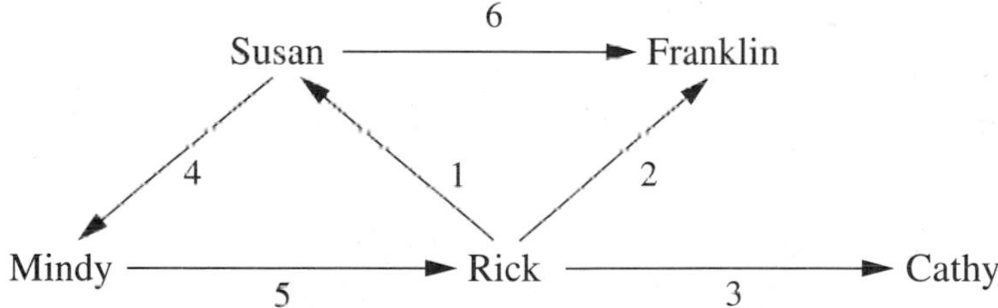

Figure 5-7: Simple Graph Consisting of Nodes and Edges

Figure 5-8 illustrates the minimal functionality associated with the `node` component. Given a `Node`, it is possible to ask for its name, find out the number of edges connected

[3] Note: these are cycles among instances, not classes.

to it, and iterate over these edges by supplying integer indices between 0 and *N*–1, where *N* is the current value returned by `Node::numEdges()`.[4]

```
// node.h
#ifndef INCLUDED_NODE
#define INCLUDED_NODE

class Edge;

class Node {
    // ...
    Node(const Node&);                            // not implemented
    Node& operator=(const Node&);                 // not implemented

  public:
    Node(const char *name);
    ~Node();
    const char *name() const;
    int numEdges() const;
    Edge& edge(int index) const;
};

#endif
```

Figure 5-8: Public Interface of `node` Component

```
// edge.h
#ifndef INCLUDED_EDGE
#define INCLUDED_EDGE

class Node;

class Edge {
    // ...
    Edge(const Edge&);                            // not implemented
    Edge& operator=(const Edge&);                 // not implemented

  public:
    Edge(Node *from, Node *to, double weight);
    ~Edge();
    Node& from() const;
    Node& to() const;
    double weight() const;
};

#endif
```

Figure 5-9: Public Interface for an `edge` Component

---

[4] It is a subtle point that supplying an integer index for iteration suggests that the underlying implementation is likely to be an array of some kind and not a linked list of edges. A naive linked-list implementation would result in quadratic runtime behavior during iteration.

An `Edge` in this system is used to connect nodes. Like nodes, edges also contain both local and network-related functionality. The network-independent information associated with the `Edge` in this example is just its weight, and the connectivity information is just the two `Node` objects to which the `Edge` is connected.

Initially we are faced with the unappealing design illustrated in Figure 5-10. `Node` uses `Edge` in its interface and vice versa. As it stands, it seems as though class `Node` and class `Edge` must be mutually dependent—otherwise how could a client possibly traverse the graph? Furthermore, there is the question of who owns the memory for these objects and who is authorized to bring instances of `Node` and/or `Edge` into and out of existence.

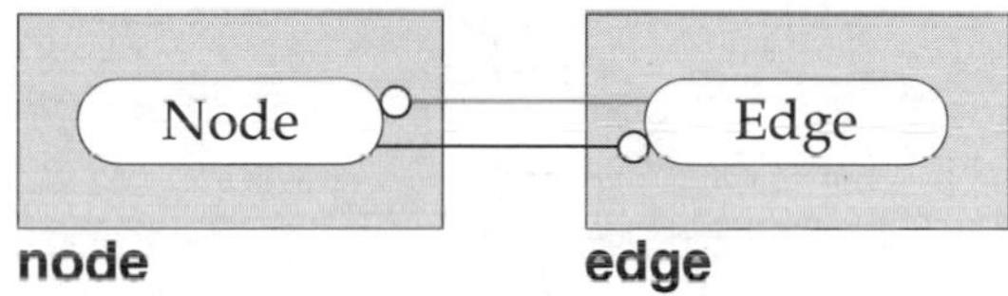

Figure 5-10: Cyclicly Dependent `node` **and** `edge` **Components**

Recall from Section 3.6 that friendship does not introduce physical dependencies by itself, but in order to preserve encapsulation it can indirectly cause physical coupling to occur. In order to avoid the breach of encapsulation and lack of modularity associated with long-distance friendships, it may be necessary to group several levelizable classes within a single component (as explained at the end of Section 5.9). A common example of this kind of coupling can be seen in virtually every container component that supplies an iterator. Invariably the iterator will be a friend of the container and therefore defined within the same component.

The above are but a few examples of the kinds of cyclic coupling that commonly arise in practice. The remainder of this chapter is devoted to developing various techniques and transformations for untangling designs that might otherwise seem to defy an acyclic physical implementation.

5.2 Escalation

Let's now return to the example involving the two cyclicly dependent components (shown in Figure 5-1): `rectangle` and `window`. Suppose that instead of having `rectangle` and `window` "know" about each other, we decide arbitrarily that rectangles are more basic than windows. We can move both conversions into class `Window`. `Window` now "uses" `Rectangle` but not vice versa, as is illustrated in Figure 5-11.

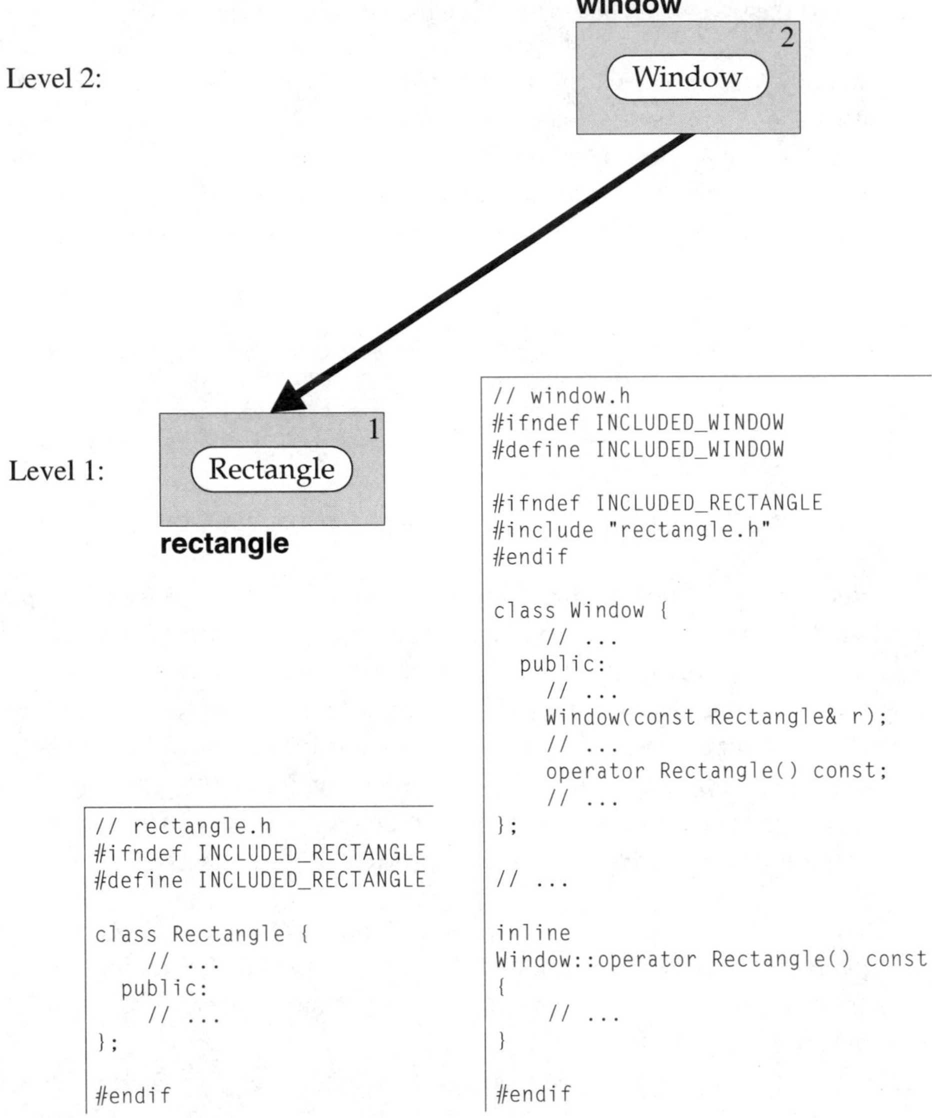


```
// window.h
#ifndef INCLUDED_WINDOW
#define INCLUDED_WINDOW

#ifndef INCLUDED_RECTANGLE
#include "rectangle.h"
#endif

class Window {
    // ...
  public:
    // ...
    Window(const Rectangle& r);
    // ...
    operator Rectangle() const;
    // ...
};

// ...

inline
Window::operator Rectangle() const
{
    // ...
}

#endif
```

```
// rectangle.h
#ifndef INCLUDED_RECTANGLE
#define INCLUDED_RECTANGLE

class Rectangle {
    // ...
  public:
    // ...
};

#endif
```

Figure 5-11: `window` **Dominates** `rectangle`

This solution requires that we change our point of view somewhat, because the `Rectangle` and `Window` classes are no longer symmetric. `Rectangle` lives at level 1, but `Window` is now defined at level 2. If we want any old box we can reuse `Rectangle` and not worry about `Window` or conversions between the classes. If we need a `Window`, however, we will have to take `Rectangle` also.

> **DEFINITION: A component `y` *dominates* a component `x` if `y` is at a higher level than `x` and `y` depends physically on `x`.**

Dominance is a property among components that is roughly comparable to the property with the same name among virtual base classes within a single derived object.[5] We introduce the concept of dominance among components now and mention that Figure 5-11 illustrates an example where component `window` *dominates* component `rectangle`. We refer to this definition of dominance in later sections.

As Figure 5-12 illustrates, component `u` dominates both components `r` and `s`. Although component `v` is at a higher level than either component `r` or component `s`, it dominates only component `t`. Component `w` dominates all five components `r`, `s`, `t`, `u`, and `v`.

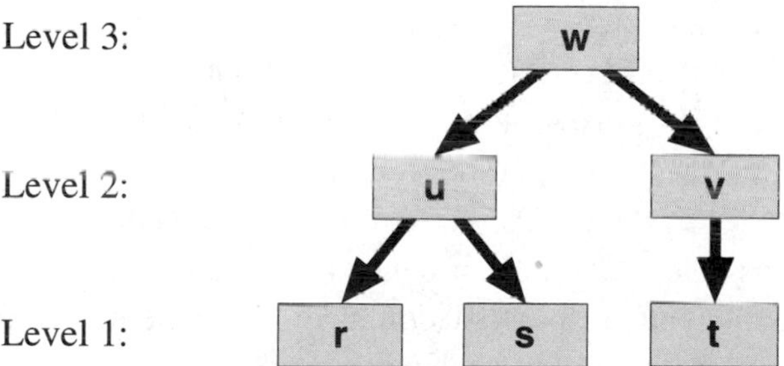

Figure 5-12: Illustration of Dominance Property for Components

The significance of dominance is that it can provide additional information beyond simple level numbers. For example, adding a dependency from a higher-level

[5] **ellis**, Section 10.1.1, pp. 204–205.

component to a lower-level component (e.g., from `u` to `t` in Figure 5-12) never introduces a cyclic dependency or changes the level numbers (as shown in Figure 5-13a).

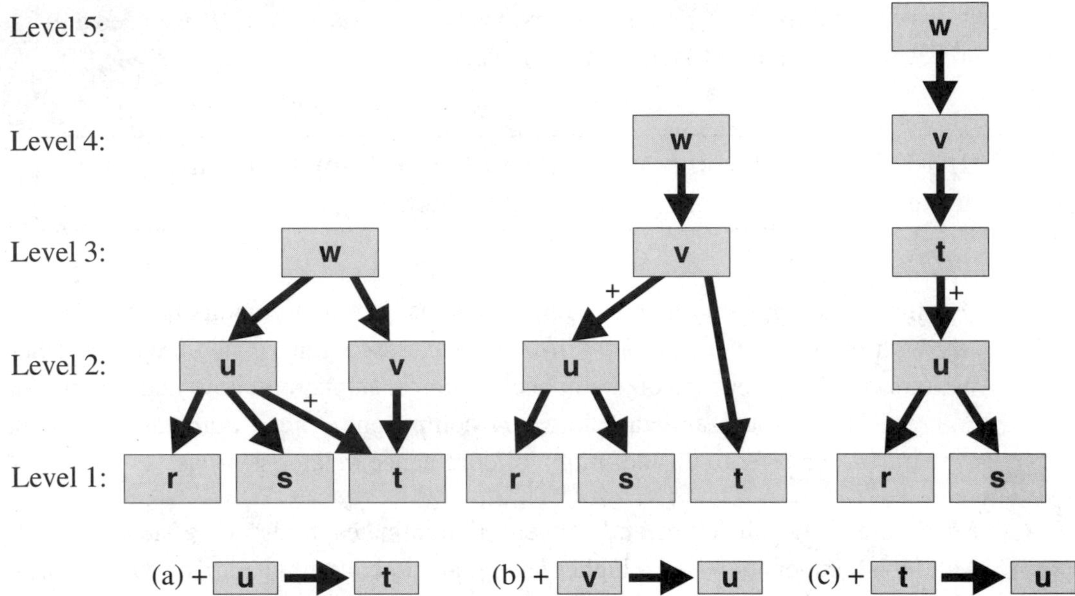

Figure 5-13: Adding a Dependency Can Cause a Change in Level Numbers

Adding a dependency between two components at the same level (e.g., from `v` to `u` in Figure 5-12) also never introduces a cycle but does affect the level number as shown in Figure 5-13b. Finally, it may even be possible to add a dependency from a lower-level component to a higher-level one (e.g., from `t` to `u` in Figure 5-12 without introducing a cyclic dependency). Adding this dependency without introducing a cycle will be possible if and only if component `u` does not already dominate component t. Here, component `u` does not dominate component `t` and the result of adding the dependency from `t` to `u` is shown in Figure 5-13c.

Of course we could have gone the other way and made `Window` the primitive object. In that case `rectangle` knows about `window` but not vice versa. This situation is depicted in Figure 5-14. Notice that in this example we have elected to move the `#include "window.h"` directive to the `rectangle.c` file, which implies that the conversion routines will *not* be inline.

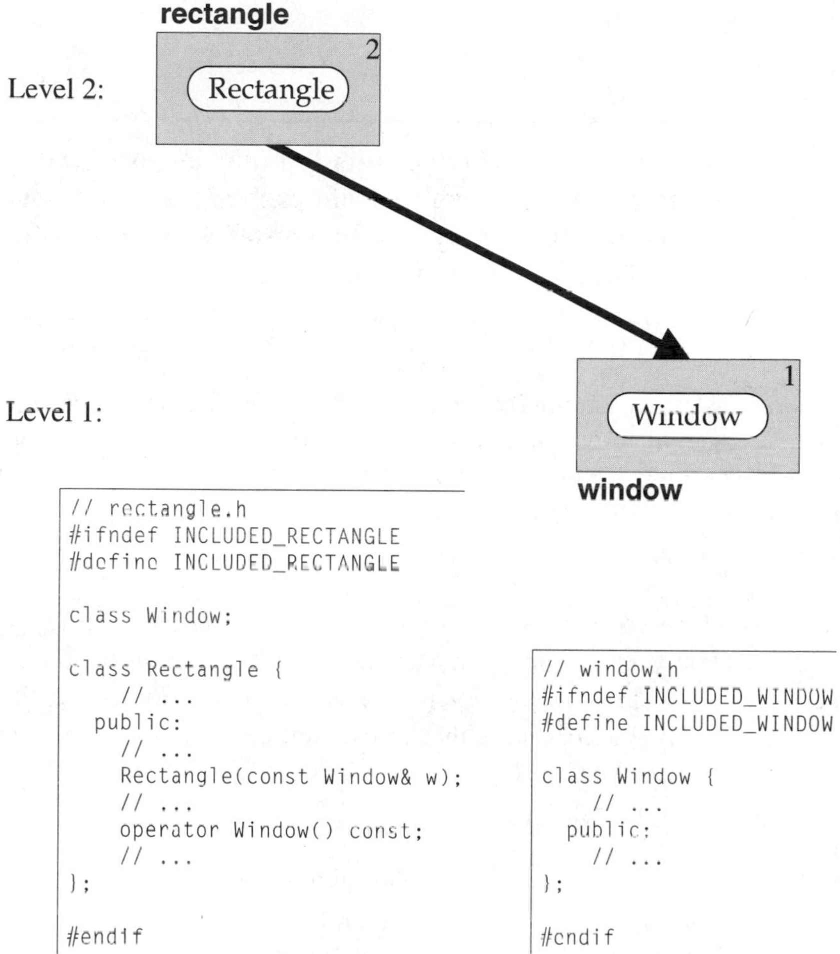

Figure 5-14: `rectangle` **Dominates** `window`

Both solutions imply that only one component can be used independently of the other. Either solution is an improvement over the original cyclicly dependent design, but we can do still better. Many clients who use these components will need one or the other but not both. Of those that do need to use both components, only some will need to convert between them. To maximize independent reusability, we can avoid having either component dominate the other by moving the cycle-inducing functionality to a higher level—a technique referred to in this book as *escalation*.

Principle

If peer components are cyclicly dependent, it may be possible to escalate the interdependent functionality from each of these components to static members in a potentially new higher-level component that depends on each of the original components.

In corporations, if two employees are not able to resolve a dispute, the common practice is to escalate the problem to a higher level. In the case of objects competing for dominance, the same solution is often effective. We can create a utility class called `BoxUtil` that knows about both the `Rectangle` and `Window` classes and then place the definition of this class in an entirely separate component, as shown in Figure 5-15.

Now clients interested in either `Rectangle` class or `Window` class are free to use either class independently. If a single client happens to use both classes but does not need to convert between them, so be it. If yet other clients require the conversion routines, they are available. However, note that conversion between `Rectangle` and `Window`, which used to be implicit, must now be performed explicitly. (See Section 9.3.1 for more on implicit conversions.)

Note that, in the previous example, we elected to use the keyword `struct` instead of `class` when defining `BoxUtil` to suggest that this type merely provides a scope for public nested types and public static member functions. In this convention, *all* members of a `struct` are public and hence there are no data members. Although creating an instance of such a type is pointless, it does no real harm. We can reduce some unnecessary clutter if we suppress our compulsion to declare the unimplemented default constructor `private`.

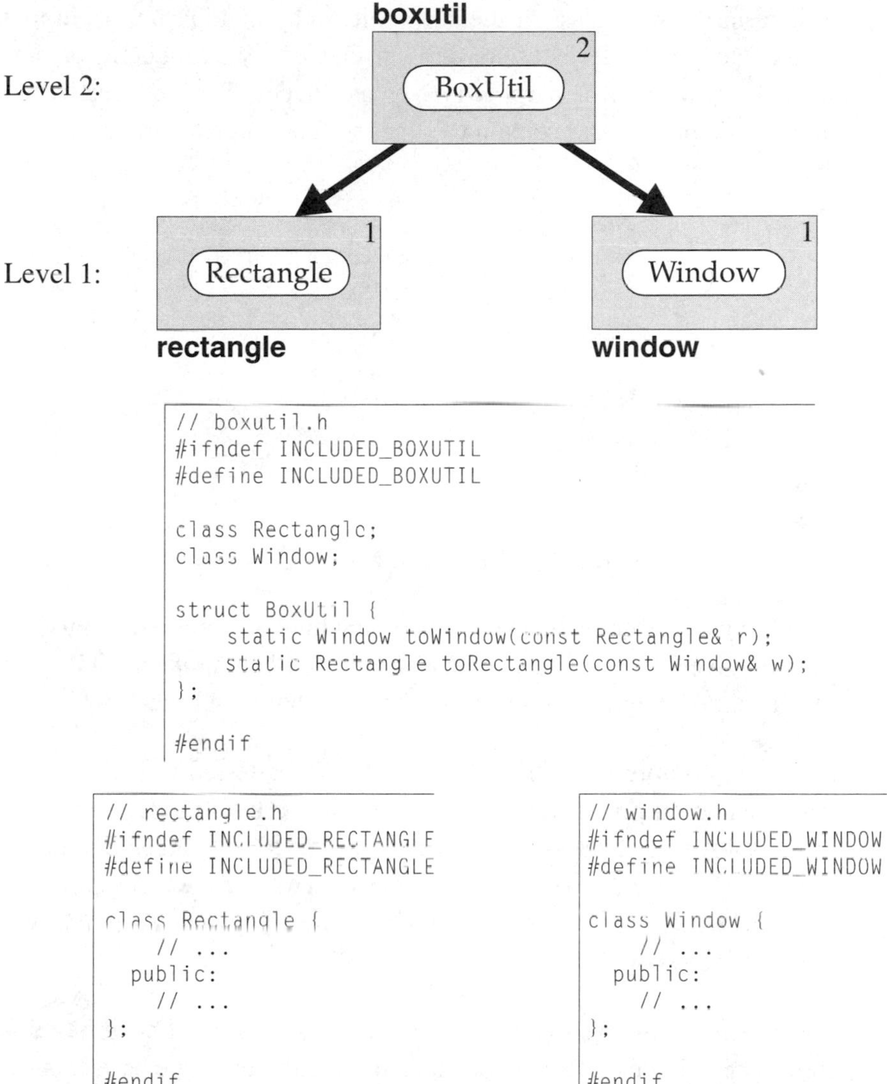


```
// boxutil.h
#ifndef INCLUDED_BOXUTIL
#define INCLUDED_BOXUTIL

class Rectangle;
class Window;

struct BoxUtil {
    static Window toWindow(const Rectangle& r);
    static Rectangle toRectangle(const Window& w);
};

#endif
```

```
// rectangle.h
#ifndef INCLUDED_RECTANGLE
#define INCLUDED_RECTANGLE

class Rectangle {
    // ...
  public:
    // ...
};

#endif
```

```
// window.h
#ifndef INCLUDED_WINDOW
#define INCLUDED_WINDOW

class Window {
    // ...
  public:
    // ...
};

#endif
```

Figure 5-15: Neither `rectangle` Nor `window` Dominates the Other

Now let's consider again the physical coupling induced by the static `create` function, defined in the base class of the shape hierarchy of Figure 5-4. Suppose we escalate `create` above the level of its derived classes by introducing a new utility class, `ShapeUtil`, whose sole purpose is to create shapes. This new class would be placed in its own component and contain the `create` function from the original `Shape` class, as shown in Figure 5-16.

```
// shapeutil.h
#ifndef INCLUDED_SHAPEUTIL
#define INCLUDED_SHAPEUTIL

class Shape;

struct ShapeUtil {
    static Shape *create(const char *typeName);
};

#endif
```

Figure 5-16: Header File for New Component `shapeutil`

By adding a new component and escalating the Uses relationship to a higher level, we have removed the cyclic dependencies among all components in the shape subsystem. The levelized diagram for the new system is shown in Figure 5-17.

It is now possible for each concrete shape to be tested in isolation. Even the partial implementation provided by class `Shape` can be tested modularly by deriving a concrete "stub" class from `Shape` in the test driver for the `shape` component. Each of the concrete shapes can now be reused independently of the rest in any combination. For example, another system is now able to reuse `circle` and `square` without having to link in `triangle`.

It is now also possible to test each of `E2`, . . . , `En` without having to link to every concrete shape. Since these components require only the shape base class interface, it may be deemed sufficient to test the incremental value added by each of the editor components `e2`, . . . , `en` on only a representative sample of all available concrete shapes.

The advantage of this new design over the original is a reduction in coupling that will translate directly into reduced development and maintenance costs while amplifying the potential for reuse. It may be difficult to appreciate the importance of this design approach when the number of implementation components in the editor, and, particularly, the number of concrete shapes, is small. The real advantage is that this new design scales up much better than the original as more editor commands and new kinds of `Shape` are added.

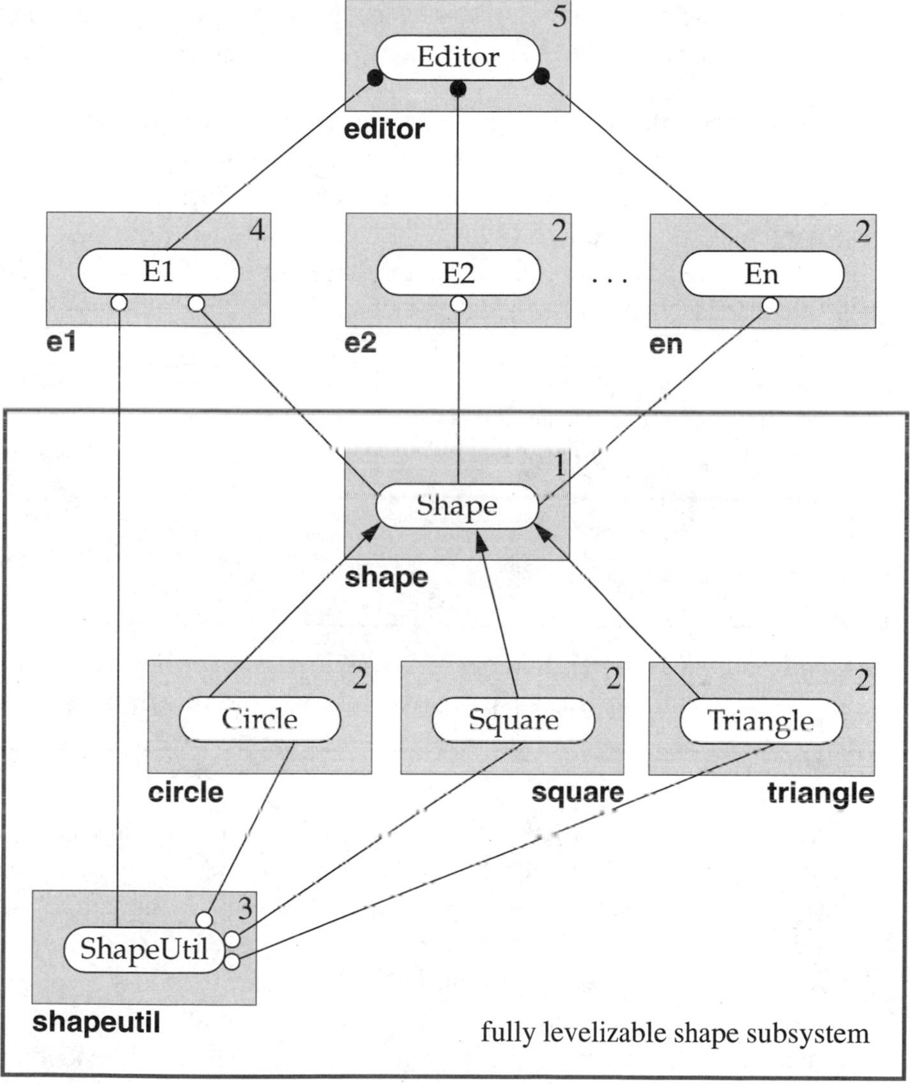

Figure 5-17: Improved Design for Shape Editor

As an objective, quantitative measure of the improvement that levelization brings to this design, let us consider four variants of the editor system. In the "scaled-down" version of this system, Figure 5-18a, both the editor and the number of shapes it works on are small (three shapes and three editor-implementation components). The numbers in the upper left corners of the component rectangles indicate the number of components that must be linked in order to test that component incrementally.

At first glance, this new design may appear to be unnecessarily complicated, but in fact it simplifies the job of both developer and client. Even with the additional component in the new design, the coupling associated with hierarchically testing the shape subsystem as measured by CCD is reduced by a full 25 percent. The coupling associated with incrementally testing the editor subsystem is reduced by 17.4 percent, giving an overall reduction in CCD of 20.5 percent.

Figure 5-18b illustrates the effect when the editor subsystem is made large (30 implementation components instead of only 3). Now the reduction in component coupling for the editor subsystem is nearly 46 percent, pushing the overall reduction in CCD to 43.3 percent.

Principle

Cyclic physical dependencies in large, low-level subsystems have the greatest capacity to increase the overall cost of maintaining a system.

Cyclic coupling at lower levels of the physical hierarchy can have a dramatic effect on the cost of maintaining clients. As can be seen in Figure 5-18c, when the shape hierarchy is made large (30 concrete types instead of only 3), the advantage of the new design, as measured by CCD, amounts not only to a reduction in coupling of over 90 percent in the shape subsystem but also a reduction of over 44 percent in the editor subsystem, for a reduction of close to 85 percent overall. When both the shape subsystem and editor are large, the overall percentage reduction in coupling continues to improve, as shown in Figure 5-18d.

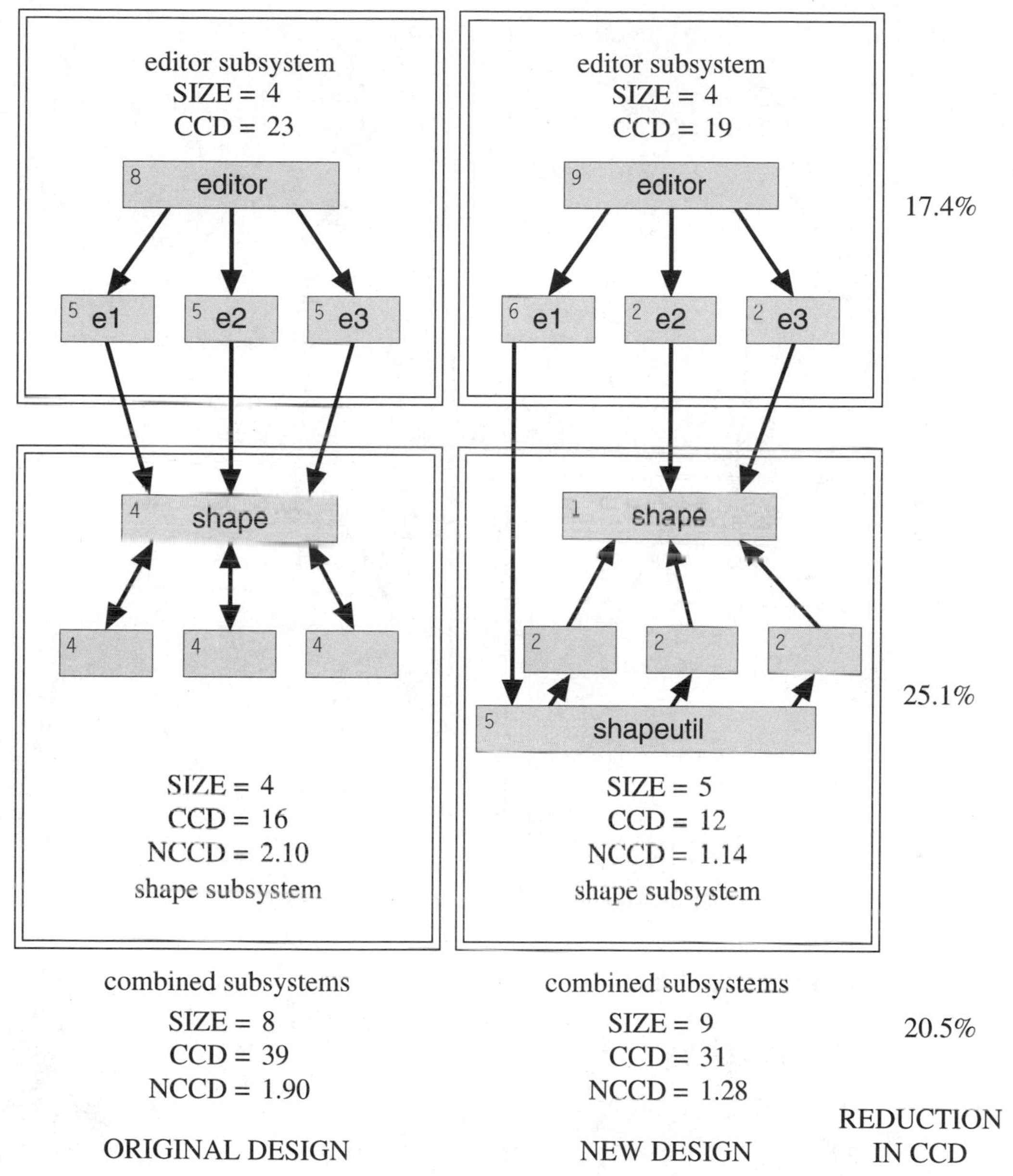

Figure 5-18a: Small Shape Hierarchy (3 Components), Small Editor (3 Components)

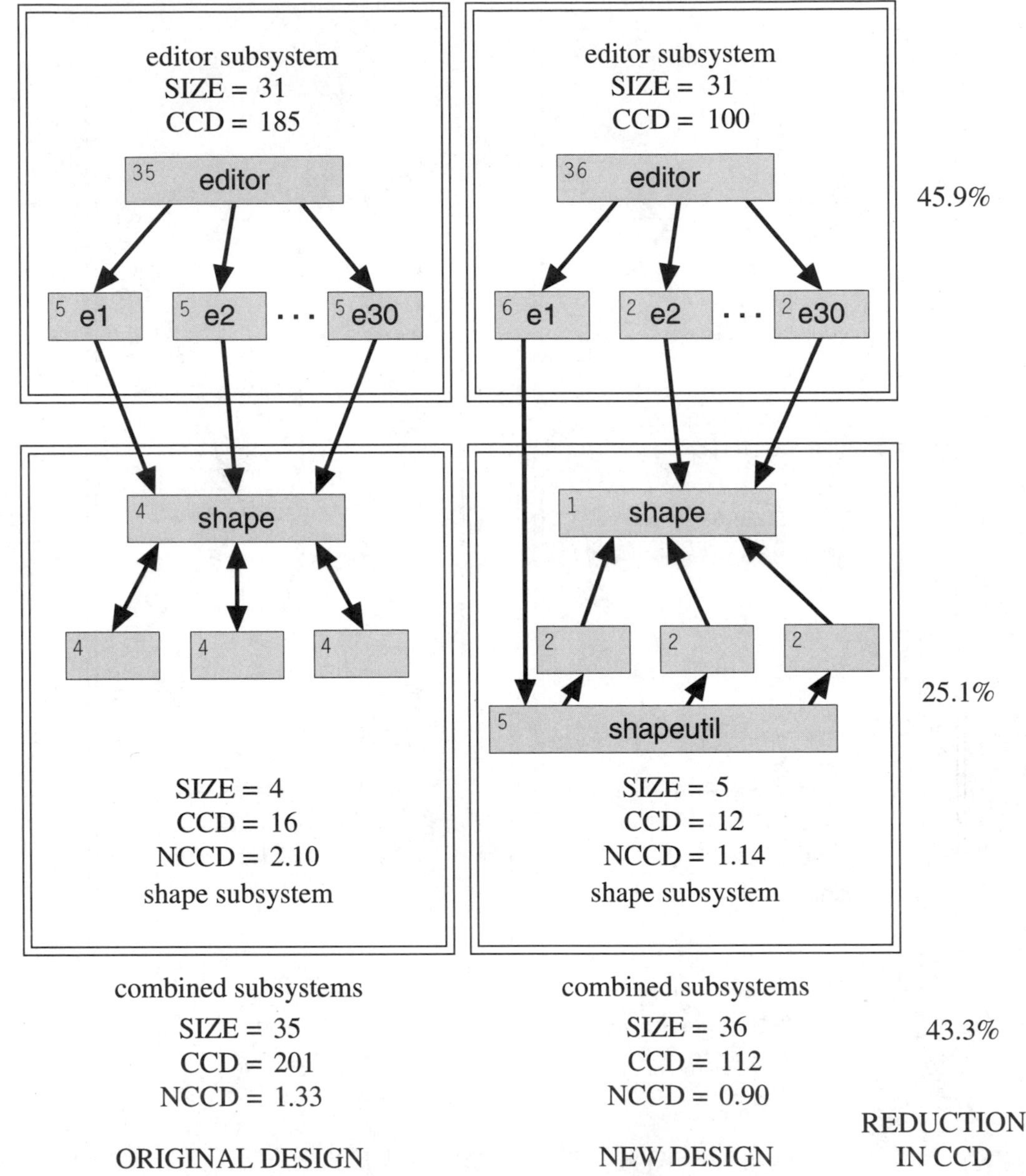

Figure 5-18b: Small Shape Hierarchy (3 Components), Large Editor (30 Components)

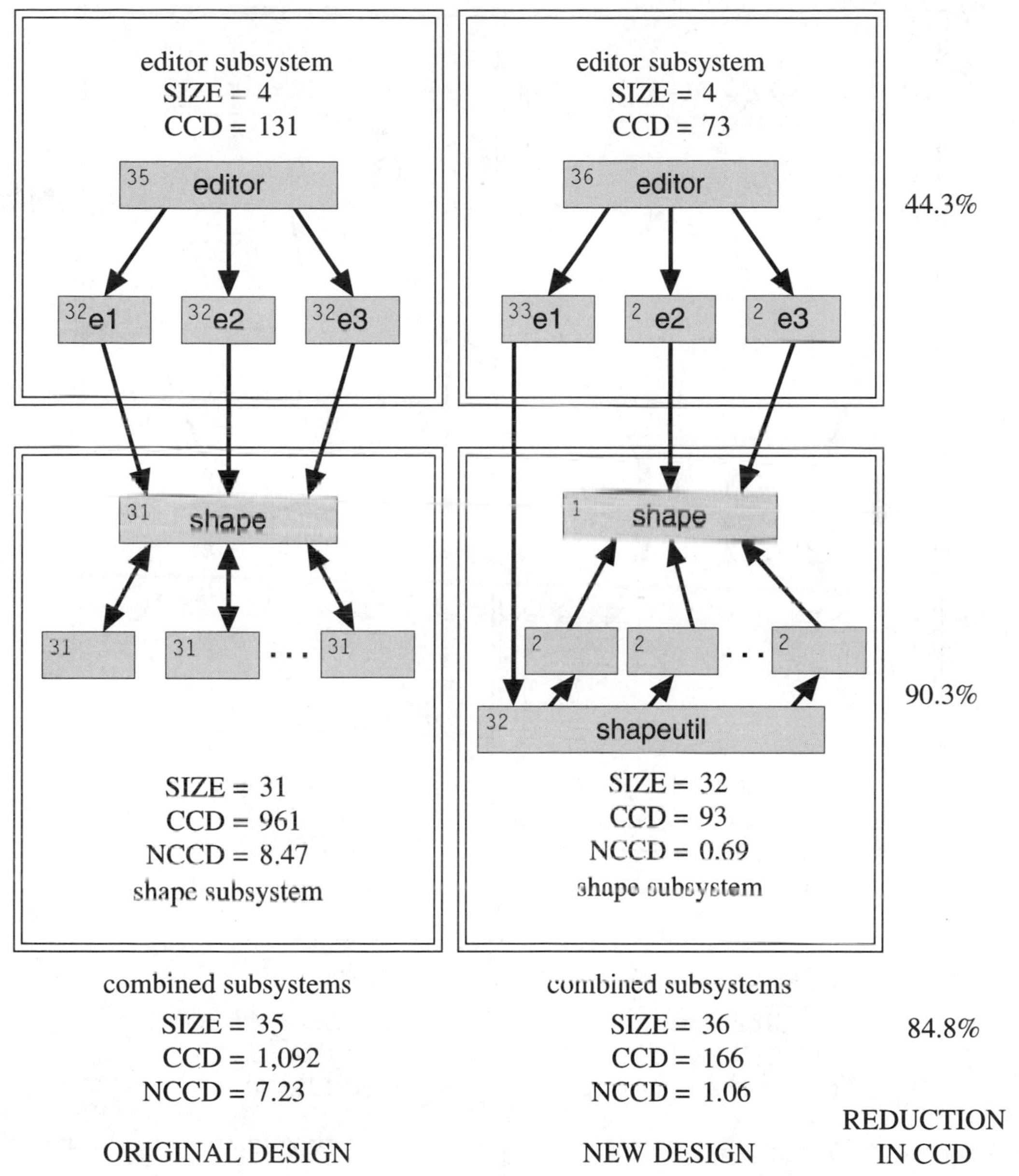

Figure 5-18c: Large Shape Hierarchy (30 Components), Small Editor (3 Components)

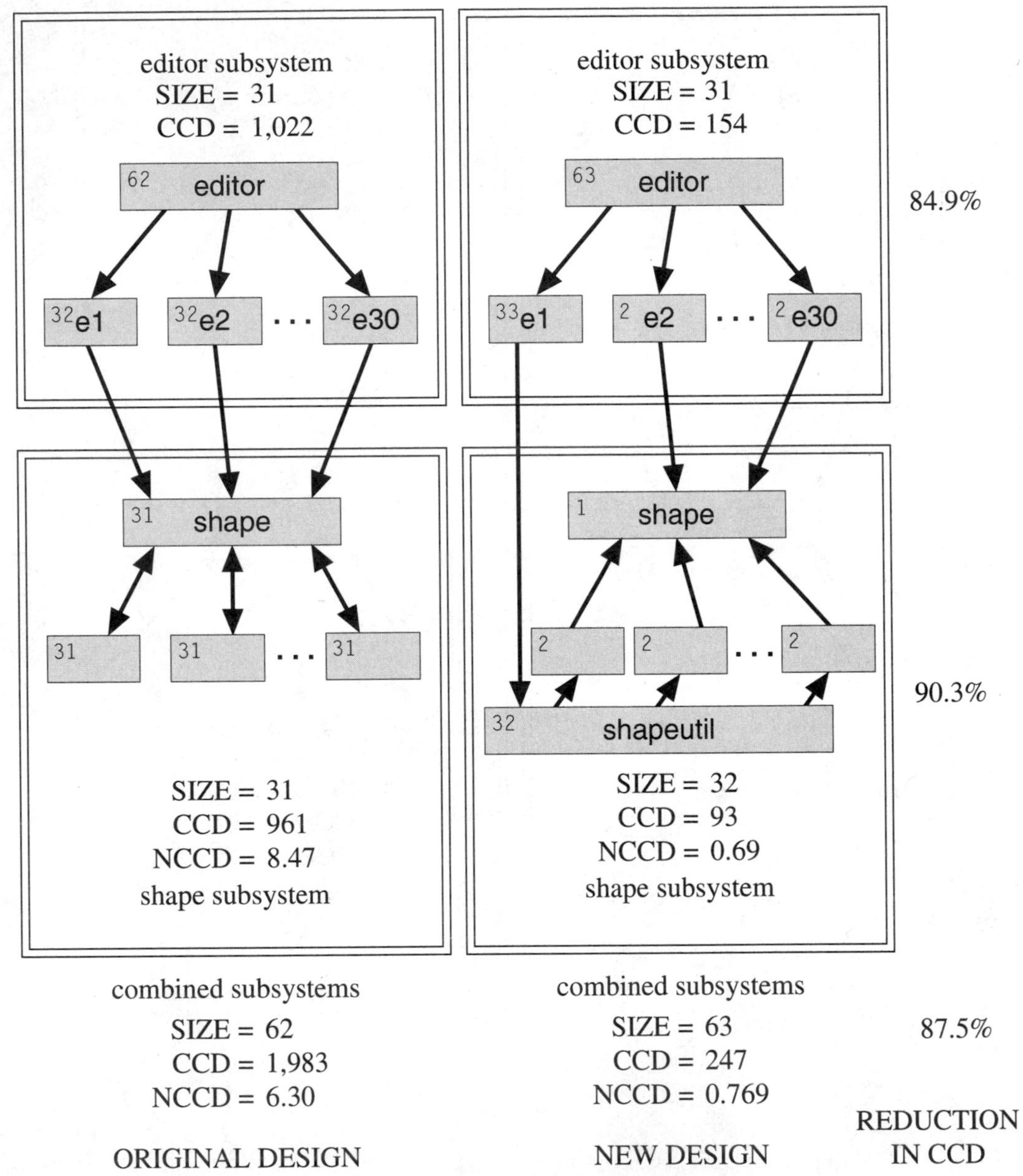

Figure 5-18d: Large Shape Hierarchy (30 Components), Large Editor (30 Components)

The important lesson to be learned from this analysis is that a high degree of coupling associated with lower-level subsystems can dramatically increase the cost of developing and maintaining clients and subsystems at higher levels.

To summarize the results of this section: escalating mutual dependencies to a higher level can be used to convert cyclic dependencies into welcome downward dependencies. The maintenance cost of a subsystem and all of its clients can be reduced significantly by avoiding unnecessary dependencies among components within the subsystem itself. At the same time, the subsystem becomes more flexible and therefore more reusable. The benefits of the improved design may not be as pronounced for smaller versions of a system.

5.3 Demotion

Until now we have endeavored to eliminate cyclic dependencies by pushing mutually dependent functionality higher in the physical hierarchy. In this section we explore the technique of pushing common functionality down to lower levels of the physical hierarchy where it can be shared and perhaps even reused. The technique of moving common functionality to lower levels of the physical hierarchy is referred to in this book as *demotion*.

Principle

If peer components are cyclicly dependent, it may be possible to demote the interdependent functionality from each of these components to a potentially new lower-level (shared) component upon which each of the original components depends.

Escalation and demotion are similar in that in either case, cyclic dependencies among components are eliminated by moving the cyclicly dependent functionality to another level in the physical hierarchy. Let us start by analyzing what happens during a more general form of escalation. As illustrated in Figure 5-19, two mutually dependent components (a) are factored into four components, (b) two of which may be mutually dependent and two of which are independent. The two higher-level components can then be combined (c) if necessary to avoid a cyclic dependency or, if cohesive, to reduce physical complexity.

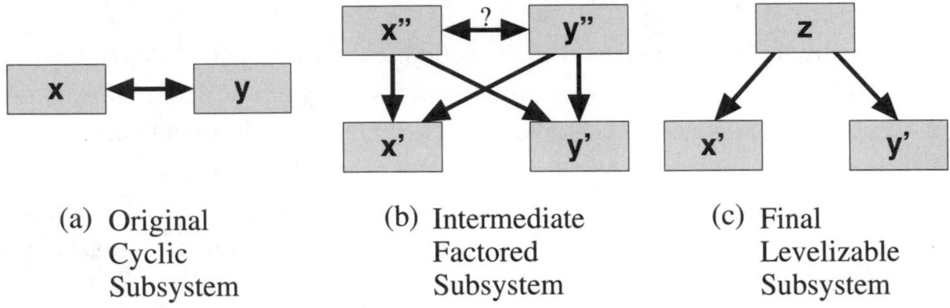

Figure 5-19: Employing Escalation to Break Cyclic Dependencies

Now contrast this with the general process of demotion. As shown in Figure 5-20, two mutually dependent components (a) are again factored into four components (b). Two of the components depend on the two other components, which may be mutually dependent. The two lower-level components can then be combined (c) if necessary to avoid a cyclic dependency or, if cohesive, to reduce physical complexity.

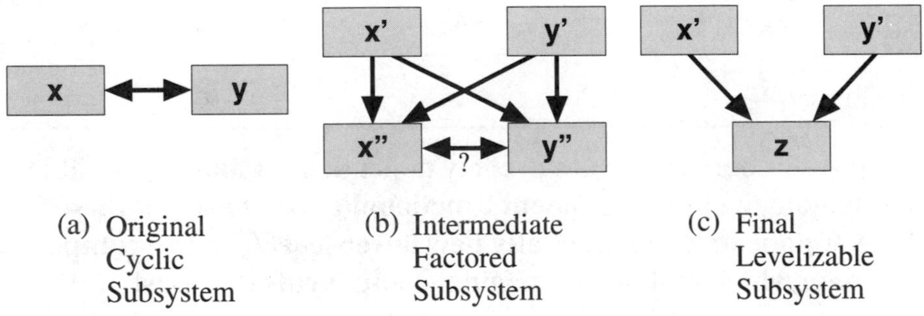

Figure 5-20: Employing Demotion to Break Cyclic Dependencies

Consider the situation shown in Figure 5-21, in which there are two geometric utility classes, `GeomUtil` and `GeomUtil2`. Each of these utilities provides a suite of functions that operate on points, lines, and polygons. External clients directly use one, the other, or both. Unlike `geomutil`, `geomutil2` is complex and depends on many other components, and even exposes some new types in its interface. Those clients that need only the basic geometric functionality provided in `GeomUtil` need not link with the `geomutil2` component.

```
// geomutil2.h
#ifndef INCLUDED_GEOMUTIL2
#define INCLUDED_GEOMUTIL2

class Line;
class Polygon;

struct GeomUtil2 {
    static int crossesSelf(const Polygon& polygon);
    static int doesIntersect(const Line& line1, const Line& line2);
    // ...
}

#endif
```

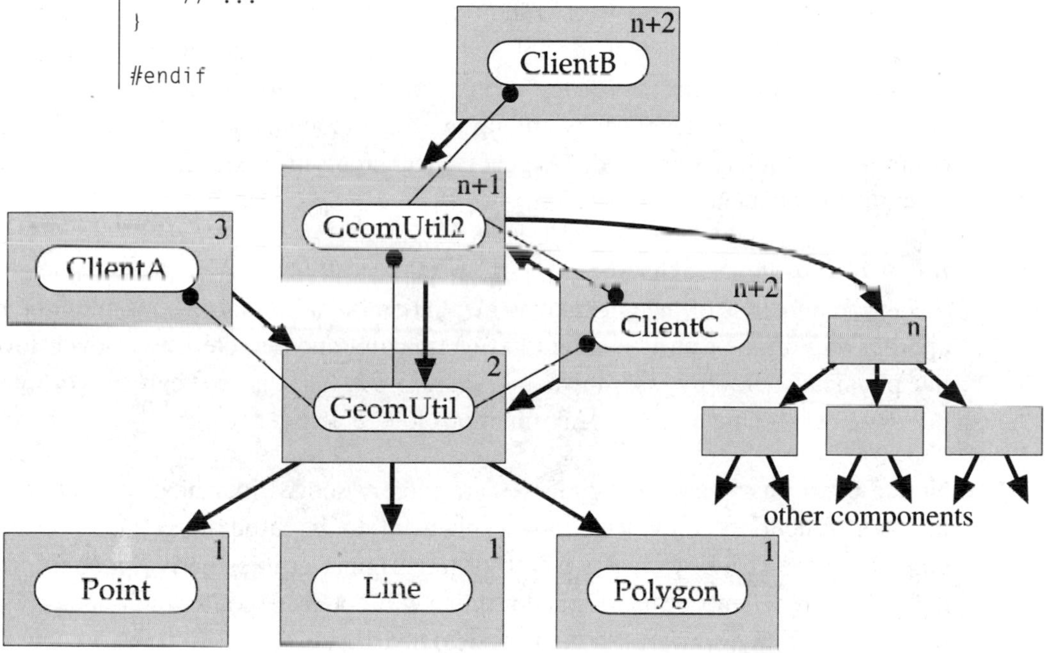

```
// geomutil.h
#ifndef INCLUDED_GEOMUTIL
#define INCLUDED_GEOMUTIL

class Point;
class Line;
class Polygon;

struct GeomUtil {
    static int isInside(const Polygon& polygon, const Point& point);
    static int areColinear(const Line& line1, const Line& line2);
    static int areParallel(const Line& line1, const Line& line2);
    // ...
}

#endif
```

Figure 5-21: Two Geometric Utility Components: `geomutil` **and** `geomutil2`

Initially these two components were levelizable, with `geomutil2` depending on `geomutil`. Unfortunately not all developers are careful about considering the physical implications of their efforts. One fine day it was discovered that, through careless enhancement, these two geometric utility components had become mutually dependent. `GeomUtil2::crossesSelf` now depends on `GeomUtil::areColinear` and `GeomUtil::isInside` now depends on `Geomutil2::doesIntersect`. What should we do?

We have a couple of alternatives. First we could repackage the functionality so that there is again a one-way dependency, and this may be the right answer. For example, we could move `doesIntersect` to `GeomUtil` and `isInside` to `Geomutil2`. Now there is no longer a cyclic dependency among these components, although clients of these components could be affected. (A general technique of repackaging components is formalized at the end of this section.)

It may also be the case that the two components have taken on distinct characteristics due to the demands of the clients who depend on them. In that case, it might be more appropriate to factor out the common functionality and demote it to a lower level in the physical hierarchy, as shown in Figure 5-22. That is, we can move both the `doesIntersect` and `areColinear` functions to `GeomUtilCore`.

Notice again that these utility classes are merely scopes in which to declare static member functions—they were never intended to be used to create objects. By employing the "trick" of making both of the original utilities derive publicly from a common core, clients of the original utilities will not need to alter their code if one or more of the utility functions they use is demoted.

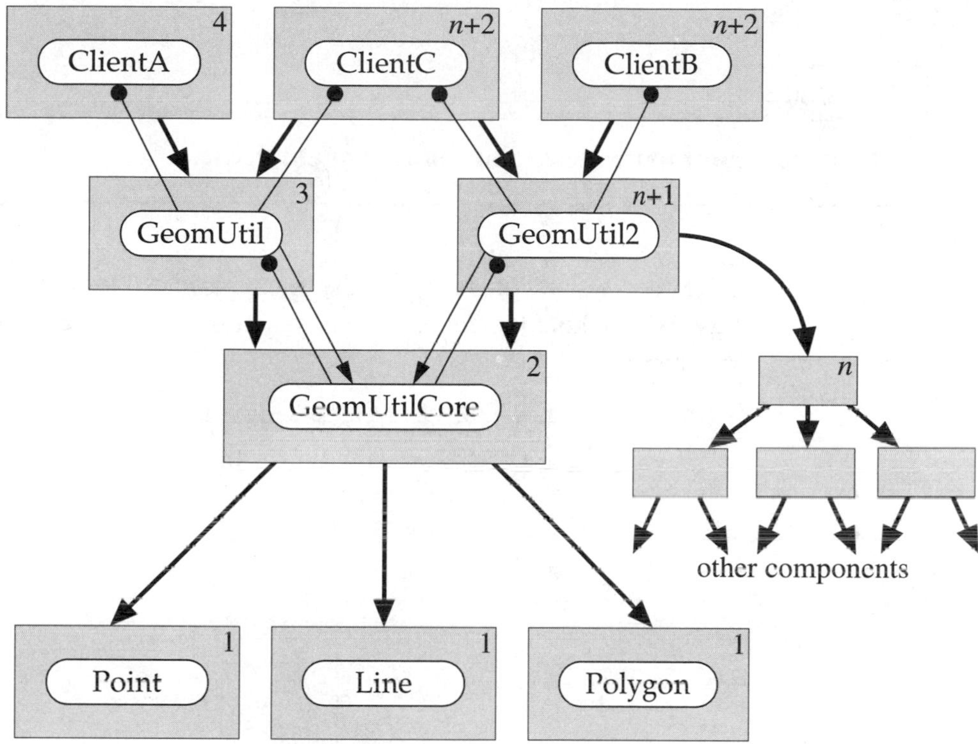

Figure 5-22: Demoting Common Functionality Among (Utility) Classes

Demotion is a useful tool for reducing the CCD of some designs even when there are no cyclic dependencies. Suppose a component x depends on only a part of another complex component y with a high CCD as shown in Figure 5-23a. If we can demote the common part of y we may be able to spare x some of the physical dependencies incurred by y (see Figure 5-23b).

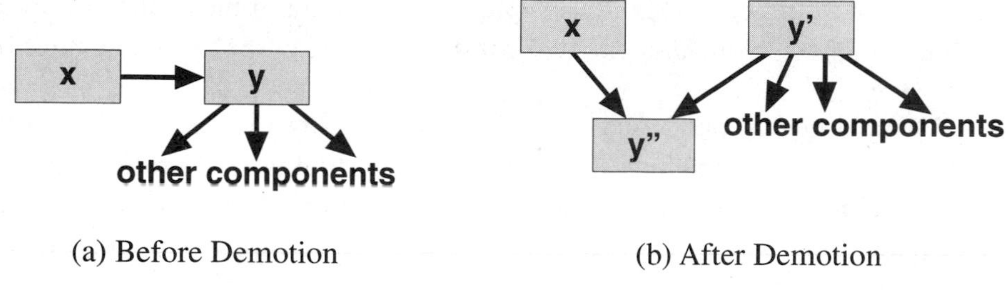

Figure 5-23: Employing Demotion to Reduce CCD

Principle

Demoting common code enables independent reuse.

Figure 5-24 illustrates a situation in which the enumerated values defined in subsystem A are used throughout the entire system, yet subsystem B is otherwise independent of subsystem A.

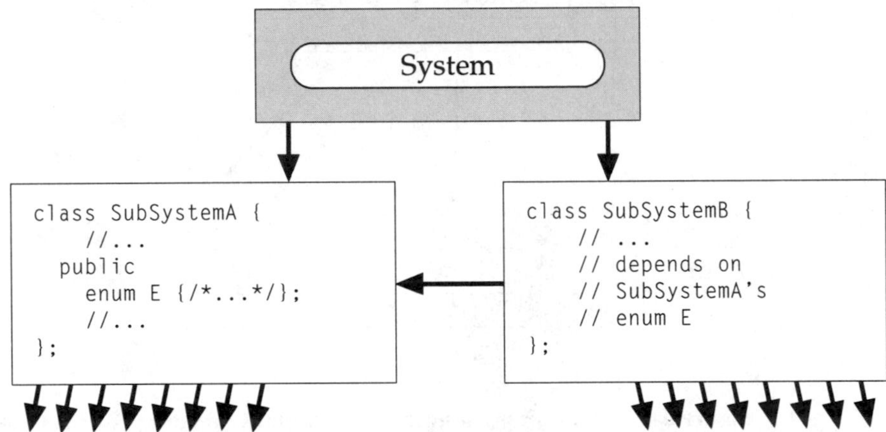

Figure 5-24: Poorly Factored System Architecture

Although there is currently no link-time dependency of subsystem B on subsystem A, this fact would not be made clear by inspecting an extracted include graph. Instead, the graph would indicate that the original architect had allowed components in subsystem B to depend, arbitrarily, on components in subsystem A. In time, normal maintenance would inevitably cause more substantial, link-time dependencies of B on A to take hold, which in turn would affect the link-time cost of maintaining subsystem B.

By creating a separate class (`struct`) for scoping the enumeration `E` originally in `SubSystemA` and moving that scoped enumeration to a separate component, we can eliminate any physical dependency of subsystem B on subsystem A. As shown in Figure 5-25, demoting enumeration `E` reduces coupling and simplifies the task of understanding the implementation of subsystem B, which, in turn, reduces the cost of maintaining the entire system.

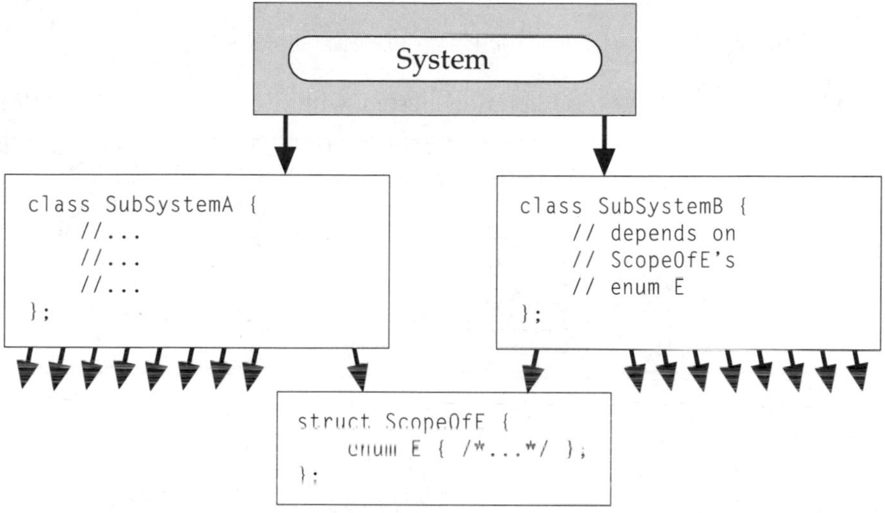

Figure 5-25: New System Architecture After Demoting the Enumeration

It may seem that placing a single enumeration in its own class is overkill. In some cases that is so, but not here. Notice that placing this tiny bit of code in its own component has freed subsystem B from the considerable maintenance burden of having to drag around all of subsystem A.

Principle

Escalating policy and demoting the infrastructure can combine to enhance independent reuse.

Another common example of an architecture that may have an unnecessarily high CCD can be found in a system that parses a text file to create a runtime data structure and then operates on that data structure to perform some desired computation.

In the architecture shown in Figure 5-26, the parser is tightly coupled to the runtime data structure in a single subsystem at the bottom of the system hierarchy. Consequently, we might expect to see a member function of the form

```
RuntimeDB::Status RuntimeDB::read(const char *fileName);
```

where `Status` is an enumeration nested within class `RuntimeDB`. Presumably this `read` function invokes a parser to load the runtime data structures with information based on the contents of the file specified by `fileName`.

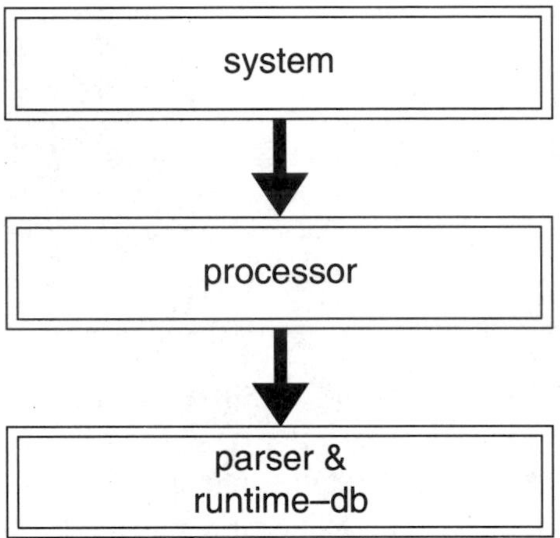

Figure 5-26: Poorly Factored Runtime Database Architecture

At the next level, the processor, which operates off the runtime database, is forced to depend on the combined parser and runtime database subsystem. The `system` component is relatively small and manages both the loading and processing of the runtime database.

Although the above architecture is levelizable, it portends some potentially severe consequences with respect to maintenance and enhancement. The development of a processor is coupled to both the parser and the runtime database, even though a parser is not needed for processing. As the system expands and we decide to add more processors, each processor must bear the unnecessary burden of linking to the parser during development.

Suppose we decide to change the format of the input file or (worse) make use of multiple formats. Now, instead of just a single read command, the runtime database must support several:

```
RuntimeDB::Status RuntimeDB::readFormatA(const char *fileName);
RuntimeDB::Status RuntimeDB::readFormatB(const char *fileName);
RuntimeDB::Status RuntimeDB::readFormatC(const char *fileName);
```

This architecture would require multiple parsers to co-exist in a single subsystem along with the runtime database, as illustrated in Figure 5-27.

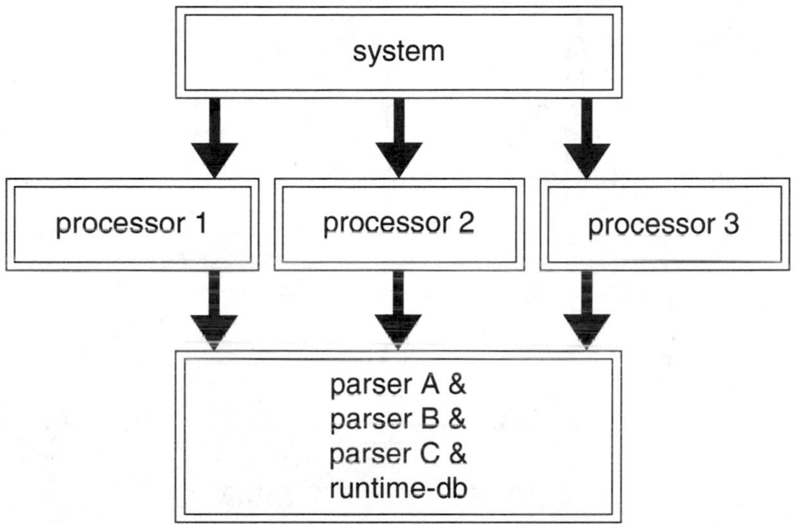

Figure 5-27: Result of Enhancing a Poor Design

The consequence of this subsystem architecture is that all existing parsers must be linked in whenever we are:

- enhancing the runtime database,
- enhancing or developing a new parser,
- enhancing or developing a new processor,
- testing any of the above, or
- reusing the runtime database in a standalone product.

In the original architecture, the database depends on the parser to load the information. However, on closer examination (see Figure 5-28), we realize that there is (or should be) an almost acyclic relationship between the runtime database and the parsers. The database is a low-level repository for information into which clients (such as parsers) deposit information and from which clients (such as processors) access and possibly manipulate information. Each parser depends on the runtime database to store the parsed information. The problem lies in the gratuitous "upward" dependency of the runtime database on a parser.

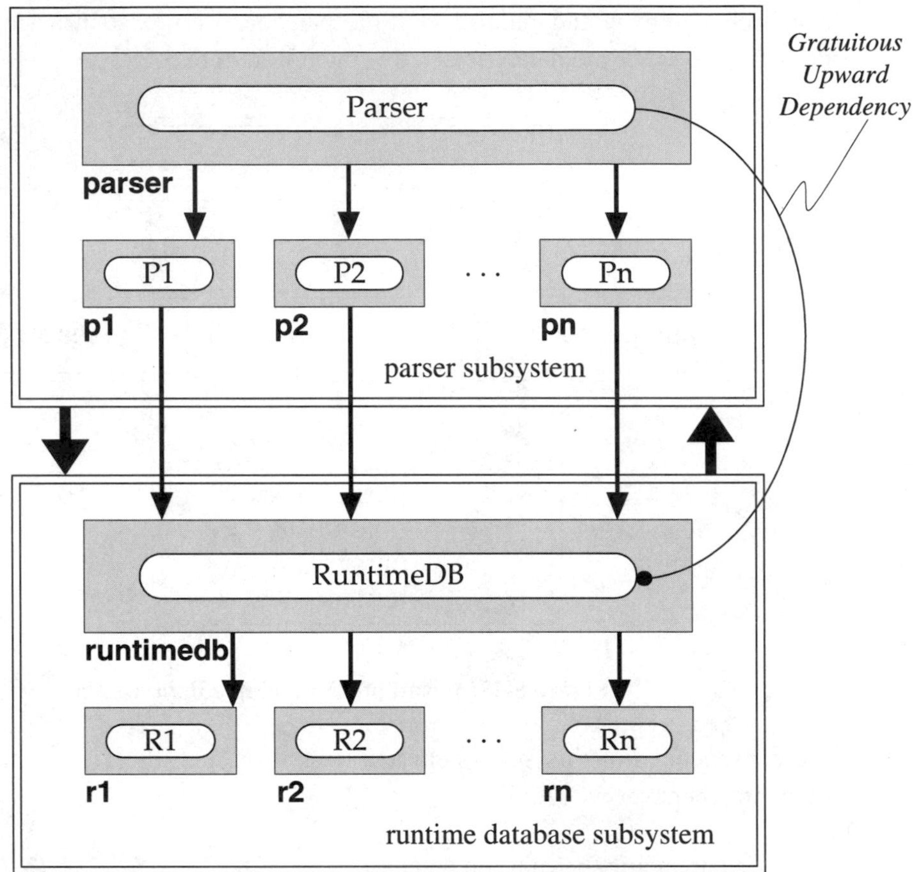

Figure 5-28: Close-Up of Poor Parser/DataBase Subsystem Architecture

Escalation and demotion combine to provide an effective solution to this problem. We can rearchitect the original system (see Figure 5-29) by first escalating the call of the parser's `read` function from the `RuntimeDB` to the system level and then demoting the common runtime database subsystem. By making the database a "dumb" repository, complete with a procedural interface for programmatically loading and retrieving information, each parser becomes "just another client" of the database. Now the system manages which files are parsed and then calls the appropriate parser, passing it a writable (non-`const`) pointer to the `RuntimeDB` object that is to be loaded:

```
ParserA::parse(RuntimeDB *db, const char *fileName);
```

If subsequent processing should not alter the runtime database but, say, merely generate reports, the system can ensure that the database is not overwritten by passing the processor a read-only (`const`) reference to the loaded `RuntimeDB`:

```
Processor1::quarterlyReport(ostrstream *ostr, const RuntimeDB& db);
```

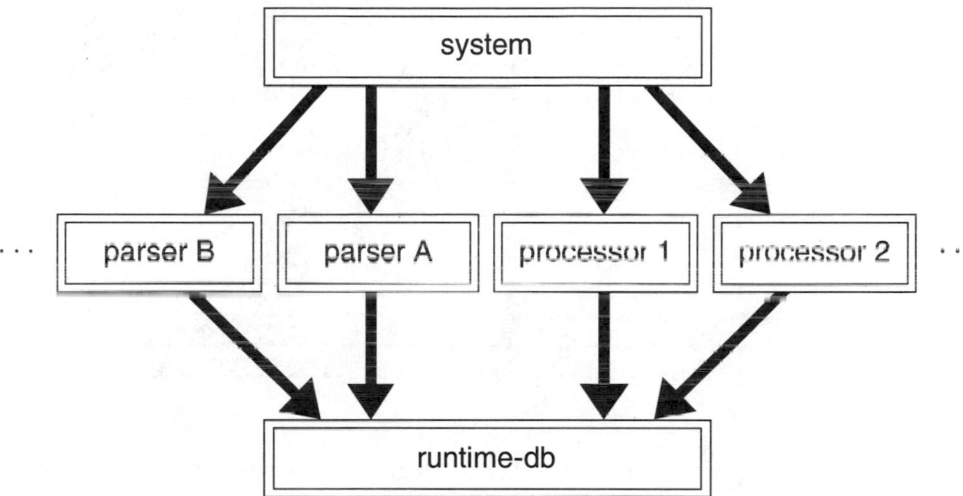

Figure 5-29: A More Maintainable System Architecture

With this new architecture, any number of independent processors can be added to the system and none of them will depend on any parser. Similarly, parsers can be replaced or added without affecting the runtime database, processors, or other parsers in any way. With this architecture it is not hard to imagine that the database, parsers, and processors could be reused in various combinations in other standalone applications (e.g., translators, archivers, and browsers).

As a final example of the power of demotion, consider the subsystem shown in Figure 5-30, in which three related components are cyclicly dependent.

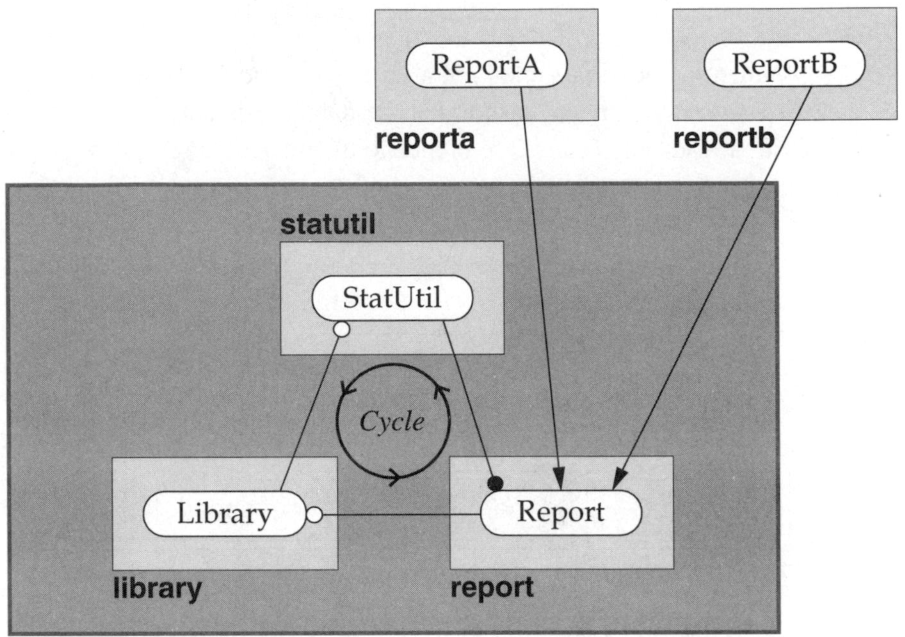

Figure 5-30: Cyclicly Dependent Library Subsystem

The `Library` contains a database of low-level information as well as a collection of heterogeneous `Report` objects. Almost all kinds of `Report` supply information that depends on aggregate statistics, calculated from the low-level data stored in the `Library`. A statistical utility class, `Statutil`, is supplied to assist in obtaining this aggregate information.[6] The common functionality implemented in the (abstract) `Report` base class uses `StatUtil`, which in turn depends on `Library`, resulting in a cyclic dependency among the `library`, `statutil`, and `report` components.

[6] Normally a *utility class* is either just a `struct` to provide a scope for a collection of related free functions or a *module* (i.e., the class contains only static data members). In either case, it is not meaningful to instantiate instances of such a class because they contain no state associated with a particular instance. See "Class Utilities" in **booch**, Chapter 5, pp. 186–187.

Principle

Factoring a concrete class into two classes containing higher and lower levels of functionality can facilitate levelization.

The problem arises in part because the single `Library` class serves as both a repository of low-level information and a collection of (higher-level) reports. Fortunately there are a couple of alternative solutions. First, by demoting the low-level repository below the rest of the subsystem, we can eliminate the cyclic coupling (as shown in Figure 5-31).

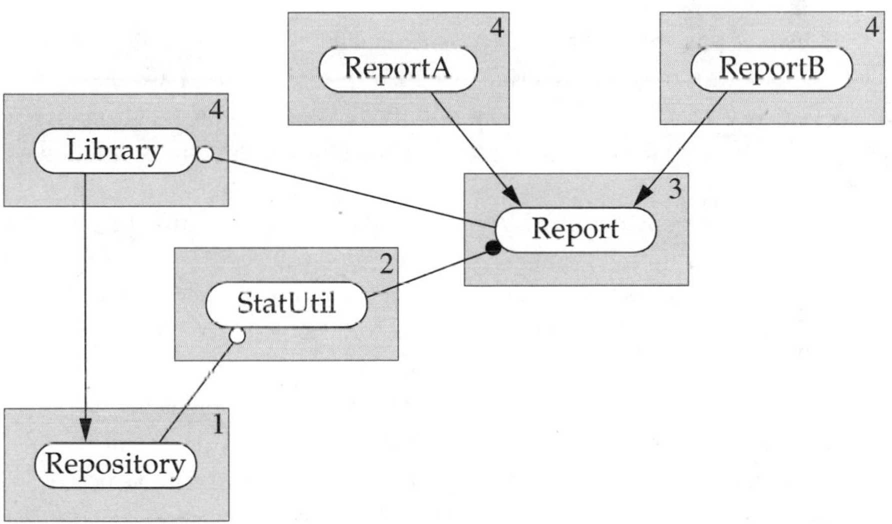

Figure 5-31: Demoting Low-Level Information in the Library Subsystem

Principle

Factoring an abstract base class into two classes—one defining a pure interface, the other defining its partial implementation—can facilitate levelization.

Another solution begins by recognizing that a single class, `Report`, has been used for two distinct purposes:

1. Providing the interface common to all reports.
2. Providing the implementation that is expected to be common to all reports.

Having a single class serve this dual role is also partially to blame for the cyclic dependency. The `Library` depends directly on the interface of the base class, `Report`, but only indirectly on its implementation, through the use of virtual functions.

Consider what would happen if we split `Report` into two classes. The first class would define the interface specified in the original `Report` class but would not implement any of the functions. That is, every function in class Report would now be declared a pure[7] virtual function. The second class, call it `ReportImp`, would derive from `Report` and provide the generic report implementation by overriding the appropriate virtual functions.

Now it is possible to break the cyclic dependency in the original system (Figure 5-30) by demoting only the interface defined in the `Report` base class below the level of Library. Class `ReportImp`, which implements common functionality and depends on `StatUtil`, remains at a higher level in the physical hierarchy, as shown in Figure 5-32.

Whether we consider these transformations to be escalation or demotion is somewhat arbitrary and unimportant. What is important is that there are two different ways in which we were able to split a single class into two classes that could then attain distinct levels in the physical hierarchy.

Which solution is better? This first solution (Figure 5-31) of factoring the `Library` class is ideal for maintenance, because the low-level repository can be developed independently of the report collection, as can the statistical utility component. The second solution (Figure 5-32) forces the entire unfactored `Library`, and therefore the low-level repository and statistical utility, to be sandwiched between the interface and partial implementation of `Report`. From this perspective, the first solution is preferable. However, there are other reasons that a single base class should define either the interface or the factored implementation but not both. Separating the interface from the (partial) implementation of a base class is discussed in detail in Section 6.4.1

[7] The destructor would be declared virtual, but not pure virtual (see Section 9.3.3).

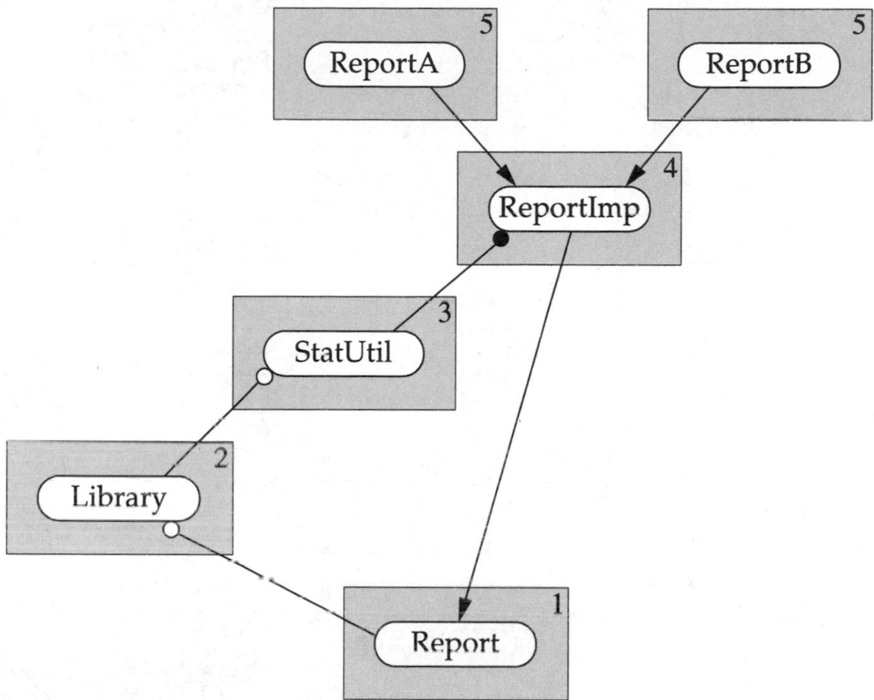

Figure 5-32: Demoting "Just" the Interface of the `Report` Base Class

Principle

Factoring a system into smaller components makes it both more flexible and also more complex, since there are now more physical pieces to work with.

An even more flexible architecture would result by adopting both transformations. Since a collection of reports makes sense as an independent abstraction, this architecture can be further improved by allowing the collection of reports to be tested and reused independently of the Repository.

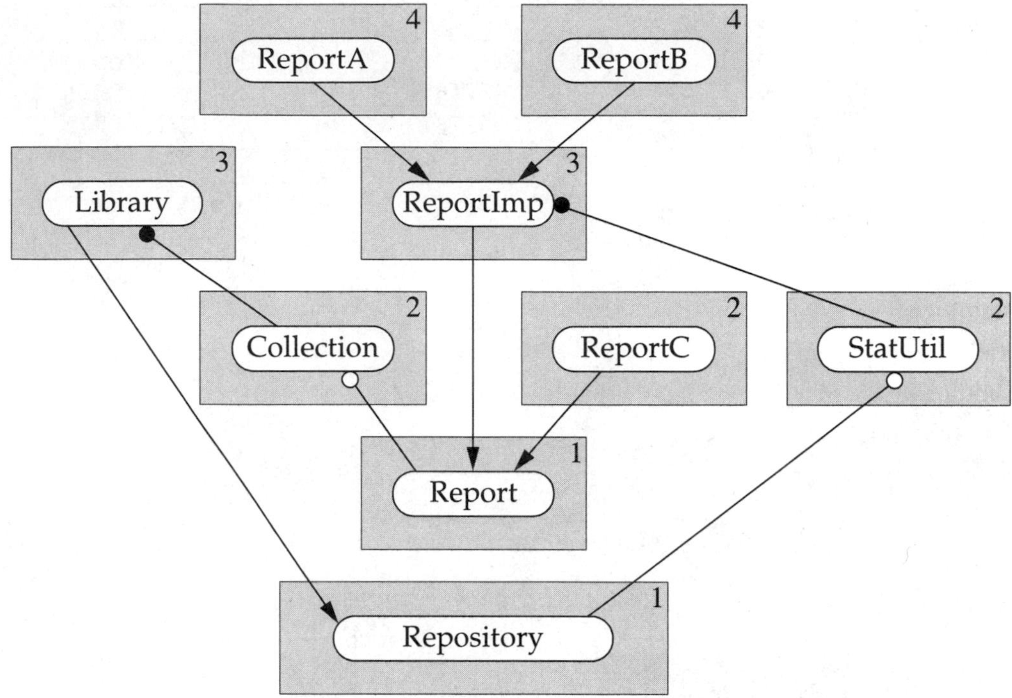

Figure 5-33: Adopting All Three Architectural Improvements

In this new architecture (shown in Figure 5-33) the physical structure exhibits more flexibility than it does in any previous architecture. To avoid unnecessary compile-time coupling, we would want to separate `Report` from its partial implementation in any case. Doing so also allow us to test `Report`, `Collection`, and `Library` by creating a very simple test-stub, `ReportC`, that does not use or depend on `StatUtil` (see Figure 5-34).

Factoring the library component is advantageous because it further reduces the physical coupling in the subsystem. The separation is particularly appropriate because we've made `StatUtil` depend only on `Repository`, while `Collection` depends only on `Report`, adding considerable flexibility to the hierarchy.

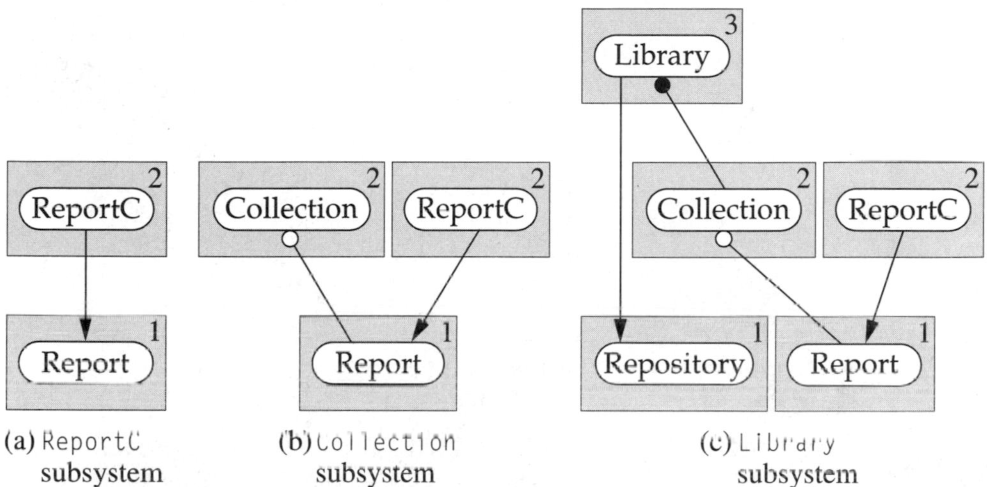

Figure 5-34: Independently Testable and Reusable Subsystems

Demoting `Repository` enables it to be tested and reused independently (Figure 5-35a) or in conjunction with `StatUtil` (Figure 5-35b). Individual, complex reports (such as `ReportA`) can be tested and reused without having to depend on a collection that may or may not eventually hold them (see Figure 5-35c).

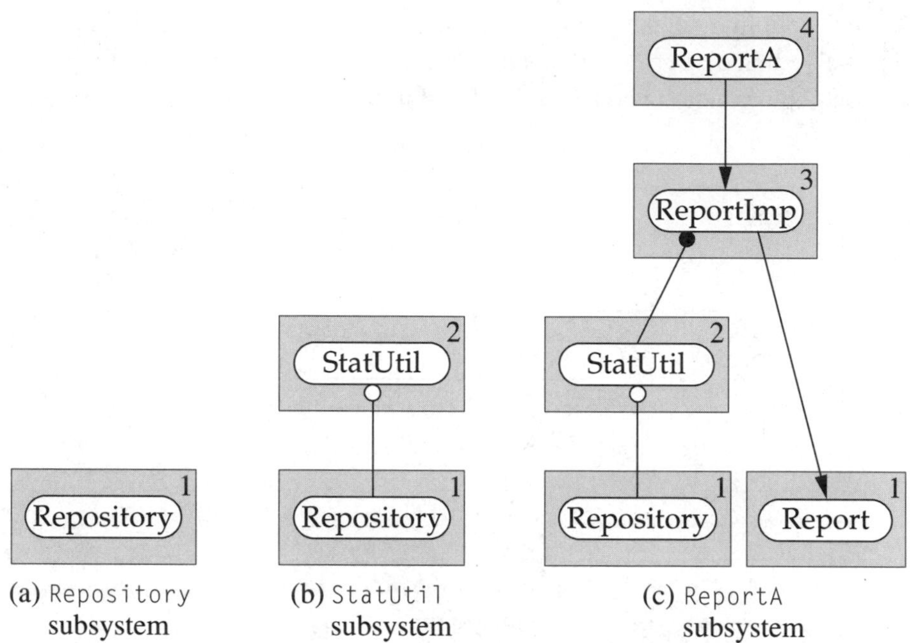

Figure 5-35: More Independently Testable and Reusable Subsystems

Escalation and demotion are closely related. What differentiates escalation from demotion in character is merely the direction in which a relatively small amount of offending functionality is moved. In fact, escalation and demotion are actually both just special cases of the more general repackaging technique illustrated in Figure 5-36.

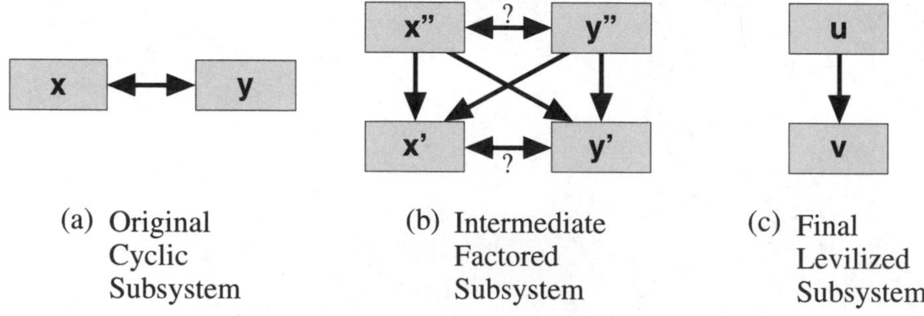

Figure 5-36: General Repackaging Technique

Here, two mutually dependent components (a) are once again factored into four components (b). Two of these components, `x'` and `y'`, may depend only on each other while the other two components, `x"` and `y"`, potentially depend on each of the other three components. The two respective pairs of, perhaps, mutually dependent components may now be recombined into two new components (c). Component `u` now depends on component `v`, which is independent. This general repackaging technique was applied informally to the components `geomutil` and `geomutil2` discussed at the beginning of this section.

To summarize: we can sometimes eliminate mutual dependencies among components by factoring commonly needed functionality and moving it lower in the physical hierarchy. Demotion is useful not only for improving cyclicly interdependent designs, but also for reducing the CCD in acyclic architectures as well. Demoting common subsystems improves both maintainability and extensibility. A properly factored system is more flexible in that its internal physical dependencies allow its components to be independently tested and reused in a wider variety of useful ways.

5.4 Opaque Pointers

Normally we assume that if a function uses an object of type `T`, it does so in a way that requires knowing the definition of `T`. That is, in order to compile the body of the function, the compiler needs to know the size and layout of the object it uses. The way a compiler learns the size and layout of an object in C++ is for the component using the object to include the header file of the component containing the object's class definition.

DEFINITION: A function `f` uses a type `T` *in size* if compiling the body of `f` requires having first seen the definition of `T`.

If a function body can be compiled having seen only the *declaration* of type `T` (e.g., `classT;`), then that function itself does *not* depend on the definition of `T`. The significance of using a type in size is that such use induces an immediate compile-time dependency on the component defining `T`. (Avoiding unnecessary compile-time dependencies is the topic of Chapter 6.) The body of a function `f` using type `T` in name but not in size typically, however, calls one or more functions in other components that, in turn, do depend on the definition of T. In this situation there would continue to be a link-time dependency of `f` on `T`.

DEFINITION: A function `f` uses a type `T` *in name only* if compiling `f` and any of the components on which `f` may depend does not require having first seen the definition of `T`.

If a function `f` and all components on which `f` depends can be compiled and linked, having seen only the *declaration* but not the definition of `T`, then `f` is said to use `T` *in name only*. For example,

```
// util.h
#ifndef INCLUDED_UTIL
#define INCLUDED_UTIL

class SomeType; // used in name only

struct Util {
    SomeType *f(SomeType *obj);
}

#endif
```

```
// util.c
#include "util.h"

SomeType *Util::f(SomeType *obj)
{
    static SomeType *lastType=0;
    return obj ? lastType = obj : lastType;
}
```

illustrates a function `f` using a type `SomeType` in name only. The significance of using a type in name only is that there is no implied physical dependency by such use—even at link time. Without the physical dependency, the coupling is all but eliminated.

Similar definitions can be constructed for a class that uses a type *in size* or *in name only*. Even more useful is that these definitions can be extended to apply to components as a whole.

DEFINITION: A component `c` uses a type `T` *in size* if compiling `c` requires having first seen the definition of `T`.

DEFINITION: A component c uses a type T *in name only* if compiling c and any of the components on which c may depend does not require having first seen the definition of T.

We use the first of these two definitions in Chapter 6. For now, we focus on the ramification of the second of these two component-level definitions. Note that, as illustrated in Figure 5-37, a component u that uses a T object in name but also depends on another component v that, in turn, uses T in size, by transitivity, cannot use T in name *only*. Component u depends physically on component v and indirectly on component t.

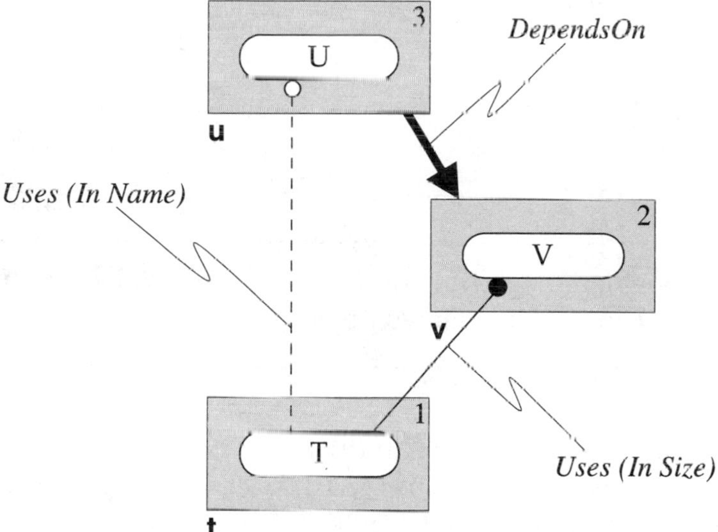

Figure 5-37: Component u Does Not Use Type T In Name *Only*

The dashed-line form of the uses notation "○- - - -" denotes that the use is "in name only" and imposes a conceptual but no physical dependency.

Here we deviate from the notation for "by-reference" dependencies suggested by Booch[8] for two reasons: (1) the logical meaning of this new In-Name-Only symbol is identical to its In-Size counterpart—it is only the *physical* implications that differ; and (2) use in name only (unlike use by reference) expressly denies any direct or indirect compile- or link-time dependency. For our purposes, three flavors of uses notation suffice:

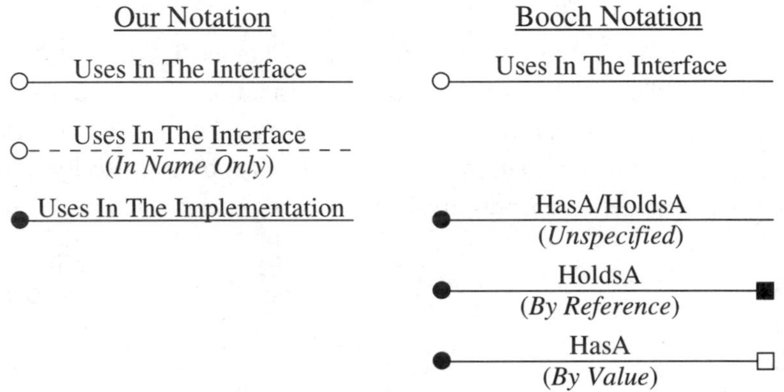

Principle

Components that use objects in name only can be thoroughly tested, independently of the named object.

Situations involving using a type in name only rarely arise naturally; they are usually contrived to avoid unwanted physical dependencies. Using a type in name only is possible when the component doing the "using" refers to the object only by pointer or reference, and never interacts with the object directly in any way other than to hold its address.

[8] **booch**, Section 5.2, Figure 14, p. 191.

```
// handle.h
#ifndef INCLUDED_HANDLE
#define INCLUDED_HANDLE

class Foo;

class Handle {
    Foo *d_opaque_p;

  public:
    Handle(Foo *foo) : d_opaque_p(foo) {}
    void set(Foo *foo) { d_opaque_p = foo; }
    Foo *get() const { return d_opaque_p; }
};

#endif
```

Figure 5-38: Handle Class that Uses `Foo` in Name Only

A pointer is said to be *opaque* if the definition of the type to which it points is not included in the current translation unit. Figure 5-38 shows a trivial example of a class that holds an opaque pointer to an instance of some class named `Foo`. The client of the `Handle` class will ultimately have to include the header file of a component that defines `Foo` in order to come up with a `Foo` object. For testing purposes, any class `Foo` will do, including even a mere class declaration as Figure 5-39 demonstrates.

```
// handle.t.c
#include "handle.h"
#include <assert.h>

main()
{
    Foo *p1 = (Foo *) 0xBAD;
    Foo *p2 = (Foo *) 0xB0B;
    Handle handle(p1);
    assert(p1 == handle.get());
    h.set(p2);
    assert(p2 == handle.get());
}
```

Figure 5-39: Trivial Test Driver for `handle` Component

The significance of this example is that it was possible to exercise the functionality of the `Handle` class completely without having to include or link to any component defining class `Foo`. Such is a litmus test for whether another type has been used not only opaquely, but also in name only.

Principle

If a contained object holds a pointer to its container and implements functionality that depends substantively on that container, then we can eliminate mutual dependency by (1) making the pointer in the contained class opaque, (2) providing access to the container pointer in the public interface of the contained class, and (3) *escalating* the affected methods of the contained class to static members of the container class.

When developing a particular application, it is common for a higher-level object to store information in objects defined at the lower levels of the physical hierarchy. If that information is in the form of a user-defined type, there is the potential for causing the subordinate object to depend on that type. As long as the subordinate does not need to make any substantive use of the type on its own, there is no need for the subordinate to include the definition of the type.

Suppose `Screen` is a container for `Widget` objects, and suppose furthermore that each `Widget` holds a pointer, `d_parent_p`, identifying the `Screen` to which the Widget belongs. Now consider the interfaces for the `widget` and `screen` components suggested in Figure 5-40, and in particular the accessor member function `numberOfWidgetsInParentScreen` of class `Widget`.

This function allows a client holding nothing but a `Widget` to find out how many other `Widget` objects there are in the `Screen` to `Which` the `Widget` belongs. From a pure usability perspective, this architecture may seem appealing; from a maintainability perspective, it is expensive.

```
// screen.h
#ifndef INCLUDED_SCREEN
#define INCLUDED_SCREEN

class Widget;

class Screen {
    Widget *d_widgets_p;
    // ...
  public:
    Screen();
    // ...
    void addWidget(const Widget& w);
    // ...
    int numWidgets() const;
    // ...
};

#endif
```

(a) Container Component `screen`

```
// widget.h
#ifndef INCLUDED_WIDGET
#define INCLUDED_WIDGET

class Screen;

class Widget {
    Screen *d_parent_p; // Screen to which
    // ...              // this widget belongs
  public:
    Widget(Screen *screen);
    // ...

    // operations involving parent screen

    int numberOfWidgetsInParentScreen() const;

    // ...
};

#endif
```

(b) Contained Component `widget`

Figure 5-40: Screen/Widget Design Causing Cyclic Dependency

The problem with the maintainability of this design is that in order to implement the `numberOfWidgetsInParentScreen` method in the `widget.c` file, we will need to "ask" the parent `Screen` for this information. Asking `Screen` anything implies having seen its definition, which is accomplished by first including `screen.h` in `widget.c`. But doing so leads to the unlevelizable situation depicted in Figure 5-41.

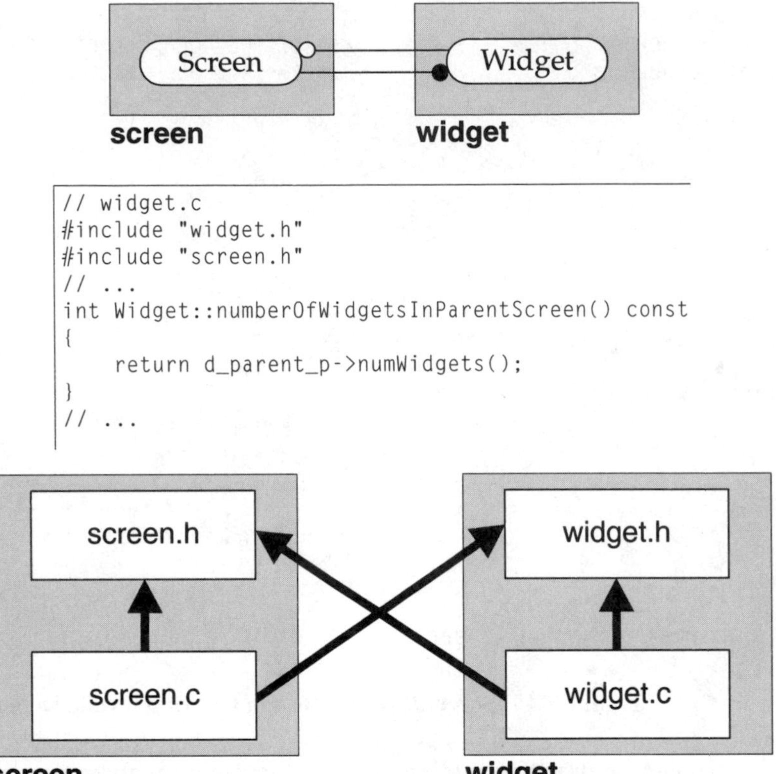

Figure 5-41: Class `Widget` "Knows About" Container Class `Screen`

The fundamental problem here is that a `Widget` is trying to do more than it should. A `Widget` has functionality that makes sense in its own context, but it cannot in general know about other `Widget` objects without asking its parent `Screen`. Consider again the analogy to a corporation. You can ask any employee, "What are you doing?" and the employee should be able to tell you. Similarly, you can always ask the employee, "Who is your boss?" In contrast, try asking the employee for the number of employees who work for his or her boss. In general the employee will not know the answer, and will need to go to the boss and ask.

Actually it is none of the employee's business how many other employees work for the boss. Consider this alternate approach. Suppose you want to know how many employees work for my boss. Instead of asking *me* that question, ask me, "Who is your boss?" I will tell you, and then you can go and ask her yourself how many employees work for her. If she wants to tell you, she will.

The use of opaque pointers (used in name only) can serve to break unwanted cyclic component dependencies. Turning back to our programming example, consider the alternate definition for the `widget` component shown in Figure 5-42. In this usage model, it is possible to ask the `Widget` for its parent `Screen`. We will then be able to ask the parent `Screen` about its other `Widget` objects (or anything else, for that matter). The principal benefit for this model, however, is that component `widget` no longer depends on component `screen` at either compile or link time. The dependency of `widget` on `screen` is now in name only.

```
// widget.h
#ifndef INCLUDED_WIDGET
#define INCLUDED_WIDGET

class Screen;

class Widget {
    Screen *d_parent_p; // screen to which this widget belongs
    // ...
  public:
    Widget(Screen *screen);
    // ...

    // operations involving parent screen

    Screen *parentScreen() const;
};

#endif
```

```
// widget.c
#include "widget.h"
#include "screen.h" // no longer needed

// ...

Screen *Widget::parentScreen() const
{
    return d_parent_p;
}
```

Figure 5-42: Modified Architecture for `widget` Component

The new component dependency graph for `screen` and `widget` is shown in Figure 5-43. With this new architecture, it is possible to test all the functionality of `widget` independently of the `screen` component. Other components that use widgets but do not care about screens need not include `screen.h` or link to `screen.o`.

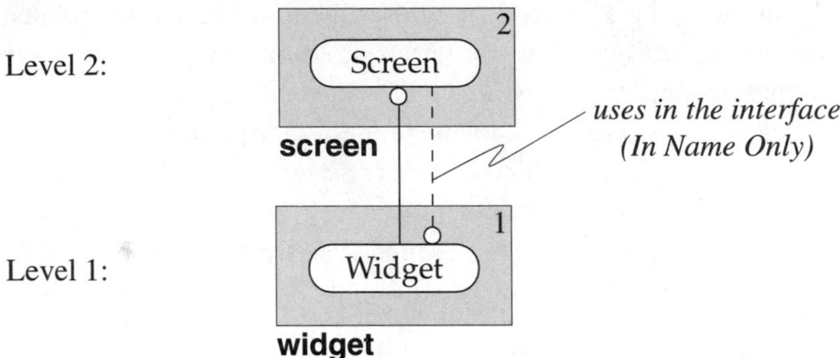

Figure 5-43: Levelizable Component Dependency for `widget` and `screen`

A small test driver that demonstrates the physical independence of `widget` on `screen` is shown in Figure 5-44.

```
// widget.t.c
#include "widget.h"
#include <iostream.h>

class Screen;      // not necessary when including widget.h

main()
{
    Screen *const screen = (Screen *) 0xbad;

    const Widget widget(screen);

    if (screen != widget.parentScreen()) {
        cout << "Error!" << endl;
    }

    // ...
}
```

Figure 5-44: Test Driver for `widget` Component in Isolation

An immediate consequence of this architectural change is that clients must perform two operations instead of one to retrieve the number of `Widget` objects in the parent `Screen`:

```
widget.parentScreen()->numWidgets()
```

For convenience, these two operations could be combined into a `static` member function of `Screen` or some other, higher-level class. Instead of saying

```
widget.numberOfWidgetsInParentScreen()
```

you would say

```
Screen::numberOfWidgetsInParentScreen(widget)
```

to obtain the value. In either case, this interface forces clients to look outside the `widget` component's interface in order to obtain the answer to their question.

Note that when moving functionality from the contained object to the container, the first argument of each new static member will be either a `const` reference or a non-`const` pointer to the contained object—depending, respectively, on whether the original member was a `const` or non-`const` function. The rationale for this style of argument passing is taken up in Section 9.1.11.

To recap: we were able to achieve an acyclic component dependency graph by making class `Widget`'s internal `Screen` pointer opaque and by moving the part of `Widget` that made substantive use of class `Screen` out of `Widget` and into the `Screen` class itself. We also exposed the `Screen` type in the public interface of `Widget` and made it necessary for clients of `widget` to look outside that component for the answers to certain kinds of questions. But in so doing, mutual physical dependency was replaced with conceptual cooperation: the lower-level object agrees only to hold on to information (specified in name only) for use at higher levels.

5.5 Dumb Data

The term *dumb data* refers to a generalization of the concept of opaque pointers. Dumb data is any kind of information that an object holds but does not know how to interpret. Such data must be used in the context of another object, usually at a higher level.

Let's consider what might be involved in implementing a simplified subsystem to model a racetrack for horses. As a starting point, we would like to be able to ask questions such as those illustrated in Figure 5-45. The top-level component should provide the capability to iterate over the races and to identify a horse by name. To make this example interesting, it should also be possible for a track to accept bets and to redeem wagers.

```
void questions(const Track& track,
               const Race&  race,
               const Horse& horse)
{
    // 1. What races do you run here?
    for (RaceIter it1(track); it1; ++it1) {
        cout << it1().number() << endl;
    }

    // 2. What time does a given race start?
    cout << race.postTime() << endl;

    // 3. What horses are running in a given race?
    for (HorseIter it3(race); it3; ++it3) {
        cout << it3().name() << endl;
    }

    // 4. What is the number of this horse?
    cout << horse.number() << endl;
}
```

Figure 5-45: Some Common Questions Asked at a Horse-Racing Track

An initial cut at the top-level track component is given in Figure 5-46. In this architecture, a `Track` holds a collection of `Race` objects and supplies a `RaceIter` to iterate over today's races at the track. The `Track` takes bets and issues (pointers to) `Wager` objects, which can be redeemed after the race is completed.

```
// track.h
#ifndef INCLUDED_TRACK
#define INCLUDED_TRACK

class Horse;
class Race;
class RaceIter;
class Track;

class Wager {
    const Horse& d_horse;
    double d_amount;
    // ...
    Wager(const Horse& horse, double amount);  // For track's use only
    Wager(const Wager&);                       // -- i.e., not for use
    Wager& operator=(const Wager&);            // by the public.
    friend Track;
```

```
  public:
    const char *horseName() const;
    int raceNumber() const;
    Track& track() const;
    double amount() const;
};

class Track {
    Race *d_races_p;
    // ...
    friend RaceIter;

  public:
    // ...
    const Race *lookupRace(int raceNumber) const;
    const Horse *lookupHorse(const char *horseName) const;
    Wager *bet(const Horse& horse, double wagerAmount);
    double redeem(Wager *bet) const;
};

class RaceIter {
    // ...
  public:
    RaceIter(const Track& track);
    void operator++();
    operator const void *() const;
    const Race& operator()() const;
};

#endif
```

Figure 5-46: Header for Top-Level Component `track`

Each `Race` object maintains the number of that race, the post time for that race, and the collection of horses running in that race. The `race` component also provides a `HorseIter` to iterate over the horses running in a specified `Race`. Given a `Race` object, it is possible to determine at which track the race will be run. A rough version of the `race` component is shown in Figure 5-47.

```
// race.h
#ifndef INCLUDED_RACE
#define INCLUDED_RACE

class HorseIter;

class Race {
    // ...
    friend HorseIter;
```

```
    public:
      Race(const Track& track, int raceNumber, double postTime);
      // ...
      int number() const;
      double postTime() const;
      const Track *track() const;
};

class HorseIter {
      // ...
    public:
      HorseIter(const Race& race);
      void operator++();
      operator const void *() const;
      const Horse& operator()() const;
};

#endif
```

Figure 5-47: Header for the Intermediate-Level Component `race`

A `Horse` is defined at the lowest level of the racetrack subsystem's physical hierarchy. A `Horse` maintains its name and number, and it can be used to determine in which race it is scheduled to run. A first cut at our leaf-level `horse` component is sketched in Figure 5-48.

```
#ifndef INCLUDED_HORSE
#define INCLUDED_HORSE

class Race;

class Horse {
      const Race& d_race;
      char *d_name_p;
      int *d_number;
      // ...
    public:
      Horse(const Race& race, const char *HorseName, int horseNumber);
      // ...
      const char *name() const;
      int number() const;
      const Race *race() const;
};

#endif
```

Figure 5-48: Header for the Leaf-Level Component `horse`

In this initial implementation, a `Wager` is implemented with only two data members as follows:

```
class Wager {
    const Horse& d_horse;
    double d_amount;
    // ...
  public:
    // ...
};
```

Holding a pointer to a `Horse`, it is possible for clients at sufficiently high levels to use the uniquely identified `Horse` to obtain a pointer to the `Race`, anywhere in the world, in which that `Horse` will run. The `Race` pointer can then be traversed, and the resulting race object used to obtain a pointer to the track where that race will be held.

The functionality for the horse racetrack system described above implies maintaining a cyclic internal data structure: Each `Track` knows the races that it holds, each `Horse` knows in which race it runs, and each `Race` knows both the track in which it is held and the horses that will participate in it. However, this data structure can be implemented with acyclic physical dependencies by using opaque pointers as shown by the component/class diagram of Figure 5-49.

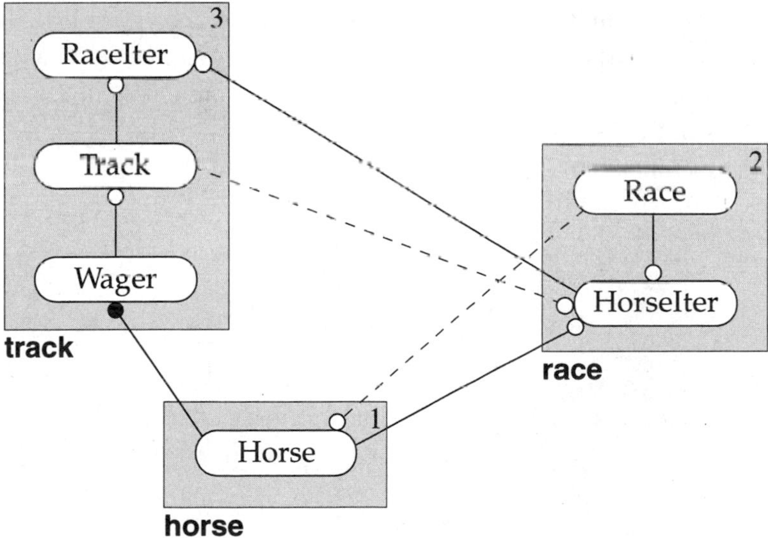

Figure 5-49: Component/Class Diagram for Racetrack Subsystem

The original architecture presented for the racetrack subsystem has no cyclic physical dependencies but is nonetheless cyclicly dependent in name. Although having two components that each know the names of one or more objects defined in the other component is not necessarily bad, there are trade-offs to be made that will be discussed shortly.

Suppose that, instead of identifying the objects in this system by their absolute addresses, we identify them in terms of indices into a sequence of objects that has meaning only in the context of the parent object.

The `Track` would then hold a sequence (array) of `Race` objects, and each `Race` would have an associated integer "index." The `Race` index would be meaningful only in the context of a `Track` object. Since the `Race` indices can be made to correspond to the publicly accessible `Race` numbers, the need for a `RaceIter` is reduced, provided we supply an accessor for `Track` to report the total number of races held today.

By the same argument, each `Horse` in a `Race` is naturally assigned a number. Given a `Race` that has a sequence of horses, we can identify the `Horse` within a `Race` by supplying its index relative to that race. We therefore can also dispense with the `HorseIter` for `Race`.

When it comes to redeeming wagers, the `Track` defines a context that is much smaller than the entire address space describable by pointers. In the original implementation, we used opaque back pointers beginning with `Horse`, and moved in a bottom-up fashion to arrive at the `Race` and finally the `Track`. In the proposed implementation, the limited context of the `Track` is exploited to identify the `Race` and `Horse` using a pair of integer indices as shown in Figure 5-50.

```
class Wager {
    const Track& d_track;
    double d_amount;
    short int d_raceIndex;
    short int d_horseIndex;
    // ...
  public:
    Wager(const Track& track,
          int horseNumber,
          int raceNumber,
          double amount);
    const Track& track() const;
    double amount() const;
    int horseNumber() const;
    int raceNumber() const;
    // ...
};
```

```
class Track {
    Race *d_races_p;
    int d_numRaces;
    // ...
  public:
    Wager *bet(int race, int horse, double amount);
    double redeem(Wager *bet) const;
    const Race *lookupRace(int raceNumber) const;
    const Horse *lookupHorse(const char *horseName) const;
    const Horse *lookupHorse(const Race& race, int horseNumber) const;
    int numRaces() const;
    // ...
};
```

Figure 5-50: Modifications to Component `track`

Observe that, because of the very limited context, we can safely use 16-bit instead of 32-bit integers. This fact could be significant if the number of outstanding wagers at any one time becomes very large. For example, on my 32-bit machine, where a double is 8 bytes long and naturally aligned,[9] the size of the wager objects drops from 24 to 16 bytes when we make the indices `short` integers—a savings of 33 percent!

Figure 5-51 illustrates the revised architecture for the racetrack subsystem. The new system is significantly simpler. This system has no cyclic dependencies between components—not even in name—and significantly fewer classes. The principal change was simply the way in which a `Horse` is identified.

Dumb data can be more convenient and occasionally more compact than opaque pointers for identifying other objects. Had the new `Wager` object identified the `Race` and `Horse` by opaque pointer instead of `short` integer index, the size of `Wager` would again be 24 instead of 16 bytes on my machine.

Another advantage is that the values stored as dumb data are not machine addresses and therefore contain meaningful values that can be tested explicitly. In the horse-racing application, the indexed approach is particularly appealing, because the indices (which are publicly accessible) do have legitimate utility in the user domain. It is not uncommon to hear a frequent patron of the track request of a parimutuel ticket agent at the betting window: "Gimme 2 bucks on number 4 in the 9th (to win)!"

---

[9] Natural alignment is discussed in Section 10.1.1.

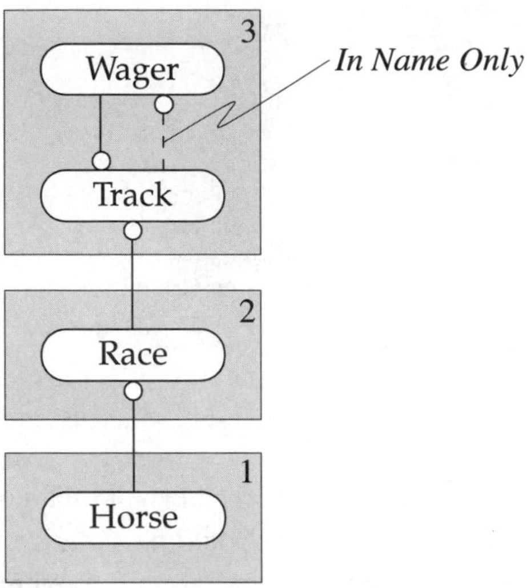

Figure 5-51: Revised Component/Class Diagram for Racetrack Subsystem

A disadvantage of the indexed approach is that it does sacrifice a fair degree of type safety compared to opaque pointers in that the `Race` and `Horse` indices are just integers. Another drawback is that this implementation forces the `Race` and `Horse` collections to be indexed rather than to remain arbitrary collections. The resulting erosion of encapsulation could easily have a negative impact on maintainability if exposed to the general public.

In situations other than our horse-racing example, the dumb-data indices used to identify subobjects in this way might very well be meaningless to clients of the subsystem. For these reasons, the use of dumb data is typically an optimized implementation technique encapsulated within a subsystem and not exposed at the higher levels of a system.

Principle

Dumb data can be used to break *in-name-only* dependencies, facilitate testability, and reduce implementation size. However, opaque pointers can preserve both type safety and encapsulation; dumb data, in general, cannot.

As a similar but more serious example, consider the task of modeling the connectivity within a circuit consisting of a heterogeneous collection of electrical components.[10] A gate-level circuit, such as the one used to introduce levelization in Figure 4-10 of Section 4.7, can be represented as a graph consisting of nodes (called *gates*) and edges (called *wires*). Each gate has a collection of electrically distinct connection points (called *terminals*). Conceptually, representing a circuit amounts to maintaining a heterogeneous collection of gates and a homogeneous collection of bidirectional wires. Each wire is attached to two distinct terminals within the circuit, establishing connectivity.

In a traditional implementation, a circuit might contain a collection of terminals, defining the primary inputs and outputs for the circuit. Each gate in the circuit would also contain a collection of terminals. Wires are not explicit objects in this model. Instead, each terminal contains a collection of pointers to (other) terminals. Pointing to another terminal implicitly establishes a connection to that terminal. In the example shown in Figure 5-52, the terminal `z` of gate `g0` is connected to the terminal `x` of gate `g1`, therefore, terminal `z` of `g0` would hold a pointer to terminal `x` of `g1`. By symmetry, terminal `x` of `g1` is also connected to terminal `z` of `g0`, so `x` of `g1` would also hold a pointer to `z` of `g0`.

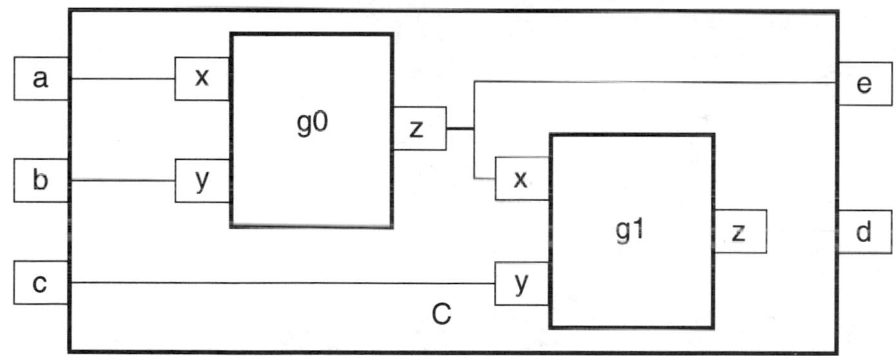

Figure 5-52: Circuit `C` Implemented in Terms of Two Gates, `g0` and `g1`

In order to traverse the graph, a `Terminal` must maintain an opaque pointer to its parent `Gate` or `Circuit`. Note that `Circuit` can be treated as just a special kind of `Gate`

[10] This example describes the application of dumb data in a very different context. The basic technique, however, is the same as for the racetrack example.

that contains instances of other gates.[11] Cyclic physical component dependencies can be avoided by using opaque pointers as shown in the partial component/class diagram of Figure 5-53 (with collection iterators omitted).

Here again there is an opportunity to break even the nominal cyclic dependencies by defining a connection "in context." If a `Circuit` contains an indexed collection (an array) of `gates`, and similarly each `Gate` contains an array of terminals, then we can identify a connection point in the context of a `Circuit` as a simple pair of integer indices.

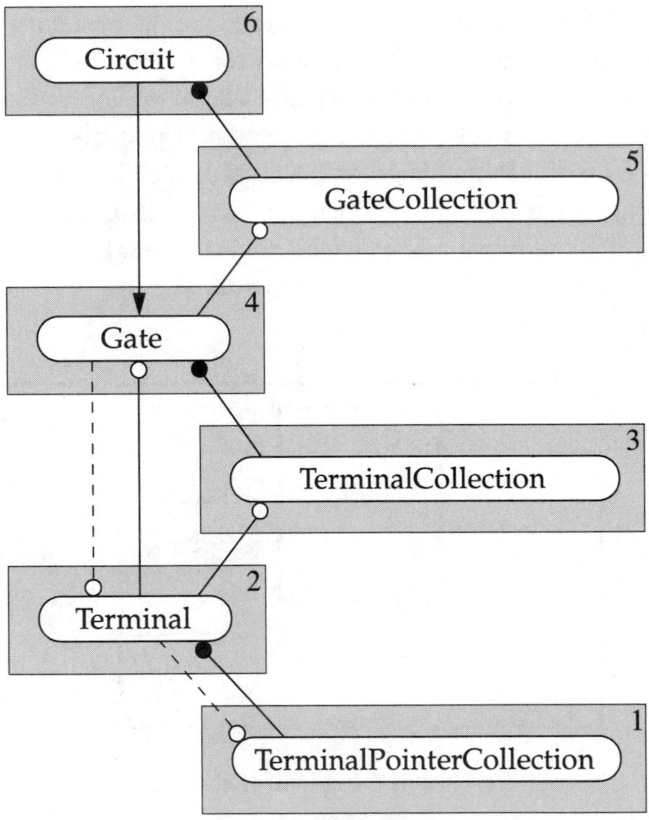

Figure 5-53: Partial Component/Class Diagram for `Circuit` Implementation

---

[11] This example illustrates another instance of recursive composition—a design pattern called *Composite* in **gamma**, Chapter 4, pp. 163–173. This pattern was seen previously in terms of `Node`, `File`, and `Directory` in Figure 4-13 of Section 4.7. The Composite design pattern has been used effectively to implement hierarchical circuit descriptions.

Consider again the example of Figure 5-52. Suppose the implementation of the circuit consists of an array of two gates, g0 and g1, with indices 0 and 1, respectively. The terminals for both g0 and g1 are x, y, and z, and happen to have indices 0, 1, and 2 respectively. We can now describe the connection point "terminal x of gate g1" as the pair of integer indices (1, 0). We can similarly describe the connection point z of g0 as the coordinate pair (0, 2).

By convention, we can identify the enclosing circuit by using an index outside the legal range for gates indices (such as –1). If the circuit's terminal a has index 0, its connection coordinates could be represented as the pair of indices (–1, 0). The complete list of connections for this circuit, described in terms of integer coordinates, is provided in Figure 5-54.

```
 C.a = (-1, 0) <-----------> ( 0, 0) = g0.x
 C.b = (-1, 1) <-----------> ( 0, 1) = g0.y
 C.c = (-1, 2) <-----------> ( 1, 1) = g1.y
g0.z = ( 0, 2) <-----------> ( 1, 0) = g1.x
g0.z = ( 0, 2) <-----------> (-1, 4) =  C.e
g1.z = ( 1, 2) <-----------> (-1, 3) =  C.d
```

Figure 5-54: Representing Connectivity Using Integer Indices

A pair of integers has no physical dependency on anything. We can therefore define a Connection class in a leaf component as follows:

```
class Connection {
    int d_gateIndex;
    int d_terminalIndex;

  public:
    Connection(int gateIndex, int instanceIndex);
    int gateIndex() const;
    int terminalIndex() const;
};
```

Figure 5-55 illustrates a completely levelizable component hierarchy in which Connection, ConnectionCollection, Terminal, TerminalArray, Gate, GateArray, and finally Circuit can be tested and verified in order.

The graph-like nature of Circuit is not evident from the subcomponents. The connectivity of the circuit is not established until the level of the component that defines the GateArray class, because it is only at that level that sufficient context exists to understand the implied graph. Users of `Circuit` need not necessarily be exposed to the lower-level `Gate` and `Terminal` classes, and may wind up "programming" the circuit by specifying gates and terminals by names that are translated to indices internally.

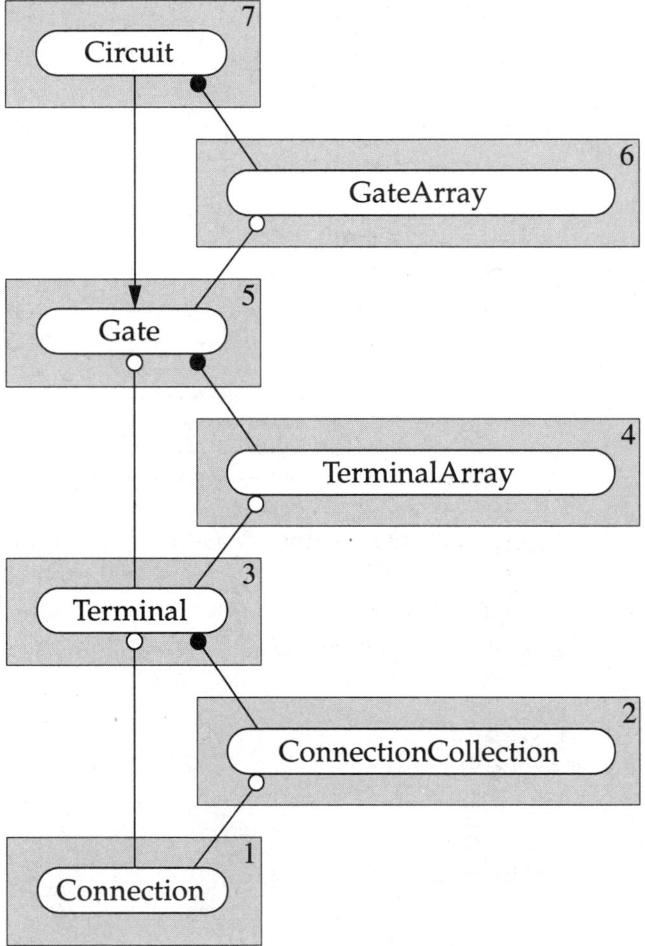

Figure 5-55: New Component/Class Diagram for `Circuit` Implementation

To conclude this section: *dumb data* is a generalization of opaque pointers that can facilitate the implementation of subsystems, in which low-level objects must implicitly refer to other low-level objects. This technique is especially indicated where these references need not be interpreted at the lower levels of the subsystem, but only in the context of some (usually) higher-level object. This restricted context can allow for more compact implementations, though it is at the expense of both type safety and encapsulation. The use of dumb data is typically a low-level implementation detail and often not exposed in the interfaces of higher-level subsystems.

5.6 Redundancy

Reuse of any kind implies some form of coupling. In some cases the coupling may be severe. In this book, *redundancy* refers to the technique of deliberately repeating code or data in order to avoid unwanted physical dependencies brought on by reuse.

Principle

The additional coupling associated with some forms of reuse may outweigh the advantage gained from that reuse.

Redundancy is indicated when the functionality exists in a separate physical unit, the amount of functionality to be reused is relatively small, and the amount of coupling that would result is so disproportionately large as to outweigh the benefit of the reuse. For cases where the amount of reuse would be substantial, it is often appropriate to demote the common code to a lower level where it can be shared.

Even within a single subsystem there is a threshold below which reuse of external functionality may not be advantageous. Consider two large components that are independent. It is possible that one of these components implements a tiny piece of functionality (such as `min`, `max`, etc.) that the other could reuse. Demoting this tiny piece of the implementation to a separate component would unjustifiably increase the physical complexity of the subsystem. Causing one of these components to depend on the other just for such a small amount of reuse would unjustifiably increase the CCD of the subsystem. Allowing one component to dominate the other reduces flexibility for adding other dependencies resulting from future enhancements. Sometimes a viable alternative to reuse is simply to repeat the code and avoid the coupling.

As a common, practical example, consider the situation illustrated in Figure 5-56, in which some low-level object, `Cell`, has a name. The name is specified when the object is constructed, cannot be changed throughout the lifetime of the object, and is destroyed when the object is destroyed. An accessor in the public interface of the object supplies the name (as a `const char *`) on request. Other than the name, there is no use made of `String` in this object.

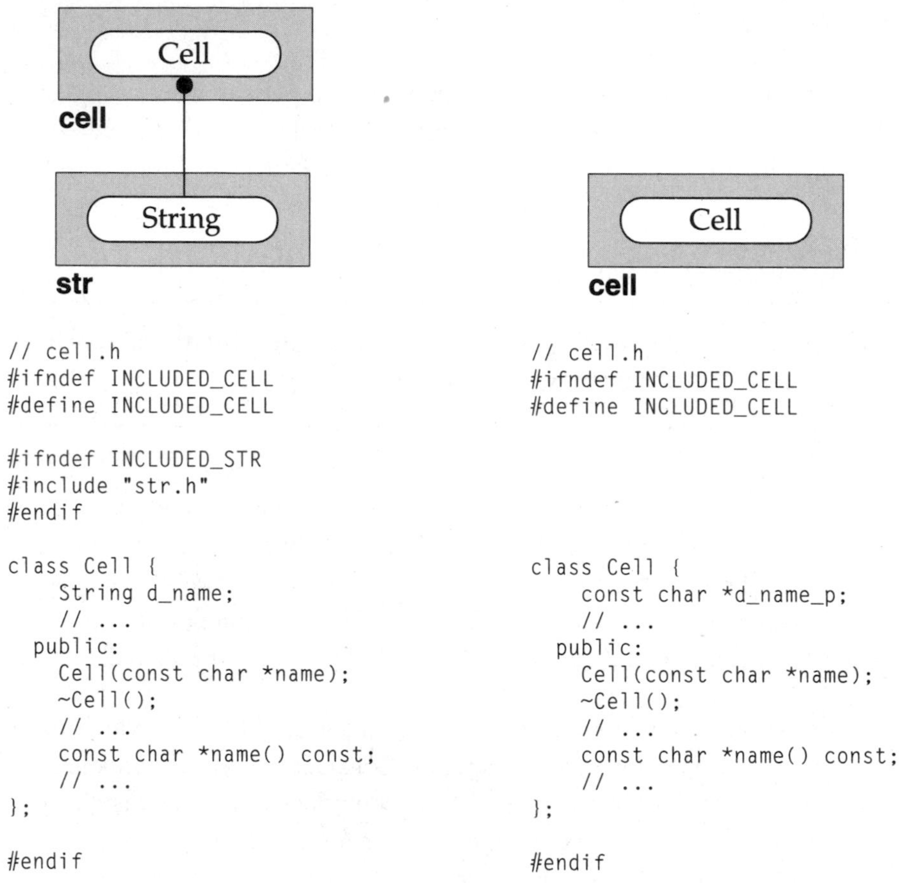


```
// cell.h
#ifndef INCLUDED_CELL
#define INCLUDED_CELL

#ifndef INCLUDED_STR
#include "str.h"
#endif

class Cell {
    String d_name;
    // ...
  public:
    Cell(const char *name);
    ~Cell();
    // ...
    const char *name() const;
    // ...
};

#endif
```

(a) Using the `String` Class

```
// cell.h
#ifndef INCLUDED_CELL
#define INCLUDED_CELL

class Cell {
    const char *d_name_p;
    // ...
  public:
    Cell(const char *name);
    ~Cell();
    // ...
    const char *name() const;
    // ...
};

#endif
```

(b) Reimplementing `String`'s Functionality

Figure 5-56: Two Ways to Implement an Object that Has a Name

The use of `String` here is an encapsulated implementation detail of the `Cell` class. The advantage of using `String` is that there is no need to use the `new` operator (directly) in the implementation of the `Cell`'s constructor, to worry about allocating the extra byte for the trailing null, or to copy the incoming `String` to the newly allocated buffer. Perhaps the biggest benefit is not having to worry about deleting this `String` in the `Cell`'s destructor.

To experienced C programmers, none of the above should present any noticeable maintenance problem. The disadvantage of depending on `String` is that it is extra baggage that must follow the `cell` component around. If `str` is not part of the same subsystem or depends on other components, then using `String` (instead of just a `char *`) could result in having to drag around other components or even libraries, further increasing the burden of using `Cell`.

As defined in Figure 5-56a, `Cell` *has* a `String` and therefore depends on component `str` in size. All clients of `Cell` will be saddled with not just a link-time but also a compile-time dependency on component `str`. This problem is avoided if `Cell` is defined as shown in Figure 5-56b. (The issues surrounding unnecessary compile-time dependencies are the subject of Chapter 6.)

In cases such as the one shown in Figure 5-56, avoiding coupling to the `str` component probably outweighs the advantages of reuse. Such would not be the case if the `cell` component makes any significant use of `String`'s capabilities (e.g., concatenation) or if `String` appeared many times in the definition of `Cell`.

Principle

Supplying a small amount of redundant data can enable the use of an object in name only, thus eliminating the cost of linking to the definition of that object's type.

Redundancy can be used effectively in a variety of ways and in conjunction with other techniques to reduce physical dependencies. In particular, choosing to use objects in name only can be effective not only for breaking cyclic dependencies within a subsystem but also for reducing the physical dependency upon other subsystems. Sometimes, however, it is necessary to supply a small amount of redundant information in order to keep certain objects opaque.

Consider the scenario illustrated in Figure 5-57. We are trying to implement a shape analyzer on top of a large shape subsystem consisting of, say, 1,000 components.

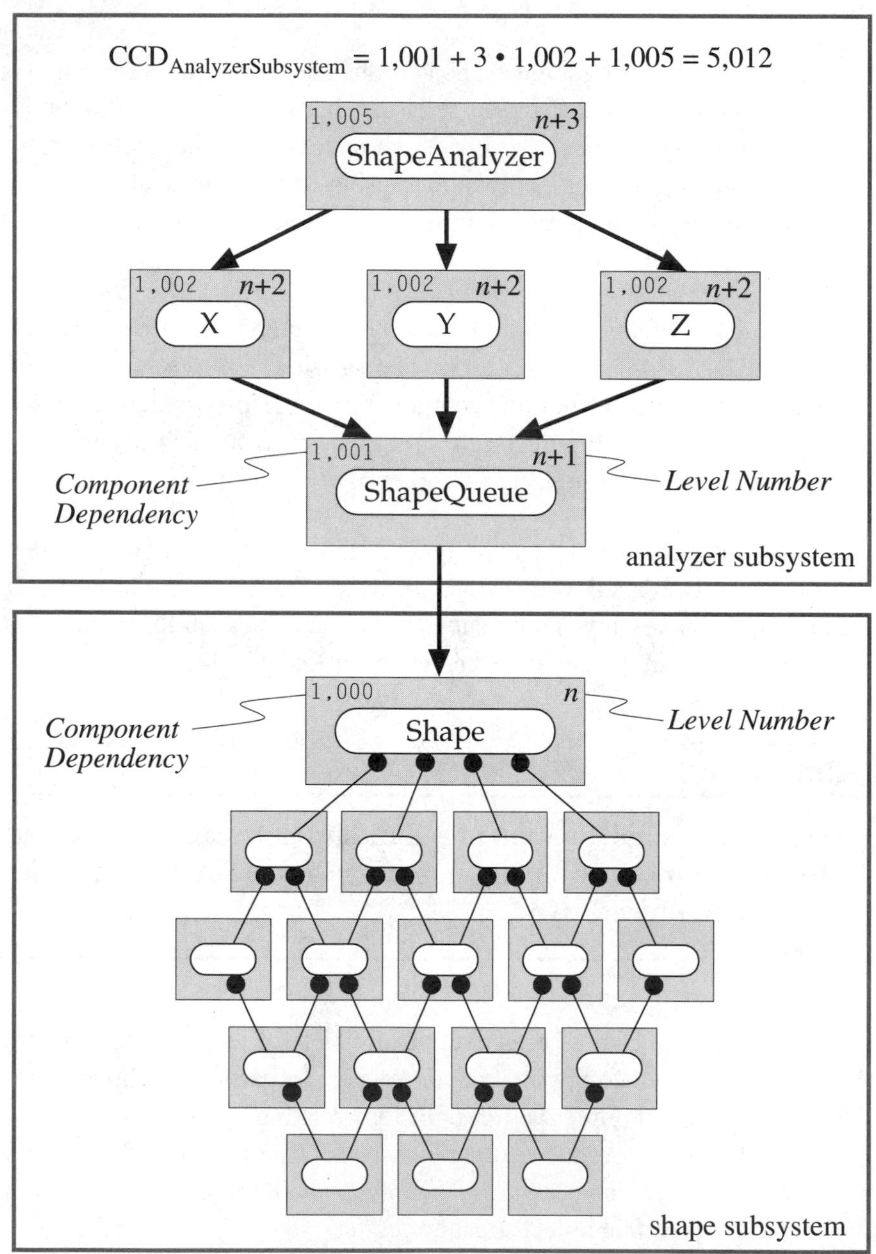

Figure 5-57: `ShapeAnalyzer` **Forced To Use Highly Coupled** `Shape` **Subsystem**

Fortunately we need to make use of only a small portion of this subsystem, in particular, the `shape` component. Unfortunately this component is fully dependent on the rest of its subsystem, giving `shape` a disproportionately large link cost (1,000 units as measured by its component dependency). The CCD for just the five components of the analyzer subsystem (that is, excluding the local link cost of maintaining the shape subsystem) is 5,013.

Often there are sophisticated container objects (such as a priority queue) that hold other objects, but that need not depend on the contained object in any substantive way. The job of the `ShapeQueue` is to maintain a heap of `Shape` objects ordered by area. The `Shape` class supplies a public member function to return its area. Designing `ShapeQueue` to use `Shape`'s `area()` member directly would tie the cost of developing and maintaining the `ShapeQueue` (and all of its clients) to the unusually large CCD imposed by `Shape`.

Figure 5-58 depicts an alternative architecture, motivated entirely by reducing the cost of maintenance and testing. Instead of having `ShapeQueue` get the area data directly from a `Shape`, a `ShapeManager` extracts this value and enters it, redundantly, along with each opaque `Shape` pointer into the `ShapeQueue`. The rest of `ShapeAnalyzer`'s implementation has been refactored so that all substantive use of class `Shape` now occurs only in the `shapemanager` component, with some additional redundant data (i.e., area) being stored in each `ShapeQueue` entry for use by components `x`, `y`, and `z`).

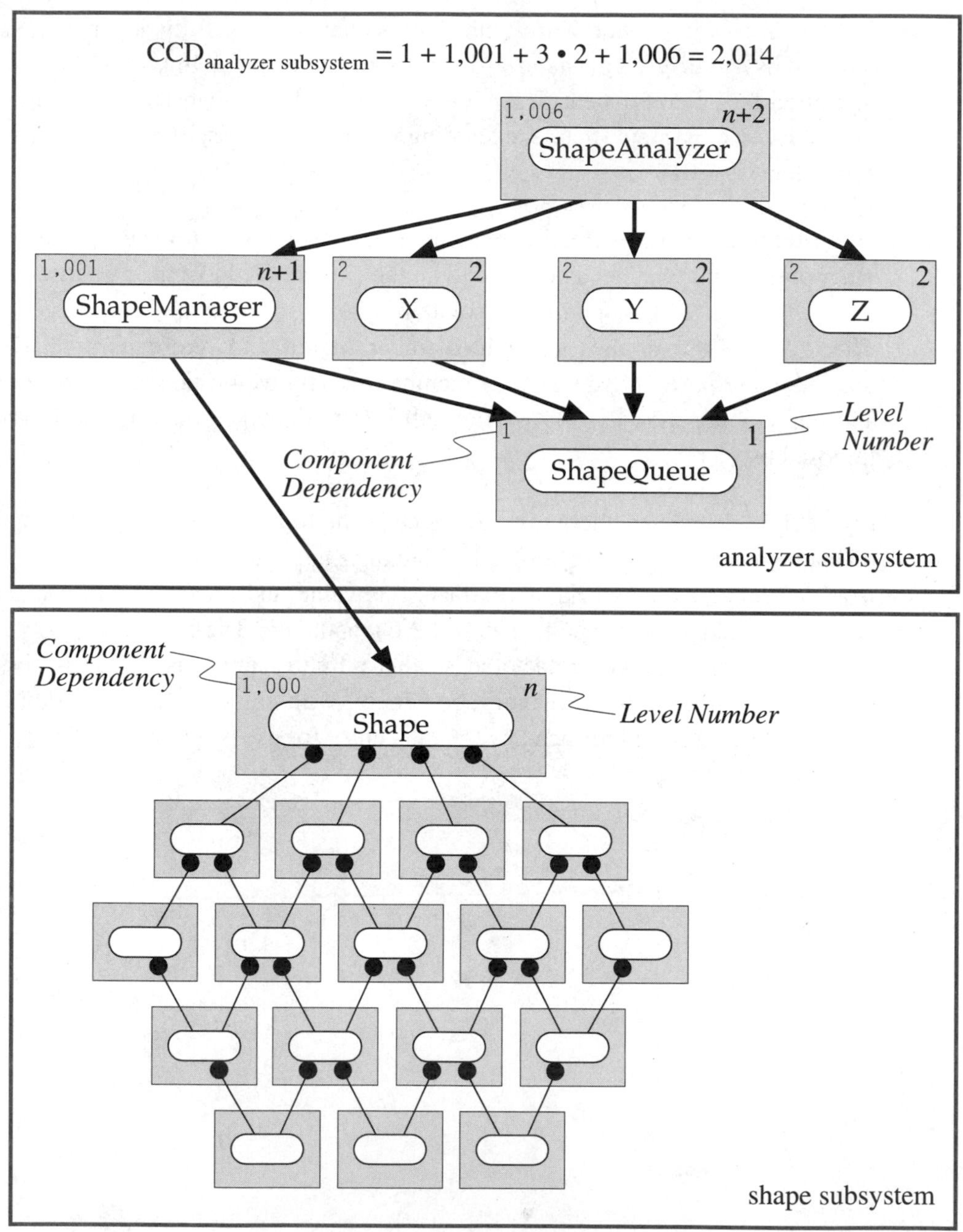

Figure 5-58: Reducing CCD by Using Redundant Data and Opaque Pointers

Principle

Packaging subsystems so as to minimize the cost of linking to other subsystems is a design goal.

The reduction in maintenance cost associated with the analyzer subsystem of nearly 60 percent is not unusual, nor is the relatively large cost associated with linking to a large, highly interdependent subsystem. A well-designed subsystem will usually contain a substantial proportion of components that do not depend on any other subsystems, and few components that depend on huge, tightly coupled subsystems such as the one containing `Shape`.

In short, reuse is rarely without cost, and its benefit must be weighed against the cost resulting from increased coupling. Very often that cost comes in the form of increased physical dependence. Techniques used to reduce physical coupling, such as opaque pointers, occasionally require providing a small amount of redundant information in order to be applied successfully. In such cases the amount of savings in terms of coupling will dictate the amount of redundancy that is tolerable.

5.7 Callbacks

A *callback* is a function, provided by a client to a subsystem, that allows that subsystem to perform a specific operation in the context of the client.

As a simple example, consider the C Library function `qsort`,[12] which is an implementation of the Quicksort algorithm:

```
#include <stdlib.h>

void qsort(const void *base,
           size_t numElements,
           size_t sizeofElement,
           int (*compare)(const void *elem1, const void *elem2);
```

[12] **plauger**, Chapter 13, pp. 357–358.

The first parameter of `qsort`, `base`, indicates the starting location of a homogeneous array of objects whose type is unknown to the `qsort` routine. The second parameter, `numElements`, indicates the number of objects in the `base` array. The third parameter, `sizeofElement`, indicates the uniform size of each element (as defined by the `sizeof` operator). The fourth and final parameter, `compare`, is a pointer to a callback function.

The `qsort` function assumes that this callback function, `compare`, will correctly determine whether the first of the objects, `elem1`, implied by its two generic pointer arguments should be considered less than, equal to, or greater than the second argument, `elem2`, by returning a negative, 0, or positive value, respectively.

To illustrate a benign use of callbacks, consider the simple problem of sorting a collection of Cartesian points based on their relative distances from the origin of a two-dimensional coordinate system. Figure 5-59a depicts an instance of this problem containing six points labeled *a* through *f*. The definition of a `Point` is given in Figure 5-59b.

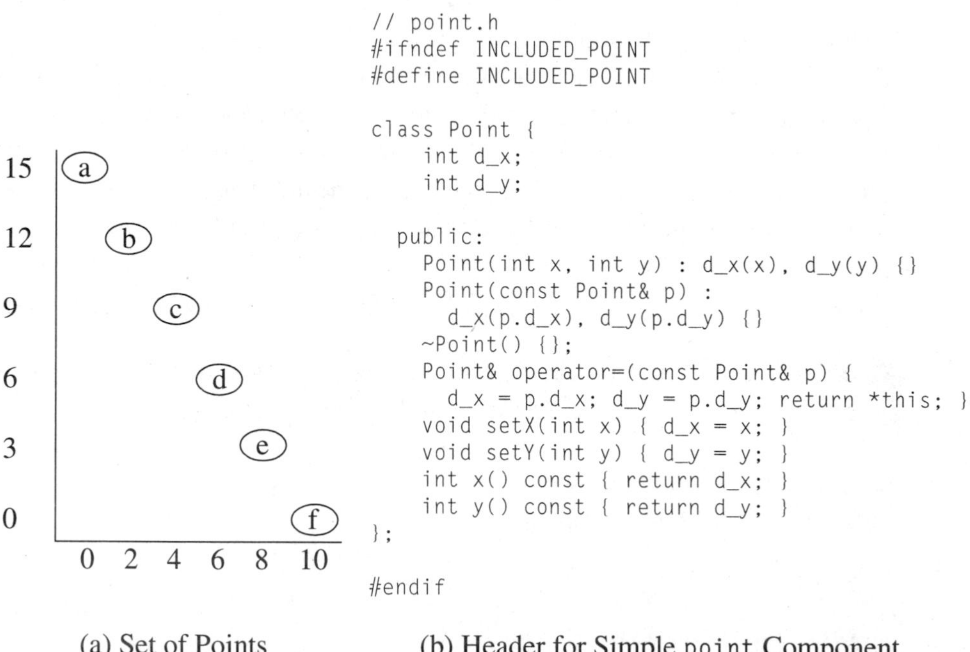


```
// point.h
#ifndef INCLUDED_POINT
#define INCLUDED_POINT

class Point {
    int d_x;
    int d_y;

  public:
    Point(int x, int y) : d_x(x), d_y(y) {}
    Point(const Point& p) :
      d_x(p.d_x), d_y(p.d_y) {}
    ~Point() {};
    Point& operator=(const Point& p) {
      d_x = p.d_x; d_y = p.d_y; return *this; }
    void setX(int x) { d_x = x; }
    void setY(int y) { d_y = y; }
    int x() const { return d_x; }
    int y() const { return d_y; }
};

#endif
```

(a) Set of Points

(b) Header for Simple `point` Component

Figure 5-59: Using Function `qsort` to Sort a Collection of `Point` Objects

The `qsort` function rearranges entries by blindly swapping one region of memory of the specified element size with another, based solely on the value returned from the callback function. The bitwise copy is performed using a function such as the C Library function `memcpy`.

In general, copying objects to new locations using `memcpy` is dangerous (see Section 10.4.2), because an object may contain a pointer or reference to itself or to other objects which it is responsible for deleting. On the other hand, it is always safe to copy and move pointers to objects using `memcpy`. Suppose we create an array of six pointers to `Point` objects and in it store the addresses of six `Point` objects representing the points in Figure 5-59a.

```
static Point a(0,15), b(2,12), c(4,9), d(6,6), e(8,3), f(10,0);
static Point *array[6] = { &a, &b, &c, &d, &e, &f };
```

In order to use `qsort`, we will need to give `qsort` a way to compare two opaque entries so it can determine their relative order. That is, given the addresses of a pair of pointers to points (of type `const void *`), we need a way of determining whether the distance from the origin to the `Point` indicated by the first memory address is less than, equal to, or greater than that of the `Point` indicated by the second address. An imperfect implementation of this callback function that suits our immediate needs is given in Figure 5-60.[13]

```
static int pointCompare (const void *addrPoint1Ptr,
                         const void *addrPoint2Ptr)
{
    // poor implementation
    const Point &p1 = **(const Point **) addrPoint1Ptr;
    const Point &p2 = **(const Point **) addrPoint2Ptr;
    int d1sq = p1.x() * p1.x() + p1.y() * p1.y(); // bad idea (overflow?)
    int d2sq = p2.x() * p2.x() + p2.y() * p2.y(); // bad idea (overflow?)
    return d2sq - d1sq;
}
```

Figure 5-60: Implementation of Callback Function Comparing Two `Point` Objects

[13] A better implementation in practice would be to use a `double` for the intermediate calculations, in order to avoid overflow. This solution is implementation dependent, and may fail on two points that are placed nearly the same (large) distance from the origin. A robust but less runtime-efficient solution would be to make use of a user-defined type (e.g., `DoubleInt`) that is guaranteed to hold at least twice as many bits as an `int`.

Programmed with the data indicating the starting location, number of entries, size of each entry, and a callback function that determines the ordinal positions of two entries in context, we can reuse this modular implementation of the Quicksort algorithm to solve our problem as shown in Figure 5-61.

```
// point.t.c
#include "point.h"
#include <stdlib.h> // qsort()
#include <iostream.h>

static int pointCompare (const void *addrPoint1Ptr,
                         const void *addrPoint2Ptr)
{
    // better (more practical) implementation
    const Point &p1 = **(const Point **) addrPoint1Ptr;
    const Point &p2 = **(const Point **) addrPoint2Ptr;
    double d1sq = p1.x() * (double) p1.x() + p1.y() * (double) p1.y();
    double d2sq = p2.x() * (double) p2.x() + p2.y() * (double) p2.y();
    return d1sq < d2sq ? -1 : d1sq > d2sq; // Warning: may fail on
                                           // points far from origin.
}

static ostream& operator<<(ostream& o, const Point& p)
{
    return o << '(' << p.x() << ',' << p.y() << ')';
}

static ostream& print(ostream& o, const Point *const *array, int size)
{
    o << '{';
    for (int i = 0; i < size; ++i) {
        o << ' ' << *array[i];
    }
    return o << " }";
}

const int SIZE = 6;

static Point a(0,15), b(2,12), c(4,9), d(6,6), e(8,3), f(10,0);

static Point *array[SIZE] = { &a, &b, &c, &d, &e, &f };

main()
{
    print(cout, array, SIZE) << endl;
    cout << "Now sort by distance from origin:" << endl;
    qsort(array, SIZE, sizeof *array, pointCompare);
    print(cout, array, SIZE) << endl;
}
```

Figure 5-61: Using a Callback to Program `qsort` **Comparison Behavior**

Realize that qsort was developed, tested, and reused many, many times, long before the Point class or this example was written. Most of the work done by the Quicksort algorithm is reusable. Only one behavior, compare, varies from one usage to the next. Supplying a callback is what enables us to factor and reuse this functionality.

Principle

The indiscriminate use of callbacks can lead to designs that are difficult to understand, debug, and maintain.

The lack of type safety in the interface of qsort is glaring. But because qsort is a stateless algorithm with a single programmable behavior, the need for a generic sorter object is controvertible. There is, however, an implied data structure. If we have reason to maintain a variety of ordered Point collections, sorted according to various comparison routines, then creating an abstract OrderedPointCollection base class (see Figure 5-62) with a corresponding iterator would prove generally useful. Doing so would also catch most type errors at compile time.

```
class OrderedPointCollection {
    // ...
  public:
    // CREATORS
    OrderedPointCollection();
    virtual ~OrderedPointCollection();

    // MANIPULATORS
    void add(Point *point);

    // ACCESSORS
    virtual compare(const Point& point1, const Point& point2) = 0;
};
```

Figure 5-62: Abstract Base Class for an Arbitrarily Ordered Point Collection

Specifying the comparison function is accomplished by deriving a simple struct:

```
struct MyPoints : OrderedPointCollection {
    compare(const Point& point, const Point& point);
    ~MyPoints(); // empty -- (see Section 9.3.3)
};
```

We can now override the comparison function in a type-safe manner as follows:

```
int MyPoints::compare(const Point& p1, const Point& p2)
{
    // better (more robust) implementation
    DoubleInt p1x = p1.x();                          // DoubleInt is a type
    DoubleInt p1y = p1.y();                          // that is at least
    DoubleInt p2x = p2.x();                          // twice as big as int.
    DoubleInt p2y = p2.y();
    DoubleInt d1sq = p1x * p1x + p1y * p1y;          // robust but slow
    DoubleInt d2sq = p2x * p2x + p2y * p2y;          // robust but slow
    return d1sq < d2sq ? -1 : d1sq > d2sq;           // robust but slow
}
```

The levelization of this system is shown in Figure 5-63. Notice that the class `OrderedPointCollection` depends on `Point` in name only, but `MyPoints::compare` depends on `Point` in size. The virtual function is acting as a "callback" because the comparison operation must be performed in the context of the `Point`'s actual definition. Unlike the callback function taking two generic pointers, the virtual function expects `const` references to `Point` objects. This in-name-only dependency of `OrderedPointCollection` on `Point` provides a welcome degree of type safety, improving maintainability while making the component easier to use.

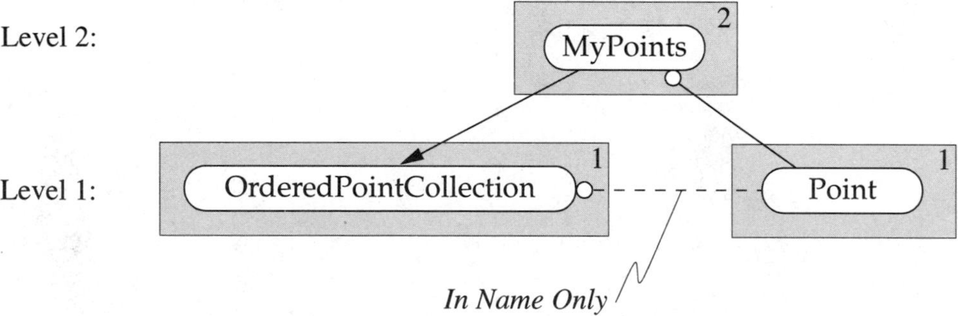

Figure 5-63: Using a Virtual Function as a Callback to Enable Factoring

Callbacks are powerful decoupling tools, but they should be used only if necessary. A mutual dependency generated by a pair of classes that call each other's member functions is a symptom of a poor design. Callbacks can sometimes be used to break the cycle, but usually this problem is better handled by repackaging the functionality.

Consider again the original, poorly factored, runtime database architecture shown in Figure 5-27. If the `read` function of each parser implements a stateless algorithm, we could conceivably pass the parsing function to the `RuntimeDB` as a callback:

```
RuntimeDB::Status RuntimeDB::read(
                    RuntimeDB::Status(*parseFunc)(const char *),
                    const char *filename);
```

However, the resulting obfuscation would probably be unjustifiable. Unlike the previous example where `OrderedPointCollection` did not depend in size on `Point`, each concrete parser would have to know all about the database in order to load it. If parsing involves state and/or a multifunction interface, the standard object-oriented approach would be to create an abstract parser base class and to derive concrete parsers for use with specific formats, as illustrated in Figure 5-64.

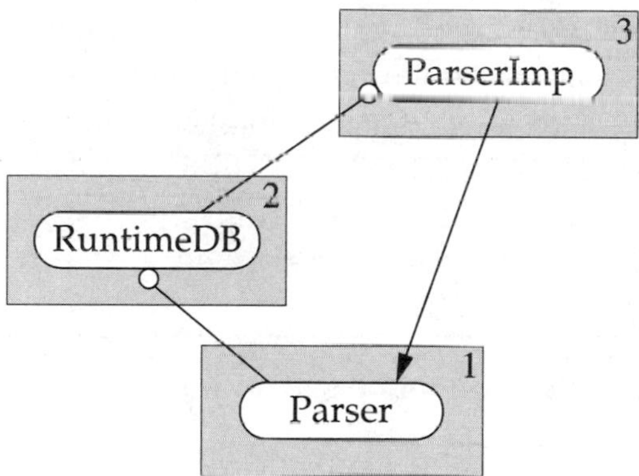

Figure 5-64: Demoting the Interface to Implement a Callback

This alternative revised architecture is better than the parser design as first presented in Section 5.3, because there is no physical coupling among individual parsers, nor is there a dependency of any processor on any parser implementation. However, this architecture is not optimal because it forces the runtime database to know about the interface common to all parsers:

```
#include "parser.h"

RuntimeDB::Status RuntimeDB::read(Parser *parser, const char *filename)
{
    parser->read(this, filename);     // virtual function call
}
```

The runtime database may be reused by other systems that have no need for parsers. Coupling the runtime database to a specific parser interface unnecessarily encumbers the subsystem, making it less general, less understandable, and less appealing to reuse. This unnecessary coupling could also adversely affect the maintainability of the runtime database if the kind of information needed during parsing is frequently updated.

The best design for this system was the revised architecture presented in Figure 5-29 of Section 5.3, which placed the database at the bottom of the system hierarchy with absolutely no dependency on parsers. That architecture allowed the database group to develop and test its subsystem in complete isolation, rather than being sandwiched between the interface and the implementation supplied by the group developing parsers. The moral of this story is that the unnecessary use of callbacks is something to be avoided.

Callbacks can also be installed statically (i.e., outside of any instance). The `new` handler[14] is an example of a static callback function with reasonable initial behavior. Clients can substitute their own function for the default in order to allow them to clean up their application in a higher-level context.

Principle

The need for callbacks can be a symptom of a poor overall architecture.

Sometimes, however, static callbacks can be used to great advantage to eliminate dependencies on large subsystems. Consider the subsystems shown in Figure 5-65, where we need to implement a heterogeneous list of planets—that is, a list of objects that are related to the base class `Planet` via inheritance. Since the list is polymorphic, each link cannot *have* a `Planet` but must instead *hold* (the address of) a `Planet`. The actual `Planet` object is allocated dynamically by the client and handed over to the list, which assumes ownership of the `Planet`'s memory from then on. When the `PlanetList` is destroyed, so are all of the `Planet` objects it contains.

---

[14] **stroustrup**, Section 9.4.3, pp. 312–314.

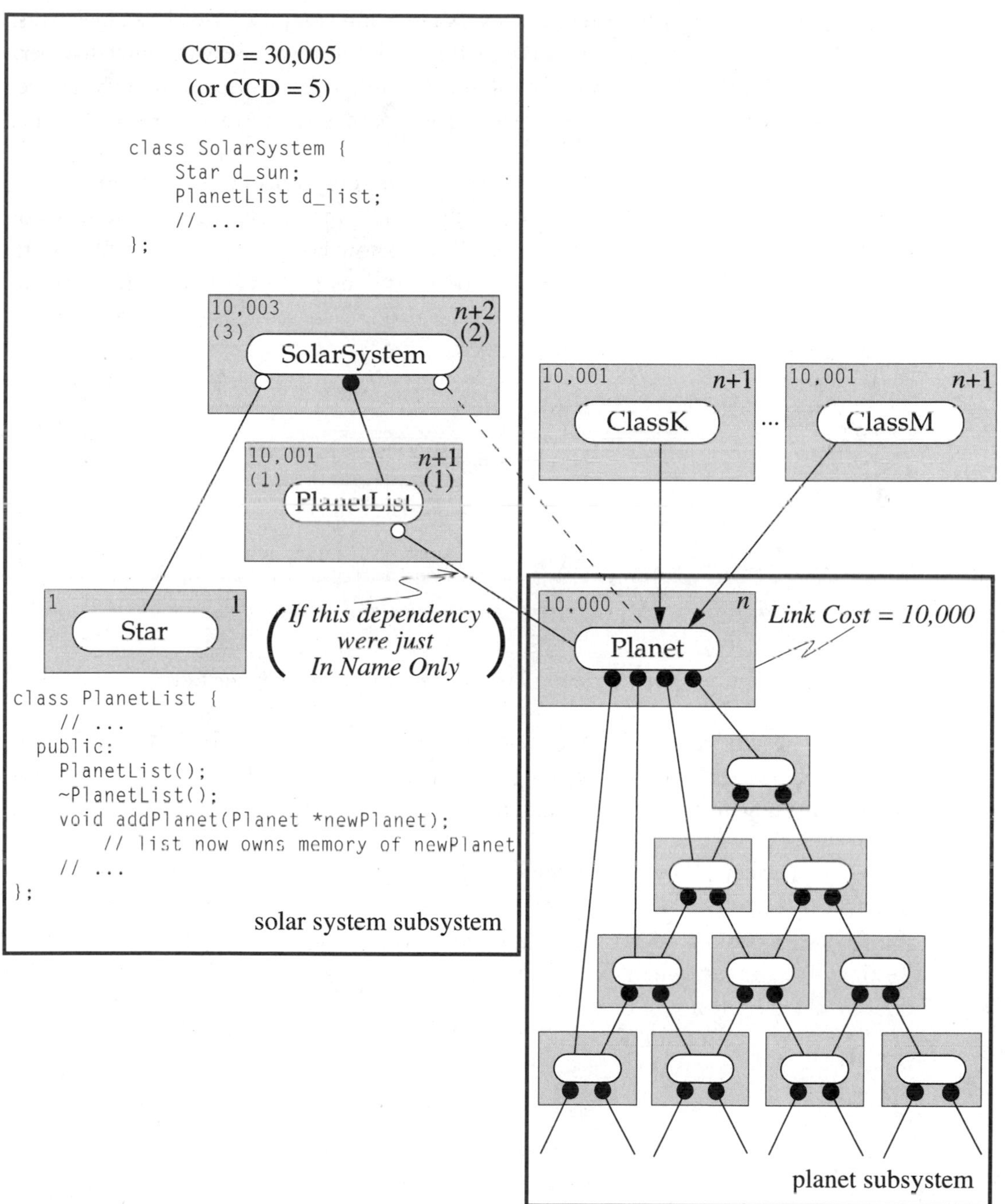

Figure 5-65: A BIG Problem

As you might well imagine, `Planet` is a very large and complex base class object with many dependencies and a correspondingly high link-time cost. We would like to avoid a physical link-time dependency of `Planetlist` on `Planet`, especially in this (admittedly unusual) case where `SolarSystem` otherwise depends on `Planet` in name only.

We could try to implement the `PlanetList` using only opaque pointers to `Planet` objects. The problem with that approach is that our `PlanetList` will not have seen the definition of class `Planet` and therefore will not know how to destroy one. We could change the specification of `PlanetList` so that it does not itself destroy the planets, and escalate that functionality to a higher level (e.g., `SolarSystem`) as suggested in Figure 5-66.

```
class SolarSystem {
    Star *d_sun_p;
    PlanetList d_list;
    static void destroyPlanets(PlanetList *list);
    // ...
  public:
    // ...
    ~SolarSystem() { destroyPlanets(&d_List); }
    // ...
};
```

Figure 5-66: Escalating Planet Destruction to a Higher Level

But in our example, even `SolarSystem` uses `Planet` in name only. Since the use of the `PlanetList` type is an encapsulated implementation detail of `SolarSystem`, it is not obvious how to escalate this functionality any higher.

With complete control over the entire subsystem, a good solution could be to demote the interface of `Planet`, as shown in Figure 5-67. Now `Planet` is just an interface, and all of the physical coupling is elevated to a higher level that does not affect `SolarSystem`. Testing `PlanetList` will now require deriving a trivial "stub" implementation for `Planet` in the `PlanetList` driver.

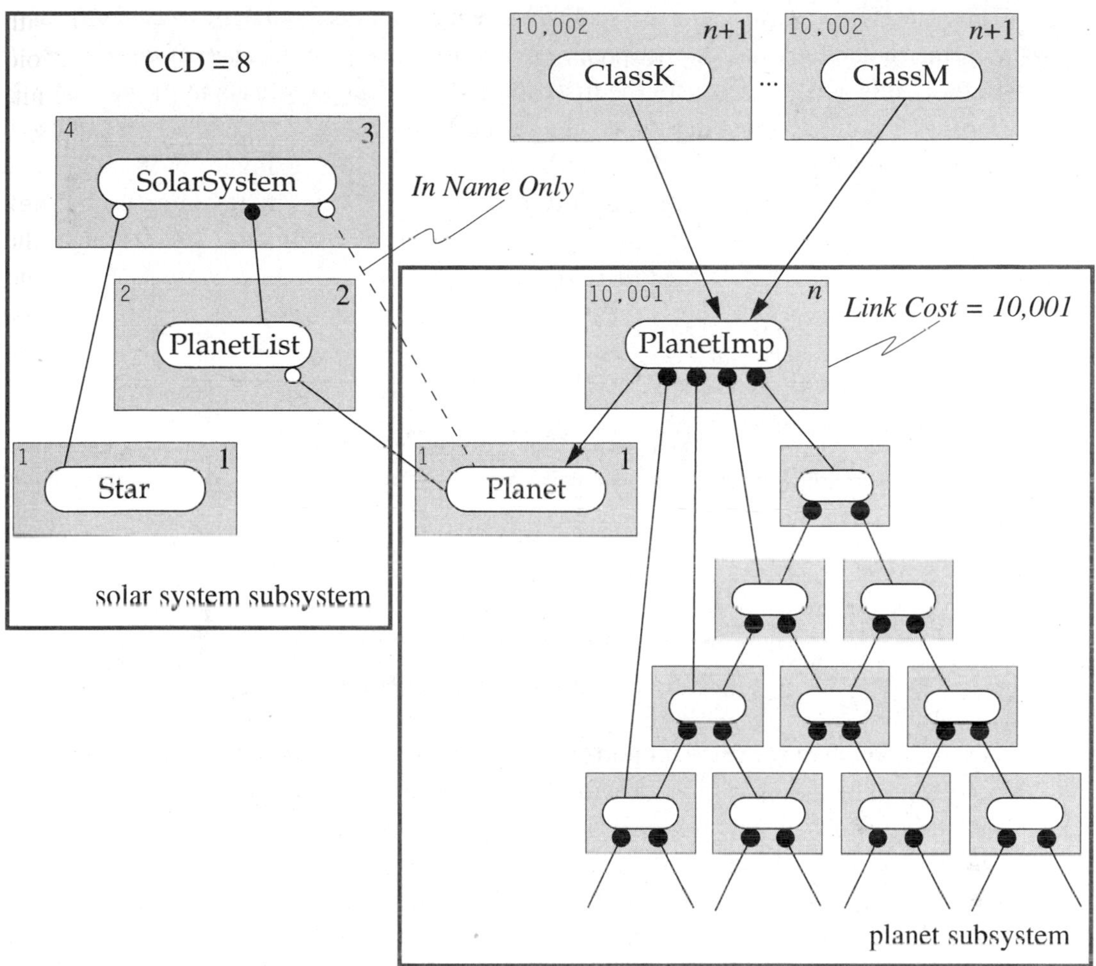

Figure 5-67: Demoting `Planet`'s Interface to a Lower Level

Unfortunately, we don't control the universe and must live with a poorly factored `Planet`. We can still break the physical dependency but it will require the use of a redundant callback function. Suppose we add a static member to class `PlanetList` of the following type:

```
typedef void DestroyPlanetFunc(Planet *);
```

The PlanetList class now has a static data member that is a pointer to a callback function that potentially has the necessary context to destroy an instance of class Planet. Before using a PlanetList for the first time, a client (who knows about Planet) should "prime" the class by calling the static method PlanetList::setDestroyPlanetFunc with the address of a suitably defined function as shown in Figure 5-68. When the PlanetList is destroyed, it can then call the destroyPlanet function on each planet that it owns.

```
// client.c
#include "client.h"
#include "planet.h"
#include "planetlist.h"
// ...
static void destroyPlanet(Planet *p) { delete p; }
// ...
Client::init()
{
    PlanetList::setDestroyPlanetFunc(&::destroyPlanet);
    // ...
};
// ...
```

Figure 5-68: Installing a Redundant Callback

A rough sketch of the relevant portions of the planetlist component is given in Figure 5-69. Class PlanetList provides a mechanism for a client at a higher level to install the callback function to destroy a Planet. When a PlanetList is destroyed, the destructor checks to see if a destroy function has been installed, and if so applies it to each Planet in the list in turn. If no callback function has been installed by the time the PlanetList is destroyed, the contained Planet objects are not destroyed and the dynamic memory associated with each Planet is "leaked." (Memory leaks are discussed in Section 10.3.5).

```
// planetlist.h
// ...
class PlanetListIter;
class PlanetList {
    // ...
    friend PlanetListIter;
  public:
    typedef void DestroyPlanetFunc(Planet *);
  private:
    static DestroyPlanetFunc *d_destroyPlanetFunc_p;
  public:
    static void setDestroyPlanetFunc(DestroyPlanetFunc *func);
    // ...
    ~PlanetList ();
    // ...
};
// ...
class PlanetListIter {
    // ...
  public:
    PlanetListIter(const PlanetList &list);
    ~PlanetListIter();
    void operator++();
    operator const void *() const;
    const Planet& operator()() const;
};
// ...
```

```
// planetlist.c
#include "planetlist.h"

PlanetList::DestroyPlanetFunc *PlanetList::d_destroyPlanetFunc_p = 0;

void PlanetList::setDestroyPlanetFunc(DestroyPlanetFunc *func)
{
    d_destroyPlanetFunction_p = func;
}

void PlanetList::~PlanetList()
{
    if (d_destroyPlanetList_p) {
        for (PlanetListIter it(*this); it; ++it) {
            (*d_destroyPlanetList_p)(it());
        }
    }
    else {
        // memory leak!
    }
}
```

Figure 5-69: Using Callbacks to Enable Independent Testing

Using callbacks in this way is not the least bit elegant. Using `PlanetList` requires knowing about low-level details with which a client should not be bothered. This approach is not recommended for public interfaces, as it can be assumed that people will forget to initialize the container class before they use it. To make matters a bit worse, `PlanetList` is not in the public interface of `SolarSystem`. It will therefore be necessary for `SolarSystem` to provide a static member such as

```
class SolarSystem {
    // ...
  public:
    static void init(void (*)(Planet *));
    // ...
};
```

that must then forward the initialization call to the `PlanetList` class.

To summarize the results of this section, a callback is a function that is supplied by a client to allow a (usually) lower-level component to take advantage of a behavior that requires a (usually) higher-level context. Virtual functions can be used to implement a type-safe callback mechanism. Callbacks are a powerful tool for breaking dependencies between cooperating classes. Callbacks are extremely important for graphics and event-based programming.

Used inappropriately, callbacks can blur the responsibility of low-level objects and result in unnecessary conceptual coupling. In general, callbacks (like recursion) can be more difficult to understand, maintain, and debug than conventional function calls. Their (pseudo) asynchronous behavior requires a different type of attention from developers. As a rule, callbacks should be treated as a refuge of last resort.

5.8 Manager Class

In the name of minimizing complexity and effort, it is easy to become too frugal with classes. Trying to implement an integer list with only a single class is a good illustration of this common mistake. One might suggest, as in Figure 5-70a, that a list could be just a pointer to a `Link` or, as in Figure 5-70b, that the link operations could be merged with the methods associated with the List itself.

The problem with approach (a) is that the level of abstraction is too low for an application to use effectively. Approach (b) fails to encapsulate private implementation details of `List`. Clients of a list abstraction will not want to be bothered with the low-level details of managing the memory of the individual links, or with ensuring that the low-level policies of a list implementation are enforced.

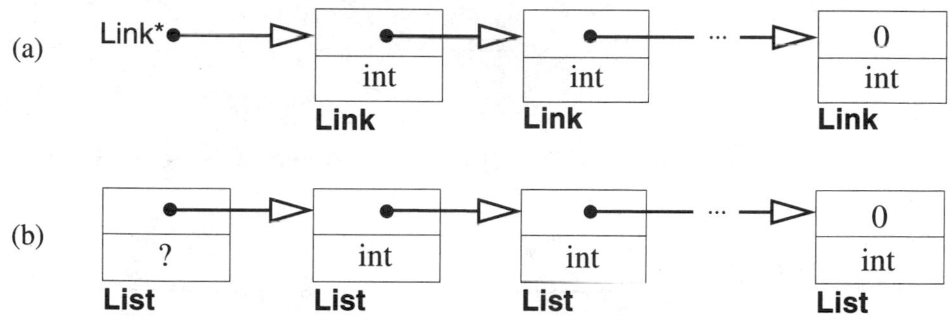

Figure 5-70: How Not to Implement a `list` Component

Even in a two-class list architecture, the role of the subordinate class can be abused. Normally, a list object itself destroys each of its links directly, but as shown in Figure 5-71, the destructor for this `List` deletes only the head `Link`. Each `Link`, in turn, recursively deletes its `d_next_p` pointer. This "elegant" approach (apart from being slower and running the risk of overflowing the program stack for long lists) makes it less clear which object owns which, primarily because instances of the same type are authorized to destroy one another. A better, more hierarchically structured way for the `List` class to clean up when it is destroyed is to traverse the list of `Link` objects and to delete each `Link` in turn, as shown in Figure 5-72.

```
class List {
    Link *d_head_p;

  public:
    // ...
    ~List() { delete d_head_p; }
              // bad idea
    // ...
```

```
class Link {
    Link *d_next_p;
    int d_data;
  public:
    // ...
    ~Link() { delete d_next_p; }
              // bad idea
    // ...
```

Figure 5-71: `List` with `Link` that Recursively Deletes the Next `Link`

```
List::~List()
{
    while (d_head_p) {
        Link *p = d_head_p;
        d_head_p = d_head_p->next();
        delete p;
    }
}
```

Figure 5-72: `List` **with Destructor that Iteratively Deletes Each** `Link`

Principle

Establishing hierarchical ownership of lower-level objects makes a system easier to understand and more maintainable.

Again the corporation analogy pertains. Regular employees do not hire and fire each other; that job is reserved for managers. The intrinsic problem is in not distinguishing between the classes used to implement an abstraction and the manager class used to enforce policy, manage memory, and coordinate the implementation classes. Note that the manager class knows about its subordinate classes, but not vice versa.

All too often the cyclic interconnection among instances of classes seems to suggest that this cyclic nature should be reflected in the physical design of a system. For small cyclicly dependent networks of objects that are inherently tightly coupled and whose definitions fit easily within a single component, there may be no reason to eliminate such cycles. That is, if it makes sense from a standpoint of usability and reuse to present two or more cohesive logical units in a single physical unit, and the functional complexity of the combined implementation does not pose an obstacle to effective testing, then there may be no problem that requires solving. On the other hand, the coupling may also be the result of not knowing how to avoid the interdependencies, or of not even having considered the issue in the first place.

As another example where the concept of a manager class proves useful, consider a simple graph consisting of nodes and edges. A graph is among the most basic of heterogeneous class networks; yet a node could be as complex as a workstation on a local area network (LAN), or a planet in a solar system. In other words, the size and complexity of the graph-independent portion of the node and/or edge might be very large compared to its network-related aspects. It is in these cases that there is considerable motivation to decouple nodes from edges.

Let us start with the situation suggested by Figure 5-10. We can illustrate the principles related to achieving a levelizable interconnected network of heterogeneous objects by attempting to develop a simple graph with the premise that `Node` and `Edge` are complex and should belong to distinct physical components.

A known effective technique for avoiding cyclic physical dependencies is to make all pointers and references to higher-level components be in name only. Perhaps we can concoct a levelizable subsystem in which `edge` dominates `node`. Our strategy will be to have `Node` hold a collection of opaque `Edge` pointers, as illustrated in Figure 5-73. Taking this approach means that all substantive questions that involve edges cannot be answered at the `node` level.

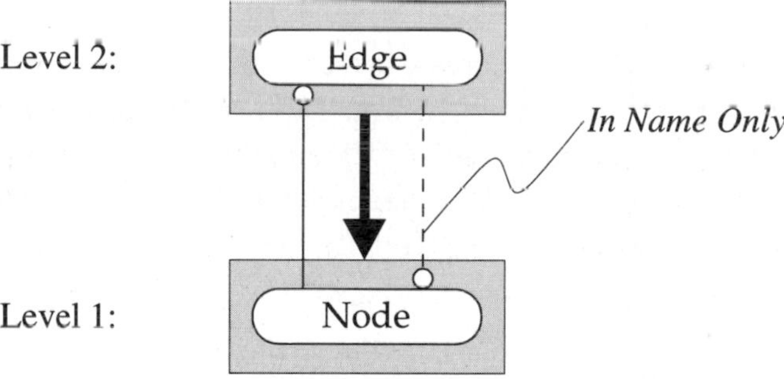

Figure 5-73: `Node` **Uses** `Edge` **In Name Only**

In the process of trying to test component `node` independently, we immediately realize some problems (refer to Figure 5-74). First, clients must not add `Edge` pointers to a `Node` directly. Otherwise the `Node` object would know about the newly added `Edge` but the Edge object would remain ignorant of its new connection to a `Node`, leaving the system in an inconsistent state. Therefore, only `Edge` objects are allowed to add an `Edge` pointer to a `Node`, but there is no way to enforce this policy with `Node` and `Edge` defined in separate components (see Section 3.6.2).

Second, testing `Node` requires creating a dummy `Edge` class in order to gain access to the private `addEdge` function—that is, we are not able to test `Node` from its intended public interface alone.

```
class Node {
    //...
    friend Edge;                    // long-distance friend
    void addEdge(Edge *edge);       // private, set only by edge
    Node(const Node&);
    Node& operator=(const Node&);

  public:
    Node(const char *name);         // Who owns the memory for nodes?
    ~Node();                        // Who is allowed to destroy them?
    const char *name() const;
    int numEdges() const;
    Edge& edge(int index) const;    // Reference hampers testing slightly
};                                  // since Edge is used in name only.
```

Figure 5-74: Problems Associated with Original Graph Design

Third, the `Node`'s `edge` function is correctly designed (from the end-user perspective) to return references and not pointers. A reference (even an opaque one), unlike a pointer, must identify the address of a valid object and therefore cannot (portably) be null or refer to an illegal address. So if we ask for an `Edge` of a newly created `Node` (which has no edges) we are in trouble. Incrementally testing `Node`'s public `edge` function at the `node` component's level requires not only creating a dummy `Edge` class to gain access to the private `addEdge` function of `Node`, but also adding actual instances of this bogus `Edge` class so that their (valid) addresses can be compared later against the lvalues returned by `edge(int)`.

Finally, it is not clear who owns the memory for `Node` instances or who is allowed to create and destroy them. For example, what happens if we try to destroy a `Node` before we have removed all of its edges? The answer is that nothing unusual happens—at least not right away. Since `Node` does not know about `Edge`, it does not know how to destroy one. Using an `Edge` to access a deleted `Node` will, of course, result in unpredictable behavior. We could pass a callback function to `Node` that knows how to delete an `Edge`, but then we must ensure that `Edge` objects are created only on the heap.

At this point our design has run out of steam. As often happens in practice, we need to step back and look at the abstraction we are trying to implement, namely a graph. Just as with `rectangle` and `window`, neither `node` nor `edge` inherently dominates the other. There is a mutual dependency involving ownership, which we need to escalate to a higher level of the system.

Figure 5-75 shows the basic architecture of the new design that will serve as a sound starting point. Class `Graph` will be responsible for managing the memory associated with instances of both `Edge` and `Node`. Nodes and edges will be added to the graph through `Graph`'s interface, as opposed to creating them independently. When a `Node` is deleted from the graph, `Graph` itself will ensure that all `Edge` objects attached to that `Node` will be deleted first. This basic design still suffers from the problem that both `Node` and `Edge` must declare `Graph` to be a `friend`. Otherwise unruly clients could, for example, add an `Edge` to a `Node` unbeknownst to either the `Edge` or the `Graph`, causing the graph subsystem to become internally inconsistent. Since we want `Node` and `Edge` to be defined in separate components, we are still not satisfied.

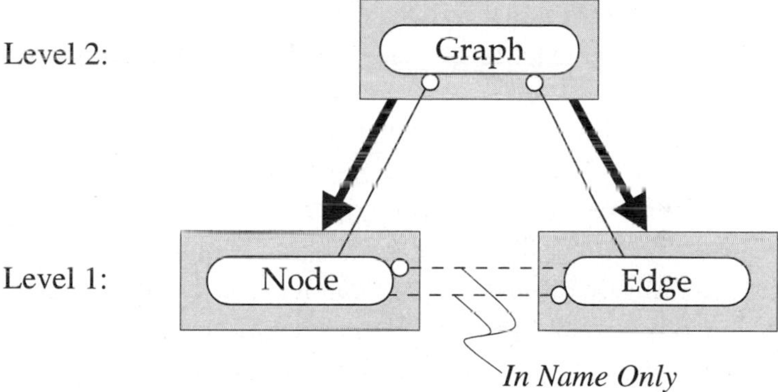

Figure 5-75: Basic Architecture of Graph Subsystem

For a simple graph, it may be entirely reasonable to place all three classes within a single component. But because our goal here is to use the graph to illustrate how to implement much more complex networks, we will not take that approach. There are (at least) two other ways to address this problem:

1. Factor out as much code as possible from the coupled system into independent components, and place the remaining, mutually dependent classes in a single component.

2. Escalate the level at which encapsulation for the entire subsystem occurs to eliminate the need for low-level friendships.

Each of these techniques is discussed in detail in the following two sections.

In summary: establishing clear ownership of cooperating objects is essential to good design. If two or more objects share mutual ownership, that functionality should be escalated to a manager class.

5.9 Factoring

Factoring means extracting pockets of cohesive functionality and moving them to a lower level where they can be independently tested and reused. Factoring is a very general and highly effective technique for reducing the burden imposed by cyclicly dependent classes. Factoring is similar to demotion except that the act of factoring does not necessarily eliminate any cycles; instead it merely reduces the amount of functionality that participates in the cycle. Factoring has the effect of escalating cyclic dependencies to a higher level where their adverse effects are less pronounced.

To demonstrate the use of factoring, suppose we are given a design consisting of three intrinsically interdependent classes `A`, `B`, and `C`, as illustrated in Figure 5-76a. Suppose further that the original logical interface is cast in stone and may not be modified. More than likely, not all of the functionality implemented in these three classes is inseparably coupled to the rest. We can use the technique of factoring to extract any independently testable implementation complexity, and thus reduce the burden of maintaining the truly cyclicly dependent portion of the code. As illustrated in Figure 5-76b, if we are successful in factoring a significant amount of the implementation into independent components, the remaining interdependent code may be small enough to justify placing it into a single component.

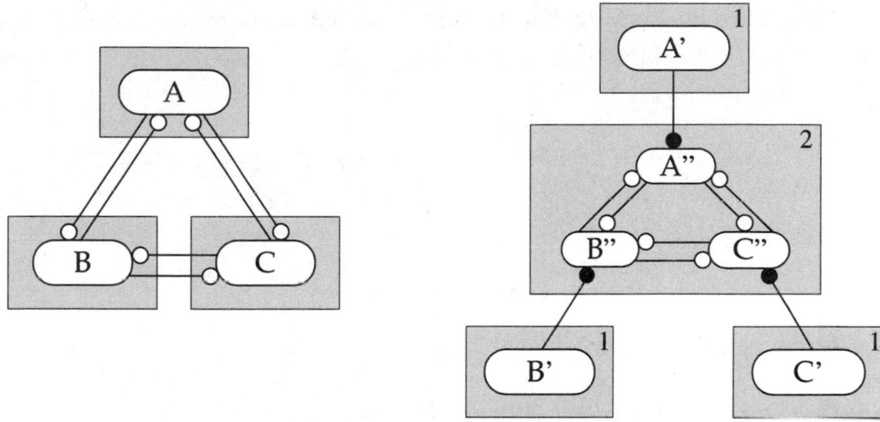

(a) Original, Unlevelizable Design (b) Factored, Levelizable Design

Figure 5-76: Factoring Out Independently Testable Implementation Details

Principle

Factoring out and demoting independently testable implementation details can reduce the cost of maintaining a collection of cyclicly dependent classes.

Fortunately, our graph example is less extreme than the hypothetical case above. We have some flexibility in our logical design, and it will turn out that the implied physical dependencies are not as severe as the hypothetical ones we are postulating. For now, let us continue to assume the worst—that is, that our initial graph subsystem is a design consisting of three intrinsically, mutually dependent classes:

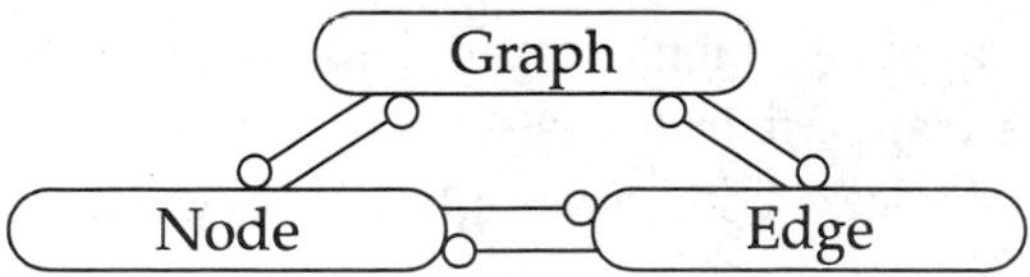

The first place to employ factoring is to separate the part of `Node` that holds graph-related data from the part of `Node` that holds graph-independent data. Inheritance is ideal for this kind of factoring. We can do the same for `Edge`. The basic idea is shown in Figure 5-77.

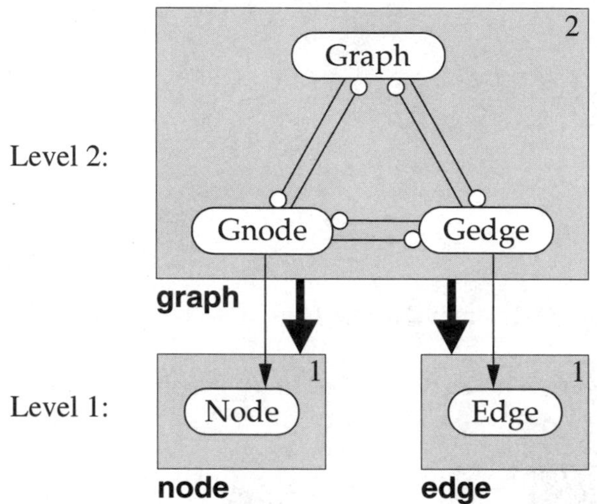

Figure 5-77: Factoring Out Network-Independent Data

In this new design, all of the tightly coupled, graph-related functionality lives in a single component, implemented using the three classes `Graph`, `Gnode`, and `Gedge`. The graph-independent data contained in `Node` and `Edge` is now pushed down to a lower level, and can be shared with other applications that are not concerned with the graph-related functionality.

Figure 5-78 illustrates the factored, network-independent portions of node and edge. In this trivial illustration a `Node` is nothing more than a name, and an `Edge` is just a `double`. But suppose for a minute that the nodes in the graph are actually cities and the edges are roads. The network component of a city, implicit in `Gnode`, is not necessary to perform many complex operations on a `Node` itself. A `Gnode` is just a special kind of `Node` that participates in `Graph` operations. Once an instance of `Gnode` has been obtained from `Graph`, it can be used anywhere in which a `Node` is required, as illustrated in Figure 5-79.

```
// node.h
#ifndef INCLUDED_NODE
#define INCLUDED_NODE

class Node {
    char *d_name_p;

  public:
    Node(const char *name);
    Node(const Node&);
    ~Node();
    Node& operator=(const Node&);
    const char *name() const;
};

#endif
```

(a) Independent node Component

```
// edge.h
#ifndef INCLUDED_EDGE
#define INCLUDED_EDGE

class Edge {
    double d_weight;

  public:
    Edge(double weight);
    Edge(const Edge&);
    ~Edge();
    Edge& operator=(const Edge&);
    double weight() const;
};

#endif
```

(b) Independent edge Component

Figure 5-78: Factored Network-Independent node and edge Components

```
class Node;
class ostream;

class Census {
    static int countPeople (const Node& node)
        // ...
};

#include "graph.h"
int g(const Gnode& gnode)
{
    return Census::countPeople(gnode); // uses only the Node portion
}
```

Figure 5-79: Reusing the Network-Independent Portion of a Node

Another advantage in factoring nodes and edges involves a concept called *value semantics*. Saying that a type has *value semantics* means that a copy constructor and (usually) an assignment operator are inherently (i.e., semantically) valid operations for a type.[15]

[15] Sometimes we choose not to implement a copy constructor (e.g., for an iterator) even when the operation could make sense. However, the abstraction itself has value semantics.

For example, consider a condominium complex that contains a fixed amount of land on which to build single-family homes. The land is divided into 25 lots, arranged in a 5-by-5 grid. The rows of lots are labeled A to E, and the columns are labeled 1 to 5 as shown in Figure 5-80.

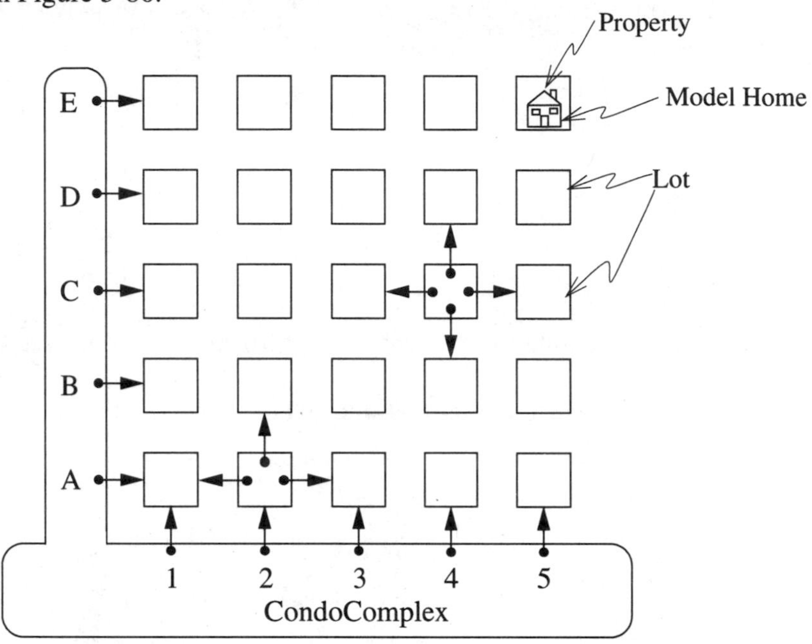

Figure 5-80: Array of 25 Lots in our `CondoComplex` Example

Each `Lot` is a separate object that maintains its own list of adjacent lots and is managed by the `CondoComplex` object. For example, `Lot` A2 holds pointers to `Lot` objects A1, B2, and A3. A `House` has value semantics because copy construction makes sense for a `House`. In other words, it makes sense to copy a `House` from `Lot` to `Lot`—that is, all houses could look exactly the same.

Suppose now that a `Property` consists of both the `House` and the `Lot` on which it sits, and that the `CondoComplex` object manages an array of `Property` objects instead of `Lot` objects. Does a `Property` also have value semantics? The answer is no, because we cannot copy one lot to another.

If we tried to assign the `Property` with `Lot` location A2 to the `Property` with `Lot` location C4, we would clobber the adjacency list associated with `Lot` C4 and invalidate the larger `CondoComplex` object. We therefore cannot make arbitrary independent copies of a Property the way we can for a House. A Property therefore does *not* have value semantics.

Although the network portion of a node (defined by Gnode) does not have value semantics, the part that is defined by Node probably does. In C++ terms, this means that the copy constructor and assignment operator of both Gnode and Gedge would necessarily be disabled (i.e., declared private), but Node and Edge could each define meaningful copy constructors and assignment operators, as shown in Figure 5-81. (The complete interface for graph is given in Figure 5-86.)

```
void f(const Graph& g)
{
    const Gnode& a = g.node("Zurich");// fine - lvalue returned
    Gnode b = g.node("London");        // error - no value semantics
    Node& c = g.node("Paris");         // fine - modifiable lvalue returned
    Node d = g.node("Tokyo");          // fine - value semantics
    a = b;                             // error - no value semantics
    c = d;                             // fine - make Tokyo look like Paris
}
```

Figure 5-81: Illustrating Value Semantics in a Graph

Principle

Where unavoidable, escalating cyclic physical dependencies to the highest possible level reduces CCD and may even enable the cycle to be replaced by a single component of manageable size.

Our second opportunity to factor comes from the observation that, in order to manage Node and Edge objects properly, Graph will need to keep track of the Gnodes an Gedge objects it allocates so that when it is destroyed, all of the memory associated with the nodes and edges of this graph can be recovered. Moreover, each Gnode will also have to keep track of the Gedge objects adjacent to it (in name only). We have the opportunity to factor out all of this functionality from the graph component classes by creating a collection of opaque pointers.

A *bag* is a kind of container that, unlike a list, does not impose an order on its elements nor, unlike a set, does it require elements to be unique. Because the semantics of a bag are not heavily specified, its implementation is left quite flexible. A `Graph` will maintain a bag of `Node` pointers and a bag of `Edge` pointers. Whether or not we have an efficient template implementation, we will want to factor this problem further by creating a bag of (generic) pointers.

Figure 5-82 shows our factored implementation of a generic bag of pointers and specialized components that take advantage of this generic container to implement bags of pointers of a specific type. We can use either layering or private inheritance to achieve the desired specialization and restore the type safety of the individual opaque pointers. Templates would be ideal, but some implementations can be very costly in terms of link time (as discussed in Section 10.4.1). For purely pragmatic reasons we may be forced to express the specialized types explicitly. Whatever the implementation, all of the function arguments are forwarded to the generic `PtrBag` class via `inline` functions in order to avoid incurring any additional overhead due to conventional function calls.

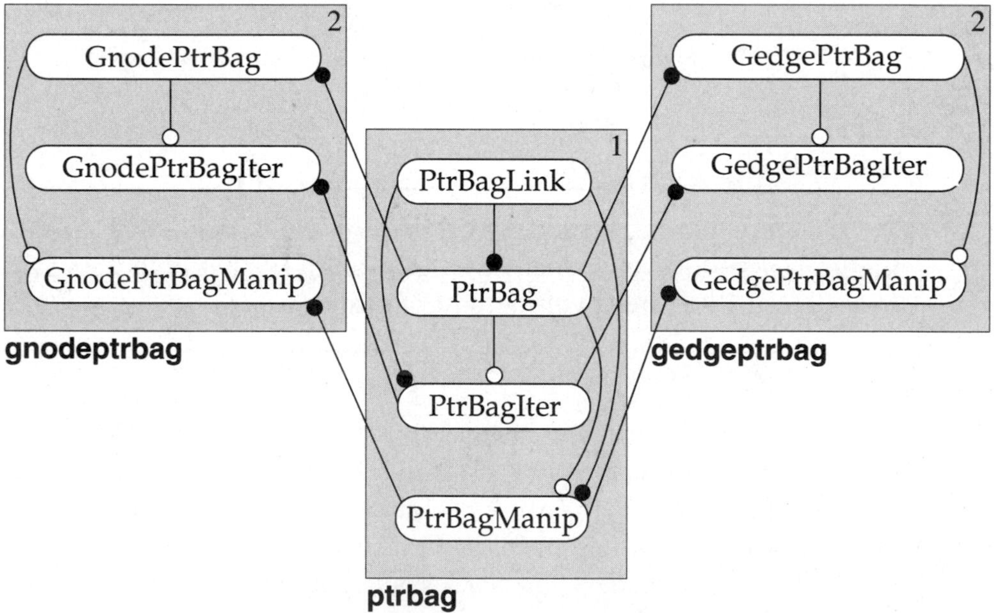

Figure 5-82: Generic `PtrBag` Container and Specializations

Figure 5-83 shows the header for a `ptrbag` component, consisting of four classes. `PtrBagLink` is a low-level implementation class whose use is an encapsulated implementation detail of the other three classes in the `ptrbag` component. We could instead have placed `PtrBagLink` in a separate component, defined it entirely within the `ptrbag.c` file, or nested it within class `PtrBag`. (The advantages and disadvantages of these and other similar design alternatives are compared and discussed in Section 8.4.)

```
// ptrbag.h
#ifndef INCLUDED_PTRBAG
#define INCLUDED_PTRBAG

class PtrBagIter;
class PtrBagManip;

class PtrBagLink {
    void *d_pointer_p;
    PtrBagLink *d_next_p;

  private:
    PtrBagLink(const PtrBagLink&);
    PtrBagLink& operator=(const PtrBagLink&);

  public:
    PtrBagLink(void *pointer, PtrBagLink *next);
    ~PtrBagLink();
    PtrBagLink *&nextRef(); // used by manipulator
    PtrBagLink *next() const;
    void *pointer() const;
};

class PtrBag {
    PtrBagLink *d_root_p;
    friend PtrBagIter;
    friend PtrBagManip;

  private:
    PtrBag(const PtrBag&);
    PtrBag& operator=(const PtrBag&);

  public:
    PtrBag();
    ~PtrBag();
    void add(void *pointer);
    void removeAll(const void *pointer);
};

class PtrBagIter {
    PtrBagLink *d_link_p;
```

```
  private:
    PtrBagIter(const PtrBagIter&);
    PtrBagIter& operator=(const PtrBagIter&);

  public:
    PtrBagIter(const PtrBag& bag);
    ~PtrBagIter();
    void operator++();
    void *operator()() const;
    operator const void *() const;
};

class PtrBagManip {
    PtrBagLink **d_addrLink_p;

  private:
    PtrBagManip(const PtrBagManip&);
    PtrBagManip& operator=(const PtrBagManip&);

  public:
    PtrBagManip(PtrBag* bag);
    ~PtrBagManip();
    void advance();
    void remove();
    void *operator()() const;
    operator const void *() const;
};

// inline function definitions omitted

#endif
```

Figure 5-83: Header File for Generic `ptrbag` Component

`PtrBag` is a container used to hold generic pointers. For this application, a redundant but convenient member function is supplied to remove all pointers with the specified value from the `PtrBag`. `PtrBagIter` is part of the logical abstraction of a bag of pointers, allowing clients to iterate over the bag, returning its contents in some unspecified order. `PtrBagManip` is similar to `PtrBagIter` except that it allows its client to modify the bag by selectively removing entries—a capability punctuated by requiring the client to supply the address of the container to be manipulated.

Most of the functions declared in `ptrbag.h` would probably be implemented inline, simply because the size of the code they generate inline is smaller than that of a function call. The few exceptions are implemented out of line, as shown in Figure 5-84. The destructor for `PtrBag` as well as the `removeAll` function have loops, making them poor candidates for inlining. The `add` function accesses the global free store, so it is useless to try to inline it for speed purposes. The `remove` function consists of enough code that calling a function will probably produce less object code than substituting the source in place. While the `remove` function call adds some execution overhead, removing edges is not expected to be a frequently executed function. After performance analysis, the `remove` function is the only one of these four that stands a chance of improvement by being declared `inline`.

```
// ptrbag.c
#include "ptrbag.h"

PtrBag::~PtrBag()
{
    PtrBagManip man(this);
    while (man) {
        man.remove();
    }
}

void PtrBag::add(void *pointer)
{
    d_root_p = new PtrBagLink(pointer, d_root_p);
}

void PtrBag::removeAll(const void *pointer)
{
    PtrBagManip man(this);
    while (man) {
        man() == pointer ? man.remove() : man.advance();
    }
}

void PtrBagManip::remove()
{
    PtrBagLink *tmp = *d_addrLink_p;
    *(PtrBagLink **)d_addrLink_p = (*d_addrLink_p)->next();
    delete tmp;
}
```

Figure 5-84: Implementation File for Generic `ptrbag` Component

The component-dependency graph for the new subsystem is shown in Figure 5-85. Look at all of the functionality that has been extracted from the cyclic group of classes buried in the `graph` component. This functionality can now be tested and reused independently of that cycle. The functionality in `gedgeptrbag` is reused in two different ways even within the `graph` component itself: once in class `Graph` to keep track of all edges, and once in class `Gnode` to keep track of connected edges. At this point we have reduced the amount of cyclicly dependent code to a manageable level of complexity appropriate for a single component—`graph`. The complexity of the graph-independent functionality identified by either `Node` or `Edge` is now segregated into independent components, that are testable *in isolation*.

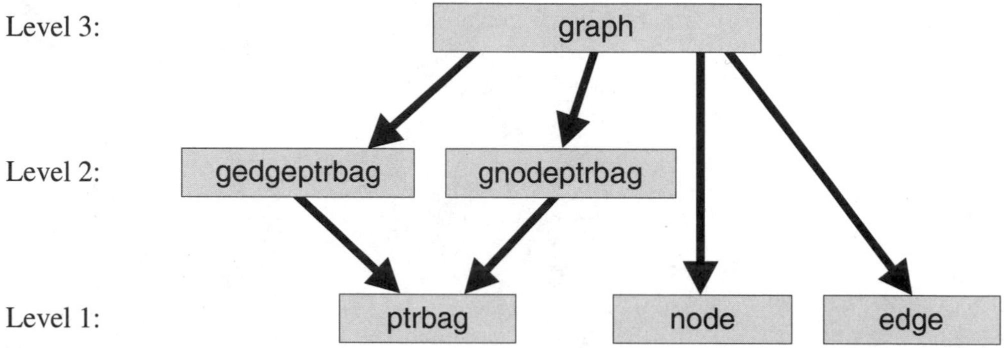

Figure 5-85: Component Dependency for a Factored Graph Architecture

Figure 5-86 gives the complete header file for the `graph` component. This implementation is efficient, flexible, and reasonably maintainable. However, using this component is not so straightforward because some of the interface (along with the implementation) has been factored out and placed in reusable components at lower levels.

```
// graph.h
#ifndef INCLUDED_GRAPH
#define INCLUDED_GRAPH

#ifndef INCLUDED_NODE
#include "node.h"
#endif

#ifndef INCLUDED_EDGE
#include "edge.h"
#endif

#ifndef INCLUDED_GNODEPTRBAG
#include "gnodeptrbag.h"
#endif

#ifndef INCLUDED_GEDGEPTRBAG
#include "gedgeptrbag.h"
#endif

class Graph;
```

```
class Gnode : public Node {
    GedgePtrBag d_edges;
    friend Graph;
    Gnode(const Gnode&);                                // not implemented
    Gnode& operator=(const Gnode&);                     // not implemented

  private:
    Gnode(const char *name);
    ~Gnode();
    void add(Gedge *edgePtr);
    void remove(Gedge *edgePtr);

  public:
    const GedgePtrBag& edges() const;
};

class Gedge : public Edge {
    Gnode *d_from_p;
    Gnode *d_to_p;
    friend Graph;
    Gedge(const Gedge&);                                // not implemented
    Gedge& operator=(const Gedge&);                     // not implemented

  private:
    Gedge(Gnode *from, Gnode *to, double weight);
    ~Gedge();

  public:
    Gnode *from() const;
    Gnode *to() const;
};

class Graph {
    GnodePtrBag d_nodes;
    GedgePtrBag d_edges;
    Graph(const Graph&);
    Graph& operator=(const Graph&);

  public:
    Graph();
    ~Graph();

    Gnode *addNode(const char *nodeName);
    Gnode *findNode(const char *nodeName);
    void removeNode(Gnode *node);

    Gedge *addEdge(Gnode *from, Gnode *to, double weight);
    Gedge *findEdge(Gnode *from, Gnode *to);
    void removeEdge(Gedge *edge);

    const GnodePtrBag& nodes() const;
    const GedgePtrBag& edges() const;
};

#endif
```

Figure 5-86: `graph` **Component Header Defining Classes** `Gnode`**,** `Gedge`**, and** `Graph`

For example, suppose you wanted to iterate over the edges connected to a particular node in a graph. You would need to get the bag of `Gedge` pointers from that `Gnode` and then use that bag to construct an instance of EdgePtrBagIter:

```
int sumOfEdgeWeights(const Gnode& gnode)
{
    int sum = 0;
    for (GedgePtrBagIter it(gnode.edges()); it; ++it) {
        sum += it()->weight();
    }
    return sum;
}
```

Conveniently, the same methodology works for obtaining all of the edges and nodes from the graph itself, as illustrated in the implementation of the output operator for a `Graph` given in Figure 5-87.

```
ostream& operator<<(ostream& o, const Graph& graph)
{
    cout << "Graph: " << endl;
    GnodePtrBagIter nit(graph.nodes());
    if (nit) {
        cout << "  Nodes:";
    }
    for (; nit; ++nit) {
        o << "   " << nit()->name();
    }
    const char *p = "  Edges:   ";
    const char *q = "           ";
    for (GedgePtrBagIter eit(graph.edges()); eit; ++eit) {
        o << endl << p << eit()->from()->name()
          << " ---(" << eit()->weight() << ")--> "
          << eit()->to()->name();
        p = q;
    }
    cout << endl << "End Graph" << endl;
    return o;
}
```

Figure 5-87: An `operator<<` for `Graph` Using Low-Level Iterators

A test driver implementing the `graph` component of Figure 5-86 is given, along with its output, in Figure 5-88. Notice that the `Gnode` pointers returned by both `addNode` and `findNode` point directly at the corresponding `Gnode` within the `Graph`. The only publicly available function in `Gnode`, `edges()`, supplies a `const` reference to its bag of `Gedge` pointers, which can then be used directly by the client to traverse the graph.

The only public functionality available in a `Gedge` provides access to the two `Gnode` objects to which the `Gedge` is connected.

```
// graph.t.c
#include "graph.h"
#include "gnodeptrbag.h"
#include "gedgeptrbag.h"
#include <iostream.h>

ostream& operator<<(ostream& o, const Graph& graph);

main()
{
    Graph g;

    {
        Gnode *n1 = g.addNode("Mindy");
        Gnode *n2 = g.addNode("Susan");
        Gnode *n3 = g.addNode("Rick");

        g.addEdge(n2, n1, 4);
        g.addEdge(n1, n3, 5);
        g.addEdge(n3, n2, 1);

        g.addNode("Franklin");
        g.addNode("Cathy");
    }

    g.addEdge(g.findNode("Susan"), g.findNode("Franklin"), 6);
    g.addEdge(g.findNode("Rick"), g.findNode("Franklin"), 2);
    g.addEdge(g.findNode("Rick"), g.findNode("Cathy"), 3);

    cout << g;
}

// Output:
          john@john: a.out
          Graph:
            Nodes:  Cathy  Franklin  Rick  Susan  Mindy
            Edges:  Rick ---(3)--> Cathy
                    Rick ---(2)--> Franklin
                    Susan ---(6)--> Franklin
                    Rick ---(1)--> Susan
                    Mindy ---(5)--> Rick
                    Susan ---(4)--> Mindy
          End Graph
          john@john:
```

Figure 5-88: Simple Test Driver Illustrating Usage of the `graph` Component

Principle

Granting friendship does not create dependencies but can induce physical coupling in order to preserve encapsulation.

In this implementation of `Graph`, private access via (local) friendship to `Gnode` and `Gedge` is essential to preserving encapsulation. This design eliminates the problems associated with long-distance friendship by physically uniting the parts of the system that need to share common implementation details via private access. In other words, by combining `Graph`, `Gnode`, and `Gedge` in a single component, the required friendships are no longer long-distance ones.

As illustrated in Figure 5-89, it turns out that `Gnode` and `Gedge` depend on each other in name only, and have no backward dependency on `Graph`. Although the three classes have no cyclic interdependencies, there is still a need for factoring. Clients of this subsystem will need to interact directly with both `Gnode` and `Gedge`. Making the entire interface of either `Gnode` or `Gedge` public would expose clients to implementation details of the `graph` component. Worse, doing so would allow clients to violate important policies enforced by the `Graph` manager class.

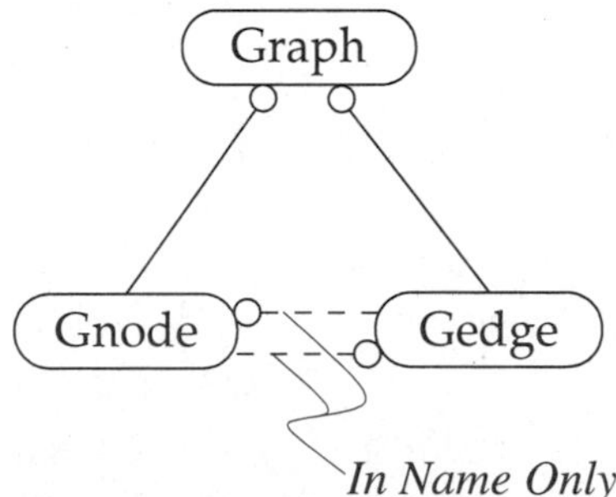

Figure 5-89: Actual Relationships Among `Graph`**,** `Gnode`**, and** `Gedge`

For example, making the `Gedge` constructor public would allow clients to bypass the `Graph` object and create instances of a `Gedge` on the program stack. There would be nothing to stop a wayward client from adding a `Gedge` created on the program stack to a legitimate `Gnode` belonging to an otherwise valid `Graph`.

To avoid these problems it is necessary to grant class `Graph` access to private functionality defined in both `Gnode` and `Gedge`. Avoiding long-distance friendship then forces us to place these intimately dependent classes in the same component. Although there is no direct physical dependency brought on by granting friendship, modularity and encapsulation dictate the effective physical coupling suggested in Figure 5-90.

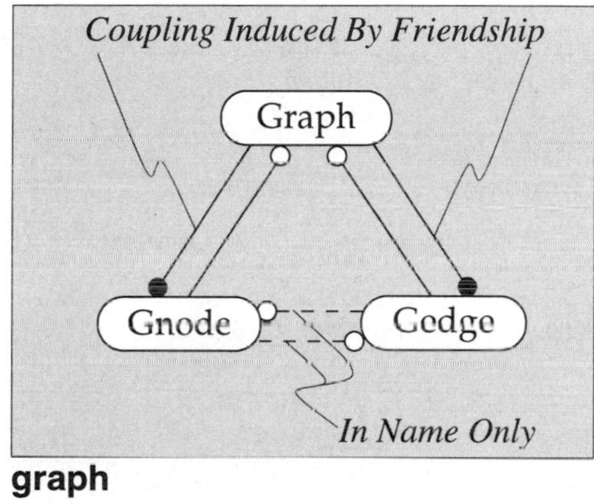

Figure 5-90: Implied Physical Coupling to Avoid Long-Distance Friendship

The fact that the physical coupling is brought about only by friendship (as discussed in Section 3.6) and not hard physical dependencies opens the door to another technique, which we will explore in the next section. For completeness, the implementation file for the `graph` component is provided in Figure 5-91.

To summarize the results of this section: factoring is a general technique that can be used to reduce the maintenance cost of designs with inherent cyclic dependencies. By relocating some of the implementation complexity to lower-level components, that functionality can be tested (and possibly reused) independently of the remaining cyclicly interdependent code. Factoring results in more flexible architectures without sacrificing runtime efficiency. When factoring the interface of a subsystem, clients may be asked to use component interfaces at lower levels of the subsystem hierarchy.

```
// graph.c
#include "graph3.h"
#include <string.h>

                // -*-*-*-*- class Gnode -*-*-*-*-

Gnode::Gnode(const char *name) : Node(name) {}

Gnode::~Gnode() {}

void Gnode::add(Gedge *edgePtr) { d_edges.add(edgePtr); }

void Gnode::remove(Gedge *edgePtr) { d_edges.removeAll(edgePtr); }

const GedgePtrBag& Gnode::edges() const { return d_edges; }

                // -*-*-*-*- class Gedge -*-*-*-*-

Gedge::Gedge(Gnode *from, Gnode *to, double weight)
: Edge(weight)
, d_from_p(from)
, d_to_p(to) {}

Gedge::~Gedge() {}

Gnode *Gedge::from() const { return d_from_p; }

Gnode *Gedge::to() const { return d_to_p; }

                // -*-*-*-*- class Graph -*-*-*-*-

Graph::Graph() {}

Graph::~Graph()
{
    for (GedgePtrBagIter eit(d_edges); eit; ++eit) {
        delete eit();
    }
    for (GnodePtrBagIter nit(d_nodes); nit; ++nit) {
        delete nit();
    }
}

Gnode *Graph::addNode(const char *nodeName)
{
    Gnode *p = new Gnode(nodeName);
    d_nodes.add(p);
    return p;
}

Gnode *Graph::findNode(const char *nodeName)
{
    for (GnodePtrBagIter it(d_nodes); it; ++it) {
        if (0 == strcmp(it()->name(), nodeName)) {
            return it();
        }
    }
    return 0;
}
```

```
void Graph::removeNode(Gnode *node)
{
    GnodePtrBagManip nodeMan(&d_nodes);
    while (nodeMan) {
        if (nodeMan() == node) {
            for (GedgePtrBagIter it(nodeMan()->edges()); it; ++it) {
                d_edges.removeAll(it());
            }
            nodeMan.remove();
        }
        else {
            nodeMan.advance();
        }
    }
}

Gedge *Graph::addEdge(Gnode *from, Gnode *to, double weight)
{
    Gedge *p = new Gedge(from, to, weight);
    d_edges.add(p);
    from->add(p);
    to->add(p);
    return p;
}

Gedge *Graph::findEdge(Gnode *from, Gnode *to)
{
    for (GedgePtrBagIter it(d_edges); it; ++it) {
        if (it()->from() == from && it()->to() == to) {
            return it();
        }
    }
    return 0;
}

void Graph::removeEdge(Gedge *edge)
{
    GedgePtrBagManip edgeMan(&d_edges);
    while (edgeMan) {
        if (edgeMan() == edge) {
            edge->to()->remove(edge);
            edge->from()->remove(edge);
            edgeMan.remove();
        }
        else {
            edgeMan.advance();
        }
    }
}

const GnodePtrBag& Graph::nodes() const { return d_nodes; }

const GedgePtrBag& Graph::edges() const { return d_edges; }
```

Figure 5-91: `graph.c` **Implementation File for** `graph` **Component**

5.10 Escalating Encapsulation

As a C++ programmer, you have no doubt encountered the notion of *encapsulation.* An interface is *encapsulating* if it makes the details of its implementation programmatically inaccessible to clients. A common misconception is that it is necessary for each individual class or component to encapsulate all implementation details and present a robust interface to the entire world. Doing so would make large, complex subsystems intolerably larger, slower, and more complicated than need be. Instead we can hide a number of useful low-level classes behind the interface of a single component (as was the case with the `p2p_router` component in Chapter 4.) We will often refer to such a component as a *wrapper.*[16]

Figure 5-92a illustrates a subsystem in which each individual component presents a public interface that is appropriate for direct use by clients in the context of using that subsystem. The encapsulation for this subsystem is enforced on a per-component basis. Figure 5-92b shows a subsystem in which some of the components defined within the subsystem are not exposed in the overall subsystem interface as defined by the wrapper component, `w`. That is, none of the types defined in components `u`, `v`, or `y` are part of either the `public` or `protected` interfaces of `w`. Although components `u`, `v`, and `y` are individually available for use by anyone, there is simply no programmatic way even to detect whether these components are used to implement `w`. Consequently, there is no programmatic way to take any advantage of the objects defined in these components when interacting with instances of this subsystem. The encapsulation for subsystem B is enforced by the wrapper component at the highest level of the subsystem.

[16] A wrapper is a component-based implementation of a design pattern known as Facade in **gamma**, Chapter 4, pp. 185–193.

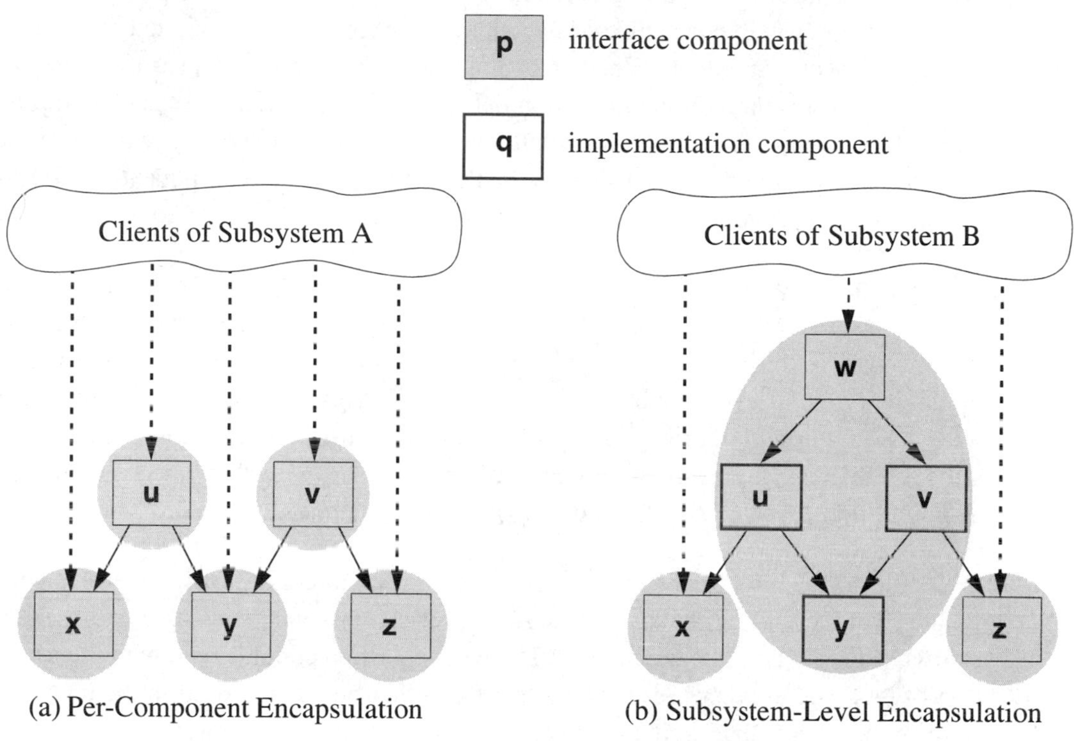

(a) Per-Component Encapsulation

(b) Subsystem-Level Encapsulation

Figure 5-92: Spheres of Encapsulation

Principle

What is and what is not an implementation detail depends on the level of abstraction within the physical hierarchy.

By analogy, a `SparkPlug` is an implementation detail of `Car`, but `SparkPlug` is used in the interface of `Engine`, which is encapsulated by `Car`. At the level of abstraction that is the inside of `Car`'s subsystem, `SparkPlug` is part of the public interface of the hierarchy of components that make up the `Car`'s implementation. At the level of abstraction of the `Car`'s client, the `SparkPlug` is hidden.

When we use a low-level library component (such as `qsort`) in the implementation of our subsystem, we do not think twice about how appropriate that component would be in the hands of our client. Whether or not we happen to make use of `qsort` will remain an encapsulated implementation detail of our subsystem. We cannot stop our clients from using `qsort` on their own; however, we can easily conceal whether or not we make use of it ourselves. This same philosophy applies to components we define within our subsystem.

Suppose that component `y` in Figure 5-92b defines the `OrderedPointCollection` of Section 5.7. Clients of our subsystem may have absolutely no need for ordered point collections, yet this component is used by other components within our subsystem to implement higher-level functionality. At the lower levels of a subsystem, components will be exchanging correspondingly lower-level information. This information, although it is an implementation detail to the end user, is well defined, predictable, and appropriate for the interfaces of low-level components.

We could try to hide `OrderedPointCollection` by making all of its interface functions private and granting specific, higher-level components, such as `u` and `v`, friend status—but why complicate matters? There is no harm a client can do with the definition of `OrderedPointCollection` so as long as this type is not used in the interfaces of the components that define the overall interface to the subsystem.[17]

The subsystem shown in Figure 5-92a is similar in structure to the factored implementation of the graph subsystem presented in the previous section. In that architecture (Figure 5-85), clients were asked to make use of lower-level components (such as `ptrbag`) in the normal course of using the subsystem.

An alternative implementation for a graph would be to provide a wrapper component through which all clients of the graph subsystem must interact in order to use the subsystem. This wrapper (like component `w` in Figure 5-92b) would not only manage the other components in the graph subsystem but would also encapsulate several implementation-level objects previously exposed to the user in the factored implementation.

Recall that in the factored implementation of the graph subsystem, both `Gnode` and `Gedge` were managed by `Graph`, meaning that `Graph` alone was authorized to create

---

[17] If an implementation class provides functions that alter static variables within the class or `.c` file, this principle may not hold.

and destroy Gnode and Gedge objects. In that implementation, both Gnode and Gedge were not encapsulated details of the subsystem; instances of these types, comprising the graph's implementation, were readily accessible through the interface of class Graph itself. To prevent clients from usurping the manager class's authority, much of the interface to both Gnode and Gedge was declared private, and Graph alone was granted friend status. Solely to avoid the breach of encapsulation that would result from long-distance friendship, we were compelled to place Graph, Gnode, and Gedge within a single component.

Principle

Escalating the level at which encapsulation occurs can remove the need to grant private access to cooperating components within a subsystem.

Always trying to force privileged communication to go on within a single component could make components ridiculously large and would defeat the advantages of a hierarchical design. If we stop worrying about the encapsulation aspect for a minute and make all of the functionality in Gnode and Gedge public, we can move each of these three classes to separate components. Because Gnode and Gedge use each other in name only, they automatically become testable independent of each other. For example, it is now easy and convenient to test directly the full functionality of the new gnode component shown in Figure 5-93.

In the factored solution, only Graph had private access to Gnode and both classes were defined in the same component. That approach eliminated the potential for improper direct use of Gnode by clients, but it precluded direct testing of Gnode as well.

With this new approach, instead of being forced to test the low-level functionality of Gnode (e.g., adding and removing Gedge pointers) indirectly through the interface of Graph, it is now possible for test engineers to verify this now-public behavior directly. However, ordinary clients will now also have direct access to this low-level functionality.

```
// gnode.h
#ifndef INCLUDED_GNODE
#define INCLUDED_GNODE

#ifndef INCLUDED_NODE
#include "node.h"
#endif

#ifndef INCLUDED_GEDGEPTRBAG
#include "gedgeptrbag.h"
#endif

class Gnode : public Node {
    GedgePtrBag d_edges;
    Gnode(const Gnode&);                     // not implemented
    Gnode& operator=(const Gnode&);          // not implemented

  public:
    Gnode(const char *name);
    ~Gnode();
    void add(Gedge *edgePtr);
    void remove(Gedge *edgePtr);
    const GedgePtrBag& edges() const;
};
#endif
```

Figure 5-93: New Individual Component `gnode` **Defining Class** `Gnode`

Originally, `Graph` was granted private access to both `Gnode` and `Gedge` to preserve encapsulation. The encapsulation was at risk only because clients of `Graph` were granted direct access to the `Gnode` and `Gedge` objects, which themselves were largely implementation details of `Graph`. If we stop exposing `Gnode` and `Gedge` in the interface of `Graph`, we can avoid this problem entirely.

Principle

Private header files are not a substitute for proper encapsulation because they inhibit side-by-side reuse.

Failing to publish header files is not the solution—that's cheating. Not granting clients access to one or more header files will make the use of certain types opaque, but these types are still programmatically accessible in name and therefore not encapsulated details. For example, an opaque pointer obtained from one part of the system could be unexpectedly reintroduced by clients into another part of the system in a way that renders the system internally inconsistent.

As Figure 5-94 illustrates, class N manages a collection of objects of type W and E. Each of these two subobjects makes use of an S object in its interface. The object S itself is an implementation detail, so clients are denied access to its header file in an effort to encapsulate its use.

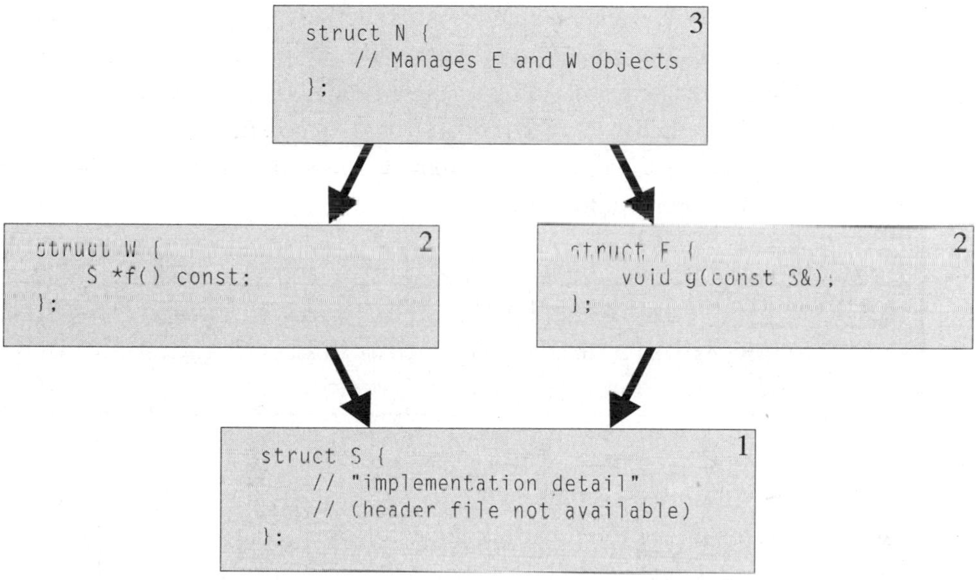

Figure 5-94: Ineffective Encapsulation by Concealing Header Files

Notice how easy it is for a client to extract an opaque S pointer from an instance of class W and use it to influence an instance of class E directly:

```
void myFunc(E *e, const W& w)
{
    e->g(*w.f());
}
```

Compare this approach with a design that properly hides its implementation details behind an encapsulating interface (i.e., a design where there is no exposure of the implementation types in the logical interface of the wrapper component for that subsystem). Even with access to all header files, there is still no programmatic way to access the low-level implementation objects hiding behind the truly encapsulating interface of the wrapper.

The advantages of proper encapsulation are many. A clear example is reuse. Trying to encapsulate an implementation type by withholding a header file effectively prevents public reuse of that implementation component. If encapsulation is done properly, clients can have side-by-side access to both low-level types and the subsystems that use them internally, with no fear that private details of the subsystem will be exposed.

Understandability and maintainability are other advantages of using proper encapsulation. Distinguishing what is and what is not a "private" header file is difficult at best. For these reasons, providing a single header file per component, which clearly and fully defines its (sole) interface, is strongly recommended. It is worth noting that withholding header files may be appropriate when the objective is not encapsulation but insulation (see Sections 6.5 and 7.4).

> **DEFINITION: In hierarchical systems, *encapsulating a type* (defined at file scope within a header file) means hiding its use, not hiding the type itself.**

Let us now return to our graph example. Successfully levelizing this new graph architecture will not be achieved by hiding the low-level implementation types of our subsystem from test engineers and/or clients. It makes no difference what others do with their own instances of these types. Rather, successful levelization of this architecture will be achieved by ensuring that there is no programmatic way to access any instance of any implementation type that is part of an instance of our subsystem.

To implement encapsulation at the subsystem level, we will need to introduce a wrapper component. Figure 5-95 gives a detailed sketch of the new architecture for the graph subsystem. The old `Graph` class has been renamed `GraphImp`, but otherwise has been left essentially unaffected. Both `Gnode` and `GraphImp` continue to make use of the factored implementations and specializations in `ptrbag` (shown as a single component in this figure). The new `graph` (wrapper) component now defines five classes to be used by clients of the subsystem.

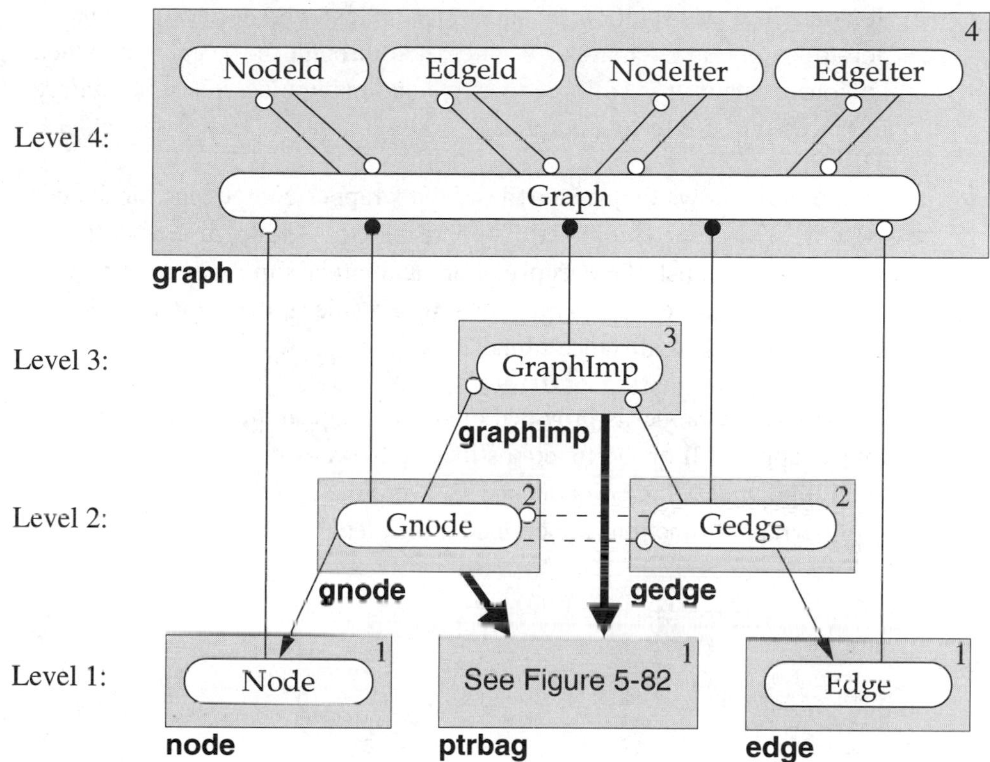

Figure 5-95: Escalating Encapsulation Using a Wrapper Component

Principle

A wrapper component can be used to encapsulate the use of implementation types within a subsystem while allowing other types to pass through its interface.

The `Node` and `Edge` classes, containing only network-independent data, are also programmatically accessible from the interface of the new `graph` component. However, from the perspective of users of the graph subsystem, the types `Gnode`, `Gedge`, and `GraphImp` and all types defined in `ptrbag` are now implementation details that are fully encapsulated by the new wrapper component.

To appreciate this solution, consider that a client who has access to `gnode.h` still cannot affect any `Gnode` that has been created through the `graph` component's interface. Of course, the user is still free to create and manipulate his or her *independent* `Gnode` instances (i.e., for testing purposes).

Figure 5-96 shows the header file of the wrapper component for the new graph subsystem. The four additional support classes (`NodeId`, `EdgeId`, `NodeIter`, and `EdgeIter`) establish the encapsulation, and either supply or require private access to `Graph`. All of these classes must therefore reside in the same component as `Graph` in order to avoid long-distance friendships.

Because this wrapper is provided only for encapsulation purposes, it is an extremely thin wrapper. All of the functions merely forward requests to the appropriate lower-level implementation components. To avoid the additional function call overhead, all of the wrapper functions are defined inline, leaving the `graph.c` file empty.

```
// graph.h
#ifndef INCLUDED_GRAPH
#define INCLUDED_GRAPH

#ifndef INCLUDED_GRAPHIMP
#include "graphimp.h"
#endif

#ifndef INCLUDED_GNODE
#include "gnode.h"
#endif

#ifndef INCLUDED_GEDGE
#include "gedge.h"
#endif

class EdgeId;                // forward declaration
class Graph;                 // forward declaration
class NodeIter;              // forward declaration
class EdgeIter;              // forward declaration

class NodeId {
    Gnode *d_node_p;
    friend EdgeId;
    friend Graph;
    friend NodeIter;
    friend EdgeIter;
```

```
  private:
    NodeId(Gnode *node) : d_node_p(node) {}
    Gnode *gnode() const { return d_node_p; }
  public:
    NodeId() : d_node_p(0) {}
    NodeId(const NodeId& nid) : d_node_p(nid.d_node_p) {}
    ~NodeId() {}
    NodeId& operator=(const NodeId& nid) { d_node_p = nid.d_node_p; return *this; }
    operator Node *() const { return d_node_p; }
    Node *operator->() const { return *this; }
};

class EdgeId {
    Gedge *d_edge_p;
    friend Graph;
    friend EdgeIter;

  private:
    EdgeId(Gedge *edge) : d_edge_p(edge) {}
    Gedge *gedge() const { return d_edge_p; }

  public:
    EdgeId() : d_edge_p(0) {}
    EdgeId(const EdgeId& eid) : d_edge_p(eid.d_edge_p) {}
    ~EdgeId() {}
    EdgeId& operator=(const EdgeId& eid) { d_edge_p = eid.d_edge_p; return *this; }
    NodeId from() const { return NodeId(d_edge_p->from()); }
    NodeId to() const { return NodeId(d_edge_p->to()); }
    operator Edge *() const { return d_edge_p; }
    Edge *operator->() const { return *this; }
};

class Graph {
    GraphImp d_imp;
    friend NodeIter;
    friend EdgeIter;

  private:
    Graph(const Graph&);                          // not implemented
    Graph& operator=(const Graph&);               // not implemented

  public:
    Graph() {}
    ~Graph() {}
    NodeId addNode(const char *nodeName)
    {
        return NodeId(d_imp.addNode(nodeName));
    }
    NodeId findNode(const char *nodeName)
    {
        return NodeId(d_imp.findNode(nodeName));
    }
```

```
    void removeNode(const NodeId& nid)
    {
        d_imp.removeNode(nid.gnode());
    }
    EdgeId addEdge(const NodeId& from, const NodeId& to, double weight)
    {
        return EdgeId(d_imp.addEdge(from.gnode(), to.gnode(), weight));
    }
    EdgeId findEdge(const NodeId& from, const NodeId& to)
    {
        return EdgeId(d_imp.findEdge(from.gnode(), to.gnode()));
    }
    void removeEdge(const EdgeId& eid)
    {
        d_imp.removeEdge(eid.gedge());
    }
};

class NodeIter {
    GnodePtrBagIter d_iter;

  private:
    NodeIter(const NodeIter&);                     // not implemented
    NodeIter& operator=(const NodeIter&);          // not implemented

  public:
    NodeIter(const Graph& graph) : d_iter(graph.d_imp.nodes()) {}
    void operator++() { ++d_iter; }
    operator const void *() const { return d_iter; }
    NodeId operator()() const { return NodeId(d_iter()); }
};

class EdgeIter {
    GedgePtrBagIter d_iter;

  private
    EdgeIter(const EdgeIter&);                     // not implemented
    EdgeIter& operator=(const EdgeIter&);          // not implemented

  public:
    EdgeIter(const Graph& graph) : d_iter(graph.d_imp.edges()) {}
    EdgeIter(const NodeId& nid) : d_iter(nid.gnode()->edges()) {}
    void operator++() { ++d_iter; }
    operator const void *() const { return d_iter; }
    EdgeId operator()() const { return EdgeId(d_iter()); }
};

#endif
```

Figure 5-96: Encapsulating Wrapper Component for Graph Subsystem

Notice that, in this interface, there is no direct access to any `Gnode` or `Gedge`. Adding or looking up a node returns a surrogate object of type `NodeId`, which holds a pointer to a `Gnode`, but under no circumstances will a `NodeId` ever let the client have access to more than just the `Node` portion of the `Gnode` it holds.

Similarly, `Gedge` is no longer exposed. Pointers to `Gedge` are now replaced by instances of type `EdgeId`. When dealing with a `Graph`, you can use an `EdgeId` just as you would have used a `Gedge` pointer. When communicating `Edge` information you can use an `EdgeId` as if it were an `Edge` pointer—nothing more.

Modifying the old test driver to accommodate the new wrapper interface requires only a few minor changes. In particular, `(Gnode *)` types are replaced by `NodeId` types and a few unnecessary `#include` directives are eliminated. The output is, of course, identical. The modified test driver is shown in Figure 5-97.

```
// graph.t.c
#include "graph.h"
#include <iostream.h>

ostream& operator<<(ostream& o, const Graph& graph);

main()
{
    Graph g;

    {
        NodeId n1 = g.addNode("Mindy");
        NodeId n2 = g.addNode("Susan");
        NodeId n3 = g.addNode("Rick");

        g.addEdge(n2, n1, 4);
        g.addEdge(n1, n3, 5);
        g.addEdge(n3, n2, 1);

        g.addNode("Franklin");
        g.addNode("Cathy");
    }

    g.addEdge(g.findNode("Susan"), g.findNode("Franklin"), 6);
    g.addEdge(g.findNode("Rick"), g.findNode("Franklin"), 2);
    g.addEdge(g.findNode("Rick"), g.findNode("Cathy"), 3);

    cout << g;
}
```

Figure 5-97: Driver Illustrating Usage of New `graph` Wrapper Component

Use of the wrapper interface is in some respects simpler than a factored implementation because most, if not all, of the available functionality is presented in a single, monolithic header file. For example, to iterate over the edges in a graph or node, we do not need to look further than the header for `graph` itself:

```
int sumOfEdgeWeights(const NodeId& nid)
{
    int sum = 0;
    for (EdgeIter it(nid); it; ++it) {
        sum += it()->weight();
    }
}
```

Wrapping has the disadvantage of making the interface less flexible and communication across it slower. A wrapped subsystem is also likely to be more costly to develop initially. However, wrapping may be the only truly effective way to achieve both levelization and encapsulation for subsystems involving many highly interdependent components.

We have come a long way from the simple two-component example of Figure 5-10 in Section 5.1.3, but the seven components in Figure 5-95 lay a strong hierarchical foundation for producing a complex yet easy-to-use and highly reliable subsystem. The topic of wrappers is continued in Section 6.4.3, where we discuss how to insulate our clients from compile-time dependency on the implementation types below our wrapper components.

To summarize this section: trying to encapsulate the implementation of a subsystem on a per-component basis can impede low-level communication and/or warp an otherwise viable design. Rather than restricting the functionality that is accessible to clients within individual classes, we can instead restrict the subset of classes exposed to clients in the interface of the overall subsystem. Using a wrapper component, we can elevate the level of encapsulation to the highest level of a subsystem. In so doing, we can eliminate the need for low-level friendships, and thereby eliminate the need for merging intimately coupled classes into a single, oversized component.

5.11 Summary

By considering the physical implications of our logical design and proactively engineering our system as a levelizable collection of components, we create a hierarchy of modular abstractions that can be understood, tested, and reused independently of the rest of our design.

Techniques for achieving levelization include the following:

• Escalation	Moving mutually dependent functionality higher in the physical hierarchy.
• Demotion	Moving common functionality lower in the physical hierarchy.
• Opaque Pointers	Having an object use another in name only.
• Dumb Data	Using data that indicates a dependency on a peer object, but only in the context of a separate, higher-level object.
• Redundancy	Deliberately avoiding reuse by repeating small amounts of code or data to avoid coupling.
• Callbacks	Using client-supplied functions that enable lower-level subsystems to perform specific tasks in a more global context.
• Manager Class	Establishing a class that owns and coordinates lower-level objects.
• Factoring	Moving independently testable subbehavior out of the implementation of complex components involved in excessive physical coupling.
• Escalating Encapsulation	Moving the point at which implementation details are hidden from clients to a higher level in the physical hierarchy.

Using these techniques to create levelizable designs tends to reduce the large, sometimes even overwhelming, logical design space, and helps to guide developers in the direction of more mainstream, maintainable architectures. Fortunately there is a serendipitous synergy between good logical design and good physical design. Given time, these two design goals will come to reinforce one another.

6

Insulation

Avoiding unnecessary compile-time dependencies is another important part of good physical design. Excessive compile-time coupling can profoundly impede our ability to maintain a system. Programmatically inaccessible implementation details that reside in the physical interface of a component cannot, in general, be modified without forcing all clients to recompile. For even moderately large projects, the cost of recompiling the entire system will inhibit any modification of the physical interface of low-level components, limiting our ability to make even local changes to the encapsulated details of their implementations.

In this chapter we present a physical process referred to in this book as *insulation*, which is analogous to the logical process commonly referred to as *encapsulation*. *Insulation* is the process of avoiding or removing unnecessary compile-time coupling.

First we establish the need for addressing insulation as part of our overall architectural design, providing both theoretical and experimental justification. Next, we identify many specific C++ constructs that can cause compile-time coupling without attempting to alleviate it. In Section 6.3, we discuss several techniques for insulating individual details of the implementation exposed via the following mechanisms:

- private base classes,
- embedded member data,
- private member functions,
- protected member functions,
- enumerations,

- compiler-generated functions,
- include directives,
- private member data, and
- default arguments.

In Section 6.4, we discuss wholesale techniques used for insulating all details of the implementation:

- protocol classes,
- fully insulating concrete classes, and
- insulating wrapper components.

Insulating very large subsystems presents a unique problem for developers. In Section 6.5, we explore implementing an ANSI C–compliant procedural interface for a very large C++ system.

Finally, in Section 6.6, we explore the conditions under which insulation is indicated. The basic runtime costs associated with insulation will be presented, along with specific conditions under which insulation is *not* appropriate. We demonstrate the process of applying insulation, and measure the runtime costs associated with various degrees of insulation.

6.1 From Encapsulation to Insulation

Insulation is a physical design issue: its logical analog is commonly referred to as *encapsulation*. In Section 2.2 we discussed encapsulation in terms of classes. In Section 3.6, we discussed encapsulation in terms of components. Then in Section 5.10, we discussed encapsulation in terms of classes defined at file scope in the header files of a hierarchical subsystem. The important aspects in each case are that:

1. Some detail is part of some entity.

2. The detail is not *programmatically* accessible through the interface defined for that entity.

Consider the header file for the `stack` component shown in Figure 6-1. The logical interface of this `Stack` class fully encapsulates its implementation. Programmatically, there is no way to distinguish this implementation from the linked-list implementation with the identical interface shown in Figure 6-2.

```
// stack.h
#ifndef INCLUDED_STACK
#define INCLUDED_STACK

class Stack {
    int *d_stack_p;
    int d_size;
    int d_length;

  public:
    Stack();
    Stack(const Stack &stack);
    ~Stack();
    Stack& operator=(const Stack &stack);
    void push(int value);
    int pop();
    int top() const;
    int isEmpty() const;
};

#endif
```

Figure 6-1: Fully Encapsulated Array-Based `Stack` **Implementation**

```
// stack.h
#ifndef INCLUDED_STACK
#define INCLUDED_STACK

class StackLink;

class Stack {
    StackLink *d_stack_p;

  public:
    Stack();
    Stack(const Stack &stack);
    ~Stack();
    Stack& operator=(const Stack &stack);
    void push(int value);
    int pop();
    int top() const;
    int isEmpty() const;
};

#endif
```

Figure 6-2: Fully Encapsulated Linked-List-Based `Stack` **Implementation**

Even though both `Stack` classes fully encapsulate their implementations, any experienced C++ programmer looking at these header files can immediately determine the general implementation strategy of these components. Each of these `stack` component headers illustrates the difficulty in concealing proprietary implementations even with encapsulating interfaces. Inline functions can exacerbate the problem by exposing clients to algorithmic details as well.

But the desire to keep component implementations proprietary is not the dominant problem for large projects. A client has a right to expect that the logical interface of a component will not change, and ideally changes made to the logical implementation of a component should not affect clients. In reality, however, the C++ compiler depends on all information in a header file, including private data. If a human being can determine the implementation strategy of a component by inspecting its header, then it is likely that clients of the component would be forced to recompile if the implementation strategy of that component changes.

Forcing clients to recompile even when only the implementation of a component changes is not a desirable physical property of a component. The more components that depend on that component, the more undesirable such compile-time coupling can become. Failing to "insulate" clients from changes to our logical implementation can have a dramatic impact on the cost of developing large projects.

Imagine a system with *N* components in which each component is compile-time dependent on all the rest. That is, compiling a component means including and parsing the definitions from the header files of all *N* components. The compile-time cost of making a change to any single header file in such a system is staggering. Instead of being proportional to the size of the component itself, the cost of compiling any single translation unit depends on the size of the entire system! As the size of the entire system increases, the cost of compiling any one component grows at a rate that is disproportionately high. As more headers are read into each translation unit, the compiler's data structures are taxed more and more heavily. That is, doubling the number of lines included in a translation unit more than doubles the time it takes to parse it (as demonstrated in Section 6.1.1).

Even for relatively small systems (say, 50,000 lines total), this type of coupling is burdensome at best; for medium and large systems, it is intolerable. For example, a `.c` file that should take only seconds to compile now takes minutes, and the total compile-time cost of a single uninsulated change is now measured not in CPU seconds but in CPU hours!

The system illustrated in Figure 6-3 consists of a base class `Shape`, a number of specific shapes derived from `Shape`, and a number of clients that depend only on the base class shape. This system has no cyclic physical dependencies and is therefore levelizable.

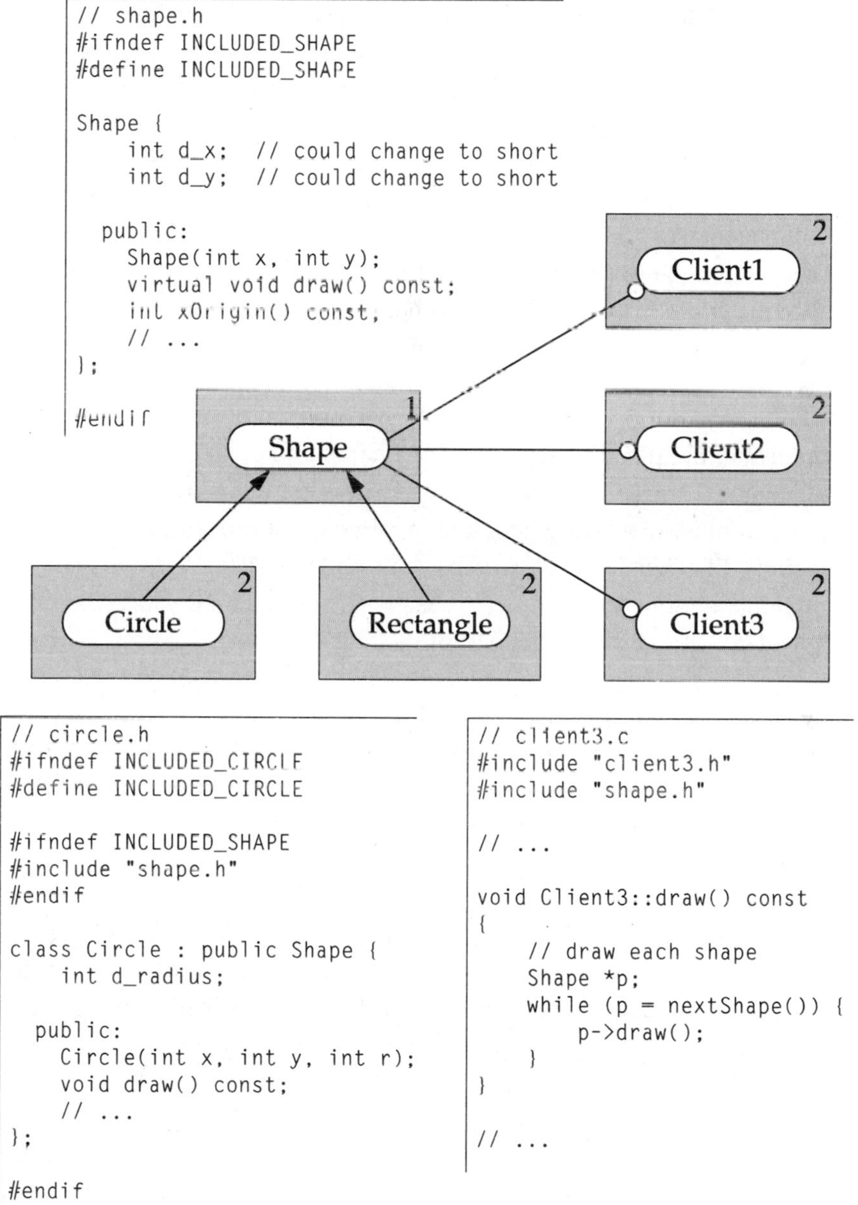
// shape.h
#ifndef INCLUDED_SHAPE
#define INCLUDED_SHAPE
Shape {
int d_x; // could change to short
int d_y; // could change to short
public:
Shape(int x, int y);
virtual void draw() const;
int xOrigin() const;
// ...
};
#endif
Client1
2
Shape
1
Client2
2
Circle
2
Rectangle
2
Client3
2
// circle.h
#ifndef INCLUDED_CIRCLE
#define INCLUDED_CIRCLE
#ifndef INCLUDED_SHAPE
#include "shape.h"
#endif
class Circle : public Shape {
int d_radius;
public:
Circle(int x, int y, int r);
void draw() const;
// ...
};
#endif
// client3.c
#include "client3.h"
#include "shape.h"
// ...
void Client3::draw() const
{
// draw each shape
Shape *p;
while (p = nextShape()) {
p->draw();
}
}
// ...

Figure 6-3: Illustration of a Compile-Time Coupled System

Originally the author of class `Shape` decided to use integers to represent the coordinates of the origin. Later the author realized that the integer range afforded by a `short int` was sufficient and that the size of `Shape` instances could be reduced significantly. The fundamental type of a private data member used to store the coordinates is clearly an implementation detail of the `Shape` class. The interface would not change, and it would continue to accept and return normal integers in the valid range (see Section 9.2). In fact, this detail is entirely encapsulated by the interface of `Shape`. Yet there is a problem.

Suppose that the author of `Shape` changes the private coordinate data type from `int` to `short int`. Which of the components in Figure 6-3 would be forced to recompile? Unfortunately, the correct answer is "all of them." Both `Circle` and `Rectangle` inherit from `Shape` and depend intimately on the internal physical layout of `Shape`. When any of `Shape`'s data members change, the internal layout of `Circle` and `Rectangle` will also have to change accordingly.

Clients of `Shape` are no better off. For one thing, the position of the virtual table pointer in the physical layout of the Shape object will almost certainly be affected by the change from `int` to `short int`. Unless the dependent code is recompiled, it simply will not work. More generally, whenever a header file is modified, all clients that include that header file must be recompiled. Therefore, whenever any part of the implementation resides in the header file of a component, the component fails to "insulate" clients from that part of its logical implementation.

DEFINITION: A contained implementation detail (type, data, or function) that can be altered, added, or removed without forcing clients to recompile is said to be *insulated*.

The term *encapsulation* conjures up an image of a clear bubble of perhaps infinitesimal thickness that surrounds the implementation of a class and protects it only from programmatic access. The term *insulation* connotes instead an opaque barrier of finite thickness that eliminates any possibility of direct interaction with the implementation of a component.

When bugs occur between internal releases of the various levels of a large system, insulating components (i.e., components that insulate clients from their implementations) are much more easily patched than non-insulating components. As long as the interface is not altered, the modified implementation can be dropped in place without having to recompile other components or worrying about headers becoming out of date. (We revisit this important topic in Section 7.6.2.)

One final testament to the value of insulation is that it can enable us to replace dynamically loaded libraries transparently. Dynamically loaded libraries are not linked into a single executable but, rather, are linked on demand into a running program. Suppose that you are the vendor of some C++-based application library. If you supply a fully insulated library implementation, then you can provide performance enhancements and bug-fixes without disturbing your clients at all. Sending them an update does not force them to recompile or even relink. All they do is reconfigure their environment to point to the new dynamically loaded library, and off they go.

In the following subsection we take a quantitative look at the cost of compile-time coupling. After that, we look at specific ways in which implementation details in C++ can become non-insulating, and then discuss transformations that can improve the degree of insulation.

6.1.1 The Cost of Compile-Time Coupling

To illustrate the severity of the problem, I devised a simple experiment.[1] I mechanically generated a varying number of simple header files, each 100 lines long. All headers were then included in an otherwise empty `.c` file. An outline of the generated files is shown in Figure 6-4.

```
// file.c                // header0.h             // header1.h             // ...
#include "header0.h"     class Class_0_0 {        class Class_1_0 {
#include "header1.h"         // ...                   // ...
#include "header2.h"     };                       };
#include "header3.h"     class Class_0_1 {        class Class_1_1 {
#include "header4.h"         // ...                   // ...
#include "header5.h"     };                       }
// ...                   // ...                   // ...
```

Figure 6-4: Experiment to Measure Compile-Time Cost

I then measured the CPU time needed to compile the `.c` file. The experiment was repeated using headers 1,000 lines long instead of 100 lines. Figure 6-5 provides the

[1] This subsection provides experimental data to corroborate the claims in the main section and may be omitted without loss of continuity.

results of running this simple experiment using the CFRONT 3.0 compiler running on a SUN SPARC 20 Workstation with 32 megabytes of memory.

The first column represents the relative size of the system where *N* represents the number of components of equal size. The next two columns represent the measured compile-time cost for headers on the order of 100 lines and 1,000 lines, respectively.

System Size: N (number of headers)	CPU seconds to parse headers	
	100-line headers	1,000-line headers
1	0.1	0.4
2	0.1	1.0
4	0.2	3.4
8	0.4	11.0
16	0.8	32.2
32	2.4	137.7
64	8.2	497.5
128	26.5	more than a day
256	98.1	
512	397.6	
1024	more than a day	

Figure 6-5: Empirical Cost of Compile-Time Coupling

If the total number of included lines is around 3,000 (30 small components or 3 large ones), doubling the number of included lines roughly triples the compile-time cost. For projects of this scale, the cost of recompiling a single `.c` file using CFRONT 3.0 is roughly proportional to $N^{1.6}$ and gets progressively worse for larger systems. A translation unit that might otherwise take only a few seconds to compile might now take several minutes.

As if this were not bad enough, because each component is compile-time dependent on every other component, an uninsulated change to any one component implies that all others must recompile as well. The cost of a single uninsulated change in a large compile-time coupled system is not proportional to N^2 but more like N^3!

If, when compiling any single translation unit, the amount of included header file information causes the compiler to exceed available physical memory, virtual memory swapping will completely overwhelm the cost of compilation, as was the case for the last entry in Column 2 and the last four entries in Column 3 of Figure 6-5. That is, for a given compiler and system configuration, there can be fairly hard limits to the absolute size of any given translation unit. For this particular configuration, 60,000 lines was practical; 100,000 lines was not.

6.2 C++ Constructs and Compile-Time Coupling

Sometimes the logical and physical decompositions of components are naturally consistent with each other. Consider a non-inline member function of a class. Its logical interface (the declaration) resides in the physical interface (the `.h` file), and its logical implementation (the function body) resides in the physical implementation (the `.c` file). In this case, the declaration merely describes the interface without exposing any more information than is necessary or desirable.

C++ does not require that all details regarding the logical implementation exist in the `.c` file. C++ allows this tight compile-time coupling for performance reasons. For a small, light-weight component implementing a stack or a list, avoiding compile-time coupling by completely insulating its implementation could have too great an impact on performance to be practical. Such light-weight components typically reach a stable state quickly and then are seldom if ever modified.

In the case of components that provide higher-level functionality such as a parser or simulator, the amount of useful work done per interface function called is often quite large. In these situations, the runtime overhead of insulating the implementation is usually neither measurable nor relevant.

It is easy in C++ to introduce implementation details inadvertently into the physical interface of a component. Whenever we place any part of the implementation of a component in its header file, we fail to insulate clients from that part of our implementation. The logical implementation is made part of the physical interface through the use of the following constructs:

- inheritance,
- layering,
- inline functions,

- private members,
- protected members,
- compiler-generated functions,
- include directives,
- default arguments, and
- enumerations.

The implications of each of these constructs with respect to compile-time coupling are explored individually in the following subsections. Our purpose now is only to expose the specific nature of the problem, but not to provide a solution just yet. Insulation techniques that systematically address all of these cases begin in Section 6.3.

6.2.1 Inheritance (IsA) and Compile-Time Coupling

Whenever one class derives from another, even privately, there can be no way to insulate clients from that fact. Even though private inheritance is considered an encapsulated implementation detail of the derived class, the physical layout of the derived object forces every client that includes the definition of the derived class to have already seen the definition of the base class. It is therefore appropriate for the header file of a derived class to include explicitly the header files containing its base classes. Whenever a base class header is modified (even if just to add a comment), UNIX utilities such as `make` will feel obliged to recompile any client of a derived class before linking that client into any new executable.

Figure 6-6 illustrates that if any change is made to the physical interface of `B`, then not only `D` but also all clients of `D` (i.e., `C1`, `C2`, and `C3`) will be forced to recompile.

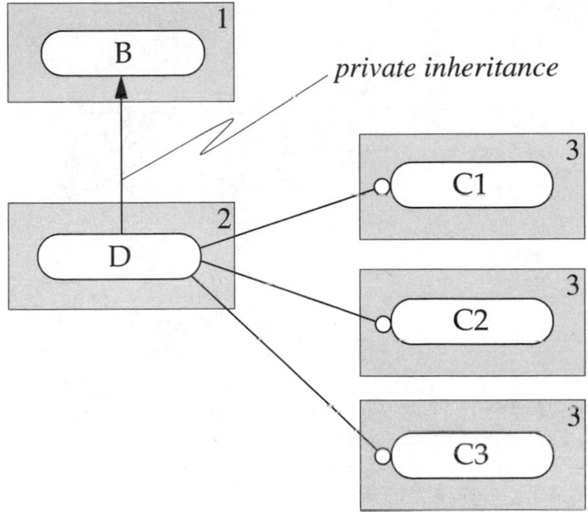

Figure 6-6: Inheritance Cannot Be Insulated from Clients

6.2.2 Layering (HasA/HoldsA) and Compile-Time Coupling

When a class embeds an instance of another user-defined type in its definition (HasA), the physical layout of the class becomes intimately dependent on the layout of that type. As a result, it will not be possible for a client to include the class definition of an object without having already seen the definitions of each of the layered subobjects embedded in that object. It is therefore appropriate for the header file of a composite object to include explicitly the header files containing the definitions of every layered object that is physically embedded within that class.

In contrast, when a class merely holds the address of an object (HoldsA), the class is not necessarily dependent on the physical layout of the held object. If so, it is appropriate for the header containing the class *not* to include the header for the held object but instead merely to declare its type.

Figure 6-7 illustrates a situation where class `Stooges` uses (in its implementation only) classes `Moe`, `Larry`, and `Curly`. Unlike classes `Larry` and `Curly`, a `Moe` is embedded in every `Stooges` object and therefore is not insulated from clients of `Stooges`. Any modification to the header file of `Moe` will necessitate the recompilation of all clients of `Stooges`.

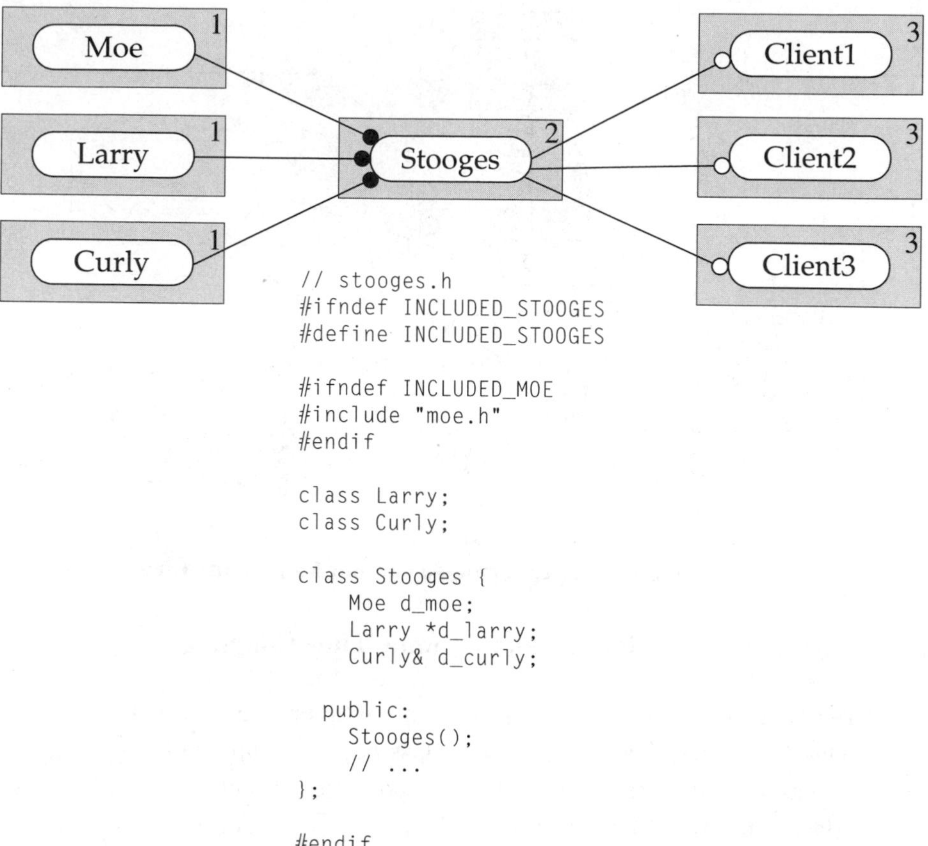


```
// stooges.h
#ifndef INCLUDED_STOOGES
#define INCLUDED_STOOGES

#ifndef INCLUDED_MOE
#include "moe.h"
#endif

class Larry;
class Curly;

class Stooges {
    Moe d_moe;
    Larry *d_larry;
    Curly& d_curly;

  public:
    Stooges();
    // ...
};

#endif
```

Figure 6-7: Embedded, Layered Objects Are Not Insulated from Clients

Every `Stooges` object also holds a pointer to an instance of a `Larry` and a reference to an instance of a `Curly`. It is not necessary for a client of class `Stooges` to know anything about the physical layout of either a `Larry` or `Curly` in order to construct an instance of class `Stooges`. It is therefore possible to modify the header file of either `Larry` or `Curly` and not have to recompile any of the clients of class `Stooges`. The physical layout and functionality of both `Larry` and `Curly` are insulated details of `Stooges`.

6.2.3 Inline Functions and Compile-Time Coupling

A function declared `inline` must be defined in the header file if it is to be substituted inline outside the current component. That requirement forces the body of the inline function to be placed in the physical interface of the component. The body of an inline function is encapsulated in that it is not programmatically accessible except by calling it via its own logical interface. Yet this part of the object's logical implementation is not insulated from clients, which has the following ramifications:

1. Any programmer that can use the component can look at the inline implementation.
2. Changing the implementation of an inline function forces all clients of the component defining the inline function to recompile.
3. Changing a function to or from an inline function also forces all clients of the component defining that function to recompile.
4. An object returned by value from an inline function is used *in size* (see Section 5.4) in the header file and is therefore never insulated from clients (although an object returned by value from a non-inline function might be). The same applies to an object used in size in the body of an inline function.
5. Therefore, when a user-defined object is passed into,[2] used in, or returned from an inline function by value, it is appropriate to include explicitly the header defining the used object in the header file defining the inline function.

Figure 6-8 illustrates ways that inlining can uninsulate otherwise insulated implementation details of class `Fred`. For example, `Fred` holds pointers to objects of type `Wilma`, `Betty`, `Barney`, and `MrSlate`, and therefore `Fred`'s object layout does not depend on the object layout of any of these types. Because member function `getWilma` returns an object of type `Wilma` by value and is declared `inline`, it *is* necessary for all clients of class `Fred` to have already seen the definition of class `Wilma`. Since member function `getBetty` is not declared `inline`, clients of `Fred` that do not need to call `getBetty` (and otherwise do not depend on type `Betty` in size) need not

[2] Passing a user-defined type into a function by value is almost never done (see Section 9.1.11).

include the header file for class Betty. In other words, clients that do not use type Betty are not forced to depend on Betty at compile time.

```
// fred.h
#ifndef INCLUDED_FRED
#define INCLUDED_FRED

#ifndef INCLUDED_WILMA
#include "wilma.h"
#endif

#ifndef INCLUDED_MRSLATE
#include "mrslate.h"
#endif

class Barney;
class Betty;

class Fred {
    Wilma *d_wilma_p;
    Barney *d_barney_p;
    Betty *d_betty_p;
    MrSlate *d_mrSlate_p;

  public:
    Fred();
    Wilma getWilma() const { return *d_wilma_p; }
    Betty getBetty() const;  // non-inline function
    const Barney& getBarney() const { return *d_barney_p; }
    double getSalary() { return d_mrSlate_p->askForRaise(); }
};

#endif
```

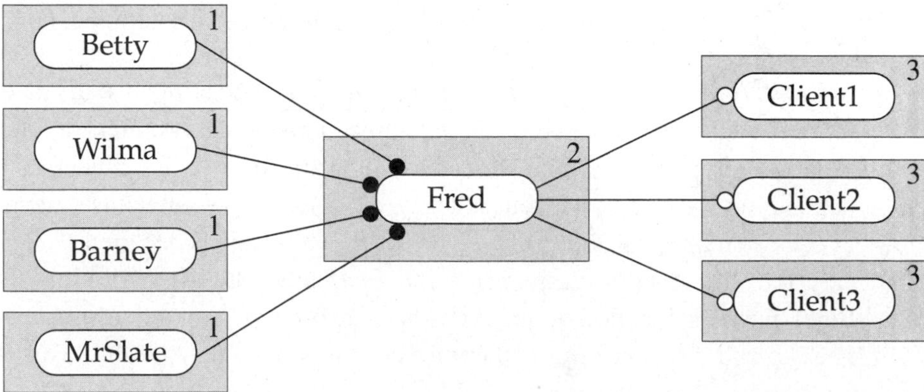

Figure 6-8: Ways that Inlining Functions Reduce Insulation

An instance of class `Barney` is returned from member function `getBarney` by reference, so unless a client depends on class `Barney` in size, there is no need for that client to include the class definition for `Barney`. Again, the client is not forced to depend on what it does not need.

Finally, the member function `getSalary` makes substantive use of the encapsulated `MrSlate` object in its implementation. Because `getSalary` is declared `inline`, all clients of `Fred` are required to have seen the definition of class `MrSlate`, whether or not they call `getSalary`. Of course, should any of the implementations of these inline functions change, all clients of `Fred` would have to recompile.

6.2.4 Private Members and Compile-Time Coupling

Each private data member of a class—although encapsulated—is not insulated from clients of that class. We have already seen several examples where modifying the implementation will require changing private data members, which in turn will require clients to recompile. For example, changing the encapsulated implementation of a `Stack` class from linked-list based to array based will force all clients of `Stack` to recompile. As we have also already seen, even a trivial code-tuning change, such as changing an `int` to a `short int`, is enough to trigger the recompilation of all clients.

We are often reminded that private member functions are encapsulated implementation details of a class, but they are not insulated implementation details—even when they are not declared `inline`. Altering so much as the signature of a private member function of a class is enough to force all clients of the component defining that class to recompile.

Figure 6-9 illustrates the problem with private members. The `d_length` member is a detail that was added presumably because it was felt that keeping track of the length was more efficient than calculating it on demand. If this assumption turns out to be false, removing `d_length` will cause all clients of this component to recompile. Similarly, the `copy` function was implemented to factor the copy operation for use in both the copy constructor and assignment operator. If we now decided to change the signature of this private helper function from `copy(const String&)` to `copy(const char *)` to enable its use in implementing the default constructor as well, all clients would again be forced to recompile.

```
// str.h
#ifndef INCLUDED_STR
#define INCLUDED_STR

class String {
    char *d_string_p;
    int d_length;
    void copy(const String& string);

  public:
    String(const char *str);
    String(const String& string);
    ~String(const char *str);
    String& operator=(const String& string);
    // ...
};

#endif
```

Figure 6-9: Private Members Are Not Insulated

6.2.5 Protected Members and Compile-Time Coupling

When considering protected members, base-class authors must now address two distinct audiences: derived-class authors and general users. Protected functions are in the interface specifically for derived classes, but are intended to be treated as implementation details by general users. Note that protected member data is rarely appropriate, especially in widely used interfaces for which insulation is a design goal.

On the surface, the protected interface provides a convenient place for prospective derived-class authors to look to determine what will be required of them. However, just as with private members, the protected interface is declared in the class definition and is therefore not an insulated implementation detail as far as general users are concerned. Modifying the protected interface of a base class in any way will force the recompilation of (1) all clients of the base class, (2) all derived classes, and (3) all clients of the derived classes.

6.2.6 Compiler-Generated Member Functions and Compile-Time Coupling

Certain basic member functions are generated automatically by the compiler, if needed, unless they are explicitly declared in a class.[3] In particular, unless a copy

[3] See **meyers**, Item 45, p. 172.

constructor is specified, the compiler will generate one with member-wise copy semantics. That is, a copy constructor will be generated that copies each member object and each base-class object according to its own individual initialization semantics.[4]

In a similar way, an implicit assignment operator also is generated if needed, copying each member object and each base class according to its own assignment semantics. A destructor will also be generated if needed, to invoke the destructors of layered and base-class objects.

In many cases, compiler-generated constructors, assignment operators, and destructors do exactly what is required. Unfortunately, if the author of a class determines a need to diverge from the compiler-generated definition, it will be necessary to introduce the appropriate member declaration into the class definition. Any such introduction of a declaration cannot be considered insulated, and any clients of the class will be forced to recompile.

```
class ComplexSymbol : public Complex {
    String d_name;

  public:
    // CREATORS
    ComplexSymbol(const String& name, double re, double im = 0.0);
    // Default copy ctor and dtor are fine.

    // MANIPULATORS
    // Default assignment operator is fine.
    // ...

    // ACCESSORS
    // ...
};
```

Figure 6-10: Relying on Compiler-Generated Functions

As shown in Figure 6-10, class `ComplexSymbol` implements copy construction, assignment, and destruction by default. If we decided to eliminate the implementation dependency of our `ComplexSymbol` on `String` and use a `char *` instead, it would be necessary to introduce a declaration for the copy constructor, assignment operator, and the destructor. In this example, the change in private data alone would force our clients to recompile; however, even if we solved that problem (and we can), introducing

[4] See **ellis**, Section 12.8, p. 295.

new declarations into the header file of our component is a change that cannot be insulated from clients.

6.2.7 Include Directives and Compile-Time Coupling

In the experiment at the beginning of this chapter (Section 6.1.1) that demonstrated the high cost of compile-time coupling, we did not even consider the possibility that each header might directly include every other header.[5] Instead we assumed that each `.c` file explicitly included every header in the system because it needed to do so. In practice, this scenario does not happen.

What is much more likely to occur is that each header file will include one or more header files that, in turn, include one or more other header files, until eventually virtually every header file in the system has been included. This is where redundant include guards (Section 2.5) help to reduce the cost of compiling by eliminating the quadratic behavior we observed in the time spent by the C++ preprocessor.

Consider the example in Figure 6-11. A `Bank` class uses a `BankCard` class and a variety of currency classes in its interface. The `Bank` class does not inherit from any other class. Let us assume that `Bank` does not have any inline functions that make substantive use of class `BankCard` or any of the currency classes. Let us further assume that class `Bank` does not embed instances of any user-defined class (HasA) in its own definition.

```
// bank.h
#ifndef INCLUDED_BANK
#define INCLUDED_BANK

#ifndef INCLUDED_BANKCARD
#include "bankcard.h"
#endif

#ifndef INCLUDED_GERMANMARKS
#include "germanmarks.h"
#endif

#ifndef INCLUDED_JAPENESEYEN
#include "japeneseyen.h"
#endif
```

---

[5] In some environments, you might encounter a limitation on the number of open source files permitted at any one time.

```
#ifndef INCLUDED_UNITEDSTATESDOLLARS
#include "unitedstatesdollars.h"
#endif

#ifndef INCLUDED_ENGLISHPOUNDS
#include "englishpounds.h"
#endif

// ...
// ...
// ...

#ifndef INCLUDED_LAKOSIANFOOBARS
#include "lakosianfoobars.h"
#endif

class Bank {
    // ...
    Bank(const Bank&);                          // We don't want to copy
    Bank& operator=(const Bank&);               // or assign banks.

  public:
    // CREATORS
    Bank();
    ~Bank();

    // MANIPULATORS
    GermanMarks          getMarks(BankCard   *cashMachineCard, double amount);
    JapeneseYen          getYen(BankCard     *cashMachineCard, double amount);
    UnitedStateDollars   getDollars(BankCard *cashMachineCard, double amount);
    EnglishPounds        getPounds(BankCard  *cashMachineCard, double amount);
    // ...
    // ...
    // ...
    LakosianFooBars      getFooBars(BankCard *cashMachineCard, double amount);
};

#endif
```

Figure 6-11: Class Using Many Types in Its Interface

Now consider a client of an instance of this `Bank` in the United States. This person is typically interested in going to the bank with his or her bank card and withdrawing some amount of money in United States dollars. A simple example of a `Person`'s withdraw member function is shown in Figure 6-12.

```
// person.c
#include "person.h"
#include "bank.h"

// ...

void Person::withdraw(double amount)
{
    d_wallet_p->putIn(d_bank_p->getDollars(d_cashMachineCard_p, amount));
}
```

Figure 6-12: Simplified Implementation of `Person`'s Withdraw Function

Picture the fictitious island republic of Lakos; its national unit of currency, the *FooBar*, is notoriously unstable and subject to change without notice. Today this country has again announced its intention to make an uninsulated change to its implementation of FooBar. The world financial community is demanding to know who will be forced to recompile.

Not only will all actual clients of `LakosianFooBars` have to recompile, but so will all other clients of `Bank`. That is, if you banked at this bank, whether or not you ever cared or had even heard about `LakosianFooBars`, any change at all to `lakosianfoobar.h` will cause software configuration management tools (such as `make`) to recompile you automatically.

To add insult to injury, there is no real need for you to be compile-time dependent on that currency! None of your code depends on that currency at compile time. So why did `bank`'s author decide to include all these header files in `bank.h` instead of `bank.c`? The answer you might receive is "for the convenience of our clients."

The author of the `bank` component believes that just in case you might need some class definition, we'll include it for you. This approach has the relatively small advantage that as long as you include `bank.h`, you will never need to include the header for `UnitedStatesDollars` or your `BankCard`. However, this approach also has the relatively large disadvantage that you will forever be at the mercy of a potentially large number of header files that you neither control nor otherwise care about.

6.2.8 Default Arguments and Compile-Time Coupling

Often a single algorithm will depend on several parameters—some with reasonable default values. Placing these default values in the header file defining the interface of the function can be more self-documenting simply because they place more information in the header file:

```
class Circle {
    // ...
  public:
    Circle(double x = 0, double y = 0, double radius = 1);
    // ...
};
```

Unfortunately, such default values become compiled in along with the interface and cannot be changed by modifying the component without forcing clients to recompile.

6.2.9 Enumerations and Compile-Time Coupling

Enumerations, CPP macros, typedefs, and (by default) non-member `const` data do not have external linkage (see Sections 2.3.3 and 2.3.4). As such, these constructs must appear in the header file of a component if they are to be used by other components (or if they appear in the body of any inline functions intended for use outside the component).

Figure 6-13 illustrates the common practice in small projects of grouping all system-wide definitions into a single component. As more components are added to the system, these components will typically include this common definitions file. Whenever the need for a new definition or return status is encountered, it is added to the `sysdefs.h` file. The more components that are added, the more opportunities there are to add to the common definitions. Whenever a common definition is added to `sysdefs.h`, almost all components in the system are forced to recompile.

Eventually the system reaches the point where making an addition to the global definitions is simply too expensive. Instead of placing a useful definition in this file, they are kept local or private. Instead of adding new specific return status values to the enumeration, preexisting codes (such as `UNSPECIFIED_ERROR`) are used over and over, even though they are vague or even inappropriate.

```
// sysdefs.h
#ifndef INCLUDED_SYSDEFS
#define INCLUDED_SYSDEFS

#ifndef INCLUDED_MATH
#include <math.h>                           // bad idea: should be insulated
#define INCLUDED_MATH
#endif
```

```
const double PI_BY_4 = M_PI/4;        // bad idea: should be class member
const double PI_BY_8 = M_PI/8;        // bad idea: should be class member

struct SysDefs {
    typedef int (*Pfdi)(double);
    typedef double (*Pfid)(int);

    enum ReturnStatus {
        SUCCESS = 0,
        WARNING,
        IOERROR,
        FILE_NOT_FOUND,
        // ...
        OUT_OF_RANGE,
        // ...
        OUT_OF_MEMORY,
        // ...
        // ...
        INVALID_GEOMETRY,
        // ...
        // ...
        // ...
        UNSPECIFIED_ERROR
    };
};

#endif
```

Figure 6-13: Component Containing Common Definitions

The problem here is that enumerations and typedefs are not implementation details but rather are plainly part of the public interface of a component. The interface of this component is not a well-organized, cohesive presentation of a single abstraction. Instead it is an eclectic hodgepodge of details. This all too common use of enumerations does not scale well as project size increases.

The compile-time coupling in this system arises because this interface is driven not from the lower levels of the physical hierarchy but from the yet-to-be-implemented higher levels. This upward dependency imposes an implicit compile-time coupling among all clients, even though these clients are in unrelated parts of the system. This example is an instance of a more general problem, involving the sharing of ownership for a component.

In the following section we discuss specific techniques for addressing this and other problems related to insulation.

6.3 Partial Insulation Techniques

Not every component should attempt to insulate its clients from every implementation detail. But, all other things being equal, it is better to insulate a client from an implementation detail than not to do so—even if only to reduce the clutter in the physical interface.

Fortunately insulation need not be an all-or-nothing proposition. Insulating one detail of the implementation can be desirable—even when other implementation details remain uninsulated. The more insulated the implementation of a component is, the less likely that changes to that implementation will force clients of the component to recompile.

Sometimes insulating an implementation detail is as easy as not insulating it. As with low-hanging fruit, we can often reap significant benefits while expending negligible effort. Other times insulation can require considerable and deliberate work. The amount of effort worth expending on insulating any given implementation detail comes down to the degree to which changes in that detail are likely to affect clients.

The following subsections provide a collection of specific techniques for selectively reducing the number of implementation details exposed in the physical interface of a component.

6.3.1 Removing Private Inheritance

Unlike public (and protected) inheritance, private inheritance is an implementation detail. One of the "advantages" of private inheritance over layering is the notational convenience of selectively exposing some but not all of the functions in the private base class to clients of the derived class via *access-declarations*[6] or *using-declarations.*[7]

Figure 6-14 illustrates how a class can privately inherit from another class and then selectively publish all members with a given name in its own interface using an access declaration.

---

[6] **ellis**, Section 11.3, p. 244.
[7] **stroustrup94**, Section 17.5.2, p. 419.

```
// base.h
#ifndef INCLUDED_BASE
#define INCLUDED_BASE

class Base {
    // ...
  public:
    Base();
    ~Base();
    void f1(int);
    void f2(double);
    int f1() const;
    double f2() const;
};

#endif
```

(a) Private Base Class Header File

```
// myclass.h
#ifndef INCLUDED_MYCLASS
#define INCLUDED_MYCLASS

#ifndef INCLUDED_BASE
#include "base.h"
#endif

class MyClass : private Base {
  public:
    MyClass() {}
    Base::f1; // access declaration
};

#endif
```

(b) Derived Class Header File

Figure 6-14: Private Inheritance and Access Declaration

The usefulness of the access declaration is dubious for a couple of reasons. It exposes a set of functions in the public interface, yet in order for a client to know what those functions are, the client must look at the header of the privately derived (implementation) class in order to know the appropriate arguments and return values. Another problem is that this class fails to insulate its client from its private base class. The client is exposed to changes in private (unpublished) functions that may not even be used in the implementation of the derived class.

One reason for using private inheritance instead of layering is to take advantage of the virtual table(s) of the base class. By overriding the behavior of the virtual functions declared in a private base class, we may be able to "customize" or "program" other behaviors that depend on the overridden behavior at the base-class level. It also is possible to invent a dummy class for derivation purposes and then proceed with layering using that dummy class. If insulation is not an issue, then private inheritance may be appropriate. If, however, this class is to become part of a more generally public interface, then a transformation from inheritance to layering is in order.

Figure 6-15 illustrates how the same logical interface as the one in Figure 6-14b can be achieved without exposing clients to the details of the implementation class. Instead of privately deriving from class `Base`, the new implementation holds an outwardly opaque pointer to class `Base`. Whenever an instance of `MyClass` is created, the appropriate constructor, declared non-`inline`, dynamically allocates a new instance of `Base` and assigns its address to the `d_base_p` member of `MyClass`. When this instance of `MyClass` is destroyed, the non-`inline` destructor will delete this instance. The assignment operator will also need to manage this base object pointer appropriately.

```
// myclass.h
#ifndef INCLUDED_MYCLASS
#define INCLUDED_MYCLASS

class Base;

class MyClass {
    Base *d_base_p;

  public:
    MyClass();
    MyClass(const MyClass& c);
    ~MyClass();

    MyClass& operator=(const MyClass& c);
    void f1(int i);

    int f1() const;
};

#endif
```

(a) Insulating Header File

```
// myclass.c
#include "myclass.h"
#include "base.h"

MyClass::MyClass() : d_base_p(new Base) {}

MyClass::MyClass(const MyClass& c)
: d_base_p(new MyClass(*c.d_base_p)) {}

MyClass::~MyClass() { delete d_base_p; }

MyClass& MyClass::operator=(const MyClass& c)
{
    if (this != &c) {
        delete d_base_p;
        d_base_p = new MyClass(*c.d_base_p);
    }
    return *this;
}

void f1(int i) { d_base_p->f1(i); }

int f1() const { return d_base_p->f1(); }
```

(b) Insulated Implementation File

Figure 6-15: Using Layering Instead of Private Inheritance

Instead of using access declarations to publish members of a private base class selectively, new member functions of `MyClass` are defined (out-of-line) to forward their calls to corresponding functions defined in class `Base`. Note that all member functions of `MyClass` that depend on `Base` in size must be declared non-`inline` if clients are to be insulated from the definition of `Base`.

In this way, class `MyClass` now insulates its clients from all organizational changes to class `Base`. Had class `Base` been abstract, then `d_base_p` would point to a dummy concrete class derived from `Base`, perhaps implemented entirely in file `myclass.c`. Note that all of this insulation is not without its cost (e.g., extra function calls and dynamic allocation), as discussed in detail in Section 6.6.1.

6.3.2 Removing Embedded Data Members

Even if performance requirements prevent us from fully insulating a class, we can still insulate clients from an individual implementation class by converting all embedded instances of that implementation class to pointers (or references) to that class and then managing those pointers explicitly in the constructors, destructors, and assignment operators of the class.

Figure 6-16 shows how we can selectively insulate clients from implementation classes by converting a HasA relationship (Figure 6-16a) to a HoldsA relationship (Figure 6-16b). In doing so we must redeclare all inline functions that formerly operated on `MyClass` data members of type `YourClass` to be non-inline. The downside of HoldsA is the increased effort required to manage the layered instance; and also the additional performance costs associated with indirection, dynamic allocation, and non-inline functions. Notice how we can continue to access performance-critical member data (such as `d_count`) via inline functions.

```
// myclass.h
#ifndef INCLUDED_MYCLASS
#define INCLUDED_MYCLASS

#ifndef INCLUDED_YOURCLASS
#include "yourclass.h"
#endif

class MyClass {
    int d_count;
    YourClass d_yours;

  public:
    // ...
    int yourValue() const
    {
        return d_yours.value();
    }

    int count() const
    {
        return d_count;
    }
};

#endif
```

(a) Before Insulating `YourClass` from Clients of `MyClass`

```
// myclass.h
#ifndef INCLUDED_MYCLASS
#define INCLUDED_MYCLASS

class YourClass;

class MyClass {
    int d_count;
    YourClass *d_yours_p;

  public:
    // ...
    int yourValue() const;

    int count() const
    {
        return d_count;
    }
};

#endif
```

(b) After Insulating `YourClass` from Clients of `MyClass`

Figure 6-16: Converting HasA to HoldsA to Improve Insulation

6.3.3 Removing Private Member Functions

Private member functions, although encapsulated logical implementation details of a class, are part of the physical interface of a component. Non-inline private member functions have external linkage; this enables functions and classes declared to be friends of this class and defined in other translation units to call them. However, as discussed in Section 3.6, befriending any function or class defined outside a component invites undisciplined clients to take advantage of private details of our class. Avoiding long-distance friendship implies that only functions and classes defined within a single component may have access to private members. Fortunately C++ (and even C) supports a more restrictive, component-wide form of access control.

Instead of making the function a private member of the class, make it a static free function declared at file scope in the `.c` file of the component.[8]

Sometimes functions are made private members not because they need private access but because the private section of the header file is a good place to store these factored helper functions. That is, some private helper functions can do all of their work using only the public interface of the class. In these cases, the transformation from private member to static free functions is easy and quickly accomplished in two steps.

The first step is to convert each private member function to a private static member by adding an appropriate writable pointer or read-only reference parameter to the function. Consider class `MyClass`, as defined in Figure 6-17a. Class `MyClass` contains two private member functions, `f` and `g`. Member `f` is a non-`const` (manipulator) function and member `g` is a `const` (accessor) function. The manipulator `f` potentially alters the object, so, in keeping with our policy (see Section 9.1.1), we will pass the instance by non-`const` pointer along with the other arguments to the function. The accessor `g` is innocuous and we will pass the instance by `const` reference along with `g`'s other arguments, as shown in Figure 6-17b.

```
// myclass.h
#ifndef INCLUDED_MYCLASS
#define INCLUDED_MYCLASS

class MyClass {
    // ...
  private:
    void f(...);
    int g(...) const;

  public:
    // ...
};

#endif
```

(a) Original Class with Private Member Functions

```
// myclass.h
#ifndef INCLUDED_MYCLASS
#define INCLUDED_MYCLASS

class MyClass {
    // ...
  private:
    static void f(MyClass *myClass, ...);
    static int g(const MyClass& myClass, ...);

  public:
    // ...
};

#endif
```

(b) Modified Class with Only Private Static Member Functions

Figure 6-17: Making Private Member Functions Static Members

---

[8] We will be able to achieve this same effect more elegantly using unnamed namespaces, as discussed in **stroustrup94**, Section 17.5.3, pp. 419–420, once this relatively new language feature becomes more widely available.

The second step is to remove these function declarations entirely from the header file, remove the member notation from function definitions in the `.c` file (shown in Figure 6-18a), and finally precede each of these definitions by the keyword `static`, as shown in Figure 6-18b. Note that this second step should not require any changes to the implementations of the other member functions defined in the `.c` file.

```
// myclass.c
#include "myclass.h"
void MyClass::f(MyClass *myClass, ...) { /* ... */ }
int MyClass::g(const MyClass& myClass, ...) { /* ... */ }
// ...
```

(a) Original Class with Private Static Member Functions

```
// myclass.c
#include "myclass.h"
static void f(MyClass *myClass, ...) { /* ... */ }
static int g(const MyClass& myClass, ...) { /* ... */ }
// ...
```

(b) Modified Class with Static Free Functions

Figure 6-18: Converting Static Member Functions into Free Functions

Unfortunately, private member functions often operate directly on other private implementation details, which can make these functions more difficult to extricate. Consider the `list` component defined in Figure 6-19. Class `List` contains three private member functions—`copy`, `clean`, and `end`—that are used repeatedly to help implement the public functionality of class `List`.

The `copy` function is already a static member, but it needs access to the auxiliary ("slave") class `Link`. Both `clean()` and `end()` depend on access to the private data member `d_head_p` that identifies the head of the list, and there are no public functions that can be used to obtain access to it. Making these three functions non-members of `List` will strip them of their privileged access to the implementations of both `List` and `Link`. Although these functions will no longer have access to the private details of either class, the callers of these functions *are* members with full access, and they are at liberty to offer up this information.

```
// list.h
#ifndef INCLUDED_LIST
#define INCLUDED_LIST

class List;
class ListIter;
class ostream;

class Link {
    int d_data;
    Link *d_next_p;
    friend List;
    friend ListIter;

    Link(const Link& link);                   // not implemented
    Link& operator=(const Link& link);        // not implemented

    // CREATORS
    Link(int data, Link *next = 0);
};

class List {
    Link *d_head_p;
    friend ListIter;

  private:
    static Link *copy(const Link *link, Link *end = 0);
        // allocate and return new copy of given list of links

    void clean();
        // destroy and deallocate entire list of links

    Link *& end();
        // return a reference to the end of the list

  public:
    // CREATORS
    List();
    List(const List& list);
    ~List();

    // MANIPULATORS
    List& operator=(const List& list);
    void append(int i);
    void append(const List& list);
    void prepend(int i);
    void prepend(const List& list);
};

ostream& operator<<(ostream& o, const List& list);

class ListIter {
    // ...
};

#endif
```

Figure 6-19a: `list.h` File for `List` Class with Private Member Functions

```
// list.c
#include "list.h"
#include <iostream.h>

                                // **********
                                // class Link
                                // **********

// CREATORS
Link::Link(int data, Link *next) : d_data(data), d_next_p(next) {}

                                // **********
                                // class List
                                // **********

// PRIVATE MEMBERS
Link *List::copy(const Link *link, Link *end)
{
    Link* linkPtr = end;
    for (Link **addrLinkPtr = &linkPtr; link; link = link->d_next_p) {
        *addrLinkPtr = new Link(link->d_data, *addrLinkPtr);
        addrLinkPtr = &(*addrLinkPtr)->d_next_p;
    }
    return linkPtr;
}

void List::clean()
{
    while (d_head_p) {
        Link *tmp = d_head_p;
        d_head_p = d_head_p->d_next_p;
        delete tmp;
    }
}

Link *& List::end()
{
    Link **addrLinkPtr = &d_head_p;
    while (*addrLinkPtr) {
        addrLinkPtr = &(*addrLinkPtr)->d_next_p;
    }
    return *addrLinkPtr;
}

// CREATORS
List::List() : d_head_p(0) {}
List::List(const List& list) : d_head_p(copy(list.d_head_p)) {}
List::~List() { clean(); }
```

```
// MANIPULATORS
List& List::operator=(const List& list)
{
    if (this != &list) {
        clean();
        d_head_p = copy(list.d_head_p);
    }
    return *this;
}

void List::append(int i) { end() = new Link(i); }

void List::append(const List& l) { end() = copy(l.d_head_p); }

void List::prepend(int i) { d_head_p = new Link(i, d_head_p); }

void List::prepend(const List& l) { d_head_p = copy(l.d_head_p, d_head_p); }

// FREE FUNCTION
ostream& operator<<(ostream& o, const List& list)
{
    o << '[';
    for (ListIter it(list); it; ++it) {
        o << ' ' << it();
    }
    return o << " ]";
}
                                        // **************
                                        // class ListIter
                                        // **************

// ...
```

Figure 6-19b: `list.c` **File for** `List` **Class with Private Member Functions**

As shown in Figure 6-20, we can modify both the `clean` and `end` helper member functions so that they, like `copy`, are declared `static` and take as arguments the private information to which they need access. Clients of these two functions must now provide a little more information when they make the call, but these functions will no longer have to rely on private access to the `List` class to do their jobs. The only problem that remains is that these functions still depend on access to the private functionality of the encapsulated Link class in order to accomplish their tasks.

```
// list.h

// ...

class List {
    // ...
  private:
    static void clean(Link *link);
    static Link *& end(Link **addrLinkPtr);
    // ...
 };

// ...
```

```
// list.c

// ...

void List::clean(Link *link)
{
    while (link) {
        Link *tmp = link;
        link = link->d_next_p;
        delete tmp;
    }
}

Link *& List::end(Link **addrLinkPtr)
{
    while (*addrLinkPtr) {
        addrLinkPtr = &(*addrLinkPtr)->d_next_p;
    }
    return *addrLinkPtr;
}

// ...
```

Figure 6-20: Passing Private Information into Static Free Functions

One solution is to make the needed functionality in the `Link` class publicly accessible. Since the use of `Link` is an encapsulated implementation detail of `List`, there is little harm that can come from allowing clients (or test engineers) to play with separate instances of the `Link` class. However, a better solution from an insulation point of view is to move the trivial definition of the `Link` class to the `.c` file and make it entirely public. Not only does this solution increase the insulation of the `list` component's implementation, but it also eliminates a lot of unnecessary clutter in its header file. The improved version of `list` is shown in Figures 6-21a and 6-21b.

```
// list.h
#ifndef INCLUDED_LIST
#define INCLUDED_LIST

class Link;
class List;
class ListIter;
class ostream;

class List {
    Link *d_head_p;
    friend ListIter;

  public:
    // CREATORS
    List();
    List(const List& list);
    ~List();

    // MANIPULATORS
    List& operator=(const List& list);
    void append(int i);
    void append(const List& list);
    void prepend(int i);
    void prepend(const List& list);
};

ostream& operator<<(ostream& o, const List& list);

class ListIter {
    // ...
};

#endif
```

Figure 6-21a: `list.h` File for `list` Component with Static Free Functions

```
// list.c
#include "list.h"
#include <iostream.h>

                              // **********
                              // class Link
                              // **********
struct Link {
    int d_data;
    Link *d_next_p;

    Link(const Link& link);                          // not implemented
    Link& operator=(const Link& link);               // not implemented

    // CREATORS
    Link(int data, Link *next = 0) : d_data(data), d_next_p(next) {}
};

                              // **********
                              // class List
                              // **********

// STATIC FREE FUNCTIONS
static Link *copy(const Link *link, Link *end = 0)
{
    Link* linkPtr = end;
    for (Link **addrLinkPtr = &linkPtr; link; link = link->d_next_p) {
        *addrLinkPtr = new Link(link->d_data, *addrLinkPtr);
        addrLinkPtr = &(*addrLinkPtr)->d_next_p;
    }
    return linkPtr;
}

static void clean(Link *link)
{
    while (link) {
        Link *tmp = link;
        link = link->d_next_p;
        delete tmp;
    }
}

static Link *& end(Link **addrLinkPtr)
{
    while (*addrLinkPtr) {
        addrLinkPtr = &(*addrLinkPtr)->d_next_p;
    }
    return *addrLinkPtr;
}
```

```
// CREATORS
List::List() : d_head_p(0) {}
List::List(const List& list) : d_head_p(copy(list.d_head_p)) {}
List::~List() { clean(d_head_p); }

// MANIPULATORS
List& List::operator=(const List& list)
{
    if (this != &list) {
        clean(d_head_p);
        d_head_p = copy(list.d_head_p);
    }
    return *this;
}

void List::append(int i) { end(&d_head_p) = new Link(i); }

void List::append(const List& l) { end(&d_head_p) = copy(l.d_head_p); }

void List::prepend(int i) { d_head_p = new Link(i, d_head_p); }

void List::prepend(const List& l) { d_head_p = copy(l.d_head_p, d_head_p); }


// FREE FUNCTION
ostream& operator<<(ostream& o, const List& list)
{
    o << '[';
    for (ListIter it(list); it; ++it) {
        o << ' ' << it();
    }
    return o << " ]";
}
                              // **************
                              // class ListIter
                              // **************
// ...
```

Figure 6-21b: `list.c` File for `list` Component with Static Free Functions

Sometimes private member functions can be converted to static free functions that are independent of the types defined in the current component. If these functions are non-trivial, it could be advantageous to attempt to verify them directly. Instead of creating a single component with inaccessible yet non-trivial static free functions, consider making two components—one with public static members used to implement the other.

Figure 6-22 illustrates the result of moving independent static functions at file scope from the `myclass.c` file and making them into publicly accessible static member functions in a separate utility component. This technique makes sense when the functions are either reusable or non-trivial, and it is especially useful when the CCD of these functions alone is very much smaller than it is for the original component.

```
// myclass.c
#include "myclass.h"
#include "myclassimputil.h"

void MyClass::func(int x)
{
    int z = MyClassImpUtil::g(x);
    // ...
    double w = MyClassImpUtil::f(z,x);
    // ...
}
```

(a) Original Component's `.c` File

```
// myclassimputil.h
#ifndef INCLUDED_MYCLASSIMPUTIL
#define INCLUDED_MYCLASSIMPUTIL

struct MyClassImpUtil {
    static int g(int y);
    static double f(int a, int b);
    // ...
};

#endif
```

(b) New Component's `.h` File

Figure 6-22: Moving Static Free Functions to Another Component

Although static functions are preferable to private members with respect to compile-time coupling, performance can become an issue, especially if there is a lot of private state information that must be passed into and out of the static functions at file scope. In such cases, other, more general forms of insulation (discussed in Section 6.4) may be preferable.

6.3.4 Removing Protected Members

What are protected members good for? That is, when is it appropriate to have protected access to class members? The simplistic answer is that protected members are appropriate when you wish to distinguish between two distinct audiences: derived-class authors and general users. The protected interface is every bit as important as the public interface when it comes to encapsulating private details (see Section 2.2), yet the protected interface is often given less attention than the public one. Realize that even though the protected interface of an individual instantiated object is not accessible by the public, anyone can derive a class that depends on these protected details.

The next question is then, "When would someone want to address two distinct audiences from within a single class?" More often than not, the answer is, "When someone is trying to do too much with a single class."

Principle

Supplying support for derived-class authors in the form of protected member functions of a base class exposes public clients of the base class to uninsulated implementation details of the derived classes.

Consider the header for the abstract base class `Shape` shown in Figure 6-23. Presumably each derived-shape object has an origin and an area, and knows how to draw itself on a given `Screen`. The screen object provides all the functionality needed to draw lines and arcs; however, writing the code to achieve this has been found to be both tedious and error prone. Knowing this, the author of the `Shape` base class has provided a suite of protected member functions to aid the derived-class author in implementing his or her own specialized `draw` function.

Figure 6-24 illustrates a derived `Rectangle` class and the implementation of its `draw` function using protected helper functions provided in the base class. The `Rectangle` is defined only by its lower-left and upper-right corners, which implicitly forces the edges of the `Rectangle` to be horizontal and vertical. The derived-class author has also defined the lower-left corner to coincide with the origin of the shape.

```
// shape.h
#ifndef INCLUDED_SHAPE
#define INCLUDED_SHAPE

#ifndef INCLUDED_POINT
#include "point.h"
#endif

class Screen;

class Shape {
  public:
    // TYPES
    enum Status { IO_ERROR = -1, SUCCESS = 0 };

  private:
    // DATA
    Point d_origin;
    Status d_drawStatus;

  protected:
    // DERIVED CLASS SUPPORT
    static double distance(const Point& start, const Point& end);
    void resetDrawStatus();
    Status getDrawStatus() const;
    void drawLine(Screen *screen, const Point& start, const Point& end);
    void drawArc(Screen *screen, const Point& center, double radius,
                                 double startAngle, double endAngle);
  private:
    Shape& operator=(const Shape&);         // not implemented
    Shape(const Shape&);                    // not implemented

  public:
    // CREATORS
    Shape(const Point& origin);
    virtual ~Shape();

    // MANIPULATORS
    void setOrigin(const Point& origin);

    // ACCESSORS
    const Point& origin() const;
    virtual double area() const = 0;
    virtual Status draw(Screen *screen) = 0;
};

#endif
```

Figure 6-23: `Shape` **Class with Protected Support for Derived-Class Authors**

```
// rectangle.h
#ifndef INCLUDED_RECTANGLE
#define INCLUDED_RECTANGLE

#ifndef INCLUDED_SHAPE
#include "shape.h"
#endif

class Rectangle : public Shape {
    Point d_upperRightCorner;

  public:
    // CREATORS
    Rectangle(const Point& lowerLeft, const Point& upperRight);
    Rectangle(const Rectangle& rect);
    ~Rectangle();

    // MANIPULATORS
    Rectangle& operator=(const Rectangle& rect);
    void setUpperRightCorner(const Point& upperRight);

    // ACCESSORS
    const Point& upperRightCorner() const;
    double area() const;
    Shape::Status draw(Screen *screen);
};

#endif
```

```
// rectangle.c
#include "rectangle.h"

// ...

Shape::Status Rectangle::draw(Screen *screen)
{
    resetDrawStatus();
    int x1 = origin().x();
    int y1 = origin().y();
    int x2 = upperRightCorner().x();
    int y2 = upperRightCorner().y();
    drawLine(screen, Point(x1, y1), Point(x1, y2));
    drawLine(screen, Point(x1, y2), Point(x2, y2));
    drawLine(screen, Point(x2, y2), Point(x2, y1));
    drawLine(screen, Point(x2, y1), Point(x1, y1));
    return getDrawStatus();
}
```

Figure 6-24: Derived `Rectangle` Shape and the Implementation of Its Draw Member

In order to draw a `Rectangle`, we will need to draw four lines. If any error occurs we will need to return `IO_ERROR` from the `Rectangle::draw` function. Our first step is to clear the draw status. We then identify the appropriate coordinates and make the necessary calls to the protected helper functions. If any error occurs along the way, these helper functions will internally set the draw status to `IO_ERROR`. When we are done, we simply return the draw status.

This is one way of doing business that is convenient for base-class authors and derived-class authors alike, but takes its toll on general clients by compile-time coupling them to numerous implementation details that they neither need nor want. This scenario is illustrated by the component/class diagram in Figure 6-25.

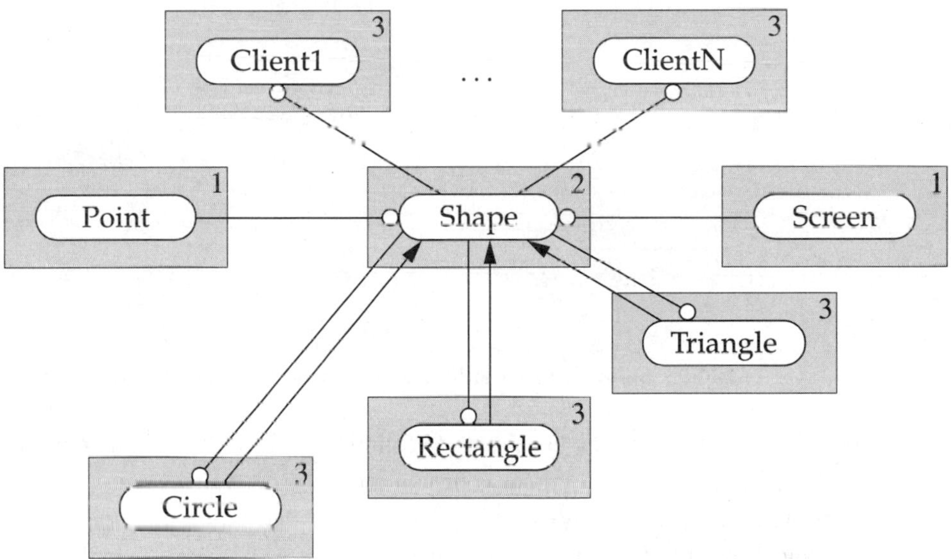

Figure 6-25: Component/Class Diagram for Original Shape System

In this case there is little justification for polluting the public interface of class `Shape` with details that only the derived-class authors care about. Suppose that instead of having each of the derived classes depend on services provided in the base class, each derived class uses a separate component (if needed) to facilitate drawing. This way, the unnecessary coupling associated with the protected members would be eliminated.

As Figure 6-26 shows, the new system is now factored so that the derived-class authors use a separate `scribe` component that the general public does not see.

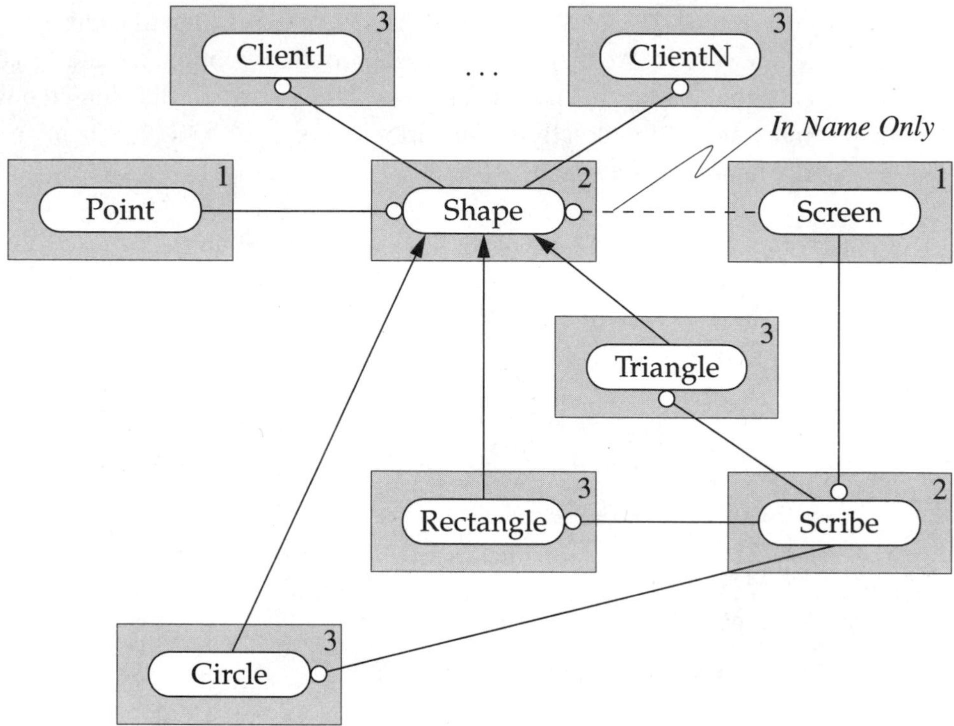

Figure 6-26: Component/Class Diagram for New Shape System

The header for the `scribe` component is shown in Figure 6-27. Since the functionality provided in this new component is no longer embedded in `Shape`, we have decided to uncouple it completely. The drawing functionality no longer depends on `Shape` in any way, and now this facility can readily be reused by objects other than those derived from `Shape` that might need to render themselves on a `Screen`.

```
// scribe.h
#ifndef INCLUDED_SCRIBE
#define INCLUDED_SCRIBE

class Screen;
class Point;

class Scribe {
    int d_hadError;
```

```
    private:
      Scribe& operator=(const Scribe&);            // not implemented
      Scribe(const Scribe&);                       // not implemented

    public:
      // STATICS
      static double distance(const Point& start, const Point& end);

      // CREATORS
      Scribe();
      ~Scribe();

      // MANIPULATORS
      void drawLine(Screen *screen, const Point& start, const Point& end);

      void drawArc(Screen *screen, const Point& center, double radius,
                                   double startAngle, double endAngle);
      // ACCESSORS
      int hadError() const;
  };

  #endif
```

Figure 6-27: New Reusable `scribe` **Component to Facilitate Drawing**

Derived-class authors will not find it difficult to use the public members of class `Scribe` instead of the protected members of the base class. Since the `scribe` component is provided only as a convenience, those who do not find its functionality useful need neither include its header nor depend on it at link time. The reimplemented `draw` function for `Rectangle` is shown in Figure 6-28. The new version of the header for the `Shape` base class is given in Figure 6-29.

Occasionally it is not feasible to remove all of the protected members of a class. Such is the case when the derived class needs access to protected services provided by a base class in order to override virtual functions.

```
// rectangle.c
#include "rectangle.h"
#include "scribe.h"

Shape::Status Rectangle::draw(Screen *screen)
{
    Scribe u;
    int x1 = origin().x();
    int y1 = origin().y();
    int x2 = upperRightCorner().x();
    int y2 = upperRightCorner().y();
    u.drawLine(screen, Point(x1, y1), Point(x1,y2));
    u.drawLine(screen, Point(x1, y2), Point(x2,y2));
    u.drawLine(screen, Point(x2, y2), Point(x2,y1));
    u.drawLine(screen, Point(x2, y1), Point(x1,y1));
    return u.hadError() ? IO_ERROR : SUCCESS;
}
```

Figure 6-28: New Implementation of `Rectangle::Draw`

An abstract base class that defines some shared functionality is sometimes referred to as a *partial implementation*. This type of factored implementation allows derived-class authors to share a common implementation, but protected functionality again places a burden on general users of the base class by exposing them to uninsulated implementation details.

```
// shape.h
#ifndef INCLUDED_SHAPE
#define INCLUDED_SHAPE

#ifndef INCLUDED_POINT
#include "point.h"
#endif

class Screen;

class Shape {
    Point d_origin;

  private:
    Shape& operator=(const Shape&);          // not implemented
    Shape(const Shape&);                     // not implemented

  public:
    // TYPES
    enum Status { IO_ERROR = -1, SUCCESS = 0 };
```

```
        // CREATORS
        Shape(const Point& origin);
        virtual ~Shape();

        // MANIPULATORS
        void setOrigin(const Point& origin);

        // ACCESSORS
        const Point& origin() const;
        virtual double area() const = 0;
        virtual Status draw(Screen *screen) = 0;
    };

    #endif
```

Figure 6-29: `Shape` **Class with Protected Member Functions Removed**

For example, Figure 6-30 illustrates a simple base class that is used both to provide a common interface and to factor the common implementation for cars. All cars have a location, yet the public cannot alter that location directly. Instead, clients must call the public member function `drive` that, in turn, will cause the location of the car to change in various ways, depending on the implementation of the actual (derived) car.

```
// car.h
#ifndef INCLUDED_CAR
#define INCLUDED_CAR

class Car {
    int d_xLocation;
    int d_yLocation;

  private:
    Car(const Car&);                        // not implemented
    Car& operator=(const Car&);             // not implemented

  protected:
    Car(int x, int y);
    int setXLocation(int x);
    int setYLocation(int y);
        // Only derived classes can set the location of a car directly.
    void move(int deltaX, int deltaY);
    static double distance1(double acceleration, double time);
    static double distance2(double acceleration, double velocity);
    double howFar(int newXlocation, int newYLocation) const;

  public:
    // CREATORS
    virtual ~Car();
```

```
    // MANIPULATORS
    virtual void drive(/* ... */) = 0;
        // Public clients alter the location of the
        // car by calling the public function drive.

    // ACCESSORS
    int xLocation() const;
    int yLocation() const;
};

#endif
```

Figure 6-30: `Car` **Base Class Containing Protected Member Functions**

Several helper functions have been supplied in the protected interface of this base class in order to aid derived-class authors in implementing the `drive` function of their own specific class. For instance, the function `move` takes relative distances and sets the new absolute location of the `Car`. Static functions `distance1` and `distance2` are independent of instance data and provide support for physical distance calculations. The `howFar` accessor function compares the current position with a specified new position and returns the as-the-crow-flies distance between the two points.

Unlike the `Shape` base class, however, `Car`'s interface defines a pure virtual function `drive` that, depending on the actual derived type of `Car`, must in turn set the value of the `Car`'s location using protected functions provided by its partial implementation.

The design of the `Car` base class couples the interface with at least a portion of the implementation. Now if a car manufacturer wants to develop an entirely new design for a car, it is forced to carry around the overhead of the partial implementation defined in the base class *whether or not it is used!*

In the case of `Car`, some of the functionality (e.g., the static functions and the `howFar` accessor) could certainly be moved to a separate utility class, as was done for `Shape`. But extricating the partial implementation from this base class requires a more comprehensive effort.

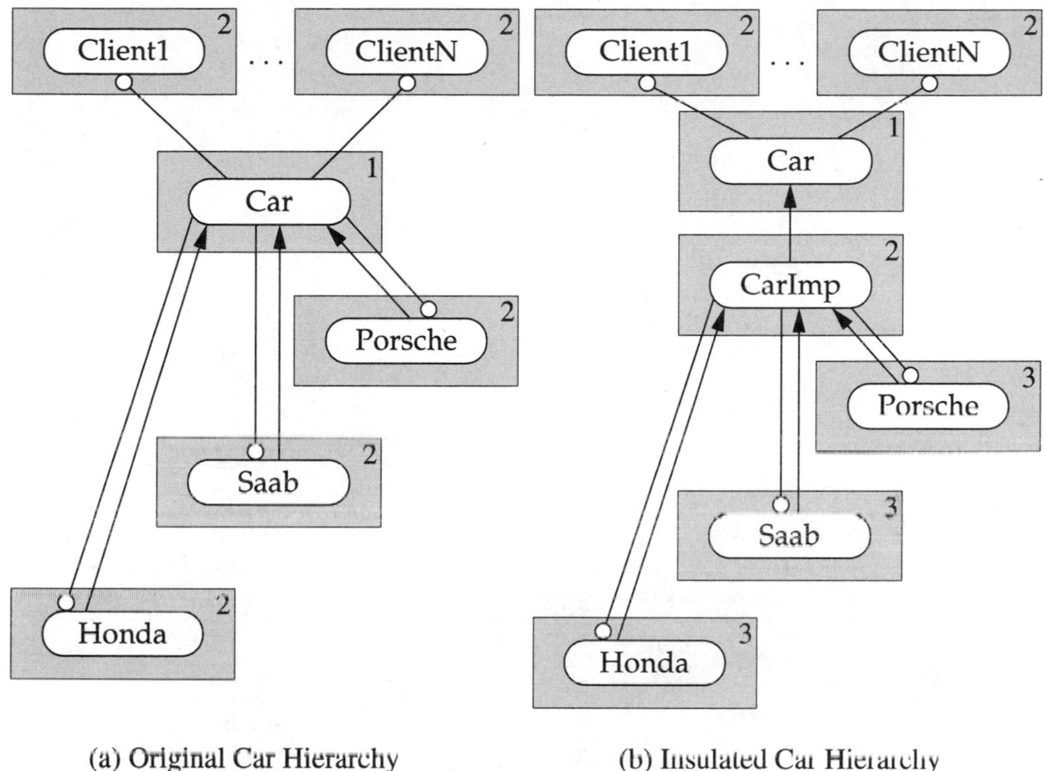

(a) Original Car Hierarchy (b) Insulated Car Hierarchy

Figure 6-31: Extracting a Protocol for Car

Figure 6-31a illustrates the component/class diagram for the original uninsulated system. By factoring the pure interface and partial implementation of `Car` into two separate classes (`Car` and `CarImp`, respectively), we will be able to separate them physically. By placing the pure interface in a separate component, we provide an insulating interface for public clients of `Car`, as illustrated in Figure 6-31b. Note that since `CarImp` derives from `Car`, further derived classes that choose to share the common implementation may continue to do so. Fortunately, changes made to the physical organization of `CarImp` cannot affect clients of `Car`. The extracted protocol for a `Car` is shown in Figure 6-32.

```
// car.h
#ifndef INCLUDED_CAR
#define INCLUDED_CAR

class Car {
  public:
    // CREATORS
    virtual ~Car();

    // MANIPULATORS
    virtual void drive(/* ... */) = 0;
        // Public clients alter the location of the
        // car by calling the public function drive.

    // ACCESSORS
    virtual int xLocation() const = 0;
    virtual int yLocation() const = 0;
};

#endif
```

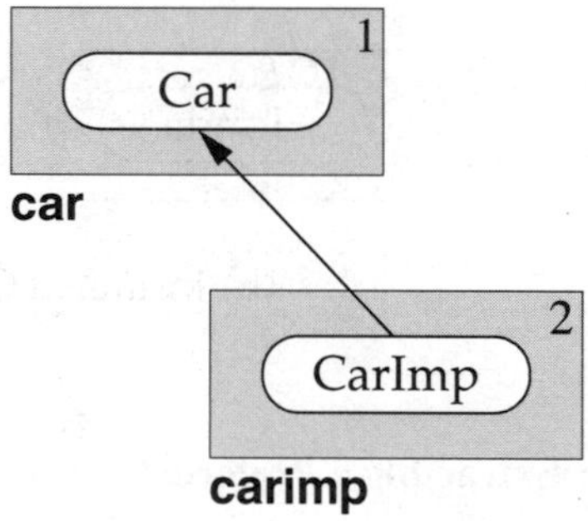

```
// carimp.h
#ifndef INCLUDED_CARIMP
#define INCLUDED_CARIMP

class CarImp : public Car {
    int d_xLocation;
    int d_yLocation;
    // ...
  public:
    // ...
    // ACCESSORS
    int xLocation() const;
    int yLocation() const;
};

#endif
```

Figure 6-32: Protocol and Partial Implementation for a Car

What we have done in order to insulate the general users from all of the implementation details is to extract a pure interface (referred to in this book as a *protocol*). Extracting a protocol is a very general and powerful technique for simultaneously achieving both levelization and insulation. Protocol classes and how to extract them are the subject of Section 6.4.1.

6.3.5 Removing Private Member Data

As you may recall, in the previous section we were able to eliminate all of the protected members from the `Shape` base class by introducing a separate facility to support the implementation of `draw` functions in derived classes. But the base class `Shape` still contained private data.

```
// myclass.h
#ifndef INCLUDED_MYCLASS
#define INCLUDED_MYCLASS

class MyClass {
    static int s_count;
    // ...
  public:
    // ...
};

#endif
```

```
// myclass.c
#include "myclass.h"
int MyClass::s_count;
// ...
```

(a) Original Class with Private Static Member Data

```
// myclass.h
#ifndef INCLUDED_MYCLASS
#define INCLUDED_MYCLASS

class MyClass

    // ...
  public:
    // ...
};

#endif
```

```
// myclass.c
#include "myclass.h"
static int s_count;
// ...
```

(b) Modified Class with Static File-Scope Data

Figure 6-33: Removing Private Static Member Data

Removing private *static* member data is relatively easy. Figure 6-33a shows a private static integer data member, `s_count`, used to track the number of active instances of `MyClass`. As long as inline member functions (or long-distance friends) do not require direct access, it is usually possible to move static member data to a static variable defined at file scope in the component's `.c` file.[9] Removing non-static member data is considerably more involved.

As we saw in Section 6.3.4, changing this encapsulated private data would force all public clients of base class `Shape` to recompile. As was done with `Car` in the previous

[9] In very rare situations, allowing components to have more than one `.c` file enables developers of reusable libraries to partition member function definitions based on usage patterns in order to reduce the runtime size of typical client programs. Allowing functions to communicate via static variables defined in the `.c` file reduces the flexibility to partition the individual member functions of a class into separate translation units (`.c` files).

section, we can factor `Shape` into two classes, one containing the pure interface and the other containing the partial implementation (including the definition of the origin data).

The component/class diagram for the factored `Shape` hierarchy is given in Figure 6-34. There are two distinct advantages to this architecture:

1. Clients of the `Shape` class are insulated from all implementation details of the actual object derived from `Shape`.

2. It is possible to derive an entirely new subtype of `Shape` without incurring any of the overhead associated with the partial implementation now defined in `ShapeImp`.

Class `Shape` no longer embeds an instance of `Point`, so clients of `Shape` are no longer forced to include the definition of `Point` in order to use a `Shape`. Derived classes can continue to share the partial implementation of `Shape` by deriving from `ShapeImp` instead of from `Shape`. As always, there is absolutely no additional runtime cost associated with extending the depth in an inheritance hierarchy. The only additional cost is that the member functions `origin` and `setOrigin`, which were statically bound, must now be invoked through the virtual calling mechanism (see Section 6.6.1).

We may decide to try an alternate partial implementation of `Shape`, `MyShapeImp`, that makes use of a pair of `short int` data members to hold the internal representation of the origin instead of a `Point`. The original architecture simply does not support this degree of reimplementation. Even if the `origin` and `setOrigin` member functions had been declared virtual, the original architecture would have forced each instance to carry around an extra data member of type `Point`.

With the new factored architecture, the choice of implementation is unrestricted. We can now provide that alternate efficient partial implementation for `Shape`, derived directly from `Shape`. Specific concrete shapes derived from `ShapeImp`, `MyShapeImp`, or even directly from Shape itself could coexist in the same running system without affecting other shapes or clients.

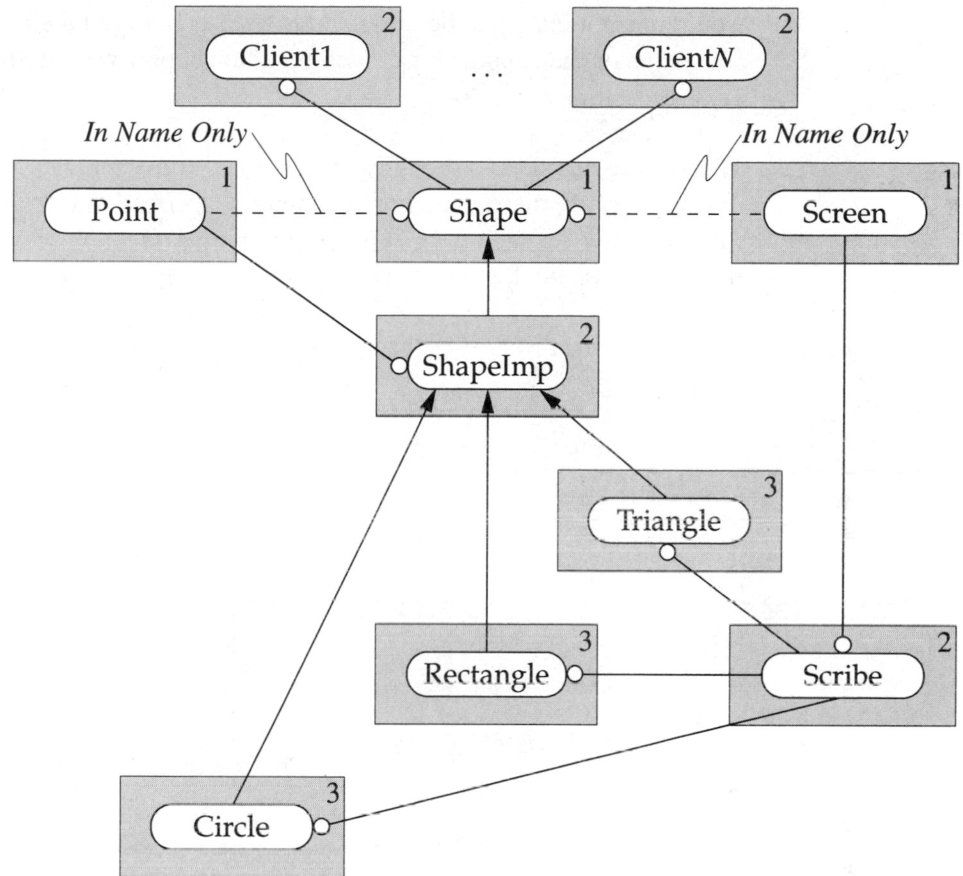

Figure 6-34: Component/Class Diagram for Factored Shape Subsystem

A protocol class for an arbitrary shape is given in Figure 6-35. Even though the `Shape` class now insulates all implementation details from its public clients, we would still opt to keep the support for drawing in a separate component for two reasons:

1. As previously mentioned, maintaining the support for drawing as a separate screen facility independent of the `Shape` hierarchy enables its reuse in rendering objects other than those derived from `Shape` (or `ShapeImp`). Embedding these support functions within `ShapeImp` would couple a spe-

cific partial implementation with more generally useful functionality. It would not, for example, be possible for `MyShapeImp` to take independent advantage of the support for drawing if that support were defined in the `ShapeImp` class.

2. The `scribe` component provides an optional service and is not an essential property of the partial implementation. Derived-class authors who find they have no need for this functionality should not only be insulated from it but should not even have to link to it during testing.

```
// shape.h
#ifndef INCLUDED_SHAPE
#define INCLUDED_SHAPE

class Point;
class Screen;

class Shape {
  public:
    // TYPES
    enum Status { IO_ERROR = -1, SUCCESS = 0 };

    // CREATORS
    virtual ~Shape();

    // MANIPULATORS
    virtual void setOrigin(const Point& origin) = 0;

    // ACCESSORS
    virtual const Point& origin() const = 0;
    virtual double area() const = 0;
    virtual Status draw(Screen *screen) = 0;
};

#endif
```

Figure 6-35: Protocol for a Shape

6.3.6 Removing Compiler-Generated Functions

Changing the definition of any compiler-generated function implies modifying the class definition to add the corresponding declaration. Any such modification would force all clients of the class to recompile. While it may be convenient to allow the compiler to generate a copy constructor, assignment operator, and/or a destructor (if needed), a truly insulating class must define these members explicitly. Often these explicitly defined functions will duplicate their default behavior. In particular, destructors will often be defined with an empty implementation. Such is the price of flexibility. (For other reasons to declare these particular functions explicitly, see Sections 9.3.2 and 9.3.3.)

6.3.7 Removing Include Directives

Unnecessary include directives can cause compile-time coupling where none would otherwise exist. There are generally three cases where a `#include` directive should appear in the header file of a component:

1. IsA: A class in this component derives from a class defined in the included file.

2. HasA: A class in this component embeds an instance of a class defined in the included file.

3. Inline: A function declared inline in this component's header file uses a class defined in the included file *in size*.

Infrequently, a header file that contains a local linkage construct (such as `enum` or `typedef` in class scope) can be another plausible excuse for including one header file in another. In general, however, there are few other situations in which placing a `#include` directive in a header file is justified.

As we saw earlier in the `Bank` example (Section 6.2.7), the `bank` component author's decision to include each of the foreign currencies was no favor at all to the clients of class `Bank`. The fact that these currencies appeared (in name) in the interface in no way implied that `Bank`'s clients needed to know their definitions in order to make good use of `Bank`. The artificial compile-time dependency of `Person` on all these foreign currencies was solely the result of the nested `#include` directives.

The transformation is simple: move all unnecessary include directives from the header file to the `.c` file, and replace them with appropriate ("forward") class declarations. The class declaration tells the client's C++ compiler that the currency represents some user-defined object type but says nothing about its internal layout. Clients of `Bank` are now insulated from changes made to types they don't use. The easily made insulating version of the `bank` component is shown in Figure 6-36.

```
// bank.h
#ifndef INCLUDED_BANK
#define INCLUDED_BANK

class BankCard;                  // class declaration instead of #include
class GermanMarks;               // class declaration instead of #include
class JapaneseYen;               // class declaration instead of #include
class UnitedStatesDollars;       // class declaration instead of #include
class EnglishPounds;             // class declaration instead of #include

// ...
// ...
// ...

class LakosianFooBars;

class Bank {
    // ...
    Bank(const Bank&);                              // We don't want to copy
    Bank& operator=(const Bank&);                   // or assign banks.

  public:
    // CREATORS
    Bank();
    ~Bank();

    // MANIPULATORS
    GermanMarks          getMarks(BankCard *cashMachineCard, double amount);
    JapaneseYen            getYen(BankCard *cashMachineCard, double amount);
    UnitedStateDollars getDollars(BankCard *cashMachineCard, double amount);
    EnglishPounds       getPounds(BankCard *cashMachineCard, double amount);
    // ...
    // ...
    // ...
    LakosianFooBars    getFooBars(BankCard *cashMachineCard, double amount);
  };

  #endif
```

Figure 6-36: Insulating Class Using Many Types in Its Interface

In general, wherever it is feasible to remove an inline function or alter a data member so as to make a `#include` directive in a header unnecessary, a positive benefit by way of reduced compile-time coupling has been realized. If this unnecessary `#include` directive is removed, however, clients that previously depended on this header file to include another will now have to be modified to include that header file directly.

6.3.8 Removing Default Arguments

It is easy enough to remove default arguments from an interface and replace them with equivalent individual functions:[10]

```
class Circle {
    // ...
  public:
    Circle(double x = 0, double y = 0, double radius = 1);
    // ...
};
```

We can change the above interface to the more insulating version as follows:

```
class Circle {
    // ...
  public:
    Circle();
    Circle(double x)                    // do we really want this?
    Circle(double x, double y);
    Circle(double x, double y, double radius);
    // ...
};
```

Upon reflection we may decide *not* to provide the identical functionality and to remove one or more of the options created for us automatically with default arguments.

We can sometimes eliminate the compile-time coupling and yet preserve the factoring of default arguments by interpreting an invalid optional value (e.g., a null pointer, a zero size, or a negative index) within the body of the function itself. Recall that in the interface for the `p2p_Router` (Figure 4-2) there was a function `findPath` that took an "optional" first argument, which was the address at which to store the result:

```
class p2p_Router {
    // ...
  public:
    // ...
    int findPath(geom_Polygon *returnValue, const geom_Point& start,
                 const geom_Point& end, int width) const;
};
```

---

[10] **ellis**, Section 8.2.6, p. 142.

By rearranging the order of arguments, we could have made this argument truly optional without hard-coding any uninsulating value in the interface:

```
class p2p_Router {
    // ...
  public:
    // ...
    int findPath(const geom_Point& start, const geom_Point& end,
                 int width, geom_Polygon *returnValue = 0) const;
};
```

Default parameters are discussed further in Section 9.1.10.

6.3.9 Removing Enumerations

Enumerations in the interface by their very nature evoke compile-time coupling. Judicious use of enumerations, typedefs, and all other constructs with internal linkage in the interface is essential to achieving good insulation.

Consider the three distinct kinds of enumerations shown in Figure 6-37. The first is a private implementation detail of the class, the second is a publicly accessible constant value, and the third is a named, enumerated list of return status values.

```
// whatever.h
#ifndef INCLUDED_WHATEVER
#define INCLUDED_WHATEVER

class WhatEver {
    enum { DEFAULT_TABLE_SIZE = 100 };                        // 1

  public:
    enum { DEFAULT_BUFFER_SIZE = 200; };                      // 2

    enum Status { A, B, C, D, E, F, G, H, I, J };            // 3

    Status doIt();
};

#endif
```

Figure 6-37: A Class Containing Three Distinct Kinds of Enumeration

The first enumeration in Figure 6-37 is inappropriately placed (unless you need a compile-time constant in the header—e.g., to implement a fixed array bound). This enumeration should either be moved to the `.c` file at file scope or, if necessary, be made a private static `const` member of the class. Representing this number as a static class data member gives both inline functions, and functions with friend status defined outside this translation unit, programmatic access to its value, without exposing a "magic number" in the header file.

The second enumeration should at least be made a private static `const` class member, and a public static (perhaps inline) accessor member function should be defined to return this value. As with most insulation techniques (see Section 6.6.1), we pay a price in runtime performance for the reduced coupling. In this case, an optimizing compiler can take advantage of known compile-time constants, such as fundamental data declared `const` at file scope, enumerators, and literals. By storing actual values (rather than addresses) directly in the instruction stream, an extra level of indirection can be avoided. By definition, however, these compile-time constants cannot be insulated from clients. Hence, any attempt to change them will inevitably force client recompilation. If this level of performance across this interface is an issue, then this component is probably at too low a level to be considered a good candidate for insulation.

Principle

Granting higher-level clients the authority to modify the interface of a lower-level shared resource implicitly couples all clients.

The third enumeration is clearly part of the interface. It may be that not all of these status values are returned by functions in this component, but rather that this component has been chosen to hold status values for other components as well. However, to reduce compile-time coupling, a much preferred approach is to distribute the status values to the appropriate components and *not* to attempt to reuse them. Distributing the enumerated status values greatly reduces coupling by allowing the enumeration to be *independent* of higher-levels in the physical hierarchy. Defining return values locally has the added value of not trying to coerce subtly different meanings into already existing status values. Each status value's meaning is local to the current object and exactly suited for its purpose. Reusing status values is but one more case where the benefit of reuse is more than offset by the coupling that ensues. A possible alternative to the definitions in Figure 6-37 is illustrated in Figure 6-38.

```
// whatever.h
#ifndef INCLUDED_WHATEVER
#define INCLUDED_WHATEVER

class WhatEver {
    static const int s_defaultBufferSize;        // 2
  public:
    static int getDefaultBufferSize();           // 2
    enum Status { A, B, C };                     // 3
    Status doIt();
};

inline int getDefaultBufferSize()                // 2
{
    return d_defaultBufferSize;
}

#endif
```

(a) `whatever.h` Header File

```
// whatever.c
#include "whatever.h"

enum { DEFAULT_TABLE_SIZE = 100 };               // 1

const int WhatEver::s_defaultBufferSize = 200;   // 2

WhatEver::Status WhatEver::doIt() { /* ... */ };
```

(b) `whatever.c` Implementation File

Figure 6-38: Alternative Definitions for the Three Enumerations of Figure 6-37

It is possible to get around the compile-time coupling of enumerations in the interface by instead passing integers or character strings. This practice does indeed remove compile-time coupling. However, having an enumeration in the interface of a function especially as a parameter, can be a useful form of coupling that helps to ensure the consistency of the program; it is not this kind of coupling that insulation seeks to eliminate.

Consider a function that returned a "bad" status value as a character string. Clients would be required to know the exact form of the string. Since this value is insulated, even determining this string the first time can be challenging for clients. Now, suppose that one of the returned strings happened to change from `ioError` to `IO_ERROR`. There would be no compiler support to help clients track down all places where the comparison value in the calling routines would need to change. Even ignoring the possibility of change, inevitable spelling errors will surely go undetected.

In general, the goal of insulation is to shield clients from the compile-time dependency associated with knowing unnecessary, encapsulated implementation details; it is not to meant to shield clients from the programmatically accessible interface or to compromise type safety.

6.4 Total Insulation Techniques

In a well-planned, well-architected system, we will know in advance which interfaces are public and which are not. This knowledge will help us to decide which interfaces should be insulating and which should not. Designing an interface to be insulating from the start is always easier and less costly than trying to insulate it after the fact.

In practice, developers may fail to consider all of the ramifications of their design decisions. Sometimes it will be necessary to insulate a particularly poorly designed class from the rest of the system, but applying individual insulation techniques would be tedious and unnecessarily costly.

Fortunately there are wholesale techniques for distancing the implementation of a class, a component, or even an entire subsystem from its interface without disturbing its working implementation. The physical motivation behind these techniques can be found in a few other texts on C++.[11] Often these techniques are motivated from an entirely logical perspective.[12] Many of them introduce one or more new components that serve as insulating interfaces for what now will become the implementation. Using these techniques, we can sometimes improve the quality of a sloppy interface so that it reaches the standard it should have met in the first place.

---

[11] **meyers**, Item 34, pp. 111–116; **murray**, Section 3.3, pp. 72–74.

[12] **gamma**, Abstract Factory, Chapter 3, pp. 87–96; Facade, Chapter 4, pp. 185–194.

6.4.1 The Protocol Class

In the ideal case, a perfectly insulating interface defines absolutely no implementation; it merely specifies an interface through which clients may access and manipulate instances of derived concrete classes.[13]

> **DEFINITION: An *abstract class* is a *protocol class* if**
>
> **1. it neither contains nor inherits from classes that contain member data, non-virtual functions, or private (or protected) members of any kind,**
>
> **2. it has a non-inline virtual destructor defined with an empty implementation, and**
>
> **3. all member functions other than the destructor including inherited functions, are declared pure virtual and left undefined.**

A *protocol class* is an *abstract class* that has no user-specified constructors, no data, and only public members. The component itself does not include any other headers except for those defining other protocols from which this protocol inherits (see Appendix A). All member functions (except the destructor) are declared pure virtual. Many compilers will need at least one non-inline function implementation in order to know in what translation unit to place the virtual function tables (see Section 9.3.3). Since the destructor is the only member function that is not declared pure virtual, it is the only viable candidate for implementing out-of-line in a protocol class.

Principle

A protocol class is a nearly perfect insulator.

---

[13] This requirement is sometimes relaxed to permit extralinguistic support for runtime type information (RTTI) as is discussed in Appendix A.

Figure 6-39 illustrates a protocol for a simple file abstraction. The `.c` file for this abstraction is nearly empty and contains only the following three lines:

```
// file.c
#include "file.h"
File::~File() {}                    // defined empty and out-of-line
```

Note that encoding the location as an integer instead of as an enumeration would have allowed us to add new integer values without requiring existing clients to recompile. In the same vein, we could then also remove or change these values without being able to detect the inconsistency at compile time. Removing compile-time coupling at the expense of compile-time type checking is typically undesirable.

```
// file.h
#ifndef INCLUDED_FILE
#define INCLUDED_FILE

class File {
  public:
    // TYPES
    enum From { START, CURRENT, END };

    // CREATORS
    virtual ~File();                    // not pure virtual!

    // MANIPULATORS
    virtual File& operator=(const File&) = 0;
    virtual void seek(int distance, From location) = 0;
    virtual int read(char *buffer, int numBytes) = 0;
    virtual int write(const char *buffer, int numBytes) = 0;

    // ACCESSORS
    virtual int tell(From location) = 0;
};

#endif
```

Figure 6-39: Protocol for a File

Instead we have chosen to define the set of valid location values explicitly in the interface. It is therefore appropriate to enumerate them in class `File`. This enumeration is in no way an implementation detail; it is strictly part of the logical interface of class `File`. That is, adding to or changing this enumeration is like adding to or changing the set of virtual functions—all derived classes and all clients would be forced to recompile.

Class `File` is abstract: it defines a complete interface but no implementation. For example, one cannot construct an object of type `File` on the program stack as an automatic variable. Somewhere, someone must derive a concrete implementation class from `File` and instantiate it. Perhaps a manager component (such as the one shown in Figure 6-40) is used to keep track of files.

```
// filemgr.h
#ifndef INCLUDED_FILEMGR
#define INCLUDED_FILEMGR

struct FileMgr {
    static File *open(const char *filename);
};

#endif
```

Figure 6-40: Header for a File Manager Component

One or more of the clients in a system may call upon the `FileMgr` in order to create an instance of `FileImp`—a concrete implementation class derived from the protocol class `File`. Once it is created, a pointer to the implementation object can be passed around the system as a pointer to an object of type `File` with no compile-time dependencies whatsoever on its implementation.

Figure 6-41 illustrates a system that uses type `File`, yet is entirely insulated from its implementation. Class `SubSys1` is the part of the system that is responsible for instantiating new objects of type `File`, and is therefore link-time, but not compile-time, dependent on class `FileImp`. Both `SubSys2` and `SubSys3` merely use the `File` protocol. These components are neither compile-time nor link-time dependent on `FileMgr` or even on `FileImp`. As such, both components `subsys2` and `subsys3` can be tested independently of `FileMgr`. These components can even be tested independently of `FileImp` if a suitable stub implementation class is supplied for the `File` protocol in the test drivers.

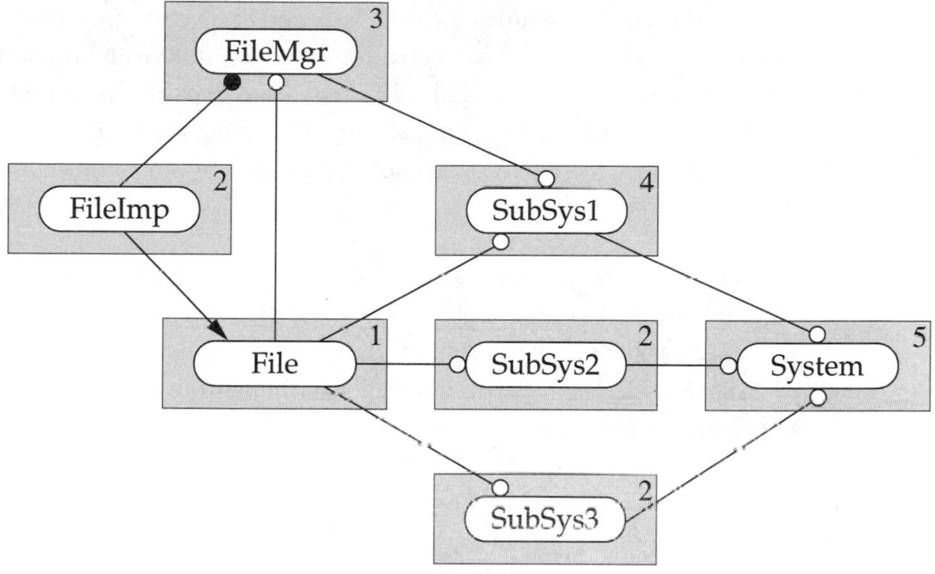

Figure 6-41: System Using a File Protocol

Principle

A protocol class can be used to eliminate both compile- and link-time dependencies.

As we saw with the library subsystem example in Figure 5-32, extracting a protocol can be used to break cyclic link-time dependencies. By physically separating the `Report`'s interface from its implementation, we allowed `StatUtil` to depend on the lower-level `Report` protocol while only the higher-level `ReportImp` partial implementation depended back on `StatUtil`. What is new and important here is that changes to the higher-level implementation component—even in its header file—can have absolutely no compile-time effect on any clients on the same or lower level of the protocol.

Sometimes we will encounter an instantiatable base class that declares some of its functions `virtual`. Often this class contains private data. Sometimes this class will contain private or protected functions. Some member functions may be declared `inline`. The class may contain static functions and enumerations intended for use by derived classes; it may contain protected (or even private) virtual functions intended for precisely that same audience. This class may even derive from or embed instances of other classes that are not programmatically accessible through the public interface of this class. In short, there may be a whole lot more going on in this class than a public client needs to know about.

Consider an instantiatable base class called `Elem` fitting the description of the previous paragraph whose usage is suggested in Figure 6-42. The public interface of `Elem` is used widely throughout the system by clients to manipulate objects of type `Elem` (or derived from `Elem`). The system architect has thoughtfully isolated the creation of `Elem` objects to a single client, `Client1`.

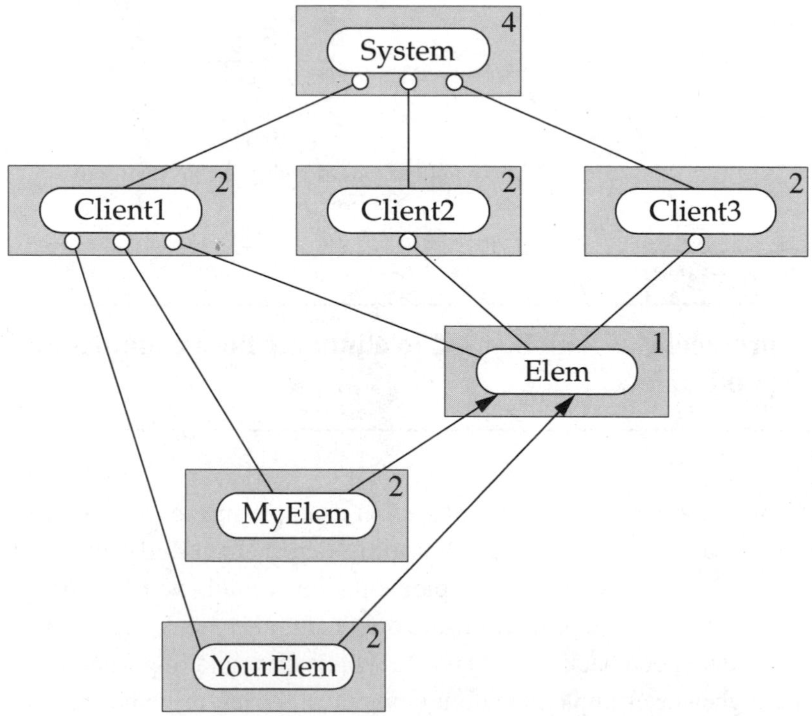

Figure 6-42: Using a Non-Insulating `Elem` Base Class

Unfortunately the intrinsic lack of insulation in the `Elem` base class exposes all clients of class `Elem` to the many unnecessary encapsulated implementation details described above. Clearly the design of the `Elem` base class is far from perfect and, ideally, it should be reworked. Reworking (like working in the first place) will require significant thought and effort. For now, we can insulate the general public from unnecessary details by extracting a protocol from class `Elem`.

As illustrated in Figure 6-43, the idea is to create a protocol class at a lower level and then to escalate static and constructor functionality to a utility class at a higher level. The protocol will contain only the information needed to access and manipulate instances of types derived from `Elem`. The utility will support all static methods, including insulated support for the creation of concrete instances of types derived from `Elem`.

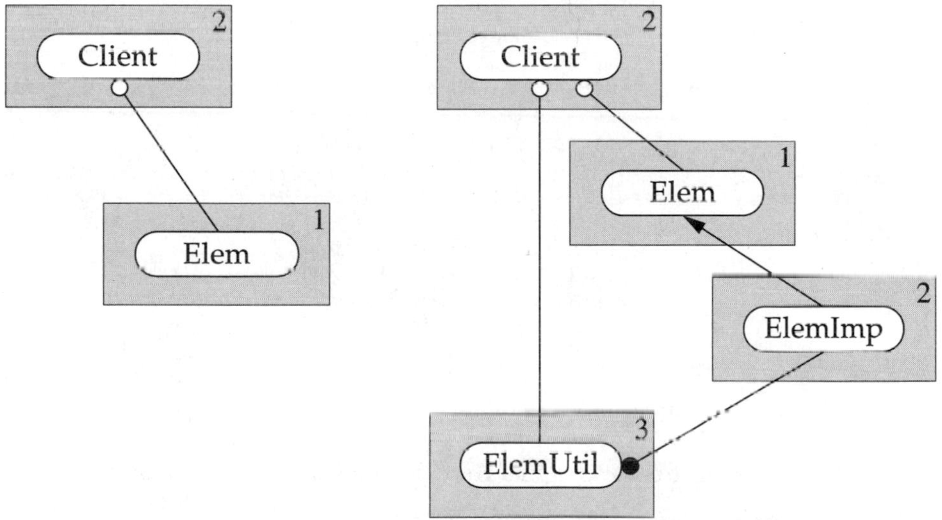

(a) Single Non-Insulating Component (b) Multiple Insulating Components

Figure 6-43: Extracting a Protocol for Base Class `Elem`

Consider the original header for class `Elem` shown in Figure 6-44.

```
// elem.h
#ifndef INCLUDED_ELEM
#define INCLUDED_ELEM
```

```
#ifndef INCLUDED_FOO
#include "foo.h"
#endif

#ifndef INCLUDED_BAR
#include "bar.h"
#endif

class Elem {
    Foo d_fooPart;
    Bar d_barPart;

  private:
    // ...
  protected:
    // ...
  public:
    enum Status { GOOD = 0, BAD, UGLY };
    Elem();
    Elem(const Foo& fooPart);
    Elem(const Bar& barPart);
    Elem(const Foo& fooPart, const Bar& barPart);
    Elem(const Elem& elem);
    virtual ~Elem();
    Elem& operator=(const Elem& elem);
    static double f1() { /* ... */ };
    static void f2(double d);
    Foo f3() const { /* ... */ };
    void f4(const Foo& foo);
    virtual const char *f5() const;
    virtual void f6(const char *name);
    virtual Status f7();
};

#endif
```

Figure 6-44: Original Header for a Highly Non-Insulating `Elem` Class

We can extract a protocol from class `Elem` as follows:

1. Copy the existing component `elem`, containing base class `Elem`, to a new name, `elemimp`, and rename the contained class to `ElemImp`. Any class that previously inherited directly from `Elem` should now be changed to inherit directly from `ElemImp`. This modification will require adjusting the inheritance portion of the class definition of any derived classes along with the `#include` directives of each component containing one or more of those classes. Derived-class constructor initialization lists may require

some adjustment as well. Note that the `Elem` type arguments and return values of all existing non-constructor members of `ElemImp` should remain of type `Elem` (i.e., should not be changed to type `ElemImp`).

2. Delete all but the public interface of the original `Elem` class. If enumerations or typedefs specified in class scope are types used in the interface of one or more non-static, public functions of `Elem`, they should remain.

3. Remove the constructors and all other static member functions from the class, but be sure to leave a virtual destructor, declared non-inline and defined empty.

4. Make all of the remaining member functions in class `Elem` pure virtual and remove their definitions.

5. Remove all `#include` directives from the `elem` component. Provide "forward" class declarations when a user-defined type is used in the interface of a pure virtual function. The new insulating `Elem` class should now appear as in Figure 6-45.

```
// elem.h
#ifndef INCLUDED_ELEM
#define INCLUDED_ELEM

class Foo;

class Elem {
  public:
    enum Status { GOOD = 0, BAD, UGLY };
    virtual ~Elem(); // defined out-of-line and empty
    virtual Elem& operator=(const Elem& elem) = 0;
    virtual Foo f3() const = 0;
    virtual void f4(const Foo& foo) = 0;
    virtual const char *f5() const = 0;
    virtual void f6(const char *name) = 0;
    virtual Status f7() = 0;
};

#endif
```

Figure 6-45: New Insulating Protocol Component `elem`

6. Modify class `ElemImp` to publicly inherit directly from class `Elem`. The header for the base class, `elem.h`, should now be included directly in the header for the partial implementation, `elemimp.h`. Each of the public non-static member functions is now declared `virtual` and should probably (although not necessarily) be declared non-`inline`. Special consideration should be given to the implementation of the virtual assignment operator

   ```
   virtual Elem& operator=(const Elem& elem)
   ```

   now inherited from class `Elem` as well as the new non-virtual operator

   ```
   ElemImp& operator=(const ElemImp& elemImp)
   ```

   defined explicitly for this concrete implementation class.

7. Remove from `ElemImp` any redundant interface information such as enumerations and typedefs that are already specified in the interface of the new protocol class, `Elem`.

   The new `ElemImp` class should now appear as in Figure 6-46. The use of `/* virtual */` indicates that the `virtual` keyword is optional. The non-inline static functions defined in the original `Elem` class were part of its interface and could have been left in the base class. However, had we done so, we would have been faced with the following unpleasant alternatives:

   - If we define the functions in the base class `Elem` to forward calls to the derived class `ElemImp`, we would violate levelization (see Section 4.7).

   - If we implement the definition of the actual `Elem` functions in the `elemimp` component, we would violate the Major Design Rule requiring components to implement the functionality they export (see Section 3.2).

   - If we implement the functions directly in the `elem.c` file, we would physically couple our protocol interface to a specific implementation, violating the definition of a protocol given earlier in this section.

```
// elemimp.h
#ifndef INCLUDED_ELEMIMP
#define INCLUDED_ELEMIMP

#ifndef INCLUDED_ELEM
#include "elem.h"
#endif

#ifndef INCLUDED_FOO
#include "foo.h"
#endif

#ifndef INCLUDED_BAR
#include "bar.h"
#endif

class ElemImp : public Elem {
    Foo d_fooPart;
    Bar d_barPart;

  private:
    // ...
  protected:
    // ...
  public:
    ElemImp();
    ElemImp(const Foo& fooPart);
    ElemImp(const Bar& barPart);
    ElemImp(const Foo& fooPart, const Bar& barPart);
    ElemImp(const ElemImp& elemImp);
    /* virtual */ ~ElemImp();
    /* virtual */ Elem& operator=(const Elem& elem);
    ElemImp& operator=(const ElemImp& elemImp);
    static double f1() { /* ... */ }
    static void f2(double d);
    /* virtual */ Foo f3() const;
    /* virtual */ void f4(const Foo& foo);
    /* virtual */ const char *f5() const;
    /* virtual */ void f6(const char *name);
    /* virtual */ Status f7();
};

#endif
```

Figure 6-46: New Implementation Component `elemimp`

It would be nice if we could retain the original interface; however, none of the above alternatives is particularly palatable.

8. To preserve levelization and to ensure complete insulation, from `ElemImp`

create yet another component, `elemutil`, containing the `struct ElemUtil`. Be sure to include `elemimp.h` in `elemutil.c`. Move all of the static member functions defined in `Elem` to `ElemImp`. Now copy all of the public static functions formerly defined in `Elem` into `ElemUtil` and reimplement them (out of line) to forward all of the client's requests to the corresponding functions now defined in class `ElemImp`.

9. Since `ElemImp` is not abstract (i.e., since it does not contain any pure virtual functions), it will be desirable to provide an insulated mechanism for clients so they can instantiate instances of type `ElemImp` without actually including the non-insulating class definition. (A separate component will be needed to insulate the creation of every object derived from class `ElemImp` as well.) For each of the constructors defined in `ElemImp`, define a new static member function in class `ElemUtil`, named `createElem`, taking precisely the same argument signature as the constructor and returning a pointer to a dynamically allocated, fully constructed instance of class `ElemImp` as a pointer to a non-`const Elem`.

   The new insulating ElemUtil class should now appear as in Figure 6-47.

```
// elemutil.h
#ifndef INCLUDED_ELEMUTIL
#define INCLUDED_ELEMUTIL

class Elem;
class Foo;
class Bar;

struct ElemUtil {
    Elem *createElem();
    Elem *createElem(const Foo& fooPart);
    Elem *createElem(const Bar& barPart);
    Elem *createElem(const Foo& fooPart, const Bar& barPart);
    Elem *createElem(const Elem& elem);
    static double f1();
    static void f2(double d);
};

#endif
```

Figure 6-47: New Insulating Utility Component `elemutil`

The modified system is illustrated in Figure 6-48. Public clients of the new `Elem` protocol will now be relieved of all the compile-time coupling formerly associated with `Elem`. All of this tight coupling has been completely isolated within the element subsystem.

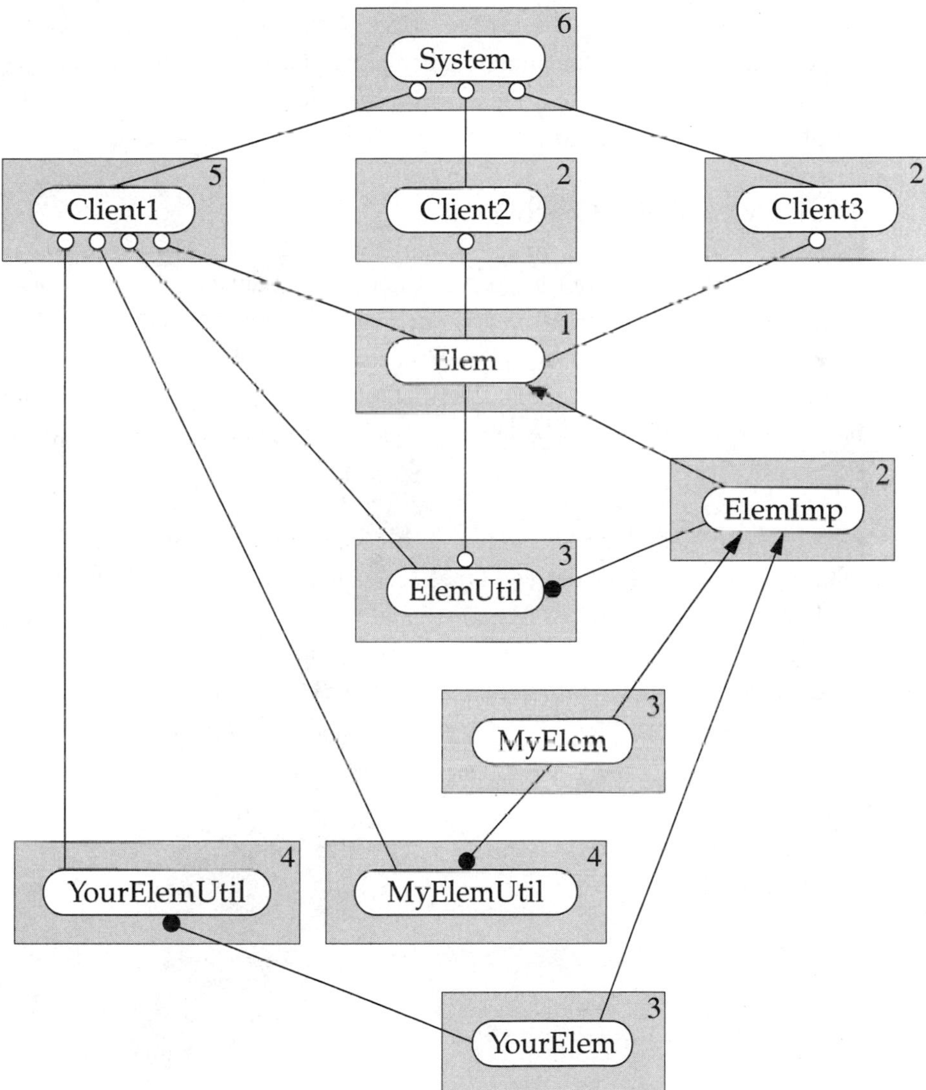

Figure 6-48: Using the New Insulating `Elem` Base Class

By providing a separate utility component with create functions to instantiate each derived class, we can continue to insulate all of our public clients from all of the complex implementation details in the `Elem` class hierarchy. This insulation applies even to clients (such as `Client1`) that endeavor to create new instances of types derived from `Elem`. Derived classes, however, continue to be at the mercy of any uninsulated changes in the `ElemImp` base class. Note that clients of derived classes providing "extra" functionality (i.e., functionality beyond what is accessible through the `Elem` protocol) unfortunately will be forced to depend on the derived class (and therefore on `elemimp`) at compile time.

6.4.2 The Fully Insulating Concrete Class

A concrete class is more than just an interface—it defines a useful object that can be instantiated as an automatic variable on the program stack. Protocol classes (discussed in Section 6.4.1) are consistent with pure object-oriented design; however, engineering is anything but pure. Sometimes we would like the insulating benefits of having a protocol and yet be able to construct an instance of the object (just like any other concrete class).

Consider the class `Example` shown in Figure 6-49. This class contains, as embedded data members, the user-defined types `A`, `B`, and `C`. All member functions are implicitly declared `inline` and the `.c` file is essentially empty. The implementation of this class is clearly not insulated from clients. Suppose we now realize that this class is going to be used widely and that the implementation is subject to change. What can we do to insulate our clients from changes to the implementation details in our example component?

```
// example.h
#ifndef INCLUDED_EXAMPLE
#define INCLUDED_EXAMPLE

#ifndef INCLUDED_A
#include "a.h"
#endif

#ifndef INCLUDED_B
#include "b.h"
#endif

#ifndef INCLUDED_C
#include "c.h"
#endif

class Example {
    A d_a;
    B d_b;
    C d_c;
    double value2() const { return d_a.value() + d_b.value(); }

  public:
    Example() {}
    Example(const Example& e) : d_a(e.d_a), d_b(e.d_b), d_c(e.d_c) {}
    ~Example() {}

    Example& operator=(const Example& e)
    {
        d_a = e.d_a;
        d_b = e.d_b;
        d_c = e.d_c;
        return *this;
    }

    double value() const
    {
        return value2() + d_c.value();
    }
};

#endif
```

```
// example.c
#include "example.h"
```

Figure 6-49: Component Containing a Non-Insulating Concrete Class

The first step is to replace all embedded data with an outwardly opaque pointer to hold that data. By removing the embedded instances, we eliminate the need of our clients to have seen the definitions of classes `A`, `B`, and `C`. We can therefore remove the explicit `#include` directives from `example.h` and replace them with class declarations. Doing so will often require defining previously inline functions out of line, which is entirely consistent with our desire to insulate.

Figure 6-50 shows how this transform would look for the `example` component. As the figure shows, the `.h` file is smaller and the `.c` file is no longer empty. Clients of component `example` are now insulated from all implementation—and even interface—changes to components `a`, `b`, and `c`.

```
// example.h
#ifndef INCLUDED_EXAMPLE
#define INCLUDED_EXAMPLE

class A;
class B;
class C;

class Example {
    A *d_a_p;
    B *d_b_p;
    C *d_c_p;
    double value2() const;

  public:
    Example();
    Example(const Example& example);
    ~Example();

    Example& operator=(const Example&);

    double value() const;
};

#endif
```

```
// example.c
#include "example.h"
#include "a.h"
#include "b.h"
#include "c.h"

Example::Example()
: d_a_p(new A)
, d_b_p(new B)
, d_c_p(new C)
{}

Example::Example(const Example& example)
: d_a_p(new A(*example.d_a_p))
, d_b_p(new B(*example.d_b_p))
, d_c_p(new C(*example.d_c_p))
{}

Example::~Example()
{
    delete d_a_p;
    delete d_b_p;
    delete d_c_p;
}

Example& Example::operator=(const Example& e)
{
    if (&example != this) {
        delete d_a_p;
        delete d_b_p;
        delete d_c_p;
        d_a_p = new A(*e.d_a_p);
        d_b_p = new B(*e.d_b_p);
        d_c_p = new C(*e.d_c_p);
    };
    return *this;
}

double Example::value2() const
{
    return d_a_p->value() + d_b_p->value();
}

double Example::value() const
{
    return value2() + d_c_p->value();
}
```

Figure 6-50: Component Containing a Partially Insulating Concrete Class

However, our clients are not entirely insulated from changes to the implementation of the `example` component itself. Specifically, clients of `example` are not insulated from the actual number of outwardly opaque pointers contained in the `Example` class definition. Adding a single instance of even a fundamental type to the private data of class `Example` would force all of its clients to recompile. Modifying the signature or return type of any private member function would have the same effect.

Principle

Holding only a single opaque pointer to a structure containing all of a class's private members enables a concrete class to insulate its implementation from its clients.

How can we completely insulate the implementation of class `Example` and still have it remain a concrete class? The answer centers around getting rid of the individual private data members and replacing them with a single opaque pointer to the class's representation.[14]

DEFINITION: A concrete class is *fully insulating* if it

1. **contains exactly one data member that is an outwardly opaque pointer to a non-`const struct` (defined in the `.c` file) specifying the implementation of that class,**
2. **does not contain any other private or protected members of any kind,**
3. **does not inherit from any class, and**
4. **does not declare any virtual or inline functions.**

[14] **murray**, Section 3.3, pp. 72–74.

```
// example.h
#ifndef INCLUDED_EXAMPLE
#define INCLUDED_EXAMPLE

class Example_i;        // fully insulated implementation
class Example {
    Example_i *d_this;

  public:
    Example();
    Example(const Example& example);
    ~Example();
    Example& operator=(const Example& example);
    double value() const;
}

#endif
```

```
// example.c
#include "example.h"
#include "a.h"
#include "b.h"
#include "c.h"

struct Example_i {
    A d_a;
    B d_b;
    C d_c;
    double value2() const { return d_a.value() + d_b.value(); }
}

Example::Example() : d_this(new Example_i) {}

Example::Example(const Example& example)
: d_this(new Example_i(*example.d_this)) {}

Example::~Example() { delete d_this; }

Example& Example::operator=(const Example& example)
{
    *d_this = *example.d_this;
    return *this;
}

double Example::value() const
{
    return d_this->value2() + d_this->d_c.value();
}
```

Figure 6-51: Component Containing a Fully Insulating Concrete Class

Figure 6-51 illustrates the result of transforming a class that does not insulate its clients from any of its implementation details to one that is fully insulating. All public inline functions are eliminated. All private member data and functions are now made part of an auxiliary `struct`, defined entirely within the component's `.c` file. Note that, in this example, the default member-wise copy semantics for the auxiliary `struct` happened to be correct and therefore were not implemented explicitly.

Principle

The physical structures of *all* fully insulating classes appear outwardly to be identical.

The important property of a fully insulated class is that changing its representation does not affect how clients perceive the physical layout of an instance, because its implementation (object layout) is always just a single opaque pointer. An instance of one fully insulating class looks the same as every instance of every other fully insulating class, regardless of its purpose or functionality. It is this property of physical uniformity that enables the arbitrary reimplementation of the class's interface without having to alter its header file in any way.

Allowing inheritance or virtual functions would affect the object layout by introducing additional data and/or additional virtual-function-table pointers. Note that inheriting from even an empty `struct` affects the size of the derived object. Thus an instance of an otherwise fully insulating class that inherits from a base class would necessarily appear physically different from an instance of a fully insulated class that does not. In other words, inheriting from a base class would increase the size of a fully insulating class beyond that of a single pointer, physically distinguishing its instances from those of other, fully insulating classes.

Principle

All fully insulated implementations can be modified without affecting *any* header file.

Another important property of being fully insulating is that the class has sole control over and access to the `struct` defining its internal representation. Letting the internal data member point directly at an instance of a class defined in a separate component would compromise our ability to make independent insulated changes to our own implementation. In order to add a private member without affecting our clients, we would be forced to alter the interface of an independently accessible, independently testable object.

When writing the implementations of member functions for a fully insulating concrete class, instead of relying on the implicit notation:

`d_c`	to mean	`this->d_c`
`value2()`	to mean	`this->value2()`

we must now use the `d_this` pointer explicitly as follows:

`d_c`	becomes	`d_this->d_c;`
`value2()`	becomes	`d_this->value2();`

The name of the data structure type (e.g., `Example_i`) and especially the name of the instance variable (e.g., `d_this`) are mostly a matter of style and need not be the same in all cases. Because the `Example_i struct` ("hidden" in the `.c` file) may contain function or static data members with external linkage, however, there is the possibility for unexpected link-time collisions with members of like-named classes defined outside this component. For this reason, the naming convention for the `struct` defining the fully insulated implementation should be disjoint from that for naming ordinary classes. Adopting the prefix of the publicly accessible class name followed by an underscore ensures that an implementation class local to a component will not collide with classes defined outside this component. You may find this kind of consistent convention helpful for identifying the representation of fully insulating classes when working on large projects.

6.4.3 The Insulating Wrapper

Wrappers were presented in Section 5.10 as a general encapsulation technique that applies not just to individual components but to entire subsystems. Instead of attempting to encapsulate within each component what would appear to a user of the subsystem as an implementation detail, we introduced wrapper components to encapsulate the use of these implementation components.

Because clients of a subsystem were not granted programmatic access to objects defined in the lower-level implementation components, we were able to force these clients to interact with the subsystem exclusively through the wrapper interface.

Here we propose to make the wrapper not only encapsulating but insulating as well. We therefore endeavor to eliminate the unnecessary clutter and compile-time coupling associated with an interface that contains irrelevant or perhaps even proprietary information.

6.4.3.1 Single-Component Wrappers

One way to produce an insulating wrapper component is to apply the total insulation technique of Section 6.4.2 to the individual objects defined in an encapsulating wrapper. We can do this without affecting any of the lower-level objects used to implement the wrapper.

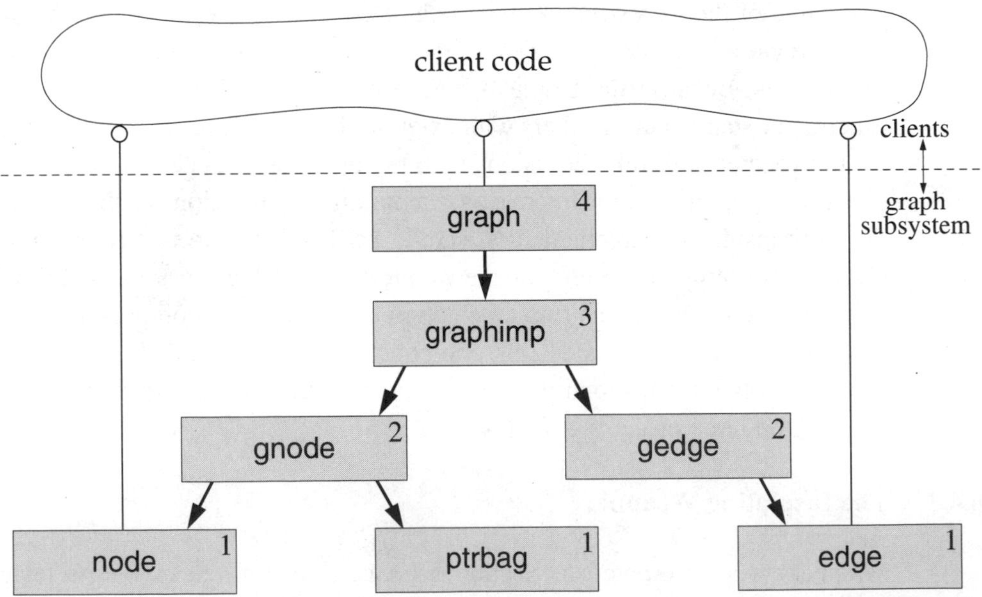

Figure 6-52: Component Dependency of Graph Wrapper from Figure 5-95

Figure 6-52 shows the component dependency for the `graph` wrapper component of Figure 5-95. As you may recall, the clients of `graph` were not permitted to access the objects defined in the implementation components: `graphimp`, `gnode`, `gedge`, and `ptrbag`. However, clients of `graph` were not insulated from changes to the headers of these components.

Let us consider insulating the `graph` wrapper component of Figure 5-95. A brute-force conversion of `graph` using the total insulation technique of Section 6.4.2 produces the header file shown in Figure 6-53. This interface does achieve total insulation, but it is at a significant cost in runtime performance due to extra dynamic memory allocations.

```
// graph.h
#ifndef INCLUDED_GRAPH
#define INCLUDED_GRAPH

class Node;                 // used in the interface of graph
class Edge;                 // used in the interface of graph

class NodeId_i;             // should be changed to:  class Gnode;
class EdgeId_i;             // should be changed to:  class Gedge;
class Graph_i;              // fully insulated implementation
class NodeIter_i;           // fully insulated implementation
class EdgeIter_i;           // fully insulated implementation

class NodeId {
    NodeId_i *d_this;       // should be changed to:  Gnode *d_node_p;
    friend EdgeId;
    friend Graph;
    friend NodeIter;
    friend EdgeIter;

  public:
    NodeId();
    NodeId(const NodeId& nid);
    ~NodeId();
    NodeId& operator=(const NodeId& nid);
    operator Node *() const;
    Node *operator->() const;
};

class EdgeId {
    EdgeId_i *d_this;       // should be changed to:  Gedge *d_edge_p;
    friend Graph;
    friend EdgeIter;
```

```
  public:
    EdgeId();
    EdgeId(const EdgeId& eid);
    ~EdgeId();
    EdgeId& operator=(const EdgeId& eid);
    NodeId from() const;
    NodeId to() const;
    operator Edge *() const;
    Edge *operator->() const;
};

class Graph {
    Graph_i *d_this;
    friend NodeIter;
    friend EdgeIter;

  private:
    Graph(const Graph&);                    // not implemented
    Graph& operator=(const Graph&);         // not implemented

  public:
    Graph();
    ~Graph();
    NodeId addNode(const char *nodeName);
    NodeId findNode(const char *nodeName);
    void removeNode(const NodeId& nid);
    EdgeId addEdge(const NodeId& from, const NodeId& to, double weight);
    EdgeId findEdge(const NodeId& from, const NodeId& to);
    void removeEdge(const EdgeId& eid);
};

class NodeIter {
    NodeIter_i *d_this;

  private:
    NodeIter(const NodeIter&);
    NodeIter& operator=(const NodeIter&);

  public:
    NodeIter(const Graph& graph);
    ~NodeIter();
    void operator++();
    operator const void *() const;
    NodeId operator()() const;
};

class EdgeIter {
    EdgeIter_i *d_this;
```

```
    private:
      EdgeIter(const EdgeIter&);
      EdgeIter& operator=(const EdgeIter&);

    public:
      EdgeIter(const Graph& graph);
      EdgeIter(const NodeId& nid);
      ~EdgeIter();
      void operator++();
      operator const void *() const;
      EdgeId operator()() const;
};

#endif
```

Figure 6-53: Header for Fully Insulating `graph` **Wrapper Component,** `graph.h`

As Figure 6-54 shows, the fully insulating version of class `NodeId` now requires dynamic allocation whenever a `NodeId` is returned by value:

```
NodeId Graph::findNode(const char *nodeName)
{
    NodeId id;                          // causes dynamic allocation
    id.d_this->d_node_p = d_this->d_imp.findNode(nodeName);
    return id;
}
```

```
// (from graph.h)

class NodeId_i;  // fully insulated
class NodeId {
    NodeId_i *d_this;
    friend EdgeId;
    friend Graph;
    friend NodeIter;
    friend EdgeIter;

  public:
    NodeId();
    NodeId(const NodeId& nid);
    ~NodeId();
    NodeId& operator=(const NodeId&);
    operator Node *() const;
    Node *operator->() const;
};
```

```
// (from graph.c)

struct NodeId_i {
    Gnode *d_node_p;
};

NodeId::NodeId()
{
    d_this = new NodeId_i;
    d_this->d_node_p = 0;
}

NodeId::NodeId(const NodeId& nid)
{
    d_this = new NodeId_i;
    d_this->d_node_p = nid.d_this->d_node_p;
}

NodeId::~NodeId()
{
    delete d_this;
}

NodeId& NodeId::operator=(const NodeId& nid)
{
    d_this->d_node_p = nid.d_this->d_node_p;
    return *this;
}

NodeId::operator Node *() const
{
    return d_this->d_node_p;
}

Node *NodeId::operator->() const
{
    return *this;
}
```

Figure 6-54: Fully Insulated Reimplementation of `NodeId` **from Figure 5-95**

Instead of insisting on total insulation for all of the wrapper classes, we can achieve most of the advantages of insulation at considerably less runtime cost if we only partially insulate the `NodeId` and `EdgeId` classes. By exposing just the names of these implementation classes in the wrapper header, we give up the flexibility to add independent members to the wrapper classes; however, we retain the right to modify the organization of `Gnode` and `Gedge` in any way we see fit.

```
// (from graph.h)

class Gnode;  // partially insulated

class NodeId {
    Gnode *d_node_p;
    friend EdgeId;
    friend Graph;
    friend NodeIter;
    friend EdgeIter;

  public:
    NodeId();
    NodeId(const NodeId& nid);
    ~NodeId();
    NodeId& operator=(const NodeId&);
    operator Node *() const;
    Node *operator->() const;
};
```

```
// (from graph.c)

NodeId::NodeId() : d_node_p(0) {}

NodeId::NodeId(const NodeId& nid)
: d_node_p(nid.d_node_p) {}

NodeId::~NodeId() {}

NodeId& NodeId::operator=(const NodeId& nid)
{
    d_node_p = nid.d_node_p;
    return *this;
}

NodeId::operator Node *() const
{
    return d_node_p;
}

Node *NodeId::operator->() const
{
    return *this;
}
```

Figure 6-55: Partially Insulated Reimplementation of `NodeId` from Figure 5-95

Figure 6-55 demonstrates how one can temper total insulation for lightweight classes to improve performance. Functions returning `NodeId` by value can now do so without the cost of allocating dynamic memory—a cost we attempt to quantify in Section 6.6.1:

```
NodeId Graph::findNode(const char *nodeName)
{
    NodeId id;  // no dynamic allocation here
    id.d_node_p = d_this->d_imp.findNode(nodeName);
    return id;
}
```

Although the runtime performance stands to benefit significantly from the partial insulation of `NodeId` and `EdgeId`, the remaining three classes—`Graph`, `NodeIter`, and `EdgeIter`—are an entirely separate matter. In each case, insulating the client of the wrapper from the implementation object requires a dynamic allocation anyway. It costs no more at runtime to allocate a `struct` containing the implementation object than it does to allocate the implementation object itself. Nor is there any additional runtime cost associated with extra indirection. We have to follow exactly one pointer—adding a theoretical offset of 0 is removed by standard *compile-time* optimization. In terms of performance, fully insulating these classes costs no more than partially insulating them, so we might as well go for it.

Notice also that `Graph`, `NodeIter`, and `EdgeIter` have each disabled both copy construction and assignment. Because the normal use of these objects requires creating and destroying them much less frequently than `NoteId` and `EdgeId`, they are naturally better candidates for insulation. The fully insulated implementations of `Graph`, `NodeIter`, and `EdgeIter`, along with the partially insulated implementations of `NodeId` and `EdgeId` corresponding to the suggested changes in the header file of Figure 6-53, are provided for reference in Figure 6-56.

```
// graph.c
#include "graph.h"
#include "graphimp.h"
#include "gnode.h"
#include "gedge.h"

NodeId::NodeId() : d_node_p(0) {}

NodeId::NodeId(const NodeId& nid) : d_node_p(nid.d_node_p) {}

NodeId::~NodeId() {}

NodeId& NodeId::operator=(const NodeId& nid)
{
    d_node_p = nid.d_node_p;
    return *this;
}
```

```
NodeId::operator Node *() const { return d_node_p; }

Node *NodeId::operator->() const { return *this; }

EdgeId::EdgeId() : d_edge_p(0) {}

EdgeId::EdgeId(const EdgeId& eid) : d_edge_p(eid.d_edge_p) {}

EdgeId::~EdgeId() {}

EdgeId& EdgeId::operator=(const EdgeId& eid)
{
    d_edge_p = eid.d_edge_p;
    return *this;
}

NodeId EdgeId::from() const
{
    NodeId id;
    id.d_node_p = d_edge_p->from();
    return id;
}

NodeId EdgeId::to() const
{
    NodeId id;
    id.d_node_p = d_edge_p->to();
    return id;
}

EdgeId::operator Edge *() const { return d_edge_p; }

Edge *EdgeId::operator->() const { return *this; }


struct Graph_i {
    GraphImp d_imp;
};

Graph::Graph() : d_this(new Graph_i) {}

Graph::~Graph() { delete d_this; }

NodeId Graph::addNode(const char *nodeName)
{
    NodeId id;
    id.d_node_p = d_this->d_imp.addNode(nodeName);
    return id;
}
```

```
NodeId Graph::findNode(const char *nodeName)
{
    NodeId id;
    id.d_node_p = d_this->d_imp.findNode(nodeName);
    return id;
}

void Graph::removeNode(const NodeId& nid)
{
    d_this->d_imp.removeNode(nid.d_node_p);
}

EdgeId Graph::addEdge(const NodeId& from, const NodeId& to, double weight)
{
    EdgeId id;
    id.d_edge_p = d_this->d_imp.addEdge(from.d_node_p, to.d_node_p, weight);
    return id;
}

EdgeId Graph::findEdge(const NodeId& from, const NodeId& to)
{
    EdgeId id;
    id.d_edge_p = d_this->d_imp.findEdge(from.d_node_p, to.d_node_p);
    return id;
}

void Graph::removeEdge(const EdgeId& eid)
{
    d_this->d_imp.removeEdge(eid.d_edge_p);
}

struct NodeIter_i {
    GnodePtrBagIter d_iter;
    NodeIter_i(const GnodePtrBag& nodes) : d_iter(nodes) {}
};

NodeIter::NodeIter(const Graph& graph)
: d_this(new NodeIter_i(graph.d_this->d_imp.nodes())) {}

NodeIter::~NodeIter() { delete d_this; }

void NodeIter::operator++() { ++d_this->d_iter; }

NodeIter::operator const void *() const { return d_this->d_iter; }

NodeId NodeIter::operator()() const
{
    NodeId id;
    id.d_node_p = d_this->d_iter();
    return id;
}
```

```
struct EdgeIter_i {
    GedgePtrBagIter d_iter;
    EdgeIter_i(const GedgePtrBag& edges) : d_iter(edges) {}
};

EdgeIter::EdgeIter(const Graph& graph)
: d_this(new EdgeIter_i(graph.d_this->d_imp.edges())) {}

EdgeIter::EdgeIter(const NodeId& nid)
: d_this(new EdgeIter_i(nid.d_node_p->edges())) {}


EdgeIter::~EdgeIter() { delete d_this; }

void EdgeIter::operator++() { ++d_this->d_iter; }

EdgeIter::operator const void *() const { return d_this->d_iter; }

EdgeId EdgeIter::operator()() const
{
    EdgeId id;
    id.d_edge_p = d_this->d_iter();
    return id;
}
```

Figure 6-56: ***Almost*** **Fully Insulated Reimplementation of graph** (`graph.c`)

If designed properly, a single wrapper component can effectively insulate clients from the organizational details of many lower-level implementation components.

6.4.3.2 Multi-Component Wrappers

Wrapping components individually is also possible, but only when direct interaction with the underlying component by clients is not required. As an instructive (but unlikely) example, consider creating the fully insulating wrapper component `pubstack` for a non-insulating, list-based `stack` component.

As illustrated in Figure 6-57, the original `stack` component exposes three classes and two operators in its header file. One of these classes, `StackLink`, is an encapsulated implementation detail of the other two classes (`Stack` and `StackIter`). The wrapper component, `pubstack`, exposes two classes, two free operators, and none of the underlying implementation details. Regardless of how `Stack` and `StackIter` are implemented, clients of the wrapper classes are insulated from all implementation details.

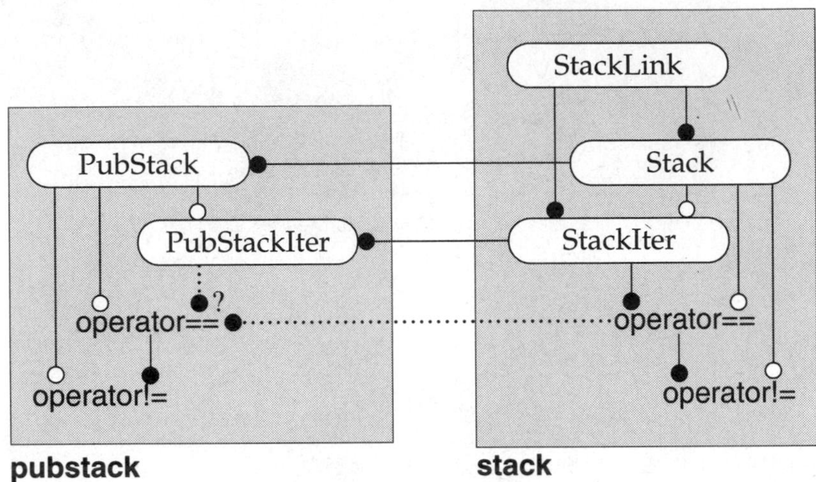

Figure 6-57: Complete Component/Class Diagram for `stack` and Its Wrapper

Figure 6-58 shows the header file for a fully insulating wrapper for a `stack` component. Each of the two wrapper classes holds only a single private opaque pointer to its own internally defined implementation structure. There are no other private or protected members of any kind in the wrapper's physical interface. All functions will be defined out of line. The friendships necessary to extract the underlying wrapped objects from other wrapper objects passed as parameters are the only implementation details in the physical interface of this wrapper component.

```
// pubstack.h
#ifndef INCLUDED_PUBSTACK
#define INCLUDED_PUBSTACK

class PubStackIter;

class PubStack_i;
class PubStack {
    PubStack_i *d_this;
    friend PubStackIter;
    // May want to grant access to improve performance and/or reuse:
    //friend int operator==(const PubStack&, const PubStack&);
```

```
  public:
    PubStack();
    PubStack(const PubStack& stack);
    ~PubStack();
    PubStack& operator=(const PubStack& stack);
    void push(int value);
    int pop();
    int top() const;
    int isEmpty() const;
};

int operator==(const PubStack& left, const PubStack& right);
int operator!=(const PubStack& left, const PubStack& right);

class PubStackIter_i;
class PubStackIter {
    PubStackIter_i *d_this;
    PubStackIter(const PubStackIter&);
    PubStackIter& operator=(const PubStackIter&);

  public:
    PubStackIter(const PubStack& stack);
    ~PubStackIter();
    void operator++();
    operator const void *() const;
    int operator()() const;
};

#endif
```

Figure 6-58: Fully Insulating `stack` **Wrapper Interface** (`pubstack.h`)

Figure 6-59 shows how the `pubstack` component is implemented. Virtually all functionality supplied by `PubStack` forwards calls out of line to the corresponding functions of the insulated implementation object, `Stack`. Each constructor of `PubStack` merely allocates an instance of its auxiliary structure, `PubStack_i`. `PubStack`'s destructor destroys this dynamically allocated instance, and all member functions simply forward their input to the corresponding members of the `Stack` object embedded in the managed instance of `PubStack_i`.

```
// pubstack.c
#include "pubstack.h"
#include "stack.h"

struct PubStack_i {
    Stack d_stack;
};

PubStack::PubStack()
d_this(new PubStack_i) {}

PubStack::PubStack(const PubStack& s)
d_this(new PubStack_i(*s.d_this)) {}

PubStack::~PubStack() { delete d_this; }

PubStack& PubStack::operator=(const PubStack& s)
{
    *d_this = *s.d_this;
    return *this;
}

void PubStack::push(int v) { d_this->d_stack.push(v); }

int PubStack::pop() { return d_this->d_stack.pop(); }

int PubStack::top() const { return d_this->d_stack.top(); }

int PubStack::isEmpty() const { return d_this->d_stack.isEmpty(); }

int operator==(const PubStack& left, const PubStack& right)
{
    PubStackIter lit(left);
    PubStackIter rit(right);
    for (; lit && rit; ++lit, ++rit) {
        if (lit() != rit()) {
            return 0;
        }
    }
    // at least one of lit and rit is now 0
    return lit == rit;
}

int operator!=(const PubStack& left, const PubStack& right)
{
    return !(left == right);
}

struct PubStackIter_i {
    StackIter d_stackIter;
    PubStackIter_i(Stack &stack) : d_stackIter(stack) {}
};
```

```
PubStackIter::PubStackIter(const PubStack& stack)
: d_this(new PubStackIter_i(stack.d_this->d_stack)) {}

PubStackIter::~PubStackIter() { delete d_this; }

PubStackIter::operator const void *() const
{
    return d_this->d_stackIter.operator const void*();
}

int PubStackIter::operator()() const
{
    return d_this->d_stackIter.operator()();
}
```

Figure 6-59: Implementation of Fully Insulating `stack` **Wrapper,** `pubstack.c`

In this example, the free `operator==` does not absolutely need to have access to the private implementation of the underlying subobject in order to implement its functionality. Instead `operator==` can implement its functionality locally via the public version of the iterator, which does have private access to the underlying implementation. If this overhead is deemed excessive, it is easy enough to declare the wrapper function

```
int operator==(const PubStack& left, const PubStack& right)
```

a friend of class `PubStack`. Doing so would grant this free operator private access to `PubStack`'s underlying `Stack` object, enabling it to invoke the corresponding, lower-level `operator==` directly:

```
int operator==(const PubStack& left, const PubStack& right)
{
    return *left.d_imp_p == *right.d_imp_p;
}
```

Anticipating the possibility of this optimization, we might choose to declare all classes and free operators that use `PubStack` in their interface to be friends of `PubStack`, thereby granting them direct access to its underlying representation object, `Stack`. For complete wrapper layers that fit within a single component (e.g., `p2p_router`, `pubstack`, `graph`), this approach is quite workable. Any implied friendships are all local to a single component and therefore neither impose additional coupling nor threaten encapsulation.

Principle

There is no way to determine programmatically from outside a component whether that component is or is not a wrapper.

Because a wrapper fully encapsulates its underlying implementation, it is not in general practical to wrap individual components. If we were to attempt to insulate a large subsystem using individual wrapper components in a way that tried to mirror the underlying implementation, the need for long-distance friendships would quickly become apparent.

Figure 6-60 illustrates the problem with wrapping components that have to interact directly. An `ElemSet` is an object that manages a collection of objects of type `Elem`. `ElemSet` has a member, `void add(const Elem&)`, that takes an element and adds a copy of its value to the set. `PubElemSet` has a similar member, `void add(const PubElem&)`, which instead takes a `PubElem` and adds a copy of its value to the set. How would you propose to implement `pubElemSet::add`? The only obvious implementation

```
void pubElemSet::add(const PubElem& elem)
{
    d_this->d_elemSet.add(elem->d_this.d_elem);
}
```

forces the higher-level `PubElemSet` to be a long-distance friend of `PubElem`, which (see Section 3.6) is a breach of encapsulation.

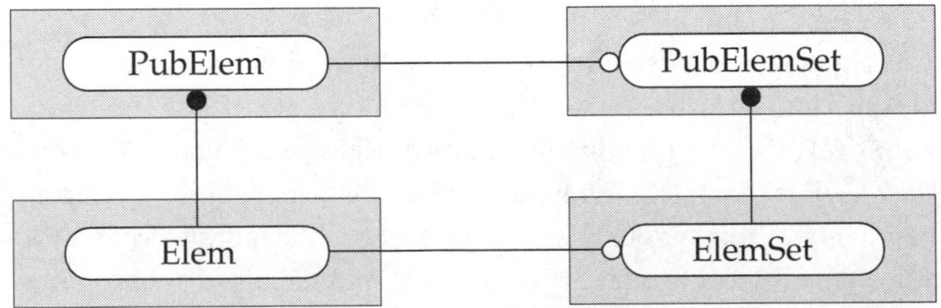

Figure 6-60: The Difficulty with Wrapping Individual Components

Forgetting for the moment the inherent problems with long-distance friendships, the sheer number of required friendships will quickly prove this strategy to be unworkable. Each wrapper type that is used as an argument to a wrapper class member (or free operator) must declare that class or operator a friend in order to allow it access to the underlying representation object being passed. As illustrated in Figure 6-61, two wrappers, `PubA` and `PubB`, are currently used in the public interface of `PubX`. `PubC`, formerly not used by `PubX`, is in the signature of a member about to be added to `PubX`. As the figure shows, adding the member function `void h(const PubC& c)` to a higher-level class, `PubX`, can force a `friend` declaration to be added to a lower-level class definition, `PubC`. This modification in turn forces that class, along with all of its clients, to recompile!

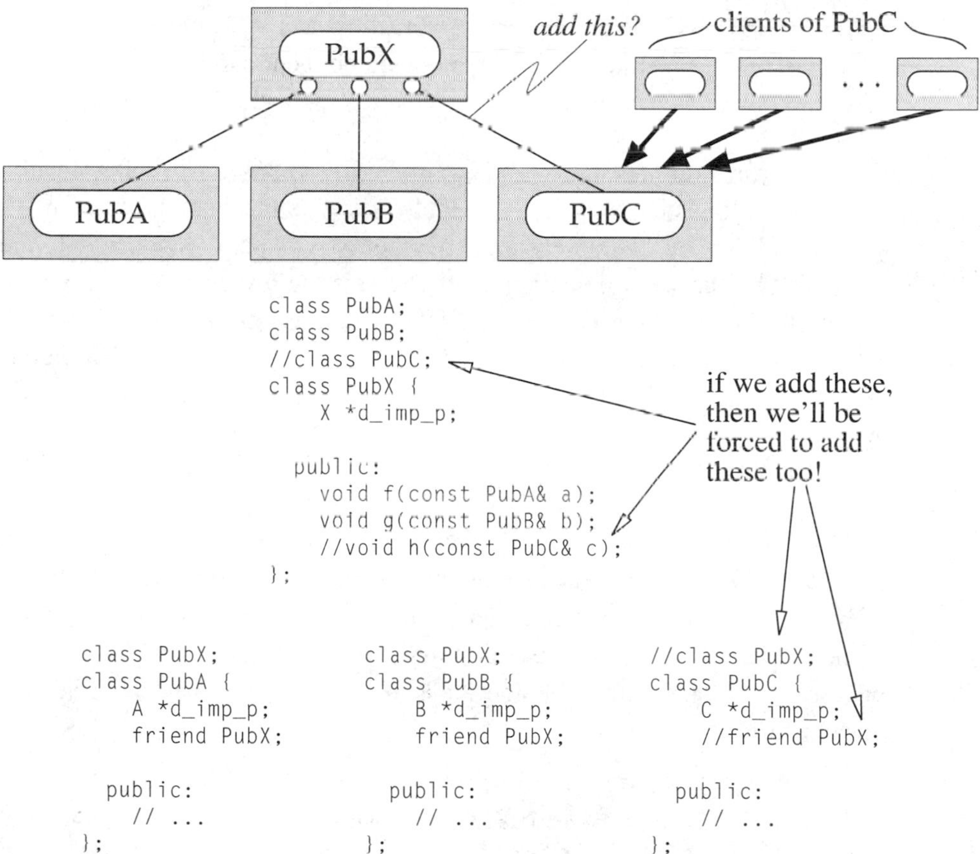

Figure 6-61: Two-Way Coupling Caused by the Uses Relation Among Wrappers

Principle

Whenever a type defined in one wrapper component is passed into a type defined in a second wrapper component, that second component will be unable to access the underlying wrapped implementation object(s); only the public functionality of the wrapper will be available.

Nonetheless, with careful design it is possible and very useful to create multi-component insulating wrappers. The secret to creating such a wrapper layer is to realize that only classes and operators within a single component can legitimately take advantage of what goes on below the interface of that component, via friendships.

Consider the component/class diagram in Figure 6-62. The low-level subsystem implementation is not only encapsulated—it is also insulated from the rest of the subsystem's clients by a relatively small number of wrapper components. In this architecture, each of the wrapper components respects the privacy of the implementation of every other component (wrapper or otherwise), and limits its access to their public interfaces. To do anything else would violate the encapsulation that we are trying to achieve in this architecture.

Wrapper objects defined within a single wrapper component are at liberty to employ friendship as needed to look below the local interfaces and manipulate the underlying representation directly. For example, suppose in Figure 6-62 that (as with `ElemSet` and `Elem`), class `E` uses class `B` in its interface and we want to expose a public version of both `E` and `B` to clients. Class `PubE` will need private access to obtain the instance of `B` encapsulated within `PubB`. We are forced to declare `PubE` a friend of `PubB`, making it necessary to place both `PubB` and `PubE` in the same wrapper component to preserve encapsulation.[15]

[15] This technique should not be construed as a general panacea for avoiding long-distance friendships among non-wrapper classes. Since wrapper classes are typically simple in nature, merging several of them in a single component does not necessarily threaten effective testability. Merging the implementation components, for example, would defeat the goals of designing a hierarchy of individual components, each with manageable complexity.

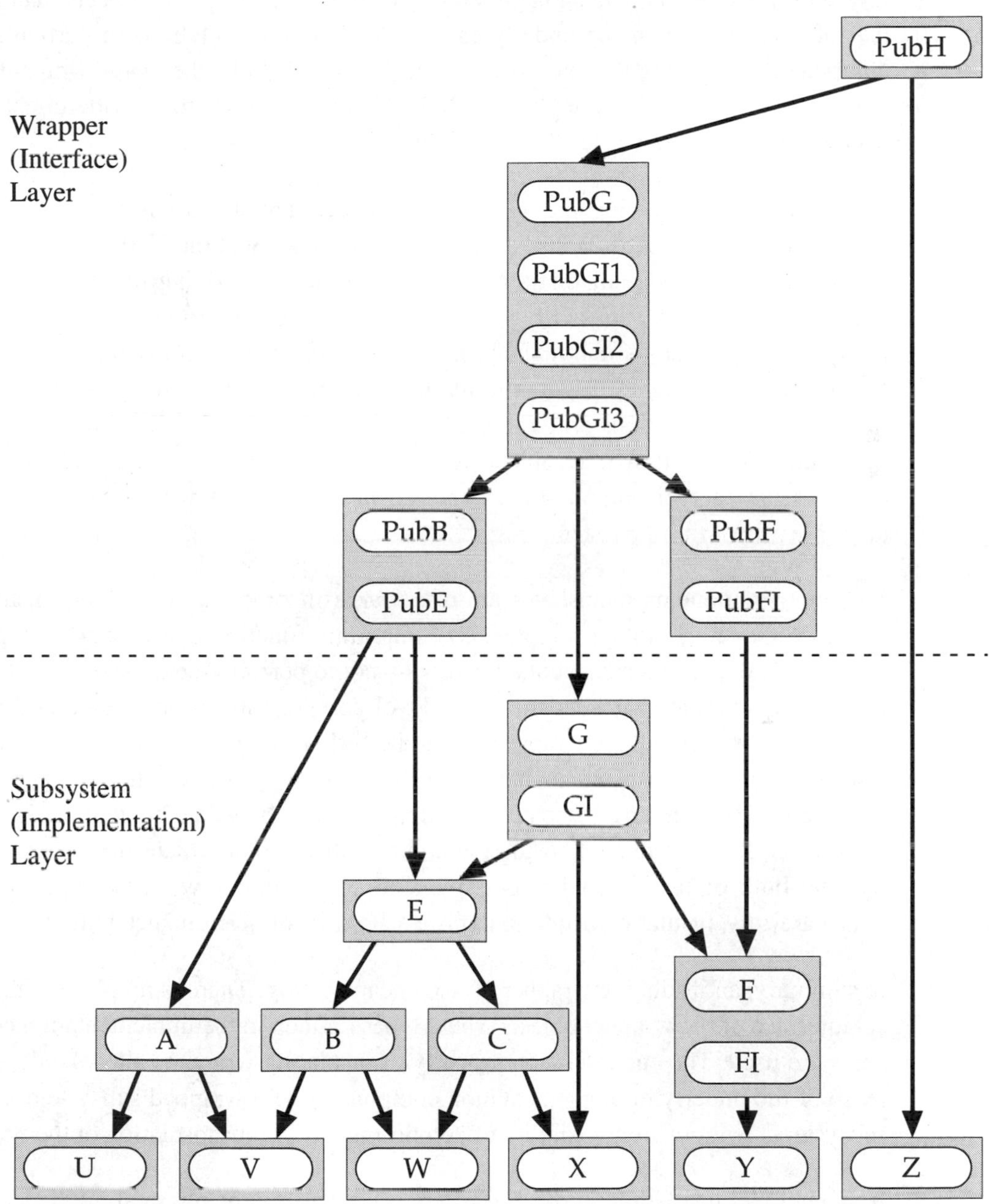

Figure 6-62: Creating an Insulating, Multi-Component Wrapper

The design goal of avoiding long-distance friendship makes it normal for wrapper-layer components to be much larger and define significantly more objects than is typical of components in the underlying, low-level implementation. In particular, the component containing the `PubG` wrapper in Figure 6-62, like the `graph` wrapper component of Section 6.4.3, supplies additional iterator classes to provide clients with insulated access to lower-level functionality.

This type of encapsulating and insulating subsystem architecture is extremely powerful. As with the encapsulating wrapper discussed in Section 5.10, we are able to impose policy by reducing direct public access to the underlying functionality. Since the insulation also occurs at a higher level, there is no need to insulate the low-level subsystem components individually. In these lower-level components, we may feel free to take advantage of tight compile-time coupling to improve performance. For instance, inline functions are commonly used to access scalar data, and objects are often embedded within other objects to avoid the overhead of dynamic allocation. In short, the impact of compile-time coupling has been dealt with "upstream" at the higher levels of the subsystem.

Wrapper components themselves are often large in order to enforce encapsulation; however, they need not be complex. One important function of a wrapper component is to delegate and coordinate complex tasks—not to perform them itself. The complex functionality implemented in the lower-level components can be tested and reused independently. Testing the wrapper should be little more than verifying that the fully tested, underlying components have been hooked up correctly. Although significant overhead may be incurred when information is passed between the wrapper layer and the low-level subsystem, choosing the appropriate level at which to insulate ensures that the bulk of the interobject communication occurs below the wrapper level. If done carefully, insulation need not impose a significant performance burden.

In summary, an insulating wrapper is also encapsulating. There is no place in the logical interface of the wrapper objects where types defined in the implementation components are used. The encapsulation property of insulating wrappers allows independent reuse of the underlying implementation components of a wrapped subsystem in other subsystems without any possibility of compromising the encapsulation of the wrapper.

If the wrapper insulation is complete, there is no place in the physical interfaces of the wrapper components where the types defined in the implementation components are even named. A partially insulating wrapper may hold pointers to objects that are themselves "first-class citizens" defined in separately accessible components. These objects can be reused independently of the wrapper and are therefore less easily modified.

In contrast, a fully insulating wrapper merely holds a pointer to a simple `struct` that defines the private implementation in its `.c` file. Because there is no independent component, there is no independent way to interact with the representation directly. Unlike a partially insulating wrapper, it is possible to add arbitrary private data without altering *any* header file.

In either case, the objects used to implement the wrapper are free to interact efficiently via their own encapsulating (but usually non-insulating) interfaces at the lower-levels of a subsystem.

Because of the potentially large number of interactions among components, it is often not feasible to wrap the individual components of a subsystem. With careful planning, however, it is possible to construct a multi-component wrapper for a subsystem. As with all other components, only the public interface of wrapper components can be accessible to other components. That is, only objects and operators defined within the same wrapper component can access each other's underlying implementation.

6.5 The Procedural Interface

Often large commercial object-oriented systems (databases, frameworks, etc.) find it necessary to supply their customers with programmatic access to a subset of the functionality available to their own internal core system developers. For example, a database may provide a high-level language interpreter (such as SQL or Scheme) to give customers interactive access to the information in the database. Often a separate interface is also provided to allow programs written by end users in C++ (or possibly even ANSI C) to manipulate the database directly. Note that by *end users* we are envisioning clients who reside outside our company or organization.

The requirements of such a programmatic interface typically include the following:

- The interface must provide the necessary functionality to manipulate the underlying system.

- The interface must not expose proprietary implementation details.

- Changes to the underlying organization must be insulated from clients.
- The overhead associated with this interface must not be excessive.

If the interface is a C++ interface, then an insulating wrapper component would be ideal. Unfortunately, not every system can be wrapped. Some systems are just too large for a set of wrapper classes to fit reasonably within a single component, and yet are too tightly interconnected to permit a properly encapsulated implementation using a multi-component wrapper. In short, if not explicitly designed as a wrapper already, it may not be feasible to create an insulating wrapper layer for an existing system without substantially altering its architecture.

If our primary goal is to insulate clients from everything that goes on underneath the facade of an insulating layer for a very large and complex system, we will have to compromise. One such compromise is to give up the true logical encapsulation of a wrapper and rely on outwardly opaque pointers with unpublished header files to achieve the encapsulation. This type of interface is commonly referred to as a *procedural interface*.

6.5.1 The Procedural Interface Architecture

The interface we are providing is typically much more abstract than those developers used to create the implementation in the first place. For the same reasons discussed in Chapter 4, it would be exceedingly difficult to ensure the reliability of such a system by testing it from the procedural interface alone. Fortunately for us, however, the complexity lies at the lower levels of the system. Our job as procedural-interface authors is to identify an appropriate subset of the types and functionality already defined in the lower-level implementation components that will allow end users to accomplish their desired application-level tasks.

Figure 6-63 is an illustration of the way a procedural interface is organized. All of the publicly accessible interface functions are independent of each other, and all of them are at a higher level than every implementation component. There is no levelization issue other than the fact that each individual interface function depends only on the underlying implementation; the procedural-interface functions should not depend on each other.

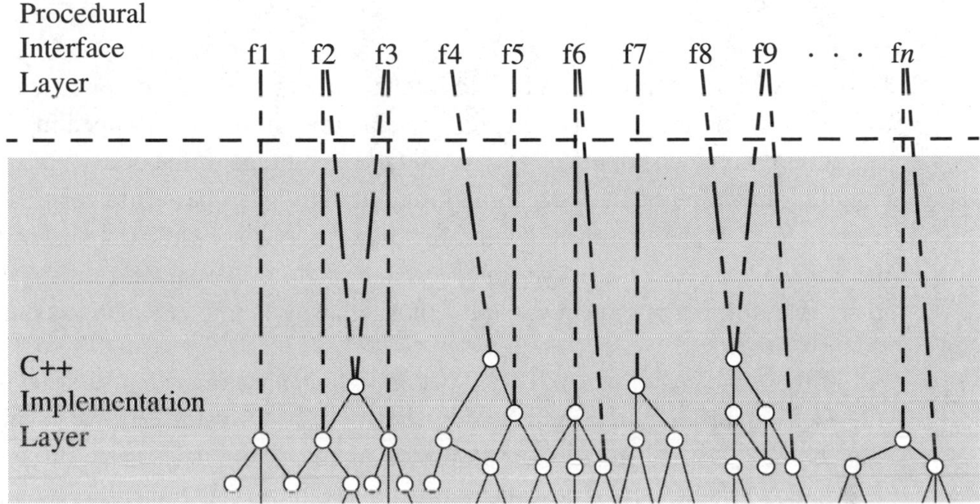

Figure 6-63: Schematic Illustration of a Procedural Interface

If we were implementing an encapsulating/insulating wrapper component, then the last thing we would want to do would be to expose the implementation types in the interface of the wrapper. But independent reuse of our implementation components by end users is likely to be irrelevant here. Forgoing independent reuse by customers is what enables us to sacrifice the logical encapsulation afforded by wrapping.

If we decide to insulate using a procedural interface, then we will not incur the overhead of creating new wrapper objects or be compelled to confine ourselves to a single component to avoid long-distance friendships. We can simply expose an appropriate subset of the underlying type names in the procedural interface without publishing their definitions.

Note that the requirements here are not the same as they were in Section 5.10. There our goal was to encapsulate the use of components; here our goal is to insulate clients from the definitions of the objects we want them to use.

Using the same type names as defined in the underlying implementation gives away little information yet preserves the type safety across the interface. End users of this interface will benefit from the compiler-enforced type safety in their own applications as well.

Besides reducing the overhead of additional classes and the compiler-enforced type safety, exposing the underlying types *in name* may have a very appealing benefit for marketing. Some customers may want to take advantage of the underlying object-oriented organization of the system, and may be willing to pay extra for this privilege. By providing these customers with a few key (protocol) base-class header files from the underlying system, it is possible to enable them to derive their own special types to be used within the system without exposing a single implementation detail.

Similarly, some customers may want better performance than an insulating procedural interface can provide. By publishing the header files of just the lowest-level, concrete objects (e.g., `Point`, `Box`, `Polygon`), preferred customers may create these objects as automatic variables and access them directly via inline functions. It is by maintaining type-name consistency across the procedural interface that all of this integration is made seamless; notice how this would not be possible with an encapsulating wrapper.

6.5.2 Creating and Destroying Opaque Objects

For the purposes of this discussion, let's assume we are to create an ANSI C–compatible interface. We therefore will be forced to use free functions—a necessary violation of a major design rule from Chapter 2. To help avoid collisions in the global name space, each of these free functions will begin with a consistent registered prefix (as discussed in Section 7.2). The ANSI C language does not support C++ references, but does support the notion of `const` versus non-`const`. Therefore all objects will be passed by pointer, and only non-`const` objects can be modified or destroyed.

Figure 6-64 depicts procedural-interface functions for creating and destroying a `Stack` object such as the one defined in Figure 3-2. Once created, the `Stack` object will remain in existence until the client explicitly destroys it with the type-safe `pi_destroyStack` function.

```
/* CREATORS */
Stack *pi_createStack();
void pi_destroyStack(Stack *thisStack);
```

Figure 6-64: Procedural Interface for Creating an Opaque Stack Object

ANSI C does not support the overloading of function names, which makes the naming process problematic—particularly for constructors. Since objects created with a procedural interface cannot be automatic variables, their creation and destruction is disproportionately more expensive than assignment. For these reasons, we may choose to omit access to copy constructors, relying instead on the default constructor and repeated use of the assignment operator.

The type safety afforded by ANSI C goes a long way toward protecting customers from shooting themselves in the foot. Because this is a C and not a C++ interface, however, there is also a greater danger that they may accidentally try to destroy something they did not allocate (and do not own), or try to destroy something they did allocate, but do so more than once. A typical example of a common memory allocation error is shown in Figure 6-65.

```
void f()
{
    Stack *s1 = pi_createStack();
    Stack *s2 = pi_createStack();

    /* ... */

    pi_destroyStack(s1);
    pi_destroyStack(s1);                /* Oops! */
}
```

Figure 6-65: The Ease of Corruption Memory in ANSI C

These kinds of customer errors are among the hardest to debug, and they can be a costly drain on a customer support organization. Fortunately there is an effective way to detect most memory allocation errors. A memory allocator that has proven highly effective at detecting and reporting memory allocation–related customer programming errors in actual products is presented in Appendix B.

6.5.3 Handles

If we are creating a procedural interface to be used by customers writing in C++ (as opposed to ANSI C), then there are better ways to handle dynamically allocated objects than just returning a pointer. One popular approach to managing dynamically allocated objects returned from functions involves a special kind of class commonly referred to as a *handle*.

DEFINITION: In this book, a *handle* is a class that maintains a pointer to an object that is programmatically accessible through the public interface of the handle class.

Basically, a *handle* is an object that is used to refer to another object.[16] Usually, a handle holds a pointer to the "held" object but contains little else, as illustrated in Figure 6-66. Unlike a wrapper, the object to which the handle refers is programmatically accessible from the interface of the handle. Handles used in this way are sometimes called *smart pointers*.[17] There are many applications for the handle pattern in C++. The `NodeId` wrapper class of Figure 5-95 acted as a handle for the `Node` portion of `Gnode` object to which it held a pointer; `EdgeId` acted similarly.

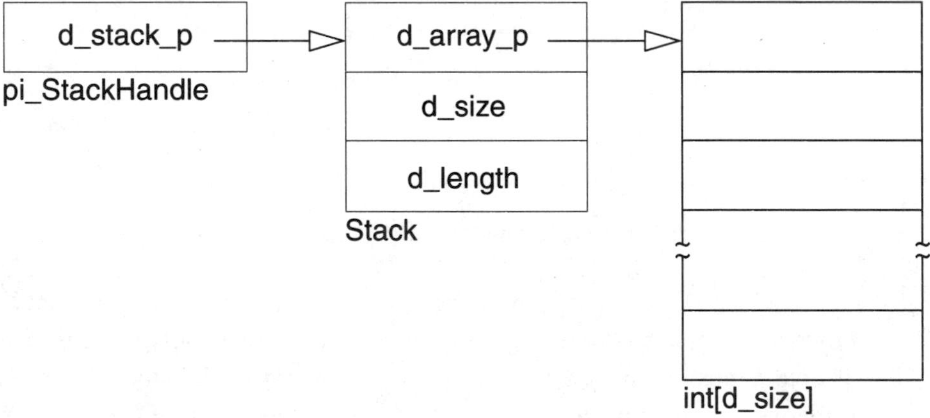

Figure 6-66: Object Diagram Illustrating `pi_StackHandle` and `Stack` Organization

A common way of *managing* a dynamically allocated object in C++ is to place its address in a separate object whose job is simply to manage it. Such a manager object is just a special type of handle object—a *manager handle*. The header file for a `Stack` manager handle is given in Figure 6-67.

---

[16] **stroustrup**, Section 13.9, p. 460.
[17] **stroustrup**, Section 7.9, p. 244.

```
// pi_stackhandle.h
#ifndef INCLUDED_PI_STACKHANDLE
#define INCLUDED_PI_STACKHANDLE

class Stack;

class pi_StackHandle {
    Stack *d_object_p;

  private:
    pi_StackHandle(const pi_StackHandle&);                  // not implemented
    pi_StackHandle& operator=(const pi_StackHandle&);       // not implemented

  public:
    // CREATORS
    pi_StackHandle();
    ~StackHandle();

    // MANIPULATORS
    void loadObject(Stack *stack);     // Not intended for public use.

    // ACCESSORS
    operator Stack *() const;          // Conversion operator to allow use
};                                     // of this object as if this were
                                       // a writable pointer to a Stack.

#endif
```

Figure 6-67: A Manager Handle for Class `Stack`

Our overall approach to creating a procedural interface involving handles is illustrated in Figure 6-68. Here, `pi_Stack` is just a `struct` (defining a namespace) containing only static member functions. These functions will serve as the C++ *procedural* interface to manipulate `Stack` objects, via outwardly opaque pointers.

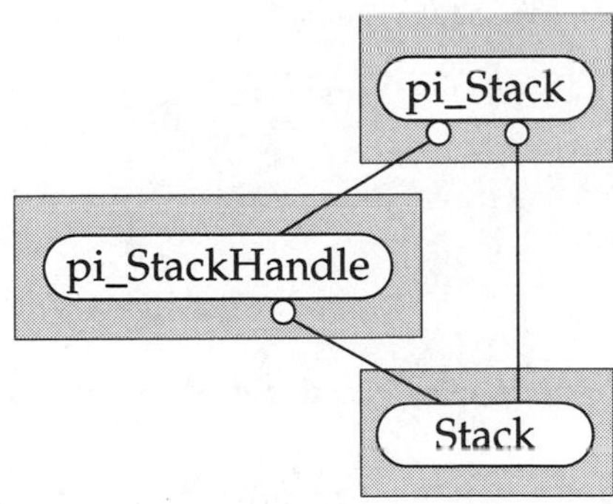

Figure 6-68: Component/Class Diagram for a Procedural Interface with Handles

```
// pi_stack.h
#ifndef INCLUDED_PI_STACK
#define INCLUDED_PI_STACK

class Stack;

struct pi_Stack {
    // (Stack Creators)
    static void create(pi_StackHandle *handleToBeLoaded);

    // (Stack Manipulators)
    static Stack *assign(Stack *thisStack, const Stack *thatStack);
    static void push(Stack *thisStack, int value);
    static int pop(Stack *thisStack);

    // (Stack Accessors)
    static int top(const Stack *thisStack) const;
    static int isEmpty(const Stack *thisStack) const;
    static int isEqual(const Stack *left, const Stack *right) const;
};

#endif
```

```
// pi_stack.c
#include "pi_stack.h"
#include "stack.h"

void pi_Stack::create(pi_StackHandle *h)
{
    h->loadObject(new Stack);
}

Stack *pi_Stack::assign(Stack *thisStack, const Stack* thatStack)
{
    *thisStack = *thatStack;
    return thisStack;
}

void pi_Stack::push(Stack *thisStack, int value)
{
    thisStack->push(value);
}

// ...
```

Figure 6-69: Procedural Interface Component `pi_stack`

Since we plan to use handles to manage memory, we will modify the stack creation function `Stack *pi_createStack()` that we used in ANSI C. In a handle-base architecture, an equivalent C++ translation of this function will take a writable pointer to a stack *handle* object as a parameter. We avoid the free functions of the ANSI C version by making this function a static member of class `pi_Stack`. The header for the entire `pi_stack` component is given in Figure 6-69.

Now, instead of returning a pointer to a dynamically allocated object directly, a `pi_StackHandle` object is first created by the client as an automatic variable. The address of this handle is then passed into the `create` function, where it is loaded with a dynamically allocated `Stack` object, as shown in Figure 6-70. Once the handle is loaded, its conversion operator allows the handle (see Figure 6-67) to be used as if it were a pointer to a `Stack`.

```
void myFunc()
{
    pi_StackHandle h;               // automatic variable
    pi_Stack::create(&h);           // load with dynamically allocated object
    for (int i = 0; i < 10; ++i) {
        pi_Stack::push(h, i);       // push 0, 1, ..., 9 on the managed stack
    }
    int x = pi_Stack::pop(h);       // pop 9 from managed stack into x
    // ...
}
```

Figure 6-70: Usage Model for a Manager Stack Handle

There is no need to implement a corresponding `destroy` function in the `pi_Stack` interface. When the handle goes out of scope, the destructor of the handle in turn destroys the contained (dynamically allocated) `Stack` object, as shown in Figure 6-71.

The scoping afforded by C++ classes and the ability to overload function names in C++ simplify the task of naming. Although the cosmetics of adding handles and scoping function names does not change the underlying nature of this interface—it is still *procedural*.

In particular, trying to make a handle look like a wrapper would be ill-advised. Consider what would happen if, instead of the current interface, we implemented the `pop` function as a non-static member of class `pi_StackHandle` (taking no arguments):

```
class pi_StackHandle {
    // ...
  public:
    // ...
    int pop();
    // ...
};
```

```
// pi_stackhandle.h
#ifndef INCLUDED_PI_STACKHANDLE
#define INCLUDED_PI_STACKHANDLE

class pi_StackHandle {
    Stack *d_stack_p;

  public:
    // ...
    ~pi_StackHandle();
    // ...
};

#endif
```

```
// pi_stackhandle.c
#include "pi_stackhandle.h"
#include "stack.h"

// ...

pi_StackHandle::~pi_StackHandle()
{
    delete d_stack_p;
}

// ...
```

Figure 6-71: Destructor for Manager Handle Destroys Its "Held" Object

The obvious semantics would be that the `pop()` member should pop and return the top element of the `Stack` object managed by this `pi_StackHandle`. Suppose, however, we are handed a pointer to a non-`const Stack` that we do not own. How could we pop it?

If, as customers, all we had at our disposal is a `pop()` member of class `StackHandle`, we would be forced to use the `loadObject()` member to put this `Stack` object pointer inside a handle before we could manipulate it. But if we did that, we would now have two agents managing the memory of the same `Stack` object!

The single purpose of the handle in a procedural interface is to manage the memory of a dynamically allocated object. Except for the `pi_Stack::create` function, which loads a `pi_StackHandle` with a newly allocated `Stack` object, *all* of the functionality defined in the `pi_Stack` procedural interface should refer directly to the underlying `Stack` and not the `pi_StackHandle`. By following this strategy, customers are never forced, or even tempted, to abuse a handle to gain access to the functionality of the underlying object.

6.5.4 Accessing and Manipulating Opaque Objects

Let us return to our assumption of ANSI C compatibility. A common hierarchical naming convention for the analog of "member functions" in a procedural interface is as follows: <prefix>_<Subject><Verb><Object>.

As a matter of consistency, it is desirable that our subject type (e.g., Stack) always appear with an uppercase first letter. Ignoring the prefix, we want the actual function name to comply with our design rule from Section 2.7 which suggests that all functions begin with a lowercase letter. To lexically distinguish these global functions from global types, we have inserted the letter f at the beginning of the actual function name. For example,

```
int Stack::pop();                     → int pi_fStackPop(Stack *);
double Angle::getDegrees() const;     → double pi_fAngleGetDegrees(const Angle *);
void List::append(const Elem&);       → void pi_fListAppendElem(List *, const Elem *);
```

Although this style of naming is entirely appropriate for the procedural interface layer, it does not necessarily translate directly to the underlying objects and member functions of the implementation layer. For example, representing the conversion functions (see Figure 5-15)

```
struct Convert {
    static Window toWindow (const Rectangle& r);
    static Rectangle toRectangle (const Window& w);
};
```

as

```
void pi_fRectangleGetWindow(const Rectangle *thisRect, Window *returnValue)
{
    *returnValue = Convert::toWindow(thisRect);
}

void pi_fWindowGetRectangle(const Window *thisWind, Rectangle *returnValue)
{
    *returnValue = Convert::toRectangle(thisWind);
}
```

would be intuitive to procedural end users, and therefore an appropriate abstraction. There is no levelization issue because each of these function depends only on implementation objects residing at lower levels in the physical hierarchy. Yet, if realized as member functions of the corresponding underlying implementation classes, this approach would quickly lead to an unlevelizable architecture. I suspect that naively trying to map this kind of naming style onto C++ classes and their member functions is a primary source of cyclic physical dependencies in many existing systems.

We now turn our attention to the class `Shape` shown in Figure 6-72. A *bounding box* is a minimal rectangle consisting of horizontal and vertical edges that circumscribe a collection of points. Every `Shape`, among other things, knows how to return (by value) a bounding box of type `Box` that contains the `Shape`.

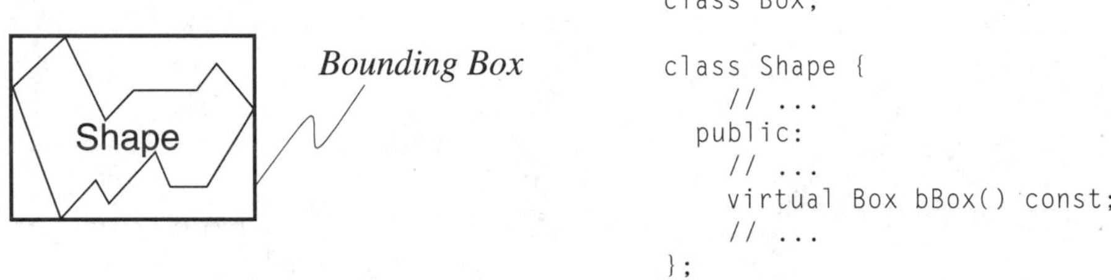
Shape
Bounding Box
class Box;
class Shape {
// ...
public:
// ...
virtual Box bBox() const;
// ...
};

Figure 6-72: Returning a User-Defined Type by Value

Because pointers are opaque, there can be no return by value for user-defined types in a procedural interface. The obvious choice is to allocate a new `Box` and return a pointer to it, as shown in Figure 6-73a. One problem with this approach is that objects returned by value are typically small objects that do not have associated dynamic memory. Dynamically allocating light-weight objects such as `Box` or `Point` every time one is accessed would create considerable unnecessary overhead. Another problem is that returning unmanaged objects would make who owned what memory confusing and increase the likelihood of leaks.

```
Box *pi_fShapeGetBbox1(const Shape *thisShape)
{
    return new Box(thisShape->bBox());
}
```

(a) Less Efficient, More Dangerous

```
void pi_fShapeGetBbox2(const Shape *thisShape, Box *returnValue)
{
    *returnValue = thisShape->bBox();
}
```

(b) More Efficient, Less Dangerous

Figure 6-73: Providing a Procedural Interface for Objects Returned by Value

Principle

In a procedural interface, having clients explicitly destroy only those objects that they explicitly create reduces confusion over ownership and can lead to improved performance.

We can avoid both the runtime overhead and confusion about ownership by sticking to the simple principle that only the objects explicitly allocated by the client of a procedural interface can be destroyed by that client—all other objects are owned and managed by the system. The preferred procedural interface function is indicated in Figure 6-73b.

The improvement in runtime efficiency in Figure 6-73b can be significant. Figure 6-74 shows two implementations of a function that returns the sum of the area of the bounding boxes for an array of shapes. For small, lightweight objects, such as Point or Box, that are obtained over and over in a single function, the cost of dynamic allocation and deallocation on every iteration of the loop (Figure 6-74a) could easily dominate the runtime cost of the function call. Instead, we can do the allocation once outside the loop (Figure 6-74b) and then reuse the allocated object over and over, resulting in a dramatic improvement in runtime efficiency.

```
double sumArea1(const Shape *shape[],
                int size)
{
    double sum = 0;
    int i;
    for (i = 0; i < size; ++i) {
        Box *box = pi_fShapeGetBbox1(shape[i]);
        sum += pi_fBoxGetArea(box);
        pi_destroyBox(box);
    }
    return sum;
}
```

```
double sumArea2(const Shape *shape[],
                int size)
{
    double sum = 0;
    Box *box = pi_createBox();
    int i;
    for (i = 0; i < size; ++i) {
        pi_fShapeGetBbox2(shape[i], box);
        sum += pi_fBoxGetArea(box);
    }
    pi_destroyBox(box);
    return sum;
}
```

Figure 6-74: Comparing Usage/Efficiency of Two Procedural Interface Models

Sometimes the system itself will allocate an object dynamically and return it to the client. In such cases, a handle class is usually provided by the underlying system to manage the memory for that object. For example, consider a `Shape` interface that is a protocol class for all kinds of `Shape` objects. Now suppose there is a class `PointIter` that is also a protocol for a variety of specific iterator objects that sequence over some collection of points. It is possible to ask an arbitrary `Shape` through its protocol to allocate a shape-specific iterator (derived from `PointIter`) and return it by loading a user-supplied instance of a `PointIterHandle`, as shown in Figure 6-75.[18]

```
class Point;

class PointIter {
  public:
    // CREATORS
    virtual ~PointIter();
```

[18] See also the Iterator design pattern in **gamma**, Chapter 5, pp. 257–71.

```
    // MANIPULATORS
    virtual void reset() = 0;
    virtual void operator++() = 0;

    // ACCESSORS
    virtual operator const void *() const = 0;
    virtual const Point operator()() const = 0;
};

class PointIterHandle {
    PointIter *d_iter_p;
    PointIterHandle& operator=(PointIterHandle&);
    PointIterHandle(PointIterHandle&);

  public:
    // CREATORS
    PointIterHandle();
    PointIterHandle(PointIter *iterator);
    ~PointIterHandle();

    // MANIPULATORS
    void loadIter(PointIter *newDynamiclyAllocatedIterator);

    // ACCESSORS
    PointIter& operator()() const;
    operator PointIter&() const;
    PointIter *operator->() const;
    PointIter& operator*() const;
};

class Shape {
    // ...
  public:
    // ...
    // ACCESSORS
    virtual void getVertices(PointIterHandle *returnValue) = 0;
    // ...
};
```

Figure 6-75: Using Handles to Manage Dynamic Memory in C++

In this example, the system is dynamically allocating an iterator object and placing it in a user-supplied handle. Since the underlying system itself is allocating the memory, the customer is not authorized to delete it. The customer is, however, authorized to create and destroy an instance of a `PointIterHandle`. The customer therefore creates a `PointIterHandle` and passes it to the `getVertices` function of `Shape`. The handle is then loaded by the system with a dynamically allocated pointer to a `PointIter`. The customer uses the object contained in and managed by the handle. When the handle is destroyed by the customer, the destructor of the handle in turn destroys the contained, dynamically allocated iterator. Reusing a handle to obtain another iterator also prompts the handle to destroy any previously installed iterator before loading the new one. An ANSI C–compatible procedural interface for the functionality of Figure 6-75 is given in Figure 6-76. The usage of such an interface is illustrated in Figure 6-77.

```
typedef struct Point Point;                          // ANSI C compatibility
typedef struct PointIter PointIter;                  // ANSI C compatibility
typedef struct PointIterHandle PointIterHandle;      // ANSI C compatibility
typedef struct Shape Shape;                          // ANSI C compatibility

                            /***** PointIter *****/
/* MANIPULATORS */
int pi_fPointIterIsValid(const PointIter *thisIter);
void pi_fPointIterGetItem(const PointIter *thisIter, Point *returnValue);

/* ACCESSORS */
void pi_fPointIterReset(PointIter *thisIter);
void pi_fPointIterAdvance(PointIter *thisIter);


                            /***** PointIterHandle *****/
/* CREATORS */
PointIterHandle *pi_createPointIterHandle();
void pi_destroyPointIterHandle(PointIterHandle *thisHandle);

/* MANIPULATORS */
/* void pi_fPointIterHandleLoadIter(PointIterHandle *thisHandle,
 *                                  PointIter *newDynamicPointIter);
 * Note: not necessary to expose this dangerous function
 */

/* ACCESSORS */
PointIter *pi_fPointIterHandleGetIter(const PointIterHandle *thisHandle);
/* Note: for a procedural interface, this one accessor is sufficient */


                            /***** Shape *****/
/* ACCESSORS */
void pi_fShapeGetVertices(Shape *thisShape, PointIterHandle *returnValue);
```

Figure 6-76: An ANSI C–Compliant Procedural Interface Involving Handles

As a procedural-interface author for a large system, you may discover a class interface that returns a dynamically allocated object directly, without placing it in a client-supplied handle. In such cases, it will be necessary for you to find (or create) such a handle of the appropriate type and require your clients to pass a non-`const` pointer to that handle into your interface function. You will then have to load the handle with the system-allocated object yourself. Doing so will preserve the principle that clients of the procedural interface are authorized to delete only what they explicitly allocate.

```
void f(Shape *shape)
{
    PointIterHandle *handle = pi_createPointIterHandle();
    Point *pt = pi_createPoint();
    PointIter *it;

    pi_fShapeGetVertices(shape, handle);
    it = pi_fPointIterHandleGetIter(handle);

    for (; pi_fPointIterIsValid(it); pi_fPointIterAdvance(it)) {
        pi_fPointIterGetItem(it, pt);
        /* do stuff with current point */
    }

    pi_destroyPoint(pt);
    pi_destroyPointIterHandle(handle);
}
```

Figure 6-77: Using an ANSI C–Compliant Procedural Interface Involving Handles

6.5.5 Inheritance and Opaque Objects

Converting between types related by inheritance is yet another aspect of writing procedural interfaces for object-oriented designs that must be addressed. The issue at hand involves how we present a type-safe, procedural interface that supports the notion of pointer conversion implied by inheritance.

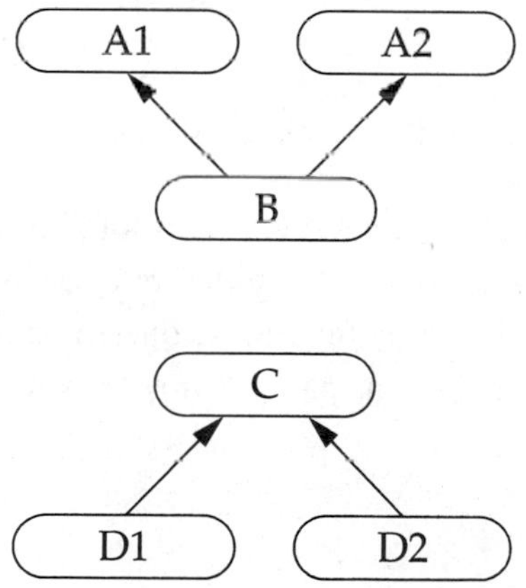

Figure 6-78: Examples of Inheritance Relationships

Consider the class diagram shown in Figure 6-78. Class `B` derives publicly from both `A1` and `A2`, which means that all of the functionality of both `A1` and `A2` is accessible through the public interface of B. Unfortunately, insulation prevents even C++ customers of a procedural interface from knowing anything about how types A1, A2, and B are related. For example, if we have a pointer to an object of type B and we want to call a member function defined in A1, we would be out of luck; this is obviously not acceptable.

Our first thought might be to duplicate the functionality defined in both A1 and A2 in B. Doing so creates a large number of redundant functions and solves only half the problem. Suppose we want to use an object of type B in a function that takes an object of type A1. Should we also make duplicates of each function for every combination of derived types? I think not.

The C++ language supports implicit (standard) conversion from pointers of a given type to pointers of another type when the first type publicly inherits (either directly or indirectly) from the second; it will be necessary to make that conversion explicit in the procedural interface.

```
A1 *pi_convertBA1(B*);
A2 *pi_convertBA2(B*);
C *pi_convertD1C(D1*);
C *pi_convertD2C(DC*);

const A1 *pi_convertConstBA1(const B*);
const A2 *pi_convertConstBA2(const B*);
const C *pi_convertConstD1C(const D1*);
const C *pi_convertConstD2C(const D2*);
```

Figure 6-79: Examples of (Standard) Conversion Functions

The explicit conversion functions corresponding to Figure 6-78 are shown in Figure 6-79. In this example, four inheritance relationships induced eight functions. Notice that there are two kinds of functions: one for const objects and one for non-const objects. Although this seems painful, it gets even worse.

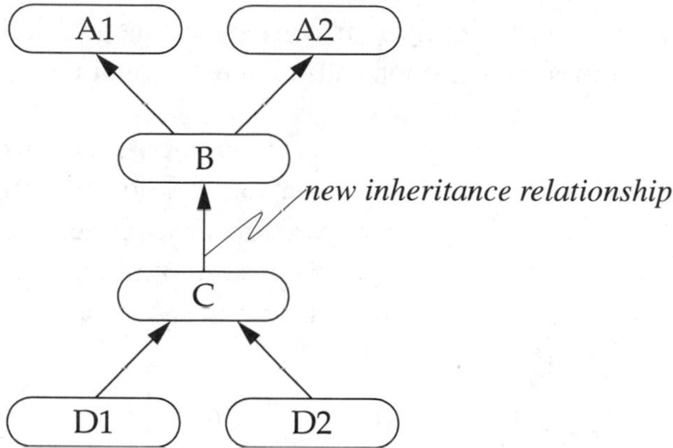

Figure 6-80: Transitivity of Conversions in Inheritance Hierarchy

Now consider what would happen if we introduced one more inheritance relationship from `C` to `B`, as shown in Figure 6-80. In addition to the obvious two additional conversion routines

```
B *pi_convertCB(C*);
const B *pi_convertConstCB(const C*);
```

the transitive nature of the IsA relation potentially introduces the following 16 conversions as well:

```
B *pi_convertD1B(D1*);
A1 *pi_convertD1A1(D1*);
A2 *pi_convertD1A2(D1*);
B *pi_convertD2B(D2*);
A1 *pi_convertD2A1(D2*);
A2 *pi_convertD2A2(D2*);
A1 *pi_convertCA1(C*);
A2 *pi_convertCA2(C*);
const B *pi_convertConstD1B(const D1*);
const A1 *pi_convertConstD1A1(const D1*);
const A2 *pi_convertConstD1A2(const D1*);
const B *pi_convertConstD2B(const D2*);
const A1 *pi_convertConstD2A1(const D2*);
const A2 *pi_convertConstD2A2(const D2*);
const A1 *pi_convertConstCA1(const C*);
const A2 *pi_convertConstCA2(const C*);
```

Although it is not absolutely necessary to supply a function to provide direct conversion from type `D1` to type `A2`, users of the procedural interface may already be annoyed by having to use one conversion function—let alone three. There is clearly a trade-off between the number of conversion-function definitions provided and the number of conversion-function calls required at runtime.

Attempting to maintain and document all of these functions by hand is expensive and error prone. Fortunately these conversion functions are trivial, regular, and easy to generate accurately using techniques similar to those employed in Appendix C for determining level numbers. Note that instead of trying to document all these conversion functions, it is far more manageable to show users how to infer the appropriate name based on the two type names:

```
<Type2> *pi_convert<Type1><Type2>(<Type1>*);

const <Type2> *pi_convertConst<Type1><Type2>(const <Type1>*);
```

To summarize: a procedural interface is entirely different from other insulation techniques presented in this chapter, and it satisfies an entirely different set of objectives. Techniques such as extracting a protocol and creating a wrapper layer serve both to encapsulate as well as insulate clients from the low-level organization of a subsystem. These other techniques enable the side-by-side reuse of low-level implementation components without any possibility of breaching the encapsulation of subsystems that use them internally.

By contrast, the primary purpose of a procedural interface is to insulate clients from all organizational aspects below a certain level. There is usually no intention of allowing customer reuse of the underlying objects—often for proprietary reasons. The main advantage of this insulation technique is that it does not require the up-front design effort that accompanies the provision of an encapsulating interface, nor does it impose the overhead of additional objects to achieve the encapsulation. The issue of long-distance friendship is eliminated because the underlying types are publicly available in name, but the header files that enable direct access to the functionality defined for these types are universally withheld from customers.

Providing a procedural interface has the distinct disadvantage that, in its pure form, clients lose the ability to extend the functionality of the system through the use of inheritance. With careful design, however, it is possible to provide a procedural interface and augment it with a few select header files to mitigate this problem. Procedural interfaces require the use of long and tedious function names to do what is normally done by members within class scope, operators, and standard conversions. Function names become even more tedious when the interface is made ANSI C compliant.

A procedural interface is neither object oriented nor particularly elegant, but it does have one big advantage: a procedural interface can *always* be used to insulate the organization of a large system from clients—even if such an interface was not considered during the early stages of the design.

6.6 To Insulate or Not to Insulate

Frequent recompilation due to changing header files is something we would like to avoid imposing on the clients of our components. Such "spontaneous" recompilations during development are both annoying and expensive.

There is little we can do to insulate our clients from the changes we make to the logical *interface* of our components—a fact that underscores the importance of getting major interfaces correct early in the design process. Batching up such changes and publishing them infrequently in the form of a software release (see Section 7.6) can reduce but not eliminate their cost.

As we have seen from the previous sections in this chapter, there are steps we can take that will reduce or even eliminate our clients' recompilation costs due to changes in the logical *implementations* of our components. But insulation itself is not without cost. Sometimes it will take more development effort to create an insulating interface for a component, and in some cases insulation could significantly degrade runtime performance.

In the following subsections we discuss the costs of insulation, when insulation is (or is not) appropriate, and what kinds of insulation techniques are best suited for particular situations that arise commonly in practice.

6.6.1 The Cost of Insulation

Insulating a class clearly can affect its runtime performance. The degree of impact depends on the class itself, the way it is used, and the techniques used to insulate it.

Principle

Although computer architectures and compilers vary, the following rule of thumb may help guide system architects in deciding whether and how to insulate at the early stages of a design.

Access	**Relative Cost of Access Alone**
By value via inline function	**1**
By pointer via inline function	**2**
Via non-inline, non-virtual function	**10**
Via virtual-function mechanism	**20**

Creation	**Relative Cost of Allocation Alone**
Automatic	**1.5**
Dynamic	**100+**

Figure 6-81 provides some hard numbers for the relative costs of various forms of function calls and object instantiation. As the figure shows, the cost of accessing data either directly or through an inline function is statistically identical. Using the CFRONT 3.0 C++ Compiler on a SUN SPARC-2 workstation with no optimization, it takes about 1/8 of a microsecond to access an integer data member (either directly or via an inline function) and assign it to another integer variable (see Figure 6-81a, c). Notice that it takes 60 percent longer on a SPARC-2 and twice as long on a SPARC-20 to accomplish this operation if the access must go through a pointer (b, d).[19]

```
struct A {
    int d_d;
    inline int i() const;
    int f() const;
    virtual int v() const;
};
```

[19] The operation becomes bound by memory-access time on the faster SPARC 20.

```
int A::i() const { return d_d; }
int A::f() const { return d_d; }
int A::v() const { return d_d; }

main ()
{
    A a, *p = &a;
    int j;
                                    //     TIME IN MICROSECONDS
                                    //     SPARC-2       SPARC-20

    j = a.d_d;                      // a.   0.124          0.040
    j = p->d_d;                     // b.   0.200          0.080
    j = a.i();                      // c.   0.125          0.040
    j = p->i();                     // d.   0.199          0.080
    j = a.f();                      // e.   0.575          0.301
    j = p->f();                     // f.   0.599          0.301
    j = p->v();                     // g.   1.076          0.543

    { A a }                         // h.   0.175          0.060
    { A *p = new A; delete p; }     // i.  11.757          5.478
}
```

Figure 6-81: Some Relative Costs of Access and Creation

For a fully insulating class, there can be no inline functions, so each access of a private member requires indirection through a pointer. The cost of accessing a data member with a regular function instead of an inline function is increased by almost a factor of four (e). Notice that the indirection now adds less than 5 percent to the total cost of the operation (f). That is, the added access cost of *not* declaring a member function `inline` dominates the small additional overhead of the indirection.

For a protocol class, there can be no non-virtual functions, and the pointer indirection is now mandatory. All function calls must go through the virtual function call mechanism. The cost of performing this same operation with a dynamically bound function instead of a statically bound function again doubles the cost of the operation (g).[20] Although the virtual-function call mechanism is somewhat slower than a direct-function call, for tiny accessor functions it can be significantly slower than accessing the data directly, using an inline function. Often, however, if one can afford to make a function non-inline, one can afford to make it virtual as well. Note that as the size of

[20] It is worth reiterating that the depth of an inheritance hierarchy does not affect the runtime performance of virtual functions. Each class maintains its own virtual table(s), so the cost of dispatching any virtual function is independent of the number of derivations in the class hierarchy.

the function grows, the runtime cost associated with executing the body of the function will soon swamp the cost of whatever calling mechanism is used; the speed improvement of inline over dynamically bound function calls will then become negligible.

A distinguishing property of a concrete class is that it can be instantiated. When an object with a fully insulated implementation is created as an automatic variable (on the program stack), its implementation structure must be allocated separately. As shown at the bottom of Figure 6-81, the cost of dynamically allocating a `struct` (on the heap) can be two orders of magnitude slower than automatic allocation (h, i). The development effort in object-specific memory management necessary to defray this cost can be significant, and class-based management techniques can lead to undesirable side effects (see Section 10.3.4.2). Even worse, the cost of dynamic allocation typically depends on the size of the application and specifically on the current utilization/fragmentation of the particular runtime dynamic memory-management system. For these reasons, full insulation for tiny, lightweight concrete classes may be contraindicated, especially for objects that are frequently created on the program stack or returned by value from functions.

6.6.2 When *Not* to Insulate

Insulating clients from changes made to encapsulated implementation details of a component in itself is good; however, not all component interfaces should be insulating.

Principle

The decision *not* to insulate the implementation of a component may be based on the knowledge that the component is not widely used.

Some components are simply not intended for general use. When the audience of a component is limited, insulation is no longer critical. In that case, the impact of changes to the uninsulated implementation may not pose any great threat. In fact some component may be specific to a subsystem that defines a few interface (wrapper) components that themselves completely insulate the entire multi-component subsystem from general users. Examples are the `p2p_router` of Chapter 4 and the `graph` wrapper of Section 6.4.3.1. Heroic efforts to insulate the implementations of each of the individual components that make up such a subsystem would be misplaced.

Principle

Unless performance is known *not* to be an issue, it may be wise to avoid insulating the implementation of low-level classes with tiny accessor functions that are used widely throughout the system.

There are two distinct ways to reduce the frequency of recompilation resulting from changes to the implementation:

1. Insulate the implementation better.
2. Make changes to the implementation less frequently.

DEFINITION: ***Light-weight*** **is a term whose meaning depends on the context in which it is used:**

- **does not depend on (many) other components,**
- **is not expensive to construct/destruct,**
- **does not allocate additional dynamic memory, and**
- **makes effective use of inline functions to access/manipulate embedded data.**

For widely used components, it is especially undesirable that clients be forced to recompile as a result of changes to encapsulated details. Yet, as we know, insulation is not free of performance cost. Small, light-weight classes such as `Point`, `Stack`, `List`, and other well-defined concrete data structures in computer science are not good candidates for insulation, even though they are used widely throughout the entire system. Insulating such classes would impose an across-the-board performance burden that, for many, would be hard to justify. In fact, for classes such as these with tiny accessor functions that are called repeatedly, the overhead of using indirection and non-inline functions could make them an order of magnitude slower, as was demonstrated in Section 6.6.1.

When the runtime cost of work done in a given function call is large relative to the cost of the call itself, insulation will not pose a significant performance problem. Therefore, if a class is widely used and its member functions are large, the implementation of that class should be insulated, regardless of any supposed performance requirements. On the other hand, highly reused, public components[21] with tiny accessor functions should probably not be insulating unless performance is clearly *not* an issue. These factors are summarized in Figure 6-82.

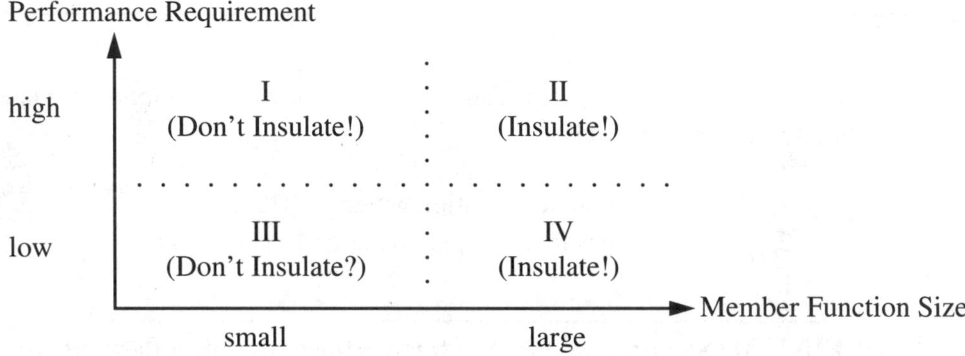

Figure 6-82: When to Insulate a Widely Used Component

Fortunately public, low-level classes are typically developed, tuned, and tested thoroughly early in the development process. After that, they are seldom if ever modified. Such intentionally non-insulating, globally used classes become almost like fundamental types in the system. Classes such as `Point`, `String`, and `List` are often used both internally and as a "medium of exchange" among the major subsystems. It is understood by developers that these highly reused types are not likely to change.

Principle

Insulating lightweight, widely used objects commonly returned by value can significantly degrade overall runtime performance.

---

[21] The term *public* here implies a low-level component or interface that is used widely throughout an entire system.

For a tiny object that does not allocate additional dynamic memory at construction, the additional cost of returning a fully insulating version of that object by value could be so severe as to affect the design of the interfaces that use it.

```
const Point pt(1,2);

Point getPointA()                                    // return by value
{
    return pt;
}

void getPointB(Point *returnValue)                   // return via parameter
{
    *returnValue = pt;
}
```

Figure 6-83 illustrates the added runtime cost of partially and fully insulating a `Point` class with respect to returning a `Point` by value from a non-inline function. Using the original non-insulating `Point` class implementation of Figure 5-59, it takes 1.52 microseconds on a SPARC 2 for a call to the `getPointA` function to return a `Point` by value. Moving all of the function definitions out of line while leaving the data members embedded in the class definition causes this time to more than double (3.39 microseconds). Fully insulating the class (implying dynamic allocation of the data) causes the function call to take 10 times as long as it would have for the non-insulating implementation. For an ultra light-weight class such as `Point`, the reduction in runtime performance incurred by insulating its logical implementation is probably unacceptable.

		Return by Value		Return via Parameter	
Description of Point Class		SPARC 2	SPARC 20	SPARC 2	SPARC 20
Original Point Class		1.52	0.75	1.16	0.52
Without Inline Functions		3.39	1.67	1.23	0.71
Fully Insulating Version:	15.82	6.96	1.49	0.73	
		(function call time in microseconds)			

Figure 6-83: The Cost of Returning a Fully Insulating `Point` Object

Instead of returning an insulating `Point` by value, we might be tempted to pass in a previously constructed `Point` object and assign to it just to avoid the overhead of the dynamic allocation associated with the construction of a temporary `Point` object. In that case, the cost of fully insulating `Point` does not exceed 30 percent on either architecture. The cost of creating one reusable instance of `Point` by the client can now be amortized over many repeated calls to functions returning points via the parameter list. This interface style is similar to the one proposed for procedural interfaces in Section 6.5.4, and is discussed further in Section 9.1.8.

Other reasons not to insulate could result from a shortage of personnel. There may be no compelling reason to insulate, and the incremental increase in development time necessary to achieve the insulation may not be deemed cost-effective. Creating a wrapper requires significant planning and effort; deadlines and a lack of experience may prevent potentially wrappable subsystems from getting wrapped properly.

Insulation may be omitted because the added physical complexity of introducing yet another component may be judged not to be worth the potential benefit that would be gained through insulation. Both protocols and wrappers involve creating a separate component to act as the interface. This separate physical entity contributes to the overall complexity of the physical architecture.

Finally, insulation is an additional, independent constraint on the implementation of a component or subsystem. Addressing this requirement leads to a somewhat more complex implementation that may be harder for some to understand and marginally more difficult to maintain than an uninsulated component or subsystem. For example, fully insulating a class requires creating a separate structure in the `.c` file and remembering to dynamically allocate and delete it during construction and destruction, respectively.

Added initial development cost, increased component count, and increased complexity are at least tenable reasons to resist unnecessary insulation. There are, however, clear overall maintenance benefits to be gained from insulation. In the absence of compelling reasons one way or the other, keep in mind that insulation is more economically removed than installed late in the development process.

Principle

For large, widely used objects, insulate early and selectively remove the insulation later if necessary.

Once a system is complete and performance analysis proves that removing the insulation from a few key components significantly improves the overall system performance, at least the benefits of the insulation will have been realized throughout the bulk of the development effort. Waiting until the end of a large project to determine empirically which components can be insulating without significant loss in performance sacrifices much of the initial maintenance benefit that insulation provides.

To summarize: insulating an interface can result in dynamically allocated memory, extra indirections, non-inline or virtual-function calls, explicit management of dynamically allocated objects, and additional translation units. The cost of insulating an interface in terms of performance, development effort, or complexity will sometimes outweigh the benefits of the insulation. On the other hand, some components are neither lightweight nor stable, and yet are available for general use throughout the system. These large, high-level, volatile, and widely used objects are prime candidates for insulation.

6.6.3 How to Insulate

In practice, there are two main ways to insulate clients from the logical implementation of a class:

1. Extract a protocol for that class.
2. Everything else:
   - Use partial implementation techniques.
   - Convert this to a fully insulating concrete class.
   - Create an insulating wrapper for the class.
   - Create a procedural interface for the class.

Because a protocol defines a pure interface, clients of the protocol not only do not depend on the implementation at compile time, but, unlike with other techniques, they need not depend on any particular implementation at link time either.

Classes that already employ virtual functions are probable candidates for "perfect" insulation by extracting a protocol class. These objects are already treated as base classes, and they already incur the extra overhead of carrying around a pointer to a virtual-function table in every instance of the class. More often than not, base classes with virtual functions are not intended to be instantiated. If a class either declares any pure virtual functions or declares all of its constructors non-`public`, the base class *cannot* be instantiated on the program stack by public clients. Therefore, the usage of such classes will be left essentially unaffected by insulating them with a protocol.

For utility classes that act as modules (e.g., `GeomUtil` in Figure 5-21), there is no need to create an instance of the class in order to use its functionality. In that case, declaring all member functions `static` and non-`inline`, and moving any static member data to the `.c` file (at file scope), obviates the overhead of instantiation and the virtual call mechanism.

For a "small" class with mostly non-trivial accessor functions such as a reasonable `String` class, total insulation might be appropriate. Notice here that the implementation of even simple functions such as equality (==) and assignment (=) potentially involves loops, additional dynamic allocation, or at minimum another non-inline function call to `strcmp` or `strcpy`. Insulating the implementation of this class would actually facilitate performance tuning by allowing different implementation strategies (e.g., reference counting and caching length) to be profiled and evaluated in the context of actual usage without having to recompile the entire system. Again, the insulation could always be removed (if necessary) much later in the development process.

Large, high-level, instantiatable objects (e.g, a circuit simulator or parser) that do not make use of inheritance or virtual functions in their interface can usually be "fully insulated" or "wrapped" with negligible impact on either size or runtime overhead. Insulation is indicated for such objects, especially when the object is intended for widespread, general use outside of the local software development group.

The `p2p_Router` shown in Figure 4-2 illustrates an ideal example of a fully insulating wrapper. The router is not a module; an instance of the router must be created and "programmed" before it can be used. The work required to construct an instance of a `p2p_Router` is not trivial, nor is the work done by the `addObstruction` function used to program it. However, the time spent using the router is completely dominated by work done in the lower levels of the router subsystem on each call to the `findPath` function. The added runtime cost of insulating the router is thus completely negligible.

As a final example, consider how we might go about insulating (someone else's) class `Solid`, whose header is shown in Figure 6-84. `Solid` is intended to be a common base class for a variety of solids but is not itself instantiatable. This intent is corroborated by observing that the constructors and assignment operator for the class are declared `protected`.

```
// solid.h
#ifndef INCLUDED_SOLID
#define INCLUDED_SOLID
```

```
#ifndef INCLUDED_IOSTREAM
#include <iostream.h>
#define INCLUDED_IOSTREAM
#endif

class Solid {
    int d_color;
    double d_scale;
    double d_density;
    ostream *d_errorStream_p;

  protected:
    // STATIC MEMBERS
    static double distance(double x1, double y1, double x2, double y2);

    // CREATORS
    Solid(ostream *errorStream, double density, double scale = 1.0);
    Solid(const Solid& solid);

    // MANIPULATORS
    Solid& operator=(const Solid& solid);
    void setColor(int color) { d_color = color; }

    // ACCESSORS
    virtual double surfaceEquation(double x, double y, double z) = 0;
        // Point(x,y,z) is on the surface when function returns
        // approximately 0 (to within some small tolerance).
    ostream& error() { return *d_errorStream_p; }
    double mass() const { return density() * volume(); }

  public:
    // CREATORS
    virtual ~Solid();

    // MANIPULATORS
    virtual void setTemperature(int degrees) = 0;
        // Changing the temperature may affect color, depending on the
        // actual object.
    void setScale(int scale) { d_scale = scale; }

    // ACCESSORS
    virtual double temperature() const = 0;
    int scale() { return d_scale; }
    int color() const { return d_color; }
    double density() const { return d_density; }
    double volume() const;
    double centerOfMassInX() const;
    double centerOfMassInY() const;
    double centerOfMassInZ() const;
    // ...
};

#endif
```

Figure 6-84: Base-Class `Solid` with Public and Protected Interface

The scale attribute of a `Solid` determines the relative size of the object. Users of `Solid` are permitted to access and modify its scale directly. The protected pure-virtual `surfaceEquation` function allows a derived class to program the unique behavior necessary to describe its own surface (parameterized by `scale()`) through an implicit equation. For example, the surface of a sphere might be described as

```
double Sphere::surfaceEquation(double x, double y, double z)
{
    return x * x + y * y + z * z - scale() * scale();
}
```

Non-virtual functions in the base class use the surface equation to compute, among other things, the `Solid`'s volume and center of mass in each spatial dimension. Making the `surfaceEquation` function protected prevents direct access to `surfaceEquation` by the public.[22]

Since it is up to the derived object to define both the behavior of getting and setting the temperature and how that affects the color of the specific object, the public `temperature` and `setTemperature` functions of `Solid` have been declared pure virtual. (Notice that the internal representation of the temperature is already insulated from clients of the base class.)

Since all objects have a color (encoded as an integer), a private integer data member and a public inline accessor are provided in the base class. General clients of `Solid` are not permitted to set the color of an instance directly. Rather, they are required to adjust its temperature, which in turn may affect the color of the object. The `setColor` manipulator function is therefore protected, so that only the derived object itself can alter the color of this instance directly.

The public interface provides several accessor functions, some of which (such as `volume`) do substantial numerical work when invoked. The protected interface provides derived-class authors with several helper functions such as `setTemperature` that may prove useful in implementing required virtual functions.

Rather than exposing the `ostream` pointer data member directly in the protected interface, the protected function `error` is supplied to provide a convenient stream refer-

---

[22] The desired effect could also have been achieved by making this virtual function private, but that would have made the tasks of the derived-class developer less obvious.

ence for reporting errors (such as setting the temperature too low or too high). The mass may play a role in determining the color, particularly for a very large, dense `Solid` such a black hole. The protected member function `mass`, which calculates the mass using members supplied in the public interface, is provided for the convenience of derived-class authors. Finally, `distance` is a function frequently used by derived-class authors. Unlike the `mass` helper function, `distance` does not depend on an instance of any class and so is made a protected static member of class `Solid`.

Clearly the original author of the `Solid` base class did not consider insulation an important design criterion, as evidenced by the casual use of inline functions. Fortunately we have several techniques available to improve the insulation of the implementation of `Solid`. These insulation improvements fall into two basic categories: total and partial.

As an exercise, let us first see what kinds of incremental improvements we can make to the class `Solid`:

```
#ifndef INCLUDED_IOSTREAM
#include <iostream.h>
#define INCLUDED_IOSTREAM
#endif
```

Without needing to think much at all, we can convert the above to `class ostream;` to eliminate unnecessary compile-time dependence on the `iostream` header and to avoid the unnecessary creation at startup of a static dummy object in every translation unit that includes `solid.h` (see Section 7.8.1.3).

```
protected:
  static double distance(double x1, double y1, double x2, double y2);
```

Since `distance` is a static function, it does not depend on the `Shape` instance data; it can easily be moved to a separate utility component.

```
protected:
  double mass() const { return density() * volume(); }
```

The calculation performed by `mass()` depends only on attributes that are accessible directly from `Shape`'s public interface. A modified, static version of the `mass` function can be moved to a separate utility component.

```
class ostream;          // already changed from #include <iostream.h>

  private:
    ostream *d_errorStream_p;

  protected:
    ostream& error() { return *d_errorStream_p; }
```

It may be possible that some derived `Solid` objects can be set to any temperature without error. The error stream function, `error()`, is just a convenience that some derived-class authors may find useful. We could simply remove the `d_errorStream_p` data member from the factored implementation (as we did with `Scribe` in the shape subsystem of Figure 6-26) and let derived-class authors implement an error stream only if needed.

```
  private:
    int d_color;
    double d_scale;
    double d_density;

  protected:
    void setColor(int color) { d_color = color; }

  public:
    int scale() { return d_scale; }
    int color() const { return d_color; }
    double density() const { return d_density; }
```

If we assume that none of the inline functions of `Solid` is called so frequently that it creates a performance problem, we can convert all inline functions to non-inline functions. Doing this will also enable us to collect all of the factored data into one `struct` defined in the `.c` file. A somewhat more insulating version of the `Solid` base class is shown in Figure 6-85.

```
// solid.h
#ifndef INCLUDED_SOLID
#define INCLUDED_SOLID

class Solid_i;               // insulated member data

class Solid {
    Solid_i *d_this;

  protected:
    // CREATORS
    Solid(double density, double scale = 1.0);
    Solid(const Solid& solid);
```

```
    // MANIPULATORS
    Solid& operator=(const Solid& solid);
    void setColor(int color)

    // ACCESSORS
    virtual double surfaceEquation(double x, double y, double z) = 0;
        // Point(x,y,z) is on the surface when function returns
        // approximately 0 (to within some small tolerance).

  public:
    // CREATORS
    virtual ~Solid();

    // MANIPULATORS
    virtual void setTemperature(int degrees) = 0;
        // Changing the temperature may affect color, depending on the
        // actual object.
    void setScale(int scale);

    // ACCESSORS
    virtual double temperature() const = 0;
    int scale():
    int color();
    double density() const;
    double volume() const;
    double centerOfMassInX() const;
    double centerOfMassInY() const;
    double centerOfMassInZ() const;
    // ...
};

#endif
```

Figure 6-85: Somewhat More Insulating Abstract Class `Solid`

At this point, to do any better we will have to use some form of total insulation technique. We cannot fully insulate the implementation of this class as it stands because of the use of virtual functions. Wrapping this class would preclude general users from deriving new kinds of `Solid` at will. Of the insulation techniques presented in this chapter, extracting a protocol is by far the best alternative here.

As with the `Car` class shown in Figure 6-30, we are unable simply to remove all of the protected functions and place them in a separate utility because of their intimate interaction with the instance itself. That is, functions in the protected interface (e.g., `setColor`) were supplied only to implement virtual functions (e.g., `setTemperature`) defined in derived classes. At the same time, these protected functions depend directly on instance information (e.g., d_color) that is accessible by clients via public functions (e.g., color) defined in this base class. It is primarily because of the virtual function dependency on intrinsic instance data that we are forced to extract a protocol to achieve total insulation.

Figure 6-86 shows the result of extracting a protocol from either the original Solid or the partially insulated version. Notice how extracting a protocol class *always* enables us to avoid exposing the protected members of the base class.

```
// solid.h
#ifndef INCLUDED_SOLID
#define INCLUDED_SOLID

class Solid {
  public:
    // CREATORS
    virtual ~Solid();

    // MANIPULATORS
    virtual void setTemperature(int degrees) = 0;
        // Changing the temperature may affect color, depending on the
        // actual object.
    virtual void setScale(int scale);

    // ACCESSORS
    virtual double temperature() const = 0;
    virtual int scale():
    virtual int color();
    virtual double density() const;
    virtual double volume() const;
    virtual double centerOfMassInX() const;
    virtual double centerOfMassInY() const;
    virtual double centerOfMassInZ() const;
    // ...
};

#endif
```

Figure 6-86: Protocol Class Solid

6.6.4 How Much to Insulate

While the implementation of p2p_Router presented in Chapter 4 is insulated, it is not "fully insulated" (as defined in Section 6.4.2) because the wrapper class holds a pointer to another class over which the component does not have sole and complete control. We would not, for example, be able to add an insulated data member to the p2p_Router class without disturbing the independently tested implementation component p2p_RouterImp.

Principle

Sometimes total insulation is no more expensive at runtime than partial insulation.

In many cases this degree of insulation may be good enough. But if p2p_router defines a very public interface, we can do better. A fully insulating p2p_router component would (forward) declare its own implementation structure (e.g., p2p_Router_i). Then, in the p2p_router.c file, struct p2p_Router_i would be defined with a single embedded member of type p2p_RouterImp:

```
// p2p_router.c
#include "p2p_router.h"
#include "p2p_routerimp.h"

struct p2p_Router_i {
    p2p_RouterImp d_imp;
};

// ...
```

Now adding a "private" data member to p2p_Router_i neither affects clients of p2p_Router nor requires changes to p2p_RouterImp:

```
// p2p_router.c
#include "p2p_router.h"
#include "p2p_routerimp.h"

struct p2p_Router_i {
    p2p_RouterImp d_imp;
    int d_moreData;       // added fully insulated detail
};

// ...
```

In this case, doing it right requires just a bit more development effort, but achieves total insulation without affecting runtime performance at all.

Principle

Sometimes the last 10 percent of the insulation is attained at the cost of a tenfold increase in runtime.

Sometimes obtaining the last little bit of insulation can be very costly. Recall from Section 6.4.3 that we opted not to insulate all of the `graph` component class completely. To do so would have caused a disproportionately high cost in terms of runtime performance. To illustrate this principle, consider the four related implementations of the graph subsystem we have seen in this and the previous chapters:

System I: Factored Objects. This subsystem corresponds to the factored implementation of Section 5.9. In this architecture, the subsystem was levelizable but clients had to know about and use lower-level components in order to use the graph.

System II: Encapsulating Wrapper. This subsystem corresponds to the encapsulating wrapper implementation of Section 5.10. In this architecture, clients can do everything necessary from a single wrapper component.

System III: Insulating Wrapper. This subsystem fully insulates the implementations of three of the five wrapper classes presented in Figure 6-53. The remaining two classes, `NodeId` and `EdgeId`, expose their respective implementation class names, `Gnode` and `Gedge`, in their physical (but not their logical) interfaces.

System IV: Fully Insulating Wrapper. This subsystem fully insulates the implementations of all five of the wrapper classes presented in Figure 6-53.

System I favored runtime performance over encapsulation. Changes to low-level interfaces could cause clients to have to rework their code. System II places a thin encapsulating wrapper over the graph subsystem. Clients are logically independent of, but not insulated from, changes to these low-level components, and could be forced to recompile. System III transforms the encapsulating wrapper of System II into an almost fully insulating wrapper. Changes to any of the underlying components cannot affect clients of the wrapper at compile time; however, it is not possible to add private data to `NodeId` (`EdgeId`) without affecting either `Gnode` (`Gedge`) or clients. System IV represents a fully insulating wrapper; arbitrary changes to any of the five wrapper-class implementations affect neither clients nor the underlying implementation components.

To illustrate the runtime cost of these various graph architectures under a spectrum of operating conditions, I created a small test program to run a series of experiments. In this program, the graph subsystem is used to create the arbitrary graph structure shown in Figure 6-87. In this graph, each edge happens to have a weight of 1, but the particular edge values will not affect the experiment.

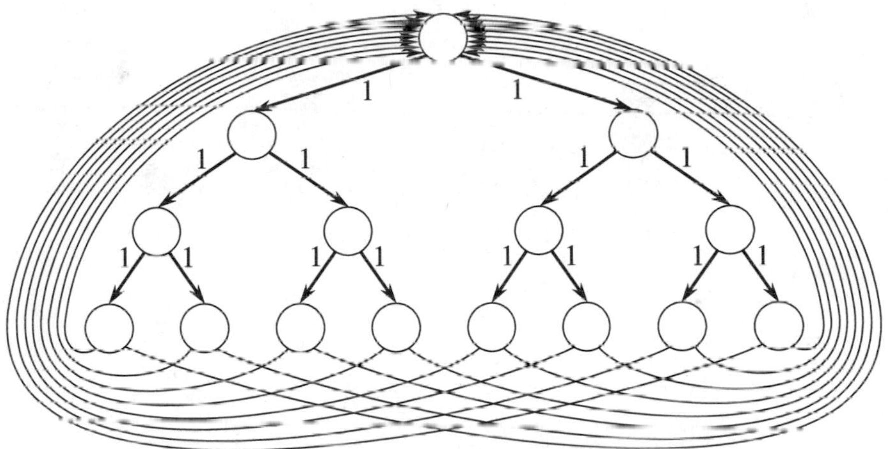

Figure 6-87 Arbitrary Graph Consisting of 15 Nodes, Each of Degree 3

After creating an instance of this graph, the program invokes a `NodeIter` to iterate over all 15 nodes in the graph, accumulating the values obtained by calling `sum` on each. The recursive function `sum` explores the graph from a specified node to a specified depth, accumulating the weights of the edges it encounters along the way. Since `sum` is exploring a binary tree, the runtime of `sum` is exponential with respect to the depth to which it searches.

The source for the actual test program is provided in Figure 6-88. The first command-line argument to the test driver indicates the depth to which `sum` is to explore the graph. The second command-line argument specifies the number of times to repeat the (identical) experiment; this second argument is used to obtain accurate time measurements for an average iteration.

```
// graph.t.c
#include "graph.h"
#include "node.h"
#include "edge.h"
#include <iostream.h>
#include <stdlib.h>

double sum(const NodeId& node, int depth)
{
    double result = 0;
    if (depth > 0) {
        for (EdgeIter it(node); it; ++it) {
            if (it().from() != node) {
                continue;
            }
            result += it()->weight();
            result += sum(it().to(), depth - 1);
        }
    }
    return result;
}

main (int argc, char *argv[])
{
    int depth = 1; int repeat = 1;
    if (argc > 1) depth = atoi(argv[1]);
    if (argc > 2) repeat = atoi(argv[2]);
    cout << "GRAPH: depth = " << depth
         << "  repeat = " << repeat << endl;

    double total;

    for (int i = 0; i < repeat; ++i) {
        Graph g;
        NodeId n = g.addNode("n");

        NodeId n0 = g.addNode("n0");
        NodeId n1 = g.addNode("n1");
        g.addEdge(n, n0, 1);
        g.addEdge(n, n1, 1);
```

```
            NodeId n00 = g.addNode("n00");
            NodeId n01 = g.addNode("n01");
            NodeId n10 = g.addNode("n10");
            NodeId n11 = g.addNode("n11");
            g.addEdge(n0, n00, 1);
            g.addEdge(n0, n01, 1);
            g.addEdge(n1, n10, 1);
            g.addEdge(n1, n11, 1);

            NodeId n000 = g.addNode("n000");
            NodeId n001 = g.addNode("n001");
            NodeId n010 = g.addNode("n010");
            NodeId n011 = g.addNode("n011");
            NodeId n100 = g.addNode("n100");
            NodeId n101 = g.addNode("n101");
            NodeId n110 = g.addNode("n110");
            NodeId n111 = g.addNode("n111");
            g.addEdge(n00, n000, 1);
            g.addEdge(n00, n001, 1);
            g.addEdge(n01, n010, 1);
            g.addEdge(n01, n011, 1);
            g.addEdge(n10, n100, 1);
            g.addEdge(n10, n101, 1);
            g.addEdge(n11, n110, 1);
            g.addEdge(n11, n111, 1);
            g.addEdge(n000, n, 1);
            g.addEdge(n001, n, 1);
            g.addEdge(n010, n, 1);
            g.addEdge(n011, n, 1);
            g.addEdge(n100, n, 1);
            g.addEdge(n101, n, 1);
            g.addEdge(n110, n, 1);
            g.addEdge(n111, n, 1);
            g.addEdge(n000, n, 1);
            g.addEdge(n001, n, 1);
            g.addEdge(n010, n, 1);
            g.addEdge(n011, n, 1);
            g.addEdge(n100, n, 1);
            g.addEdge(n101, n, 1);
            g.addEdge(n110, n, 1);
            g.addEdge(n111, n, 1);

            total = 0;
            for (NodeIter it(g); it; ++it) {
                total += sum(it(), depth);
            }
        }

        cout << "total = " << total << endl;
    }
```

Figure 6-88: Test Driver for Measuring Runtime Efficiency of Graph Subsystems

	Running Time on SUN SPARC 20 (in CPU Seconds)			
Depth	Factored (Original) System I	Encapsulating Wrapper System II	Mostly Insulating Wrapper System III	Fully Insulating Wrapper System IV
0	0.0018	0.0018	0.0020	0.0033
	(100%)	(100%)	(111%)	(183%)
1	0.0019	0.0020	0.0026	0.0115
2	0.0022	0.0024	0.0050	0.0381
3	0.0026	0.0031	0.0086	0.0675
4	0.0033	0.0043	0.0144	0.1023
5	0.0046	0.0063	0.0248	0.1438
	(100%)	(137%)	(539%)	(3,126%)
6	0.009	0.014	0.063	0.334
7	0.016	0.025	0.120	0.609
8	0.027	0.044	0.213	1.054
9	0.048	0.078	0.380	1.836
10	0.121	0.202	0.998	4.895
	(100%)	(167%)	(825%)	(4,045%)
11	0.23	0.38	1.91	9.37
12	0.41	0.68	3.40	16.42
13	0.74	1.22	6.06	28.94
14	1.92	3.22	15.95	77.87
15	3.69	6.15	30.51	148.44
	(100%)	(167%)	(827%)	(4,023%)
16	6.6	10.9	54.4	262.2
17	11.8	19.4	97.0	462.4
18	30.7	51.5	255.1	1245.5
19	58.9	98.5	488.1	2374.4
20	105.8	175.2	870.6	4194.8
	(100%)	(166%)	(823%)	(3,965%)

Figure 6-89: Runtime Cost of Various Graph System Architectures

The test driver was run for depths ranging from 0 to 20 with a repeat value of 1,000 (depth 0–5), 100 (depth 6–10), 10 (depth 11–15), and 1 (depth 16–20) on each of the four systems described above.[23] The results of this very illuminating experiment are given in Figure 6-89.

When the depth of the graph traversal is specified as `0`, no graph traversal takes place. Most of the time is spent in building up and tearing down the graph structure. These kinds of operations are inherently relatively expensive; as the first line of Figure 6-89 indicates, the effects of encapsulating and even insulating are negligible and small, respectively. When fully insulating, we incur a runtime cost that is 83 percent higher than our cost when not insulating. This is because of the very pronounced increase in the cost of returning a fully insulating `NodeId` by value from `NodeIter`.

As we increase the depth of the graph, the cost of traversing it begins to affect overall performance. Functions that are used to read the information in a graph are much smaller and do much less work per call than those used to construct the graph. These lightweight functions, however, are called many, many times in the course of traversing the graph.

At a depth of 5, it takes 2.5 times as long for the experiment to run on System I as it took at a depth of 0; however, many times that number of additional function calls are occurring. If these small functions are made disproportionately expensive, the runtime performance will suffer. At this same depth, the encapsulated System II now experiences an increase of 37 percent compared to the runtime for the unwrapped System I. The partial insulation of System III causes the experiment to take 5 times as long. The dynamic allocations brought on by totally insulating `NodeId` and `EdgeId` in System VI have cost us a factor of 30!

At a depth of 10, it takes 100 times as long for the experiment to run on System I as it did at a depth of 0. The time spent calling those "little" functions now dominates the runtime cost. For an encapsulating wrapper (System II), this experiment will run about 67 percent longer. For an insulating wrapper (System III) it will take over 8 times as long, and for a fully insulating wrapper (System IV), it will take fully 40 times as long.

---

[23] The test driver was trivially altered to accommodate the slightly different interface of System I.

By scanning down Figure 6-89 from this point, we can see that we have reached the other asymptote; increasing the depth does not further spread the respective runtime performance ratios of these graph subsystem variants.

What lessons can be learned from this experiment?

1. Insulating the implementation of an object whose functions already do a substantial amount of work below the insulating layer will have no noticeable effect on runtime performance (suggesting that the level of insulation is appropriate).

2. Encapsulating a subsystem with a wrapper whose functions do a non-trivial amount of work below the encapsulating layer will have a negligible effect on runtime performance (suggesting that the level of encapsulation is appropriate).

3. Providing even an encapsulating wrapper for lightweight functions that are called frequently can have a significant effect on overall performance (perhaps suggesting that the level of encapsulation should be escalated).

4. Providing an insulating wrapper for lightweight functions that are called frequently can have an overwhelming effect on overall performance (forcing the level of insulation to be escalated).

5. Providing a totally insulating wrapper for tiny objects that are frequently returned by value can have a devastating effect on overall performance (forcing the degree of insulation to be reduced and/or the level of insulation to be escalated).

6.7 Summary

In this chapter, we introduced the concept of *insulation* as the physical analog of the logical concept commonly referred to as *encapsulation*. An implementation detail of a component is insulated if it can be changed without forcing clients of the component to recompile.

Several constructs were identified that could potentially result in undesirable compile-time coupling:

- ***Inheritance*** and ***Layering*** force the definitions of the inherited or embedded object to be seen by the client.

- ***Inline Functions*** and ***Private Members*** expose the implementation details of this object to clients.

- ***Protected Members*** expose the protected details to public clients.

- ***Compiler-Generated Functions*** force an implementation change to affect the declared interface.

- ***Include Directives*** artificially create compile-time coupling.

- ***Default Arguments*** expose the default value to clients.

- ***Enumerations*** cause unnecessary compile-time coupling due to improper placement and/or inappropriate reuse.

All other things being equal, it is better to insulate a particular implementation detail from a client than not—even if other details remain uninsulated. Partial implementation techniques are used to reduce the extent of compile-time coupling without incurring all of the overhead that total insulation could imply:

- Removing ***private inheritance*** by converting WasA to HoldsA.

- Removing ***embedded data members*** by converting HasA to HoldsA.

- Removing ***private member functions*** by making them static at file scope and moving them to the `.c` file.

- Removing ***protected member functions*** by creating a separate utility component and/or extracting a protocol.

- Removing ***private member data*** by extracting a protocol and/or moving static data to the `.c` file at file scope.

- Removing ***compiler-generated functions*** by explicitly defining these functions.

- Removing ***include directives*** by removing unnecessary include directives or replacing them with (forward) class declarations.

- Removing ***default arguments*** by replacing valid default values with invalid default values or employing multiple function declarations.

- Removing ***enumerations*** by relocating them to the `.c` file, replacing them with `const` static class member data, or redistributing them among the classes that use them.

For widely used interfaces, avoiding all compile-time dependency on the underlying implementation details is highly desirable. Three general insulation approaches were discussed to insulate clients from all implementation details:

- ***Protocol Class:*** Creating an abstract "protocol" class is a general insulation technique for factoring the interface and implementation of an abstract base class. Not only are clients insulated from changes to the implementation at compile time, but even link-time dependency on a specific implementation is eliminated.

- ***Fully Insulating Concrete Class:*** A "fully insulating" concrete class holds a single opaque pointer to a private structure defined entirely in the `.c` file. This `struct` contains all of the implementation details that were formerly in the private section of the original class.

- ***Insulating Wrapper Component:*** The concept of an encapsulating wrapper component (from Chapter 5) can be extended to a fully insulating wrapper component. Wrappers are typically used to insulate several other components or even an entire subsystem. Unlike a procedural interface, a wrapper layer requires considerable up-front planning and top-down design. In particular, care must be taken in the design of a multi-component wrapper to avoid the need for long-distance friendships.

A *procedural interface* is a collection of functions that sit on top of an existing collection of components and expose a subset of the functionality to end users. A procedural interface is an alternative to total insulation. Unlike the three total insulation techniques presented in this chapter, a procedural interface is neither logically encapsulating nor entirely insulating. A procedural interface does have the unique advantage of working on very large systems that may not have been designed with a procedural interface in mind.

Generally if a component is used widely throughout a system, its interface should be insulating; however, not all interfaces should be insulating. For example, insulation may not be practical, particularly for lightweight, reusable components. Common reasons for choosing *not* to insulate a component include the following:

- *Exposure*: The number of clients may be known to be small.
- *Time to access data*: The class may have embedded data and make effective use of tiny inline functions to access it.
- *Time to create objects*: A tiny class (e.g., `Point`) may not already allocate dynamic memory.
- *(Initial) development cost*: There may be no compelling reason to insulate; the extra development effort may not be cost-effective.
- *Number of components*: Insulation may require yet another component (e.g., to hold a protocol or wrapper), increasing maintenance costs.
- *Component complexity*: An insulated implementation (e.g., a "fully insulated" `struct` defined in the `.c` file) may be harder to understand and maintain than an uninsulated implementation.

7

Packages

A large project can span many developers, several layers of management, and even multiple geographic sites. The physical structure of the system will reflect not only the logical structure of the application but also the organizational structure of the development team that implements it. Large systems require hierarchical physical organization beyond what can be accomplished by a levelizable hierarchy of individual components alone. In order to encompass more complex functionality, we need to introduce a unit of physical design at a higher level of abstraction. This chapter addresses the physical structure needed to support the development of very large systems. In particular, we introduce a macro unit of physical design referred to in this book as a package.

A package aggregates a collection of related components into a logically cohesive physical unit. Each package has an associated *registered* prefix that immediately identifies both files and file-scope logical constructs as belonging to that package. After presenting the semantics and physical structure of packages in the first two sections, we apply the concept of levelization at the package level in Section 7.3. Here we discover that many of the techniques that applied at the component level also work when applied to entire packages. At the same time, new issues that must be addressed separately emerge. In Section 7.4, we explore the concept of insulation at the package level, in terms of improving the usability of complex subsystems for clients. Then, in Section 7.5, we extend the envelope of project size by hierarchically grouping packages. In Section 7.6, we discuss the process of releasing a stable snapshot of a system. One possible directory structure for releasing a large system is presented. We then examine a technique known as *patching* for updating published software between releases. Next, in Section 7.7, we examine the role of `main()` in an object-oriented software system, along with the special privileges and responsibilities of owning the "top" of a program. Finally, in Section 7.8, we examine the first few moments in the life of a program's execution. It is at this time that potentially all file-scoped static data is initialized.

In large systems, static initialization can lead to unacceptably long invocation times. We take a look at four alternative initialization strategies, comparing their relative strengths and weaknesses as we go. We also address the need to clean up before program exit in order to facilitate memory regression testing.

7.1 From Components to Packages

In Chapter 3 we introduced the component as the smallest unit of physical design. A typical component contains one, two, or even several classes, often accompanied by appropriate free operators. Normally a component consists of many hundreds of lines of C++ source code and comments, with the `.h` and `.c` files often of comparable length. Occasionally a low-level definition component will have fewer than a hundred lines and an empty `.c` file. Sometimes wrapper components for large subsystems or machine-generated components will be measured in the thousands of lines. As a rule of thumb, however, several hundred to a thousand lines is a good practical size for components in terms of effective comprehension, testing, and reuse.

As we saw with the `p2p_router` example in Chapter 4, we can build fairly complex subsystems using only a handful of components. In that example, the implementation of high-level functionality declared within a single component interface was distributed across a hierarchy of components that greatly improved its testability. A system consisting of tens of thousands of lines can be supported easily without further partitioning. But what if our systems are much bigger than this? Suppose they consist of hundreds of thousands of lines of code. How would we address the physical organization of literally hundreds of components? As ever, we will address complexity with the tried-and-true: abstraction and hierarchy.

When designing a system from the highest level, there are almost always large pieces that it makes sense to talk about abstractly as individual units. Consider the design of an interpreter for a large language (such as C++) shown in Figure 7-1. Each of the subsystems described in that design is likely to be too large and complex to fit appropriately into a single component. These larger units (indicated in Figure 7-1 with a double box) are each implemented as a collection of levelizable components.

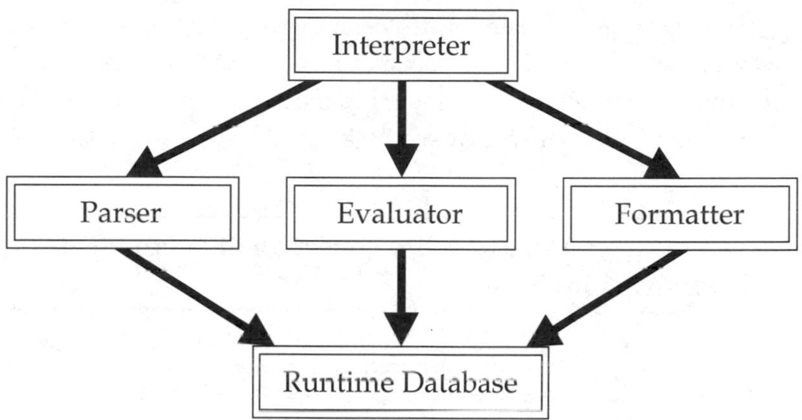

Figure 7-1: High-Level Interpreter Architecture

The dependencies in Figure 7-1 between these larger units represent an *envelope* for the aggregate dependencies among the components that comprise each subsystem. For example, the runtime database is an independent subsystem; it has no dependencies on any external components. Each of the parser, evaluator, and formatter subsystems has components that depend on one or more components in the runtime database, but none of the components in any of these three subsystems depends on any components in the other two parallel subsystems. The top-level interpreter consists of components that depend on components within each of the three parallel subsystems (and perhaps directly on components within the runtime database). Carefully partitioning a system into large units and then considering the aggregate dependencies among these units is critical when distributing the development effort for projects across multiple individuals, development teams, or geographical sites.

Although the design of Figure 7-1 would not be considered a large project, it could easily be assigned to more than one developer. There is a natural partitioning that would allow several developers to work on this project concurrently. After the runtime database is designed, there would be an opportunity for three concurrent development efforts to begin on the parsing, evaluating, and formatting functionality. Once these pieces start to fall into place, the implementation and testing of the top-level interpreter can begin.

Until now, we have discussed these separate subsystems as conceptual units with no actual physical partitions. If the entire project is expected to require only 20,000 lines of code and is being implemented by a single developer, there may be no compelling need to partition the overall architecture into distinct physical units. However, if the design is, say, 80,000 lines of code or if more than one developer will be working on the project at any given time, there is a much greater need for the conceptual physical partitioning to become concrete.

<u>DEFINITION</u>: A *package* is a collection of components organized as a physically cohesive unit.

The term *package* refers to a generally acyclic, often hierarchical collection of components that together have a cohesive semantic purpose. Physically, a package consists of a collection of header files along with a single library file containing the information in the corresponding object (`.o`) files. A package might consist of a loosely coupled collection of low-level, reusable components, such as the original Standard Components library from AT&T,[1] and now the new Standard Template Library (STL) developed at Hewlett-Packard.[2] A package might also consist of a special-purpose subsystem intended for use by only a single client, such as the `p2p_router` subsystem from Chapter 4.

Figure 7-2 illustrates one possible organization for packages within a file system. In this organization, all packages exist at the same level in the directory structure regardless of their physical interdependencies. All headers (required outside a given package) are placed in a single, system-wide directory called `include`. A library file corresponding to each package is placed in a single systemwide directory called `lib`.

Each package directory contains files holding the source code for components associated with that package. As illustrated schematically in Figure 7-2, package `pk` contains *n* components: `pk_c1`, `pk_c2`, . . . , `pk_cn` in its source directory. Each component (e.g., `pk_ci`) has an associated header file (`pk_ci.h`), an implementation file (`pk_ci.c`), and an individual test driver (`pk_ci.t.c`) that can be used to exercise the functionality implemented in the component incrementally. Note that to be effective,

[1] **stroustrup94**, Section 8.3, pp. 184–185.

[2] STL has been accepted as part of the ANSI/ISO (Draft) C++ Standard (see **musser**).

these hierarchical test drivers should be considered as much a part of the system source code as the components they test. These drivers can be easily distinguished from the implementation files by their `.t.c.` suffix.

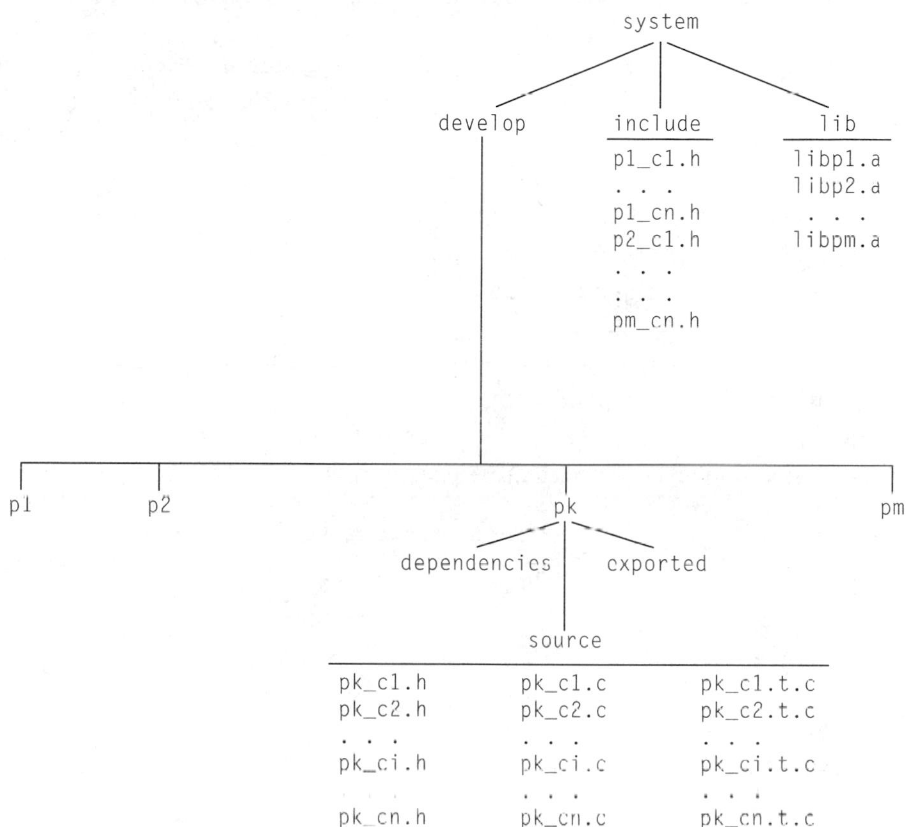

Figure 7-2: A Simple Development Organization for Packages

In addition to the source directory, there are two files under each package directory. The `dependencies` file holds the names of all other packages upon which this package is authorized to depend. That is, in order to use this package, clients will *not* have to include or link to any other component defined in another package unless that package is named in the dependencies file associated with this package. Although package dependencies seldom change, it does occasionally happen. Specifying these dependencies is the job of the system architect; verifying them is a process that can and should be automated.

The `exported` file contains a list of component headers that are to be placed in the systemwide include directory of Figure 7-2 for use by general clients. Since not all headers defined in a package are intended for use by external clients, the set of exported headers may be a proper subset of the components defined within the package.

Placing headers used outside a package in a single systemwide include directory makes it convenient to specify where to look for exported header files. Exporting only the subset of headers needed by other packages reduces the clutter through which clients must wade in order to use the product. Placing these headers in a single directory can also improve a client's compile-time efficiency with respect to looking in multiple package directories (see Section 7.6.1). Placing library files in a single directory simply makes using them more convenient.

Until now, we have addressed levelization only at the component level. Recall from Section 4.7 that components that do not depend on any other (local) components are assigned a level of 1. By *local* we were referring to components defined in our package; components defined in other packages were assigned a level of 0.

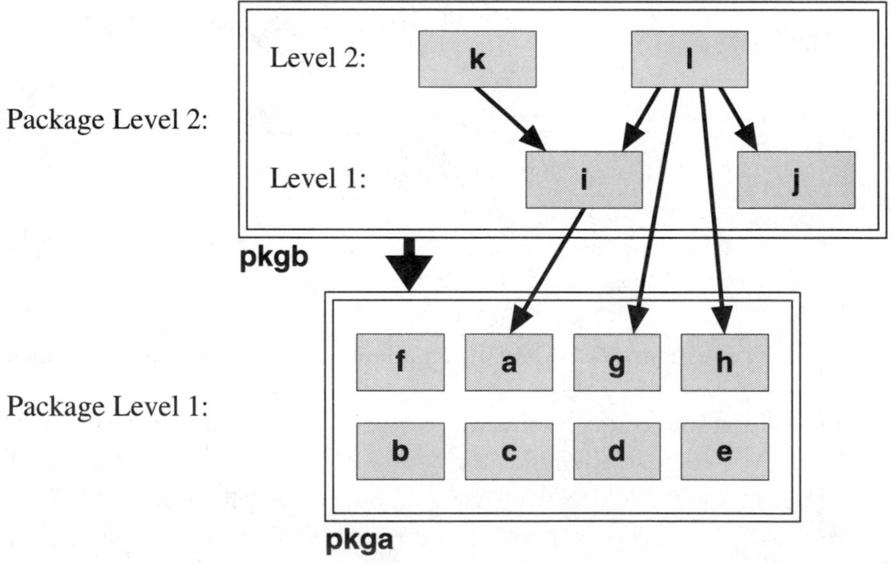

Figure 7-3: Dependencies on Components in Other Packages

Figure 7-3 illustrates the way we have all along been treating the dependencies of our subsystem (`pkgb`) on another subsystem (`pkga`). When testing our own package hierarchically, we assume that components defined outside our package are already tested and known to be internally correct. We therefore can assign to each of these external components a level number of 0 with respect to our local components. Components within our own package (e.g., i and j) that do not depend on any other components local to this package are defined to have a level of 1. Components that depend locally on components at level 1 but no higher (e.g., k and l) are at level 2.

DEFINITION: A package x *DependsOn* another package y if one or more components in x DependsOn one or more components in y.

Just as relationships between logical constructs defined within components imply physical dependencies (see Section 3.4), dependencies among packages are implied by the individual dependencies among the components that comprise them. In Figure 7-3, for example, component i in pkgb DependsOn component a in pkga and component l in pkgb DependsOn components g and h in package pkga. Therefore according to the definition, pkgb DependsOn pkga. Provided pkga does not depend back on pkgb, we can assign level numbers to these packages as a whole, just as we did for the individual components within a package.

Packages provide a powerful mechanism of abstraction for developers and architects alike. Figure 7-4a shows a collection of 20 components, a through t, grouped into four packages: pkga, pkgb, pkgc, and pkgd. Each package defines a high-level architectural unit consisting of a cohesive hierarchy of cooperating components, united for a common purpose.

In contrast, Figure 7-4b shows the identical system represented as an unpackaged, levelizable collection of individual components. The modularity and the abstraction of the high-level architecture are gone; we have lost the semantic value attached to these high-level partitions created during the process of the top-down design.

As Figure 7-4a shows, the individual component dependencies across package boundaries of Figure 7-4b have been abstracted away and replaced with overall package dependencies. For example, the dependencies of component p on component d and component q on components e and f shown in Figure 7-4b are collectively represented in Figure 7-4a by the package dependency of pkgc on pkga.

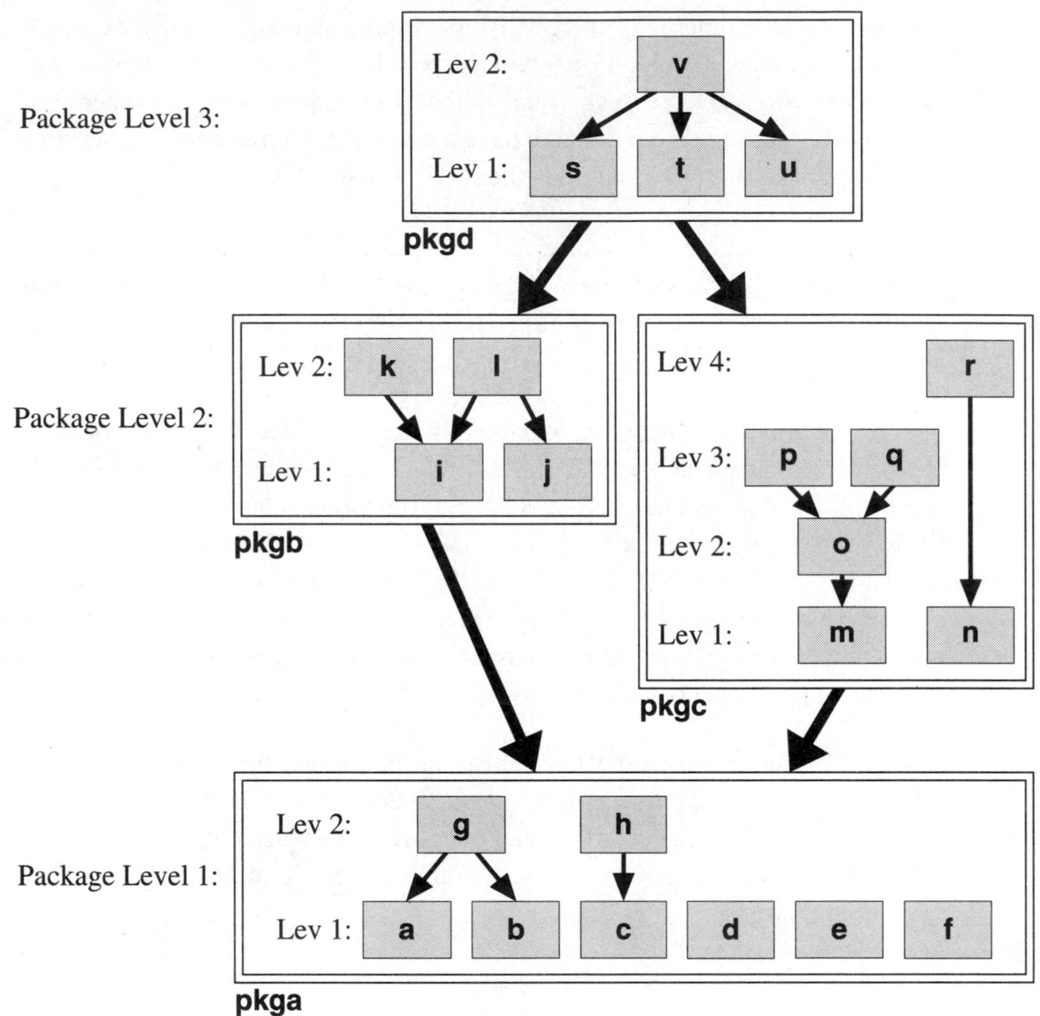

(a) Top-Down Decomposition of a System into Packages of Components

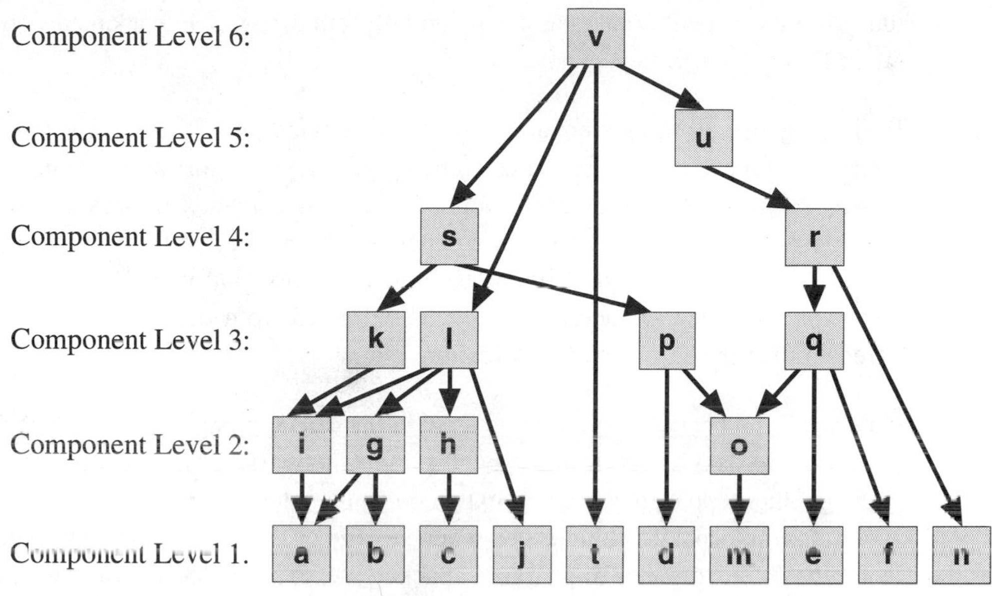

(b) Equivalent Unpackaged System

Figure 7-4: Two Different Views of a System

Notice that the local component level numbers within each package of Figure 7-4a still begin with level 1. This is again because dependencies on other packages are treated as "primary inputs" (see Section 4.7) and, for the purposes of hierarchical testing, are presumed to be correct. As is common, each of these packages contains leaf components (i.e., components such as t that do not depend on any other components in the system). In an unpackaged system (Figure 7-4b), these leaf components would all have an absolute component level of 1. Consequently there is a tendency for many components to fall to the lower levels of the unpackaged diagram, perhaps obscuring their purpose. It is by packaging these leaf components along with their clients that we are able to improve the modularity of the system.

Often a package will hold dozens of components. While a typical component might consist of 500 to 1,000 lines of source code, a typical package might encompass anywhere from 5,000 to 50,000 lines of source. Decomposing large designs into cohesive packages of manageable size greatly simplifies the development process. For developers, comprehending up to a few dozen components and their detailed interdependencies within a package (as in Figure 7-4a) is significantly easier than understanding the arbitrary dependencies among potentially hundreds of unpackaged components (as in Figure 7-4b).

Packaging also allows system architects to understand, discuss, and develop the overall architecture of a large system at a much higher level of abstraction than would otherwise be possible. For example, an architect can delineate the responsibility of a package and then specify acceptable dependencies among entire packages as part of the overall system design without having to address individual components. The actual package dependencies can later be extracted from the source code and compared against the architect's specification.

Having all the packages at the same level in the directory structure makes them easily accessible to developers. Using special-purpose tools (see Appendix C), the physical package interdependencies can be extracted from and compared against the architect's specification located within the dependencies file of the development structure shown in Figure 7-2. Note that to guarantee package-level levelization when testing a new version of a package, only those packages named in the dependencies file should have their exported headers made available for inclusion or their libraries files supplied in the link command.

The partitioning of components into packages is governed by more than just some arbitrary threshold of size or complexity. Identifying package-sized units of cohesive functionality is a natural consequence of top-down design. As with class dependencies within a single component, component dependencies within a package are often more numerous and intricate than dependencies across package boundaries. Because of their more localized nature, the physical character of dependencies among components within a package often involves more compile-time coupling than their inter-package counterparts. In fact, some components defined in a package may be merely insulated implementation details of other components defined in the same package; the headers for these implementation components would probably not be made available outside of the package.

Packaging also reflects the development organization. Typically, a package will be owned/authored by a single developer. The impact of change within a package can be well understood by its owner and dealt with both consistently and effectively. Changes across package boundaries affect other developers and perhaps even the entire system. Therefore, highly coupled parts of the system are often better off being part of a single package.

The degree to which parts of the system are likely to be reused as a unit also plays a role in the packaging of components. In the example of Figure 7-1, the runtime database may be used by a suite of tools, while the three parallel subsystems are used only once. Even if the runtime database were very small in comparison to these other parts of the system, it could make sense to place this low-level subsystem in its own package to avoid tying its reusable functionality to any of the other less-often-used packages. (An analogous argument was presented for demoting enum E in Section 5.3, Figures 5-24 and 5-25.)

To summarize: a package is an aggregate unit of physical design. Like a component, a package serves as a cohesive unit of related functionality fulfilling a common purpose. Packages serve as both abstractions for architects and partitions for developers. Package composition is determined by several factors, including semantic cohesion, the nature of physical dependencies, the organization of the development team, and the potential for independent reuse.

7.2 Registered Package Prefixes

As was discussed in Section 2.3.5, the only logical entities declared at file scope in header files are classes, structs, unions, and free operators. The reason given for this restriction was to reduce the opportunity for name collisions. When only a single developer is involved, it is not hard to avoid name collisions simply by following this strategy. Namespaces (as discussed in Section 7.2.2) can be used to counter a disorganized proliferation of global names resulting from the integration of completely independent development efforts. However, when dealing with many developers working across multiple sites on a large unified system, a more structured approach is required.

7.2.1 The Need for Prefixes

The approach taken here, which ensures unique global class names, requires that each package be associated with a unique *registered* prefix consisting of two to five characters. When a package is first created, its prefix is *registered* with some company-wide authority or service so that no other package developer will inadvertently reuse it. Each construct in the header file declared at file scope is prepended with the package prefix. The `.c` and `.h` files implementing this component are also each prepended with the same prefix. It is by prepending each global name with this registered prefix that we are able to guarantee that similar names defined in distinct packages cannot possibly collide.

Major Design Rule

Prepend every global identifier with its package prefix.

For example, a package of geometric primitives would consist of a number of independent reusable components. A component defining a basic point would not be named `point` but would instead be named `geom_point`, where "geom" is the unique registered prefix associated with the `geom` package. The class defining a geometric point would not be called `Point` but instead would be called `geom_Point`.[3]

Each identifier declared at file scope *must* be preceded by a registered prefix in order to ensure the avoidance of name conflicts across package boundaries. Although only classes, structs, unions, and free operators are allowed at file scope, extraordinary circumstances (such as the ANSI C–compliant interface of Section 6.5.4) could force an exception to this rule. If for some reason we were to declare a function, variable, enumeration, or typedef at file scope in a header file, we would still want to make sure to prepend each of its file-scope identifiers with the appropriate package prefix. This independent design rule is illustrated in Figure 7-5.

[3] Note that for the purposes of the convention for distinguishing type names from non-type names as presented in Section 2.7, we have elected not to treat the prefix as part of the identifier. An equivalent and equally valid convention would be to capitalize the prefix instead (e.g., `Geom_point`). Capitalizing `Point` rather than `Geom` merely emphasizes that `geom_Point` is a `Point` *type* in the `geom` *package*.

```
// geom_polygon.h              // Filenames are always all lowercase.
#ifndef GEOM_POLYGON           // CPP macros are always all uppercase.
#define GEOM_POLYGON           // Hence, the prefix must be case insensitive.

enum geom_Color { geom_RED, geom_GREEN, geom_BLUE };
    // Proscribed global enumeration must still use package prefixes.

typedef short int geom_Int16;
    // Proscribed global typedefs must still use package prefixes.

class geom_Polygon {
    // Global class definitions are not a design rule violation.
};

int operator==(const geom_Polygon& left, const geom_Polygon& right);
    // Global operators are not a design rule violation.

geom_area();
    // Proscribed global functions must still use package prefixes.

double geom_scaleFactor;
    // Proscribed global variables must still use package prefixes.

#endif
```

Figure 7-5: Even Proscribed Constructs at File Scope Require Prefixes

Identifiers declared within class scope need not have package prefixes because the enclosing class (which is prefixed) provides a natural shield against collisions as well as a suitable grouping for related functionality. Similarly, identifiers with internal linkage, declared and used entirely within a single `.c` file, also need not use prefixes. That is, the scope of a typedef, enumeration, static variable, or static (or inline) free function specified within a `.c` file is limited to a single translation unit and therefore cannot collide with an identical short name defined locally within another translation unit. Static class member data and non-inline member functions have external linkage. It is therefore appropriate to use package prefixes for class names even when the class itself is defined and used entirely within a single `.c` file. Otherwise we run the risk that such a hidden class will produce external symbols that at link time might collide with those of a class hidden in the `.c` file of a component belonging to some other package.[4]

---

[4] Note that prefixes are not strictly necessary for hidden classes, provided that the developer ensures that all aspects of linkage for the hidden class are internal. A generally useful extension to the package-prefix technique for naming classes with external linkage that are private to a component was presented in the context of fully insulating classes at the end of Section 6.4.2.

Major Design Rule

Prepend every source file name with its package prefix.

Names generated by the compiler are sometimes geared to the name of the source file itself. In CFRONT, file names are used as a basis for naming both the virtual tables and also for naming the entry points for initializing and destroying instances of user-defined types defined at file scope—both of which have external linkage. Therefore, to avoid link-time conflicts, it is important that all source files in the system have unique names. The library containing all of the `.o` files for the `geom` package would also be adorned in some manner with the "geom" prefix (e.g., `libgeom.a` on a Unix system).

For many systems, harsh limitations on file-name length make prepending unique prefixes painful. If the limitation is eight characters or fewer, the file names could get rather cryptic. On some systems (e.g., Unix), file-name length is not a problem except for archaic constraints placed on the length of the name of a `.o` file that can be placed in a library archive file. The names of the corresponding `.c` files may need to be constrained to some relatively small length (as low as 14 characters on some Unix-based systems). In this case we can either make the `.h` files correspondingly short to match the `.c` file, or we can provide some sort of external cross reference to allow longer header file names to be associated with shorter (abbreviated) implementation file names. On my Unix system I use symbolic links to achieve this mapping during development.

7.2.2 Namespaces

In July of 1993, the ANSI/ISO Committee adopted the namespace construct designed by Bjarne Stroustrup to aid in resolving collisions between global identifiers with the same name.[5] For example,

---

[5] **stroustrup94**, Section 17.1, p. 400.

```
namespace geom {
    class Point { /* ... */ };
    Point& operator==(const Point& left, const Point& right);
    class Polygon { /* ... */ };
    // ...
}
```

defines a namespace `geom`. The constructs declared within the braces are placed within their own scope and therefore will not collide with either global names or names declared in any other namespace. While *using directives* are supplied primarily to ease transition, the intent is always to use explicit qualifications via *using-declarations*:[6]

```
void mySpace::Class::f()
{
    geom::Point p(3,2);
    // ...
}
```

As you can see, both namespaces and registered prefixes can be used in similar ways to avoid name conflicts among classes developed within a single company. Neither, however, can serve as a complete substitute for the other.

When dealing with C++ application libraries supplied from two distinct vendors, there are several potential problems. As described in Appendix B, if the compilers used to develop these libraries are not compatible, you're out of luck. But even if you can get both vendors to supply compatible libraries (architecture, operating system, and compiler/linker), there is no central authority with which to register prefixes; thus there is a distinct possibility that globally defined names will collide. Herein lies the power of the namespace construct.

Placing all library code developed by a company within a single namespace wrapper makes it impossible to ensure that even the unlikely event of matching both prefixes and identifiers can be overcome merely by explicit qualification. Suppose two companies, SDL and SCI, both supply geometric library software. Each company decides to create a "unique" package prefix called `geom`. Obviously, there is a possibility that one or more of the geometric names (e.g., `Point`, `Line`, `Polygon`) within those packages will coincide.

---

[6] **stroustrup94**, Sections 17.4.2, p. 408 and 17.4.5.3, p. 414.

```
// sdl/geom_point.h
#ifndef INCLUDED_SDL_GEOM_POINT
#define INCLUDED_SDL_GEOM_POINT
namespace SDL {

class geom_Point {
    // ...
  public:
    geom_Point(int x, int y);
    geom_Point(const geom_Point& point);
    ~geom_Point();
    geom_Point& operator=(const geom_Point& point);
    void setX(int x);
    void setY(int y);
    int x() const;
    int y() const;
};

int operator==(const geom_Point& left, const geom_Point& right);
int operator!=(const geom_Point& left, const geom_Point& right);

}

#endif
```

```
// sci/geom_point.h
#ifndef INCLUDED_GEOM_POINT
#define INCLUDED_GEOM_POINT

class geom_Point { /* ... */ }

int operator==(const geom_Point& left,
               const geom_Point& right);
int operator!=(const geom_Point& left,
               const geom_Point& right);

#endif
```

```
// my_class.c
#include "my_class.h"
#include <sdl/geom_point.h>
#include <sci/geom_point.h>

void my_Class::f() {
    SDL::geom_Point p(1,2);
    ::geom_Point q(3,4);
    // ...
}
```

Figure 7-6: Using Namespaces to Resolve Name Conflicts Among Vendors

If one (or both) of these companies has the foresight to place their code within a single companywide namespace, the identifier name conflict-resolution problems disappear.[7]

The technique of combining package prefixes and namespaces to resolve name conflicts among multiple vendors is illustrated in Figure 7-6. Even though SCI did not choose to use namespaces, we can still access their `geom_Point` class by prepending the scope resolution operator (`::`) to designate true file scope. Notice that SDL has protected itself, but SCI is at risk if some other vendor or one of its clients did not choose to take these precautions.

Because the C++ language supports the arbitrary nesting of namespaces,[8] we could have elected to resolve interpackage name collisions within our company by replacing package prefixes with package namespaces. For example,

```
void f
{
    SDL::geom_Point pt;             // package prefix
    // ...
}
```

would instead be written

```
void f
{
    SDL::geom::Point pt;            // package namespace
    // ...
}
```

As we will soon see, however, replacing package prefixes with package namespaces is ill advised.

As of the writing of this book (May 1996), the namespace feature of the C++ language was not generally available. Even if it were, it would not affect the need for prefixes, which have many advantages beyond simply avoiding name collisions. A package serves a cohesive purpose that unites the components within it. Each package tends to take on its own character. This phenomenon is due in part to the intrinsic nature of the package and also to the subtle variations in style promulgated by its author. By identifying a component or class as belonging to a particular package, you immediately

---

[7] We could still have problems if compiler-generated symbols with external linkage are generated based on the file name (as is the case in some implementations).

[8] **stroustrup94**, Section 17.4.5.4, pp. 415–416.

provide a context that aids in understanding its broader purpose.[9] In time, the package prefix will be the first thing to catch your eye when reading application code that depends on components from multiple packages.

Principle

The dominant purpose of a prefix is to identify uniquely the *physical* package in which the component or class is defined.

In addition to its semantic cohesion, a package is also a physical unit. An important function of a package prefix is to identify where in the file system the definition of a given class or component can be found. Package prefixes also make searching for "use" of a particular package much easier. There are many other trivial advantages to package prefixes. For example, if you forget to link-in a particular package, the nature of the problem will be immediately obvious, as illustrated in Figure 7-7.

```
john@john: CC -g geom_iter.o  geom_util.o  geom_file.o  geom_print.o \
-o a.out -L/home/sys/lib -lxref  -lne  -llst  -lcrx
ld: Undefined symbol
    ___ct__10stdc_ErrorFCQ2_10stdc_Error8errorNumPCciT2
    stdc_AssocList::operator=(const stdc_AssocList&)
    stdc_AssocList::operator+=(const stdc_AssocList&)
    stdc_AssocList::operator+=(const stdc_NameValue&)
    stdc_AssocList::setAssociation(const stdc_NameValue&)
    stdc_PIcontext::pop() const
    stdc_PIcontext::push() const
    operator==(const stdc_AssocList&,const stdc_AssocList&)
    stdc_AssocListIter::operator()() const
    stdc_Error::operator=(const stdc_Error&)
    stdc_PIcontext::~stdc_PIcontext()
    operator<<(ostream&,const stdc_Error&)
    stdc_AssocList::~stdc_AssocList()
    ___vtbl__14stdc_AssocList
    stdc_Error::~stdc_Error()
Compilation failed
john@john:
```

Figure 7-7: Link-Time Errors Resulting from Missing the `stdc` Package Library

[9] For this and other views on segmenting the global namespace, see **stroustrup94**, Sections 17.4.1, p. 406; and 17.4.5.5, pp. 416-417.

Much more important, a package, like a component, represents a cohesive unit. As with component-level design, the logical and physical design of a package are tightly interleaved. It is important when discussing packages and, in particular, their physical interdependencies, that the logical and physical properties of each package coincide.

7.2.3 Preserving Prefix Integrity

The purpose of a prefix is to provide a hierarchical identification for the physical location of the definition of a component or global logical construct. For well-designed packages with cohesive functionality, the package prefix contributes semantic as well as physical information. Using the prefix to identify only semantic properties defeats its primary purpose of forcing similarly prefixed cohesive logical functionality to be packaged together in the same physical library.

Principle

Ideally, a package prefix will connote cohesive logical and organizational characteristics in addition to denoting the physical library in which a component or class is defined.

Sometimes there may be a great temptation to distribute logically related units across multiple physical libraries and to assign these logical units a common package prefix. For example, a given package (`pub`) might provide a set of low-level, reusable container types. Each of these components and each of the types defined therein would begin with the prefix `pub_`. Now suppose we are developing our own application package (`xr2e`) and discover we need a new type, `Btree`, which happens to have similar characteristics (low level, container, reusable) to those found in the `pub` package. What should we do?

We might be tempted to call this component `pub_btree` and place it in our own library to reflect its logical relationship to the `pub` package. This urge should be suppressed. The fact that all components with a given package prefix reside in a single physical library is too valuable to both understanding and managing the organization of large systems to be sacrificed.

Instead we have two viable alternatives—each with its own advantages:

1. Call it `xr2e_Btree` and place it in our own package.
2. Call it `pub_Btree` and place it in the `pub` package.

Probably the easier thing to do is simply to call the class `xr2e_Btree` and define it in a component that is part of our own package. Implementing this object locally reduces the likelihood that it will be reused—which can be both good and bad. By defining the `Btree` within the same package, we retain ownership and therefore need not be as concerned about making changes or enhancements to it should it suit our needs to do so.

The potential for reuse is not always obvious *a priori*. It may be that we believe that no one else will need a `Btree` type, so we'll just write it and keep it for ourselves. If others think this way and the `btree` component turns out to be truly reusable, we may eventually see several redundant versions of a `Btree` popping up in our system. As a rule, if we see three or more comparable versions of a `btree` component in our system, the component may very well be a good candidate for reuse. At this point, we should probably evaluate the impact of consolidating our system by moving a single, unified version of `Btree` to the more public `pub` package (and changing its prefix to `pub_`).

Often, we will believe that a component is reusable only to find that it is not needed by others. Placing such deadweight in highly reusable packages is worse than delaying the entry of potentially reusable components into the `pub` package. It is almost always easier to make functionality more rather than less public. If in doubt, it is better to defer adding a component to a widely used package until empirical evidence warrants it.

If we are convinced at the outset that a component absolutely belongs in another package, then we will need to talk to the developer responsible for maintaining that package. If your proposal is compelling, as it might well be for a `Btree`, the owner of `pub` may agree to write the `btree` component for you and place it in the `pub` package for all to use. Note that you will now be just another customer of the `pub` package, and give up the right to add intrusive special customizations to the `pub_btree` component.

Scheduling constraints may force you to write the component yourself and hand it over (along with its incremental test driver) to the `pub` package developer. After a careful review, this developer will assume ownership, and again you will become just like any other client with no special privileges.

The important trade-off here is that if you create a component redundantly, then you can make it exactly what you want it to be. You will not have to negotiate with other package developers, and you may be able to avoid additional package dependencies. If you hand this component over to some other package developer, you relinquish responsibility for and control over its functionality. If the component is not inherently reusable, the cost to you and to others of sharing it will probably outweigh any benefit. If the component is a good candidate for reuse, then it could be in everyone's best interest to have it defined and maintained in a single, semantically cohesive, lower-level package where it can be found and reused easily.

While the notion of a translation unit is well defined in the C++ language, the notion of a package is entirely the work of the system developers, and its implementation is dependent on the particular operating system. Because packages are not part of the language, it is up to system architects and developers to create these cohesive partitions within a large system, almost entirely on their own.

Computer-aided software engineering (CASE) tools such as browsers help to uncover many detailed properties and interdependencies among a large collection of classes. Good tools are an important part of the design process, but they are not a substitute for the thoughtful partitioning of semantically cohesive functionality into distinct physical units. Even the fanciest runtime environment would be hard pressed to convey as quickly the same semantic information afforded by consistently tagging logically cohesive global constructs with their physical package prefix.

The registered prefix convention for all global identifiers and files is admittedly painful at first. In time, most people not only adjust to it but come to depend on it during their daily development efforts. The advantages afforded by registered package prefixes are well worth the extra effort for developing very large projects.

7.3 Package Levelization

By analogy, a component is to its package as a planet is to its solar system. Each component describes a physical entity, and each package describes a cohesive aggregate of these physical entities. The physical coupling among the nearby components within a package is typically more acute than the coupling between components in distinct packages.

7.3.1 The Importance of Levelizing Packages

As you recall, avoiding cyclic dependencies among individual components was an important design goal because it aided in incremental comprehension, testing, and reuse.

Major Design Rule

Avoid cyclic dependencies among packages.

Avoiding cyclic dependencies among packages is a major design rule for the following reasons:

1. Development. When linking the entire system or any portion thereof, it will be necessary to specify the order in which package libraries are called upon to resolve undefined symbols. If the envelope of dependencies among components within individual packages is acyclic, there will be at least one order that will be guaranteed to resolve all symbols during linking. In Unix, cyclic dependencies among packages imply that it will be necessary to include one or more libraries at least twice in the link command. Doing so increases the time necessary to link a subsystem by forcing one or more libraries to be searched multiple times. Worse, minor changes to the calling sequence of functions could cause the library order required by the link command to change, thus causing the link to fail. It then becomes a non-trivial exercise to determine a new library linking sequence that does not result in undefined symbols.

2. Marketing. Often a system will have a basic functionality and several optional add-on packages of functionality, as is illustrated in Figure 7-8. If the system itself depends on any one of these add-on packages, then that add-on is not optional and must be shipped with the system. If any of the add-on packages are mutually dependent, they cannot be marketed and sold as truly independent options.

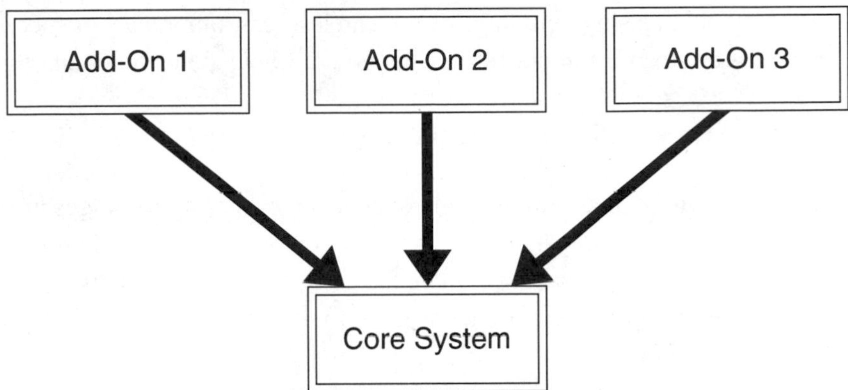

Figure 7-8: Acyclic Package Dependencies Provide Flexibility

3. Usability. Even if marketing is not an issue, users will not want to have to link-in a huge library or several large libraries just to use some simple functionality of the basic system (or just one of the supposedly independent applications). Minimizing package interdependencies reduces the number of libraries that must be linked into an application, which can in turn help to reduce the ultimate size of the executable image (both in core and on disk).

4. Production. To support concurrent development in very large systems, it is effective to have a staged release process (as discussed in Section 7.6). Acyclic hierarchies of packages are collected into even larger architectural units called *groups*. Group levelization is then used to partition these groups into *layers*, which are then released in levelized order from bottom to top. Allowing cyclic dependencies among packages would impede our ability to form groups and therefore to make staged releases.

5. Reliability. Design for testability dictates that there be a way to test a large system incrementally and hierarchically. Avoiding cyclic dependencies among the macroscopic parts of the system is merely a natural consequence of this paradigm.

Although we might be serene enough to tolerate cyclic dependencies among a few components within a single package due to carelessness, ignorance, or special circumstance, we must be steadfast in our resolve to avoid cyclic dependencies among packages.

7.3.2 Package Levelization Techinques

The techniques for avoiding cyclic dependencies among packages are similar to those for avoiding cyclic dependencies among components. The basic goal is to ensure that, if the components in package `b` depend on services supplied by components in package `a`, then components in package `a` do not depend either directly or indirectly on components in package `b`.

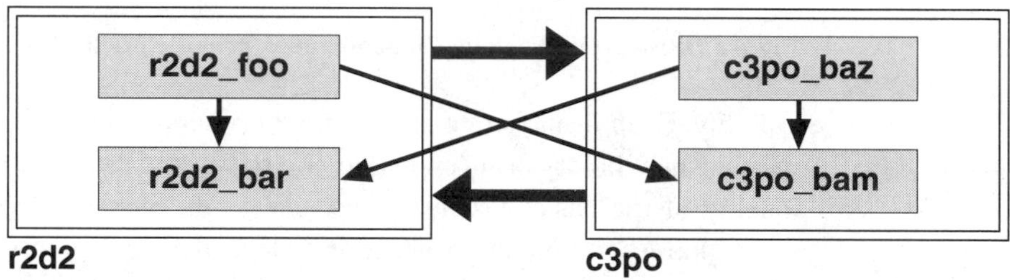

Figure 7-9: Two Mutually Dependent Packages

Figure 7-9 illustrates a situation in which two packages, `r2d2` and `c3po`, have become interdependent. This problem is entirely analogous to the problem we encountered in Figure 5-3, where logical constructs in both `rectangle` and `window` caused a mutual dependency between these two components.

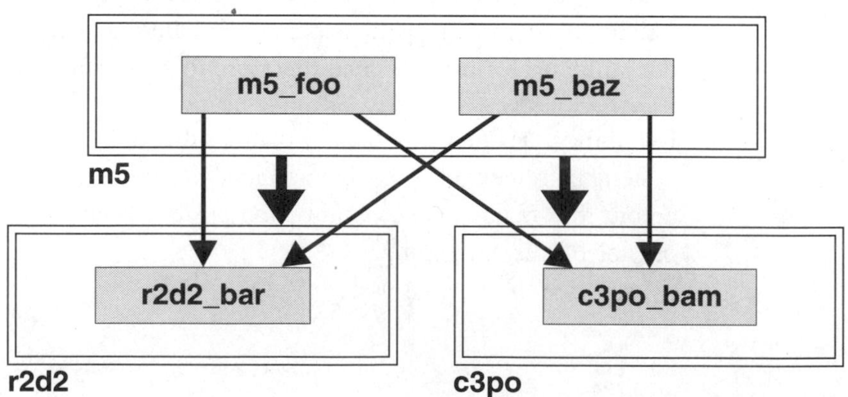

Figure 7-10: Escalating Mutual Dependencies Between Packages

Fortunately, remedies analogous to those given in Section 5.2 for untangling the `rectangle` and `window` component dependencies apply here also. For example, we could escalate two of the components contributing to mutual package-level dependency to a higher package level, as shown in Figure 7-10. Or we might decide to apply the more general repackaging technique shown in Figure 5-36 to come up with two entirely new packages.

Principle

It is not necessarily possible to assign a single package prefix to the subset of components used directly by clients of a multi-package subsystem.

The purpose of a package is to unite closely related collections of components into modular physical entities that can be referred to abstractly and reused effectively. Figure 7-11 shows a hierarchy of components whose dependencies form a binary tree. Clearly these components are levelizable. As discussed in Section 7.2.3, however, all components with the same package prefix should belong to the same physical library. Consequently, the packages implied by these prefixes are not levelizable, as illustrated in Figure 7-12.

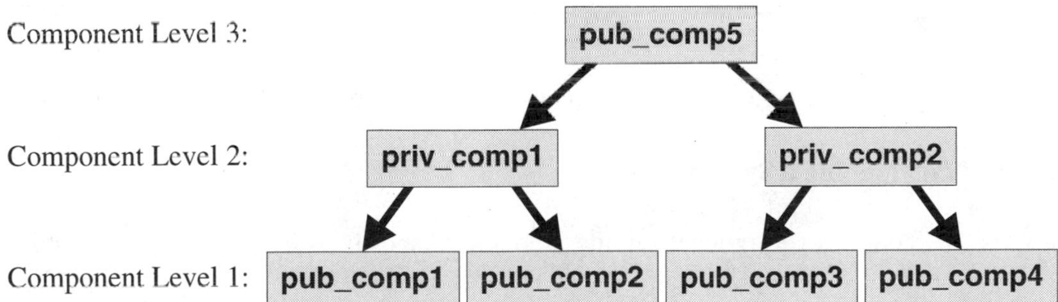

Figure 7-11: Implied Cyclic Package Dependencies

The problem identified by Figure 7-12 can arise in practice when a single prefix is assigned to a conceptual presentation package—that is, a package containing everything directly usable by clients of a multi-package subsystem. If this presentation package defines both protocol classes (which are inherently very low level) and wrapper components (which are inherently very high level), it will not be possible to interleave components from separate, intermediate-level implementation packages and maintain a levelizable package hierarchy. The solution to this common problem is simply to provide two separate packages for presentation to clients. One package will reside at the bottom of the package hierarchy and contain components that define only protocol classes; the second will reside at the top of the subsystem and define only wrappers.

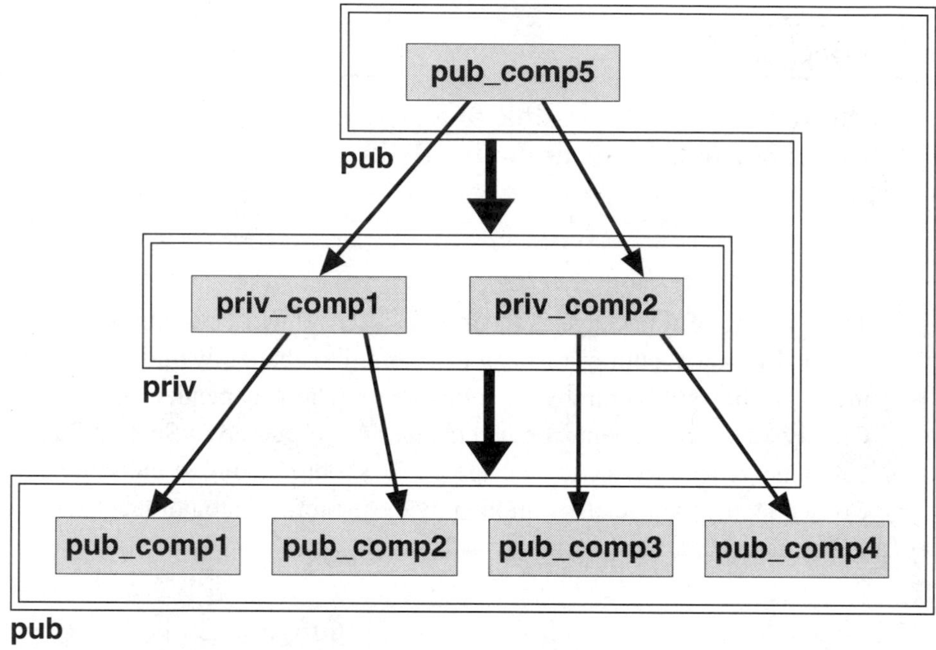

Figure 7-12: Levelizable Component Hierarchy; Unlevelizable Package Hierarchy

7.3.3 Partitioning a System

Although ensuring levelizability among packages is essential, that alone is not sufficient. For example, Figure 7-13a illustrates a bottom-up approach to packaging in which we have merely taken the unpackaged design of Figure 7-13b and carefully diced it into packages whose aggregate dependencies on other packages form an acyclic graph. But simply partitioning a sea of levelizable components into an otherwise arbitrary set of levelizable packages does not address an important aspect of design: cohesion. To be effective, a package should consist of components and logical entities that have related semantic characteristics, tight coupling, or otherwise make sense to be packaged together and treated abstractly at a higher level.

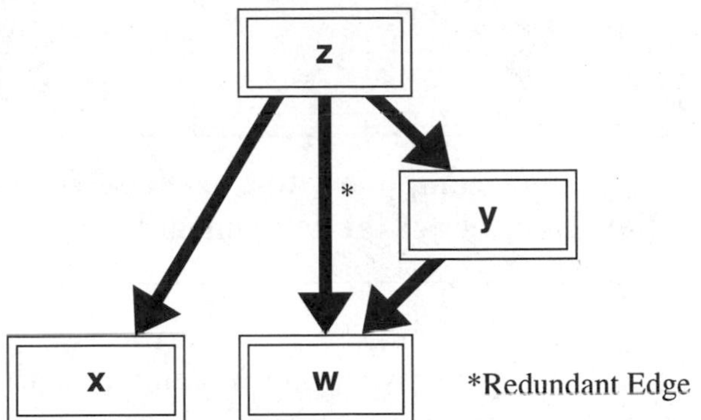

(a) Abstract Package-Level Dependency Diagram

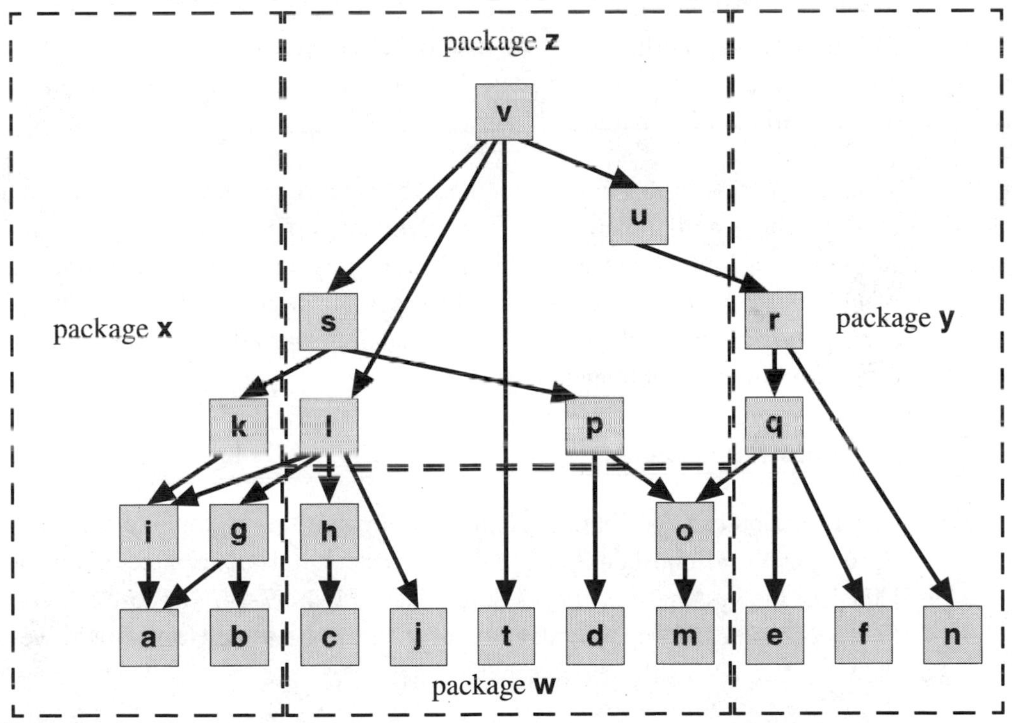

(b) Detailed Package/Component Dependency Diagram

Figure 7-13: Less Useful, Physically Partitioned System (Compare with Figure 7-4)

Principle

When adding a new component to a package, both the logical and physical characteristics of the component should be considered.

As discussed in terms of subsystems in Section 5.7, dependency is also a factor that should be considered when incorporating components into packages. Suppose a given package is lightweight in character, depending on no other packages. Suppose further that adding a single, logically cohesive component would force clients of that package to link with ten other packages. Even if the logical cohesion of the component is ideal for the package, the impact of the additional dependencies would probably override any other consideration. Both logical and organizational cohesion should be considered as defining the character of a package.

A better solution in this case would be to create a separate package for this new component, with a similar, perhaps, but not identical prefix that conveys the similar nature of the logical semantics yet distinguishes the physical dependency implications. By placing this heavyweight component in a separate package, clients of the light-weight package will not be saddled with the overhead of unwanted and oppressive dependencies on libraries they do not need.

7.3.4 Multi-Site Development

The geographical distribution of the development team coupled with interpackage dependencies will influence how package ownership is distributed among developers. Consider the system of packages described in Figure 7-14. Suppose our company has two geographically separate development sites, N and S. How should we distribute the workload across these two separate sites?

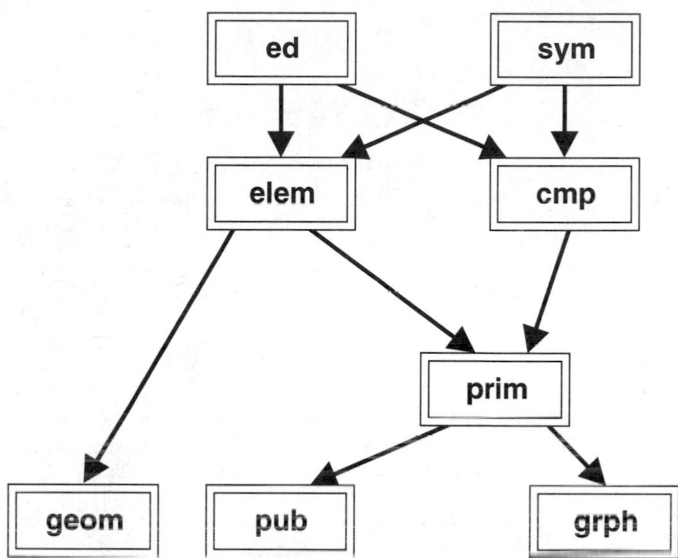

Figure 7-14: System of Packages and Their Physical Dependencies

Logistically, it makes sense that the package dependencies across sites be minimized to whatever extent is possible in order to reduce inefficiencies associated with intersite communication. Consider the package development distributions proposed in Figure 7-15. Distribution (A) is pathologically bad, with seven direct package dependencies across sites. Dividing the diagram with a vertical line (B) illustrates another inappropriate partition with five direct intersite dependencies. Dividing the diagram with a horizontal line (C) may provide an optimal solution with a cost of only three long-distance direct dependencies. Both (D) and (E) also provide potentially optimal solutions if the complexity of packages and/or available resources at each site are not evenly distributed.

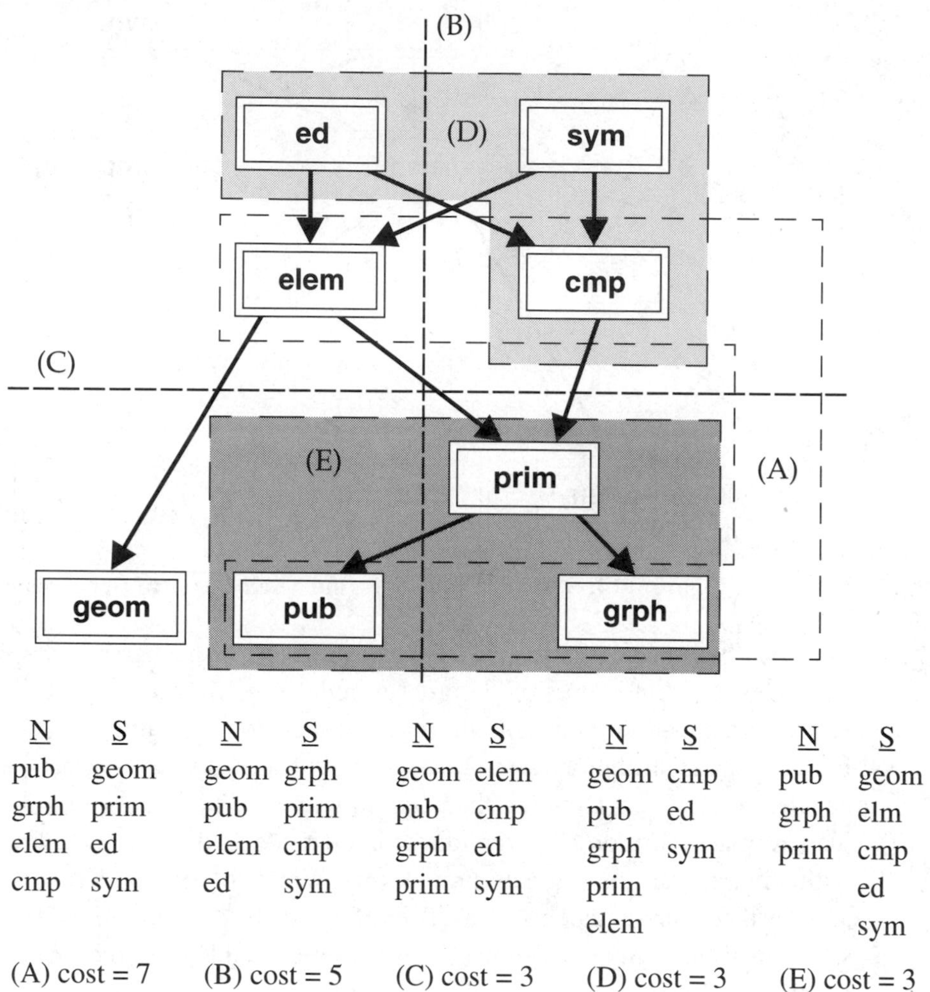

Figure 7-15: Potential Package Development Assignments Across Sites

Identifying packages and delineating their interdependencies can affect the success of larger projects. Minimizing the cost of interpackage dependencies should be at the forefront of every architect's mind throughout the design process. Most important, avoiding the high cost of cyclic dependencies among packages is essential if the flexibility and maintainability of the system are to be preserved.

To summarize: partitioning a system into a levelizable collection of packages is critical to the success of a large project. Most of the techniques discussed in Chapter 5 for achieving a levelizable collection of components apply equally well to packages. Apart from the coupling brought about by long-distance friendships, the same reasoning that enabled us to reduce CCD can be used to reduce the cost of interpackage dependencies. Whenever we can take advantage of these techniques to reduce package interdependencies, we are making significant improvements toward the flexibility and maintainability of the overall system.

7.4 Package Insulation

Packages present a higher level of abstraction than components. For packages with a horizontal dependency structure, such as `geom` (see Section 4.13), we must export most of the individual component header files in order to make the package functionality usable by clients (see Figure 7-16a). Even though placing these physically independent components in a single package does not hide any additional details, we can still benefit from the ability to refer to the aggregate of these components abstractly as `geom`—a benefit that should not be underestimated.

Principle

Minimizing the number and size of exported header files enhances usability.

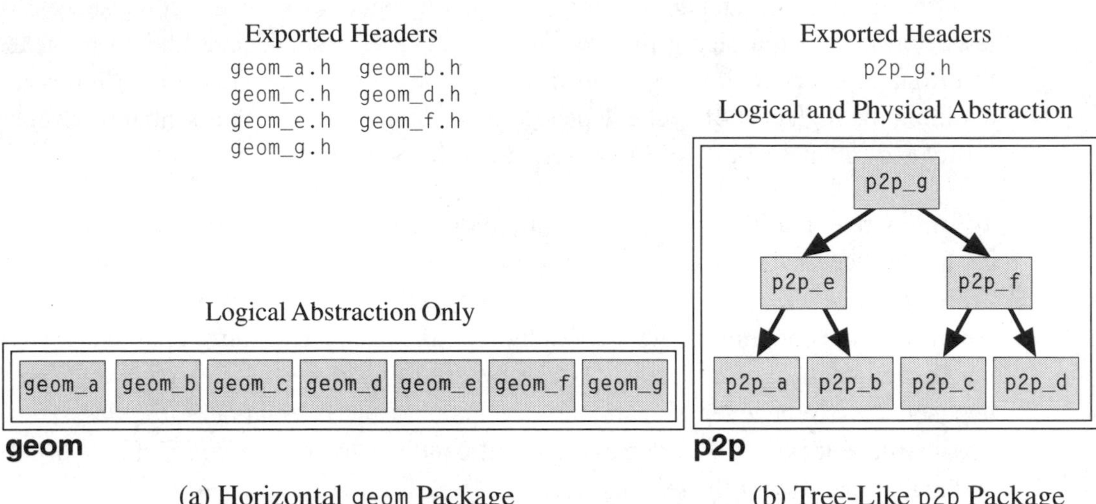

(a) Horizontal `geom` Package (b) Tree-Like `p2p` Package

Figure 7-16: A Package Is a Logical and Potentially a Physical Abstraction

In the case of tree-like packages, such as `p2p`, that sport a small number of insulating wrapper components, we can gain not only the conceptual abstraction but also a physical abstraction as well. It is by not exposing superfluous information in the form of unnecessarily exported header files, as illustrated in Figure 7-16b, that this physical form of abstraction is realized.

As with a good component interface, the fewer details we expose in the interface of a package, the easier it is for the package developer to maintain and tune its implementation. Minimizing the size of the physical interface to which the client is exposed can also improve usability. Although the surface area of a horizontal package is inherently large, this need not be the case for a tree-like package.

A package implementing a complex, application-specific subsystem, such as `p2p`, typically represents a substantial amount of functionality. The implementation of the subsystem may span dozens of components. In order for clients to use this package, a non-empty subset of the components must have their header files exported (i.e., made available to components defined outside this package). Although package developers and test engineers will always have access to all headers, regular clients of a package need not necessarily be exposed to headers whose use is encapsulated.

Answering "yes" to any of the following questions for a particular component defined in a given package implies that the header for that component must be exported:

1. Do clients of this package need access to this component in order to use any part of the functionality provided by this package as a whole?

2. Does any other exported component in this package fail to insulate its clients from this components definition?

3. Do other packages need access to this component, (e.g., to reuse its functionality independently in their own implementations)?

Consider a package such as `p2p` that is implemented hierarchically and presents its public functionality entirely through the interface of only a small collection (one in this case) of wrapper components. These wrapper components must be exported to the global include directory (see Figure 7-2) in order for external clients to use the package. However, there may be no need to export the header files of the remaining components.

Notice that we are not proposing to withhold header files here for the purpose of encapsulating details, but rather as a means of reducing the clutter that clients must wade through in order to use our package. Whether or not we export the implementation component header files depends on whether or not they are needed (or useful) for purposes other than creating the `.o` files that belong to this package's library.

If a wrapper component is encapsulating but not insulating (see Section 6.4.3) it may be necessary for the client's compiler to have seen the definition of one or more of its implementation components in order to compile the wrapper interface. If so, you will be forced to export implementation headers, your clients will depend on them at compile time, and your flexibility to make changes to them will be impeded.

Finally, in the process of implementing our package, we may have accidentally created one or more implementation components that other developers find useful in implementing their own packages. In that case, we may generously decide to publish the header files for these components. In doing so we enable reuse, but also enable additional interpackage coupling. This coupling could potentially have an adverse effect on our ability to maintain our own package, and could introduce new package level dependencies that were not authorized by the system architect. Such additional package-level dependencies would further constrain the levelizability of the entire system.

If a component header is not exported, our clients remain entirely insulated from it. We may feel free to make any changes to it that we like. Once a header file is exported, changes we make to its interface potentially affect many others who are attempting to reuse its functionality. Even if we preserve the functionality, making any change whatsoever to an exported component's header file will annoyingly force clients who include this header to recompile. This example illustrates yet another situation in which reuse may not necessarily be a good thing.

In practice, there are likely to be a few low-level (horizontal) packages that export a relatively large number of logically related and probably widely used component headers. Most of the remaining packages would then implement sophisticated functionality that operates on common, low-level types. Ideally these higher-level packages would export relatively small, high-level interfaces in the form of insulating wrapper component headers.

7.5 Package Groups

In very large systems (involving many hundreds of thousands of lines of C++ code), even a package is not at a high enough level of abstraction to be useful in discussing overall system architecture. During the process of top-down design, architects will identify major portions of the system. Each of these major subsystems will be implemented by a team of developers; each subsystem will consist of a cohesive collection of packages called a *group*.

> **DEFINITION: A *package group* is a collection of packages organized as a physically cohesive unit.**

Just as related components were collected into packages, so are related packages collected into groups. An individual package is appropriately owned and maintained primarily by a single developer, but a package group is usually owned by the project manager (or principal engineer) of the development team that is charged with its implementation.

The same principles that applied to the composition of individual packages and the interdependencies among them (such as logical cohesion and avoiding cyclic dependencies) apply to package groups as a whole. Like packages, groups should carry a well-defined architectural significance that governs what is (and what is not) appropriate to belong to that group. For example, if a group is entitled "core functionality," we should resist placing packages that are not true to that label within this group.

> **<u>DEFINITION</u>: A package group `g` *DependsOn* another package group `h` if one or more packages in `g` DependsOn one or more packages in `h`.**

Consider the large system shown in Figure 7-17. Although this system will consist of some 40 packages (500,000 lines) when complete, its functionality naturally divides into five vertically arranged package groups. Each of these groups consists of several packages. Not only are these packages individually levelizable, but the dependencies among entire groups as defined above are also acyclic. That is, groups at higher levels contain packages that depend on packages in groups at lower levels, but never vice versa.

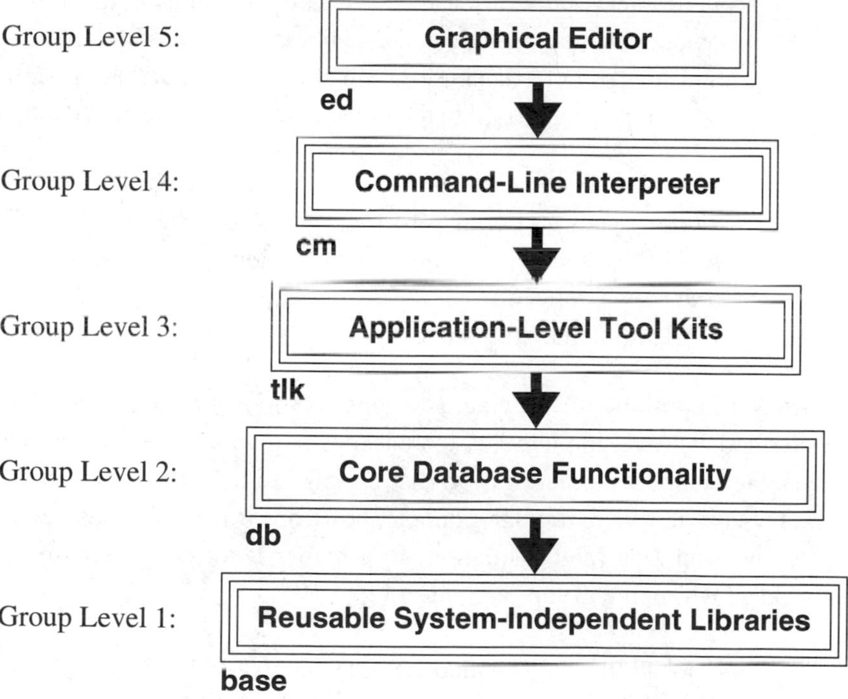

Figure 7-17: A Large-System Architecture

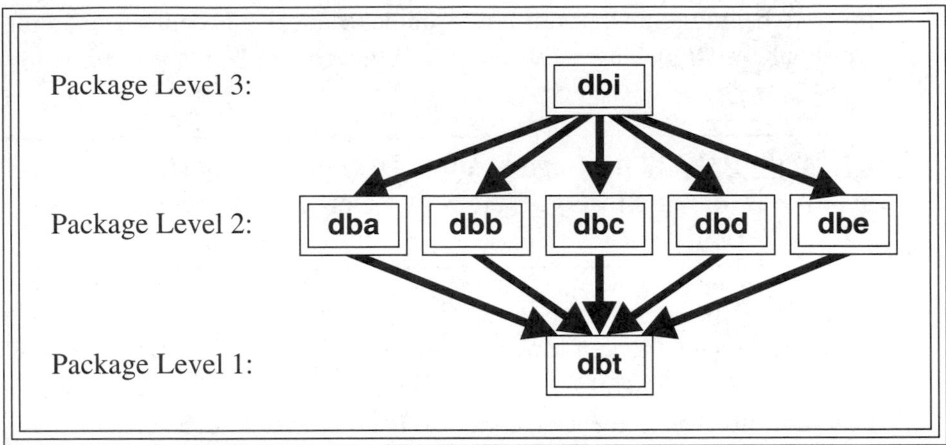

Figure 7-18: Package Organization of Core Database Group

There are good reasons for wanting to merge individual package libraries into a single large group library. Many of these reasons are analogous to those for merging the `.o` files of components into a single package library. Consider the internal, package-level organization for the core database group shown in Figure 7-18. In this architecture, there are several packages used in the implementation of the core database functionality.

At the lowest level of the core database group, the `dbt` package represents a horizontal collection of types and protocols used throughout the group and by its clients. At the next level are a set of five independent implementation packages. A single package `dbi` provides a collection of wrapper components to present the combined functionality of the implementation packages to clients in higher-level groups.

Often it is possible to provide a wrapper component for a subsystem directly in an intermediate-level implementation package (e.g., `dba`), thereby having to expose only a single component header from that package to the rest of the group. As happens to be the case in this particular example, however, it is sometimes necessary to escalate the encapsulation (and insulation) to a higher level—in this case, to a higher-level package within the group (e.g., `dbi`).

With the exception of the low-level types and protocols defined in `dbt`, the entire functionality of the core database group is accessible through the wrapper components provided in `dbi` alone. Because `dbi` is an encapsulating and insulating package of wrapper components for dba, dbb, dbc, dbd, and dbe, there is no compelling reason to provide clients of this group with the headers for components defined within these implementation packages. Once we have built the dbi package library, exporting these headers to higher-level groups would serve only to clutter the global include directory. Note again that exposing these headers is not an issue of encapsulation, but one of insulation and abstraction.

After building the database group, we will make available to clients of the group only the subset of headers defined in the dbi and dbt packages. As a convenience to our clients, we will combine *all* of our individual package libraries into a single group library file with the associated prefix db,[10] and make that file publicly available.

To clients of our core database, it will now appear as if we had implemented the database as a single package, db, with two related prefixes: dbi and dbt. There may now be a temptation to rename both dbt and dbi to the simpler db; but this would be a mistake. Within the collection of packages that comprise the core database group, we may be looking at literally hundreds of thousands of lines of code. For some, this would be considered a large system in its own right. If we change the prefix names of these components, we give up an important maintenance property of our system—the prefix identifies the package where the source can be found. Furthermore, we lose our protection against namespace collisions between these two packages.

If our solution to these problems is then to combine these two packages into a single low-level package, we have given up package levelization and any reasonable ability to develop and test our system hierarchically. We are back to the problem illustrated in Figure 7-12. From a purely practical point of view, we must remember not to lose sight of maintainability in our efforts to please the aesthetics of our clients (or ourselves).

---

[10] Note that this name too must be registered to avoid collisions between other group and package library names.

Principle

Demoting protocols and escalating wrappers within a package group can help to avoid cyclic dependencies between exported (presentation) packages and unexported (implementation) packages.

Step back for a moment and notice that the protocols are part of the lowest-level package (`dbt`), not part of the presentation package (`dbi`). Escalating wrappers and demoting protocols is a general and effective technique that can help to avoid cyclic dependencies between the public and private packages within a group.

Low-level package partitions continue to serve many useful purposes, even though most clients will not be concerned about internal partitioning. For example, during the development process, it is inevitable that bugs will occur. It may then be useful to link with versions of individual packages that have been compiled to contain debuggable symbols. For very large systems, trying to link and debug many packages using the debuggable versions can produce very large executables and make the entire process exceedingly slow. The amount of disk space alone needed to hold an executable in which every component in a group has been compiled with the debug option can pose a significant development burden. Highly effective, commercially available tools[11] used to detect low-level coding errors at runtime can produce executables literally three times their normal size that run an order of magnitude slower. Having only two alternatives—all or none—for linking with such large, special-purpose group libraries is often not practical.

Fortunately most developers, working either within a package group or directly above it, will probably have a good idea as to which individual packages within the group are likely to be the ones causing the problem. These developers will know how to adjust their link command to pull in only the appropriate special-purpose package libraries, leaving access to the remaining package libraries unaffected. Providing the ability to select individual specially built package libraries from within a group helps

[11] An example of a particularly effective tool is Purify, from Pure Software Corporation.

to widen the envelope of systems that can be developed with a given set of tools on a given hardware platform.

The size and structure of package aggregates is not bounded. In the example of Figure 7-7, these groups of packages took the form of a vertically arranged sequence. As we will see in the next section, this vertical arrangement of groups somewhat simplifies the internal release process. In a yet-larger system (i.e., in excess of a million lines of source code), groups might form a tree-like or DAG-like structure (see Figure 7-19)—perhaps to reflect the engineering management structure of the development effort. Of course, in an actual design, the group dependencies would probably not be as regular as the one shown in the figure.

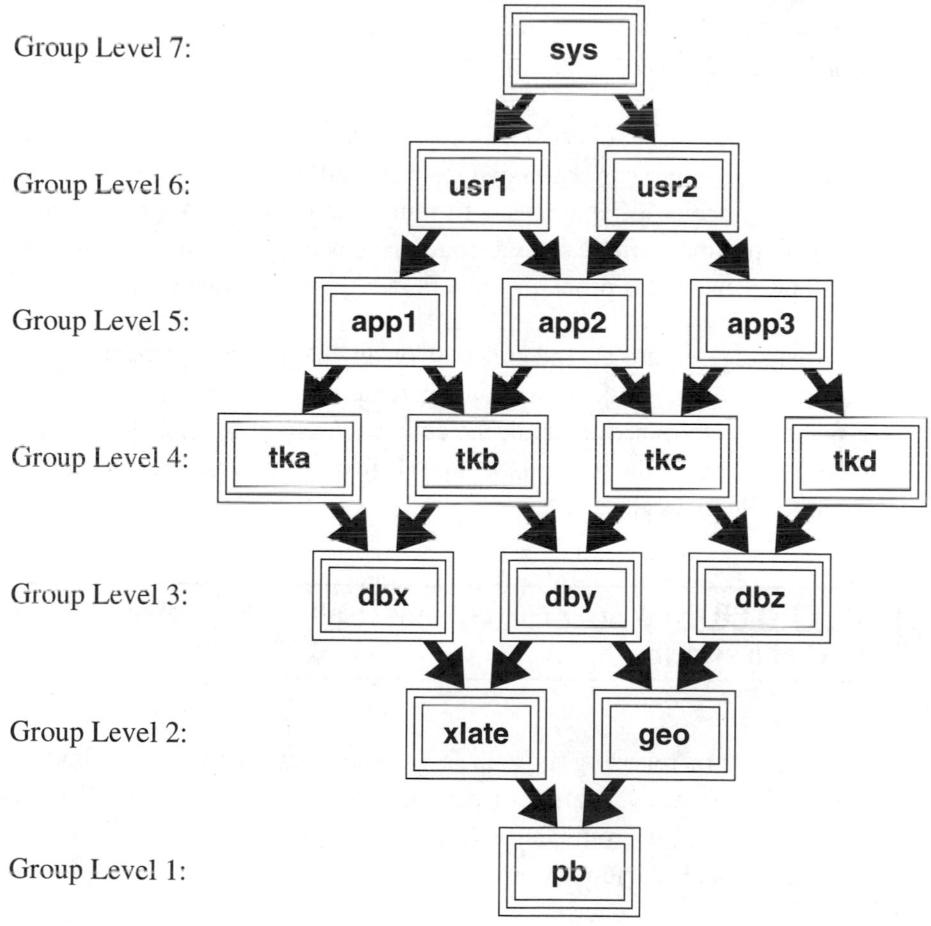

Figure 7-19: Hypothetical Very Large System with DAG-Like Group Dependencies

In short, groups of packages are analogous to packages of components. A group should consist of packages that are logically cohesive or otherwise make sense as a single cohesive physical unit. As it does with packages, the defined purpose of a group should govern its contents; what is not germane should not be part of the group. Of course, dependencies among groups of packages should form a directed acyclic graph. Although a package is an appropriate size for being owned and implemented by a single developer, a group would be more likely to be owned by a project manager and implemented by a development team. From a client's point of view, a group looks just like a single huge package with a collection of closely related prefixes; however, in all cases the integrity and uniqueness of each individual package within each group should be preserved. Access to individual special-purpose package-level libraries is needed during development.

7.6 The Release Process

As one of many developers working concurrently on a large project, it can be difficult to determine why your regression tests are failing—was it the change you just made to this package or a change made to some lower-level package? Developing software in an environment where spontaneous changes can occur affects productivity even for small projects, and is probably unworkable for most larger projects.

Internal releases are an integral part of any large development project. Groups of packages are the smallest unit of functionality that are normally released. At some regular predetermined interval, the code for a group of packages (e.g, the core database group, `db`, of the previous section) is frozen[12] and the process of building a stable internal release begins.

> **DEFINITION: A *layer* corresponds to all package groups at a given level of a system.**

The process of releasing a group is accomplished in an orderly, bottom-up fashion, governed by the levelization of the packages within the group. The packages at the lowest level in the group are built and tested in isolation. Once these packages pass their individual, component-level hierarchical regression tests, level-2 packages can

[12] The liberty to make arbitrary updates to this version of the software is suspended.

be built and tested, linking only with level-1 packages. The process of rebuilding a system is markedly similar to the way the individual components within a package are developed and tested, but on a larger scale.

The levelization of package groups has a special significance in the release process. All groups at each level in the system are collectively called a *layer*. For systems with vertically arranged groups (see Figure 7-17), each layer consists of only a single group. For larger systems with more complex group arrangements (see Figure 7-19), a given layer may consist of several groups. To ensure consistency across the entire system, it is important that all groups on which a given group `g` depends have been released before code for `g` is frozen and `g` is released. For example, group `dby` in Figure 7-19 is at level 3. The `dby` group cannot update its dependencies to the new version of group `geo` until the `xlate` group has also been released. In contrast, group `dbz` depends only on group `geo` and hence need not wait for the `xlate` group to be released in order to start the update process.

By definition, all groups on a given level are independent of each other. The release process for each of these groups can occur independently. Although not all groups at the next higher level will depend on all groups at the previous level, tracking individual group dependencies during the release process may be more effort than it is worth. We can simplify the release process while ensuring the consistency of the entire system simply by insisting that all groups on a given level are released before beginning the release process for groups at the next higher level.

When the release process for all groups on this layer is complete, the availability of the new package groups is announced. Developers working on the next higher layer continue to use the previous release of the lower-level layer until they reach a convenient stopping point. After rerunning their own regression tests one last time, these developers may now—at their leisure—adjust their environments to refer to the newer release of the lower-level software.

At this point the developers may have to make changes to their own code to accommodate any interface changes made to lower-level package groups since the last release—a process sometimes referred to as *porting*.[13] Obviously, with good planning

[13] The term *porting* applies to moving a software system to a new platform. This new platform can take the form of new hardware, a new operating system, or a new version of the lower layers of the system itself.

such changes will be minimized. After a few minor adjustments, developers should be able to rerun their regression tests to verify that changes to the lower-level software have not altered the nature of the needed functionality. These developers can now resume development, using the new stable release of the software. At some point these clients will in turn freeze their code and go through a similar release process.

Notice how a client of the immediately preceding layer is not forced to respond immediately when a new release is published. Experience has shown that providing some slack between the release of successive layers is an effective way to manage internal releases within a large system.

7.6.1 The Release Structure

Figure 7-20 shows one way to organize the development hierarchy for the system presented in Figure 7-18. This development-directory structure supports multiple releases and the notion of header files shared among packages that are not exported outside the group. At the root of the directory structure there are the five group directories corresponding to the five groups in the system of Figure 7-17; each group has a subdirectory structure similar to the one shown here for the core database group, `db`. Beneath the `db` directory are subdirectories holding the past several parallel release structures of this group; the release illustrated in Figure 7-20 for the `db` group is release 1.6.3.

Under the group's release directory are four directories and a file. The directories are `dependencies`, `source`, `include`, and `lib`, and the file is `exported`. The dependencies directory indicates the names and release versions of the other groups on which this group depends. On a Unix-based system, each of these dependencies may be represented by a symbolic link that refers back to the specific release of the lower-level group used to build this group. Providing these references allows the include and link directories of clients to remain relative as they update a single pointer from the old to the new release of a group.

The source subdirectory is organized in the same way as it was the for the much simpler package-development structure shown in Figure 7-2. As Figure 7-20 indicates, all of the source for each package within the group lives under a directory corresponding to its package prefix, which makes it easy for developers to locate packages defined within the group. Unfortunately, locating packages defined *outside* the group now becomes more difficult. This problem can be addressed by having packages within a group extend a common group prefix (e.g., dba or dbb) or, less desirably, by identifying the group location in the global package registry. There is an additional issue involving "prefix prefixes"—that is, how does anyone know that dbq is not a legal prefix for some new package not in group db?

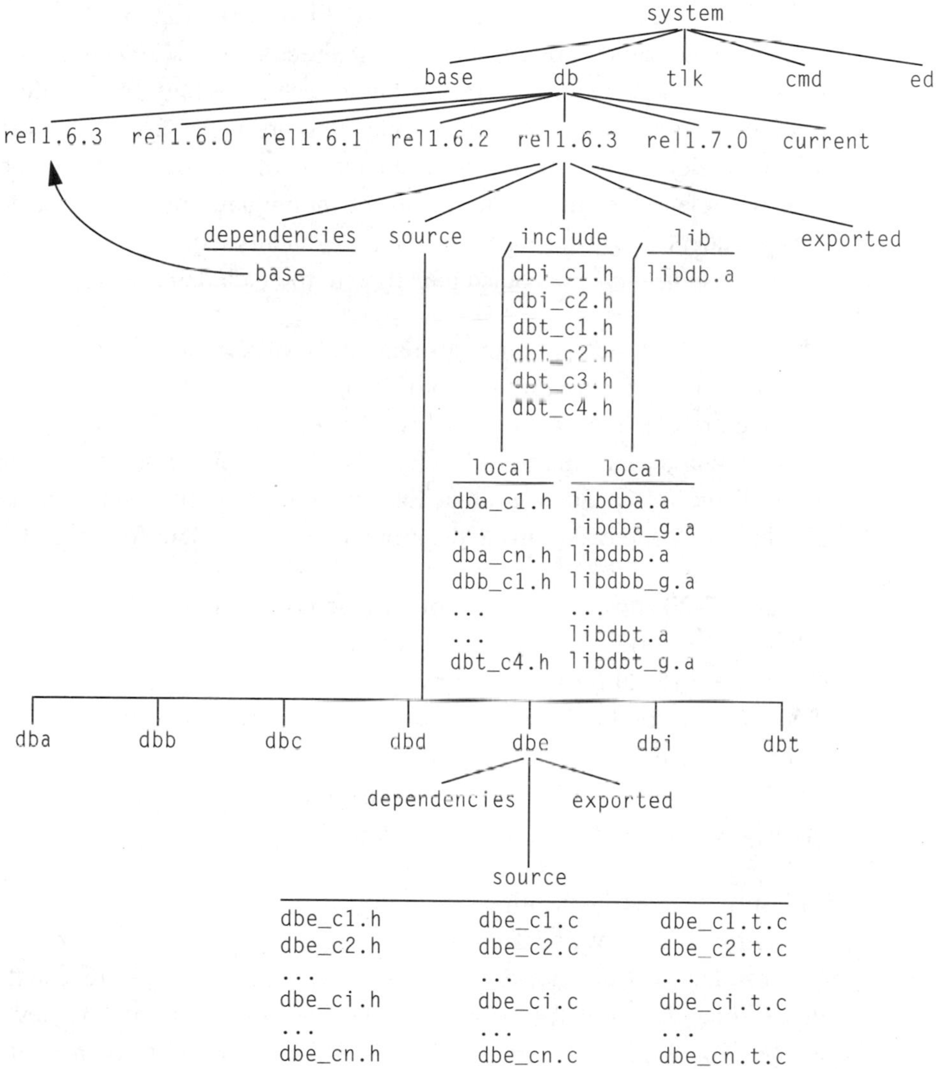

Figure 7-20: A Development Directory Hierarchy for Package Groups

Configuration control must be an integral part of the development process. Systems such as SCCS and RCS will need to be integrated into the development environment. Even more powerful systems are also commercially available, but a detailed discussion of the use of such tools is beyond the scope of this book.

The include directory is now more complex in order to support the notion of exported versus local headers for this group. The subdirectory `local` under `include` is similar to the global include area of Figure 7-2, but is accessible only from within the `db` group. This local directory contains header files that are necessary to support interpackage communication within this group. The contents of the file `exported`, defined directly under the release for the group, identifies individual components or entire packages whose headers are to be made available to clients external to this group. During a release, these headers are copied directly into the included directory for the group.[14]

Finally, the `lib` directory is now also more complex in order to support the notion of a single group library. Again the subdirectory `local` under `lib` is similar to the global `lib` directory of Figure 7-2 in that this subdirectory holds all of the various versions of the individual package library files. Instead of containing library files corresponding to each package, `lib` contains a single library file representing their union. Providing just a single library file makes using the group more convenient for general clients.

As Figure 7-20 shows, more than one version of each individual package library may be built. The suffix `_g` is used to indicate that the library has debugging symbols. Many other special forms of libraries may exist as well, for purposes such as performance monitoring or runtime memory-bounds checking. If the group is large, it may not be practical to use or even build special-purpose libraries for the entire group. Instead, developers will typically identify the individual packages within the group that they would like to analyze more carefully.

Releasing a group using this development directory structure is straightforward. The entire directory and file structure (except for the files contained under the `include` and `lib` directories) for this group and release is repeated under a new release (e.g., `system/db/rel1.7.1`). The dependencies for this new release (e.g., `system/db/rel1.7.1/dependencies/base`) are adjusted to point to the new release of the lower-level software (e.g., `system/base/rel1.7.1`). Each package in this group is then copied to the new release, rebuilt, and tested in levelized order.

---

[14] Symbolic links or the equivalent may replace actual copies.

As each package is built, header files that are to be exported from the package for use by other packages within this group are placed in the local include directory (e.g., `system/db/rel1.7.1/include/local/dba_c3.h`). At the same time, each version of the individual package libraries is placed in the local lib directory for this group (e.g., `system/db/rel1.7.1/lib/local/libdba.a`) Once all packages local to this group have been built, the package libraries are combined into a single library and placed in the lib directory (e.g., `system/db/rel1.7.1/lib/libdb.a`). Only those headers that clients of this group will need in order to use the group are then exported to the include directory (e.g., `system/db/rel1.7.1/include/dbi_c1.h`).

The directory `current` is not published but is reserved for ongoing development. Although changes to published versions are infrequent and carefully controlled (see Section 7.6.2), changes to the `current` (development) version may be expected to occur frequently.

We can extend this directory structure to support multiple platforms by providing an addition node in the hierarchy just before any machine-dependent files. For example,

```
system/db/rel1.7.1/lib/libdb.a
```

would instead become

```
system/db/rel1.7.1/lib/sun4os4/libdb.a
```

or

```
system/db/rel1.7.1/lib/hppaux9/libdb.a
```

to reflect the desired combination of machine architecture and operating system.

Principle

Minimizing the time it takes to recompile after a source-code change can significantly reduce the cost of development.

The cost of compiling is partially a function of the number of header files in an include directory, but is even more dependent on the number of directories the compiler has to search in order to locate all required header files. On most systems, it is significantly faster to compile components when all of the header files reside in just a few directories than if the headers are distributed across many individual (package-level) include directories.

To make the cost of an excessive number of individual include directories concrete, I devised an experiment to compare the overhead of compiling a single component using individual package include directories, group include directories, layer include directories, and a single global directory. I made several order-of-magnitude assumptions:

- 10 `#include` directives per component
- 10 components per package
- 10 packages per group
- 10 groups per layer
- 10 layers per system

The experiment was repeated for systems containing 1, 10, 100, 1,000, and 10,000 components on structures with varying numbers of include directories. Figure 7-21 contains the results of running the experiment both with the CFRONT compiler on a SUN SPARC 10 workstation and also with the native C++ Compiler on an HP 7000 workstation.

For reference, compiling an otherwise empty component that depends on only a single package include directory takes approximately 1 CPU second to compile on the SUN and 0.2 CPU seconds on the HP. As the system size increases, the cost of compiling increases modestly on the SUN and only negligibly on the HP. For systems on the order of 1,000 components, the cost of compiling a component using individual package include directories can use nearly twice the CPU time on the SUN and 4.5 times the CPU time on the HP. For larger systems, the overhead of using individual package include directories is even more pronounced—roughly an order of magnitude for the SUN and nearly so for the HP.[15]

[15] Note that actual elapsed "wall" time can overwhelm even the CPU time when compiling components that depend on a large subsystem. For example, the wall time to compile a component against a 1,000-component system distributed across 100 individual package include directories was 22.1 seconds on the SUN and 4.8 seconds on the HP. When the system consisted of 10,000 components, the wall time to compile a single component grew to 225.5 seconds on the SUN and 209.2 seconds on the HP.

Subsystem Size in Number of Components	Number of Include Directories				Number of Include Directories			
	1	10	100	1000	1	10	100	1000
10	1.0 (100%)				0.2 (100%)			
100	1.0 (100%)	1.0 (100%)			0.2 (100%)	0.2 (100%)		
1,000	1.1 (100%)	1.1 (100%)	2.0 (182%)		0.2 (100%)	0.2 (100%)	0.9 (450%)	
10,000	1.4 (100%)	1.4 (100%)	2.3 (164%)	15.1 (1,079%)	0.2 (100%)	0.2 (100%)	0.9 (450%)	15.2 (760%)
	CPU Time on SUN SPARC 10				CPU Time on HP 735			

Relative to Using a Single Include Directory

Time in CPU Seconds

Figure 7-21: Compilation Time/(Overhead) Due to Multiple Include Directories

Reducing the amount of time it takes to recompile and relink can have a significant impact on productivity. Fortunately, there are a couple of ways we can reduce this problem for large systems short of buying a faster piece of hardware. The most effective method is to reduce the number of header files via insulation, as discussed in Chapter 6. Another method, which will have a lesser (but still significant) impact, is to reduce the number of include directories that a compiler needs to search during a given compilation. One such way is to propagate the headers exported from lower-level groups (identified by file `dependencies`) into a dependent group's own exported headers directory, perhaps with additional filtering defined in file `exported`.

As Figure 7-22 illustrates, not all the headers exported by the `base` and `db` layers are needed by clients of the `tlk` layer. Instead of having `tlk` simply publish just its own headers, `tlk` could republish the necessary subset of lower-level exported headers in addition to its own exported headers. In this way we can avoid forcing its clients to specify the separate include directories for both `base` and `db`. Now clients of the `tlk` layer need specify only one include directory in order to access the `tlk` layer functionality. Here again, it is insulation that enables us to reduce the number of headers we expose to our clients to improve their rate of compilation.

system/base/rel1.7.1/include	system/db/rel1.7.1/include	system/tlk/rel1.7.1/include
pub_c1.h	dbi_c1.h	tlk1_c1.h
pub_c2.h	dbi_c2.h	tlk1_c2.h
usr_c1.h	dbt_c1.h	tlk1_c3.h
pub_c2.h	dbt_c2.h	tlk2_c1.h
usr_c3.h	pub_c1.h	tlk3_c1.h
	pub_c2.h	tlk3_c2.h
	usr_c1.h	dbi_c1.h
		dbt_c1.h
		pub_c1.h

Figure 7-22: Minimizing a Client's Cost of Including Headers

Another alternative is to make the client group responsible for "prefetching" all of its required headers into a single include directory before attempting to compile. Requiring the client to create a special-purpose directory to efficiently reuse a subsystem in effect makes such a subsystem less reusable. This second approach seems less friendly, since it forces the client to do more work to use the subsystem; however, it can have its advantages in a hostile environment.

7.6.2 Patches

Making changes to a release is potentially disruptive to development, and so it is important to preserve the stability of a release once it is created. Sometimes a critical bug will be detected in a stable release that cannot wait until the next release to be fixed. Repairing the bug and rebuilding the entire system from scratch is both disruptive and time consuming, especially for the potentially large client population. If the problem is in the implementation, it is often much more cost-effective to *patch* it.

<u>DEFINITION</u>: A *patch* is a local change to previously released software to repair faulty or grossly inefficient functionality within a component.

The simplest, safest, and most common kind of patch involves making changes to only the `.c` file of a component. After the `.c` file is modified and compiled, the resulting `.o` file may then (on a Unix system) be placed before a library file in the link command to supplant an existing `.o` file. Of course, clients can choose whether or not to link-in these patch files—for some, the fix may not be worth the loss in stability.

Principle

A patch must not affect the internal layout of any existing object.

Not every bug can be patched. Fortunately, if the header file for the component is not exported, the layout of such an object can be known only to the components within the package. In such cases, the bug can almost always be fixed by providing one or more patch files to solve the problem. However, even if the header file is exported, there are a number of bugs that can be patched without having to rebuild the entire system. The more insulated the implementation of a component, the more likely that it can be patched without affecting components outside the package.

Consider the non-insulating class `Example` shown in Figure 6-49, implemented entirely inline. If the header for `Example` is exported, there is no way we could hope to patch a bug in it. Any change we would make to the implementation of class `Example` would force the recompilation of all clients that use it. Compare this now to the fully insulating `Example` class of Figure 6-51, which has no inline functions, no inheritance, and exposes only a single opaque pointer to its data. It is virtually certain that we could patch any purely implementational problem, thus avoiding the need for clients of this class to recompile.

Ideally a patch does not require modifying any header files at all. Modifying information in an exported header file has the potential to affect an unbounded number of clients; such changes are therefore best avoided. Although risky, there are a number of repairs we can make that will not invalidate our release, even though it may mean altering the existing exported header files. If we can guarantee that the effects of these local changes are link compatible and do not invalidate the release, we can save the considerable expense and effort of a second release.

The following kind of changes are relatively safe:

- Altering the body of a non-inline function.
- Altering any construct in the `.c` file with internal linkage.

- Adding a new exported header file to the release.
- Adding a `friend` declaration to a class.
- Relaxing an existing access specifier (e.g., from `protected` to `public`).
- Adding a new non-virtual function to a class (risky).
- Adding a class or free operator to a header (risky).

Note that the last four examples require modifying a header file. After such a change, this header file should be artificially backdated to prevent unnecessary recompilations by clients. The last two examples are risky because of the possibility of introducing an ambiguity from function or operator overloading in a header file that has already been included by some client. Had the last example been introduced in a new and separate header file, there would be no chance that the construct would affect any existing usage.

The following changes can potentially corrupt a release:

- Adding, reordering, modifying, or removing any data members.
- Adding, reordering, or removing any virtual function.
- Changing the signature or return value of any function.
- Adding, reordering, modifying, or removing any inheritance relationships.
- Altering any construct in the header with internal linkage.
- Reducing the access of a class member (e.g., from protected to private).
- Introducing an access specifier between adjacent data members.[16]

The lists presented here are not complete, but should give the idea and flavor of the kinds of changes that, if made carefully, can be accomplished locally via patches. The only real requirements are that:

1. We ensure link-time compatibility after the patch.

2. We avoid causing our clients to recompile because of changes in header-file time stamps.

3. We are sure that the system would successfully rebuild if we were to try to do so.

---

[16] See **ellis**, Sections 9.2, p. 173; and 11.1, pp. 241–247.

There is much more to creating an effective development environment than can be presented here. The techniques used will depend on the operating system. Organizations similar to those illustrated in Figure 7-20 have been used successfully on Unix-based systems to develop very large projects.

7.7 The `main` Program

When we write a program in C++, we are required by the language to provide a unique definition of the function `main` to interface with the operating system and, in particular, to process any command line arguments. However, when we invest tens, hundreds, or even thousands of staff years to create a C++ system, there is no single top to the system. That is, invariably there are several executables, each with its own `main` procedure, that together comprise the system. Instead of producing a single program, our design methodology has created a hierarchical collection of reusable subsystems. Many of these subsystems will be used in standalone input verifiers, translators, viewers, report generators, output analyzers, and so on. The number of individual "main" programs is likely to grow as the system evolves and matures.

Principle

Factoring independently testable and potentially reusable functionality out of a translation unit that defines `main` enables essentially the entire implementation of the program to be reused in a yet larger program.

The purpose of a translation unit defining `main` (other than a hierarchical test driver) is to provide a C++ subsystem with a command line interface, interpret environment variables, and manage global resources—nothing more. A common mistake is to place far too much code in a file that defines `main`. Such code cannot be tested incrementally from a C++ test driver, nor can it be reused within a larger C++ program.

For example, consider a program designed to perform some sort of desktop publishing function—say a glossary generator, illustrated in Figure 7-23. The function of a glossary generator is to read an input document and store it as a set of unique words. This input is filtered against a second input defining a set of blocking words. Blocking words are common words (such as *and*, *this*, *a*, etc.) that are likely not to be appropriate for a glossary. Next, the remaining set of words is compared against a third input, a thesaurus, that in this context represents a mapping of aliases or alternate forms to more common or basic terms. For example, *method* is another name for *member function* in C++. Finally, all basic terms that are not blocked or aliased must be defined in a fourth input—a dictionary. A *dictionary* is a mapping from a set of common terms to their respective definitions. The outputs of the glossary generator are a list of undefined terms and the alphabetized subset of the definitions in the dictionary corresponding to recognized terms.

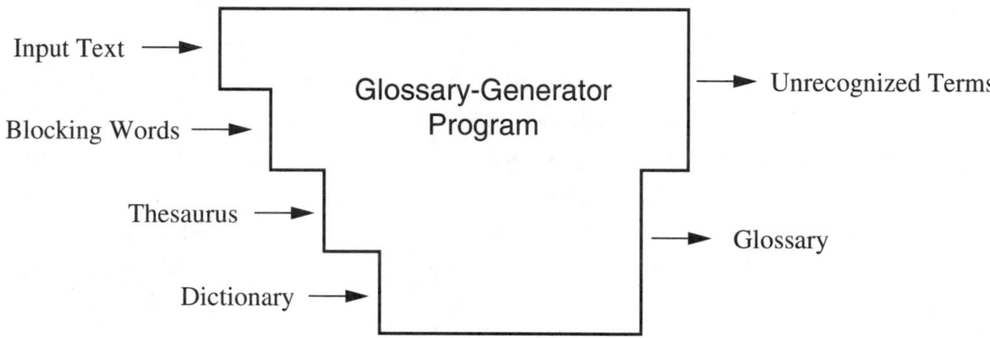

Figure 7-23: Glossary-Generator Program

Where should we begin the design of this program? In a top-down approach we should probably begin with `main`, right? Perhaps. However, we should be diligent in our efforts to factor out the implementation of functionality provided by `main` into independently testable and potentially reusable components. (Recall the technique of factoring to reduce complexity of unmanageably large components presented in Section 5.9.) How we will import the information from the command line is only one of our concerns. Another important question we should be asking is how the underlying functionality might some day conveniently be integrated into a larger program (e.g., a desktop publishing framework). To achieve a modular design, we must simultaneously address the underlying programmatic interface and the standalone command-line interface for the immediate end user.

A central piece in the design of a glossary-generator program is very likely a glossary-generator object defined in a glossary-generator component, such as the one illustrated in Figure 7-24. In order to use a glossary-generator object, we first need to program it with blocking words, aliases, and dictionary definitions. Explicit manipulator functions in the dtp_GlossGen class are provided for these purposes. After the glossary generator is programmed, we can load the individual words of the input text into the glossary-generator object using the addTextWord manipulator function. Once we are done loading all the input text for the document, we will create an iterator to sequence over the glossary definitions in alphabetical order. A second iterator is provided to allow us to sequence over any undefined terms. Having completed processing on a first document, we may wish to pass several related documents through the same generator. The clearInputWords manipulator allows us to start again with a new document while retaining the previously programmed blocking words, aliases, and definitions.

```
// dtp_glossgen.h
#ifndef DTP_INCLUDED_GLOSSGEN
#define DTP_INCLUDED_GLOSSGEN

class dtp_GlossDefIter;
class dtp_GlossUndefTermIter;

class dtp_GlossGen_i;                    // fully insulated implementation
class dtp_GlossGen {
    dtp_GlossGen_i *d_this;

    friend dtp_GlossDefIter;
    friend dtp_GlossUndefTermIter;

  private:
    // NOT IMPLEMENTED
    dtp_GlossGen(const dtp_GlossGen&);
    dtp_GlossGen& operator=(const dtp_GlossGen&);

  public:
    // CREATORS
    dtp_GlossGen();
    ~dtp_GlossGen();

    // MANIPULATORS
    int addBlockingWord(const char *blockingWord);
    int addAlias(const char *alias, const char *keyTerm);
    int addDefinition(const char *keyTerm, const char *definition);
    int addTextWord(const char *textWord);
    void clearInputWords();
};

class dtp_GlossDefIter_i;                // fully insulated implementation
class dtp_GlossDefIter {
    dtp_GlossDefIter_i *d_this;
```

```
  private:
    // NOT IMPLEMENTED
    dtp_GlossDefIter(const dtp_GlossDefIter&);
    dtp_GlossDefIter& operator=(const dtp_GlossDefIter&);

  public:
    // CREATORS
    dtp_GlossDefIter(const dtp_GlossGen& glossaryGenerator);
    ~dtp_GlossDefIter();

    // MANIPULATORS
    void operator++();

    // ACCESSORS
    operator const void *() const;
    const char *keyTerm();             // Provides an association
    const char *definition();          // (keyTerm, definition) so
                                       // we choose not to define an
                                       // operator()() here.
};

class dtp_GlossUndefTermIter_i;        // fully insulated implementation
class dtp_GlossUndefTermIter {
    dtp_GlossUndefTermIter_i *d_this;

  private:
    // NOT IMPLEMENTED
    dtp_GlossUndefTermIter(const dtp_GlossUndefTermIter&);
    dtp_GlossUndefTermIter& operator=(const dtp_GlossUndefTermIter&);

  public:
    // CREATORS
    dtp_GlossUndefTermIter(const dtp_GlossGen& glossaryGenerator);
    ~dtp_GlossUndefTermIter();

    // MANIPULATORS
    void operator++();

    // ACCESSORS
    operator const void *() const;
    const char *operator()() const;   // Returns just the current undefined
};                                     // term so operator()() is ok here.

#endif
```

Figure 7-24: Insulating Interface for a Glossary-Generator Wrapper Component

Our `main` will still need to create a `dtp_GlossGen` object and then translate input from (files referenced by) the command line into `dtp_GlossGen` member function calls in order to program this object appropriately. However, we may elect to use any number of input grammars in order to program the glossary generator. It would therefore be inappropriate to tie the programmatic interface of the glossary generator to any one syntax. Instead, we create a separate component responsible for reading some given input, parsing that input, and exercising the glossary-generator component accordingly. The highest levels of the glossary generator program's component architecture are shown in Figure 7-25.

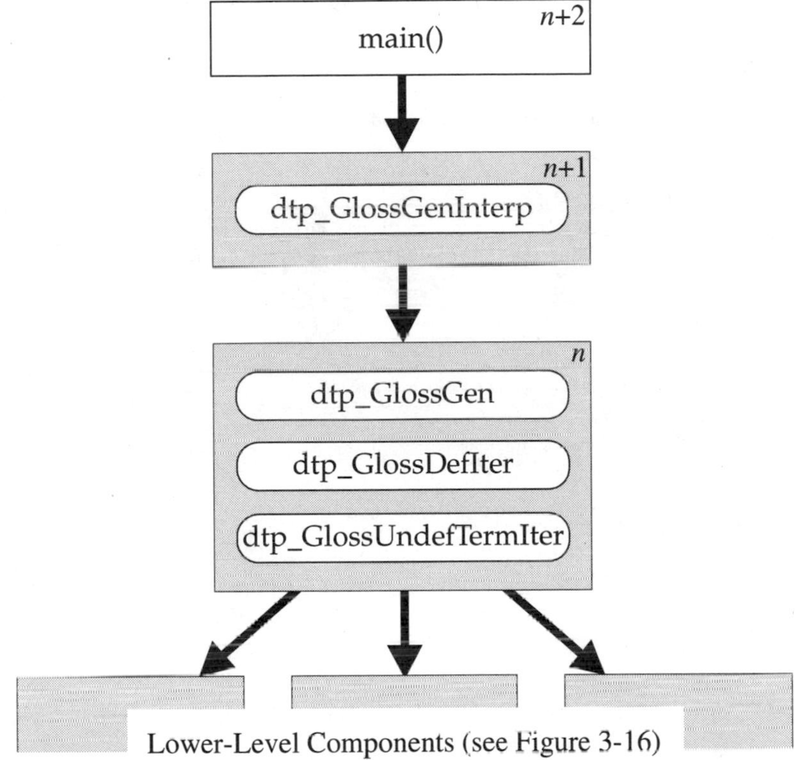

Figure 7-25: High-Level Glossary Generator Program Architecture

The job of the interpreter component, illustrated in Figure 7-26, is to attach itself to a glossary-generator object and then exercise that object accordingly, based on commands found in a specified input file or stream. The interpreter object itself is programmed with two pieces of information:

1. The address of the glossary generator it is to manipulate.

2. The error output stream to which the interpreter is to report detailed syntax error messages.

```
// dtp_glossgeninterp.h
#ifndef DTP_GLOSS_GEN_INTERP
#define DTP_GLOSS_GEN_INTERP

class dtp_GlossGen;
class ostream;
class istream;

class dtp_GlossGenInterp_i;
class dtp_GlossGenInterp {
    dtp_GlossGenInterp_i *d_this;

  private:
    // NOT IMPLEMENTED
    dtp_GlossGenInterp(const dtp_GlossGenInterp&);
    dtp_GlossGenInterp& operator=(const dtp_GlossGenInterp&);

  public:
    // CREATORS
    dtp_GlossGenInterp(dtp_GlossGen* glossGen);
        // create an interpreter

    ~dtp_GlossGenInterp();
        // destroy this interpreter

    // MANIPULATORS
    void setErrorStream(ostream& errorStream);
        // Set output stream to which detailed errors will be reported.
        // By default, this stream is cerr.

    // ACCESSORS
    int exercise(const char *fileName = "-") const;
        // Parses commands from the specified input file.  Returns
        // -1 on I/O error, 0 on success, and 1 on syntax error.
        // The default "-" stands for "standard input" (i.e., cin).

    int exercise(istream& input, const char *fileName = 0) const;
        // Parse commands from the specified input stream.  Returns
        // -1 if an I/O error occurs; otherwise returns the line
        // number of the first syntax error.  If successful, this
        // function returns 0.  The second argument is used only
        // for the purpose of identifying the input source when
        // formatting syntax error messages to the error stream.
};

#endif
```

Figure 7-26: Fully Insulating Interpreter Component for Glossary Generator

Two accessor functions of the interpreter are provided to exercise the functionality of the associated glossary-generator object. The first simply takes a file name and opens it if possible. This function then calls the second (more primitive) form, which takes an open stream and an optional "file" name to be used in formatting error messages. The lower-level function is exposed in the interface so that the source of the stream need not be an actual file. Note that these two member functions do not affect the state of the interpreter; they affect only the state of the glossary generator.

Finally, all that is left to do in `main` is to create these two objects and sequence through a set of command-line arguments. If no command-line arguments are specified, `cin` should be assumed by default. A tiny standalone main driver for the glossary generator program is shown in Figure 7-27. This driver illustrates a reusable pattern, suitable to a variety of standalone applications.

```
// dtp_glossgeninterp.t.c
//
// Usage: a.out [ <file name> | - ]*
//
// Example:
//
//      john@john: a.out stuff.abc such.def -
//
//      The above command line will first read input from the file
//      "stuff.abc", then read input from the file "such.def", and
//      finally read from standard input (cin).

#include "dtp_glossgeninterp.h"
#include "dtp_glossgen.h"

const char *const defaultArgs[] = { "", "-" };    // has internal linkage
const int defaultNumArgs = sizeof defaultArgs / sizeof *defaultArgs;

main(int argc, char *argv[])
{
    int status = 0;
    const char *progName = argv[0];
    int numArgs = argc > 1 ? argc : defaultNumArgs;
    const char *const *args = argc > 1 ? argv : defaultArgs;

    dtp_GlossGen glossaryGenerator;
    dtp_GlossGenInterp interpreter(&glossaryGenerator);

    for (int i = 1; i < numArgs && 0 == status; ++i) {
        status = interpreter.exercise(args[i]);
    }

    return status;
}
```

Figure 7-27: A Standalone Main Driver for Glossary Generator and Interpreter

Ownership of `main` comes with both privilege and responsibility. There is only one `main` in a given program. It is this piece of code that should be responsible for reading environment variables and establishing global resources. The person who owns `main` owns the global name space. For example, there is no harm if the file containing `main` defines or accesses external global variables, fails to use package prefixes, and so forth. To ensure our ability to integrate arbitrary subsystems, however, no other part of the system should pollute the global name space or attempt to usurp a global resource.

Guideline:

In general, avoid granting one component license that, if also taken by other components, would adversely impact the system as a whole.

This (Kant-like) philosophy implores that unless we define `main`, we should not attempt to do something that, if others did it also, would have a negative consequence for the overall system.

Excessive use of inline functions is just one example of the kind of behavior that can lead to subtle integration problems down the road. By cavalierly declaring inappropriately large member functions inline, we can often improve the runtime performance of our own object in isolation or within a small subsystem. However, this runtime improvement is obtained at the cost of repeated code and increased executable size.

When such selfishly architected subsystems are integrated into larger subsystems, the increased code size begins to show its adverse effect. Hardware mechanisms designed to improve the performance of commonly used routines are defeated by the excessive repetition of inline code. The increased program size reduces the percentage of the executable that the operating system can keep in core, which leads to increased swapping. At some level of integration, many of these objects will actually begin to run more slowly (as a result of the excessive inlines) than they would have run had some of the larger functions been declared non-`inline`. The end result of this selfishness is a net decrease in overall system performance.

Another case in which a lack of diligence by individual developers can adversely affect an integrated system involves the indiscriminate use of non-local static objects, as discussed in Section 7.8. Yet another specific case of avoiding such egocentric behavior on the part of a component or subsystem is discussed in the context of class-specific memory management in Section 10.3.4.2.

Major Design Rule

Only the `.c` file that defines `main` is authorized to redefine global `new` and `delete`.

An important special case of this philosophy is that only the owner of `main` can be authorized to redefine the global operators `new` and `delete`. Components that do not define `main` are proscribed from such unilateral behaviors. Otherwise two independent subsystems, each redefining a unique resource (such as global `operator new`), would not be link compatible.

To summarize: there is no top when designing a large system. The purpose of `main` is only to provide a C++ subsystem with an interface to the command line, interpret environment variables, and manage global resources—nothing more. Factoring functionality provided by `main` into separate components facilitates hierarchical testing and enables easier integration into yet larger systems. The `.c` file that defines `main` owns the global name space and is exempt from certain design rules that pertain to ordinary components. For components that do not define `main`, care should be taken not to take liberties that, if also taken for other components, could compromise the system as a whole.

7.8 Start-Up

The elasped time between when a program is first invoked and when the thread of control enters `main` is referred to in this book as *start-up*. It is during this time that potentially *all* non-local static objects in every translation unit are constructed, as illustrated in Figure 7-28.[17]

---

[17] According to the C++ language specification (**ellis**, Section 3.4, p. 19), all non-local static objects within a translation unit must be constructed prior to the first use of any function or object defined within that translation unit; in practice, however, *all* such initializations can and commonly do occur at start-up.

DEFINITION: *Start-up time* (also known as *invocation time*) is the time between when a program is first invoked and when the thread of control enters `main`.

```
// my_component.c
#include "my_component.h"                    // defines class my_Class
#include "pub_list.h"                        // defines class pub_List
#include <sys/types.h>                       // declares typedef time_t
#include <sys/time.h>                        // declares ::time()

// static object at file scope
static pub_List list;                        // constructed at start-up

// static data member initialized by function call
static time_t startUpTime = time(0);         // called at start-up

// static object in class scope
pub_List my_Class::d_List;                   // constructed at start-up

// ...
```

Figure 7-28: Initialization of Non-Local Static Variables at Start-Up

Since the order of initialization between non-local static objects defined in separate translation units is implementation dependent, special care must be taken to ensure that such static objects are initialized before they are used. When the intent is to provide a single instance of a globally accessible object, our stated aversion to global data (Section 2.2) leads us to look for an alternative. Instead of creating an instance of an object at file scope with external linkage, we can usually achieve our purpose with a logical construct commonly referred to as a *module* and implemented in C++ as a class containing only static members.[18]

[18] A *module* can also refer to a physical entity that is similar to a component, but that has a procedural interface. Note that, in ANSI C, the only way to implement a logical module is as a physical module (i.e., as a separate translation unit defining static data at file scope). For more about modules, see **stroustrup**, Section 1.2.2, p. 16.

Guideline

Prefer modules to non-local static instances of objects, especially when:

1. **Direct access to the construct is needed outside a translation unit.**
2. **The construct may not be needed during start-up or immediately thereafter and the time to initialize the construct itself is significant.**

The need to ensure the proper initialization of static constructs before they are used is well documented.[19] What is less commonly appreciated is the magnitude of the combined impact such initializations can have on start-up time. For small programs, initializing a few static constructs at start-up would probably have no noticeable impact on a user's perception of the time needed to invoke the program. However, the larger a system is, the more opportunity there is for independent static constructs to require initialization during start-up.

Principle

The construction of each non-local static objects in a program potentially contributes to invocation time.

Since every static object defined at file scope or within class scope is potentially constructed before `main` is entered, a very large system whose components regularly define such static objects could take an unacceptably long time to bring up. In fact, there are documented cases of very large (supposedly interactive) systems where naively ignoring the cost of initialization at start-up has resulted in invocation times in excess of 10 minutes!

[19] **ellis**, Section 3.4, p. 20; **meyers**, Item 47, p. 178.

Non-local static objects are initialized and destroyed automatically by the C++ runtime system; their indiscriminate use by individual components is a form of egocentric behavior that degrades the invocation performance of integrated systems. Although there is nothing we can do to stop these static instances from being initialized at start-up, there is considerable flexibility about how and when modules are initialized. Fortunately, it is always possible to transform a single global instance of an object into a module that, when initialized, dynamically allocates that object.[20] Once initialized, the module can successfully return a reference to the dynamic object it now holds.

7.8.1 Initialization Strategies

There are at least four different techniques that can be used to ensure that a module is initialized before it is used:

- Wake-up initialized
- Explicit `init` function
- Nifty counter
- Check every time

Each of these initialization strategies has its own advantages and disadvantages; the best choice will depend on several factors:

- The time required to initialize the module
- The likelihood that the module will actually get used
- The amount of work done per module function call
- The frequency with which calls to module functions are made
- The number of components that use the module directly
- Whether there is a need to free/reallocate resources before the program exits

7.8.1.1 The Wake-Up Initialized Technique

By far the best way to initialize a module is to try to have the module "wake up" in an initialized state. For example, using this wake-up approach, a global registry module might be implemented as a list of record links, as shown in Figure 7-29.

---

[20] See the Singleton design pattern in **gamma**, Chapter 3, pp. 127–138.

```
// ax_registry.h
#ifndef INCLUDED_AX_REGISTRY
#define INCLUDED_AX_REGISTRY

class ax_RecordLink;
class ax_Record;

class ax_Registry {
    static ax_RecordLink *d_list_p;

  public:
    static void addRecord(ax_Record *record);
        // Add record to registry; registry now owns the record.

    static void cleanup();
        // Free all dynamicly allocated memory; reset to empty.

    // ...
};

#endif
```

```
// ax_registry.c
#include "ax_registry.h"
ax_RecordLink *ax_Registry::d_list_p = 0;
// ...
```

Figure 7-29: Module that Wakes Up Already Initialized

As long as all the static data members are fundamental types (pointers,[21] integers, doubles, arrays of characters, etc.), they will be initialized at load time (i.e., prior to start-up) without affecting invocation time. Had we instead embedded a `pub_List` object (i.e., not just a pointer) as a static member of class `ax_Registry`, then that member would get initialized automatically (during start-up), incurring a runtime cost.

7.8.1.2 The Explicit `init` Function Technique

Not all modules can wake up initialized. More generally, some components may define modules or contain static constructs that must be initialized at runtime before they can be used. One way to enable this initialization is to provide each such component with an `init` function, as illustrated in Figure 7-30. This `init` function must be called (at least once) before the static constructs provided by the component can be used. The `init`-function approach is quite flexible in that the initialization can be deferred until

[21] A non-local static pointer to a user-defined type can be initialized at load time; in particular, initialization to 0 is common.

well after the start-up phase and invoked only if and when the component is actually needed.

```
// ax_table.h
#ifndef INCLUDED_AX_TABLE
#define INCLUDED_AX_TABLE

class ax_RecordLink;
class ax_Record;

class ax_Table {
    static ax_RecordLink **d_array_p;
    static int d_size;

  public:
    static void init(int size);
    static void cleanup();
    static int addRecord(const ax_Record& record);
    // ...
};

#endif
```

```
// ax_table.c
#include "ax_table.h"
#include "pub_List.h"
#include <memory.h>                    // declare memset
// ...

static pub_List s_list;                // global within this
                                       // component only

ax_RecordLink **ax_Table::d_array_p;

int ax_Table::d_size;

void ax_Table::init(int size)
{
    if (d_array_p) return;
    d_size = size;
    d_array_p = new ax_RecordLink *[size];
    memset(d_array_p, 0, size * sizeof *d_array_p);
}

// ...
```

Figure 7-30: Providing a Component with an Explicit `Init` Function

Although flexible, the explicit-`init`-function approach is quite error prone; clients commonly forget to initialize a component before using it, often resulting in a fatal runtime error. To mitigate this problem, we might provide a distinguished component at the package level (e.g., `ax_package`) with an `init` function that initializes any component requiring runtime initialization defined within this package. At the same time it could also call the `init` functions for all other packages upon which this package depends.

Principle

Initializing components on which you do not otherwise directly depend can significantly increase CCD.

The package-level `init`-function approach has some serious drawbacks. First, there is the obvious maintenance burden of ensuring that the `init` function of every contained component and of every package upon which these components depend gets called by the package-level init function. Much more problematic is that initializing the entire package can dramatically increase coupling, potentially drawing in many components at link time that are not otherwise needed. It is for this latter reason that the use of package-level `init` functions are best avoided—especially for a generally reusable package with a horizontal dependency structure. Instead, it is preferable for components that depend directly on other components requiring explicit initialization to initialize such components *individually*. The client component may in turn supply an init function for use by its own direct clients, or instead may incorporate some other initialization technique. Maintaining the initialization graph at a fine level of granularity helps to keep the CCD of a system to a minimum.

7.8.1.3 The Nifty Counter Technique

When static objects use other static objects, the initialization problem becomes more complex. For the sake of illustration, suppose that the global `pub_List` object of Figure 7-30 itself makes use of a static construct that also requires runtime initialization (e.g., for class-specific memory management, as discussed in Section 10.3.4). Trying to create a `pub_List` as a static object at start-up before the `pub_List`'s static memory management has been initialized could easily cause a fatal runtime error. Since the relative order of these two initializations is implementation dependent, special precautions must be taken.

```
// pub_list.h
#ifndef INCLUDED_PUB_LIST
#define INCLUDED_PUB_LIST

// ...

class pub_List {
    // ...
};

struct pub_ListInit {
    pub_ListInit();
    ~pub_ListInit();
} pub_listInit;

#endif
```

```
// pub_list.c
#include "pub_List.h"

// ...

static int s_niftyCounter = 0;

pub_ListInit::pub_ListInit()
{
    if (0 == s_niftyCounter++) {
        // init pub_List's static constructs
    }
}

pub_ListInit::~pub_ListInit()
{
    if (0 == --s_niftyCounter) {
        // clean-up pub_List's static constructs
    }
}
```

Figure 7-31: Using Nifty Counters to Ensure Initialization Before Use

Instead of the error-prone `init`-function approach, we might consider using the nifty-counter approach.[22] In this approach, a dummy static instance of an initialization class is placed in the header file of a component at file scope, as shown in Figure 7-31. Part of the purpose of this static instance is to count the number of other components that include this component's header. Each static instance of this dummy object included by a translation unit will be constructed during start-up (in some order). The first time a static instance of the dummy object is constructed, the static count is increased from 0 to 1, and the dummy object knows to initialize its component.[23] Each subsequent time a dummy instance is constructed, the only effect is to increment the static count.

[22] The nifty-counter approach is discussed in **ellis**, Section 3.4, pp. 20–21.

[23] Note that the use of any non-inline function defined within a translation unit will trigger the construction of all non-local static instances defined within that translation unit.

At program exit, the process is reversed; the destructor for each dummy object decrements the static count. When this count reaches 0, the dummy object knows it is OK to clean up the component. `iostream` uses the nifty-counter technique to ensure that `cin`, `cout`, `cerr`, and `clog` are initialized before they are used.

The beauty of the nifty-counter approach is that it is foolproof. It is not possible to use a component requiring runtime initialization without first including its header. Doing so causes a dummy object to get constructed, which in turn forces an uninitialized component to become initialized. All this happens *before* the translation unit that included the component's header can make use of the newly supplied declarations to access the component. Thus a class that employs the nifty-counter method of initialization may safely be instantiated statically, even if the class itself uses other non-local static objects that also employ this technique.

Another benefit of using the nifty-counter approach is that only those components in a package that are actually needed in order to link are initialized. The runtime cost of the nifty-counter initialization mechanism itself is negligible except for pathological designs containing *N* components depending directly on *M* modules, where both *N* and *M* are large. Normally this overhead is not large when compared with the construction of the first static object that does the real work of initializing the component.

The major disadvantage of using nifty counters is that even components that only *might* be used at runtime are initialized at start-up anyway. For dynamic libraries that are loaded into a running program on demand, a non-local static initialization often requires dragging these libraries in at start-up, which defeats the purpose of demand loading. If the amount of work done during the initialization itself is large (e.g., loading a multi-dimensional table), it would be wise to consider using another technique that allows us to defer this initialization until later in the execution of the program.

Non-local static objects are commonly used to load a collection of independent concrete types into a global registry at start-up. However, linking to some library implementations (such as archive files on a Unix system) will not incorporate a translation unit's `.o` file unless there is an explicit reference to an external symbol that is resolved by this `.o` file.

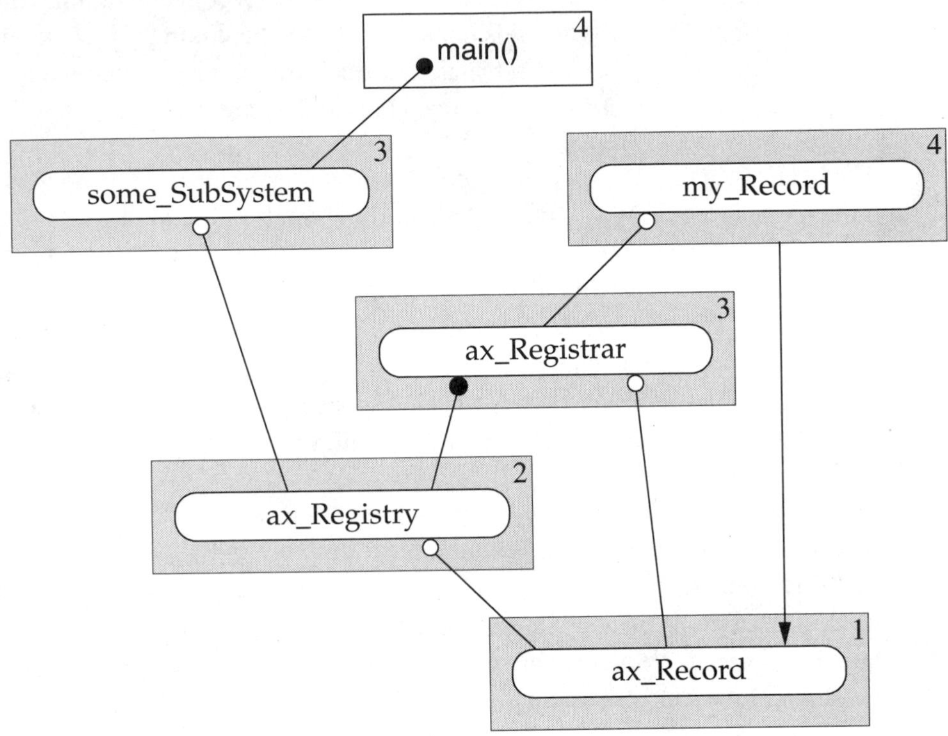

Figure 7-32: Component/Class Diagram of System with Automatic Initialization

Consider the system illustrated in Figure 7-32. An `ax_Registry` (see Figure 7-29) is a module that acts as a global repository for various kinds of concrete records (e.g., `my_Record`) derived from the protocol class `ax_Record`. Since it is expected that there will be many different record subtypes, a special helper class, `ax_Registrar`, is available to aid in the automatic addition of concrete record types into the global registry at start-up. Component `ax_registrar` is presented in Figure 7-33.

```
// ax_registrar.h
#ifndef INCLUDED_AX_REGISTRAR
#define INCLUDED_AX_REGISTRAR

class ax_Record;

struct ax_Registrar {
    ax_Registrar(ax_Record(*)());
    ~ax_Registrar();
};

#endif
```

```
// ax_registrar.c
#include "ax_registrar.h"
#include "ax_registry.h"

static int s_niftyCounter = 0;

ax_Registrar::ax_Registrar(ax_Record(*cfp)())
{
    ++s_niftyCounter;
    ax_Registry::add((*cfp)());
}

ax_Registrar::~ax_Registrar()
{
    if (--s_niftyCounter <= 0) {
        ax_Registry::cleanup((*cfp)());
    }
}
```

Figure 7-33: `ax_Registrar` **Object Used to Register Records at Start-Up**

To register an instance of a record type such as `my_Record`, a non-local static instance of the `ax_Registrar` class is defined in the `.c` file of component `my_record` as shown in Figure 7-34. Merely linking `my_record.o` into an executable image is enough to guarantee that it is registered in the global record registry of the system. But if `my_record.o` is part of a Unix library archive, there is no explicit reference to draw it in at link time. That is, linking to concrete records defined in a collection of `.o` files will work as expected, but, unless explicitly referenced, linking to the same objects defined in a Unix library archive will have *no effect*; after start-up the global registry will be empty!

```
// my_record.h
#ifndef INCLUDED_MY_RECORD
#define INCLUDED_MY_RECORD

#ifndef INCLUDED_AX_RECORD
#include "ax_Record.h"
#endif

class my_Record : public ax_Record {
    // ...
  public:
    static ax_Record *create();
    my_Record();
    // ...
};

#endif
```

```
// my_record.c
#include "my_record.h"
#include "ax_registry.h"

static ax_Registry s_dummy(&my_Record::create);

ax_Record *my_Record::create()
{
    return new my_Record;
}

// ...
```

Figure 7-34: Using `ax_Registrar` **to Register** `my_Record`

If concrete record objects reside in such a library archive, there must be some explicit link-time dependency in order to draw them in. One solution is to provide an empty non-inline `init` function to be called by `main`. However, we can avoid the dependency of derived-record objects on the registry by escalating the registration process to a higher level (e.g., `main`). In so doing we both improve flexibility and reduce the CCD. The modified architecture using explicit initialization is shown in Figure 7-35.

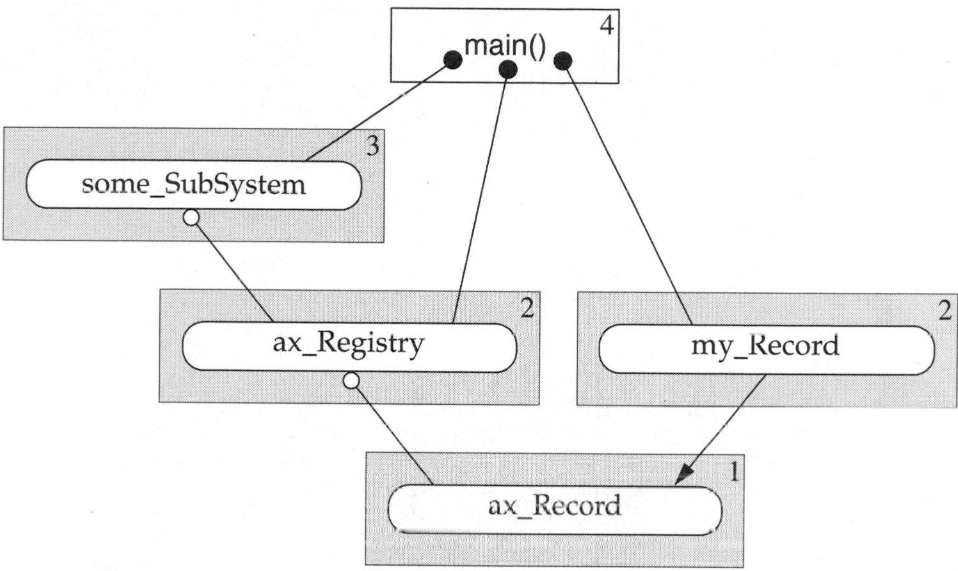

Figure 7-35: Component/Class Diagram of System Using Explicit Initialization

Identifying which particular derived-record types are to be incorporated in a given executable must be done somewhere. The appropriate types can either be installed explicitly by the component that defines `main` or externally to the program through configuration management. The fact that a seemingly elegant initialization technique will fail to work properly when incorporated into certain libraries underscores the importance of physical design.

7.8.1.4 The Check-Every-Time Technique

The larger the program, the less likely it is that we will use all of the functionality it provides. Infrequently used subsystems may still require significant work to initialize at runtime. As with insulation, if each function call of a component already performs a non-trivial task, adding a small amount of additional runtime overhead on each call will probably not noticeably affect runtime performance.

```
// ax_ledger.h
#ifndef INCLUDED_AX_LEDGER
#define INCLUDED_AX_LEDGER

class ax_Record;

class ax_Ledger {
    // ...
  public:
    static int addRecord(const Record& record);
    static void cleanup();
    // ...
};

#endif
```

```
// ax_Ledger.c
#include "ax_ledger.h"
// ...

static s_initFlag = 0;

static void init()
{
    s_initFlag = 1;
    // initialize component's static constructs
}

inline void s_checkInit()
{
    if (!s_initFlag) {
        init();
    }
}

int ax_Table::addRecord(const Record& record)
{
    checkInit();
    // now go ahead and add a record
}

void ax_Table::cleanup()
{
    // clean-up component's static constructs
    s_initFlag = 0;
}

// ...
```

Figure 7-36: Check Every Time and Initialize if Necessary

Using the check-every-time technique illustrated in Figure 7-36, we do not need to initialize the component explicitly. Instead, we make sure that each function within the component that depends on internal static constructs first checks whether the component has been initialized; if not, the function initializes the component immediately. The advantages of the check-every-time approach are that it is also foolproof (for clients, anyway) and that initialization need not occur at start-up. By deferring the initialization until needed, we reduce invocation time and pay at runtime only for what we use. `iostream` employs this technique to allocate buffer space for a stream object the first time it is used (see Section 10.3.3). The disadvantage of checking on every function call is that it is often not practical for heavily used, lightweight objects. We must also remember to include this initialization check whenever we add a new function to our component.

7.8.2 Clean-Up

Often just exiting the program will accomplish what our general users want; however, as responsible developers, we must always consider the testability of our designs. There are several ways of verifying that our code does not "leak" memory; however, holding onto memory indefinitely is sometimes hard to distinguish from an actual leak—especially in regression tests. Constructs, such as multiple inheritance, that cause dynamically allocated memory to be managed by a pointer to anywhere other than the beginning of the allocated block make it difficult even for sophisticated tools to distinguish legitimate use from leaked memory.

Major Design Rule

Provide a mechanism for freeing any dynamic memory allocated to static constructs within a component.

By providing a clean-up function for each component containing static variables or objects that might harbor dynamically allocated memory, we help to ease the burden of detecting memory leaks. This requirement is presented as a major design rule because a single non-compliant component could affect the testability of any component that needs it.

One mixed blessing of the nifty-counter approach is that the destructor of the dummy object can be used to initiate the clean-up of a static construct automatically. This is good news for quality assurance, but it can present a burden for users who would prefer, for performance reasons, simply to exit. Fortunately we can always supply a "switch" in order to program whether clean-up is actually to occur at program exit. The benefit of providing this extra clean-up capability is an extra measure of quality; the only real cost is that of additional development time and of a small amount of extra complexity in the interface.

7.8.3 Review

To summarize this entire section: initializing modules and non-local static objects at start-up can make the time to invoke a large program unacceptably long. Although we cannot affect the point in the program at which these static instances are initialized, it is always possible to transform a single global instance of an object into a module. An effective way to ensure initialization without runtime cost is to design the module or component to wake up initialized by having only fundamental static data members (which are initialized at load time). Another approach to reducing invocation time is to defer initialization until it is actually needed. This deferred initialization can be accomplished using individual `init` functions or with initialization checks built into every access. The `init`-function approach is the most flexible and also the most error prone, but it may be necessary when the individual access functions are lightweight and called frequently. Explicit initialization is also required when attempting to link-in self-initializing components stored in a Unix-style library upon which there is no explicit link-time dependency. The check-every-time approach is foolproof for clients and especially appropriate when the work done in each function call is already substantial. Finally, if we know we are likely to need a component initialized immediately upon invocation and its functions are lightweight and called frequently, the nifty-counter approach may be the best choice after all. In all cases, providing a mechanism to free any dynamic memory held by static constructs (before the program exits) will facilitate regression testing for memory leaks.

7.9 Summary

In this chapter we formalized the notion of a *package* as an aggregate cohesive unit of physical design. A package is a natural consequence of top-down design that serves as both an abstraction for architects and as a partition for developers. Every package consists of an acyclic hierarchy of cooperating components. The file names for each component within a package and each global construct defined within that component should begin with the *registered* prefix allocated to that package. The dominant purpose of this prefix is to identify in which package the definition of a given component or class can be found. Consistent use of package prefixes partitions the global name space, which avoids name conflicts during package integration.

Dependencies between components within a package form a levelizable hierarchy. To test components hierarchically within a package, components contained within other packages are presumed to be correct; each external component has a level number of 0 with respect to local components. Components that do not depend on other components within the same package are defined to have a local component level number of 1. However, if package boundaries were removed, these components would not necessarily have an absolute component level of 1. Local components that do not depend on any other components within the system (called *leaf components*) have both a local and an absolute component level of 1. Placing these leaf components within the packages that use them helps to improve the modularity and reusability of the system.

Dependencies among packages are defined by the envelope of the individual dependencies between the components that comprise the packages. For reasons relating to development, marketing, usability, production, and reliability, it is required that the aggregate dependencies among packages are acyclic. Packages with acyclic dependencies form a levelizable hierarchy that is completely analogous to component levelization. Most of the techniques discussed in Chapter 5 for reducing the coupling between individual components apply to packages as a whole. In particular, escalation, demotion, and factoring are commonly used to reduce the development costs associated with interpackage dependencies.

Insulation at the package level includes reducing the number (and size) of header files that must be exported for clients to use the package. Insulating clients of a package from a particular component contained within the package requires that the component itself is not used directly by external clients of the package as a whole, all exported components that use this component insulate its definition from external clients, and the individual component is not independently reused by other packages. Whenever we insulate our clients from the underlying complexities of a subsystem, we are likely to have improved both its usability and maintainability.

Just as packages partition a system into levelizable hierarchies of components, package groups partition a large system into levelizable hierarchies of packages. Principles, such as logical cohesion and avoiding cyclic dependencies, that applied to the composition of individual packages and the interdependencies among them apply also to package groups as a whole. The library file for individual packages may be merged into a single group library file for the convenience of clients at higher levels; however, specially instrumented versions of individual package libraries should continue to be made externally accessible during development. Every package used in a system *must* continue to have a unique associated prefix irrespective of any package grouping.

Internal releases are an integral part of any large development project. A directory structure capable of supporting versioned releases was presented in Section 7.6.1. Very large systems can be partitioned into horizontal bands of package groups called *layers*. A layer corresponds to all groups on a given level. A levelizable system can be released in stages, starting at the bottom layer (group level 1) and progressing to higher-level groups. To improve insulation, abstraction, and compile-time performance for our clients, we may choose to export only a subset of all headers needed to compile a given package, group, or layer.

A *patch* is a local change to a previously released version of software. Making a patch is typically less expensive and far less disruptive than re-releasing the entire system. Our ability to patch a release is directly related to the degree to which implementation details are insulated from clients. Types of changes that probably can and cannot be realized with patches were presented in Section 7.6.2.

For a large software system written in C++, there is usually no "top"—no single program that defines the system. The purpose of `main` is only to provide a command-line interface, interpret environment variables, and manage global resources.

Factoring the underlying functionality provided by `main` into separately testable and reusable components facilitates integration into yet larger subsystems. Only the `.c` file `main` can take unilateral global actions; components that do not define `main` should avoid egocentric behavior that might compromise the integration process down the road.

Start-up is defined as the time from the moment a program is invoked until the thread of control enters `main`. It is during this period that *all* non-local static objects defined throughout the entire program are constructed. Naively ignoring the cost of such initialization can result in unacceptably long invocation times. A module can be implemented in C++ as a class containing only static members, and is preferable to a nonlocal static instance, especially when the cost of initialization is high and the need for the object is not immediate.

Four separate techniques for initializing static constructs were presented:

1. *Wake up initialized*: The static data member is of a fundamental type, which can be initialized at load time.

2. *Explicit* `init` *function*: The `init` function for a component must be called explicitly before the component can be used.

3. *Nifty counter*: A static instance of a dummy object defined in the header file of the component guarantees intialization before use (at start-up).

4. *Check every time*: Initialization occurs on demand (i.e., the first time any function in the component is called).

The choice of initialization technique will depend on several factors, including:

- The "weight" of the component
- If and when the component is likely to be used
- The cost of initializing the component itself

Effective regression testing for memory leaks dictates that we provide a way to free dynamic memory associated with static constructs—even if this feature is not required by the application itself.

PART III: LOGICAL DESIGN ISSUES

Until now, the focus has been primarily on concepts that pertain to physical design (e.g., components, levelization, insulation, and packages). Although good physical design is critical to the success of larger projects, fundamental logical design issues should be addressed by any project team early in the development process.

Logical design is a more mature and well-understood discipline than physical design. Consequently, the presentation in this part takes on a different flavor. Where possible, other readily accessible books are cited to help minimize redundancy. Part III of this book is a terse "reference manual" on the effective logical design of components.

Design patterns describe reusable micro-architectural units of cooperating components. There are countless design patterns in use in large software systems. This level of logical design is, for the most part, beyond the scope of this book; however, many of the most common design patterns are cataloged elsewhere and are readily accessible.

In this final part of the book, we limit ourselves to the design and implementation of individual components. C++ provides an almost overwhelming logical design space. This extra freedom can make finding an optimal design more complicated than is warranted by the functionality implemented by the component. Our goal is therefore to simplify the interface of each component and eliminate redundant degrees of freedom that unnecessarily complicate the logical design space.

In Chapter 8 we take a high-level look at component design—this time from a logical perspective. We consider the familiar concept of encapsulation and characterize conditions under which total encapsulation may be prohibitively expensive. We also identify and contrast various ways in which to implement auxiliary objects used only within the implementation of a component.

In Chapter 9 we focus our attention on the abundant issues that confront the component-interface author as individual behaviors are cast into the syntax of C++ operators and member functions. Whether to implement a particular behavior as a member or free operator, whether to make it virtual, how to pass in a particular argument, and how to return a value are just some of the 14 separate issues addressed. The consequences of using the various flavors of integers (e.g., `short`, `unsigned`, `long`) in the interface are also presented. We then take a close look at the issues surrounding special-case functionality such as conversion operators, compiler-generated behaviors, and—in particular—the destructor.

In Chapter 10 we tour some of the issues that face implementors of objects in a large-system environment, with one eye toward performance and the other toward reliability. Highlights include the selection and ordering of individual member data and the effective implementation of individual functions. A large part of this chapter is devoted to a quantitative analysis of the efficient customized management of an object's memory. We see that object-specific memory management can be more efficient than the conventional class-specific techniques, while avoiding the potential problem of soaking up memory in long-running programs. Finally, we explore the pitfalls of memory management in the context of generic, template-based container classes and then briefly contrast the applicability of templates with design patterns.

8

Architecting a Component

An individual object is usually too small to capture a complete concept. For an object to be effective it may require free operators, or even entire friend classes, in order to capture the essential behavior of an abstraction. An *abstraction* is an abstract specification of objects and functions that cooperate to serve some useful purpose. A *component* is a concrete representation of that specification. A component is therefore also the fundamental building block of logical design.

Encapsulation, like insulation, can be a matter of degree. The costs associated with complete encapsulation can often be prohibitively expensive. Sometimes we can attain considerable performance gains without any real loss in flexibility by settling for almost complete encapsulation. How and when to make this trade-off requires careful deliberation.

A component will occasionally need to define and use in its implementation auxiliary objects that are not intended for direct use by clients. C++ provides several techniques for implementing such classes, each with advantages and disadvantages. There are sound reasons for choosing exactly one of these approaches in most cases. Establishing the selection criteria is all that is needed. In this chapter we consider several high-level aspects of component interface design. We discuss the type and amount of functionality that is appropriate for the component as a whole as well as for the individual objects it contains. We characterize the costs associated with complete encapsulation, and present ways to reduce that cost. Finally, we survey the many ways to implement auxiliary objects within a component, and provide a rationale for making an implementation choice based on the properties emphasized by the particular usage model.

8.1 Abstractions and Components

In Chapter 3 we introduced components as atomic units of physical design. Everything placed in the header file of a component is made available at once. This physical cohesion makes a component (not a class) the smallest unit of design that is independently reusable across executable programs.

The component level is also the appropriate level for detailed logical interface design. When you, as a user, take advantage of a component implementing, say, a list abstraction (see Figure 6-19) you are probably using more than the functionality provided in the `List` class itself. For example, writing a simple output statement such as

```
cout << "list = " << list << endl;
```

involves the use of a free operator (i.e., `operator <<`) that is not part of the logical interface of any class. The `ListIter` class provides functionality, that is, an intrinsic part of the list abstraction, yet this functionality is not supplied by the interface of class `List` directly.

DEFINITION: An *abstraction* is an abstract specification of a collection of objects and related behaviors that fulfills a common purpose.

According to Stroustrup,[1] an appropriate definition of an *abstract data type* (*ADT*) is a formal abstract specification of a single object. A class (interface and implementation) would then be a concrete specification of this object. By analogy, an abstraction is also an abstract specification, with a component being the analogous concrete specification.

Principle

A *class* is a concrete specification of an ADT; a *component* is a concrete specification of an abstraction.

---

[1] **stroustrup**, Section 1.2.3, pp. 18–19.

In other words, a *component* is the realization of not just a type, but of a self-consistent microcosm of functionality that, taken as a whole, comprises what we call an *abstraction*. It is the entire abstraction, not just a single ADT, that defines a useful logical partition of the functionality within a system that is implemented by a component.

8.2 Component Interface Design

There are several aspects to the quality of a well-designed component interface.[2] At a minimum, the interface must be sufficient for intended clients to make efficient use of the abstraction that the component was designed to support. Consider a component implementing a set abstraction. The ability to

1. determine membership in the set,
2. iterate over the members of the set, or
3. remove a given member from the set

may or may not be necessary for any particular client. However, without the additional ability to add members to the set, this component will be of little use to anyone.

Principle

- **Private interfaces should be *sufficient*.**
- **Public interfaces should be *complete*.**
- **Class interfaces should be *primitive*.**
- **Component interfaces should be *minimal* yet *usable*.**

---

[2] **booch**, Section 3.6, p. 136.

If a component is not intended for public use, then, as suggested in Section 1.8, the minimal subset of functionality that does the job efficiently for its known fixed set of clients is, by definition, *sufficient.* At the other end of the spectrum, if a component is intended to be reused widely in various situations throughout a system, then we cannot necessarily know ahead of time what subset of the functionality will be needed.[3] A *complete* interface enables all operations commonly expected by users of a given abstraction to be accomplished in an efficient manner. The more remote our clients, the more likely we are to opt to err on the side of generality by trying to make the interface complete.[4]

Principle

Where practical, deferring the implementation of unneeded functionality reduces the cost of development and maintenance, and avoids prematurely committing to a precise interface or behavior.

Often a complete interface requires a more involved implementation strategy than one that would be sufficient for any individual client. Hence, a complete interface may be more expensive to implement. The more general implementation may also run more slowly than a specialized version, perhaps even on the most basic and frequently used operations.[5] Hence, a complete interface may be more expensive at runtime. A more complete interface is usually larger and more complex, incorporating less frequently used features. A larger or more complex interface makes it more difficult for clients to find and use basic features. Hence, a complete interface may be more expensive to use. Since a complete interface is more expensive according to a variety of measures, it is wise to be sure that a complete interface is warranted before implementing one.

---

[3] *Accidental reuse* implies use in situations other than for which a component was originally intended. *Intentional reuse* implies (among other things) a desire on the part of the component author to provide a complete interface and a robust implementation. If you were to link to a component that is part of a standard library of "reusable" components (e.g., STL), would you be *using* it or *reusing* it? What about `iostream`?

[4] See **meyers**, Item 18, p. 62.

[5] For example, template-based container classes that must work correctly when parameterized by arbitrary user-defined types cannot take the same liberties with bit-wise copy routines (such as `memcopy`) as could a container designed exclusively for fundamental types (see Section 10.4.2).

Between the two extremes of sufficient and complete can lie a wide middle ground. For example, it is generally true that assigning the state of one iterator to that of another is almost never performed in practice. Hence, an iterator's assignment operator can usually be declared private and left unimplemented, without affecting the usability of the component. This deliberate omission saves development time and code size, yet leaves open the possibility of adding that functionality without causing existing clients to rework their code.

DEFINITION: An operation defined on an object is *primitive* if implementing that operation efficiently implies having direct access to private details of the object.

When selecting functions for the interface of a class, our goal should be to strive for a minimum set, using *primitiveness* as a criteria. Clearly, adding and deleting members of a set are independent primitive operations. The ability to iterate over the members of a set enables a client to determine membership, suggesting that membership itself is not an independent primitive operation. However, it is likely that determining membership via iteration is fundamentally *much* less efficient than it would be if implemented with direct private access to the internal representation (e.g., by binary search). If determining membership is likely to be a frequently used operation, it would almost certainly qualify for primitive status.

Even a potentially significant performance benefit is a legitimate reason to treat an operation as primitive. Consider the `String` class of Figure 6-9. We are not sure whether we are going to have a `d_length` member in the class or not. If we do, then we will surely want to provide a primitive `length()` accessor function. If we decide against, then we will simply have `length()` forward its call to the standard C library function `strlen(const char *)` along with the underlying representation. In the latter case, there is no actual performance gain; however, unless we provide the `length()` member, there is no way to give clients the maximum benefit afforded by each implementation as we experiment back and forth between the two. Whether or not we have a `d_length` member should in no way force clients to rework their code; such considerations are part of the subtle art of encapsulation.

Principle

Keeping the functionality to a practical minimum enhances both usability and reusability.

When selecting functions for the interface of a component, our goal is again to strive for minimality, but with an eye toward usability. Supplying every conceivable operation for an abstraction in a component interface increases its girth, overwhelms its clients, and adversely effects its usability. For example, we could provide non-primitive support for replacing the top entry on the `Stack` of Figure 3-2. Although potentially useful to a few clients, most would find such functionality superfluous.

By the same argument, we could also have omitted the tests for equality in the `stack` component of Figure 3-2. Since these tests are implemented as free, non-friend functions, `operator==` and `operator!=` could instead be implemented by any developer who needs them. But if many users are developing applications that will work together in a large system, it is desirable to avoid having each user rewrite the same functions within each subsystem. Such redundancy wastes development time, executable size, and, consequently, execution time. Finding the appropriate non-primitive functionality to add to a component to make it most useful is a design goal. Often the smallest interface that accomplishes this goal is optimal.

Principle

Minimizing the use of externally defined types in a component's interface facilitates reuse in a wider variety of contexts.

The term *coupling* applies to both logical and physical designs. Physical coupling comes from placing logical entities in the same component or by creating a physical dependency of one component upon another. Logical coupling arises from types used in the interface of one component that are defined or supplied by other components.

As with physical coupling, logical coupling is best kept to a minimum. Reducing the number of external types used in the logical interface often makes a component easier to use and to maintain.

Suppose you are creating a very public interface and you need to accept character string inputs. Which interface in Figure 8-1 do you feel is more general? Your clients may have their own string class which they are accustom to using. Every general-purpose string class will know how to generate a `const char *` representation. The interface of Figure 8-1a will force your clients to use class `my_String`; the interface of Figure 8-1b will not.

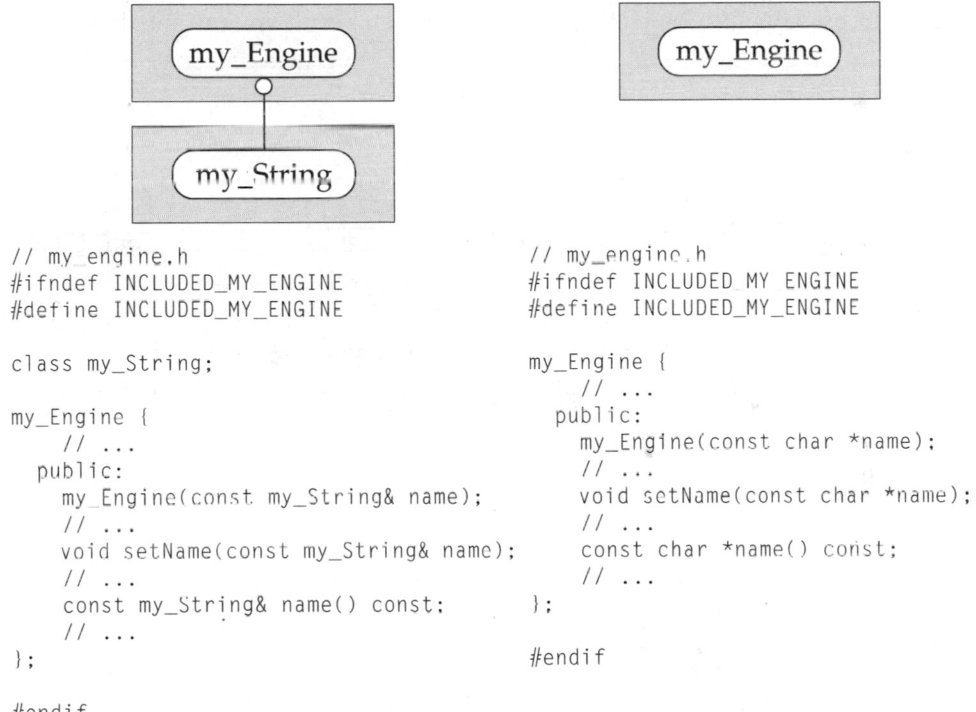


```
// my_engine.h
#ifndef INCLUDED_MY_ENGINE
#define INCLUDED_MY_ENGINE

class my_String;

my_Engine {
    // ...
  public:
    my_Engine(const my_String& name);
    // ...
    void setName(const my_String& name);
    // ...
    const my_String& name() const;
    // ...
};

#endif
```

(a) Using `my_String` in the Interface

```
// my_engine.h
#ifndef INCLUDED_MY_ENGINE
#define INCLUDED_MY_ENGINE

my_Engine {
    // ...
  public:
    my_Engine(const char *name);
    // ...
    void setName(const char *name);
    // ...
    const char *name() const;
    // ...
};

#endif
```

(b) Using `const char *` in the Interface

Figure 8-1: Avoiding Logical Coupling

The consequences of this form of logical coupling would have been even more severe had we instead elected to depend on some other non-standard component-library type (e.g., `your_String` in the interface). Until an ANSI/ISO standard string component is universally available, there will continue to be an advantage to preferring `const char *` over any other string representation in a ubiquitious interface.

In short, there are a number of high-level questions we must ask ourselves when designing the interface of a component. The most important questions is, "How public is this component?" If it will be reused in lots of different and unpredictable ways, it will need to have a reasonably complete interface. If the component is intended for private use within a package (and will not be exported), the interface should be sufficient—nothing more. In all cases we can improve the maintainability of our classes if we design their interfaces to contain only primitive functionality, pushing off useful but non-primitive functionality into separate operators or classes without private access. Finally, logical coupling often can result in unwanted physical coupling; avoiding the use of unnecessary types in the interface of a component that are defined outside that component can help to alleviate this coupling.

8.3 Degrees of Encapsulation

Encapsulation can be harder to achieve than it might at first seem. Like total insulation, total encapsulation can also be prohibitively expensive at runtime.

Figure 8-2 is an example of poor encapsulation.[6] Instead of taking an argument, each manipulator function returns a writable reference to a private data member.

```
// bad_point.h
#ifndef INCLUDED_BAD_POINT
#define INCLUDED_BAD_POINT

class bad_Point {
    int d_x;    // (may change to short later)
    int d_y;    // (may change to short later)

  public:
    // CREATORS
    bad_Point(int x, int y) : d_x(x), d_y(y) {}
    bad_Point(const bad_Point& p) : d_x(p.d_x), d_y(p.d_y) {}

    // MANIPULATORS
    bad_Point& operator=(const bad_Point& p) {
        d_x = p.x(); d_y = p.y(); return *this; }
    int& x() { return d_x; }    // bad idea
    int& y() { return d_y; }    // bad idea
```

[6] See **meyers**, Item 30, pp. 100–102.

```
        // ACCESSORS
        int x() const { return d_x; }
        int y() const { return d_y; }
    };

    #endif
```

Figure 8-2: Example of Poor Encapsulation

Figure 8-3 shows a trivial test driver for the `bad_Point` interface.

```
// bad_point.t.c
#include "bad_point.h"
#include <iostream.h>

ostream& operator<<(ostream& o, const bad_Point& p)
{
    return o << '(' << p.x() << ", " << p.y() << ')';
}

main()
{
    bad_Point pt(1,2);
    cout << pt << endl;
    pt.x() = 5;
    cout << pt << endl;
}
```

Figure 8-3: Test Driver for Poor `bad_Point` Interface

When run on the example as shown in Figure 8-2, this driver produces the following output (as expected):

```
john@john: a.out
(1, 2)
(5, 2)
john@john:
```

But now suppose we change the type of the private data members in `bad_Point` from `int` to `short`:

```
class bad_Point {
    short d_x; // OK, we changed "private" data
    short d_y; // so what?

  public:
    // ...
```

and rerun the experiment. The results have now changed to the unexpected:

```
john@john: a.out
(1, 2)
(1, 2)
john@john:
```

The problem is that the reference returned in the interface (`int&`) is inconsistent with the type of data returned (`short`). As a result, a temporary `int` is created and a writable reference to that temporary is returned. We could modify the interface functions to instead return a `short&`, but then we would have modified the interface in response to an implementation change—thereby propagating the problem to our clients.

A properly encapsulating version of the interface for `bad_Point` (like `geom_Point` in Figure 4-3) would define the manipulators to take the new value of the member to be set as a parameter:

```
main()
{
    bad_Point pt(1,2);
    cout << pt << endl;
    //pt.x() = 5;              // Returning writable reference replaced
    pt.setX(5);                // by function taking value of x coordinate.
    cout << pt << endl;
}
```

The resulting output is again as expected—regardless of whether the data members are declared `int` or `short`:

```
john@john: a.out
(1, 2)
(5, 2)
john@john:
```

Principle

A good test for encapsulation is to see whether a given interface will simultaneously support two significantly different implementation strategies without modification.

In the bad_Point example, doing it right costs nothing extra; however, in some cases, total encapsulation can be more expensive. Consider the two potential implementation strategies for a geom_Box, shown in Figure 8-4. Implementation (a) stores the lower-left and upper-right corners of the box as points embedded in the geom_Box. It is therefore possible to return both the lower-left and upper-right corners by const reference. The center point is not stored, and so it must be calculated and returned by value. Likewise, both the length and width must be calculated on demand. Implementation (b), however, stores the center point along with the width and height of the geom_Box. The center point is returned efficiently by const reference, while the lower-left and upper-right corners must be calculated and returned by value. Length and width now require no calculation, but—being fundamental types—they are returned most efficiently by value.

```
class geom_Box {
    geom_Point d_lowerLeft;
    geom_Point d_upperRight;

  public:
    // ...
    const geom_Point& lowerLeft() const;
    const geom_Point& upperRight() const;
    geom_Point center() const;
    int width() const;
    int height() const;
};
```

(a) Stores Lower-Left and Upper-Right Corners

```
class geom_Box {
    geom_Point d_center;
    int d_width;
    int d_height;

  public:
    // ...
    geom_Point lowerLeft() const;
    geom_Point upperRight() const;
    const geom_Point& center() const;
    int width() const;
    int height() const;
};
```

(b) Stores Center, Width, and Height

Figure 8-4: Two Implementation Strategies for a geom_Box Class

Principle

A fully encapsulating interface may impose a significant performance burden on a given implementation.

Part of the advantage of one implementation over the other is in avoiding the expense of constructing the most frequently accessed point and instead returning it efficiently by reference. Strictly speaking, however, these two interfaces, though similar, are not programmatically identical. For example, in implementation (b), it is possible to take the address of the center point, while in implementation (a) it is not. Encapsulating all aspects of the implementation would necessitate returning all three points (i.e., from `lowerLeft`, `center`, and `upperRight`) by value, or passing in the address of a previously constructed point whose value is to be assigned. In the case of `geom_Box`, a fully encapsulating interface would eliminate much of the performance gain of one implementation over another.

A classic example where encapsulation is not complete can be found in virtually any general-purpose string class, which for efficiency will invariably provide direct access as a `const char *` to its internal null-terminated string representation. Clearly this interface constrains the internal implementation, forcing it to maintain a valid null-terminated string representation as long as the string object is not modified or deleted. However, a more encapsulating interface turns out to be too expensive or inconvenient to be popular.

Another example where the interface constrains the implementation for efficiency can be found in an unbounded array abstraction in which a writable reference to an indexed object is returned. As illustrated in Figure 8-5a for an array of points, this style of interface forces the implementation to maintain the same space for a `geom_Point` object once it has been referenced. Any attempt by the array to relocate the object would invalidate references held by clients.

```
class geom_PointArray {
    // ...
  public:
    // ...
    geom_Point& operator[](int index);
    const geom_Point& operator[](int index) const;
    // ...
};
```

Figure 8-5a: Partially Encapsulating Interface (Array A)

By contrast, a naive, fully encapsulated version would provide functions to get and set a particular element, as illustrated in Figure 8-5b. Notice that this interface is completely general. There is nothing to stop us from storing the points internally as, say, two parallel arrays of integers. We might decide to implement some kind of in-core compression scheme for points. We might even think about swapping part of a large array out to disk.

```
class geom_PointArray {
    // ...
  public:
    // ...
    geom_Point point(int index) const;
    void setPoint(const geom_Point& point, int index);
    // ...
};
```

Figure 8-5b: Naive Fully Encapsulating Interface (Array B)

Principle

Passing in the address of a previously constructed object to be assigned the return value (called *return by argument*) can improve performance while preserving total encapsulation.

Although this new interface does nothing to limit our implementation choice, the runtime cost of using this fully encapsulating interface could be substantially more expensive—even when the two underlying implementations are identical. For less lightweight elements (i.e., being significantly larger, having a non-inline copy constructor, or requiring dynamic memory allocation at construction), a fully encapsulating version of the interface could be prohibitively expensive at runtime.

Fortunately, there is another fully encapsulating form of the interface that does afford some relief for "heavier" objects, particularly when accessing their values. Returning an object by value will result in construction (and destruction) of at least one temporary of the indexed type. As Figure 8-5c illustrates, we can pass in a writable pointer to an existing object instead of returning the object by value. Assigning the value of the existing object (just once) can often be accomplished with relative efficiency.

```
class geom_PointArray {
    // ...
  public:
    // ...
    void getPoint(geom_Point *returnValue, int index) const;
    void setPoint(const geom_Point& point, int index);
    // ...
};
```

Figure 8-5c: Alternate Fully Encapsulating Interface (Array C)

To make this all concrete, I created a single *experimental* version of a `PointArray` class with all three modes of access available simultaneously. The contents of Figure 8-6 were placed at the top of a driver file used to compare the relative performance of these three modes of operation.

```
// pointarray.t.c
#include "point.h"
#include <memory.h>                // memcpy()

class PointArray {
    Point **d_array_p;             // array of pointers to Point objects
    int d_size;                    // current physical size of "unbounded" array
    Point d_dummy;                 // not static to avoid construction at startup

  private:
    void resize(int maxIndex);  // extend array of Point pointers when needed

    PointArray(const PointArray& array);                // not implemented
    PointArray& operator=(const PointArray& array);     // not implemented

  public:
    // CREATORS
    PointArray(int size) : d_array_p(0), d_size(0), d_dummy(0,0)
    {
        resize(size - 1);                                // Code reuse is good.
    }

    ~PointArray();

    // MANIPULATORS
    Point& operator[](int index)                        // ARRAY A
    {
        if (index >= d_size) {
            resize (index);
        }
        return *d_array_p[index];
    }

    void setPoint(const Point& point, int index)        // ARRAY B & C
    {
        if (index >= d_size) {
            resize (index);
        }
        *d_array_p[index] = point;
    }

    // ACCESSORS
    int size() const { return d_size; }                 // ARRAY A, B, C
```

```
    const Point& operator[](int index) const            // ARRAY A
    {
        return index >= d_size ? d_dummy : *d_array_p[index];
    }

    Point point(int index) const                        // ARRAY B
    {
        return index >= d_size ? d_dummy : *d_array_p[index];
    }

    void getPoint(Point *returnValue, int index) const // ARRAY C
    {
        *returnValue = index >= d_size ? d_dummy : *d_array_p[index];
    }
};

PointArray::~PointArray()
{
    for (int i = 0; i < d_size; ++i) {
        delete d_array_p[i];
    }
    delete [] d_array_p;
}

void PointArray::resize(int maxIndex)
{
    int newSize = maxIndex + 1;
    Point **p = d_array_p;
    d_array_p = new Point *[newSize];
    memcpy (d_array_p, p, d_size * sizeof *p);
    delete p;
    for (int i = d_size; i < newSize; ++i) {
        d_array_p[i] = new Point(0,0);
    }
    d_size = newSize;
}
```

Figure 8-6: Experimental `PointArray` Class Implementation

The first test was to compare the relative efficiency of reading the *x* coordinate of the first 1,000 points of the array and accumulating this value in the variable sum. This experiment was run for each of the three array interfaces as presented in Figure 8-7. To illustrate the effect the "weight" of the object can have on the interface, the three different `Point` implementations used in the experiment of Figure 6-83 were reused here as well.[7]

[7] Data presented represents fully optimized code.

```
main()
{
    int arraySize = 1000;
    int sum = 0;
    PointArray array(arraySize);
    const PointArray& constArray = array;   // Provide a const reference to
    // ...                                  // enable the invocation of the
                                            // const version of operator[]
// INTERFACE A:
    {
        for (int j = 0; j < arraySize; ++j) {
            sum += constArray[j].x();
        }
    }

// INTERFACE B:
    {
        for (int j = 0; j < arraySize; ++j) {
            sum += constArray.point(j).x();
        }
    }

// INTERFACE C:
    {
        Point pt(0,0);
        for (int j = 0; j < arraySize; ++j) {
            constArray.getPoint(&pt, j);
            sum += pt.x();
        }
    }
}
```

Figure 8-7: Experimental `PointArray` "Reading" Driver

Figure 8-8 provides the results of comparing these three different interfaces styles for accessing `Point` objects within the same array. Using the original `Point` class (line 1) with all its functions declared inline, the cost of total encapsulation is only minimally more for the naive encapsulation of ARRAY B (111%) and nonexistent for the full encapsulation of ARRAY C (100%). Removing the inline functions from the contained `Point` type (line 2) makes both constructing and assigning to `Point` objects somewhat more expensive. Part of the runtime advantage of ARRAY C (168%) over ARRAY B (271%) is that the `Point` assignment is occurring exactly once per array access without the extra constructor (and destructor) calls generally needed to return an object by value. For a contained object that allocates dynamic memory on construction (line 3), the cost of construction (1,673%) well exceeds the cost of assigning the new value in place (169%). From this data we conclude that there can be substantial gains in performance for fully encapsulated classes if we return heavyweight objects through the argument list instead of by value.

Line	Description of Point Class	Partially Encapsulating ARRAY A	Totally Encapsulating ARRAY B	Also Totally Encapsulating ARRAY C
1.	Original Point Class (light)	0.222 (100%)	0.247 (111%)	0.222 (100%)
2.	Without Inline Functions (medium)	0.296 (100%)	0.802 (271%)	0.497 (168%)
3.	Fully Insulating Version (heavy)	0.369 (100%)	6.173 (1,673%)	0.622 (169%)

loop time in milliseconds on SUN SPARC 20
(time as percentage of Array A's time)

Figure 8-8: Relative Costs of Accessing a `PointArray` Element

The second test was to compare the relative efficiency of setting the *x* coordinate of the first 1,000 points of the array while leaving the *y* coordinate unchanged. Note that interface A allows us to accomplish this operation directly, while interfaces B and C force us to first get the current value of the entire point. This experiment, illustrated in Figure 8-9, was also run for each of the three array interfaces and for each of the three `Point` implementations. The results are tabulated in Figure 8-10.

```
main()
{
    arraySize = 1000;
    PointArray array(arraySize);
    PointArray& nonConstArray = array; // provide non-const reference.
    // ...

// INTERFACE A:
    {
        for (int j = 0; j < arraySize; ++j) {
            nonConstArray[j].setX(j);
        }
    }
```

```
    // INTERFACE B:
        {
            for (int j = 0; j < arraySize; ++j) {
                nonConstArray.setPoint(Point(j, nonConstArray.point(j).y()), j);
            }
        }

    // INTERFACE C:
        {
            Point pt(0,0);
            for (int j = 0; j < arraySize; ++j) {
                nonConstArray.getPoint(&pt, j);
                nonConstArray.setPoint(Point(j, pt.y()), j);
            }
        }
}
```

Figure 8-9: Experimental `PointArray` "Writing" Driver

Line	Description of Point Class	Partially Encapsulating ARRAY A	Totally Encapsulating ARRAY B	Also Totally Encapsulating ARRAY C
1.	Original Point Class (light)	0.162 (100%)	0.403 (249%)	0.336 (226%)
2.	Without Inline Functions (medium)	0.242 (100%)	1.451 (503%)	1.118 (418%)
3.	Fully Insulating Version (heavy)	0.385 (100%)	12.901 (3,551%)	6.669 (1,732%)

loop time in milliseconds on SUN SPARC 20
(time as percentage of Array A's time)

Figure 8-10: Relative Costs of Manipulating a `PointArray` Element

Based on the results of this experiment, we can conclude that providing a writable reference to the contained object can have profound performance benefits that increase dramatically with the weight of the object. For fully insulating classes, some degree of relief is provided by returning the original value through the argument list.

Principle

Settling for less than full encapsulation is sometimes the right choice.

Fully encapsulating interfaces should be a design goal. However, if performance is also a design goal, then extravagant implementation choices must be ruled out regardless of the degree of encapsulation. By making reasonable assumptions, we can achieve superior performance while preserving the flexibility we need in order to modify our implementation within appropriate limits.

As a final aside, we should note a subtle problem with the interface of the unencapsulated version of this array. There are two versions of the `[]` operator:

```
operator[](int index)
```

and

```
operator[](int index) const.
```

The first of these operators can potentially resize the array; the second cannot. If this array were implemented as a "sparse array," the space for a `Point` (or a significantly bigger object) might deliberately be left unallocated until referenced by the non-`const` version of `operator[]`. With this interface, the act of merely "reading" a non-`const` array object will implicitly populate it. It would be far more practical to skip the operator overloading and choose distinct *function* names for these operations. Doing so would make this array far less prone to subtle misuse that could result in grossly excessive allocations of memory.

To summarize: encapsulation is a cornerstone of good object-oriented design; its goal is to minimize the logical dependency of clients on the details of an implementation across an interface. More complete encapsulation affords implementors greater flexibility in their choice of implementation. Yet, like insulation, total encapsulation for a very low-level object can be prohibitively expensive at runtime.

If performance is a design goal, then certain implementation choices (e.g., object compression and swapping to disk) must be ruled out anyway. By making reasonable assumptions, learned through experience, we can attain most of the benefit of encapsulation without incurring excessive and unnecessary runtime cost. When total encapsulation is appropriate, we can sometimes reduce its runtime cost by passing in a previously constructed object to load instead of returning the object by value.

8.4 Auxiliary Implementation Classes

Often a component will make use of one or more tiny *auxiliary* classes in its implementation that are not programmatically accessible in the interfaces of the principal classes defined in that component. Two characteristics help to distinguish an auxiliary implementation class from other kinds of classes:

1. The class is intended for the sole purpose of implementing a component and is not intended for direct use (or reuse) outside that component.

2. The class is trivial and may not warrant direct testing.

The `Link` class of the list component shown in Figure 6-19 is a case in point. There are a variety of ways to realize such implementation classes, each with its advantages and disadvantages. In this section we explore the pros and cons of a variety of design options.

Consider a simple integer list class shown in Figure 8-11a. Class my_Link is an implementation detail of my_List, and is not programmatically accessible from my_List. In this implementation, the auxiliary class definition is placed in the header file of the component defining the primary class. This straightforward approach is the simplest and most common method of implementing components using such auxiliary classes.

```
// my_list.h
#ifndef INCLUDED_MY_LIST
#define INCLUDED_MY_LIST

class my_Link {
    int d_data;
    my_Link *d_next_p;

  public:
    // ...
};

class my_List {
    my_Link *d_head_p;
    // ...
  public:
    // ...
};

#endif
```

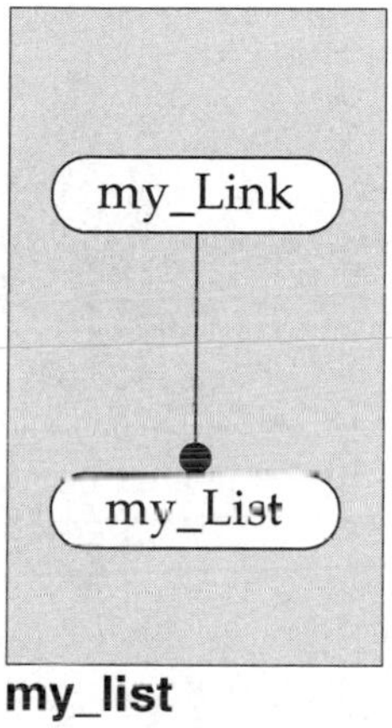

Figure 8-11a: (Original) File Scope Implementation of my_Link **(A)**

We could put the link class in its own component, as illustrated in Figure 8-11b. This arrangement has the advantage of allowing us to test (and even reuse) my_Link independently of my_List. But for tiny implementation classes such as my_Link, the coupling brought about by reuse along with the extra physical complexity of a second component makes this an unlikely choice.

```
// my_list.h
#ifndef INCLUDED_MY_LIST
#define INCLUDED_MY_LIST

class my_Link;

class my_List {
    my_Link *d_head_p;
    // ...
  public:
    // ...
};

#endif
```

```
// my_link.h
#ifndef INCLUDED_MY_LINK
#define INCLUDED_MY_LINK

class my_Link {
    int d_data;
    my_Link *d_next_p;

  public:
    // ...
};

#endif
```

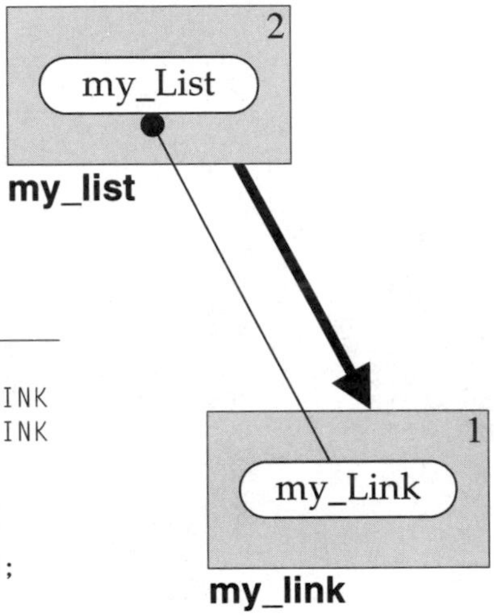

Figure 8-11b: Separate Component Implementation of my_Link (B)

We could declare my_List a friend of class my_Link and make all of the link's functions private, as suggested in Figure 8-11c. Making my_Link a "slave" class of my_List prevents clients of component my_list from using my_Link directly; however, access for direct testing is also precluded.

```
// my_list.h
#ifndef INCLUDED_MY_LIST
#define INCLUDED_MY_LIST

class my_List;

class my_Link {
    int d_data;
    my_Link *d_next_p;
    friend my_List;
    // ...
};

class my_List {
    my_Link *d_head_p;
    // ...
  public:
    // ...
};

#endif
```

my_Link
my_List
my_list

Figure 8-11c: Slave Class Implementation of `my_Link` **(C)**

We could make the `my_Link` class a local definition, contained entirely within the `.c` file, as illustrated in Figure 8-11d. This design would serve to insulate clients from `my_Link`. However, in addition to precluding direct testing, this design would also preclude inlining any members of `my_List` that made substantive use of `my_Link`. If component `my_list` had also contained an iterator, not being able to inline iterator functions might have significantly degraded runtime performance.

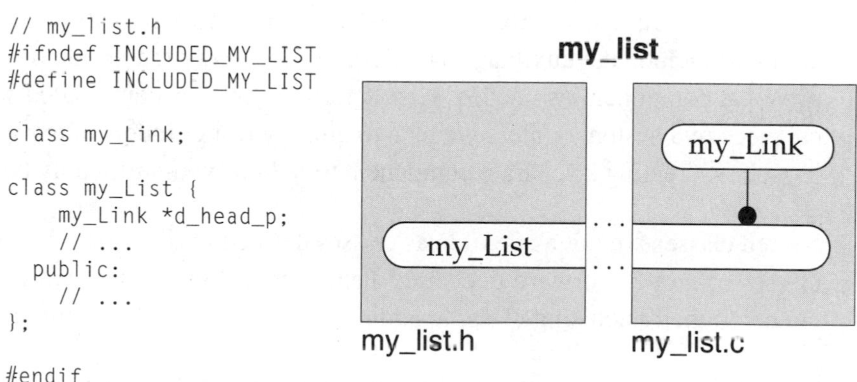

```
// my_list.h
#ifndef INCLUDED_MY_LIST
#define INCLUDED_MY_LIST

class my_Link;

class my_List {
    my_Link *d_head_p;
    // ...
  public:
    // ...
};

#endif
```


Figure 8-11d: Local Class Implementation of `my_Link` **(D)**

Finally, we could make the my_Link class a private (or public) nested class whose definition is contained entirely within class my_List, as illustrated in Figure 8-11e. This implementation would not insulate clients from the details of my_Link, but it would permit members of my_Link to be used in the bodies of inline members of my_List (and my_ListIter). Making my_Link a nested class avoids affecting the global name space; making it private makes it encapsulated and therefore not directly usable (or testable).

```
// my_list.h
#ifndef INCLUDED_MY_LIST
#define INCLUDED_MY_LIST

class my_List {
    class my_Link {
        int d_data;
        my_Link *d_next_p;

      public:
        // ...
    };

    my_Link *d_head_p;
    // ...
  public:
    // ...
};
```

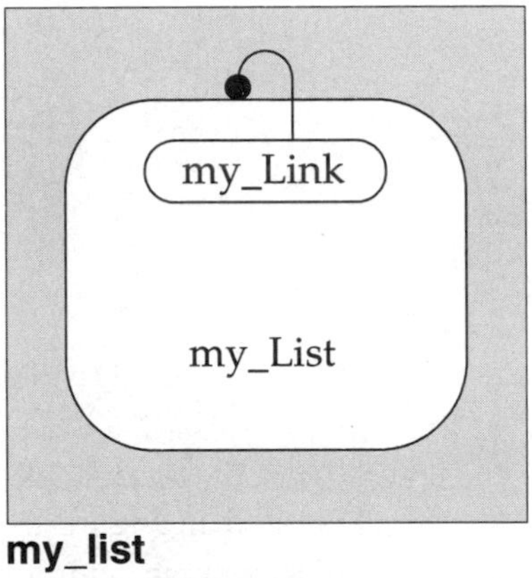

Figure 8-11e: Nested Class Implementation of my_Link **(E)**

The advantages of each of the implementation alternatives for the my_Link class presented in this section are summarized in Figure 8-12. Placing my_Link in a separate component (implementation B) is clearly the most flexible, allowing the component author to include the auxiliary class definition in either the .c file or the .h file of the principal component as needed. However, there is a cost associated with each physical piece of a system. Unless we plan to directly test or independently reuse the auxiliary class, creating a separate component to hold it would probably be unwarranted.

Nested classes are not as flexible as classes defined at file scope. For example, nested classes cannot be forward declared;[8] hence, nested classes cannot be insulated from clients of their enclosing class. In addition, nested types are notationally cumbersome

[8] The ANSI/ISO committee has adopted a proposal to allow the forward declaration of nested classes in C++. See **stroustrup94**, Section 13.5, pp. 289–290.

and cause excessive clutter in the physical interface. The syntax of the nested implementation inhibits our conveniently transplanting the auxiliary class to the `.c` file or to another component, should we later decide to insulate or reuse it.

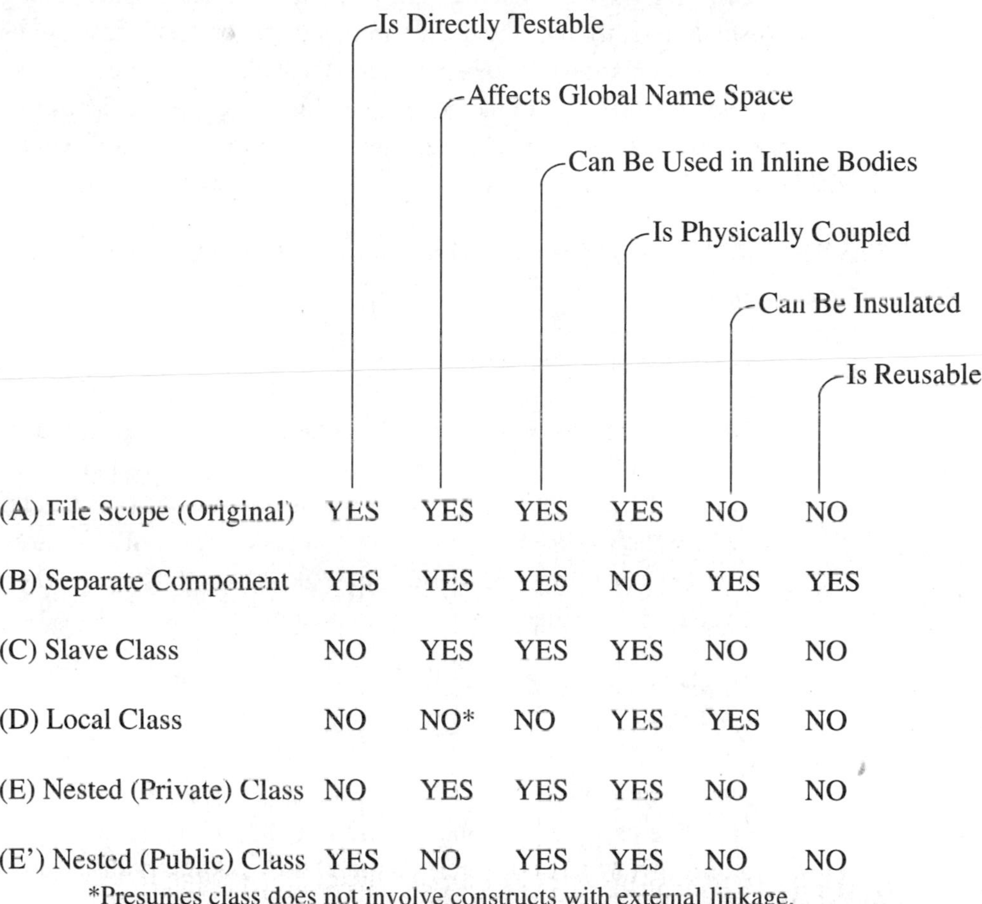

	Is Directly Testable	Affects Global Name Space	Can Be Used in Inline Bodies	Is Physically Coupled	Can Be Insulated	Is Reusable
(A) File Scope (Original)	YES	YES	YES	YES	NO	NO
(B) Separate Component	YES	YES	YES	NO	YES	YES
(C) Slave Class	NO	YES	YES	YES	NO	NO
(D) Local Class	NO	NO*	NO	YES	YES	NO
(E) Nested (Private) Class	NO	YES	YES	YES	NO	NO
(E') Nested (Public) Class	YES	NO	YES	YES	NO	NO

*Presumes class does not involve constructs with external linkage.

Figure 8-12: Summary of Various Auxiliary Class Implementation Advantages

The original implementation (A) and the public nested implementation (E') have similar properties. The one benefit of the nested public design is that it does not affect the global name space. Considering the disadvantages of nested classes described above, if you're going to make a nested class public, why not just prefix its name and define it at file scope in the `.h` file (as in implementation A)?

Though not insulated, private nested classes are truly encapsulated and cannot be accessed by clients of the primary objects, nor can they be directly tested. The slave class implementation (C) is almost identical to the private nested class implementation (E), except that the class itself is part of the global name space, though still not usable or testable directly. The local class implementation (D) is also similar to a private nested implementation (E), except that the local classes are insulated from clients and therefore cannot be used in the bodies of inline functions of the primary classes. For more on classes without external linkage, see Section 3.2 (immediately following the discussion of Figure 3-7).

The best choice in any given situation will depend on the answers to the following three questions:

x. Does the auxiliary component warrant direct testing?

   In our `list` component, the `Link` class will automatically be tested with 100 percent coverage just by testing the `List` class under normal conditions; there is no practical advantage to testing `Link` directly. In cases where the auxiliary class is more complex, we should probably allow for direct access, which would eliminate slave (C), local (D), or private nested (E) auxiliary class implementations.

y. Does the component expose inline functions that require access to the auxiliary class?

   If the component's header does not define inline functions that make substantive use of an auxiliary class, that class can be insulated from clients and is often best implemented locally (D). However, if the auxiliary class is complex enough to warrant direct testing, the class should be implemented using either (A) or (B).

z. Will the component be used widely?

   If the component is used only in the implementation of a single subsystem, then there may be no need to get fancy. The original implementation (A) will often be a good choice.

A decision tree to aid in making the decision is provided in Figure 8-13.

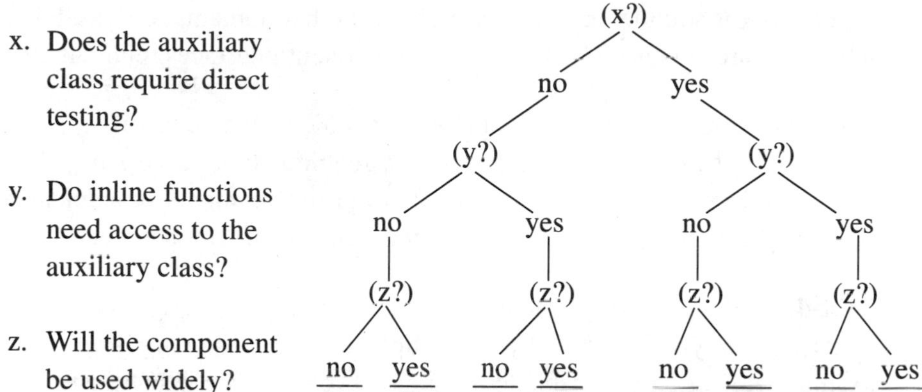

*The header for the auxiliary class is included in the `.h` file instead of the `.c` file of the principal component.

Figure 8-13: Deciding Which Auxiliary Class Implementation to Use

To sum up: defining auxiliary classes in the same header file as the primary classes is common; often this approach is adequate, if not optimal. Where possible, we would like to insulate auxiliary classes from our clients by hiding them in the `.c` file or, if necessary for testing, placing them in a separate component. For lightweight components that are widely used, we may be forced to use slave or private nested classes to enforce our sole ownership of the auxiliary class. This section is intended as a guideline and is not a substitute for the application of common sense.

8.5 Summary

Components serve jointly as effective units of both logical and physical design. An abstraction is an abstract specification of closely related objects and (operator) functions; a component (interface and implementation) is the corresponding concrete realization.

There are several competing aspects to consider when creating the high-level specification for a component. For components designed as part of a specific subsystem, we require only that the interface be sufficient for its intended clients. For components that will be used for various purposes throughout a large system, we expect the interfaces to be complete. By *sufficient* we imply that the interface is suitable for solving a particular instance of a problem in some domain. By *complete* we mean that the interface is suitable for solving an arbitrary problem in that domain. Both usability and maintainability are enhanced by keeping all component interfaces minimal.

Operations defined as members of individual objects should be *primitive*. An operation is primitive if its efficient implementation requires direct access to private details of the class. Operations that are useful but not primitive should be implemented outside of the object in terms of primitive functions, and should not be granted friend status.

User-defined types used in the interface of a component imply a strong logical dependency on that type. As with physical coupling, logical coupling is best minimized. For example, it is often preferable to use a `const char *` parameter instead of some particular string class in order to avoid unnecessary logical coupling, especially if the interface will be used by a variety of clients in many different contexts.

Encapsulation is a property of an object that enables the implementation of that object to be modified without affecting its logical interface. Sometimes total encapsulation can be prohibitively expensive. However, encapsulation, like insulation, need not be absolute in order to be useful. Often we can make reasonable assumptions that allow us to achieve our performance goals, and still preserve sufficient encapsulation to allow us to continue to modify the implementation within reasonable limits. If total encapsulation is required, we can sometimes achieve a sizable performance gain by passing in a previously constructed object as a writable argument to be loaded with the result, rather than returning the result by value. The performance gain for *return by argument* over *return by value* is even more pronounced for heavyweight objects that manage internal dynamic memory.

When implementing a component, there is often a need to create one or more auxiliary classes. These classes are not accessible through the interface(s) of the primary object(s) defined in the component. These classes are implementation details of the component and are simple enough that they may not require independent testing. The following strategies have been identified for implementing auxiliary classes:

- At file scope in the `.h` file.
- In a separate component.
- As a slave class of one or more primary classes.
- In the `.c` file of the component.

- As a private (or public) nested class of a primary class.

Figure 8-12 identifies the various advantages of these implementation strategies for auxiliary classes with respect to the following questions:

- Is the auxiliary class directly testable?
- Does the auxiliary class affect the global name space?
- Can the auxiliary class be used in inline function bodies?
- Is the auxiliary class physically coupled?
- Can the auxiliary class be insulated from clients?
- Is the auxiliary class independently reusable?

Figure 8-13 provides a decision tree that can be used to select the appropriate implementation for an auxiliary class based on the context in which it will be used.

9

Designing a Function

The goal of function design is to provide safe, easy, and efficient access to the behaviors defined by an abstraction. The C++ language provides great latitude when it comes to specifying the interface at the function level. Whether to make a function an operator, whether it should be a member or free operator, how arguments should be passed, and how values should be returned are all part of this level of the design process. There are reasons beyond style that play a role in making these design decisions, many of which we touch on in this chapter.

The C++ language places a variety of flavors of fundamental integer types (such as `short`, `unsigned`, `long`, etc.) at our disposal. These types represent yet another degree of freedom that, if used thoughtlessly, can complicate and even weaken an interface.

A user-defined conversion operator allows the compiler to convert implicitly to or from a user-defined type. Careful design requires weighing the possible advantages of implicit conversion against ambiguities and potential for errors caused by the resulting degradation in type safety. Certain other functions, if not explicitly specified, will be defined automatically by the compiler if needed. Deciding when these compiler-generated function definitions are good enough requires thoughtful consideration.

In this chapter we provide a framework in which to design the interface of a component, but at the level of detail of an individual function. We examine the excessively large design space available to component authors and identify design decisions that have shown themselves to be either beneficial or counter productive. We see how many unnecessary degrees of freedom in the design space of the functional interface can be eliminated without any loss in effectiveness. The resulting framework can then help guide us toward simpler, more uniform, and more maintainable interfaces.

9.1 Function Interface Specification

There is a list of issues one must address when specifying the interface of a function in C++ in accordance with the ground rules presented in Chapter 2:

1. Operator or non-operator function?
2. Free or member operator?
3. Virtual or non-virtual function?
4. Pure or non-pure virtual member function?
5. Static or non-static member function?
6. `const` or non-`const` member function?
7. Public, protected, or private member function?
8. Return by value, reference, or pointer?
9. Return `const` or non-`const`?
10. Argument is optional or required?
11. Pass argument by value, reference, or pointer?
12. Pass argument as `const` or non-`const`?

There are two organizational issues that, although not part of the logical interface, must also be addressed:

13. Friend or non-friend function?
14. Inline or non-inline function?

There is a great deal of interplay among these issues; typically the answer to one question will imply or at least affect the answer to another. In what follows we address each of these issues individually, and provide guidelines for making optimal design decisions.[1]

9.1.1 Operator or Non-Operator Function

Apart from the compiler-generated operators (e.g., assignment), the only reason to make a function an operator is for the notational convenience of the client. Note that,

[1] See also **meyers**, Item 19, p. 70.

unlike function notation, operator notation is not context sensitive; the resulting function call resolution of an operator invoked from a member function will be the same as if invoked at file scope.[2] When used judiciously, operator overloading has a natural and obvious advantage over the functional notation—especially for user-defined logical and arithmetic types.

```
#include "pub_intset.h"
#include <iostream.h>

main()
{
    pub_IntSet a, b, c, d, e, f;

    a += 1; a += 3; a += 5; a += 7;
    b += 1; b += 2; b += 3; b += 4;
    c = a + b; d = a*b; e = a - b;


    f = a*b*c + b*c*d + c*d*e;















    cout << f << endl;
}
```

(a) With Operator Overloading

```
#include "pub_intset.h"
#include <iostream.h>

main()
{
    pub_IntSet a, b, c, d, e, f;

    a.add(1); a.add(3); a.add(5); a.add(7);
    b.add(1); b.add(2); b.add(3); b.add(4);
    c = pub_IntSet::or(a, b);
    d = pub_IntSet::and(a, b);
    e = pub_IntSet::sub(a, b);
    f = pub_IntSet::or(
        pub_IntSet::or(
            pub_IntSet::and(
                pub_IntSet::and(a, b),
                c
            ),
            pub_IntSet::and(
                pub_IntSet::and(b, c),
                d
            )
        ),
        pub_IntSet::and(
            pub_IntSet::and(c, d),
            e
        )
    );

    pub_IntSet::print(cout, f) << endl;
}
```

(b) Without Operator Overloading

Figure 9-1: Two Usage Models for an Integer Set Abstraction

Consider the two different usage models shown in Figure 9-1, corresponding to two different interfaces for an integer set component, `pub_intset`. Figure 9-1a illustrates how operator notation can be used effectively. The nature of the set abstraction makes

[2] **ellis**, Section 13.4.1, p. 332.

the meanings of these operators intuitive, even for developers not familiar with this particular component. Figure 9-1b shows the equivalent computation using the more bulky function call notation.[3]

Principle

Readability (more than ease of use) should be the primary reason for employing operator overloading.

In this integer set application, the operator notation clearly enhances both readability and ease of use. By *readability*, we mean the ability of a software engineer to discern, quickly and accurately, the intended behavior of a body of unfamiliar source code. *Ease of use* refers to how easily a developer can use the object effectively to create new software. Any typical body of source code is read many more times than it is written ("For most large, long-lifetime software systems maintenance costs exceed development costs by factors ranging from 2 to 4"[4]), so it makes practical sense to favor readability over ease of use in the long run.

Guideline

The semantics of an overloaded operator should be natural, obvious, and intuitive to clients.

It is easy to come up with cute and easy-to-use applications for operators that have no intuitive meaning for developers unfamiliar with your component. Sophomoric antics, such as defining unary `operator~` as a member of a string class to reverse the string in place, are obviously out of place in a large-scale development environment. The litmus test for determining when to supply operator notation should be whether

[3] We have made some of the member functions static to enable the same symmetric implicit conversion of arguments, as do the corresponding operators (see Section 9.1.5). The indentation style of the deeply nested function calls in Figure 9-1b is borrowed from languages such as LISP and CLOS where such constructs occur frequently.

[4] **sommerville**, Section 1.2.1, p. 10.

there is a natural and intuitive meaning—immediately obvious to new clients—that improves (or at the very least maintains) the level of readability.[5]

Guideline

The syntactic properties of overloaded operators for user-defined types should mirror the properties already defined for the fundamental types.

At a semantic level, it is quite difficult to provide specific guidelines as to what is and what is not intuitive. However, at a syntactic level we can make a number of strong and well-defined statements based on the implementation of the fundamental types in the language.

Principle

Patterning the syntactic properties of user-defined operators after the predefined C++ operators avoids surprises and makes their usage more predictable.

In the C++ language, every expression has a value. There are two basic types of values, called *lvalues* and *rvalues*.[6] An lvalue is a value whose address can be taken. If an lvalue can be on the "left" of an assignment statement, it is said to be a *modifiable* lvalue; otherwise it is said to be a *non-modifiable* lvalue.[7] An rvalue cannot be assigned to nor can its address be taken.[8] The simplest lvalued expression is a variable identifier itself. Unless the variable is declared `const`, it is a modifiable lvalue.

[5] See also **cargill**, Chapter 5, p. 91.

[6] Originally these terms came from classic C: the term *lvalue* meant that the value of an expression could appear on the left of an assignment statement while an *rvalue* could appear only on the right. With the advent of `const` in C++ and ANSI C, lvalues are now divided into two flavors: modifiable and non-modifiable (see **stroustrup**, Section 2.1.2, p. 46–47).

[7] **ellis**, Section 3.7, p. 25–26.

[8] Bit fields are an exception in that they can appear on the left of an assignment statement, yet according to the ARM (**ellis**, Section 9.6, p. 184), the address of a bit field may not be taken. The same is true for unnamed temporaries of a user-defined type (see Section 9.1.2).

Certain operators, such as assignment (=) and its variations (`+=  -=  *=  /=  ^=  &=  |=  ~=  %=  >>=  <<=`), pre-increment (`++x`), and pre-decrement (`--x`) all return modifiable lvalues when applied to fundamental types. These operators *always* return a writable reference to the modified argument. For example the hypothetical definition of these operators for the fundamental type `double` (if implemented as a C++ class) might look as shown in Figure 9-2.

```
class double {                              // Note: not legal C++
    // ...
  public:
    double() {}
    double(int);
    double(const double&);
    ~double() {}

    double& operator=(const double& d);
    double& operator+=(const double& d);
    double& operator-=(const double& d);
    double& operator*=(const double& d);
    double& operator/=(const double& d);

    double& operator++();                   // pre-increment ++x
    double& operator++();                   // pre-decrement --x
    double operator++(int);                 // post-increment x++
    double operator--(int);                 // post-decrement x--

    double *operator&();                    // unary address operator
    const double *operator&() const ;       // unary address operator
};

double operator+(const double& d);          // unary +
double operator-(const double& d);          // unary -

int operator!(const double& d);             // unary logical "not"

int operator&&(const double& left, const double& right);
int operator||(const double& left, const double& right);

double operator+(const double& left, const double& right);
double operator-(const double& left, const double& right);
double operator*(const double& left, const double& right);
double operator/(const double& left, const double& right);

int operator==(const double& left, const double& right);
int operator!=(const double& left, const double& right);
int operator< (const double& left, const double& right);
int operator<=(const double& left, const double& right);
int operator> (const double& left, const double& right);
int operator>=(const double& left, const double& right);
```

Figure 9-2: Hypothetical Implementation of Fundamental Type `double`

Other operators shown in Figure 9-2 return an rvalue because there is no appropriate lvalue to return. In the case of symmetric binary operators (such as + and *), the value to be returned is neither the left argument nor the right argument but a new value derived from both; consequently the return must be by value.[9] Equality (== !=) and relational (< <= > >=) operators always return an `int` type rvalue of either `0` or `1`; clearly neither of the input arguments would be appropriate to return here either. The post-increment and post-decrement operators are an interesting special case in that they are the only operators that modify the object and yet have no appropriate lvalue to return:

```
double double::operator++(int)          double double::operator--(int)
{                                       {
    double tmp = *this;                     double tmp = *this;
    ++*this;                                --*this;
    return tmp;                             return tmp;
}                                       }
```

As a more subtle example, consider the two usage models corresponding to a generic symbol table abstraction shown in Figure 9-3. In both cases, a symbol table—parameterized by type `int`—is constructed, two symbols are added, and the value of symbol "foo" is looked up by name. Since it is entirely possible that a symbol with the specified name does not exist in the table, it is not appropriate for the function doing the lookup to return its result by value or reference; hence the value is returned by pointer. (Notice how and to what degree we have just taken liberty with encapsulation.) But compare this usage with what we normally expect when we apply `operator[]` to a fundamental array of `int`. We expect to get back a reference to the indexed value, not a pointer which may be null. This difference in usage between the `operator[]` in Figure 9-3a and the usage of `operator[]` for fundamental types tends to make the function call notation of Figure 9-3b preferable in this case. Reserving the operator notation for those cases where the syntax closely mirrors the corresponding fundamental syntax reinforces the effectiveness of operator overloading.

---

[9] For a more detailed explanation, see **meyers**, Item 23, pp. 82–84.

```
#include "gen_symtab.h"

main()
{
    gen_SymTab<int> s;
    s("foo", 1); // operator()
    s("bar", 2); // (bad idea)
    const int *val = s["foo"];
    // ...
```

(a) With Operator Overloading

```
#include "gen_symtab.h"

main()
{
    gen_SymTab<int> s;
    s.add("foo", 1);
    s.add("bar", 2);
    const int *val = s.lookup("foo");
    // ...
```

(b) Without Operator Overloading

Figure 9-3: Two Usage Models for a Generic Symbol Table Abstraction

Figure 9-4 summarizes the declarations of most C++ operators as they would be if applied to fundamental types. (The fundamental operators `->` `->*` `()` and `,` provide little insight.)

```
                                        // operators with similar declarations
class T {
    T& operator++();                    // ++x --x (prefix)
    T operator++(int);                  // x++ x-- (postfix)

    T* operator&();                     // &x (unary)
    const T* operator&() const;         // &x (unary)

    T& operator=(const T&);             // = += -= *= /= %= <<= >>= &= ^= |=
};

T operator-(const T&);                  // - + ~ (unary)
int operator!(const T&);                // ! (unary)

T operator+(const T&, const T&);        // + - * / << >> % & ^ |
int operator==(const T&, const T&);     // == != < <= > > =
int operator&&(const T&, const T&);     // && ||

// if the type is pointer-like (i.e., P = T*)

class P {
    T& operator[](int) const;           // indexed array access (binary)
    T& operator*() const;               // pointer dereference (unary)
};

// if type is pointer-to-const-like (i.e., PC = const T*)
class PC {
    const T& operator[](int) const;     // indexed array access (binary)
    const T& operator*()const;          // pointer dereference (binary)
};
```

Figure 9-4: Summary of Properties of Some Fundamental Operators

Notice that unary operators that do not modify their arguments are *not* fundamentally members. For example, unary `operator!` works perfectly on a user-defined type such as an `ostream` even though there is no `!` operator defined for this type:

```
#include "iostream.h"
void g(ostream& out)
{
    if (!out) {
        cerr << "output stream is bad" << endl;
        return;
    }
    // ...
}
```

The code above works because an `ostream` knows how to convert itself implicitly to a fundamental type (`void *`) for which the `!` operator is defined. If `operator!` were treated as a member of a hypothetical `void*` class definition, no user-defined conversion could occur and the above code would result in a compile-time error.

If we want to disable implicit conversion of the argument to the "free" unary `operator!`, we can remain consistent with these guidelines simply by making the `!` operation a member function—e.g., `obj.not()` instead of an operator.[10]

9.1.2 Free or Member Operator

The decision of whether to make an operator function a member or a free function is entirely defined by whether implicit type conversion of the leftmost operand is desirable. If the operator modifies this operand, such conversion is definitely *not* desirable.

Principle

The C++ language itself serves as an objective and relevant standard after which to model user-defined operators.

Consider what could happen if we defined the concatenation operator (+=) for a string class to be a free function instead of emulating the approach taken for the fundamental

[10] See also **murray**, Section 2.5, p. 44.

types. As Figure 9-5 illustrates, making `operator+=` a free function has enabled the implicit conversion of its left-hand `const char *` operand to a temporary `pub_String` (denoted here as `t005`) with `foo` as its value. Even though this temporary would be an rvalue for fundamental types, it is the temporary `pub_String` object that then has the value `"bar"` concatenated to it (and is not a compile-time error).[11] As this behavior would likely surprise and annoy our clients, we would be wise to suppress it.

```
// pub_String.h
// ...
class pub_String {
    // ...
  public:
    pub_String(const char *str);
};

pub_String& operator+=(pub_String& left, const pub_String& right);
    // free-function definition of concatenation for strings

// ...
```

```
#include "pub_string.h"

void f()
{
    pub_String a("tar");
    const char *b = "foo";
    pub_String c("bar");
    b += c; // has no effect
```

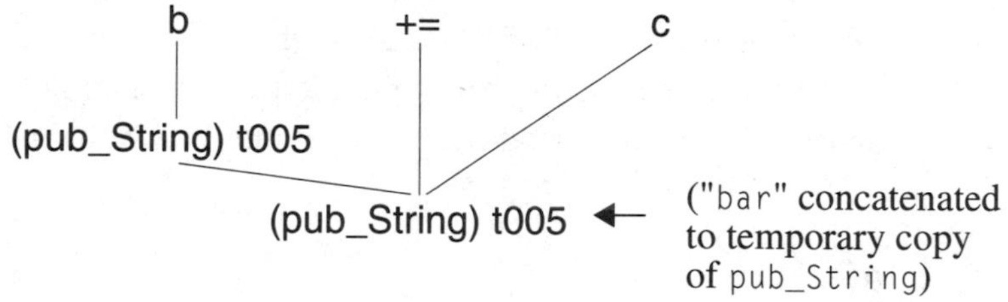

```
    a += b += c; // a now holds "tarfoobar"
                 // but b remains unaffected.
}
```

Figure 9-5: Result of Implementing `operator+=` as a Free Function

[11] The C++ Language currently permits the modification of unnamed temporaries of user-defined type. See **murray**, Section 2.7.3, pp. 53–55.

On the other hand, we expect certain operations (e.g., + and ==) to work regardless of the order of their arguments. Consider `operator+`, which is used to concatenate two strings and return its result by value. The language allows us to define `operator+` as either a member or a non-member. The same goes for `operator==`. If we elect to define these operators as members, then we will subject our clients to the following anomalous behavior:

```
void f()
{
    pub_String s("foo"), t("");
    int i;

    t = s + "bar";                  // ok
    t = "bar" + s;                  // error
    i = s == "bar";                 // ok
    i = "bar" == s;                 // error
}
```

The problem is that

```
pub_String::operator+(const String& right)
```

and

```
pub_String::operator==(const String& right)
```

enable a `char *` to be implicitly converted to a `pub_String` on the right via a constructor of the form

```
pub_String::pub_String(const char *)
```

while no such conversion on the left is possible.[12] Making these operators free solves the symmetry problem until we add the conversion operator

```
pub_String::operator const char *() const
```

to the `pub_String` class.

Figure 9-6 illustrates a problem brought about merely by adding a conversion (cast) operator from a `pub_String` to a `const char *`. Strangely, the two apparently similar operators == and + are not identical with respect to overloading as (naively) we would

---

[12] **ellis**, Section 13.4.2, p. 333.

like to believe. The difference lies in the fact that there are now two ways to interpret the == operator:

1. Implicitly convert the `char *` to a `pub_String` and compare using `operator==(const String&, const String&)`.

2. Implicitly convert the `pub_String` to a `const char *` and compare using the built-in == for pointer types.

The problem does not exist for the + operator because there is no way to "add" two pointer types in C++; hence there is no ambiguity.

```
// pub_String.h
// ...
class pub_String {
    // ...
  public:
    pub_String(const char *pcc);
    // ...
    operator const char *() const;    // <== new conversion operator
};

int operator==(const String& left, const String& right);
String operator+(const String& left, const String& right);

// ...
```

```
#include "pub_String.h"

void f()
{
    pub_String s("foo"), t("");
    int i;

    t = s + "bar";          // ok
    t = "bar" + s;          // ok
    i = s == "bar";         // error (ambiguous)
    i = "bar" == s;         // error (ambiguous)
    i = strlen(s);          // ok
}
```

Figure 9-6: Ambiguity Resulting from both Conversion Operators

In a real-world string class, we would never rely on the implicit conversion to obtain the string value for fear that the extra construction and destruction would unduly affect our performance. Instead, we would define separate overloaded versions of `operator+` to handle each of the three possibilities as efficiently as possible, thus sidestepping these ambiguity problems.

Principle

Inconsistencies in overloaded operators can be obvious, annoying, and costly to clients.

As Figure 9-7 illustrates, in order to accept a `const char *` on the left of the == operator, we are forced to make at least one of the equality operators functions a free function.

```
class pub_String {
    // ...
  public:
    pub_String(const char *pcc);
    operator const char *() const;
    int operator==(const char *pcc) const; // bad idea: (asymmetric)
        // Allows for user-defined conversion only for the
        // argument on the right side of the operator.
};

int operator==(const pub_String& left, const pub_String& right);
int operator==(const char *left, const pub_String& right);
    // Allows for user-defined conversion on both the
    // left and right arguments symmetrically.


struct Foo {
    Foo();
    operator const pub_String& () const;
        // Implicitly convert a Foo to a pub_String.
};

struct Bar {
    Bar();
    operator const char *() const;
        // Implicitly convert a Bar to a (const char *).
};
```

```
void g()
{
    Foo foo;
    Bar bar;
    if (bar == foo) {         // ok:      Bar =to=> (const char *)
        // ...                            Foo =to=> (const pub_String&)
    }
    if (foo == bar) {         // error:   Foo =NO=> (const pub_String&)
        // ...                            Bar =to=> (const char *)
    }
}
```

Figure 9-7: Result of Implementing `operator==` as a Member Function

As long as we are supplying all three versions of the `operator==` function, what harm could it do to make one a member? The harm is that a lack of symmetry could surprise our clients. In the event that one object can be implicitly converted to `pub_String` and the other to a `const char *`, we would still expect the order of comparison to be unimportant. That is, if `bar == foo` compiles, then so should `foo == bar` (and produce the identical result at runtime). However, if the

```
int operator==(const pub_String&, const char *);
```

version is not available as a free function, then there is no way for the following implicit conversions to occur:

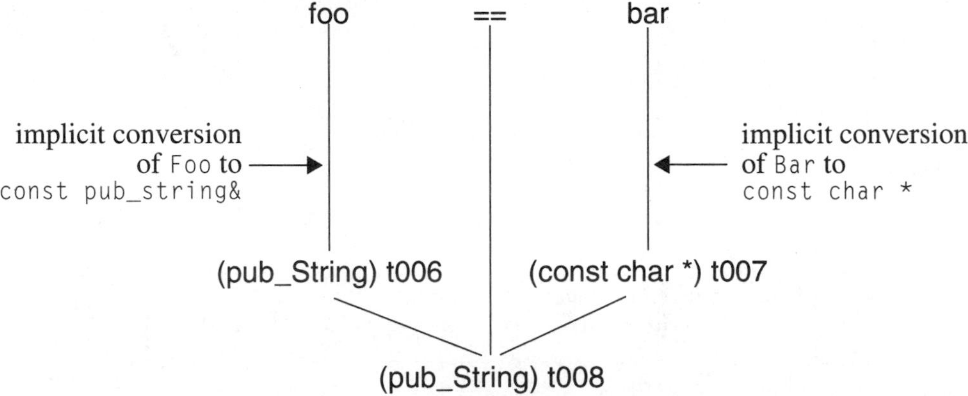

The conclusion is that `operator==` should *always* be a free function, regardless of what other functions are involved. The same reasoning holds for the other binary operators that do not modify either operand and return their result by value.

The example set forth by the language itself is an impartial and useful model that clients can exploit to infer basic syntactic and axiomatic properties of operators. The goal of modeling the fundamental operations is not to enable implicit conversions unnecessarily, but rather symmetrically to avoid surprises. If operator overloading is used to any great extent, it is reasonable to expect that the abstraction is suitable for reuse in a variety of situations. Clients of reusable components will appreciate a consistent and professional interface—devoid of syntactic surprises. Note that the C++ language requires that the following operators be members:[13]

`=`	Assignment
`[]`	Subscript
`->`	Class member access
`()`	Function call
`(T)`	Conversion ("cast") operator
`new`	(static) allocation operator
`delete`	(static) deallocation operator

9.1.3 Virtual or Non-Virtual Function

Dynamic binding enables member functions accessed through a base class to be determined by the actual subtype of the object, as opposed to the type of the pointer or reference used in the call. A function must be declared `virtual` in order to be dynamically bound. Only member functions can be virtual in C++. However, the conclusion that polymorphic behavior of an operator requires it to now become a member where it would otherwise have been a free function is erroneous.

Principle

Syntactic issues, such as symmetric implicit conversion for binary operators, need not be compromised in order to achieve polymorphic behavior.

---

[13] **ellis**, Section 12.3c, p. 306; **stroustrup94**, Section 3.6.2, pp. 82–83.

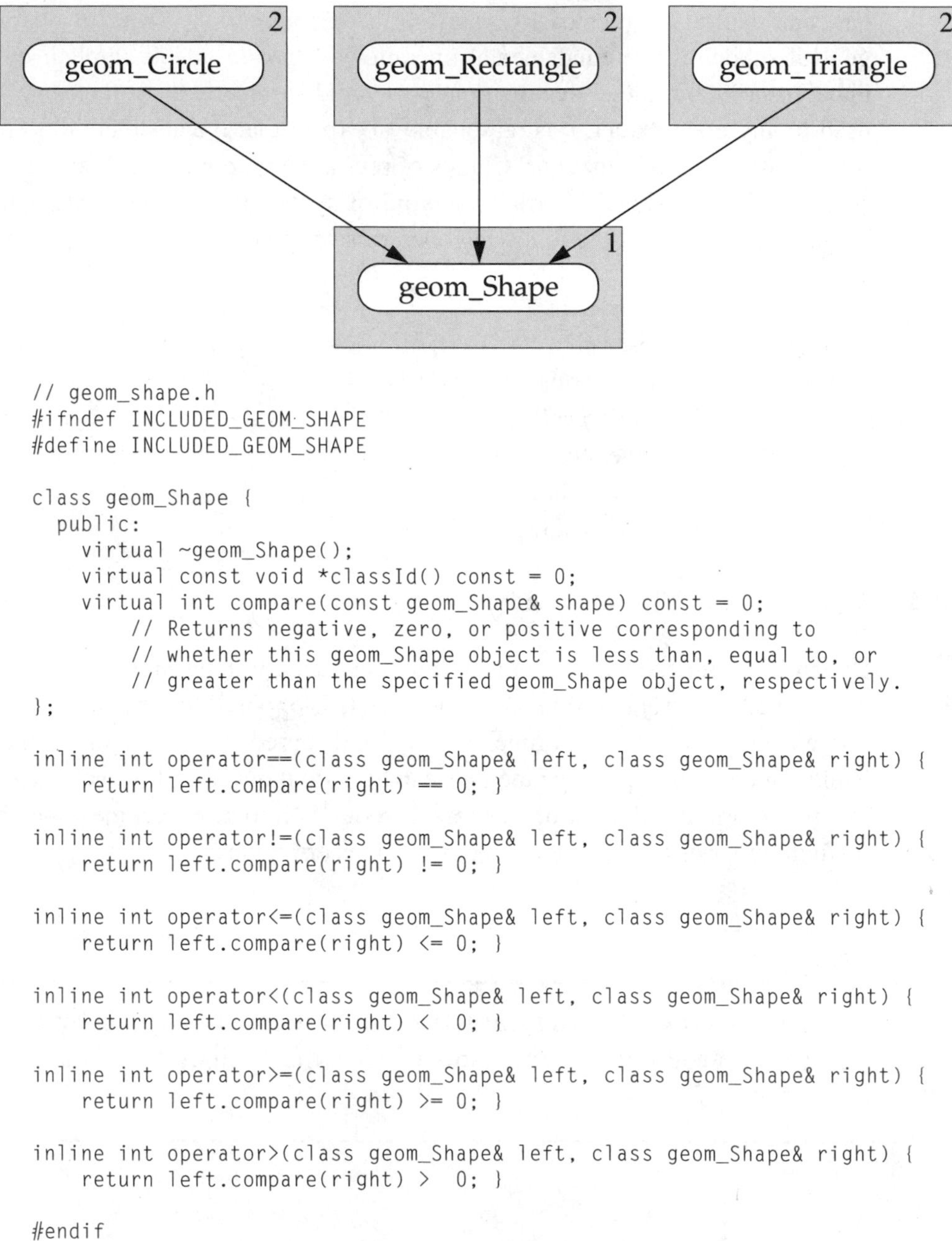


```
// geom_shape.h
#ifndef INCLUDED_GEOM_SHAPE
#define INCLUDED_GEOM_SHAPE

class geom_Shape {
  public:
    virtual ~geom_Shape();
    virtual const void *classId() const = 0;
    virtual int compare(const geom_Shape& shape) const = 0;
        // Returns negative, zero, or positive corresponding to
        // whether this geom_Shape object is less than, equal to, or
        // greater than the specified geom_Shape object, respectively.
};

inline int operator==(class geom_Shape& left, class geom_Shape& right) {
    return left.compare(right) == 0; }

inline int operator!=(class geom_Shape& left, class geom_Shape& right) {
    return left.compare(right) != 0; }

inline int operator<=(class geom_Shape& left, class geom_Shape& right) {
    return left.compare(right) <= 0; }

inline int operator<(class geom_Shape& left, class geom_Shape& right) {
    return left.compare(right) <  0; }

inline int operator>=(class geom_Shape& left, class geom_Shape& right) {
    return left.compare(right) >= 0; }

inline int operator>(class geom_Shape& left, class geom_Shape& right) {
    return left.compare(right) >  0; }

#endif
```

Figure 9-8: Polymorphic Comparison of Shapes Using Free Operators

Figure 9-8 illustrates how symmetric operators can and should continue to remain free even in the presence of polymorphic behavior. Instead of making each of the six equality and relational operators virtual members of the class, a single virtual compare member is provided. These six operators will now continue to behave symmetrically with respect to any implicit conversion.

Equality operators often make sense even when the relational operators do not (think of a point abstraction). Sometimes sorting a heterogeneous collection allows for more efficient access. In such cases, any ordering (even an arbitrary one) can be useful. The virtual `classId()` method in Figure 9-8 enables derived types to define their own runtime type identifier.[14] Using this identifier, shapes of the same type can be sorted according to their own internal ordering, while ordering across concrete types can be defined by some different (perhaps arbitrary) comparison. An implementation of a `geom_Circle`, which participates in a total order on shapes, is provided succinctly for reference in Figure 9-9.

[14] See **ellis**, Section 10.2, pp. 212–213.

```
// geom_circle.h
#ifndef INCLUDED_GEOM_CIRCLE
#define INCLUDED_GEOM_CIRCLE

#ifndef INCLUDED_GEOM_SHAPE
#include "geom_shape.h"
#endif

class geom_Circle : public geom_Shape {
    static const void *d_classId_p;
    double d_radius;

  public:
    geom_Circle(double radius) : d_radius(radius) {}
    geom_Circle(const geom_Circle& circle) : d_radius(circle.d_radius) {}
    ~geom_Circle(const geom_Circle& circle);
    geom_Circle& operator=(const geom_Circle& circle) {
                       d_radius = circle.d_radius; return *this; }
    const void *classId() const { return d_classId_p; }
    int compare(const geom_Shape& shape) const;      // virtual
    int compare(const geom_Circle& circle) const;    // non-virtual
};

inline int operator<(class geom_Circle& left, class geom_Circle& right) {
    return left.compare(right) < 0; }

// ... (definitions of other 5 symmetric operators omitted)

#endif
```

```
// geom_circle.c
#include "geom_circle.h"
const void *geom_Circle::d_classId_p = &d_classId_p; // runtime type id
geom_Circle::~geom_Circle() {} // empty & out-of-line (see Section 9.3.3)

int geom_Circle::compare(const geom_Shape& shape) const
{
    return shape.classId() == d_classId_p ?
        compare((const geom_Circle&) shape) :   // compare instances
        d_classId_p < shape.classId() ? -1 : 1; // compare types
}

int geom_Circle::compare(const geom_Circle& circle) const
{
    return d_radius < circle.d_radius ? -1 : d_radius > circle.d_radius;
}
```

Figure 9-9: Implementation of Polymorphic Comparison for `geom_Circle`

Principle

Virtual functions implement variation in behavior; data members implement variation in value.

More generally, virtual functions are used to describe variation in behavior across types derived from a common base class. Data members, however, are sufficient for describing variation in value without having to resort to inheritance.[1] For example, we would not define a protocol class `art_Color`, and then derive classes `art_Red`, `art_Blue`, and `art_Yellow`; a single (perhaps fully insulating) concrete `art_Color` class that stores one of a number of enumerated colors is probably a more appropriate design. However, virtual functions are an effective technique for breaking both compile-time and link-time dependencies (see Section 6.4.1). For that reason, a single concrete class might be derived from an `art_Color` protocol.

DEFINITION:

Hide: **A member function *hides* a function with the same name declared in a base class or at file scope.**

Overload: **A function *overloads* the name of another function with the same name defined in the same scope.**

Override: **A member function *overrides* an identical function declared virtual in a base class.**

Redefine: **The default definition of a function is irretrievably replaced by another definition.**

[1] See **cargill**, Chapter 1, pp. 16–19.

Finally, there are four similar terms that are commonly used (and misused) to describe a function and its effect on other functions (*hide*, *overload*, *override*, and *redefine*) that we define here for reference. Distinct functions with the same name are said to be *overloaded* only if they are declared in the same scope. When a member function in a derived class is declared with the identical interface of a function declared virtual in a base class, that function is said to *override* the base class function. In all other cases, a function name *hides* all identically named functions in an enclosing scope, regardless of their argument signatures. Functions hidden in a named scope are not directly accessible, but can be accessed via the scope resolution operator (`::`). However, when we *redefine* a function (e.g., global `new` or class specific unary `&`), we replace its definition; the previous definition is no longer accessible from the program.[16]

Guideline

Avoid hiding a base-class function in a derived class.

We should be careful not to hide the definitions of any base-class functions in derived classes. In particular, we should never supply a new definition for a non-virtual function in a derived class, since that would make the function sensitive to the type of any pointer or reference from which the function might be called.[17] Allowing the type of the pointer or reference to affect which behavior is invoked is counterintuitive, subtle, and error prone. Hiding functions defined in base classes does not protect them from use; it merely makes such use more cumbersome. We can always fiddle with the pointer or use the scope resolution operator to call the hidden member. A better idea is simply never to hide a member function in the first place. An example of a design pattern involving virtual functions, multiple inheritance, and runtime type identification can be found in Appendix C.

---

[16] **ellis**, Section 10.2, p. 210, and Section 13.1, p. 310.

[17] See **meyers**, Item 37, pp. 130–132.

9.1.4 Pure or Non-Pure Virtual Member Function

Declaring a virtual function to be pure forces the concrete derived-class author to supply a definition. If failing to supply a specific behavior in a derived class is likely to be an error, then the virtual function should be declared pure in the base class.

Protocol classes (see Section 6.4.1) are useful for achieving both levelization and insulation in inheritance hierarchies. We want to avoid defining any behavior in the protocol class itself; making all of the member functions (except the destructor) pure virtual enables us to avoid defining any of them.

An abstract class derived from a pure protocol is sometimes referred to as *partial implementations*. Protocol functions that are not declared in the derived class are inherited as pure virtual. Some functions in a partial implementation may have a useful default behavior, but they should not necessarily default automatically. As illustrated in Figure 9-10, both defining a virtual function and declaring it pure forces a derived-class author to enable the default behavior explicitly.[18]

```
#include <iostream.h>

struct Base {                          // *** Base Class ***
    virtual void f() = 0;
    virtual ~Base();
};

Base::~Base() {}


struct Partial : Base {                // *** Partial Implementation ***
    virtual void f() = 0;              // declaration of pure virtual function
    ~Partial();
};

void Partial::f()                      // definition of pure virtual function
{
    cout << "Partial::f" << endl;
}

Partial::~Partial() {}
```

[18] See **ellis**, Section 10.3, p. 214.

```
struct Derived : Partial {        // *** Concrete Derived Class ***
    Derived() {}
    void f();
    ~Derived();
};

void Derived::f()
{
    cout << "Derived::f" << endl;
    Partial::f();                 // explicit call of pure virtual function
}

Derived::~Derived() {}


main()
{                                 // *** Main Program ***
    Base *b = new Derived;
    b->f();
}

// Output:
//      john@john: a.out
//      Derived::f
//      Partial::f
//      john@john:
```

Figure 9-10: Forcing Default Behavior to Be Enabled Explicitly

8.5.2 Static or Non-Static Member Function

The obvious reason for making a function a static member of a class is that it does not depend on any particular instance of an object:

```
class my_Widget {
    static int d_instanceCount;
    // ...
  public:
    static int instanceCount() { return d_instanceCount; }
    // ...
};
```

Principle

Static member functions are commonly used to implement non-primitive functionality in a separate *utility* class.

Escalating functionality to a higher level may require making it a static member function of a type defined in some other component (see Figure 5-15). If the function is a convenience function that does not require private access, we might consider making the function a static member of a separate class to emphasize its non-primitive status.

```
class geom_Point { /* ... */ };

struct geom_PointUtil {
    static int compareMagnitude(const Point& a, const Point& b);
        // Compare the distance of each point from the origin,
        // and return a negative, zero, or positive value
        // depending on whether the magnitude of a is less than,
        // equal to, or greater than that of b, respectively.
};
```

Notice that by making the `compareMagnitude` a static function, we retain symmetry with respect to the implicit conversion of its arguments. Had we instead declared `compareMagnitude` a non-static member of `geom_Point`, there could be cases where `a.compareMagnitude(b)` would compile but `b.compareMagnitude(a)` would not (see Section 9.1.2)

Though rarely necessary, we could grant private access while retaining this symmetry just by moving the static method inside the `geom_Point` class itself.

9.1.6 `const` Member or Non-`const` Member Function

A member function should be declared `const` in order to remove unnecessary restrictions on its use wherever this is appropriate.[19] There are two notions of `const`-ness: *logical* and *physical*. Logical `const`-ness is more nebulous and refers to what the user is meant to perceive as `const`; changes to the internal organization that are programmatically undetectable by the client are considered logically `const`. On the other hand, the C++ language enforces physical `const`-ness. A member function can be declared `const` so long as it (1) does not modify the bits contained directly in the structure that defines the class, or (2) does not return a non-`const` pointer or reference to any data member embedded in that structure.

Figure 9-11 illustrates how physical `const`-ness is enforced in C++. A `const` member function is permitted to modify and return a writable reference to memory that is held

---

[19] See **meyers**, Item 21, pp. 73–78.

and managed by an object. Since all of the functions defined above cause or enable side effects that are programmatically accessible by clients, none would be considered logically `const` functions.

```
class ex_String {
    char *d_str_p;

  public:
    // ...
    makeNull()              { d_str_p = 0; }      // physically non-const
    makeEmpty()       const { d_str_p[0] = 0; }  // physically const

    char *&getRepRef()      { return d_str_p; }  // physically non-const
    char * getRep() const { return d_str_p; }  // physically const
};
```

Figure 9-11: The C++ Language Enforces Physical `const`-ness Only

<u>DEFINITION</u>: An object is `const`-*correct* if a function taking only a single argument that is a `const` reference to that object is not able, without explicit casting, to obtain a non-`const` reference to that same object (or a portion thereof) from within the function body.

Guideline

Every object in a system should be `const`-correct.

Deciding what is and what is not `const` behavior of an object is an important part of the design of its class (see Section 10.3.1). Care must taken to ensure that there are no loopholes that could allow a client to circumvent that decision. Returning writable access to an object's internal representation from a `const` member function can short-circuit the ability of the compiler to help ensure that a `const` object is not modified.[20]

---

[20] **meyers**, Item 29, pp. 96–99.

Principle

Returning a non-`const` object from a `const` member function can rupture the `const`-correctness of a system.

```
class te_Node {
    // ...
  public:
    // ...

    // MANIPULATORS
    void setValue(double v);




    // ACCESSORS
    const char *name() const;
    te_Node *parent() const;
    te_Node *child1() const;
    te_Node *child2() const;
};
```

a) Not `const` Correct

```
class te_Node {
    // ...
  public:
    // ...

    // MANIPULATORS
    void setValue(double v);
    te_Node *parent();
    te_Node *child1();
    te_Node *child2();

    // ACCESSORS
    const char *name() const;
    const te_Node *parent() const;
    const te_Node *child1() const;
    const te_Node *child2() const;
};
```

b) `const` Correct

Figure 9-12: Illustrating `const`-Correctness

When designing the system, it is easy to inadvertently provide ways in which a non-`const` version of a reference to an object can be obtained from a `const` reference to that same object. For example, Figure 9-12 provides two definitions of a `te_Node` used to implement a binary tree. Figure 9-12a defines `const` member functions that return writable access to the parent and each child. A function taking a reference to a `const te_Node` could easily modify this supposedly `const` value, without ever resorting to a cast, as follows:

```
void f(const te_Node& readonlyNode)
{
    if (readonlyNode->child1()) {
        te_node *writableNode = readonlyNode->child1()->parent();
        writableNode->setValue(-9.99E99);
    }
}
```

In the context of a system, an object that does not allow a non-`const` reference to an object to be obtained from a `const` reference to that same object alone (either directly or indirectly) is said to be `const`-*correct*. Figure 9-12b defines a class that does not provide a way to obtain writable access from a `const` reference through indirect means. This implementation is `const`-correct because it preserves the intent of what can and cannot be done with a `const te_Node` alone.

<u>DEFINITION</u>: A system is `const`-*correct* if there is no way (without using an explicit cast) for a function taking only `const` reference arguments to any subset of objects within the system to obtain a writable reference to any of these objects (or any portions thereof) from within the body of the function.

In other words, given an arbitrary function:

```
void f(const T1& a1, const T2& a2, ..., const TN& aN)
{
    // There is simply no way for me to get hold of a
    // writable reference to any of a1, a2, ..., aN or
    // any portion thereof (short of casting away const).
}
```

Guideline

A system should be `const`-correct.

`const`-correctness is a property that extends beyond a single class or component and applies to an entire system. For example, class `Node` in Figure 5-8 is suspect because it contains a function

```
Edge& Node::edge(int index) const;
```

that allows a client to obtain a modifiable `Edge` from a `const Node`. Even if `Edge` were to have been careful to perpetuate the `const`-ness as shown here:

```
Node& Edge::to();                    Node& Edge::from();
const Node& Edge::to() const;        const Node& Edge::from() const;
```

as long as we can obtain a non-`const` reference to a `Node` from a non-`const Edge`, the subsystem is not `const`-correct:

```
void f(const Node& readonlyNode)
{
    if (readonlyNode->numEdges() > 0) {
        Edge& writableEdge = readonlyNode->edge(0);
        Node& writableNode = (&writableEdge->to() == this) ?
                               writableEdge->to() :
                               writableEdge->from();

        // writableNode is a writable reference to readonlyNode!
    }
}
```

In a heterogeneous network of objects, a `const` member of one type can be exploited to undermine the `const`-correctness of another. The problem can be illustrated graphically, as shown in Figure 9-13a. In this conversion graph, every type in the system has both a non-`const` and a `const` representation. Converting from the non-`const` (down) to the `const` version of a type is automatic. Member functions of a type *X* that return a pointer or reference to a type *Y* are represented in the conversion graph with the appropriate directed edge from the appropriate version (i.e., `const` or non-`const`) of type *X* to the appropriate version of type *Y*.

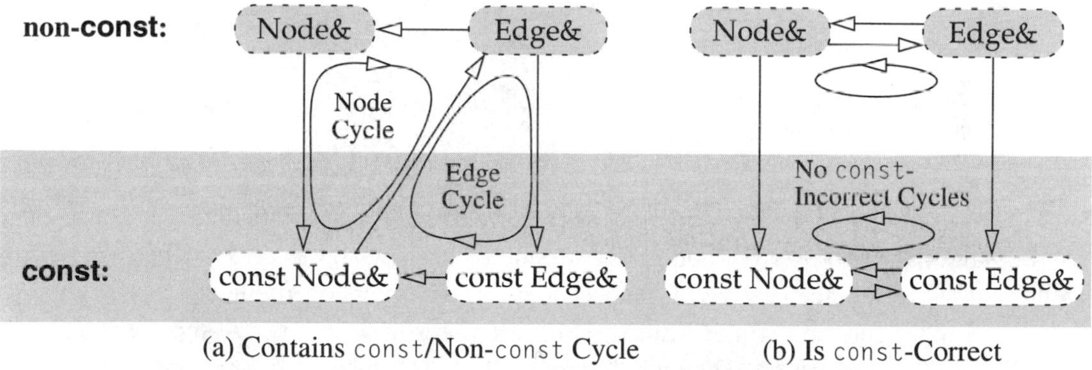

(a) Contains `const`/Non-`const` Cycle (b) Is `const`-Correct

Figure 9-13: Establishing `const`-Correctness Graphically (see Figure 9-12)

Since `Edge` defines a `const` member that returns a reference to a `const Node`, there is a directed edge from `const Edge&` to `const Node&`. The non-`const` version of this method is treated analogously. The problem is that `Node` contains a `const` member that returns a non-`const Edge` reference—hence the upward sloping diagonal entry in

Figure 9-13a. This diagonal entry introduces a cycle that contains both the `const` and the non-`const` versions of `Node`. Consequently, given a `const` reference to a `Node`, we can potentially obtain a non-`const` reference to the identical `Node`. A similar cycle involves both versions of `Edge`, so a `const Edge` reference could be converted to non-`const` without the use of a cast.

<u>DEFINITION</u>: A system is `const`-*correct* if its conversion graph contains no cycle that involves both the `const` and non-`const` versions of any one type.

The conversion graph shown in Figure 9-13b reflects the definition of `Node` given in Figure 9-12b. There are conversion cycles between `Node&` and `Edge&`, and also between `const Node&` and `const Edge&`. However, there is no one cycle that involves both versions of either type; this small subsystem is `const`-correct. This interpretation of `const`-correctness generalizes to apply to an entire system.

It is possible that an object may supply `const` information, such as a name that could then be used to look up a writable version of the same object in some non-`const` container object:

```
void g(te_Tree *t, te_Node& readonlyNode)
{
    te_Node *writableNode = t->lookup(readonlyNode.name());
    writableNode->setValue(-9.99E99);
}
```

The above is not a violation of `const`-correctness because the `const` object alone is not enough to obtain a non-`const` version of itself. Had the `te_Tree` been passed by `const` reference, we would expect that a `const` version of the `te_Tree::lookup` member function would instead return a pointer to a `const te_Node`, ensuring the `const`-correct system shown in Figure 9-14.

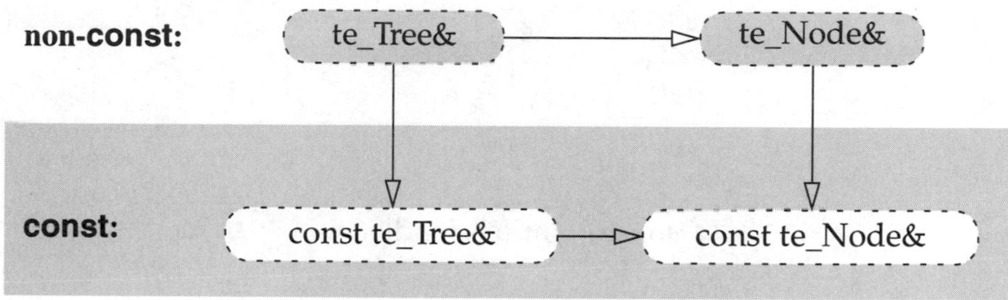

Figure 9-14: A `const`-Correct Implementation of `te_Tree` and `te_Node`

There are situations where we do want a `const` member to return a non-`const` reference or pointer to another type. In the `PointIterHandle` of Figure 6-75, we are able to access a writable version of the contained `PointIter` from a reference to a `const` handle:

```
PointIter *PointIterHandle::operator->() const;
```

The intent here was to emulate the semantics of a writable pointer passed by value—that is, you can modify the indicated object but you cannot change the handle itself to refer to a different object.[7] However, as Figure 9-15 illustrates, this subsystem *is* `const`-correct because there is no way to obtain a writable `PointIterHandle` reference from either kind of `PointIter`.[8]

---

[7] The usefulness of a `const` iterator obtained from a handle passed to a function by `const` reference is dubious.

[8] Note that verifying `const`-correctness for a system can be done through static analysis; however, because violating `const`-correctness can depend on the underlying object (instance) network, it is possible to have a `const`-correct system that cannot statically be proven to be so. Such systems are more expensive to maintain and much harder to validate.

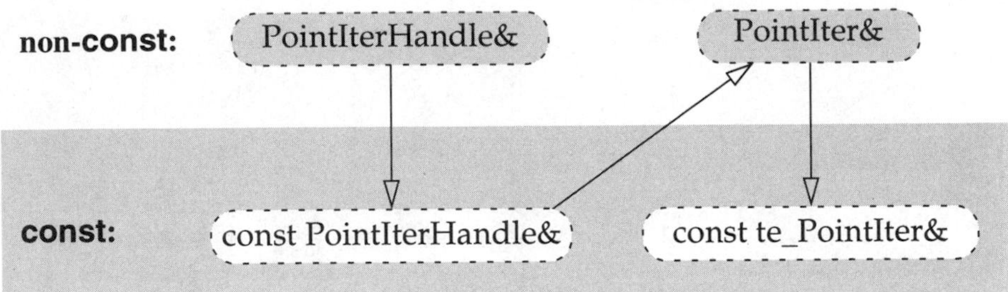

Figure 9-15: A `const`-Correct Implementation of `PointIterHandle` and `PointIter`

Ignoring `const`-correctness implies that an argument passed to a function by `const` reference may "legitimately" be modified within that function. Respecting `const`-correctness improves the consistency of the system and enables the compiler to detect a wider class of errors at compile time than would otherwise be possible.

Guideline

Think twice (at least) before casting away `const`.

Casting away `const`-ness serves to undermine all the benefits we worked so hard in this section to achieve.

8.5.4 Public, Protected, or Private Member Function

Member functions intended for direct use by general clients must be declared `public`. Free operators such as the equality or relational operators may be implemented in terms of a primitive member function (see Figure 9-21). If this primitive member function is not public, the dependent free operators will need to be declared friends of the class, which lessens maintainability and enables abuse (see Section 3.6).

Principle

Member functions that are not public expose general users to uninsulated implementation details.

Private member functions are intended for use within a class and by friends of a class. Since friendship outside a component is discouraged, there is often little advantage to non-virtual private member functions over static free functions defined at file scope in the `.c` file (see Section 6.3.3). One common valid use of a private non-virtual member function is to factor out complex but seldom needed behavior from an otherwise tiny and frequently called inline function. For example, class `my_Stack` in Figure 10-13 uses the private non-inline member `growArray()` to implement the public inline `push` method:

```
inline
void my_Stack::push(int value)
{
    if (d_sp >= d_size) {
        growArray();
    }
    d_stack_p[d_sp++] = value;
}
```

Without using private methods, we would be forced either to implement the entire `push` method out-of-line with a significant cost in performance, or to violate encapsulation by making the `growArray` method public. Trying to implement the entire `push` function inline is probably out of the question.

Private virtual functions make sense when the behavior defined in a derived class is used only by members and friends of the base class. A potential use of a private virtual function can be found in the `surfaceEquation` member of class `Solid` described in Section 6.6.3 (see Figure 6-84).

Principle

All virtual and protected functions are intended for consideration by derived-class authors.

Protected member functions are explicitly earmarked for derived-class authors. Protected member functions expose general clients to implementation details and are often best avoided (see Section 6.3.4). Although private virtual function are not accessible to derived classes, derived-class authors may be expected to supply definitions for these functions; in this sense, private virtual functions are exceptional:

```
class Base {
  private:
    virtual void programMe();
};

class Derived : public Base {
  public:
    void programMe();     // The derived class itself cannot call this
                          // function through the base-class interface;
                          // yet even clients of the derived class's public
                          // interface are able to access this function.
};
```

8.5.5 Return by Value, Reference, or Pointer

The issue of whether to return by value or not comes down to whether there is something within the object or argument list suitable to reference. For example, there is no reasonable implementation[9] of

```
pub_String& operator+(const pub_String& left, const pub_String& right);
```

As we saw in Section 8.3, returning an object by value preserves total encapsulation but can be significantly more expensive at runtime than returning a pointer or reference. For non-operator functions, we have the additional option of returning an object through the argument list. Return by argument is usually more efficient than return by

[9] See **meyers**, Item 23, pp. 82–84; Item 31, pp. 102–105.

value, and yet it is still fully encapsulating. The four ways to return a (`Foo`) value are summarized in Figure 9-16.

```
Foo v(...);                         // return by value
const Foo& r(...);                  // return by reference
const Foo *p(...);                  // return by pointer
int a(Foo *retVal, ...);            // return by argument

int a(Foo& retVal, ...);            // bad idea (see Section 9.1.11)
```

Figure 9-16: Four Ways to Return a Value from a Function

In cases where the function may fail, return by value or reference may not an option.[24] Sometimes we can return the value by pointer, which can be 0 on failure. Another option is to return an integer status to indicate success or failure, and to return the object itself through the argument list.

Guideline

For functions that return an *error status*, an integral value of 0 should always mean success.

For functions that return an error status as either an `int` or some enumerated type, it is convenient to have a way of knowing whether or not this function worked[25] without having to inspect some header file to determine the appropriate success value for this particular function. Traditionally, a status of zero indicates success, a non-zero status indicates failure, and the particular non-zero value may be used to provide additional information to clients.

---

[24] Sometimes it may make sense to return an object in a class-defined "invalid" state.

[25] Note that a function such as `fclose` performs an operation and returns an *error status* regarding the outcome of that operation. A function such as `isalpha` merely answers a yes-or-no question with no preconceived notions of success or failure. Consequently, `fclose` returns an error status, while `isalpha` does not.

Principle

Often there is exactly one way for a function to work and several ways for it to fail; as clients, we may not care why it failed.

Very often, clients will not care why an operation failed; in such cases a simple test for non-zero status is sufficient, as indicated in Figure 9-17. In some cases, this convention may allow us to avoid including an additional header enumerating the error conditions, thereby reducing unwanted compile-time coupling.

Although redundant, this 0 initializer indicates that the value of the enumerator is not arbitrary.

```
int f(...)
{
    enum { GOOD = 0, BAD, UGLY } status = GOOD:

    if (0 != g(...)) {
        status = BAD;
        // ...
    }

    if (GOOD == status && 0 != h(...)) {
        status = UGLY;
        // ...
    }

    // ...

    return status;
}
```

Figure 9-17: 0 == Success for All Functions that Return Status

For non-`const` member functions, returning a non-`const` reference to the object itself is always a viable option. Returning a pointer or reference to an internal part of the object potentially limits the implementation choice; its impact on encapsulation should be considered carefully (see Section 8.3).

Principle

Returning a dynamically allocated object by loading a modifiable handle argument is less prone to memory leaks than returning that object by non-`const` pointer.

For polymorphic objects such as `geom_Shape` (see Figure 9-8), it is not possible to return an object by value. Returning a clone (dynamic copy) of the object by non-`const` pointer places the burden of deallocation on the client, and is prone to memory leaks. The use of a reference here would be obscure and inappropriate (see Section 9.1.11). A preferred approach for returning newly allocated polymorphic objects would be to pass in a pointer to a handle (see Section 6.5.3) explicitly designed to hold a pointer to the base class `geom_Shape`:

```
class geom_ShapeUtil {
    void create(geom_ShapeHandle *handle, const char *typeName);
        // Create a new shape of the type specified by typeName and
        // load it into the handle passed in via a non-const pointer.
};
```

Guideline

Functions that answer a yes-or-no question should be worded appropriately (e.g., `isValid`) and return an `int` value of either `0` ("no") or `1` ("yes").

Finally, it is helpful for functions that explicitly answer a yes-or-no question to be worded to indicate this fact—`isAcute()`, `hasProtocol(id)`, `areParallel(line1, line2)`, and so forth. —and to return an `int` value of `0` for "no" and 1 (nothing else) for "yes." By emulating the behavior of built-in operators such as == that return Boolean values, we help to make the semantics of these common functions clear. Sometimes clients will depend on the `1` value where they need not:

```
if (1 == angle.isAcute()) { /* ... */ }
```

If you cache this value as a flag in the object, you might be tempted to return a masked bit that could have some non-Boolean value (e.g., `8`). Converting a non-Boolean value `x` to a Boolean value `y` is as simple as `y = !!x`. An appropriate implementation of `isAcute` might look as follows:

```
int geom_Angle::isAcute() const
{
    return !!(d_flags & ACUTE_MASK);
}
```

Since the ANSI/ISO committee has adopted `bool` as a distinct integral type in C++, we should probably consider returning `bool` instead of `int` in such cases once this new fundamental type becomes generally available:[26]

```
bool geom_Angle::isAcute()const
{
    return d_flags & ACUTE_MASK;
}
```

At least now the conversion to a Boolean value is implicit and automatic.

9.1.9 Return `const` or Non-`const`

In an effort to eliminate unnecessary restrictions, we strive to take `const` operands and return non-`const` results while maintaining `const`-correctness.[27]

Guideline

Avoid declaring results returned by value from functions as `const`.

Results returned from a function by value are rvalues. In the case of fundamental types, declaring an rvalue `const` is redundant, confusing, and can interfere with template instantiation:

```
const int f(); // redundant use of const
```

---

[26] **stroustrup94**, Section 11.7.2, pp. 254–255.

[27] **meyers**, Item 21, pp. 73–78.

An rvalue of a user-defined type (e.g., an object returned by value from a function) can be manipulated by non-`const` member functions; an object returned by value as `const` cannot. This latter behavior is a "corner" of the language that is both contentious and may not be implemented consistently across current compilers and platforms. Since the value returned is a copy anyway, exploiting the notion of a `const` versus a non-`const` rvalue is typically unnecessary.

In general, returning a value by `const` pointer or reference is less restrictive on the implementation than returning a non-`const` pointer or reference. In the sparse array implementation of `PointArray` (discussed in Section 8.3), for example, it is convenient to return a `const` reference to a dummy empty object. If the reference were non-`const`, we would be forced to allocate a new object at that location. Note that `const` member functions are obliged not to return non-`const` objects that would violate `const`-correctness (see Section 9.1.6).

8.5.7 Argument Optional or Required

Having just one function body is often easier to maintain than several overloaded versions.[14] In most cases it is easy enough to use inline functions to create overloaded versions that, in effect, allow optional arguments to be located in the middle of an argument list.[15]

Principle

Default arguments can be an effective alternative to function overloading, especially where insulation is not relevant.

Figure 9-18 contrasts the use of overloaded functions with that of default arguments for factoring common code within a constructor call. As shown in Figure 9-18a, factoring the implementations of several overloaded constructors requires the use of an auxiliary function `init`, since one constructor cannot usefully be called from another.[16] Such factoring does not allow us to take advantage of the initialization lists

[14] See **cargill**, Chapter 2, p. 32; Chapter 3, p. 65; and Chapter 4, p. 87.

[15] **ellis**, Section 8.2.6, p. 142.

[16] **meyers**, Item 24, pp. 85–87.

of the constructors. The use of inline functions in Figure 9-18a to forward calls from several overloaded functions (sometimes referred to as *inline forwarding*) eliminates the potential overhead of nested function calls. At the same time, inline forwarding negates the insulating value of having separate overloaded functions implemented out-of-line.

```
geom_Point {
    int d_x;
    int d_y;

  private:
    void init (x, y);

  public:
    geom_Point ();
    geom_Point (int x, int y);
    // ...
};

geom_Point operator+(const Point&,
                     const Point&);

inline
void geom_Point::init(int x, int y)
{
    d_x = x;
    d_y = y;
}

inline
geom_Point::geom_Point()
{
    init(0, 0);
}

inline
geom_Point::geom_Point(int x, int y)
{
    init(x, y);
}
```

(a) Using Overloaded Functions

```
geom_Point
    int d_x;
    int d_y;

  public:
    geom_Point(int x = 0, int y = 0);

    // ...
};

geom_Point operator+(const Point&,
                     const Point&);

inline
geom_Point::geom_Point(int x, int y)
: d_x(x)
, d_y(y)
{
}
```

(b) Using Default Arguments

Figure 9-18: Factoring Common Constructor Code

Figure 9-18b illustrates a great economy of notation compared to factoring constructor function bodies. Note, however, that these two implementations are not identical with respect to the construction of a `geom_Point` from an `int`:

```
void g()
{
    geom_Point a = 5;
    a = a + 10;
}
```

The implementation in Figure 9-18a does not allow a `geom_Point` to be constructed from a single argument, and so precludes the non-intuitive initialization and implicit conversion above. Using two default arguments to implement the default constructor as in Figure 9-18b subtly introduces an undesirable integer conversion operator that allows the above code to compile silently (see Section 9.3.1).

Default arguments can be more self-documenting, more compact, and more easily understood by clients than multiple overloaded functions because they place more information in the header file. As such, default arguments are at odds with the goal of insulation. For more information about how to reduce compile-time coupling when using default arguments, see Section 6.3.8.

One important use of default arguments is to allow developers to append additional parameters to functions conveniently, without breaking any preexisting programs that use them.

Guideline

Avoid default arguments that require the construction of an unnamed temporary object.

Passing user-defined types as default arguments is cumbersome at best; not all objects make sense as defaults. Constructing a temporary object to pass in by default, like passing an object by value, is expensive and should be avoided.

9.1.11 Pass Argument by Value, Reference, or Pointer

Passing user-defined types by value is unnecessary and expensive. This practice is so costly that it has contributed to the perception that the C++ language itself is slow.[31]

[31] For more justification, see **meyers**, Item 22, pp. 78–82.

Minor Design Rule

Never pass a user-defined type (i.e., `class`, `struct`, or `union`) to a function by value.

Instead of passing a user-defined type by value, pass it by `const` reference. In the absence of global variables, the semantics are essentially identical in practice, but the runtime performance is superior. Enumerations and all fundamental types are most efficiently passed by value.

When it comes to returning a value through the argument list, there are two mind sets:

1. `void f(my_Object& result, ...); // return by non-const reference`
2. `void f(my_Object *result, ...); // return by non-const pointer`

Wherever feasible, we would like to use the language itself to express our intention instead of relying on a comment. The C++ language definition states that a pointer may be null but that a reference may not. Returning a value through a modifiable reference argument makes the semantics clear: the object to receive the value *must* be supplied by the client. Any documentation to reiterate this requirement would be unnecessary and redundant. Consequently there is no need to test for a null reference—and there is no portable way to do so anyway. Returning an object by non-`const` pointer can therefore be reserved exclusively for results that are truly optional; that is, the pointer is always tested inside the function, and if a null pointer is supplied, the result is not loaded into the object.

In the other camp,[18] classical theory discourages functions that modify their arguments; such functions are known to be more difficult to maintain. Remember that, historically, most of the cost incurred over the life of a system is in maintenance and enhancement—not initial development. Allowing functions to modify their arguments by reference makes it more difficult for software engineers maintaining an

[18] **stroustrup**, Section 2.3.10, p. 62.

unfamiliar body of code to know whether an argument passed into a function (apparently by value) could potentially be modified.

The expressive power of writable references applies only if you happen to look at the appropriate header file. From looking at just the client code in Figure 9-19, it is not at all clear what caused the value of the `my_String` variable `name` initialized with `"Laurel"` to come to hold the (incorrect) value `"Hardy"`.

```
void g(int i, int j)
{
    my_String name("Laurel");
    // ...
    int s = my_Stuff::funcX(name, i);
    // ...
    int t = your_Problem::funcY(name, j);
    // ...
    int u = their_Thing::funcZ(name, i + j);
    // ...
    cout << "name = " << name << endl;
}

// Output:
//     name = Hardy
```

Figure 9-19: Modifying Function Arguments via Writable References

Functions that actually do modify their arguments are relatively scarce. By adopting the guideline of modifying function arguments only through non-`const` pointers, we make such functions easy to spot from the client code. Figure 9-20 shows that only one of the three functions that operate on name could legitimately have modified its value; in this example, we can look in only one place instead of three, simply by virtue of having followed this guideline.

Guideline

Be consistent about returning values through arguments (e.g., avoid declaring non-`const` reference parameters).

```
void g(int i, int j)
{
    my_String name("Laurel");
    // ...
    int s = my_Stuff::funcX(name, i);
    // ...
    int t = your_Problem::funcY(&name, j);
    // ...
    int u = their_Thing::funcZ(name, i + j);
    // ...
    cout << "name = " << name << endl;
}

// Output:
//      name = Hardy
```

Figure 9-20: Modifying Function Arguments Only via Writable Pointer

Figure 9-21 demonstrates that even in the body of a function that takes a non-`const` pointer argument, we need look no further than the definition of this function (rather than the header files declaring each called function) to infer which called functions might modify that argument.

```
void f(my_String *name, i, j)
{
    int s = my_Stuff::funcX(*name, i);          // should not modify name
    // ...
    int t = your_Problem::funcY(name, j);       // potentially modifies name
    // ...
    int u = their_Thing::funcZ(*name, i + j);   // should not modify name
    // ...
}
```

Figure 9-21: Nesting Functions that Return via Writable Pointer

Historically, passing objects by pointer and passing objects by reference have not always been equivalent when it came to user-defined conversions. Until the C++ language definition changed for release 2.0 of CFRONT,[33] a function taking a non-`const` reference to `your_Class` would allow its argument to undergo a user-defined conversion to a temporary *before* the return-by-argument assignment could occur. The value would therefore *not* be returned to the caller, and this error would have gone undetected until runtime. By contrast, a function taking a non-`const` pointer never permitted user-defined conversion to occur; a type error would always have been detected at

[33] **stroustrup94**, Section 3.7, p. 86.

compile time. The latter is the desired behavior and is consistent with that of member operators such as `operator=`, which will not implicitly convert the object that they modify (see Section 9.1.2).

It is worth noting that standard pointer conversions continue to work as expected when passing the object to be modified via non-`const` pointer. In other words, passing the address of a derived object to a function taking a pointer to one of its public base classes makes sense and the conversion will occur implicitly. It is only the unwanted, user-defined conversion that is suppressed by requiring the client to pass the modifiable argument's address. Fortunately, most current compilers will at least warn you when a user-defined conversion causes a temporary to be bound to a non-const reference parameter.

The C language does not permit function arguments to be modified directly; C++ does. When first using C++, classic C programmers will often forget to insert the `const` qualifier before a reference parameter where appropriate, leaving a reader to wonder whether the function author intended the argument to be modifiable or not. Discouraging *any* use of non-`const` references in function arguments makes the intent clear (or the defect immediately obvious).

Proponents of passing function arguments by modifiable reference would argue that a reference is self-documenting in that there is no question about whether a valid object must be supplied, whereas a pointer argument leaves this possibility open. Again, the only way to know what is expected is to look at the header file for each function called (and that could mean many header files).

Forcing the client to pass the address for a modifiable argument often requires the client to type the extra keystroke "&". However, this extra keystroke is worth its weight in gold when it comes to advertising that a function call can potentially modify its argument. And because most functions do *not* modify their parameters, almost all function calls can quickly be eliminated from suspicion.

Returning an argument by non-`const` pointer is a general and context-independent technique; the syntactic anomaly alerts clients to the special nature of the argument. Any notational convenience of passing a modifiable argument into a function by non-`const` reference is outweighed by the need to avoid costly surprises. However, non-`const` reference parameters continue to have their place in operator functions (e.g., `operator+=`) and well-entrenched idioms such as streams, which make no sense unless the stream can be modified. The context of the stream idiom makes the semantics of their usage relatively clear, compared with returning some little-known object through a modifiable reference.

Guideline

Avoid storing the address of any argument to a function in a location that will persist after the function terminates; pass the address of the argument instead.

Another related issue is that passing a user-defined type by `const` reference is so common that we might never suspect the importance of a particular value's being an lvalue. Consider the scenario of Figure 9-22. An infinite precision integer type `my_BigInt` is defined that can be constructed from a fundamental `int` type. The `my_BigIntSet` is a homogeneous collection that stores only the address of the object supplied to its `add` function. Suppose a naive user tries to create a function `g` that adds three integers to the set. Each integer is implicitly converted to a temporary `my_BigInt`, which is guaranteed to remain valid only until the function returns; the temporary can be destroyed *any* time thereafter until exiting the scope in which the temporary was created.[34] If the second temporary `my_BigInt` is no longer valid by the time the `isMember` method of `my_BigIntSet` is invoked, a memory reference through a bad pointer value could easily cause this program to crash!

```
class my_BigInt {
    // ...
  public:
    my_BigInt(int i);
    // ...
};

class my_BigIntSet {
    const my_BigInt **d_set_p;
    int d_size;                         // physical size
    int d_length;                       // cardinality
```

[34] **ellis**, Section 12.2, p. 268.

```
    public:
      // ...
      void add(const ni_BigInt& bi);  // bad idea: should pass by pointer
          // Stores the address of this object in the set.

          int isMember(const my_BigInt& bi) const;
              // Returns 1 if bi is a member of the set; else 0.

      };

  void g()
  {
      my_BigIntSet set;
      set.add(1);                      // Address of temporary my_BigInt Added
      set.add(2);                      // Address of temporary my_BigInt Added
      set.add(3);                      // Address of temporary my_BigInt Added
      set.isMember(2);                 // core dump?!
  }
```

Figure 9-22: Retaining the Address of a Reference Argument in a Function

Without careful scrutiny of the class definitions, the client has absolutely no warning that the address of the object (and not a copy of the object) will be retained. Had we instead defined the `add` function of `my_BigIntSet` to take a `const` pointer, we would have alerted the client that this function considers the lvalue to be important, and—at the same time—documented that fact directly in the declaration itself.[35] The modified usage model for `my_BigIntSet` is illustrated in Figure 9-23.

```
class my_BigIntSet {
    // ...
  public:
    // ...
    void add(const ni_BigInt *bi);
    // ...
};

void g ()
{
    my_BigIntSet set;
    set.add(1);                  // compile time error!
    set.add(&2);                 // compile time error!
    // ...
```

Figure 9-23: Making the Need for an Lvalue Explicit

---

[35] This recommendation, called the *Linton convention*, is presented in **murray**, Section 9.2.4, pp. 213–215.

Storing the address of an argument to a function is bad form. If the argument is passed by value, it is represented as a local automatic variable and the address will become invalid as soon as the function returns. If the argument is passed by `const` reference, we have no guarantee that it does not refer to a temporary. Passing the argument by `const` pointer instead of by `const` reference suppresses the implicit creation of a temporary, which is desired behavior when we plan to hold onto that address. Exceptions to this guideline do occur in very common idioms when it is obvious from context (e.g., an iterator) that the address of the object *must* be stored. Note that when a function stores the address of a non-`const` argument for later modification, the two guidelines presented in this section (e.g., modifiable + lvalue) both apply; in this case, the object should *always* be passed by non-`const` pointer.

Minor Design Rule

Never attempt to delete an object passed by reference.

Beyond modification, functions that delete an object should always take a non-`const` pointer to that object and never a non-`const` reference. In order to delete an object, you must supply a pointer to the delete operator. Taking the address of an object to be deleted is error prone; some compilers (e.g., CFRONT) will generate a warning message, cajoling the developer to add an extra assignment (or worse, a cast) to a pointer variable. Even more compelling is the fact that the C++ language specification permits the value of a deleted pointer to be adjusted (e.g., to 0) by the compiler.[22] A null (or invalid) reference is not permitted in the language.[23]

Using pointer instead of reference arguments to capture the semantic properties mentioned in this section has yet another benefit in terms of maintenance. If a function that previously did not modify or take the address of an argument should suddenly be changed to do so, all clients of that function would be forced to examine their code before they could recompile. This is exactly what we want! Making such significant semantic changes with syntactic compatibility could silently lead to subtle bugs and very unpleasant surprises.

---

[22] **ellis**, Section 5.3.4, p. 63.

[23] **cargill**, Chapter 6, p. 125; **ellis**, Section 8.4.3, p. 153.

9.1.12 Pass Argument as `const` or Non-`const`

Whenever a pointer or reference passed to a function refers to the object as `const`, it widens the audience of potential clients who can take advantage of this function.

Guideline

Whenever a parameter passes its argument by reference or pointer to a function that neither modifies that argument nor stores its writable address, that parameter should be declared `const`.

As a rule, whenever we can reasonably pass a pointer or reference argument as `const`, we should.[38]

Guideline

Avoid declaring parameters passed by value to a function as `const`.

An argument passed to a function by value is a copy. Declaring the parameter `const` makes its value immutable in the function body:

```
void f(const int i)             // bad idea
{
    // ...
    ++i;                        // compile-time error
    // ...
}
```

Whether or not this local copy is changed is an implementation detail of the function; declaring it `const` exposes this decision in the interface, compromising not only insulation but also readability. This is not an issue for user-defined types since we never pass them by value anyway (see Section 9.1.11).

---

[38] See **meyers**, Items 21–22, pp. 73–82.

Guideline

Consider placing parameters (except perhaps those with default arguments) that enable modifiable access before parameters that pass arguments by value, `const` reference, or `const` pointer.

Except for (optional) parameters with default arguments added after a function is already in use, parameters that allow their arguments to be modified should precede parameters whose arguments are passed by value, `const` reference, or `const` pointer. Apart from making where to look for modifiable arguments more uniform, this recommendation is admittedly arbitrary; however, it is a classic style that is language independent, predates C++ (and even C), and has proven useful over the years.

8.5.10 Friend or Non-Friend Function

Friendship, even within a single component, affects maintenance cost.

Principle

Avoiding unnecessary friendships (even within the same component) can improve maintainability.

Before making an individual operator a friend, consider whether there is a primitive member function that can be used to implement that operator. For example, we can often implement free `operator+` in terms of the primitive member `operator+=` (see Section 3.6) without making `operator+` a friend. Similarly, a single public member function `compare` can be used to implement all six of the free equality and relation operators (`==  !=  <=  <  >=  >`) (see Section 9.1.2). Typically an iterator class with private access can be used to implement a free output `operator<<` of a container type (such as a set, list, etc.), obviating individual friendships and enhancing user extensibility.

Guideline

Avoid granting friendship to individual functions.

In general, whenever we decide we need a free operator, we should be cognizant of what primitive functions we might use to implement that operator. Making a free operator a friend could compromise encapsulation (see Section 3.6).

9.1.14 Inline or Non-Inline Function

From Section 6.2.3 we know that inline functions affect insulation. Apart from exposing the implementation, large inline functions can increase executable size, potentially making an integrated system run slower than if some of these functions had been declared non-inline. If insulation is not an issue, the first question is whether the object code resulting from the body of the function is larger or smaller than the non-inline function call. If the inline object code is no bigger than a function call, inlining will not increase executable size.

Guideline

Avoid declaring a function `inline` whose body produces object code that is larger than the object code produced by the equivalent non-inline function *call* itself.

For functions that merely get and set data members, it is often reasonable to use an inline function without first acquiring performance data. For function bodies that generate more object code than the corresponding non-inline function call, performance analysis at the system level should precede the decision to define the function inline. Passing additional arguments to a function increases the amount of code generated for a non-inline function call. Therefore, an inline function taking several arguments could justify a somewhat larger function body before profiling.

If a function is called frequently and performance is critical, the next question to ask is, "From how many distinct locations can the function be called?" If access to the function is restricted and the function is known to be called from only a few distinct locations, then inlining is not likely to be an issue with respect to executable size. If the function is large and may be called from many locations, the function is not likely to be a candidate for inlining.

Guideline

Avoid declaring a function `inline` that your compiler will not generate inline.

Finally, inlining is merely a hint to the compiler; there is no way to ensure that a function will actually be `inline`'d. Whenever we take the address of a function declared `inline`, we force a static (non-inline) version of the function to be generated in the translation unit where the address was taken. If a function declared `inline` is too large or too complex, it might not inline; the metrics that control this are compiler dependent.

When a function does not inline, the compiler defines a static version of the inline function in each translation unit that uses the inline. These multiple static copies may cause the executable to be bigger and run more slowly than if the function had been declared non-inline. Fortunately, there are usually ways to ask a compiler to report functions that do not inline.[39]

A dynamically bound function call cannot be generated inline; however, a virtual function call can be inlined when the virtual call mechanism is disabled by using the scope resolution operator (`::`). A virtual function call can also be inlined if the compiler can determine the exact type of the concrete object (e.g., when the function is called from the object itself instead of through a pointer or reference). In any event, the compiler will be forced to implement a non-inline version of the virtual function in order to store its address in the virtual tables. If we are not careful, far more than one static copy of this function could be generated (see Section 9.3.3).[40]

---

[39] See **meyers**: Item 33, pp. 107–110.

[40] See also **murray**, Section 9.13.2, p. 244.

9.2 Fundamental Types Used in the Interface

In Chapter 3 we discussed the uses relation in terms of user-defined types. In this section we address the use of various fundamental types in the interface of a function.

9.2.1 Using `short` in the Interface

The C++ language requires that variables declared of type `char` or `short` be promoted automatically to type `int` before participating in an expression. That is, no direct use of `char` or `short` values can be made in an expression apart from determining their size (`sizeof`) or taking their address (unary `&`).

Guideline

Avoid using `short` in the interface; use `int` instead.

Figure 9-24a illustrates that before a `char` or a `short` is used in a binary expression, it is first automatically promoted to a temporary of type `int`. Irrespective of any overloaded function call resolution, the same automatic promotion to `int` values also occurs implicitly during a function call as indicated in Figure 9-24b. The type `int` in C++ typically corresponds to the fundamental integer size supported by the underlying computer hardware. For most commercially available workstations, an `int` is (at least) 32 bits.[41]

---

[41] In what follows I am assuming a 32-bit (or larger) architecture. If you are working on a 16-bit machine or an embedded system, some of the statements in this section will not apply.

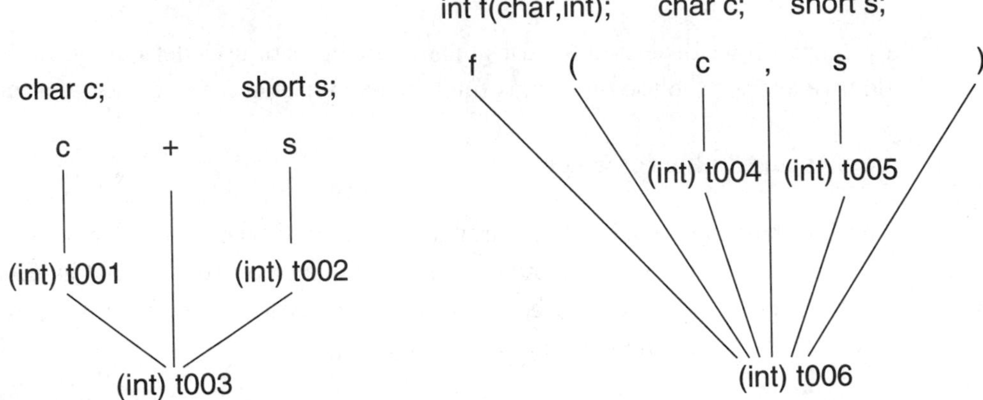

(a) Integral Promotion in Binary Operation (b) Integral Promotion in Function Call

Figure 9-24: Result of Integral Promotion

Figure 9-25 illustrates a class that uses `short` instead of `int` in its interface. Why might we want to do such a thing? The motivation comes from a desire to express intent directly in the declaration and avoid having to resort to comments. If we declare that a parameter is a `short`, no one would ever try to pass in anything larger and so we don't have to check it ourselves, right?

```
class my_Point {
    short d_x;
    short d_y;

  public:
    // CREATORS
    my_Point(short x, short y);
    my_Point(const my_Point& p);
    my_Point();

    // MANIPULATORS
    my_Point& operator=(const my_Point& p);
    void x(short x);
    void y(short y);

    // ACCESSORS
    short x() const;
    short y() const;
};
```

Figure 9-25: Using `short` Integers in the Interface (Bad Idea)

Principle

Specifying design decisions directly in the code instead of relying on comments is a design goal; designing robust interfaces that are safe to use and easy to maintain will occasionally compete with this goal.

The fact of the matter is that documenting information in the header file that is useful only when looking directly at the header file itself can be of limited utility when it comes to maintenance (see Section 9.1.11). Clients will pass an integer literal or expression regardless of how we attempt to document it in the header; declaring the integer to be a `short` simply causes the truncation to occur outside the function rather than inside, making it impossible for the function itself to detect an overflow error. To the client, the perception is the same: the function doesn't work.

Consider the answers to the following questions:

1. Does using a `short` in the interface ensure at compile time that overflow will not occur at runtime?

   No. The C++ language allows arithmetic overflow to occur silently at runtime.

2. Does using `short` in the interface allow for overflow detection?

   No. If the interface accepted an `int`, we could at least detect a coordinate that is out of range of the implementation; at a minimum, passing an `int` would allow us to assert the precondition.

3. Does using `short` in the interface serve to encapsulate or un-encapsulate the implementation?

   Exposing `short` in the interface limits the size of the coordinates that any implementation can accommodate and eliminates our ability to detect overflow; limiting implementation choice is a symptom of reducing encapsulation.

4. Does using `short` in the interface improve or degrade efficiency?

   If anything, the argument may have to have its high-order bits masked off, requiring additional work and therefore reducing runtime efficiency.

5. Does using `short` in the interface interfere with overloaded function resolution?

   Yes. According to the rules of the language, converting an `int` to a `short` is a standard conversion just like converting an `int` to a `double`. That is, if two functions were named `f`, one taking a `short` and the other taking a `double`, the call `f(10)` would be ambiguous.

6. Does using `short` in the interface interfere with template instantiation?

```
template<short N>
class pub_BitVec {
    int d_bits : N;

  public:
    BitVec();
    int operator[](int i);
    void set(int i);
    void clear(int i);
    void toggle(int i);
};
```

Figure 9-26: Template Class Parameterized by `short`

   Yes. According to the rules of template instantiation, the type of a template must match the argument exactly; a template parameterized by a `short` such as `pub_BitVec` in Figure 9-26 will not be instantiated when declared with an integer literal or any compile-time constant integral expression:

```
BitVec<2> v1;                   // expecting short got int
BitVec<short(2)> v1;            // ok.
BitVec<5 - 3> v2;               // expecting short got int
BitVec<short(5 - 3)> v1;        // ok.
```

9.2.2 Using `unsigned` in the Interface

The C++ language requires that binary operators involving one `unsigned` integer first convert the other integer to `unsigned` before performing the operation. Usually this is not a problem; however, when it is, it's not at all easy to debug.

Guideline

Avoid using `unsigned` in the interface; use `int` instead.

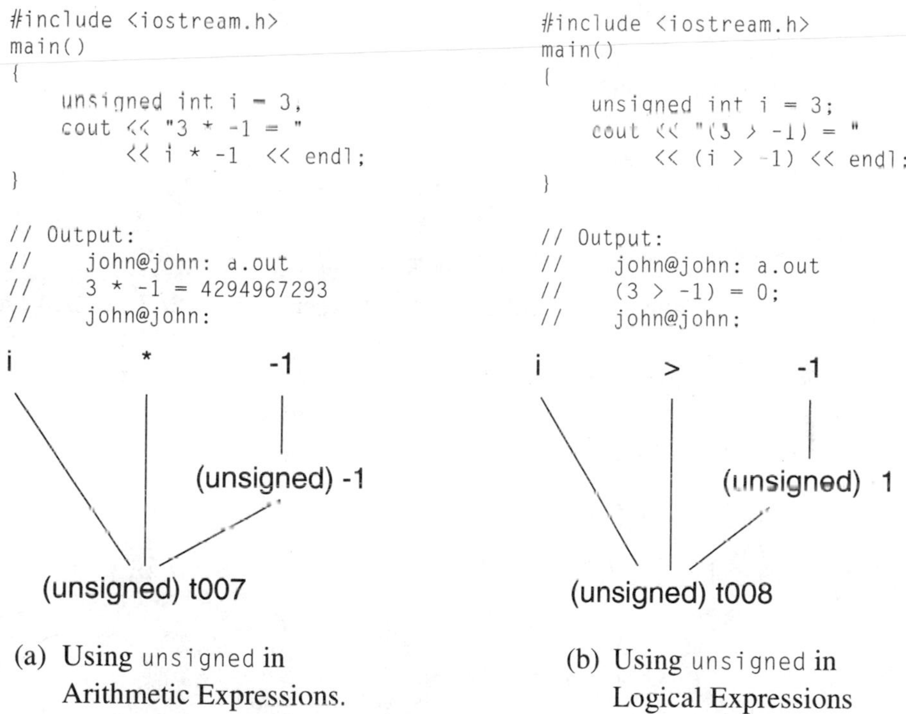

```
#include <iostream.h>
main()
{
    unsigned int i = 3;
    cout << "3 * -1 = "
         << i * -1  << endl;
}

// Output:
//     john@john: a.out
//     3 * -1 = 4294967293
//     john@john:
```

```
#include <iostream.h>
main()
{
    unsigned int i = 3;
    cout << "(3 > -1) = "
         << (i > -1) << endl;
}

// Output:
//     john@john: a.out
//     (3 > -1) = 0;
//     john@john:
```


(a) Using `unsigned` in Arithmetic Expressions.

(b) Using `unsigned` in Logical Expressions

Figure 9-27: Mixing `int` with `unsigned` in Binary Expressions

Figure 9-27a illustrates that when a `signed` and an `unsigned` value are involved in a binary operation, the bit pattern of the `signed` number is silently reinterpreted as an `unsigned` number. No actual temporary is created. For most integer representations, the result is the largest number that will fit in an `unsigned` (e.g.,

$2^{32} - 1 = 4294967295$). This number is then multiplied by 3, which causes the `unsigned` to overflow; the result is therefore printed as $(3 \bullet (2^{32}-1)) \bmod 2^{32} = 2^{32} - 3$. In Figure 9-27b precisely the same reasoning applies. The `unsigned` value again causes the bit pattern of the `signed` value to be reinterpreted to a huge `unsigned` value, the comparison is made, and—for many—produces unexpected results.

```
class my_Array {
    int *d_array_p;
    unsigned short d_size;      // bad idea: Short used in implementation
                                //           only, but see Section 10.1.2.
  public:
    // CREATORS
    Array(unsigned int size);
    Array(const Array& array);
    ~Array();

    // MANIPULATORS
    Array& operator=(const Array& array);
    int& operator[](unsigned int i);

    // ACCESSORS
    int operator[](unsigned int i) const;
    unsigned int size() const;
};
```

Figure 9-28: Using `unsigned` Integers in the Interface (Bad Idea)

One might argue that we deserve what we get when we mix negative and unsigned integers. Perhaps—when *we* do it. But consider the seemingly innocent `my_Array` class shown in Figure 9-28.

```
#include <assert.h>
#include <iostream.h>
void printForwardMovingAverage(const my_Array& a, int width)
{
    assert(width > 0);
    const int N = width - 1;
    int total = 0;
    for (int i = -N; i < a.size(); ++i) {
        if (i + N < a.size()) {
            total += a[i + N];
        }
        cout << i << '\t' << double(total)/width << endl;
        if (i >= 0) {
            total -= a[i];
        }
    }
}
```

Figure 9-29: Innocent Client Function to Print the Forward Moving Average

As a client of the `my_Array` class, I have written the function shown in Figure 9-29, which takes an instance of `my_Array` and prints its forward moving average of specified width. As a responsible developer, I whipped up the little test driver shown in Figure 9-30 to verify that my function worked—and it did not.

```
// test.c
# include <stdlib.h>  // atoi()

main(int argc, char *argv[])
{
    const int SIZE = argc > 1 ? atoi(argv[1]) : 4;
    const int WINDOW = argc > 2 ? atoi(argv[2]) : 2;
    my_Array array(SIZE);
    for (int i = 0; i < SIZE; ++i) {
        array[i] = 1;
    }
    printForwardMovingAverage(array, WINDOW);
}
```

Figure 9-30: Test Driver for `printForwardMovingAverage` Function

The output I expected for the default values (an array of `SIZE` 4 containing all 1's and a `WINDOW` width of 2) was supposed to look as shown in Figure 9-31a; the disappointing reality is shown in Figure 9-31b.

```
john@john: a.out
-1       0.5
 0        1
 1        1
 2        1
 3        0.5
 john@john:
```

(a) Expected Output

```
john@john: a.out
john@john:
```

(b) Actual Output

Figure 9-31: Driver Output for `printForwardMovingAverage` Function

Even though we know better than to mix `unsigned` and `int`, one does not always check a header for each integer value that is returned. In this case, it was `size()` that did us in. The problem is again that comparing a negative number with an `unsigned int` will usually go the wrong way, as illustrated again in Figure 9-32.

```
#include <iostream.h>
main()
{
    my_Array a(10);
    cout << "size = " << a.size() << endl;
    if (a.size() > -1) {
        cout << "size is positive or zero." << endl;
    }
    else {
        cout << "size is negative!!!" << endl;
    }
}

// Output:
//      john@john: a.out
//      size = 10
//      size is negative!!!
//      john@john:
```

Figure 9-32: Comparing an `unsigned int` Return Value Against a Negative `int` Value

All we need to do to repair the damage in this case is to replace the line

```
for (int i = -N; i < a.size(); ++i) {
```

in Figure 9-29 with the pair of lines

```
const int S = a.size(); // work-around for returning unsigned
for (int i = -N; i < S; ++i) {
```

and the function will operate correctly.

Principle

Occasionally comments work better than trying to express an interface decision directly in the code (e.g., `unsigned`).

Bugs occurring from the use of `unsigned` in the interface are frustrating and notoriously hard to detect. Looking at the problem with a debugger, it can seem that the `if` statement itself in Figure 9-32 must be broken. It is often quite a stretch to guess that the return value of the function is declared `unsigned` and is implicitly converting some other negative number to a positive value as a result of a binary comparison operation.

Consider the answers to the following questions:

1. Does using `unsigned` in the interface ensure at compile time that negative numbers will not be passed in at runtime?

   No. The C++ language allows the bit pattern to be reinterpreted silently at runtime.

2. Does using `unsigned` in the interface allow for the possibility of checking for negative values?

   Yes, but you have to coerce the `unsigned` back to an `int` internally.

3. Does using `unsigned` improve or degrade runtime efficiency?

   It typically has no effect.

4. Does using `unsigned` increase the size of the positive integer that can be stored?

   Yes—by 1 bit. This extra bit is rarely useful. If the extra capacity is needed, there is a risk of losing data when the `unsigned` is converted back to an `int` (see Section 10.1.2).

5. Does using `unsigned` in the interface increase or decrease the likelihood of user error?

   It increases it. Without looking at the header file, there is no safety advantage, since the conversion is done silently. Naively using an unsigned return value in an expression that involves a negative `int` value will cause the client's code to break at runtime.

6. Does using `unsigned` in the interface serve to encapsulate or unencapsulate the implementation?

   Exposing `unsigned` in the interface effectively limits the values that any implementation will accommodate, thereby reducing encapsulation.

7. Does using `unsigned` in the interface interfere with overloaded function

resolution?

Yes. According to the rules of the language, converting an `int` to an `unsigned` is a standard conversion, just like converting an `int` to a `double`. That is, if two functions were named `f`, one taking an `unsigned` and the other taking a `double`, the call `f(10)` would be ambiguous.

8. Does using `unsigned` in the interface interfere with template instantiation?

   Yes. We encounter a problem for precisely the same reason as when parameterizing a template with a `short` (see Section 9.2.1).

9.2.3 Using `long` in the Interface

Although in this book we cavalierly assume that an `int` holds at least 32 bits, in fact only 16 bits are needed to satisfy the ANSI requirement for type `int`.[42] If you are working on a 16-bit machine, the following guideline clearly does not apply.

Guideline

Avoid using `long` in the interface; `assert(sizeof(int) >= 4)` and use either `int` or a user-defined large-integer type instead.

The C++ language defines a `long` integer to be at least as large as an `int`. A `long int` means "the biggest integer you have"; an `int` means "the biggest integer that is efficient" (typically the natural word size of the computer). On a 16-bit machine, a `long` is probably a double word (32 bits). On most commercially available compilers for 32-bit workstations, a `long` is a single 32-bit word. On 64-bit architectures, an `int` will probably continue to be set at 32 bits for compatibility with existing programs, while a `long` might be 64 bits. If portability is an issue, any assumption that a `long int` is more than 32 bits is a recipe for failure (not every machine you may want to port to will have a 64-bit `long int`).

---

[42] **ellis**, Section 3.2.1c, p. 28.

Figure 9-33 illustrates a component that uses `long int` instead of `int` in the interface. Why might we want to do such a thing? Usually the answer to this question is something like, "I want it to hold the biggest integers it can." For small projects on small machines, this reason might be sufficient. For large projects running on industrial-strength workstations on multiple platforms, the `int` is either big enough or it isn't—if you're not sure, then it isn't. Fortunately, the C++ language enables us to define a larger integer type ourselves.

```
class my_Point {
    long int d_x;
    long int d_y;

  public:
    // CREATORS
    my_Point(long int x, long int y);
    my_Point(const my_Point& p);
    my_Point();

    // MANIPULATORS
    my_Point& operator=(const my_Point& p);
    void x(long int x);
    void y(long int y);

    // ACCESSORS
    long int x() const;
    long int y() const;
};
```

Figure 9-33: Using `long` Integers in the Interface

Whenever we initialize, assign, or pass a `long int` value where an `int` value is expected, we are forcing a standard conversion that has the potential to lose information (if it didn't, there would be no reason to use `long` in the first place). The compiler may warn clients of these "lossy" conversions, as illustrated in Figure 9-34. We could always tell our clients how to suppress these warnings by sprinkling their code with casts—just kidding!

```
int r(int x, int y);

void g()
{
    my_Point p(3, 2);              // fine, int converted to long.
    int j, i = p.x();              // warning: long assigned to int
    j = p.y();                     // warning: long assigned to int
    double d = r(p.x(), p.y());    // warning: argument 1: long passed as int
                                   // warning: argument 1: long passed as int
}
```

Figure 9-34: Mixing Types `int` and `long`

Consider the answers to the following questions:

1. Does using a `long` in the interface ensure increased capacity over an `int`?

   Not on all platforms. Often an `int` and a `long` are the same size. If you depend on increased capacity, your code will not be portable.

2. Does using `long` in the interface hinder usability?

   Yes. A potentially large number of warning messages could inundate clients (see also question 3).

3. Does using `long` in the interface interfere with overloaded function resolution?

   Yes. According to the rules of the language, converting an `int` to a `long` is a standard conversion, just like converting an `int` to a `double`.[43] That is, if two functions were named `f`, one taking a `long` and the other taking a `double`, the call `f(10)` would be ambiguous.

4. Does using `long` in the interface interfere with template instantiation?

   Yes. We encounter a problem for precisely the same reason as when parameterizing a template with a `short` (see Section 9.2.1).

9.2.4 Using `float`, `double`, and `long double` in the Interface

The C++ language enables floating-point computation to occur in each of the three floating-point types:

- float,
- double, and
- long double.

[43] Going from `int` to `long` is *not* an integral promotion; rather it is a standard conversion. Converting an `int` to a `long` and its (`const`/`volatile`) equivalents is the only "non-lossy" standard conversion in the language.

Guideline

Consider using `double` exclusively for floating-point types used in the interface unless there is a compelling reason to use `float` or `long double`.

Historically, C required all floating-point expressions to be of type `double` and did not support `long double`. ANSI C introduced the ability to do arithmetic directly with `float` values. Most C library calls pass and return a floating-point value as a `double`. These days, much of the computer hardware is optimized to make `double` floating-point calculations run as quickly as possible. In fact, a double precision multiply on my machine is an order of magnitude faster than an integer multiply (which is implemented as a subroutine).

Principle

In most cases that arise in practice, the only fundamental types you need in order to represent integer and floating-point numbers in the interface are `int` and `double`, respectively.

The same issues of consistency, error checking, operator overloading, and template instantiation that applied to the integer types apply to floating-point types as well.

8.7 Special-Case Functions

There are a few special member functions that warrant some discussion. Conversion operators (i.e., single-argument constructors and "cast" operators) and compiler-generated functions (such as the copy constructor, the assignment operator, and, in particular, the destructor) deserve specific mention.

8.7.1 Conversion Operators

Implicit conversions compete with type safety, can introduce ambiguities, and in general increase the cost of maintaining a program. Any time we create a constructor that can take a single argument, we enable an implicit user-defined conversion. Defining a conversion operator other than a constructor, referred to in this book as a *cast operator*, also enables implicit conversion. An example of each of these forms can be found in Figure 9-35.

```
pub_String {
    // ...
  public:
    pub_String(const char *cptr, int maxSizeHint = 0);  // "cast constructor"
    // ...
    operator const char *() const;                      // "cast operator"
};
```

Figure 9-35: The Two Forms of User-Defined Conversion Operators in C++

Principle

Constructors that enable implicit conversion, especially from widely used or fundamental types (e.g., `int`), erode the safety afforded by strong typing.

A constructor accepting a single argument, sometimes called a *cast constructor*, can contribute to surprises by enabling an unexpected conversion. Consider the two-dimensional table component sketched in Figure 9-36.

```
// d2_table.h
# ifndef INCLUDED_D2_TABLE
# define INCLUDED_D2_TABLE

class d2_Entry;
class d2_RowIter;
class d2_ColIter;
```

```
class d2_Table {
    // ...
    friend d2_RowIter;
    // ...
  public:
    d2_Table();
    // ...
};

class d2_RowIter {
    // ...
    friend d2_ColIter;
    // ...
  public:
    d2_RowIter(const d2_Table& table);  // takes a d2_Table
    operator const void *() const;
    void operator++();
};

class d2_ColIter {
    // ...
  public:
    d2_ColIter(const d2_RowIter&);      // takes a d2_RowIter!!!
    operator const void *() const;
    void operator++();
    const d2_Entry& operator()() const;
};

#endif;
```

Figure 9-36: Sketch of Two-Dimensional `d2_table` Component

The intent is that a client will apply a row iterator to the table and, for each row position, reapply a new column iterator to that row iterator.

As the function in Figure 9-37 shows, editor cut-and-paste can introduce bugs: `cit(t)` on the indicated line should have been `cit(rit)`. As long as our code is "type-safe," we stand a good change of detecting such bugs at compile time—but not here! What actually happens is that each instantiation of the second iterator forces an implicit conversion of the `d2_Table`, `t`, to an unnamed temporary of type `d2_RowIter` (which happens to be positioned at the first row of the table). There is no guarantee that this temporary row iterator will remain valid while the column iterator operates; but if it does, the table will appear as if the contents of all rows are identical to the first.

```
void g(d2_Table& t)
{
    for (d2_RowIter rit(t); rit; ++rit) {
        for (d2_ColIter cit(t); cit; ++cit) {       // <-- oops!!! "cit(t)"
                                                    // should be "cit(rit)"
            cout << cit() << endl;  // print (ith row, jth col) table entry
        }
    }
}
```

Figure 9-37: (Mis)using the `d2_table` Component

A cast constructor taking a user-defined type is less likely to be a problem in practice than constructors taking a single fundamental type—especially an integral type. For example, consider the situation depicted in Figure 9-38. A `gr_Graph` provides its clients with the ability to look up a particular node either by name or id. Unfortunately, a `gr_NodeId` knows how to construct itself from an arbitrary integer. The apparent type safety afforded by `gr_Graph`'s overloaded `lookupNode` methods does little to detect the error in function `f`. The problem is that the extra "*" at the indicated line turns the character string name, `names[0]`, into the ASCII value of its first character; this value is promoted to an `int` and then implicitly converted to some bogus `gr_NodeId`. It is anyone's guess what happens next. The error would have been detected at compile time had `gr_NodeId` not enabled an implicit conversion from an integral type. (A similar problem results from the use of default arguments in Figure 9-18b.)

```
class gr_Node;

class gr_NodeId {
    int d_index;

  public:
    // gr_NodeId(int index);       // there goes type safety
    // ...
};

class gr_Graph {
    // ...
  public:
    // ...
    const gr_Node *lookupNode (const char *name) const;
        // lookup a node in the graph by name
    const gr_Node *lookupNode (const gr_NodeId& id) const;
        // lookup a node in the graph by id
};
```

```
void f(const char *names[], const gr_Graph& g)
{
    const gr_Node *node = g.lookupNode(*names[0]);  // <-- oops!!! didn't
                                                     // want * in *names[0]
    if (node) {
        cout << *node << endl; // all is well, print the node
    }
    else {
        cout << "Program Error: What happened to the node!!!" << endl;
        assert(0);     // node with this name should be there
    }
}
```

Figure 9-38: (Mis)using `gr_Graph` to Look Up a `gr_Node` by Name

Guideline

Consider avoiding "cast" operators, especially to fundamental integral types; instead, make the conversion explicit.

In general, explicit conversion functions are more readable and much safer than implicit conversions. Although cast constructors are a necessary part of doing business, cast operators are a form of implicit conversion that is more easily avoided: we can *always* supply an explicit conversion function to do the work of a cast operator.

As we saw in Figure 9-6, providing `pub_String` with both a cast constructor and a cast operator (for implicit conversion to and from a `const char *`) led to ambiguities that required further effort to resolve. Had we replaced the cast operator with a member function such as `const char *str() const;` with the identical implementation, no ambiguity would have occurred.[44]

In very limited, well-understood situations, implicit conversions can increase usability.[45] Automatically converting a `pub_String` to a `const char *` and converting an arbitrary object to a `const void *` (as a test for validity) seem to be reasonably safe uses of implicit conversion. Arguably, the client code would be clearer if forced to call explicit members such as `str()` and `isValid()`. What makes these conversions

---

[44] See **meyers**, Item 26, p. 89.
[45] See **stroustrup**, Section 7.3.2, pp. 232–233.

reasonable is the lack of surprise potential. Passing a `pub_String` to a function expecting a `const char *` is almost always a reasonable thing to do because the semantics of the two types are so tightly coupled. Implicitly converting to a `const void *` is safe because the only useful thing you can do with the result is compare it to 0.

Clear misuses of implicit conversion involve converting an object to an unrelated or more widely usable type—especially a fundamental type. For example, having a specific object such as `gr_NodeId` convert itself to an `int` representing its internal index is entirely inappropriate and virtually eliminates any type-safety advantage of having represented the value as a class. A `geom_Point` that knows how to convert itself to a double representing its magnitude would also be inappropriate, especially since explicit conversion (e.g., using `pt.magnitude()`) is safer, is more readable, and is an interface alternative that is always available.

9.3.2 Compiler-Generated Value Semantics

The C++ language requires that the compiler automatically generate the definitions of certain basic member functions, if needed, unless they are already explicitly declared in the class (see Section 6.2.6). Most commonly of interest are the generated copy constructor and assignment operator.

Guideline

Explicitly declare (either public or private) the constructor and assignment operator for any class defined in a header file, even when the default implementations are adequate.

When considering whether or not to declare a copy constructor or assignment operator explicitly, the first question to ask is whether we intend this object to support value semantics (see Section 5.9). For some objects, such as `Gnode` in Figure 5-81, value semantics do not make sense. For other objects, such as iterators, value semantics make sense but are often not necessary for a sufficient interface (see Section 8.2). In either case, we should explicitly inhibit the use of such value-semantic functions by declaring them `private` and deliberately leaving them undefined.[46]

If value semantics are to be supported, the next issue is whether the compiler-generated constructor and/or assignment operator would do the right thing.[33] If the default definitions are not correct, we will need to declare these members and define them ourselves. Otherwise, we must determine the likelihood that the default definitions might become invalid, and determine also the cost to our clients of making an uninsulated change to our interface if they do. If the expected cost is too high, we would again opt to define these operations ourselves rather than use the default implementation.

Finally, for very local objects where the compiler-generated implementations make sense and insulation is not an issue, we might allow these function definitions to default. In particular, allowing default copy and assignment semantics is often appropriate for classes defined entirely within a `.c` file. However some clients of an exported class definition that relies on default semantics may be left with this nagging doubt: is the default implementation really good enough, or did the author simply fail to address this issue?

Note that some current implementations of C++ do not allow generated `operator=` to be called via function notation, nor its address to be taken, as required by the language.[34] Such failings by compilers bolster the argument in favor of always declaring an exposed class's value-semantic operators explicitly.

8.7.3 The Destructor

The destructor is an important function with many unique responsibilities; we enumerate them here.

Minor Design Rule

In every class that declares or is derived from a class that declares a virtual function, explicitly declare the destructor as the first virtual function in the class and define it out of line.

---

[32] **meyers**, Item 27, pp. 92–93.
[33] **ellis**, Section 12.8, p. 295; and **meyers**, Item 11, pp. 34–37.
[34] **ellis**, Section 12.8, p. 296.

The destructor is responsible for destroying the object and freeing any resources (e.g., dynamic memory) currently managed by that object. When a class declares a function `virtual`, it is advertising itself as a base class—what other reason could there be for declaring a function `virtual`? Derived classes may accrue resources even when the base class has none. Conversely, in order to ensure that the derived class destructor is called, even from a base-class pointer or reference, the base-class destructor must be declared `virtual`.[49]

In an efficient implementation of dynamic binding, we would hope that there would be only a single copy of any virtual table in the entire program. The question is, "In which unique translation unit will the compiler deposit the virtual table definition(s) for a given class?" The trick employed by CFRONT (and many other C++ implementations) is to place the external virtual tables in the translation unit that defines the lexically first non-inline virtual function that appears in the class (if one exists).

The cost of ignorance can sometimes be truly staggering. Figure 9-39 depicts a real-life problem that went undetected in a large project for quite some time. The story begins with the fact that the popular `core_String` class is derived from `core_StringBase` that contains virtual functions, including of course a virtual destructor. The `core_String` class, not allocating any additional resources, failed to declare a destructor at all. The compiler is required to generate a destructor for the derived class and place it in a virtual table for the derived class.

```
class core_StringBase {
    // ...
  public:
    // ...
    virtual ~core_StringBase();
    // ...
    virtual int length();
    virtual operator const char *() const;
};

class core_String : public core_StringBase {
    int d_length;
```

[49] **ellis**, Section 12.4, p. 278.

```
    public:
      core_String(const char *cptr);
      core_String(const core_String& string);
      core_String& operator=(const core_String& string);
      int length() { /* ... */ }
};
```

Figure 9-39: Failing to Define at Least One Virtual Function Out of Line

Not being given any clue as to where to place a unique global copy of the virtual table, the compiler placed a copy of the table in every translation unit that included the `core_String` header. To add insult to injury, there was also no unique place to generate a non-inline version of the destructor; hence, a static copy of the destructor was placed in every translation unit along with the virtual tables. Finally, every inline virtual function (e.g., `length`) was also denied a unique home for its out-of-line implementation. A static version of each inline virtual function was also placed in every translation unit that included the `core_String` class.

The problem was finally detected when the Unix "nm" utility was run on the executable and a histogram of static names turned up thousands of static function definitions, each with the same name, but defined in separate translation units. Declaring the destructor for `core_String` and implementing it out of line solved all of the problems. This behavior is cryptic and implementation dependent; however, this is our current reality.

In the style we have followed throughout this book, creators precede any other non-static member functions. Thus, the first virtual member function encountered is invariably the destructor. Also, in order for the address of a destructor to be placed in a virtual function table, there must be at least one version of the destructor defined out of line anyway. The requirement that there must be at least one virtual function declared non-inline, coupled with the natural lexical position of the destructor within the class, makes the destructor the natural choice to be declared virtual and defined out of line.

In rare cases (e.g., a deep inheritance hierarchy), performance may be improved by defining empty destructors inline, in which case some other function in the class *must* be declared a virtual, non-inline function to avoid generating redundant tables.

Guideline

In classes that do not otherwise declare virtual functions, explicitly declare the destructor as non-virtual and define it appropriately (either inline or out-of-line).

For classes that do not otherwise declare virtual functions, implementing a virtual destructor is not likely to be appropriate. Making the destructor alone virtual would, in most implementations, increase the size of each instance by the size of a pointer. For small objects such as `geom_Point`, the increase in cost could be 50 percent. One solution for guarding against memory leaks is that a class derived from a base class with a non-virtual destructor should avoid managing additional resources that must be released when the object is destroyed.[50]

For classes that do not require virtual functions, there is still a reason to require that the destructor be declared explicitly. Calling the destructor of a fundamental type explicitly is legal C++:[51]

```
int i;
i.int::~int();        // legal C++; does nothing
```

Attempting an explicit call to the destructor of an object that does not explicitly declare one and for which none has been generated doesn't work on several current compilers. Since it is not possible to take the address of a destructor, a destructor is generated for a class that does not explicitly declare one only when a base class or embedded member object has a destructor.[52] This fact has implications for template-based container objects that attempt to call the destructor of the parameterized type explicitly (Figure 10-33b provides a useful workaround). For consistency, it should be possible to destroy any object in place, regardless of whether or not a destructor has been defined.

---

[50] **meyers**, Item 14, pp. 42–48.
[51] **ellis**, Section 12.4, p. 280.
[52] **ellis**, Section 12.4, p. 277.

9.4 Summary

C++ provides an enormous amount of flexibility in describing the function-level interface. There are at least 14 separate questions we must address as we design each function. Each of these decisions evokes additional considerations that must be resolved in context:

1. Operator or non-operator function?

   Operator:
   - The operator notation improves usability (readability in particular).

   Non-Operator:
   - The operation on the user-defined type does not syntactically mirror the same operation on the fundamental types.

2. Free or member operator?

   Free:
   - We want to enable implicit user-defined conversion for its leftmost argument.
   - It is syntactically symmetric (e.g., `==` `<` `+`).

   Member:
   - We want to disable implicit user-defined conversion for its leftmost argument.
   - It modifies an argument (e.g., `=` `+=` `*=` `++`)
   - The language requires membership (e.g., `()` `[]` `->`).

3. Virtual or non-virtual function?

   Virtual:
   - Its behavior must be able to be overridden in a derived class.

   Non-virtual:
   - It is a symmetric operator function (e.g., `!=` `>=` `|`).
   - It is a unary operator function that should support user-defined conversion of its argument (e.g., `!` `+` `-`).
   - Its behavior can be implemented as variation in the value of member data.

4. Pure or non-pure virtual member function?

    Pure:

    - Not overriding its behavior in a derived class is likely to be an error.
    - Physically decoupling the interface from the implementation is important.
    - The class will be used by many clients.
    - The class defines a protocol.

    Non-pure:

    - Default behavior makes sense.
    - Its default behavior is correct in many cases.
    - The class will not be widely used.

5. Static or non-static member function?

    Static:

    - It uses a `struct` solely to scope the name of the function.
    - It implements non-primitive behavior escalated from a lower-level object
    - Symmetry with respect to user-defined conversion is needed among all of its arguments.

    Non-Static:

    - It depends on data contained within a specific instance of the class.
    - It is an operator function.

6. `const` or non-`const` member function?

    `const`:

    - It does not modify bits embedded in the `class` or `struct`.
    - It modifies only *physical* values that are never programmatically accessible by clients.

    Non-`const`:

    - It modifies logical values, even though the compiler says `const` would be legal.
    - It returns a non-`const` version of a type that could violate `const`-correctness.

- It is static.

7. Public, protected, or private member function?

Public:

- It is intended for direct use by the general public.

Protected:

- It is intended for use only by derived-class authors.

Private:

- It is a non-virtual implementation detail (especially to factor the implementation of a public inline function).
- It is a virtual function that must be programmed but that need not be accessed by derived classes.

8. Return by value, reference, or pointer?

Value:

- There is no preexisting object available to return.
- Preserving total encapsulation, is important.

Reference:

- There is always something to return.
- We are returning access to a polymorphic object whose memory is managed elsewhere.

Pointer:

- There *may* be something to return.
- The function may fail.

Argument:

- We want to return a newly allocated polymorphic object in a handle that will manage the object, reducing the likelihood of memory leaks.
- We want to preserve total encapsulation while returning heavy-weight objects more efficiently than by value.
- We want to return more than one item.
- Both status and a value must be returned.

9. Return `const` or non-`const`?

Const:

- We are returning a pointer or reference to a data member of the class.

- Returning non-`const` would violate `const`-correctness.
- We are returning a reference to a shared *dummy* object (e.g., a zero entry in a sparse array).

Non-`const`:

- We are returning by value.
- We are providing direct writable access to a contained object (e.g., in an array).

10. Argument optional or required?

Optional:

- We have added a new argument to existing code.
- There is a single algorithm.
- We want our code to be self-documenting.
- The default argument is an invalid value.

Required:

- This is a widely used interface.
- The default value is a user-defined type.
- Insulation is important.

11. Pass argument by value, reference, or pointer?

Value:

- It is a fundamental or enumerated type.

Reference:

- It is a user-defined type that is not modified.

Pointer:

- It is modified.
- Its address is taken.
- It is deleted.
- It may be omitted.

12. Pass argument as `const` or non-`const`?

`const`:

- It is a user-defined type passed by reference.
- It is never modified, but is passed by pointer (because a null value is sometimes appropriate).

Non-`const`:

- It (e.g., an enumeration or fundamental type) is

passed by value.

13. Friend or non-friend function?

    Friend:

    - Enforcement of encapsulation is not an issue (rare).

    Non-friend:

    - There is a member function (e.g., `compare`) or friend class (e.g., `StackIter`) available that is suitable for implementing it (e.g., `operator==`).

14. Inline or non-inline function?

    Inline:

    - The size of the inline function *body* would be smaller than the size of the non-inline function *call*.
    - Performance is measurably critical, and it is reasonably small or called from only a few places.

    Non-inline:

    - It will not inline.
    - It is useful only when dynamically bound.
    - Insulation is important.

There are many alternative integral types available for use in the interface of functions: `short`, `unsigned`, `long`, etc. In practice, on a 32-bit machine, the only integral type we need in the interface is `int`. Using any other type is potentially inefficient, unencapsulating, error prone, or just plain annoying to use.

There are three alternative floating-point types available in C++: `float`, `double`, and `long double`. Traditionally all floating-point arguments in C were converted to `double` before being passed as arguments. Most hardware is geared to handle `double` values as efficiently as possible. Unless there is a compelling reason to do otherwise, all floating-point numbers should be expressed as `double` in the interface.

Conversion operators (e.g., single-argument constructors and cast operators) compete with compile-time type safety. Constructors that take a single argument enable implicit user-defined conversion. However, such constructs are a necessary part of many interfaces. On the other hand, cast operators are easily avoided, simply by providing explicit conversion functions. Occasionally usability is enhanced by implicit conversion. In most cases, however, implicit conversion is a liability, particularly when it involves a fundamental integral type.

The C++ compiler automatically generates certain undefined functions (if needed). There are a variety of reasons for not relying on the default behavior, particularly when the interface is used widely throughout the system. Many implementations of C++ depend on there being at least one virtual function defined out of line. In our style, this will always be the destructor. Some current compilers do not allow explicit calls to destructors that are not explicitly declared. In practice, it is wise to define the destructor of *every* class explicitly. For classes with no virtual functions, define the destructor inline or out of line as appropriate. For classes with virtual functions, define the destructor out of line. For protocol classes (see Section 6.4.1.) the destructor should be empty.

10

Implementing an Object

The cavernous realm of object implementation alternatives is made ever more vast by good (i.e., small, encapsulating) interfaces. Making a design error here is far less costly than errors at higher levels of design because the problem is confined to a tiny portion of the overall system. Yet there are still several ways in which even individual implementation techniques can combine during system integration to affect the overall success of a project.

A program must run in an environment with finite resource (e.g., memory). Classes with many instances active at a single time put a premium on the size of their objects. The sizes and order of their individual data members will affect this size. Custom memory-management techniques can sometimes be used to double runtime performance, but they can also cause a system, over time, to soak up much more memory than is actually necessary.

In this final chapter, we examine some basic principles relating to the organizational details of implementing classes in C++. We even proffer some suggestions on implementing individual member functions. In the remainder of the chapter, we examine several issues relating to custom memory management.

Although memory management is a complex topic, it is a necessary concern of most high-performance systems. We look at several detailed examples and experiments that compare the relative merits of some common memory-management organizations. In particular, we explore the performance advantages of class-specific management techniques, and then discuss potential problems that can be caused when classes using these techniques are integrated into larger systems. We then present object-specific memory management as a preferred alternative—one that avoids many of these problems while achieving essentially the same runtime performance as the class-based technique. Finally we discuss memory management in the context of templates, and provide a detailed example of how to implement truly general-purpose container objects.

10.1 Member Data

In this section we discuss logical and organizational issues pertaining to the choice and ordering of data members within a class.

10.1.1 Natural Alignment

Many common RISC-based microprocessors depend on instances of fundamental types being naturally aligned. Being *naturally aligned* means that instances of built-in types such as `int`, `double`, and `char *` cannot reside at just any address, but instead must be aligned on an *N*-byte address boundary where *N* is the size of the object.

> **DEFINITION: An instance of a fundamental type is *naturally aligned* if its size divides the numerical value of its address.**

Since `sizeof(char)` is 1, a `char` may be stored at any addressable location in memory. If `sizeof(short)` is 2, it cannot be stored at an "odd" address; instead it must be stored at an "even" address, sometimes referred to as a *half-word boundary* (on a 32-bit machine). Integers and pointers, which often have sizes corresponding to the word size of the computer, would have to be stored at a word boundary (e.g., a 4-byte boundary on a 32-bit machine). A `double`, which is often larger than the word size of a machine, would normally be stored on a two-word boundary.[1]

---

[1] Often a `double` can be stored on an odd-word boundary (as opposed to an even-word boundary) without disastrous consequences. However, on some architectures, failing to follow natural alignment for a `double` can result in a significant decrease in performance.

DEFINITION: An instance of an aggregate type is *naturally aligned* if the alignment of the subtype with the most restrictive alignment requirement divides the address of the aggregate.

An instance of an array of a given type has the same alignment requirement as that of the type itself. Satisfying natural alignment for a user-defined type means satisfying the alignment requirements of the most restrictive embedded subtype. Figure 10-1 gives some examples of natural alignment on a typical 32-bit machine.

Assume `sizeof(char *) = sizeof(int)` = 4 and `sizeof(double)` = 8.

```
struct A {              struct B {              struct C {
    char d_c;               char d_c;               double d_d;
};                          char d_ac[3];           char *d_pc_p;
                        };                          int d_i;
                                                };

   sizeof(A): 1            sizeof(B): 4            sizeof(C): 16
alignment(A): 1         alignment(B): 1         alignment(C):  8
```

Figure 10-1: Size and Natural Alignment of Various User-Defined Types

Principle

The order in which data members are declared can affect object size.

The C++ language guarantees that in the absence of intervening access specifiers (e.g., `public`, `protected`, and `private`), the memory for non-static data members will be allocated with increasing address values corresponding to their order of declaration within the structure; however, they need not be contiguous.[2] Alignment within

[2] **ellis**, Section 9.2, p. 173.

a structure can cause gaps at both the middle and end of a structure (but never at the beginning). As a rule, one can assume natural alignment when it comes to organizing the layout of a `class` or `struct`; however, one should not depend on it.

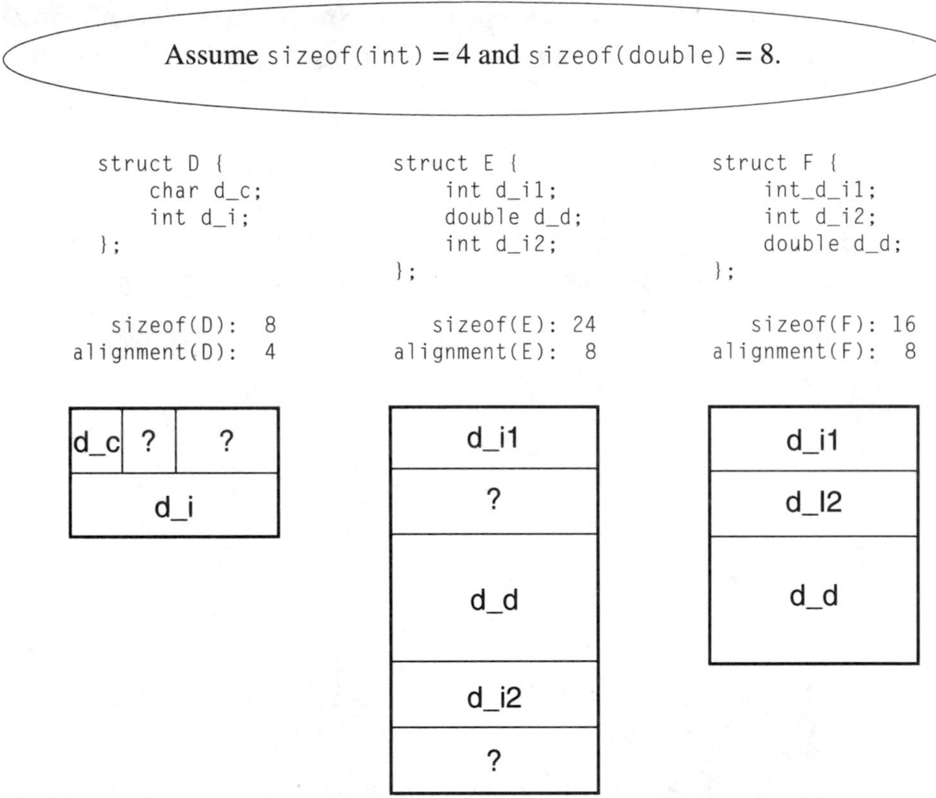

Figure 10-2: User-Defined Types with Holes

Figure 10-2 gives the size, natural alignment, and corresponding object layout of three user-defined types. Type `D` has a hole in the middle because the second data member is forced to reside on a word boundary. Type `E` has two holes: the first hole is caused because the `double`, `d_d`, is forced to start on a double word (8-byte) boundary. The second hole at the end is to ensure that each element in an array of `E` objects is also aligned:

```
given:   E a[N], b;  // N is compile-time const with value > 0
then:    assert(sizeof a == N * sizeof b);
```

Considering the order in which data members are declared (to reduce object size) becomes important when there will be many instances of the type active at one time. We can reorganize the data members of type `E` in Figure 10-2 to eliminate the holes; the result is type `F`, which is 33 percent smaller.

Whenever we attempt to allocate an object in place using the placement syntax for overloaded global operator `new`, we must make sure to do so at a properly aligned location. We may assume that global `new` returns addresses that will work for the most restrictive possible boundary. But we must be careful to avoid code such as the following:

```
#include <new.h>   // declare placement syntax
// ...
char *buf = new char[sizeof(Stack[100])];
Stack *p = new(&buf[1]) Stack;              // bus error!
```

An example of ensuring proper alignment within a buffer is given in Figure B-5 of Appendix B.2.

10.1.2 Fundamental Types Used in the Implementation

We argued in Section 9.2 that it is wise to restrict the selection of fundamental types used in the interface. The use of unusual fundamental types in the implementation brings up a separate set of issues.

Guideline

Use `short` instead of `int` in the implementation as an optimization only when it is *known* to be safe to do so.

```
class win_Point {
    short d_x;
    short d_y;

  public:
    win_Point(int x, int y);
    // ...
};
```

Figure 10-3: Using `short` in the Implementation

Figure 10-3 illustrates a reasonable use of `short` in the implementation of an object, assuming that the specification of this class states that the values of both *x* and *y* must be in the range [0, . . . , 1,023] at all times. On a 32-bit architecture where `sizeof(short)` is 2, we stand to fit the entire object in a single 32-bit register. The potential performance implications in both space and runtime may justify the use of `short` in this case. (For a more easily ported approach, see Section 10.1.3.) Justifiable uses of `unsigned` apart from low-level bit-shifting operations[3] are much harder to come by.

Guideline

Consider not using `unsigned` even in the implementation.

```
class pub_Array {
    int *d_array_p;
    unsigned int d_size;

  public:
    pub_Array(unsigned int size);
    // ...
};
```

(a) An Array Class

```
class core_String {
    char *d_string_p;
    unsigned short d_length;

  public:
    // ...
    int length() const;
    // ...
};
```

(b) A String Class

Figure 10-4: Inappropriate Use of `unsigned` and `short` in the Implementation

Figure 10-4 shows two classes in which the use of `unsigned` and `short` is misplaced (assuming a standard 32-bit architecture). In Figure 10-4a, the internal size is made `unsigned` to accommodate an array of up to 2^{32} integers, presumably to avoid the possibility of overflow. This decision has prompted the class author to expose the `unsigned int` in the interface as well. Even ignoring the adverse effect on the interface, the reasoning that leads to using `unsigned` in this example is twice fallacious. First, there is no way operator `new` is going to find space for anywhere near 2^{32} (about 4 billion) contiguous integer-sized objects (for the foreseeable future at least). Second, unless a pointer variable is larger than an `int`, the virtual address space limits the

---

[3] **ellis**, Section 5.8, p. 74.

total number of integers: $2^{32} \div$ `sizeof(int)` $\leq 2^{30}$. In other words, a (signed) `int`, which can hold positive values of up to $2^{31} - 1$, is more than big enough.

Principle

Using `unsigned` in the implementation to "gain a bit" is an indication that the fundamental integral type is not large enough to be safe.

In Figure 10-4b, the `core_String` class defines its internal size to be a `short` because it does not expect the length of a string to exceed several thousand. The internal variable is then made `unsigned`, just in case this value exceeds 32,767. Apart from the loss in maintainability discussed in Section 9.2.2, in all but pathological cases, if 32,767 isn't known to be large enough, then 65,535 is suspect as well. Making a `short` value `unsigned` "just in case" is tempting fate—it is usually better to use an `int` than to risk disaster. The misuse of `short` in this case is made even more ridiculous because natural alignment will create a hole where the other half of an `int` could have been placed; using a `short` here saves nothing.[4]

As with any localized, code-tuning effort, the decision to use alternate fundamental integral types (e.g., `short`, `char`) to optimize the storage within an object is best deferred until after the object is working, has been functionally tested, and performance analysis data is available. A suite of thorough regression tests will help to ensure that we do not optimize the correctness out of our implementation.[5]

10.1.3 Using `typedef` in the Implementation

Typedefs are often helpful for expressing complex function declarations. Typedefs also have a very useful place in the definitions of certain basic types that assume a precise number of bits in the representation.

---

[4] For further discussion regarding the inappropriate use of fixed-size arrays in the implementation, see **murray**, Section 9.2.2, pp. 210–212.

[5] See also **murray**, Sections 9.9–9.10, pp. 234–235; and **cargill**, Chapter 7, p. 138.

Sometimes we know exactly how many bits we need. For example, when we want to store information persistently (on disk) that is shared across heterogeneous platforms, we want to make sure that our basic data types hold no more and no less precision than needed. Figure 10-5a shows a systemwide header file that isolates the definitions of types with absolute sizes. When porting to a new platform, we need change only this one file in order to ensure that objects that assume absolute sizes are handled correctly. For example, Figure 10-5b shows a `geom_Point` class that requires exactly 32 bits for each coordinate. Typically, an `int` corresponds to the word size of the machine. Even on a 64-bit architecture we need only 32 bits for compatibility with other architectures—why waste the space?

```
// sys_type.h
#ifndef INCLUDED_SYS_TYPE
#define INCLUDED_SYS_TYPE

struct sys_Type {
    typedef signed char Int8;
    typedef short Int16;
    typedef int Int32;
    typedef unsigned char Uint8;
    typedef unsigned Uint16;
    typedef int Uint32;
    typedef float Float32;
    typedef double Float64;
};

#endif
```

(a) System-Wide Definitions File

```
// geom_point.h
#ifndef INCLUDED_GEOM_POINT
#define INCLUDED_GEOM_POINT

#ifndef INCLUDED_SYS_TYPE
#include "sys_type.h"
#endif


class geom_Point {
    sys_Type::Int32 d_x;
    sys_Type::Int32 d_y;

  public:
    Point (int x, int y);
    // ...
};

#endif
```

(b) Fixed-Size `geom_Point` Class

Figure 10-5: Using `typedef` to Specify Fixed Size in the Implementation

In case you thought that only functions are worth testing, consider the test driver for the `sys_type` component shown in Figure 10-6. Exercising this driver before any other ensures that components that depend on fixed-size data types are not "fooling themselves." We have isolated our configuration assumptions to a single file. Compile-time coupling is not a problem here since the common information derives from the lower-level compiler and the architecture of the machine (which is fixed), and not from any higher-level extensible collection of components (which could change).[6]

[6] Section 6.2.9 deals with enumerations and compile-time coupling.

```
// sys_type.t.c
#include "test_util.h"          // define TEST_ASSERT, etc.
#include "sys_type.h"
main()
{
    TEST_BEGIN
    TEST_ASSERT(1 == sizeof(Int8));
    TEST_ASSERT(2 == sizeof(Int16));
    TEST_ASSERT(4 == sizeof(Int32));
    TEST_ASSERT(1 == sizeof(Uint8));
    TEST_ASSERT(2 == sizeof(Uint16));
    TEST_ASSERT(4 == sizeof(Uint32));
    TEST_ASSERT(4 == sizeof(Float32));
    TEST_ASSERT(8 == sizeof(Float64));
    TEST_END
}
```

Figure 10-6: Testing a `typedef`

10.2 Function Definitions

Once we are down to the level of implementing functions, most of our decisions are localized. The cost of making a poor decision is therefore small, because changing it typically does not affect a large amount of code. Even so, there are a few general points to keep in mind when writing function bodies.

10.2.1 Assert Yourself!

Documenting the conditions under which the behavior of a function is undefined is an important part of developing the interface. Comments in the interface are passive, and do nothing to warn of a programming error at runtime. As discussed in Section 1.3, we can use both comments and assert statements in combination to achieve light-weight maintainable code.

In longer functions, there are sometimes several paths that can lead to the same statement; often this statement assumes internal conditions. Figure 10-7 illustrates a situation in which either the `if` or the `while` might not be entered. In any case, the stated condition that follows the if statement must hold true and is backed up by an assert statement.

```
// ...

if (!q) {
    while (p && 0 != strcmp(name, p->name())) {
        p = p->next();
    }
}

// Either q is true, or p now points to the first element
// with the specified name if one exists.
assert (q || !p || 0 == strcmp(name, p->name()));

// ...
```

Figure 10-7: Commenting/Asserting an Internal Invariant

These kinds of internal self-checks do more than merely detect errors at runtime. The practice of explicitly identifying an assumption encourages a crispness of thinking that typically makes the logical flow of the function easier for others to follow.[7]

In systems that monitor critical functionality, we might be reluctant to remove the assert statements even in production code; however, forcing the entire program to abort when a programming error causes an object to enter an inconsistent state is clearly not acceptable either. The natural extension of an assert statement would be to `throw` an exception derived from a base class such as `sys_ProgrammingError`. In this case, instead of automatically exiting, fault-tolerant systems could be designed to `catch` and recover from such errors at whatever level had sufficient context to do so. Failing to catch the error would degenerate to an abort. Notice that by using exceptions we have, in effect, "escalated" the responsibility of handling the error to a higher-level component (see Section 5.2).

10.2.2 Avoid Special Casing

Obtaining code coverage is one common criterion used to measure the effectiveness of tests. But the more paths there are through a function, the more difficult it can be to assure ourselves that the function is reliable under all conditions.

---

[7] See also **murray**, Section 9.2.1, pp. 208–210.

Principle

Algorithms that naturally include their boundary conditions are often simpler, shorter, and easier to understand and to test than algorithms that treat boundary conditions as a special case.

For example, developers sometimes choose to use a pair of pointers when walking a list to be modified. This approach requires treating the empty list as a special case (or always maintaining a dummy first link). Instead of using the pointer to the current link as a state variable, consider instead maintaining the address of the current link, as was done for the `PtrBagManip` class shown in Figure 5-83.

Figure 10-8a shows an implementation that maintains both a pointer to the current link and a pointer to the previous link; the `d_prevLink_p` pointer will be used to update the `d_next_p` field of the previous link when the current link is removed. If the current link happens to be the first link in the list, `d_prevLink_p` will be 0, and we will need to update the root of the list instead; we therefore retain a writable pointer to the `PtrBag` itself.

The implementation of Figure 10-8a is straightforward but inelegant, complicated by unnecessary state and algorithmic complexity. Equivalent functionality is accomplished with the implementation in Figure 10-8b. Removing the first element in this implementation is handled in just the same way as removing any other element.

Implementation (b) requires only one state variable, and the complexity of removing a node is significantly reduced.

Principle

A variety of problems can be solved by adding an extra level of indirection.

```
class PtrBagManip {
    PtrBag *d_bag_p;
    PtrBagLink *d_Link_p;
    PtrBagLink *d_PrevLink_p;

  public:
    // ...
    void remove();
    // ...
};

void PtrBagManip::remove()
{
    PtrBagLink *tmp = d_Link_p;
    d_link_p = d_link_p->next();
    if (d_prevLink_p) {
        d_prevLink_p->nextRef() = d_link_p;
    }
    else {
        d_bag_p->d_root_p = d_link_p;
    }
    delete tmp;
}
```

(a) Treating the Boundary Condition as a Special Case

```
class PtrBagManip {
    PtrBagLink **d_addrLink_p;

  public:
    // ...
    void remove();
    // ...
};

void PtrBagManip::remove()
{
    PtrBagLink *tmp = *d_addrLink_p;
   *d_addrLink_p = (*d_addrLink_p)->next();
    delete tmp;
}
```

(b) Treating the Boundary Condition as Part of the Main Algorithm

Figure 10-8: Avoiding Special-Case Code

The technique of maintaining *the address of* a pointer instead of the pointer itself is a terse but powerful idiom for manipulating a variety of list-like structures:

```
struct Link { Link *d_next_p; Link(Link *next) : d_next_p(next) {} // ...

class List { Link *d_head_p; void modify(); // ...

static int q(const Link& x);     // 1 if some condition on x holds; else 0

void List::modify()              // some function that modifies the list
{
    Link **ppl = &d_head_p;      // starting at the beginning
    while (*ppl && !q(*ppl)) {   // while not at end and item not found
        ppl = &(*ppl)->d_next_p; // advance the (address of the) pointer
    }
    assert(!*ppl || q(*ppl));    // ppl points to last or desired Link *

    // ...                       // insert before, remove, etc. using *ppl
```

The extra level of indirection allows us to insert an element into an ordered list without having to maintain two pointers or treat the empty list as a special case:

```
*ppl = new Link(*ppl);              // inserting before an item is easy
```

Removing a specific Link from a list is also facilitated:

```
if (*ppl) {                         // if found we can unlink and delete item
    Link *item = *ppl;
    *ppl = (*ppl)->d_next_p;
    delete item;
}
```

This idiom (or its for-loop equivalent) is used to implement the private functions copy and end in the List class shown in Figure 6-19b, and is also used extensively to implement a hash-based symbol table (Figure 10-11) in the following section.

10.2.3 Factor Instead of Duplicate

In Section 5.6 we argued that reuse of small functions could result in physical coupling that is not worth the benefit of a factored implementation. However, within a single well-designed component, there is little justification for replicating code. Often construction, destruction, and assignment will share common algorithms. As with the `List` class shown in Figure 6-19, it can be useful to define a small set of more primitive functions to factor out commonality from this basic public functionality, as indicated in Figure 10-9.

Default Constructor:		`init();`	
Copy Constructor:		`init();`	`copy();`
Assignment Operator:	`clean();`	`init();`	`copy();`
Destructor:	`clean();`		

Figure 10-9: Factoring Common Creator/Assignment Functionality

It is interesting to note that the assignment operator is not completely primitive; it can be implemented in terms of the destructor and the copy constructor, which are primitive:

```
#include "new.h"                // declare placement syntax

T& T::operator=(const T& that)
{
    if (this != &that) {        // check for x = x
        T::~T();                // destroy object in place
        new(this) T(that);      // construct object in place
    }
    return *this;               // return reference to this object
}
```

This observation has implications for template-based container-class design (see Section 10.4.2).

Another example of factoring can be found in the implementation of a basic symbol-table component. A symbol table is a specialization of an associative array that supports a mapping from a key (most often a character string) to some value (in this case, the user-defined type `my_Value`).

Figure 10-10 shows the header file for a simple implementation of a symbol table. This implementation uses closed hashing and so is implemented using a dynamically allocated array of `my_SymTabLink` pointers (`d_table_p`) of size derived from `maxEntriesHint` (`d_size`). There are four basic operations provided: add if not found, set whether or not found, remove and report if found, and lookup. Each of these operations can be implemented separately, as shown in Figure 10-11a. However, each of these functions basically requires locating the pointer to the symbol (implemented as a `my_SymTabLink`). Note that only the `remove` method requires the address of the pointer; both `add` and `set` can always add a new symbol to the front of the list for a given hash slot, and `lookup` never adds a new symbol.

Principle

Factoring generally reusable functionality within a component can reduce code size and improve reliability with only a modest loss in runtime performance.

```
// my_symtab.h
#ifndef INCLUDED_MY_SYMTAB
#define INCLUDED_MY_SYMTAB

class my_Value;
class my_SymTabLink;
class my_SymTabIter;

class my_SymTab {
    class my_SymTabLink **d_table_p;                  // closed hash table
    int d_size;                                       // size of hash table
    friend my_SymTabIter;

  private:
    my_SymTab(const my_SymTab&);                      // not implemented
    my_SymTab& operator=(const my_SymTab&);           // not implemented

  public:
    // CREATORS
    my_SymTab(int maxSymbolsHint = 0);                // see Section 10.3.1
        // Optionally specify approx. number of entries (default =500).
    ~my_SymTab();

    // MANIPULATORS
    my_Value *add(const char* name);
        // Adds a symbol to the table only if name is not already present.
        // Returns a pointer to the internal value if added, and 0 otherwise.

    my_Value& set(const char* name);
        // Adds a symbol to the table if not already present.  Returns a
        // reference to the internal value of a symbol with specified name.

    int remove(const char *name);
        // Removes a symbol from the table.  Returns 0 if the symbol with
        // the specified name was found, and non-zero otherwise.

    // ACCESSORS
    my_Value *lookup(const char *name) const;
        // Returns a pointer to an existing symbol's value, or 0 if
        // a symbol with the specified name cannot be found.
};

my_SymTabIter { /* ... */ };

#endif
```

Figure 10-10: Partial Header for Basic Symbol-Table Abstraction

```
// my_symtab.c
# include "my_symtab.h"

static int hash(const char *name) { /* ... */ }
```

```
my_Value *my_SymTab::add(const char *name)
{
    int index = hash(name) % d_size;
    my_SymTabLink *&slot = d_table_p[index];
    my_SymTabLink *p = slot;

    while (p && 0 != strcmp(p->name(), name)) {
        p = p->next();
    }
    if (!p) {
        slot = new my_SymTabLink(name, slot);
        return &slot->value();
    }
    else {
        return 0;
    }
}
```

```
my_Value& my_SymTab::set(const char *name)
{
    int index = hash(name) % d_size;
    my_SymTabLink *&slot = d_table_p[index];
    my_SymTabLink *p = slot;

    while (p && 0 != strcmp(p->name(), name)) {
        p = p->next();
    }
    if (!p) {
        p = slot = new my_SymTabLink(name, slot);
    }
    return p->value();
}
```

```
// my_symtab.c
# include "my_symtab.h"

static int hash(const char *name) { /* ... */ }

static my_SymTabLink *&
locate(my_SymTabLink **table, int size, const char *name)
{
    int index = hash(name) % size;
    my_SymTabLink **pp = &table[index];
    while (*pp && 0 != strcmp((*pp)->name(), name)) {
        pp = &(*pp)->next();
    }
    return *pp;
}
```

```
my_Value *my_SymTab::add(const char *name)
{
    my_SymTabLink *& p = locate(d_table_p, d_size, name);
    if (p) {
        return 0;
    }
    p = new my_SymTabLink(name, p);
    return &p->value();
}
```

```
my_Value& my_SymTab::set(const char *name)
{
    my_SymTabLink *& p = locate(d_table_p, d_size, name);
    if (!p) {
        p = new my_SymTabLink(name, p);
    }
    return p->value();
}
```

```
int my_SymTab::remove(const char *name)
{
    enum { FOUND = 0, NOT_FOUND };

    int index = hash(name) % d_size;
    my_SymTabLink **pp = &d_table_p[index];
    while (*pp && 0 != strcmp((*pp)->name(), name)) {
        pp = &(*pp)->next();
    }
    if (*pp) {
        my_SymTabLink *q = *pp;
        *pp = q->next();
        delete q;
        return FOUND;
    }
    else {
        return NOT_FOUND;
    }
}
```

```
my_Value *my_SymTab::lookup(const char *name) const
{
    int index = hash(name) % d_size;
    my_SymTabLink *p = d_table_p[index];

    while (p && 0 != strcmp(p->name(), name)) {
        p = p->next();
    }
    return p ? &p->value() : 0;
}
```

(a) Reimplementing Specific Functionality

```
int my_SymTab::remove(const char *name)
{
    enum { FOUND = 0, NOT_FOUND };
    my_SymTabLink *& p = locate(d_table_p, d_size, name);
    if (!p) {
        return NOT_FOUND;
    }
    my_SymTabLink *q = p;
    p = q->next();
    delete q;
    return FOUND;
}
```

```
my_Value *my_SymTab::lookup(const char *name) const
{
    my_SymTabLink *& p = locate(d_table_p, d_size, name);
    return p ? &p->value() : 0;
}
```

(b) Reusing More General Functionality

Figure 10-11. Implementing a Symbol Table Class

The equivalent functionality can be implemented more succinctly, as shown in Figure 10-11b. The implementation is smaller and the performance is comparable, though not quite as good. If, after performance analysis, we find that `lookup` is taking a noticeable amount of time, we might reasonably choose to reimplement that function independently of the more general `locate` function (but not before profiling).[8]

Incidentally, the term *symbol table* is somewhat of a misnomer. Although this abstraction is in some sense a collection of symbols, the notion of a symbol in this component is implicit; there is no "Symbol" type exposed in this symbol-table component's logical interface. An efficient symbol table is not entirely trivial to implement, as discussed in Section 10.3.5.

10.2.4 Don't Be Too Clever

At my first job out of college, I was told of a legendary programmer whose knowledge of FORTRAN was without peer. This thoughtful fellow was concerned that some of the most obscure constructs of the language were not getting their fair share of use. He therefore made it his business to see that each of these constructs was adequately represented in production software, even if it meant a bit more work for himself and others. I wish I could have met the man; alas, he was let go just before I joined the company.

Guideline

When designing a function, component, package, or entire system, use the simplest techniques that are effective.

Anyone understanding this book is clearly not a novice programmer. In fact, you probably know the C++ language inside and out. Knowing the language well is essential to being an expert C++ software engineer—there is no doubt about that. But knowing the rules of the language itself is only a fraction of the overall knowledge required for designing large systems. Mastering the Annotated C++ Reference Manual (ARM) will allow you to know what each of the C++ constructs does, but not the frequency with

---

[8] See **cargill**, Chapter 7, p. 138.

which they are used in day-to-day programming. Using the most common approach that solves a problem effectively makes the software easier to read and maintain. As they say in medical school, "When you see hoofprints, think horses not zebras."

10.3 Memory Management

Memory management is an important aspect of high-performance designs. Under certain conditions, real performance benefits can be achieved through the allocation of memory in a more restricted context. At the same time, memory is a global resource; inappropriate use of memory management by individual classes (as with excessive use of inline functions) can adversely affect the performance of an integrated system.

The syntax and language issues of memory management in C++ are fairly involved; fortunately these details are well covered elsewhere.[9] In this section we present a variety of issues pertaining to the design of customized memory management. We make explicit the difference between logical and physical state values. The impact of certain specific physical parameters on performance is analyzed. Several variants of a class-specific memory manager are presented, and their relative performance and impact on the system are discussed. Testability issues are also addressed. We conclude that the use of an *object*-specific, rather than a *class*-specific, approach to memory management is preferable in most cases.

10.3.1 Logical versus Physical State Values

In many implementations in which an object manages dynamic memory directly, there will be two distinct kinds of data members that define the "state" of the object: *logical* and *physical*.

> **<u>DEFINITION</u>: A value associated with the state of an object is a *logical value* if it contributes to the intended semantics (i.e., the essential behavior of the ADT) for that object; otherwise it is a *physical value*.**

---

[9] See, for instance, **meyers**, Items 5–10, pp. 18–33.

Principle

For a fully encapsulating interface, every programatically accessible value is a logical value.

The definition of *logical value* is in terms of semantics and not programmatic accessibility because encapsulation is regularly violated in the name of efficiency. Just because an object fails to encapsulate a particular value in practice does not imply that it contributes to essential behavior. Although the intention of a component author is less objectively measurable than the values that are accessible through a component's interface, this essential behavior tends not to depend as much on the implementation choice as the set of programatically accessible values.

Guideline

Avoid allowing programmatic access to *physical* values.

Consider the implementation of the `pub_String` class shown in Figure 10-12. The state of this string includes the address of a managed array of characters and its contents, the physical size of that array, and the logical length of the string contained in that array. String length contributes to the semantics of a string abstraction and is therefore a logical value (regardless of whether it is stored or calculated). In contrast, the size of the internal array used to hold the string need not be exactly one more than the length; its precise value is important to the physical state of the object but not to its logical state.

A goal of encapsulation is to hide all of the physical state while making the logical state readily available through the interface. In the case of the string class, the contents of the dynamic array from location zero up through the length of the string are part of its logical state; the remainder of the array and the address of the array itself are part of its physical state.

```
class pub_String {
    char *d_str_p;              // dynamic array of characters
    int d_size;                 // physical size of array
    int d_length;               // logical length of string

  public:
    pub_String(const char *str, int maxLengthHint = 0);
    // ...
    pub_String& operator+=(const pub_String& str);
    // ...
    int length() const { return d_length; }
    operator const char *() const { return d_str_p; }
};
```

Figure 10-12: One Possible Implementation of a String Class

As we know from Section 8.3, this string class is not fully encapsulating because its cast operator exposes a physical value (i.e., the address of the array). As a rule, we would like to avoid providing programmatic access to physical values through the interface of an object. Efficiency and even practicality will, at times, compete with this goal. However, what is and what is not considered a physical value depends on the level of abstraction (see Section 5.10).

Sometimes, for (perceived) performance reasons, we will feel compelled to allow the client to help our class do its job. Clearly it is not appropriate to expose the size of the internal array of a general-purpose string in its interface. We can, however, provide a mechanism for a client who knows ahead of time how big a string will become to give a "hint" to the object.

In Figure 10-12, for example, an optional second argument in the constructor of the `pub_String` class can serve as a hint to its implementation. Note that this hint does not restrict the length of the string that this `pub_String` object is required to accommodate; the client is always entitled to exceed the value indicated by a hint without error. If this hint is heeded, the physical size of the string array might be set to `maxLengthHint+1` at construction. Now perhaps subsequent use of the += operator will not require resizing the string, potentially improving runtime performance.

Principle

A *hint* is write-only.

A hint passed as an argument in a member function is just that—a hint (just like `register` or `inline`). What the object does with the hint is its own business. An object is absolutely free to ignore a hint, and there should be no programmatic way to determine the effect of having provided a hint. Conversely, an inaccurate hint value may well degrade the performance of an object, but it should not affect any logical behavior.

Principle

The best hints are not tied directly to a specific implementation.

The best hints are those associated with the abstraction itself rather than with any particular implementation. Notice that the hint is called `maxLengthHint` and not `sizeHint`.

Whether or not an argument should be treated as a hint depends on the level of abstraction. For a hash-table abstraction, we would probably make the number of slots explicit and provide an accessor for that value. For a hash-table-based implementation of a symbol-table abstraction (Figure 10-10), we might instead provide the hint `maxSymbolsHint`.

Guideline

The result of calling a `const` member function should not alter *any* programmatically accessible value in the object.

Logical values are closely tied with logical `const`-ness (see Section 9.1.6). If a member function is declared `const`, it is its duty not to modify any logical value. For the same reasons, a `const` member should avoid modifying any physical value that happens to be programmatically accessible (e.g., the address of the array in the string class).

```
pub_String str("foo", 1000);
// ...
const char *pcc = str;
if (str.length() < 10) {            // const member length() resizes array
    cout << pcc << endl;            // ?? behavior is undefined!
```

```
}
```

For example, suppose that, in some implementation, a call to `length()` caused the dynamic array to be reallocated (say to a "more appropriate" size). Then the result of calling this `const` member function would invalidate the `const char *` pointer and the subsequent output operation would be undefined.

Principle

Two instances of a type that supports value semantics are equal (==) if all of their individual respective logical values are equal; they are not equal (!=) if any of their individual respective logical values are not equal.

Logical value is also directly tied to the notion of equality. For objects that support value semantics (see Section 5.9), distinct objects may be defined to have equal value. That is, the definition of equality is that of logical equality rather than physical equality. In the case of a `pub_String` object, two strings are equal if they have the same length *n* and the contents of the first *n* corresponding characters of their respective internal arrays are equal. Because `pub_String` exposes some of its physical state, we can find differences in logically equal `pub_String` objects:

```
pub_String s1("foo");
pub_String s2("foo");

const char *p1 = s1;
const char *p2 = s2;
const char *p3 = s1;

s1 == s2                // yes
p1 == p2                // no
p1 == p3                // yes
```

10.3.2 Physical Parameters

The design space for physical values can be large. In this section, we examine the organizational design space of the simple array-based integer stack whose header file is shown in Figure 10-13.

```
// my_stack.h
#ifndef INCLUDED_MY_STACK
#define INCLUDED_MY_STACK

class my_Stack {
    int *d_stack_p;                           // dynamic array
    int d_size;                               // physical size
    int d_sp;                                 // logical depth

  private:
    void growArray();                         // increase physical size
    my_Stack(const my_Stack&);                // not implemented
    my_Stack& operator=(const my_Stack&);     // not implemented

  public:
    my_Stack(int maxDepthHint);               // hint: probable maximum depth
    ~my_Stack();
    void push(int value);
    int pop() { return d_stack_p[--d_sp]; }
    int top() { return d_stack_p[d_sp-1]; }
    int isEmpty() const { return d_sp <= 0; }
};

inline
void my_Stack::push(int value)
{
    if (d_sp >= d_size) {
        growArray();                         // note use of private member function
    }
    d_stack_p[d_sp++] = value;
}

#endif
```

Figure 10-13: Header File for an Array-Based Stack Component

First, let's consider the hint of the expected maximum stack depth. Recall that a hint is only a suggestion; the stack implementation could choose to ignore it entirely. On the other hand, the hint may be in error; the implementation must not fail if the hinted maximum depth is exceeded. However, if the stack is given a tight upper bound on the number of elements it will be required to hold at any given time, the implementation will be able to use this information to improve performance.

Figure 10-14 illustrates the implementation of the `my_Stack` functions that affect the management of the dynamic array. At the top of the file, two enumerated physical parameter values, `INITIAL_SIZE` and `GROW_FACTOR`, characterize the performance trade-offs in this component. In the absence of a hint, the initial size of the array will be set to `INITIAL_SIZE`. Whenever the stack becomes full, a new array whose size is a multiple of the previous size will be allocated; the value of this multiplier is specified by `GROW_FACTOR`.

Knowing the size of the array in advance enables the implementation to avoid reallocation. The extent of the improvement is not necessarily as significant as it might first appear. By using the `GROW_FACTOR` approach to resize the array, it takes only O(log(N)) reallocations of the `d_stack_p` array in order to handle a stack of depth N. Further, the number of integer copies that have to be done in order to reach this size is only O(N), and not O(N log(N)) as one might naively expect.[10]

```
// my_stack.c
#include "my_stack.h"
#include <memory.h>  // memcpy()
#include <assert.h>

enum { INITIAL_SIZE = 1, GROW_FACTOR = 2 };

my_Stack::my_Stack(int size)
: d_size(size > INITIAL_SIZE ? size : INITIAL_SIZE)
, d_sp(0)
{
    d_stack_p = new int[d_size];
    assert(d_stack_p);
}

my_Stack::~my_Stack()
{
    delete [] d_stack_p;
}

void my_Stack::growArray()
{
    int *p = d_stack_p;
    d_size *= GROW_FACTOR;
    d_stack_p = new int[d_size];
    assert(d_stack_p);
    memcpy(d_stack_p, p, d_sp * sizeof *d_stack_p);
    delete [] p;
}
```

Figure 10-14: Implementation File for an Array-Based Stack Component

---

[10] See **murray**, Section 8.3.2, pp. 173–174.

Because of the exponential nature of the GROW_FACTOR, its precise value does not affect performance as much as it affects space. Having a GROW_FACTOR of 2 means that at most twice as much space will be allocated for the array as needed. If we were to change the GROW_FACTOR to 4, it would mean that up to 75 percent of the array could go unused. A potentially more space-efficient but much less robust approach would be to have a linear GROW_SIZE instead of an exponential GROW_FACTOR, by making the changes to the stack's implementation shown in Figure 10-15.

```
// my_stack.c
#include "my_stack.h"
#include <memory.h>  // memcpy()
#include <assert.h>

enum { INITIAL_SIZE = 0, GROW_SIZE = 100 };                // modified

my_Stack::my_Stack(int size)
: d_size(size > INITIAL_SIZE ? size : INITIAL_SIZE)
, d_sp(0)
{
    d_stack_p = d_size > 0 ? new int[d_size] : 0;          // modified
    assert(d_stack_p || d_size <= 0);                      // modified
}

my_Stack::~my_Stack()
{
    delete [] d_stack_p;
}

void my_Stack::growArray()
{
    int *p = d_stack_p;
    d_stack_p = new int[d_size += GROW_SIZE];              // modified
    assert(d_stack_p);
    memcpy(d_stack_p, p, d_sp * sizeof *d_stack_p);
    delete [] p;
}
```

Figure 10-15: Using a Fixed GROW_SIZE **Instead of an Adaptive** GROW_FACTOR

To demonstrate the relative effect of these physical parameters under simulated operation, I created the performance test driver shown in Figure 10-16. The usage pattern is deliberately designed to cause the stack to grow quickly. On each iteration of the loop, the current value of the loop index is pushed onto the stack three times and then the stack is popped once. Note that the depth of the stack grows by 2 on each iteration.

```
// my_stack.t.c
#include "my_stack.h"
#include <stdlib.h>    // atoi()
#include <iostream.h>

main(int argc, const char *argv[])
{
    register int repeat = argc > 1 ? atoi(argv[1]) : 0;
    cout << "repeat = " << repeat << '\t';
    my_Stack s;

    for (register int i = 0; i < repeat; ++i) {
        s.push(i);
        s.push(i);
        s.push(i);
        int value = s.pop();
    }
}
```

Figure 10-16: Trivial Performance "Stress" Test Driver for `my_stack`

The results of running the driver of Figure 10-16 for perturbations of individual physical parameter values are presented in Figure 10-17. The first row represents 4,000 iterations of the loop for each of eight physical configurations. Each successive row doubles the number of iterations, up to 8,192,000 iterations. The first two columns represent the alternative of using a fixed `GROW_SIZE`. This non-adaptive approach will inevitably exhibit quadratic runtime behavior for unexpectedly large stacks; for large values of `GROW_SIZE`, it can be excessively wasteful of memory for small stacks.

Hinting the correct maximum depth up front is clearly a win when you know this value *a priori*. In the absence of information, any particular value for `INITIAL_SIZE` could either be wasteful of space or too small to make any difference. The runtime performance is not a sensitive function of the actual value of the `GROW_FACTOR` because the array adapts geometrically; however, excessive space demands could result from a grow factor larger than 2. Notice that on the final row of the table, a grow factor of 4 or 8 is actually faster than guessing a size that is just over half the final value and then having to copy that half to a new array (guessing the correct value of 16,384,002 produces the optimal result of 7.0).[11]

---

[11] The extra 2 in the initial size is to allow the queue to push three times and pop once on the final two iterations of a loop of the same size without forcing a reallocation to occur.

(GROW_SIZE):	100	10,000						
INITIAL_SIZE:	0	0	1	128,002	1,024,002	8,192,0022	1	1
GROW_FACTOR:			2	2	2	2	4	8
Iterations	I	II	III	IV	V	VI	VII	VIII
4,000	0.0							
8,000	0.4							
16,000	1.8							
32,000	9.5	0.0						
64,000	51.0	0.1	0.0	0.0	0.0	0.0	0.0	0.0
128,000	254.6	0.6	0.1	0.1	0.1	0.1	0.1	0.1
256,000	1074.5	2.7	0.3	0.2	0.2	0.1	0.3	0.2
512,000		11.0	0.7	0.6	0.4	0.4	0.4	0.4
1,024,000		42.9	1.4	1.2	1.0	0.8	1.1	0.9
2,048,000		170.8	2.7	2.4	2.3	1.6	2.0	2.2
4,096,000			5.4	5.1	5.2	3.3	4.6	3.9
8,192,000			10.7	10.7	10.5	9.0	8.3	7.2

CPU Seconds Running (Optimized) on SUN SPARC 20 Workstation

Figure 10-17: Relative Performance for Various Physical Parameter Settings

The `INITIAL_SIZE` and `GROW_FACTOR` approach is quite general, and applies to a wide variety of array-like objects that must dynamically expand as need demands. During initial development, choosing an `INITIAL_SIZE` of 1 and a `GROW_FACTOR` of 2 is a good way to ensure that new code is exercised thoroughly. Later on, after performance analysis, these numbers can be adjusted if necessary to provide marginal performance improvements.

As a final note, the usage pattern presented here favors the `GROW_FACTOR` approach. For objects that grow slowly over time to reach a stable running size, `GROW_SIZE` may occasionally prove to be preferable. A major disadvantage with `GROW_SIZE` is that we cannot place an upper bound on surplus memory usage as a percentage of the actual memory required over a wide range of sizes (as we can for `GROW_FACTOR`). If an upper bound of 50 percent unused memory is too high, we can always resort to a fractional `GROW_FACTOR`. For example, a `GROW_FACTOR` of 1.1 would limit the potential excess memory usage to only 10 percent while preserving its geometrically adaptive nature. The only caveat is that the combination of `INITIAL_SIZE` and `GROW_FACTOR` must be chosen so that the first resizing increases the current size by at least 1. Unless there is going to be a large number of my_Stack objects active at any given time, this level of concern over excess memory usage is probably not warranted.

10.3.3 Memory Allocators

Memory allocators are a topic rich with theory that is well beyond the scope of this book. In this section we confine ourselves to a discussion of two very basic but useful allocators that we use in subsequent sections.

```
// pub_blocklist.h
#ifndef INCLUDED_PUB_BLOCKLIST
#define INCLUDED_PUB_BLOCKLIST

class pub_BlockLink;

class pub_BlockList {
    pub_BlockLink *d_blockList_p; // linked list of allocated blocks
    pub_BlockList(const pub_BlockList&);             // not implemented
    pub_BlockList& operator=(const pub_BlockList&); // not implemented

  public:
    // CREATORS
    pub_BlockList();
        // Create an empty list of allocated blocks of memory.

    ~pub_BlockList();
        // Destroy this object and all associated blocks of memory.

    // MANIPULATORS
    void *allocate(int bytes);
        // Allocate block of memory of specified number of bytes.

    void release();
        // Free all blocks of memory allocated through this object.
};

#endif
```

Figure 10-18: Interface for Simple Block-Allocator Component

The pub_BlockList allocator shown in Figure 10-18 provides a convenient mechanism for keeping track of all global memory requested through the object's allocate function. In effect, the allocator owns and manages the memory so you do not need to keep individual track of it. Once you know that all the memory is no longer in use, you can free it all by calling the release member. When the pub_BlockList is destroyed, it automatically frees all memory allocated by it. For completeness a trivial implementation of the pub_BlockList block memory allocator is presented in Figure 10-19.

```
// pub_blocklist.c
#include "pub_blocklist.h"
#include <assert.h>

// (LOCAL) AUXILIARY CLASS
class pub_BlockLink {
    void *d_block_p;             // block of storage
    pub_BlockLink *d_next_p;     // pointer to next link (or null)
    pub_BlockLink(const pub_BlockLink&);
    pub_BlockLink& operator=(const pub_BlockLink&);

  public:
    pub_BlockLink(void *block, pub_BlockLink *next) :
                               d_block_p(block), d_next_p(next) {}
    ~pub_BlockLink() { delete [] d_block_p; }
    pub_BlockLink *next() const { return d_next_p; }
};

pub_BlockList::pub_BlockList() : d_blockList_p(0) {}

pub_BlockList::~pub_BlockList() { release(); }

void pub_BlockList::release()
{
    while (d_blockList_p) {
        pub_BlockLink *q = d_blockList_p;
        d_blockList_p = d_blockList_p->next();
        delete q;
    }
}

void *pub_BlockList::allocate(int bytes)
{
    void *p = new char[bytes];
    assert(p);
    d_blockList_p = new pub_BlockLink(p, d_blockList_p);
    return p;
}
```

Figure 10-19: Implementation of Simple Block-Allocator Component

Principle

Instrumenting global operators `new` and `delete` is a simple but effective way to understand and test the behavior of dynamic memory allocation within a system.

A common property of sophisticated memory allocators is that they are often complex and notoriously error prone, yet have tiny interfaces that make them difficult and costly to test. Fortunately, as test authors we own `main` (see Section 7.7). Hence, we know we can always take advantage of redefining global `new` and `delete` to suit our own needs.[12,13]

Figure 10-20 illustrates how global `new` and `delete` can be exploited to gain confidence that the allocator is operating as expected. On each call, redefined global operator `new` simply announces the fact that it was called and what size block of memory was requested. Each call to redefined global operator `delete` echoes the address about to be freed. As for the test itself, the `main` driver creates an instance of the `pub_BlockList` allocator, uses it to allocate two blocks, releases these blocks, allocates one more block, and allows the allocator to go out of scope.

```
// pub_blocklist.t.c
#include "pub_blocklist.h"
#include <iostream.h>
#include <stdio.h>
#include <malloc.h>

void *operator new(size_t sz)
{
    void *p = malloc(sz);
    printf("\t...new(%d): %x\n", sz, p);
    return p;
}

void operator delete(void *addr)
{
    printf("\t...delete(%x)\n", addr);
    free(addr);
}

main()
{
    cout << endl << "TEST DRIVER FOR: pub_blocklist" << endl << endl;
    {
        printf("pub_BlockList b();\n");
        pub_BlockList b;

        printf("b.allocate(100);\n");
        b.allocate(100);

        printf("b.allocate(200);\n");
        b.allocate(200);
```

---

[12] **ellis**, Section 5.3.3, p. 60.

[13] See also **murray**, Section 9.7.2, pp. 226–229.

```
        printf("b.release();\n");
        b.release();

        printf("b.allocate(100);\n");
        b.allocate(100);

        printf("b.pub_BlockList::~pub_BlockList()\n");
    }
    printf("end of test\n");
}
```

Figure 10-20: Trivial Development Test Driver with Instrumented `new` and `delete`

The results of running this simple driver on my machine are given in Figure 10-21.

```
john@john: a.out
        ...new(64): 6520
        ...new(64): 65f8
        ...new(64): 6640
        ...new(64): 6688
        ...new(1024): 66d0

TEST DRIVER FOR: pub_blocklist

pub_BlockList b();
b.allocate(100);
        ...new(100): 6ad8
        ...new(8): 6b48
b.allocate(200);
        ...new(200): 6b58
        ...new(8): 6c28
b.release();
        ...delete(6b58)
        ...delete(6c28)
        ...delete(6ad8)
        ...delete(6b48)
b.allocate(100);
        ...new(100): 6ad8
        ...new(8): 6b48
b.pub_BlockList::~pub_BlockList()
        ...delete(6ad8)
        ...delete(6b48)
end of test
john@john:
```

Figure 10-21: Output from Running Trivial Development Test Driver on My Machine

By "listening in" we stand to learn a great deal about how the global system operates. Notice that before the test banner even prints, five allocations (which are never released) have already occurred. The first four are a direct result of including `iostream.h` with its nifty counter initialization for `cin`, `cout`, `cerr`, and `clog` (see Section 7.8.1.3). The fifth allocation occurs as a result of using `cout` for the first time (an example of check-every-time initialization, discussed in Section 7.8.1.4).

Principle

Using `iostream` when instrumenting global `new` and `delete` can cause undesirable side effects.

Because `iostream` uses global operator `new`, we want to avoid using `iostream` when redefining the global operator `new` itself. Regressing to the use of the more primitive `stdio` avoids recursion when instrumenting global operators `new` and `delete`.

A cursory examination of the rest of the output tells us that our toy implementation of the block allocator is working as expected. Each allocation causes two blocks to be allocated: one for the memory itself and one for the link that manages it. Releasing the two blocks causes the same four addresses that were previously allocated to be deleted. Finally, reallocating a block on my machine returned the *same address* as the first time—a sign that the memory really was freed. However, a different address would not necessarily imply a problem on other platforms. Note that a more sophisticated allocator would probably make only a single allocation for both the link and the block itself.

A second type of allocation scheme, referred to as *pool allocation*, is ideal for allocating the memory for a large number of fixed-size objects. A pool allocator can be implemented using a block allocator in its implementation to keep independent track of large blocks of memory. Pool allocation will be discussed further in the context of a specific example in Section 10.3.4.2, but is provided here for reference in Figure 10-22.[14]

[14] See also **stroustrup**, Section 13.10.3, pp. 472–474 (note that the original printing of that section contained substantive coding errors).

```
// pub_pool.h
#ifndef INCLUDED_PUB_POOL
#define INCLUDED_PUB_POOL

class pub_BlockList;
class pub_Pool {
    pub_BlockList *d_blockAllocator_p;        // * is for insulation
    const int d_objSize;
    const int d_chunkSize;
    int d_instanceCount;                      // help detect memory leaks
    struct Link { Link *d_next_p; } *d_freeList_p;
    void replenish();

  private:
    pub_Pool(const pub_Pool&);                // not implemented
    pub_Pool& operator=(const pub_Pool&);     // not implemented

  public:
    // CREATORS
    pub_Pool(int objectSize, int chunkSize = 0);
        // Create an allocator for a pool of specified size.
        // Optionally specify chunkSize in terms of the number
        // of objects for which space is to be allocated each
        // time the pool is replenished.

    ~pub_Pool();
        // Destroy pool AND ALL ASSOCIATED BLOCKS OF MEMORY.

    // MANIPULATORS
    void *alloc();
        // Allocate block of memory of specified number of bytes.

    void free(void *obj);
        // Return the address to the local free pool.

    void dryUp();
        // Release all dynamically allocated memory from this pool.
};

inline
void *pub_Pool::alloc()
{
    if (!d_freeList_p) {
        replenish();
    }
    Link *p = d_freeList_p;
    d_freeList_p = p->d_next_p;
    ++d_instanceCount;                        // help detect memory leaks
    return p;
}

inline
void pub_Pool::free(void *obj)
{
    Link *p = (Link *) obj;
    p->d_next_p = d_freeList_p;
```

```
    d_freeList_p = p;
    --d_instanceCount;                         // help detect memory leaks
}

#endif
```

Figure 10-22a: A Pool Allocator Interface

```
// pub_pool.c
#include "pub_pool.h"
#include "pub_blocklist.h"
#include <assert.h>

enum { DEFAULT_CHUNK_SIZE = 100 };

pub_Pool::pub_Pool(int objSize, int chunkSize)
: d_freeList_p(0)
, d_objSize(objSize >= sizeof(Link) ? objSize : sizeof(Link))
, d_chunkSize(chunkSize > 0 ? chunkSize : DEFAULT_CHUNK_SIZE)
, d_blockAllocator_p(new pub_BlockList)
, d_instanceCount(0) // help detect leaks
{
    assert(objSize > 0);
    assert(d_blockAllocator_p);
}

void pub_Pool::dryUp()
{
    d_blockAllocator_p->release();
    d_freeList_p = 0;
}

pub_Pool::~pub_Pool()
{
    if (0 == d_instanceCount) {                // help detect leaks
        delete d_blockAllocator_p;
    }
    assert(0 == d_instanceCount);              // really help detect leaks
}

void pub_Pool::replenish()
{
    int size = d_chunkSize * d_objSize;
    char *start = (char *) d_blockAllocator_p->allocate(size);
    assert(start);
    char *last = &start[(d_chunkSize - 1) * d_objSize];
    for (char *p = start; p < last; p += d_objSize) {
        ((Link *)p)->d_next_p = (Link *)(p + d_objSize);
    }
    ((Link *)last)->d_next_p = 0;
    d_freeList_p = (Link *) start;
}
```

Figure 10-22b: A Pool Allocator Implementation Using a Block Allocator

10.3.4 Class-Specific Memory Management

The C++ language enables us to take over the dynamic memory allocation process on a class-by-class basis by redefining class-specific operators `new` and `delete`. Anyone allocating a dynamic instance of the class will automatically receive a pointer to memory provided by the class-specific allocator.

Sometimes a higher-level manager object will use a lower-level class whose instances must be dynamically allocated and deallocated repeatedly throughout the life of the manager. Special-purpose allocators for these subordinate objects can often be used to more than double the overall speed of the manager.

In this section we examine the use of a class-specific memory allocation strategy in the context of a simple *priority queue* (also know as a *heap*) for instances of `geom_Point`. We also observe some potential problems related to leak detection and integration within a large system. A generally useful solution to the integration problem can be found in the object-specific allocation strategy presented in Section 10.3.5.

The interface for the `my_PointQueue` class is given in Figure 10-23. The constructor for this point queue allows us to provide a physical hint about how large we expect the queue to grow. Points are added to the queue via the `push` method, prioritized by a cost that is the method's second argument. The point with the current lowest cost is returned by argument via the `pop` method, along with its associated cost, which is returned by value.

```
// my_PointQueue
#ifndef INCLUDED_MY_POINTQUEUE
#define INCLUDED_MY_POINTQUEUE

class geom_Point;
class my_PointQueueEntry;

class my_PointQueue {
    my_PointQueueEntry **d_heap_p;          // physical array
    int d_size;                             // physical size
    int d_length;                           // logical length

  private: // not implemented
    my_PointQueue(const my_PointQueue&);
    my_PointQueue& operator=(const my_PointQueue&);
```

```
  public:
    // CREATORS
    my_PointQueue(int maxLengthHint = 0);  // physical hint (see Section 10.3.1)
    ~my_PointQueue();

    // MANIPULATORS
    void push(const geom_Point& point, double cost);
    double pop(geom_Point *returnValue);
        // Undefined if length is 0.

    // ACCESSORS
    int length() const { return d_length; }
};

#endif
```

Figure 10-23: Interface File for Priority-Queue Component `my_pointqueue`

The implementation of this priority queue makes use of an auxiliary class, `my_PointQueueEntry`, which is derived from `geom_Point` and holds the value of the associated cost. This auxiliary class is defined locally in the `.c` file of the component. The complete implementation of the priority queue is provided for reference in Figure 10-24; however, our concern is with the memory-management issues and not the data structure itself.[15]

Much of the runtime cost associated with operating the queue is in the dynamic allocation and deallocation of instances of `my_PointQueueEntry` during successive pushes and pops. In addition, the work done in each `push` and `pop` of a priority queue is substantial when compared to the respective operation in the `my_Stack` object discussed in Section 10.3.2. The effect of particular values for `START_SIZE` and `GROW_FACTOR` here is virtually undetectable compared with the cost of allocation and other overhead; for large queues, however, the degradation in performance resulting from the use of a fixed `GROW_SIZE` would still be keenly felt.

[15] See **aho83**, Sections 4.10–4.11, pp. 135–145.

```
// my_pointqueue.c
#include "my_pointqueue.h"
#include "geom_point.h"
#include <memory.h>          // memcpy()

// STATIC FILE SCOPE DEFINITIONS WITH INTERNAL LINKAGE
inline int parent(int i) { return (i + 1) / 2 - 1; }
inline int firstChild(int i) { return (i + 1) * 2 - 1; }
enum { INITIAL_SIZE = 1, GROW_FACTOR = 2 };

// (LOCAL) AUXILIARY CLASS
class my_PointQueueEntry : public geom_Point {
    double d_cost;

  private:
    my_PointQueueEntry(const my_PointQueueEntry&);
    my_PointQueueEntry& operator=(const my_PointQueueEntry&);

  public:
    // CREATORS
    my_PointQueueEntry(const geom_Point& point, double cost)
    : geom_Point(point), d_cost(cost) {}
    ~my_PointQueueEntry() {}

    // ACCESSORS
    double cost() const { return d_cost; }
};

my_PointQueue::my_PointQueue(int size)
: d_length(0)
, d_size(size > INITIAL_SIZE ? size : INITIAL_SIZE)
{
    d_heap_p = new my_PointQueueEntry *[d_size];
}

my_PointQueue::~my_PointQueue()
{
    while (--d_length >= 0) {
        delete d_heap_p[d_length];
    }
    delete [] d_heap_p;
}

void my_PointQueue::push(const geom_Point& point, double cost)
{
    if (d_length >= d_size) {
        my_PointQueueEntry **tmp = d_heap_p;
        d_heap_p = new my_PointQueueEntry *[d_size *= GROW_FACTOR];
        memcpy(d_heap_p, tmp, d_length * sizeof *d_heap_p);
        delete [] tmp;
    }

    my_PointQueueEntry *newNode = new my_PointQueueEntry(point, cost);
    int n = d_length++;
```

```
    // SIFT UP

    while (n > 0) {
        int p = parent(n);
        if (d_heap_p[p]->cost() <= newNode->cost()) {
            break;
        }
        d_heap_p[n] = d_heap_p[p];
        n = p;
    }

    // n is now the index at which to insert the new node

    d_heap_p[n] = newNode;
}

double my_PointQueue::pop(geom_Point *returnValue)
{
    assert(length() > 0);
    *returnValue = *d_heap_p[0];
    double cost = d_heap_p[0]->cost();
    delete d_heap_p[0];

    int n = 0;
    my_PointQueueEntry *newNode = d_heap_p[--d_length];

    // SIFT DOWN

    while (1) {
        int c = firstChild(n);
        if (c >= d_length) {
            break;                      // no children
        }

        if (c + 1 < d_length) {         // two children
            if (d_heap_p[c+1]->cost() < d_heap_p[c]->cost()) {
                ++c;                    // adjust to second child
            }
        }

        // c is index of minimum child, whether first or second

        if (d_heap_p[c]->cost() >= newNode->cost()) {
            break;                      // all children are not smaller
        }
        d_heap_p[n] = d_heap_p[c];
        n = c;
    }

    // n is now the index at which to insert the new node

    d_heap_p[n] = newNode;
    return cost;
}
```

Figure 10-24: Implementation File for Priority-Queue Component `my_pointqueue`

10.3.4.1 Adding Custom Memory Management

By default, each `my_PointQueueEntry` object is allocated using the general-purpose global allocator associated with global operators `new` and `delete`. However, we can improve performance by creating our own allocation scheme that exploits the fact that all instances of a particular class have the same size: the `sizeof` the class.

Figure 10-25 demonstrates how we can create a customized memory-management system that reduces the frequency with which we must access the relatively slow global allocator. Instead of requesting space for one instance at a time, we allocate enough space for a number of instances (specified by `CHUNK_SIZE`). Each large block is conceptually broken into `CHUNK_SIZE` contiguous smaller blocks that are then sewn together into a linked list and rooted in the static class member `s_freeList_p`.

Now the first call to the class-specific `new` causes a large global allocation; however, the next `CHUNK_SIZE - 1` allocations can be accommodated simply by detaching an available block from the free list. When an instance of the `my_PointQueueEntry` class is deleted, its fixed-sized memory block is pushed on to the front of the free list for use in a subsequent reallocation.[16]

```
// ...
#include <stddef.h>  // size_t
// ...
enum { INITIAL_SIZE = 1, GROW_FACTOR = 2, CHUNK_SIZE = 100 };
struct Link { Link *d_next_p; };                      // no external linkage

// AUXILIARY CLASS (WITH SOME EXTERNAL LINKAGE)
class my_PointQueueEntry : public geom_Point {
    static Link *s_freeList_p;                          // external linkage
    static void replenish();                            // external linkage
    double d_cost;

  private:
    my_PointQueueEntry(const my_PointQueueEntry&);              // not impl.
    my_PointQueueEntry& operator=(const my_PointQueueEntry&);  // not impl.
```

[16] See also **murray**, Section 9.12.3, pp. 238–242.

```
    public:
      // STATICS
      void *operator new(size_t)
      {
          if (!s_freeList_p) {
              replenish();
          }
          assert(s_freeList_p);
          Link *p = s_freeList_p;
          s_freeList_p = p->d_next_p;
          return p;
      }
      void operator delete(void *addr, size_t)
      {
          ((Link *) addr)->d_next_p = s_freeList_p;
          s_freeList_p = (Link *) addr;
      }

      // CREATORS
      my_PointQueueEntry(const geom_Point& point, double cost) :
                                       geom_Point(point), d_cost(cost) {}
      ~my_PointQueueEntry() {}

      // ACCESSORS
      double cost() const { return d_cost; }
  };

  Link *my_PointQueueEntry::s_freeList_p = 0;

  void my_PointQueueEntry::replenish()
  {
      int size = CHUNK_SIZE * sizeof(my_PointQueueEntry);
      char *start = new char[size];
      char *last = &start[(CHUNK_SIZE - 1) * sizeof(my_PointQueueEntry)];
      for (char *p = start; p < last; p += sizeof(my_PointQueueEntry)) {
          ((Link *)p)->d_next_p = (Link *)(p+sizeof(my_PointQueueEntry));
      }
      ((Link *)last)->d_next_p = 0;
      s_freeList_p = (Link *) start;
  }
```

Figure 10-25: Typical Customized Class-Specific Memory-Management Scheme

To demonstrate the relative effectiveness of this allocation scheme under simulated operation, I created a performance test driver (show in Figure 10-26), similar to the one used to test `my_Stack` in Figure 10-16. On each iteration of the loop, three points with arbitrary associated values are pushed into the queue and then the current point with the lowest value is popped out. Note that the length of the queue grows by 2 on each iteration.

```
// my_pointqueue.t.c
#include "my_pointqueue.h"
#include "geom_point.h"
#include <iostream.h>
#include <stdlib.h>          // atoi()

main(int argc, const char *argv[])
{
    int repeat = argc > 1 ? atoi(argv[1]) : 0;
    cout << "repeat = " << repeat << "\t";

    my_PointQueue q;
    geom_Point p(0,0);

    for (int i = 0; i < repeat; ++i) {
        int x = i * i * i * i * i;
        q.push(p, x % 9999);
        q.push(p, x % 7777);
        q.push(p, x % 3333);
        double cost = q.pop(&p);
    }
}
```

Figure 10-26: Trivial Performance "Stress" Test Driver for `my_PointQueue`

The results of running the driver of Figure 10-26 for individual perturbations of the `CHUNK_SIZE` parameter are presented in Figure 10-27. The first row represents 1,000 iterations of the loop for each of eight physical configurations. Each successive row doubles the number of iterations, up to 1,024,000 iterations. The first two columns represent the effect of using a fixed `GROW_SIZE` and preallocating the maximum size of the queue array, respectively (as we did for `my_Stack` in Section 10.3.2). Again we see (column I) that the non-adaptive approach (without class-specific memory management) produces a severe performance problem for larger queue sizes. On the other hand, pre-allocating the entire queue array up front (column II) has only a negligible runtime performance benefit over the simple grow-factor approach (column III) advocated in Section 10.3.2.

By adding class-specific memory management to allocate space for just two `my_PointQueueEntry` objects at a time (column IV), we achieve a significant improvement over allocating individual `my_PointQueueEntry` objects using global operator `new` (column III). Allocating space for four entries at a time (column V) improves matters further. Note that when using block allocations, not only does the runtime improve, but the substantial spatial overhead required to manage individual, globally allocated blocks of memory is reduced as well.

(GROW_SIZE):	100							
INITIAL_SIZE:	0	1,024,002	1	1	1	1	1	1
GROW_FACTOR:		2	2	2	2	2	2	2
CHUNK_SIZE:				2	4	10	100	1000
Iterations	I	II	III	IV	V	VI	VII	VIII
1,000	0.0	0.0	0.0					
2,000	0.1	0.1	0.1	0.0	0.0	0.0	0.0	0.0
4,000	0.4	0.2	0.2	0.1	0.1	0.1	0.1	0.1
8,000	1.2	0.5	0.5	0.3	0.3	0.3	0.3	0.2
16,000	4.1	1.1	1.1	0.6	0.6	0.6	0.5	0.5
32,000	10.9	2.4	2.5	1.3	1.2	1.2	1.2	1.2
64,000	29.9	5.0	5.1	2.7	2.6	2.5	2.5	2.5
128,000	87.2	10.6	11.1	5.7	5.5	5.4	5.3	5.3
256,000	296.1	22.3	22.6	11.9	11.3	11.1	10.9	10.9
512,000		47.1	47.9	24.2	23.6	23.4	23.1	22.6
1,024,000		101.2	104.3	51.1	48.3	48.1	47.9	47.3

CPU Seconds Running (Optimized) on SUN SPARC 20 Workstation

Figure 10-27: Relative Performance for Various Values of `CHUNK_SIZE`

As we approach a `CHUNK_SIZE` of 100 entries (column VII) we see diminishing returns. The fact that we have amortized the cost of global allocations over at least *N* local allocations makes the effective cost of a local allocation (at most) just a little more than 1/*N* of a global allocation. When deallocation is tightly and more evenly interleaved with allocation, this class-specific allocation technique becomes even more attractive (and the slower the global allocator, the more impressive will be the improvement).

10.3.4.2 Hogging Memory

Customized class-specific allocators of this type frequently have the following problem: they tend to collect memory throughout the execution of a program, but they never give that memory back to the global allocator. In this allocation scheme, the static `s_freeList_p` part of the component wakes up initialized to 0. Once the program starts running, the memory blocks from the static free list may be shared by multiple my_PointQueue instances, so no single queue object may free the common pool. This implementation violates the major design rule of Section 7.7, which requires that we provide some way to release memory allocated to static variables before the program exits. Consequently, it is difficult to use automated tools to determine whether or not the program has lost track of this memory.

Principle

Class-specific allocation schemes that never give back their memory make the automated detection of memory leaks much more difficult.

In order to comply with the design rule, we could keep independent track of all memory blocks allocated for my_PointQueueEntry objects; we could then return these blocks to the global allocator once we were sure that no outstanding instances of my_PointQueueEntry remain. Figure 10-28 shows a factored reimplementation of the auxiliary my_pointQueueEntry class that accomplishes this goal. Instances of class my_PointQueueEntry are managed by reusing the prepackaged pub_pool component of Figure 10-22. The static s_allocator member of type pub_Pool is initialized at start-up. All memory for dynamic instances of my_PointQueueEntry will come from this static allocator object instead of the global allocator. At the end of the program, no instances of my_PointQueue will remain; it will therefore be safe for the static pub_Pool object to release this memory back to the global allocator when the pool is destroyed.

```
// ...
#include "geom_point.h"
#include "pub_pool.h"
// ...
enum { INITIAL_SIZE = 1, GROW_FACTOR = 2, CHUNK_SIZE = 100 };

// AUXILIARY CLASS (WITH SOME EXTERNAL LINKAGE)
class my_PointQueueEntry : public geom_Point {
    static pub_Pool s_allocator;                          // external linkage
    double d_cost;

  private:
    my_PointQueueEntry(const my_PointQueueEntry&);               // not impl.
    my_PointQueueEntry& operator=(const my_PointQueueEntry&);  // not impl.
```

```
  public:
    // STATICS
    void *operator new(size_t)
    {
        return s_allocator.alloc();
    }
    void operator delete(void *addr, size_t)
    {
        s_allocator.free(addr);
    }

    // CREATORS
    my_PointQueueEntry(const geom_Point& point, double cost) :
                                       geom_Point(point), d_cost(cost) {}
    ~my_PointQueueEntry() {}

    // ACCESSORS
    double cost() const { return d_cost; }
};

pub_Pool my_PointQueueEntry::s_allocator(sizeof(my_PointQueueEntry),
                                                         CHUNK_SIZE);
```

Figure 10-28: Reusing the `pub_Pool` Allocator to Implement `my_PointQueueEntry`

If you examine the listing of the `pub_Pool` allocator in Figure 10-22a, you will see that it maintains its own internal instance count. Attempting to destroy the pool while there are outstanding instances is considered by this particular allocator to be a programming error. In such cases, the pool refuses to give back any of its allocated blocks—deliberately leaking memory. If any one instance is leaked, all instances are leaked; now we can much more easily detect the problem with automated tools. For emphasis, this error condition is "documented" in the `pub_Pool`'s destructor with an assert statement.

It is worth pointing out that this implementation of `my_PointQueueEntry` is safe because the static instance of `pub_Pool` lives in the same translation unit as the managing `my_PointQueue` object and is therefore guaranteed to be initialized before it is used. However, consider the example in Figure 10-29 and assume that `my_PointQueueEntry` is instead defined in a translation unit separate from `my_PointQueue`. If the static initialization of `main.o` at start-up takes place before the static initialization `my_pointqueueentry.o`, the behavior will be undefined (and probably not pretty). Whenever a static instance of an allocator is physically separated from the translation unit that defines a manager object, we will need to take extra precautions to ensure that an instance of the manager created during start-up is well behaved.[17]

```
// main.c
#include "my_pointqueue.h"

int f()
{
    my_PointQueue q;
    q.push(geom_Point(1,2), 3.0);
    return 4;
}

int i = f();    // occurs at startup

main() {}
```

Figure 10-29: Subtle Undefined Behavior Resulting from Static Initialization

Principle

Class-specific memory allocators tend to soak up globally allocated memory, thereby increasing overall memory usage.

In isolation, class-specific memory allocators tend to work very well. This implementation does not violate any design rules, and yet in the context of a large system, the class-specific allocation approach has potentially serious consequence with respect to integration. During the course of program execution, instances will be created and destroyed; at certain times, there may be many instances of a given class—at other times, relatively few. Class-specific allocation causes the total memory requirement to increase because each class stubbornly holds onto the maximum amount of memory it has used at any time throughout the history of the execution of the program. Memory stored in private allocators is not available for general use. Over time, each individual pool reaches and holds its "high-water mark."

Figure 10-30 shows a typical memory-usage pattern for a system that contains multiple static pools. Initially at start-up the pools are empty. During the first phase of pro-

---

[17] See **meyers**, Item 47, pp. 178–182.

cessing, pools A and B are used fairly heavily, with pools D and E receiving only minimal use. By phase II, instances associated with pools A and B are no longer needed. Pool C is used heavily and pool D receives moderate use. In phase III of processing, only instances that make use of pool E are in high demand. Even though the active objects in the system never require more than 25 megabytes, the total memory usage has exceeded that value threefold. If only a few classes use a class-specific allocation strategy, there may not be a problem. However, in a large-system environment, "a few" is difficult to enforce.

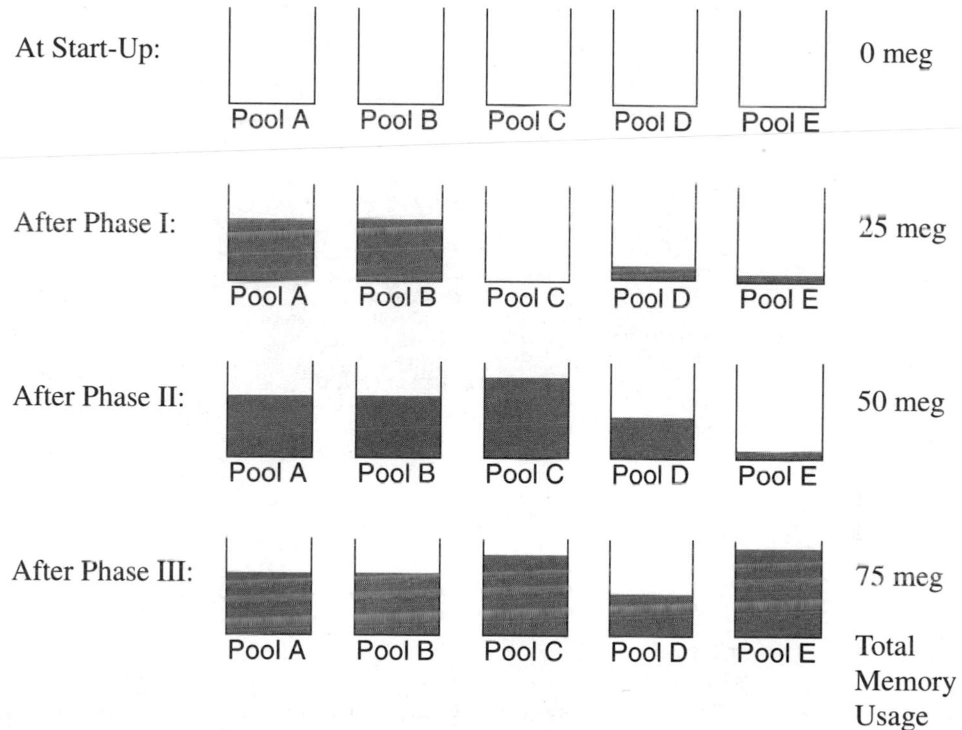

Figure 10-30: Typical Memory-Usage Pattern due to Class-Specific Allocation

We could try to improve this situation by augmenting the previous implementation to institute an instance-counting scheme as illustrated in Figure 10-31. The theory is that when the instance count reaches 0, it is safe to release all the blocks in the pool and start over. Unfortunately, one single static instance of this class, or a class that makes use of an instance of this class, is enough to pin the entire pooled memory in the private static allocator for the duration of the program.

```
// AUXILIARY CLASS (WITH SOME EXTERNAL LINKAGE)
class my_PointQueueEntry : public geom_Point {
    static pub_Pool s_allocator;                           // external linkage
    static int s_instCount;                           // new; external linkage
    double d_cost;

  private:
    my_PointQueueEntry(const my_PointQueueEntry&);               // not impl.
    my_PointQueueEntry& operator=(const my_PointQueueEntry&);  // not impl.

  public:
    // STATICS
    void *operator new(size_t)
    {
        ++s_instCount;                                                  // new
        return s_allocator.alloc();
    }
    void operator delete(void *addr, size_t)
    {
        s_allocator.free(addr);
        if (--s_instCount <= 0) {                                       // new
            s_allocator.dryUp();                                        // new
        }                                                               // new
    }

    // CREATORS
    my_PointQueueEntry(const geom_Point& point, double cost) :
                                        geom_Point(point), d_cost(cost) {}
    ~my_PointQueueEntry() {}

    // ACCESSORS
    double cost() const { return d_cost; }
};

pub_Pool my_PointQueueEntry::s_allocator(sizeof(my_PointQueueEntry),
                                                            CHUNK_SIZE);
int my_PointQueueEntry::s_instCount = 0;                                // new
```

Figure 10-31: Providing Some Automatic Clean-up for a Class-Specific Allocator

Principle

The indiscriminate use of class-specific memory management is a form of egocentric behavior that can adversely affect the overall performance of an integrated system.

The root of the problem is that we are relying on a low-level object to do more than it can reasonably do. The solution to this problem—like so many others in this book—is again to escalate the allocation responsibility to a higher level where it can be implemented more effectively.

10.3.5 Object-Specific Memory Management

Independent instances of classes should have independent behavior.[18] The concept applies both functionally and organizationally. Class-specific memory management does not have the context to know when part of its pool is safe to delete. On the other hand, each client object knows the context in which the subordinate objects will be used, and so it is in a much better position to say when they are no longer needed.

Principle

An object-specific memory allocation scheme has enough context to know when a subset of instances, allocated to and managed by a particular object, is no longer needed and can be freed.

The concept of escalating the responsibility of allocation is similar to the discussion in Section 5.8 regarding a linked list where the links deleted themselves recursively (see Figure 5-71). In that case we made the analogy that regular employees did not hire and fire each other. Here we deify the manager and say that our ultimate fate is entirely in the hands of our maker.

Guideline

Prefer object-specific over class-specific memory management.

In the case of `my_PointQueue`, we can solve the memory coupling problem simply by escalating the responsibility of allocation from the auxiliary class `my_PointQueueEntry`

[18] See **cargill**, Chapter 6, p. 119.

to the container object my_PointQueue itself. To convert the *original* (non-optimized) my_pointqueue component (shown in Figures 10-23 and 10-24) to allocate instances of the auxiliary class on a per-client basis, we need to have a unique pool allocator for each client object. We will therefore add a pub_Pool * data member to the my_PointQueue class in file my_pointqueue.h as follows:

```
// my_pointqueue.h
// ...
class pub_Pool;                          // <- add this
// ...
class my_PointQueue {
    pub_Pool *d_allocator_p;             // <- add this
    // ...
```

Notice that we thoughtfully avoided directly embedding the allocator as a data member so as not to force our clients to include the pub_Pool header. The allocator itself is managed by the my_PointQueue instance. Incidentally, the following guideline is just common sense.

Guideline

Use a non-const *pointer* data member to hold *managed* objects.

We will need to use the *placement syntax* of global operator new[19] (declared in new.h) in order to place instances of the my_PointQueueEntry class on the custom-sized memory blocks provided by the pool allocator. We will again need to include the definition of the pool and specify the desired CHUNK_SIZE as follows:

```
// my_pointqueue.c
// ...
#include "pub_pool.h"                         // <- add this
#include <new.h>                              // <- add this
// ...
enum { INITIAL_SIZE = 1, GROW_FACTOR = 2, CHUNK_SIZE = 100 };
// ...                                        // ^^^ add this ^^^ (again)
```

The constructor must now allocate a pub_Pool to initialize the d_allocator_p data member.

[19] **ellis**, Section 5.3.3, p. 60; see also **murray**, Section 9.5, p. 222.

```
my_PointQueue::my_PointQueue(int size)
: d_length(0)
, d_size(size > INITIAL_SIZE ? size : INITIAL_SIZE)
, d_allocator_p(new pub_Pool(sizeof(my_PointQueueEntry))) // <- add this
{
        d_heap_p = new my_PointQueueEntry *[d_size];
}
```

Now we need to modify the destructor. Even though the managed object has an empty destructor, we still need to free each pointer explicitly; this particular pool allocator is itself counting each instance that we free in order to help detect memory leaks.

Change:

```
my_PointQueue::~my_PointQueue()
{
    while (--d_length >= 0) {
        delete d_heap_p[d_length];
    }
    delete [] d_heap_p;
}
```

to look like:

```
my_PointQueue::~my_PointQueue()
{                                  // This loop turns out not to be needed for
    while (--d_length >= 0) {     // a pool that does not track instances.
        d_heap_p[d_length]->my_PointQueueEntry::~my_PointQueueEntry();
        d_allocator_p->free(d_heap_p[d_length]);
    }
    delete [] d_heap_p;
    delete d_allocator_p;
}
```

The last two changes involve methods `push` and `pop`. To *push* a new value, we must change the line that performs the push operation to use the placement syntax of operator `new` as follows:

Change:

```
my_PointQueueEntry *newNode = new my_PointQueueEntry(point, cost);
```

to look like:

```
my_PointQueueEntry *newNode =
    new(d_allocator_p->alloc()) my_PointQueueEntry(point, cost);
```

Finally, we need to change the line that deletes the entry to instead *destroy but not delete* the object, and then return its memory to the object-specific allocator as follows:

Change:

```
delete d_heap_p[0];
```

to look like:

```
d_heap_p[0]->my_PointQueueEntry::~my_PointQueueEntry();
d_allocator_p->free(d_heap_p[0]);
```

Destroying the object is optional if the entry object's destructor does nothing; however, it must always be freed. If we were to replace `pub_Pool` with another type of pool allocator (e.g., one without instance tracking), all of the entries remaining in the queue could be freed more efficiently simply by deleting the allocator.

Minor Design Rule

Avoid depending on the order in which data members are defined in an object during initialization.

As a brief aside, notice that `d_heap_p` is not part of the initialization list in the constructor for `my_PointQueue`. That is, we could have written

```
my_PointQueue::my_PointQueue(int size)
: d_length(0)
, d_size(size > INITIAL_SIZE ? size : INITIAL_SIZE)
, d_heap_p(new my_PointQueueEntry *[d_size])          // bad idea
{
}
```

However, the order in which data members are initialized is defined by the order in which they are declared in the definition of the class and not the order in which they appear in the initialization list.[20] There is no guarantee that `d_size` is or will continue

[20] For a different opinion on how to address this problem, see **meyers**, Item 13, pp. 41–42.

to be declared before `d_heap_p` in the class definition (see Figure 10-23). This kind of error is subtle and can be difficult to debug.

Instead of depending on this order, we can usually make direct use of the incoming expression (e.g., `size`), which we know is valid. In this case, `size` is mixed in with a conditional expression to produce `d_size` (which is the value we actually want). Rather than repeat the conditional expression, we put the initialization code in the assignment body (at no additional cost in performance).[21]

Principle

If we can exploit knowledge about a specific client's usage pattern, we can often write more effective allocators for its managed objects.

Getting back to our main topic: both class-specific and object-specific pool-based allocation strategies have comparable runtime performance characteristics under most circumstances. However, with an object-specific allocation strategy, each instance of the manager object is autonomous; that is, one instance of `my_PointQueue` does not affect another. When a `my_PointQueue` object is destroyed, all of its resources are returned to the system for redeployment. We have attained our runtime performance without soaking up a valuable global resource: memory.

As a second example, consider how we might optimize the allocation of the memory for a symbol table (see Figure 10-10). If the symbol table is implemented as a hash table of fixed-size symbols, we might make use of pool allocation. The more difficult problem is how to improve the efficiency of allocating strings. Creating a class-specific string allocator would probably do only slightly better than a completely general-purpose allocator.

On the other hand, if we associate the memory of the strings with a symbol-table object, we are in a much better position to write an optimized, special-purpose string allocator. For example, we can use an object-specific block allocator to obtain a large block of memory and then peel off pieces in the exact size required. Because this allo-

[21] See **meyers**, Item 12, pp. 37–41.

cator is being designed in the context of a manager object, we may know something specific about its intended usage pattern. For example, we may know that symbols are rarely (or never) deleted from the table. Using a general class-specific string allocation scheme, we would be forced to deal with the overhead of individually deleted strings, whether or not we needed it. In a symbol table, we can simply let these strings go, knowing full well that they will be recovered by the block allocator when the symbol table itself is destroyed.

Guideline

Consider providing a way to switch between block allocations and individual allocations of dynamic memory.

Relying on object-specific block allocators to improve performance is not foolproof. If not carefully used, block allocators have a nasty habit of masking memory leaks so that they go undetected by memory analysis tools. Consider again the object-specific pool-allocation strategy for `my_PointQueue`. Suppose I inadvertently forgot to free the object once it was popped:

```
double my_PointQueue::pop(geom_Point *returnValue)
{
    assert(length() > 0);
    *returnValue = *d_heap_p[0];
    double cost = d_heap_p[0]->cost();
    d_heap_p[0]->my_PointQueueEntry::~my_PointQueueEntry();
    // d_allocator_p->free(d_heap_p[0]); // oops! (forgot this line)

    // ...
}
```

<u>DEFINITION</u>: A *memory leak* occurs when a program loses the ability to free a block of dynamically allocated memory.

Strictly speaking, the programming error above does not result in a memory leak because the object's block allocator still retains a pointer to the memory; practically speaking, the object has lost the use of this memory. If we are using an instance-tracking allocator such as pub_Pool, we will discover that a "leak" has occurred as soon as the my_PointQueue object is destroyed. Otherwise, the memory will be returned only when the object itself is destroyed and we will never know that anything went wrong; however, the amount of memory required by the object may turn out to be grossly excessive.

Memory management is a fairly involved affair. If we are going to enjoy its benefits, we should safeguard ourselves from its woes. One way to do this is to provide some sort of switch that allows a test engineer to disable the optimized allocation strategy and revert to individual calls to the global operators new and delete. The desired effect can be accomplished using conditional compilation, as shown in Figure 10-32. The same effect can be accomplished at runtime with a static procedural interface or at start-up by reading environment variables.

```
#ifndef DEBUG_ALLOC
    my_PointQueueEntry *newNode =
        new(d_allocator_p->alloc()) my_PointQueueEntry(point, cost);
#else
    my_PointQueueEntry *newNode = new my_PointQueueEntry(point, cost);
#endif

// ...

#ifndef DEBUG_ALLOC
    d_heap_p[0]->my_PointQueueEntry::~my_PointQueueEntry();
    d_allocator_p->free(d_heap_p[0]);
#else
    delete d_heap_p[0];
#endif
```

Figure 10-32: Conditionally Compiling Out Optimization to Detect Memory Leaks

Providing the ability to run unoptimized has two advantages:

1. It allows computer-aided software engineering (CASE) tools such as Purify (or even instrumented versions of operators new and delete) to pinpoint internal memory leaks.

2. It lets you know exactly how much time and space your memory-management strategy is actually saving you.

10.4 Using C++ Templates in Large Projects

Conceptually, templates provide a qualitative leap in the possibilities for reuse—particularly in the category of common, low-level container objects. Their expressive power makes templates a welcome and highly anticipated feature of the language. Unfortunately, many existing compilers have suffered from serious efficiency and/or coupling problems that would make the introduction of templates into a large-project environment highly questionable. In this section, we mention problems surrounding two template implementation strategies for C++ compilers and then consider memory-management issues related to the development of template-based container classes touched on in earlier chapters.[22]

10.4.1 Compiler Implementations

Most compilers implement templates in one of two ways:

1. CFRONT-Like: When templates are encountered in a program, a system-wide repository is created to provide information that is shared among translation units.

2. MACRO-Like: The source code for both the header and the implementation of the template component must be made available to clients.

In the approach taken by CFRONT, a "simulated" link is performed to determine what undefined symbols can be resolved via template instantiation. In the normal mode, resolving these symbols can (and typically does) result in new undefined symbols being generated from the bodies of newly instantiated functions. This process repeats until the simulated link does not turn up any new undefined symbols. The number of simulated links could be as large as the depth of the function-call hierarchy, making template development in this mode very expensive in terms of link time. Students taking my object-oriented design course at Columbia University have encountered times of as long as 15 minutes to compile a single list template component and link it with its test driver using CFRONT 3.0 on a SUN SPARC 2 workstation.

Techniques such as avoiding templates that make in-size use of their parameterized objects and linking to pre-instantiated libraries help to lessen the added link-time cost

---

[22] See also **stroustrup**, Chapter 8, pp. 255–292; and **murray**, Chapters 7–8, pp. 141–203.

but do not eliminate it. Unfortunately, the use of just a single template on some platforms is enough to dramatically affect link time.

The MACRO approach does not suffer from excessive link time, but does create a problem with respect to insulation. Having to make implementation source available to clients also means that the code can no longer be treated as proprietary.

In spite of their obvious value, as of the writing of this book (May 1996) I continue to hear horror stories about the use of templates in large projects that confirm my own experiences with increased development time, particularly link time. With the recent adoption of the Standard Template Library (STL)[23] by the ANSI/ISO committee, the need for generally available compilers with efficient and robust support for templates becomes even more urgent.

As an avid C++ programmer, I eagerly await the next wave of C++ compilers, which I sincerely hope will address these shortcomings more effectively for large projects.[24]

10.4.2 Managing Memory in Templates

Writing good template-container classes is significantly more difficult than writing the equivalent container for a specific object. While writing a template, we must be aware that the parameter type could be either a fundamental type or a user-defined type that itself manages dynamic memory. It is not possible to derive directly from a fundamental type, nor is it in general possible to use a bitwise copy (e.g., `memcpy`) to move a user-defined type. In what follows, we explore some of the intricacies involving memory management in template classes.

---

[23] For more information about STL, see **musser**.

[24] For more on potential compiler implementation strategies for templates, see **stroustrup94**, Section 15.10, pp. 365–378.

Principle

Embedding the actual parameter type in a dummy parameterized type (e.g., `gen_StackItem<T>` for a `gen_Stack<T>`) allows us to treat fundamental types as if they were user-defined types with respect to inheritance, and to enable address and allocation functionality that might not be available in all user-defined types.

To solve the derivation problem from fundamental parameter types shown in Figure 10-33a, we can always create a dummy template `struct` that contains (HasA) the parameterized type. We can then derive from this dummy type as illustrated in Figure 10-33b, add class-specific `new` and `delete`, reestablish a private address-of (unary `&`) operator, or do anything else we might like with a cooperative user-defined type.

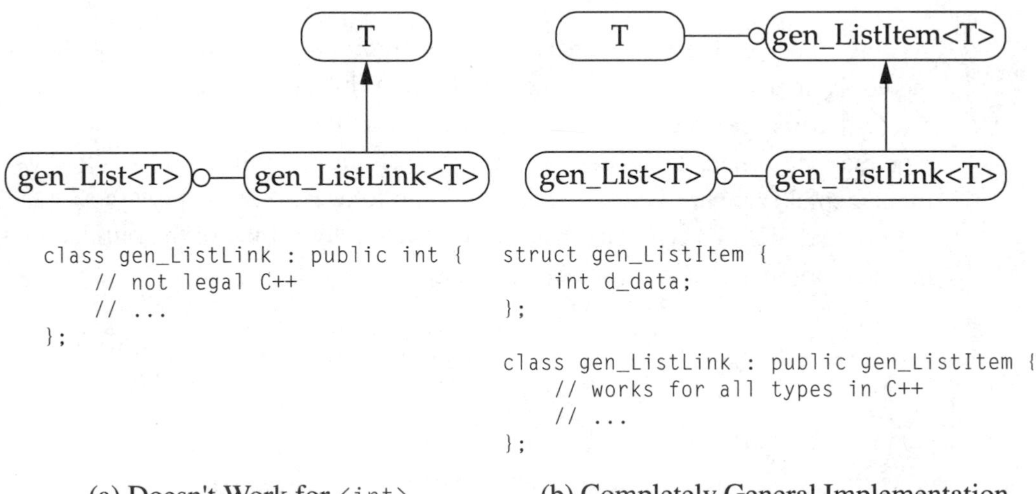


```
class gen_ListLink : public int {
    // not legal C++
    // ...
};
```

```
struct gen_ListItem {
    int d_data;
};

class gen_ListLink : public gen_ListItem {
    // works for all types in C++
    // ...
};
```

(a) Doesn't Work for `<int>`   (b) Completely General Implementation

Figure 10-33: Enabling Derivation from Arbitrary Parameter Types

Principle

In general, an object cannot be copied (or moved) using a bitwise copy.

In the general case, copying objects to new locations using `memcpy` is dangerous because the object may contain a pointer or reference to another subordinate object that it owns. After making a bitwise copy, there would be two instances of the object, each thinking that it alone is responsible for deleting the memory of the same subordinate objects. Destroying both instances would result in deleting the subordinate object twice (i.e., a programming error).

Even moving the original object using a bitwise copy cannot be done safely in general. Being careful not to call the original object's destructor ensures that subordinate objects will not be deleted twice, but does not address particularly fussy objects that may hold pointers that are self-referential (e.g., a circular linked list where the list class has an embedded link). Avoiding bitwise copies of objects is particularly important to remember when implementing containers using C++ templates.

Whether `memcpy` will work in copying a particular object is clearly an implementation detail and subject to change. Allowing one object (the template) to depend on the implementation of another (the parameterized type) in this way is not only a violation of encapsulation, but is also prone to subtle and insidious memory errors as the system evolves.

Principle

In general, an object cannot be copied or moved to uninitialized memory using that object's assignment operator.

To illustrate these points, let's consider trying to convert the integer `Stack` shown in Figure 3.2 to a template-based `Stack` of arbitrary objects. Instead of jumping right into template notation, it is often useful to start by replacing each occurrence of the original stack item type (`int`) with a typedef (`T`) as shown in Figure 10-34. Using template notation from the start may make your template more difficult to debug and is likely to increase your development time. Once you have gotten the `Stack` to work on a couple of different fundamental types (e.g., `int` and `double`) and at least one heavyweight user-defined type (e.g., `pub_String`), it will be a simple matter to convert to C++ template notation.

```
// stack.h
#ifndef INCLUDED_STACK
#define INCLUDED_STACK

typedef int T;                    // <= Stack item type T, currently an int

class StackIter;

class Stack {
    T *d_stack_p;
    int d_size;
    int d_sp;
    friend StackIter;

  public:
    Stack();
    Stack(const Stack &stack);
    Stack& operator=(const Stack &stack);
    ~Stack();
    void push(const T& value);
    T pop();
    const T& top() const;
    int isEmpty() const;
};
// ...
#endif
```

Figure 10-34: Converting a Class to a Template Class (see Figure 3.2)

The first thing we might do is figure out how to allocate the array:

```
// stack.c
#include "stack.h"
#include <memory.h>  // memcpy()

enum { START_SIZE = 1, GROW_FACTOR = 2 };

Stack::Stack()
: d_stack_p(new T[START_SIZE])                              // oops!
, d_size(START_SIZE)
, d_sp(0)
{}
```

This is no good! We are implicitly allocating *and initializing* all the objects in the physical array. This could be grossly inefficient—especially for a heavyweight type. Instead, try this:

```
Stack::Stack()
: d_stack_p((T*) new char[START_SIZE * sizeof *d_stack_p])  // ok
, d_size(START_SIZE)
, d_sp(0)
{}
```

Next, we want to try to implement the Stack's copy constructor. The original code looked like this:

```
Stack::Stack(const Stack& s)
: d_stack_p(new T[s.d_size])
, d_size(s.d_size)
, d_sp(s.d_sp)
{
    memcpy(d_stack_p, s.d_stack_p, d_sp * sizeof *d_stack_p);
}
```

We now "thoughtfully" modify the above code to look like this:

```
Stack::Stack(const Stack& s)
: d_stack_p((T*) new char[s.d_size * sizeof *d_stack_p])
, d_size(s.d_size)
, d_sp(s.d_sp)
{
    for (int i = 0; i < d_size; ++i) {
        d_stack_p[i] = s.d_stack_p[i];                       // oops!
    }
}
```

We have just introduced a subtle bug that will not reveal itself until we instantiate this Stack with a type that has a meaningful destructor. Notice that the stack item on the left is uninitialized garbage. If we were to parametrize our template with pub_String, consider how the following pub_String assignment operator might behave inside the above loop:

```
pub_String & pub_String::operator=(const pub_String& string)
{
    if (this != &string) {
        delete d_string_p;                                   // yowza!
        d_string_p = init(string.d_string_p);
    }
    return *this;
}
```

Minor Design Rule

When implementing memory management for a general, parameterized container template, be careful *not* to use the assignment operator of the contained type when the target of the assignment is uninitialized memory.

Since the left size is uninitialized memory, the contents of the location will probably not match the address of the `pub_String` object on the right; if the memory location corresponding to `d_string_p` happens not to be 0, the memory-allocation system will be corrupted. Using assignment to copy parameter types to uninitialized memory when writing template-based container classes is a surprisingly common error.

Guideline

When implementing memory management for a completely general, parameterized container that manages the memory for its contained objects, assume that the parameterized type defines a copy constructor and a destructor—nothing more.

Copying an arbitrary object can be done legitimately only by the use of its copy constructor. Moving an arbitrary object can be done only by the use of its copy constructor, followed by an explicit call to its destructor:[25]

[25] Note that most but not all objects with a copy constructor also implement an assignment operator. However, an assignment operator can be simulated with a destructor and a copy constructor (see Section 10.2.3).

```
#include <new.h>  // declare placement syntax

Stack::Stack(const Stack& s)
: d_stack_p((T*) new char[s.d_size * sizeof *d_stack_p])
, d_size(s.d_size)
, d_sp(s.d_sp)
{
    for (int i = 0; i < d_sp; ++i) {
        new(&d_stack_p[i]) T(s.d_stack_p[i]);   // ok
    }
}
```

When destroying the stack, we must control exactly which contained instances we do and do not destroy. The behavior of the original code

```
Stack::~Stack()
{
    delete [] d_stack_p;                         // no good!
}
```

would now be undefined, and could wind up leaking memory. Instead, we must destroy each *active* stack item explicitly as follows:

```
Stack::~Stack()
{
    for (int i = 0; i < d_sp; ++i) {
        d_stack_p[i].T::~T();
    }
    delete [] (char *) d_stack_p;                // ok
}
```

The rest of this story follows along the same lines. The `push` method will require placement syntax; the `pop` method will require an explicit call to the parameter type's destructor (a complete stack template component is provided for reference in Figure 10-35). The moral of the story is that when writing templates, we are forced to think about an entirely new dimension of constraints that simply did not exist for specific types. Any assumptions that we make about the parameterized type could affect the usefulness of the template, if not its correctness. However, it is reasonable for more specialized template classes (e.g., `gen_Set` and `gen_OrderedList`) to specify the functions and operations required of their respective parameter types.

```
// stack.h
#ifndef INCLUDED_STACK
#define INCLUDED_STACK

template<class T> class StackIter;

template<class T>
struct StackItem {
    T d_item;
    StackItem(const T&);
    ~StackItem(){}  // Some compilers need this (see Section 9.3.3).
};

template<class T>
class Stack {
   StackItem<T> *d_stack_p;
    int d_size;
    int d_sp;
    friend StackIter<T>;

  public:
    Stack();
    Stack(const Stack<T>& stack);
    ~Stack();
    Stack& operator=(const Stack<T>& stack);
    void push(const T& value);
    T pop();
    const T& top() const;
    int isEmpty() const;
};

template<class T>
class StackIter {
    StackItem<T> *d_stack_p;
    int d_sp;
    StackIter(const StackIter<T>&);              // not implemented
    StackIter& operator=(const StackIter<T>&);  // not implemented

  public:
    StackIter(const Stack<T>& stack);
    ~StackIter();
    operator const void *() const;
    const T& operator()() const;
    void operator++();
};

#endif
```

Figure 10-35a: Template `stack` Component Interface (`stack.h`)

```
// stack.c
#include "stack.h"
#include <new.h>      // declare placement syntax
#include <memory.h>   // memcpy()
#include <assert.h>

enum { START_SIZE = 1, GROW_FACTOR = 2 };

template<class T>
StackItem<T>::StackItem(const T& item)
: d_item(item)
{
}

template<class T>
Stack<T>::Stack()
: d_stack_p((StackItem<T> *) new char[START_SIZE * sizeof *d_stack_p])
, d_size(START_SIZE)
, d_sp(0)
{
}

template<class T>
Stack<T>::Stack(const Stack<T>& s)
: d_stack_p((StackItem<T> *) new char[s.d_size * sizeof *d_stack_p])
, d_size(s.d_size)
, d_sp(s.d_sp)
{
    for (int i = 0; i < d_sp; ++i) {
        new(d_stack_p + i) StackItem<T>(s.d_stack_p[i]);
    }
}

template<class T>
Stack<T>::~Stack()
{
    for (int i = 0; i < d_sp; ++i) {
        d_stack_p[i].StackItem<T>::~StackItem();
    }
    delete [] (char *) d_stack_p;
}

template<class T>
Stack<T>& Stack<T>::operator=(const Stack<T>& s)
{
    if (&s != this) {
        for (int i = 0; i < d_sp; ++i) {
            d_stack_p[i].StackItem<T>::~StackItem();
        }
        if (d_size < s.d_size) {
            delete d_stack_p;
```

```
            d_stack_p = (StackItem<T> *)
                                    new char[s.d_size * sizeof *d_stack_p];
            d_size = s.d_size;
        }
    }
    d_sp = s.d_sp;
    for (int i = 0; i < d_sp; ++i) {
        new(d_stack_p + i) StackItem<T>(s.d_stack_p[i]);
    }
    return *this;
}

template<class T>
void Stack<T>::push(const T& v)
{
    if (d_sp >= d_size) {
        StackItem<T> *p = d_stack_p;
        d_size *= GROW_FACTOR;
        d_stack_p = (StackItem<T> *) new char[d_size * sizeof *d_stack_p];
        for (int i = 0; i < d_sp; ++i) {
            new(d_stack_p + i) StackItem<T>(p[i]);
            p[i].StackItem<T>::~StackItem();
        }
        delete [] (char *) p;
    }
    new(d_stack_p + d_sp++) StackItem<T>(v);
}

template<class T>
T Stack<T>::pop()
{
    assert(d_sp > 0);
    StackItem<T> tmp = d_stack_p[d_sp - 1];
    d_stack_p[--sp].StackItem<T>::~StackItem();
    return tmp.d_item;
}

template<class T>
const T& Stack<T>::top() const
{
    assert(d_sp > 0);
    return d_stack_p[d_sp - 1].d_item;
}

template<class T>
int Stack<T>::isEmpty() const
{
    return d_sp <= 0;
}
```

```
template<class T>
StackIter<T>::StackIter(const Stack<T>& stack)
: d_stack_p(stack.d_stack_p)
, d_sp(stack.d_sp)
{
}

template<class T>
StackIter<T>::~StackIter()
{
}

template<class T>
StackIter<T>::operator const void *() const
{
    return d_sp > 0 ? this : 0;
}

template<class T>
const T& StackIter<T>::operator ()() const
{
    assert(d_sp > 0);
    return d_stack_p[d_sp - 1].d_item;
}

template<class T>
void StackIter<T>::operator++()
{
    assert(d_sp > 0);
    --d_sp;
}
```

Figure 10-35b: Template `stack` **Component Implementation** (`stack.c`)

Guideline

Where possible, implement templates on top of a factored reusable `void *` **pointer type using inline functions to reestablish type safety.**

The expressive power of templates hides the fact that duplicate object code is being generated for the non-inline functions of each and every instantiated template type. Wherever possible, we would like to be able to factor common functionality rather than have the size of our executables grow unnecessarily. Container classes such as `GnodePtrBag` (in Figure 5-82) are ideal candidates for template implementation: all of the real code can be factored into a single non-template type (e.g., `PtrBag`), and templates can provide the pointer type safety (through inline functions) without generating any redundant object code.[26] Consistently following this guideline can make a huge difference in the size of an executable program.

10.4.3 Patterns versus Templates

Whenever we are able to capture reusable behavior in a concrete form by using templates, we stand to improve the modularity and reliability of our system. The availability of standard libraries such as STL makes the benefits of reuse immediate and obvious. Templates are especially useful for describing generic container classes such as arrays, sets, AVL trees, and priority queues, whose implementations are virtually independent of the type of objects they contain.

Although templates are powerful tools that address some problems well, not all commonality can be characterized concretely in the form of a template. A higher-level concept is that of a *design pattern*.[27]

DEFINITION: A *design pattern* is an abstract organization of classes or objects that has repeatedly proven effective at solving similar kinds of problems in diverse application areas.

A design pattern is a micro architecture embedded within a larger design. One of the most common patterns is that of iterator, yet iteration alone does not lend itself to a template realization. A design pattern abstracts a recurring design structure. A pattern will typically span several components. Less specific than an abstraction, a design pattern captures a higher-level behavior that characterizes a part of a subsystem without necessarily delineating detailed operations. Because of the high level at which a design pattern is expressed, it can be reused again and again in only superficially different ways.

All experienced developers, whether or not they know it, use patterns in their designs. The use of design patterns is a natural consequence of experience: we look back at what we have done in similar situations and repeat what worked. Over time we begin

---

[26] **stroustrup**, Section 8.3.2, pp. 264–265; see also **murray**, Section 8.6.1, pp. 188–190.
[27] See **gamma**.

to amass strategies for organizing objects and learn under what circumstances a given strategy is applicable.

So why then is identifying design patterns as such useful? Simply put, to facilitate and expedite the development process. Experience takes considerable time and effort to accumulate. It took more than a millennium for the best minds in the world to advance the state of mathematics from the acceptance of negative numbers to the discovery of calculus in the 17th century. Yet much of this eclectic mathematical information is presented to students in an organized format, often before they leave high school.

As it is with more established disciplines such as mathematics, so it should be with object-oriented software engineering. Providing computer professionals with a variety of useful solutions and characterizing the conditions under which they apply allows practitioners to advance the state of the art instead of continually rediscovering the wheel.

Having a catalog of design patterns can be of value when you need to determine a way of solving an architectural problem and you lack the experience to know which among several design alternatives would be most efficacious in your particular situation. If the trade-offs have already been documented, it would be foolish not to incorporate that information in your decision. In cases where no acceptable solution seems forthcoming having a "thesaurus" of known-to-be-useful configurations can often provide the catalyst needed to arrive at an appropriate architecture in a timely manner.

Principle

Design patterns are an effective way of communicating reusable concepts and ideas at an architectural level.

In addition to being effective solutions in their own right, design patterns provide a lexicon—a vocabulary through which architects can readily communicate their ideas at a high level. Although a good mnemonic name is useful, sometimes having any name at all is better than having to describe the pattern each time you need to communicate it.

We have made repeated use of several simple design patterns throughout this book. For example:

- Providing a collection of non-primitive functions as instance-independent (`static` in C++) members of a separate *utility* class is useful to facilitate both the levelization of components and the minimality of class interfaces.

- Extracting a pure interface from an (abstract) class and placing this *protocol* class in a component separate from the remaining (partial) implementation that now derives from it allows clients to use this interface without being forced to depend on any particular implementation at either compile or link time.

- Embedding the private members of a concrete class in a `struct` defined entirely within its component's `.c` file enables the class to *fully insulate* clients from its implementation (C++ language specific).

- Encapsulating the details of sequencing through the parts or members of a principle class by providing a separate *iterator* friend class in the same component improves maintainability without restricting the number of concurrent clients.

For those familiar with them, each of the terms *utility*, *fully insulating*, *protocol*, and *iterator* immediately brings to mind a significant amount of abstract organizational information that obviates the accompanying description. For those unfamiliar, each of these terms provides a name that can be used to retrieve the details of the pattern (see the index).

Principle

Design patterns, like the design process itself, address both logical and physical issues.

Many of the patterns described in this book are C++ language specific and motivated by the desire to achieve a sound physical design. These are *physical design patterns*. A levelizable collection of components, each consisting of a single interface (`.h`) file and a single implementation (`.c`) file, is among the most fundamental of these patterns.

By contrast, *logical design patterns* are ostensibly language independent and address issues that arise as part of the logical design process (e.g., Iterator).

The book entitled *Design Patterns: Elements of Reusable Object-Oriented Software* by Gamma, Helm, Johnson, and Vlissides is published in the same series as this one and is its logical/architectural complement. In it 23 useful patterns, synthesized from actual working systems, are presented in sufficient detail to be immediately useful. As with all other good designs, each pattern naturally suggests implementation as a levelizable hierarchy of collaborating components. As a sample, I have provided an additional and very useful design pattern that I call *protocol hierarchy* (see Appendix A).

10.5 Summary

In this chapter we have discussed a diverse collection of topics pertaining to the implementation of individual objects in C++. Alignment requirements can cause gaps to appear in the physical layout of objects. Reordering internal data can sometimes decrease instance size, which is especially important for classes that are expected to have many instances active at a single time.

In an effort to minimize object size, we will sometimes use `short` or `char` fundamental types to represent integral member data, but only when we are sure that overflow will not occur. Attempting to use `unsigned` to obtain an extra bit is an indication that the integral type is *not* large enough to be safe. In general, the use of `unsigned` is error prone and not recommended.

Typedef declarations can be used as aliases for fundamental types of a specific size (e.g., `Int32`, `Float64`) for consistency in the implementation of objects that will be shared across platforms such as is done in object-oriented databases.

At the level of implementing individual functions, the cost of making a poor decision is relatively small because the effects of that decision are usually localized in a tiny portion of the system. However, the following practices are recommended:

- Use assert statements to help verify and document the assumptions you are making throughout the implementation of complex functions.

- Try to incorporate boundary conditions into the basic algorithm rather than treat a boundary condition as a special case.

- Within a single component, try to avoid repeating blocks of code; instead, refactor these blocks into locally reusable subroutines.

- In general, try to find the simplest solution that solves the problem effectively.

Logical state values contribute to the essential behavior of an object, while physical values are solely an artifice of a particular implementation choice. As a rule, we will try to avoid providing programmatic access to physical values.

A *hint* is additional information supplied by a client to an object to enable that object to improve performance. Like `inline` or `register`, a hint is only a suggestion, and should not affect the logical state of an object.

Customized dynamic memory management can be complex to implement but is often necessary to achieve high performance. The design space for managing dynamically allocated memory can be quite large. In Section 10.3.2, we explored two approaches of expanding the size of an internal array:

- `GROW_FACTOR`: Increase the array size by a multiplicative factor.

- `GROW_SIZE`: Increase the array size by adding a fixed increment.

`GROW_FACTOR` was shown to be more robust with respect to performance over a wide range of array sizes. The runtime performance of `GROW_SIZE` for unexpectedly large arrays was unacceptable slow. Although `GROW_SIZE` was potentially more frugal in space requirements, a `GROW_FACTOR` of G will never allow the array to exceed the optimal allocation by more than a factor of G. Except for pathological cases, `GROW_FACTOR` is almost always a good first choice for implementing expanding arrays.

In Section 10.3.3, we examined two types of memory allocators:

- A *block allocator* keeps track of each allocated block of potentially varying size and provides a mechanism for deallocating all memory at once when it is no longer needed.

- A *pool allocator* maintains a free pool of fixed-size blocks. When the pool is dry, the block allocator is called to replenish the pool. When the pool is destroyed, all blocks are deallocated.

We observed that there is much to be gained when developing and using memory allocators by instrumenting the global operators `new` and `delete`. Note that we will use functionality declared in `stdio.h` instead of `iostream.h` in the bodies of global memory operators, since `iostream` depends on global `new` for its own dynamic allocations.

Class-specific memory allocation implies that the class itself contains static variables to help manage the memory of instantiated objects, usually by holding a list of unused chunks of memory sized appropriately for that particular object. It is not uncommon for runtime performance to double as a result of this kind of optimization.

Class-specific memory-management schemes also have an important drawback in that they rarely give the memory they allocate back to the runtime system. Although this memory is not leaked, it is not available for general use. A large system with many class-specific memory managers can soak up far more memory than is necessary.

Object-specific memory management solves many of the problems intrinsic to the class-specific approach, with essentially the same runtime performance characteristics in most cases. The managing object has the context to know what the usage pattern of the managed object is likely to be. The manager is therefore in a much better position than the *class* of the subordinate to manage that object's memory optimally. In addition, when the manager is destroyed, all memory associated with subordinate objects is returned to the runtime system and is again generally available. The result is a more robust system that tends not to hang on to (much) more memory than it needs at any one time.

Block-allocation techniques are effective at improving runtime performance, but they can mask coding errors that result in failing to reuse individual instances that have been deallocated. Such errors are not memory leaks, but they can subtly degrade the spatial performance characteristics of complex objects. Providing a mechanism for switching between block and individual allocations enables us to test for this illusive yet common problem either by instrumenting global `new` and `delete` or by using commercially available tools.

Templates are an important part of the expressive power of the C++ language. Many existing compiler implementations suffer from serious flaws: either the link process is intolerably long, or their implementations cannot be insulated from clients. The adoption of STL heightens the need for compilers with efficient and robust support for templates in large projects.

Implementing a template-based container class is significantly more difficult than implementing the equivalent container for a specific object. Generally reusable template classes must work with both fundamental types and user-defined types. It is not possible to inherit directly from a fundamental type, nor is it, in general, correct to use bitwise copy (e.g., `memcpy`) on user-defined types. A common error is the use of the parameterized object's assignment operator to copy the object to uninitialized memory. When implementing the most general container classes, we may assume that the parameterized object has a copy constructor and a destructor, but nothing more.

Template syntax improves the modularity of the source code, but if used naively it can generate an enormous amount of redundant object code. By implementing templates on top of generic pointer algorithms to reestablish type safety, we can substantially reduce the potential for generating excessive code and for having to endure unbearable link times.

Templates address a certain class of problems, but not all commonality can be expressed using templates. Patterns are a higher level of design abstraction used to describe a commonly recurring micro-architecture embedded within a larger design. Design patterns provide a lexicon for efficiently expressing reusable design ideas. The *Design Patterns* book, which is part of this series, catalogs 23 of the most common patterns used in industry. Another useful example of a design pattern, *protocol hierarchy*, is provided for reference in Appendix A.

Appendix A

The Protocol Hierarchy Design Pattern

Recognizing and reusing common design patterns is essential to the effective development of large, high-quality software systems. An important pattern for object-oriented database applications called *Protocol Hierarchy* is described in this appendix. This pattern is presented in a format similar to 23 other useful patterns cataloged and explained in *Design Patterns: Elements of Reusable Object Oriented Software*.[1] Note that patterns in that book are identified by name and page number for easy reference (e.g., Composite (163) appears on page 163 of *Design Patterns*).

---

[1] **gamma**.

PROTOCOL HIERARCHY — Class Structural

Intent

Organize a heterogeneous collection of loosely related object types into a logical hierarchy. A diverse and dynamic population of clients will each be able to manipulate a maximal subset of instances created from an *extensible* set of largely disparate types safely and uniformly.

Also Known As

Safe Casting

Motivation

It is typical for clients to write applications that work with a collection of fundamental types. Treating each type as a special case is tedious and hard to maintain or extend. The ability for clients to treat a wider variety of objects uniformly makes it easier for clients to write more general applications that are also easier to maintain.

Database and graphical applications will often require that the objects on which they operate implement certain common functionality. In order for an object to participate transparently in a particular application, it must derive from a protocol class that declares this required functionality.

For example, an object database requires that each concrete persistent object implement functionality to "write itself" in a machine-independent format to a byte stream and also to read itself back from such a stream. This common functionality can be factored into an abstract base class (`DbPersistent`) as follows:

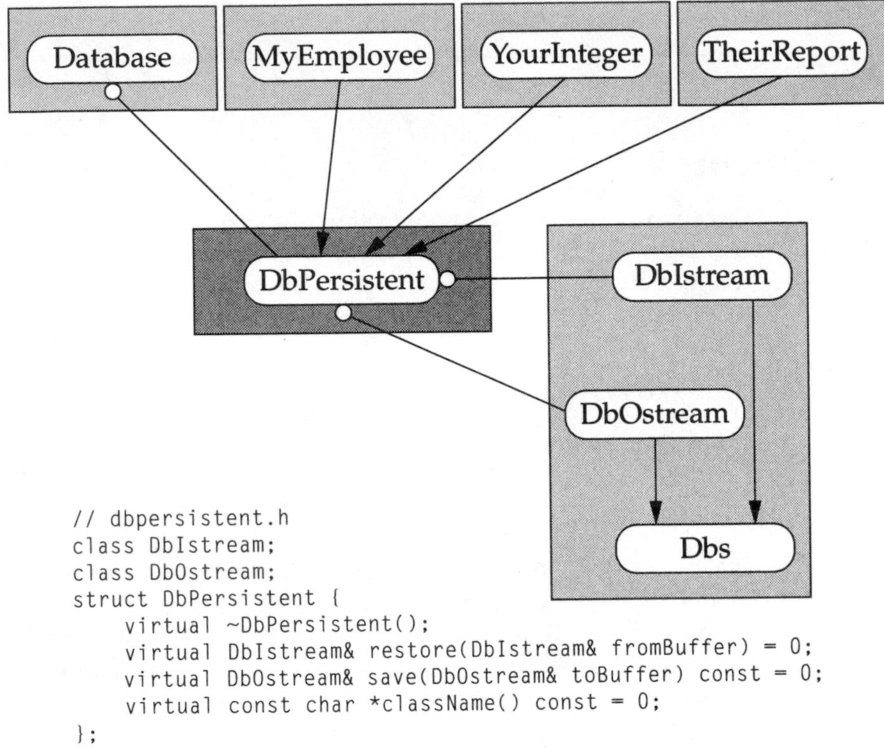


```
// dbpersistent.h
class DbIstream;
class DbOstream;
struct DbPersistent {
    virtual ~DbPersistent();
    virtual DbIstream& restore(DbIstream& fromBuffer) = 0;
    virtual DbOstream& save(DbOstream& toBuffer) const = 0;
    virtual const char *className() const = 0;
};
```

Now clients (e.g., `Database`) can treat all persistent objects uniformly without having to cast down to the particular type.

A potential problem is that apart from the required functionality, there may be little that the individual types have in common. In the case of an object database, many persistent objects may have nothing whatsoever in common except the functionality that permits them to be saved to disk.

One way to accommodate this diverse functionality is to have the root base class contain the union of all operations defined on any subclass. This approach leads to what is called a *fat interface*.[2] A fat interface implies that there are operations that can be called through the base class that do not make sense for some derived objects. In such cases it will be necessary either to first check to see if the particular object supports the operation, or test the return status of the method to see if it succeeded. In either event, we are not able to treat all objects uniformly, and there is the potential to invoke an unsupported operation inadvertently.

---

[2] **stroustrup**, Section 13.6, pp. 452–454.

Apart from losing uniformity and compile-time type-safety, the fat-interface approach means that adding any new operation in a subclass would force the base class, *all* existing subclasses, and *all* their respective clients to recompile.

Defining an enumerated value for each type is also not the answer. This technique, sometimes called "switching on type," forces all clients to know about every type. Adding a new type implies modifying some low-level component that enumerates all of the available types, again forcing all existing subclasses and their clients to recompile (see Section 6.2.9). In order for clients to manipulate the new type, however, each client will also be forced to modify source code by adding the corresponding case to each switch. Consequently, switching on type makes extending the set of types very expensive.

In some similar patterns such as Composite (163), a specific function—e.g., `const Derived *Base::derived() const`—is sometimes provided to test the base class to see if it is of a particular derived type and if so to return a valid pointer to that type, and `0` otherwise. (The use of the `dynamic_cast` construct if available would be preferable.) Having a base type return one of its derived types in its interface creates a cyclic dependency between the base and derived types. Adding a new derived type would also require adding yet another test member function to the base class, which would force all other derived classes and all of their clients to recompile. This new type would not automatically be handled by existing clients. Therefore these clients would then have to be modified in order to accommodate the new type.

Instead, we can organize our loosely related concrete types using a hierarchy of pure abstract (protocol) types whose parents share common interface characteristics, but which contain *none* of the implementation. This hierarchy of protocols acts as a kind of decision tree that allows clients to descend to the level of specificity of operations required for their application without casting all the way to a particular concrete type. Each client will then be able to operate on a maximal set of related objects using a common protocol, while preserving a high degree of compile-time type safety. Moreover, we will be able to add new protocols and new concrete types without disturbing existing protocols, concrete objects, or clients.

Extending the database example, consider an editor subsystem that manipulates persistent *graphical* objects. Each graphical object has a location and can be moved in a uniform manner. Each graphical object must be able to render itself on a given screen. It therefore makes sense to introduce a protocol for graphical editor objects as follows:

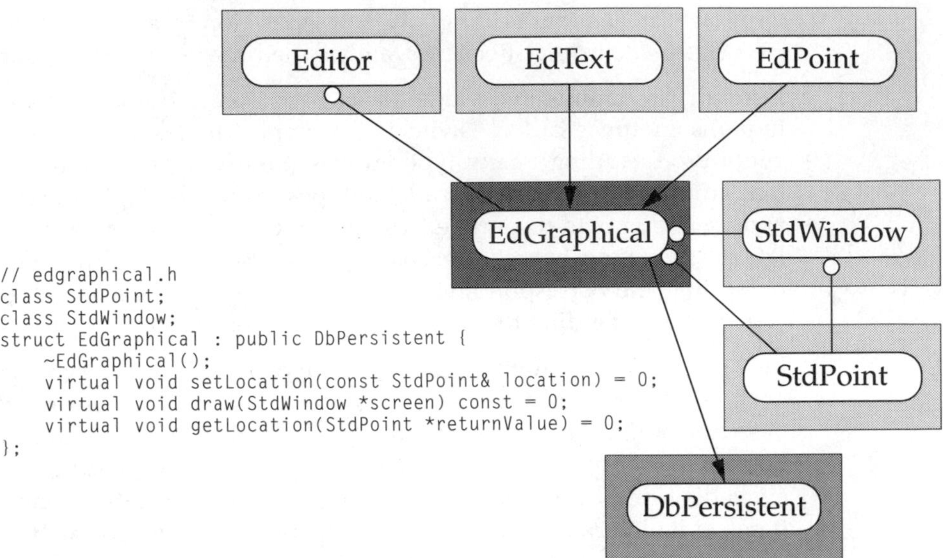


```
// edgraphical.h
class StdPoint;
class StdWindow;
struct EdGraphical : public DbPersistent {
    ~EdGraphical();
    virtual void setLocation(const StdPoint& location) = 0;
    virtual void draw(StdWindow *screen) const = 0;
    virtual void getLocation(StdPoint *returnValue) = 0;
};
```

Certain operations make sense for a wide subclass of graphical objects called *geometric* objects—i.e., objects that represent closed shapes. For example, we can reasonably ask for the area of either a polygon or a circle, but not of text. This commonality can be captured with a protocol as follows:

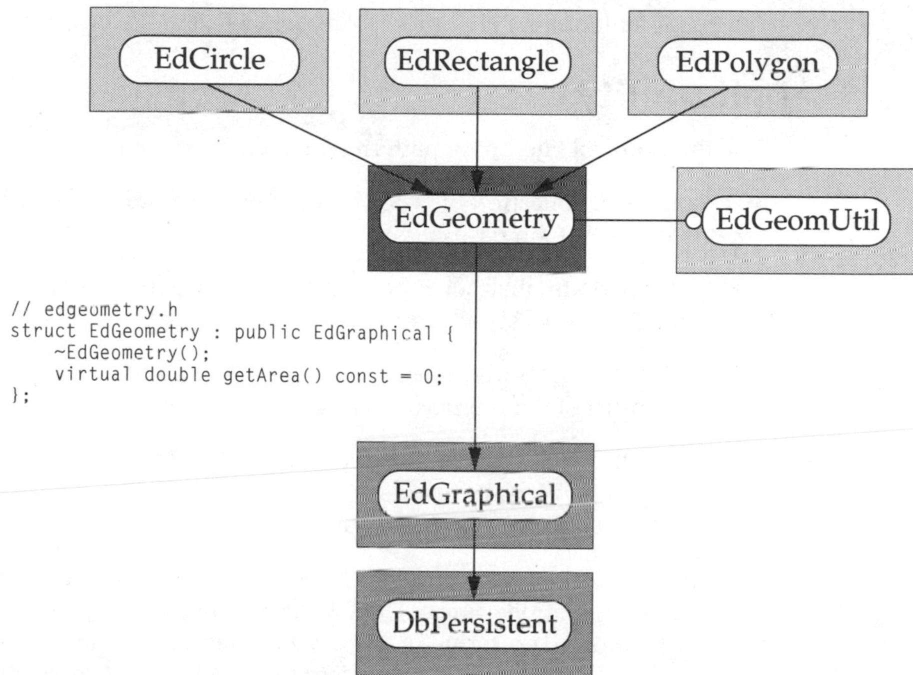
EdCircle
EdRectangle
EdPolygon
EdGeometry
EdGeomUtil
// edgeometry.h
struct EdGeometry : public EdGraphical {
~EdGeometry();
virtual double getArea() const = 0;
};
EdGraphical
DbPersistent

Now a `struct` (e.g., `EdGeomUtil`) containing non-primitive geometric utility functions that require a sensible notion of area would take arguments of type `EdGeometry` instead of `EdGraphical`.

However, there are other ways in which distinct kinds of geometric objects can be modified that are entirely different. For example, we can change the radius of a circle but not of a polygon. And we can add a vertex to a polygon but not to a circle. In such cases we may be forced to cast all the way to a concrete class or to use a more flexible, runtime-based approach. In practice, however, most applications will be able to operate effectively using a more general, protocol interface.

Each of the protocols is a pure abstract class that contains no data and defines no substantive functionality. In other words, each protocol inherits only the interface from its parent(s).[3] This characteristic is an integral part of the pattern because it avoids imposing any implementation baggage on either clients or derived class authors. In order for the Protocol Hierarchy pattern to work, a developer of a concrete object derived from a protocol must guarantee that *all* of

[3] It is possible to extend the protocol hierarchy to have more than one root protocol (see implementation note 5).

the indicated behavior is implemented with semantics that are consistent with the documentation for that protocol as well as all of its ancestors.

Applicability

Use the Protocol Hierarchy pattern when

- a diverse collection of types inherits only a small subset of their interfaces from a common base class.
- intermediate abstract types derived from a root base class can allow a wider range of objects to be treated uniformly by clients.
- the ability to handle a particular subclass of objects as a special case leads to a significant overall performance improvement.[4]
- the collection of objects is extensible and is expected to grow over the life of the system. We must be able to extend the hierarchy without affecting existing protocols, concrete classes, or clients.
- the basic operations required by each object are primitive and stable. If the set of operations is expected to grow, and these new operations can be implemented in terms of the public interface of the concrete objects, consider using the Visitor (331) pattern instead of, or in addition to, Protocol Hierarchy.
- the existing hierarchy of protocols is relatively stable. The addition of new concrete leaf types is not expected to cause a substantial refactoring of the hierarchy; however, additional intermediate abstract protocol classes may be inserted into the hierarchy at the cost of recompiling all derived protocol and leaf classes, along with all of their respective clients, but *without* having to rework existing code.

Structure

A protocol hierarchy uses inheritance to create intermediate protocols, that enable loosely related concrete leaf types to be treated uniformly by clients where possible.

---

[4] **stroustrup**, Section 13.5, pp. 442–443.

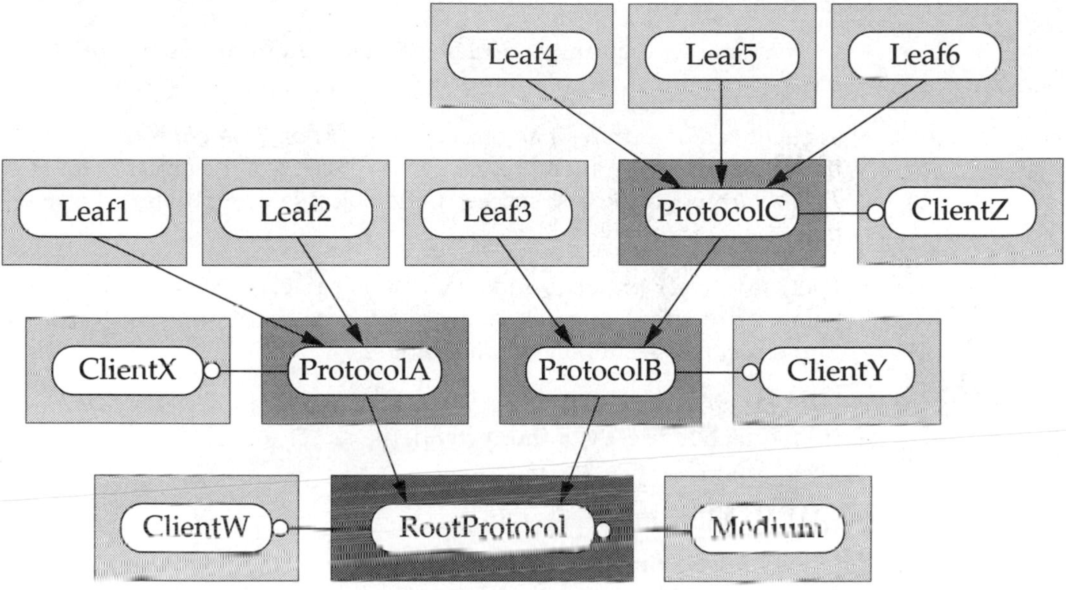

Participants

- RootProtocol (`DbPersistent`)
  - the root of the protocol hierarchy.
- Medium (`DbIstream`, `StdWindow`)
  - a type used in the interface of a protocol.
- Protocol (`EdGraphical`, `EdGeometry`)
  - defines a common intermediate interface that allows clients to use derived concrete leaf types uniformly.
- Leaf (`MyEmployee`, `EdPoint`, `EdCircle`)
  - a concrete type that implements the functionality defined in the protocols from which it inherits (either directly or indirectly).
- Client (Database, Editor, GeomUtil)
  - an application that uses the appropriate protocol to interact with the most general set of objects supporting the behavior required for this application.

Collaborations

- Clients operate uniformly on all objects derived from an appropriate protocol through that protocol's interface.
- A client can determine if an object of type *Root Protocol* is appropriate for its consideration by attempting a `dynamic_cast` of the object to the desired *Protocol* type. If the cast succeeds, the object is compatible; otherwise, the object is incompatible.
- Each (abstract) protocol and (concrete) leaf class may need to provide behavior to simulate a `dynamic_cast` where that language feature is not implemented (see implementation note 2).
- Each concrete leaf class must perform *all* behavior indicated by any protocol from which it directly or indirectly derives.

Consequences

Using the Protocol Hierarchy pattern has the following benefits and liabilities:

1. *Avoids fat interfaces*. For systems where the alternative is a root interface that is the union of the interfaces of all derived types, a protocol hierarchy reduces compile-time coupling while promoting type safety.
2. *Avoids ad-hoc down-casting*. Protocol Hierarchy provides a well-organized, reusable collection of intermediate-level interfaces that obviate always having to cast down to a specific *concrete* type.
3. *Is levelizable*. Protocol Hierarchy avoids having a base class know about any of its derived classes (see implementation note 2). It also avoids creating a closed system in which only those who can modify the source code of the base class can extend the system.
4. *Is naturally insulating*. Clients that interact only with the abstract protocol types in the hierarchy are never forced to recompile as a result of changes to the encapsulated implementation details of the concrete leaf classes (see Section 6.4.1).
5. *Is modular and easy to extend*. Adding new concrete objects to a well-designed protocol hierarchy affects no other components (e.g., concrete types, protocols, or clients). Slipping a new concrete type under an existing protocol immediately enables clients working off that protocol (or any of its base protocols) to manipulate instances of the new type transparently.

6. *Can improve efficiency.* If measurement demonstrates a bottleneck in the system and one leaf or protocol class is especially common, then providing a more efficient, special-purpose algorithm for such types may be justified. Dynamic casting requires at least one virtual function call and therefore has a non-trivial cost. However, when a client intends to make several function calls, casting all the way to the concrete leaf type can sometimes improve runtime performance significantly by enabling direct use of inline functions (see Section 6.6.1).

7. *Requires inheritance hierarchy.* This approach requires that all of the objects participating in the protocol hierarchy are related by inheritances to (at least) one root base class (compare with the Visitor (331) pattern, which does not require these objects to be related). Note also that the fixed set of methods declared in a protocol hierarchy corresponds to primitive behaviors defined by virtual functions in the concrete leaf objects. (By contrast, the extensible operations of the Visitor pattern must be implemented in terms of the public interfaces of these objects.)

8. *Requires some global knowledge.* In order to come up with a useful protocol hierarchy, it is necessary to have some idea of the applications that will make use of the intermediate protocols as well as the kinds of objects that will participate in the hierarchy.

9. *Is expensive to restructure.* Adding intermediate protocols to an existing hierarchy will require recompiling all types that derive (directly or indirectly) from the new protocol as well as all of their clients. But in contrast to other techniques (such as switching on type), clients would not be forced to rework their code to take advantage of new types of objects introduced into the hierarchy. On the other hand, removing a protocol from the hierarchy could result in serious consequences for an existing client base. In general, it is not feasible to remove a protocol that has become established in a large system.

Implementation

There are many issues to consider when implementing the Protocol Hierarchy pattern:

1. *Protocols factor interface, not implementation.* It is a cruel irony that the more general the interface, the more complex the underlying data structure must be in order to represent arbitrary instances. For example, representing an arbitrary polygon requires an unbounded amount of space. In contrast, a rectangle (which is a kind of polygon with vertical/horizontal edges) can always be represented with just two points (e.g., `d_lowerLeftCorner` and

d_upperRightCorner). To avoid burdening more specific concrete objects with unnecessarily general implementations, it is imperative that no protocol define any data members or behavior of any kind (except as needed in implementation note 2).

Sometimes we will encounter an attribute of a protocol (e.g., color) that all derived classes must support. Rather than define this attribute as a data member of the protocol, we can define a parallel (implementation) hierarchy to accommodate such attributes—suggested by the Bridge (151) pattern. In so doing, we can preserve the separation of interface from implementation, achieve total insulation, and still provide support for implementing complex concrete types.

2. *Dynamic casting*. The C++ Language Draft Standard now supports run-time type information (RTTI) in the form of built-in dynamic_cast and typeid operations.[5] In cases where the dynamic_cast feature of C++ is not available, it will be necessary to supply extralingual support for safely casting to the more specific protocols and concrete types in the protocol hierarchy.[6] One effective approach for simulating dynamic_cast—originally termed "safe casting"—requires that every class T (abstract or concrete) in a protocol hierarchy with root protocol R define a pair of static functions:[7]

```
class T {
    // ...
  public:
    static T *T::dynamicCast(R& object);
    static const T *T::dynamicCast(const R& object);
    // ...
};
```

Each of these functions returns a pointer to an object of type T only if the actual object is of type T or has T as a (direct or indirect) base class; otherwise a value of 0 is returned. The argument to every dynamicCast function in the hierarchy is always of root type R in order to maximize the number of object types that can be safely reinterpreted.

---

[5] **stroustrup94**, Section 14.2, pp. 306–336.

[6] **stroustrup**, Section 13.5, pp. 442–451.

[7] Two versions of this function are needed in order to preserve const correctness (see Section 9.1.6).

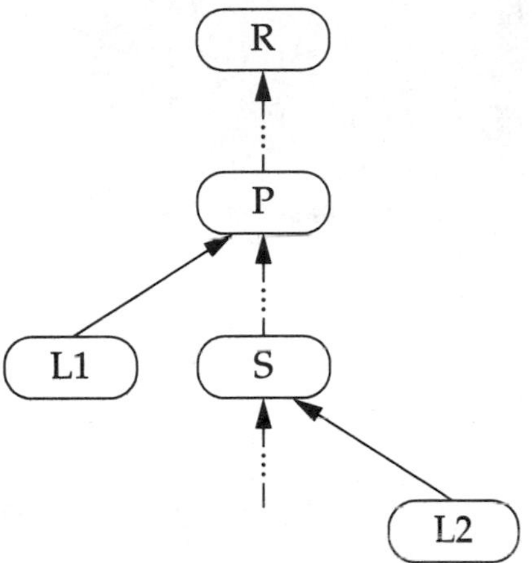

When a client wishes to determine if a particular instance derived from protocol P is also derived from a subprotocol S, the dynamicCast function corresponding to protocol S can be used as follows:

```
void client(const P& p)
{
    const S *s;
    if (s = S::dynamicCast(p)) {  // assignment (=) is intentional
        // p is a kind of S; treat specially using valid s.
        s->functionDefinedOnlyForTypeS();
    }
    else {
        // p is not an S; treat generically using p.
        p.functionDefinedForTypeP();
    }
}
```

Implementing the dynamicCast functions requires the support of a virtual function, hasProtocol, declared public in the root protocol R. The purpose of hasProtocol is to determine whether or not this concrete object is an instance of a leaf type derived from the specified class (or an instance of the class itself). Since some C++ compilers do not yet implement the typeid operation,[8] there may be no built-in way of identifying the type of an object at runtime. To address this deficiency, we will employ a variation of the following trick.[9] We can associate with each class T the address of a unique static member of the class:

---

[8] **stroustrup94**, Section 14.2.5, pp. 316–317.
[9] **ellis**, Section 10.2, pp. 212–213.

```
// t.h
class T {
    static const void *const s_typeId;    // external linkage
    // ...
};

// t.c
const void *const T::s_typeId = &s_typeId;// external linkage
// ...
```

But to improve insulation and avoid external symbols we can achieve the same effect by moving `s_typeId` to the `.c` file as a `static` (i.e., internal linkage) variable at file scope (assuming one hierarchy type per component):[10]

```
// t.c
const void *const s_typeId = &s_typeId;    // internal linkage
```

The virtual function `hasProtocol(const void *)` will return `1` if its argument is equal to the `s_typeId` of the object itself or is equal to the `s_typeId` of some base class of the object. The definition of the `hasProtocol` function for each derived type `T` is (in general) implemented as follows:[11]

```
int T::hasProtocol(const void *typeId) const
{
    return typeId == s_typeId
        || DirectBase1::hasProtocol(typeId)
        || DirectBase2::hasProtocol(typeId) // For multiple roots
        // ...                              // see implementation
        || DirectBaseN::hasProtocol(typeId) // note 5.
    ;
}
```

In the above example, `T` must be derived directly from protocol `DirectBase1`. In the presence of multiple roots (see implementation note 5) a class may derive from more than one protocol and therefore must check each of its (multiply inherited) immediate base classes as indicated for `DirectBase2, ..., DirectBaseN`.

---

[10] Note that a pointer that is itself declared `const` at file scope—e.g., `void *const p;`—has internal linkage. Note also that a pointer of type `const void *` can hold the address of *any* (non-member) object, including the address value of any pointer object (e.g., `const void **`).

[11] In some implementations, the `hasProtocol` function takes a user-defined type (e.g., `TypeId`) constructed from the unique address in order to preclude passing an arbitrary address to that function.

The `dynamicCast` static member functions for an arbitrary derived type `T` can now be implemented as follows:

```
T *T::dynamicCast(R& object)
{
    return object.hasProtocol(s_typeId) ? (T *) &object : 0;
}
const T *T::dynamicCast(const R& object)
{
    return object.hasProtocol(s_typeId) ? (T *) &object : 0;
}
```

Since only the root of the hierarchy `R` is used by a specific `dynamicCast` function, only `R::hasProtocol` need be public. All `hasProtocol` functions in derived classes may be declared protected to help reinforce proper usage.

3. *Optimizing with a static cast*. Sometimes a client will have enough global context to know that a `dynamicCast` (or `dynamic_cast`) will succeed. In such cases we can sometimes measurably improve performance by resorting to a type unsafe cast (or `static_cast`).[12] Such optimizations are inherently error prone. A reasonable compromise is to combine the two forms of cast with an assert statement as follows:

```
void knowledgeableClient(const R& object)
{
    const T *p;
    assert(p == T::dynamicCast(object));
    p = (T *) &object;
    // use valid pointer of type (const T *)
    // ...
}
```

During development, programming errors will be detected and immediately reported. The redundant error checking can then be removed easily from production code to eliminate this unnecessary performance burden.

4. *Implementing protocol destructors*. Although a protocol contributes no instance data of its own, it is necessary that its (empty) destructor be declared `virtual` and defined out-of-line to avoid the proliferation of unwanted static copies of both the destructor function and the protocol class's virtual table(s) (see Section 9.3.3). If `dynamic_cast` is simulated as described in implementation note 2, the `hasProtocol` function can assume this role so that the destructors for protocol classes need not be defined.

---

[12] The use of `dynamic_cast` and `static_cast` on pointers to classes in an inheritance hierarchy is discussed in **stroustrup94**, Section 14.3.2.1, p. 330.

5. *Multiple root protocols.* It is technically possible for a protocol to possess more than a single parent protocol and for a protocol hierarchy to possess multiple roots:

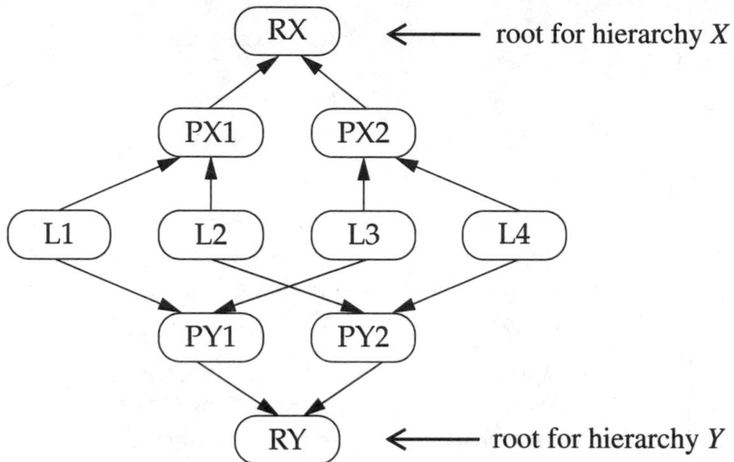

In the above example, `L1`–`L4` represent four concrete leaf classes. Protocol `PX1` (or `PX2`), derived from root protocol `RX`, can be used to treat `L1` and `L2` (or `L3` and `L4`) uniformly. Providing a second root `RY` allows us to derive two new protocols (`PY1` and `PY2`) which allow us to treat `L1` and `L3` (or `L2` and `L4`) uniformly.

The value of multiple roots in a protocol hierarchy is limited for a number of reasons:

- Each class requires two `dynamicCast` functions per root: one for `const` objects and one for non-`const` objects.
- Each new root adds one additional virtual table pointer to each concrete object instance.
- Finding the appropriate position of a concrete leaf class in a multi-rooted protocol hierarchy is more difficult than for a hierarchy with one root.
- Using protocols to achieve all arbitrary groupings would require an exponential number of roots. Circuit elements, for example, could be categorized based on whether or not they are graphical, electrical, or composite. If these three attributes are independent, providing protocols for every combination would require eight roots. Instead of organizing attributes into a decision tree at compile time, we can aggregate attributes into categories at runtime. Instead of a `hasProtocol` function, we would use a

function such as `hasCategory` to determine if a given object is appropriate to a given application. This more dynamic approach solves a problem that is similar to the one addressed by the Decorator (175) pattern.

- The use of virtual base classes would allow a protocol to be derived from a root protocol in more than one way:

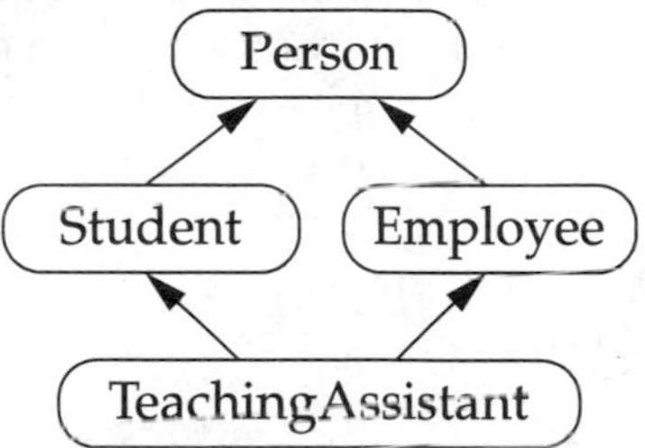

In the above example, a `TeachingAssistant` is derived from the `Person` protocol along two distinct paths: `Student` and `Employee`. The C++ language does not permit conventional casting to work in the presence of virtual base classes (although `dynamic_cast` will work when the derive class can be determined unambiguously).[13] With reconvergence in the inheritance hierarchy, the runtime cost of doing a `dynamicCast` (as implemented in implementation note 2) could potentially become exponential in the depth of the protocol hierarchy:

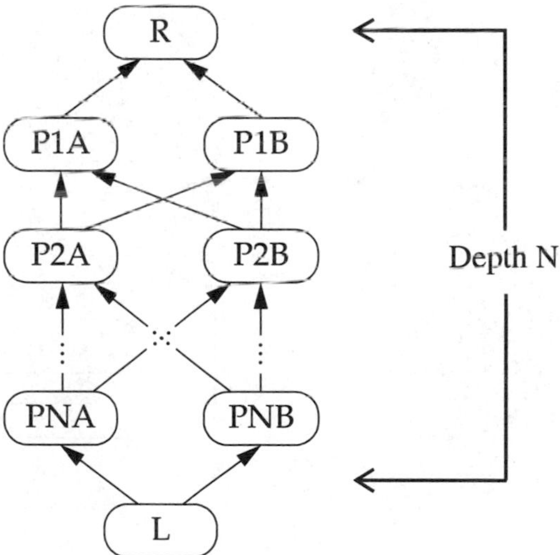

[13] **stroustrup94**, Section 14.2.2.3, pp. 312–313.

In the protocol hierarchy above there are N levels separating the leaf class `L` from the root protocol `R`. Assuming the cast ultimately fails, a naive depth-first search for the specified protocol would traverse 2^N distinct paths from `L` to `R`.

6. *Multiple inheritance*. An effective use of multiple inheritance is to merge an existing (low-level) class defining non-virtual functionality into a protocol hierarchy. In this approach, we derive a new concrete leaf class by inheriting from both the existing concrete class and the appropriate abstract protocol. We then use the functionality supplied by the concrete base class as needed to implement the virtual functions of the protocol. Using multiple inheritance in this way is an instance of the class form of the Adapter (139) pattern.[14]

   For example, we might choose to implement the leaf type `EdCircle` by inheriting from both the abstract `EdGeometry` protocol and a concrete `StdCircle` type with no virtual functions (and perhaps many inline functions) provided in a low-level standard library package such as `std`:

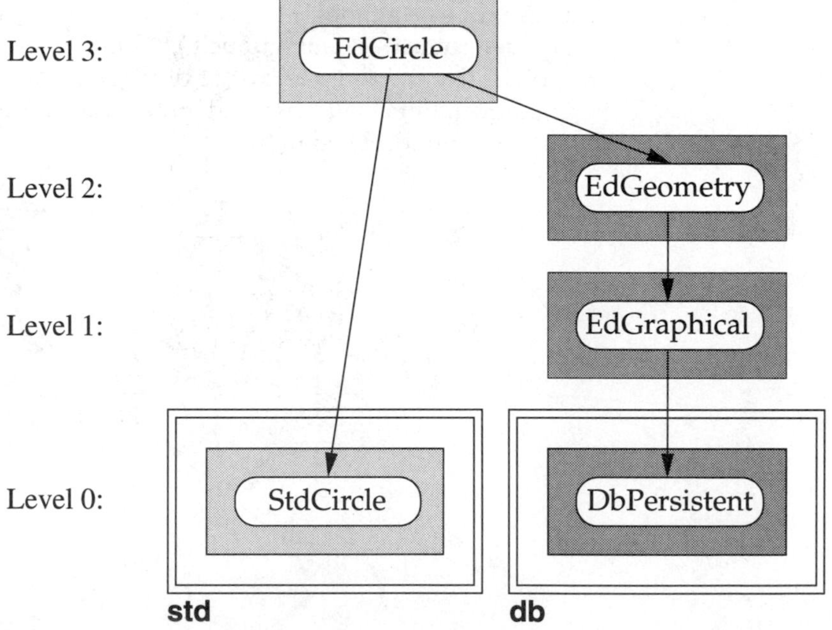

[14] A simple example of object i/o using multiple inheritance can also be found in **stroustrup94**, Section 14.2.7, p. 322.

Class `EdCircle` then needs only to implement the virtual functions defined in the protocol hierarchy, often in terms of the functions provided (perhaps under a different name) in the low-level `StdCircle` class.

7. *Media*. As a rule, it is wise not to use a type that participates in a protocol hierarchy as a *medium* (i.e., in the interface of other types in that same hierarchy). For example, consider the interface of `EdGraphical`. In order to get/set the location of a graphical object, we need to supply some sort of point object. `EdPoint` is a kind of `EdGraphical`. If we were to supply an `EdPoint` for this purpose, we would create a cyclic dependency between `EdPoint` and `EdGraphical`:

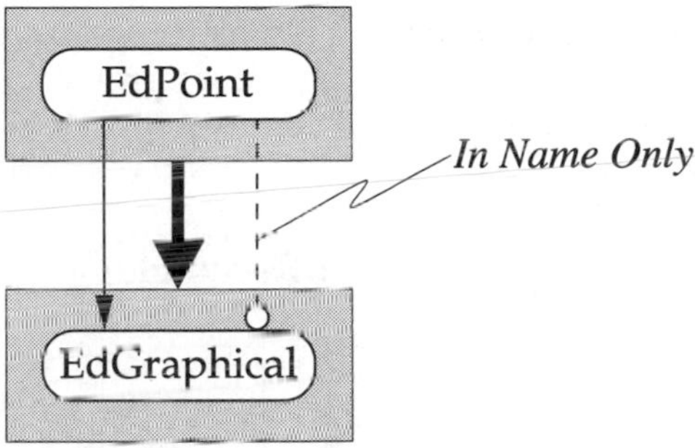

Because `EdGraphical` is only a protocol, its dependency on `EdPoint` is in name only. But consider what happens when two or more concrete leaf types appear in the `EdGraphical` protocol. Suppose `EdGraphical` also supplies functionality to return the bounding box of the graphical object as an `EdRectangle`:

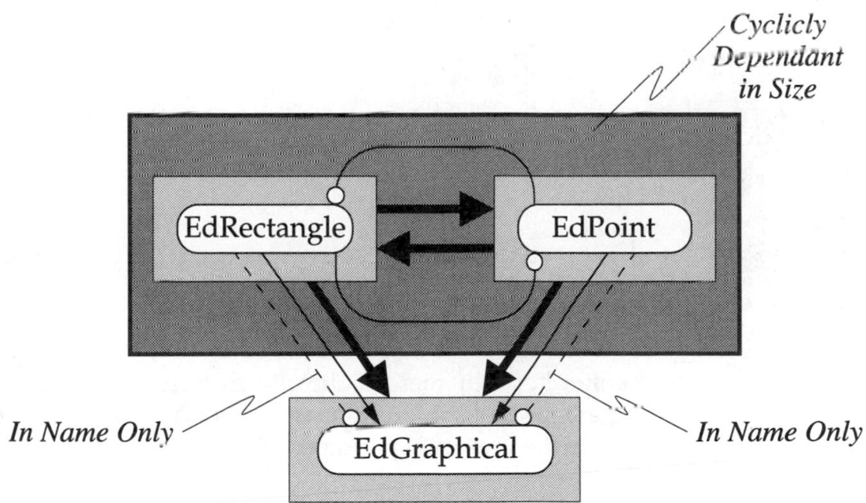

Since both `EdRectangle` and `EdPoint` are required to implement all functionality declared in the `EdGraphical` protocol, each must make substantive use of all types named in that protocol. This use results in a cyclic physical dependency that grows larger with each new leaf type named in the protocol.

Implementing a leaf class by inheriting from both a concrete type implemented in a lower-level library and the appropriate protocol (as suggested in implementation note 6) solves this levelization problem. Low-level concrete types are used to pass complex information between members of the protocol hierarchy. Public inheritance automatically allows each concrete type in the protocol hierarchy to be used as if it were a low-level library type. Providing a constructor to create a concrete protocol type from a low-level library type allows protocol and non-protocol types to interact seamlessly:

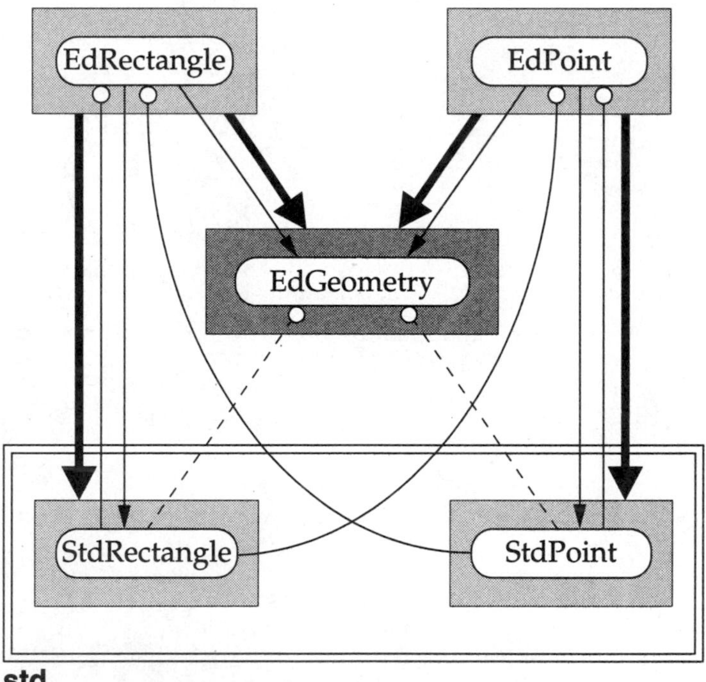

Sometimes functionality required by the protocol of a concrete leaf type cannot be implemented directly in terms of the corresponding low-level type because such an implementation would violate the internal levelization of the low-level package.

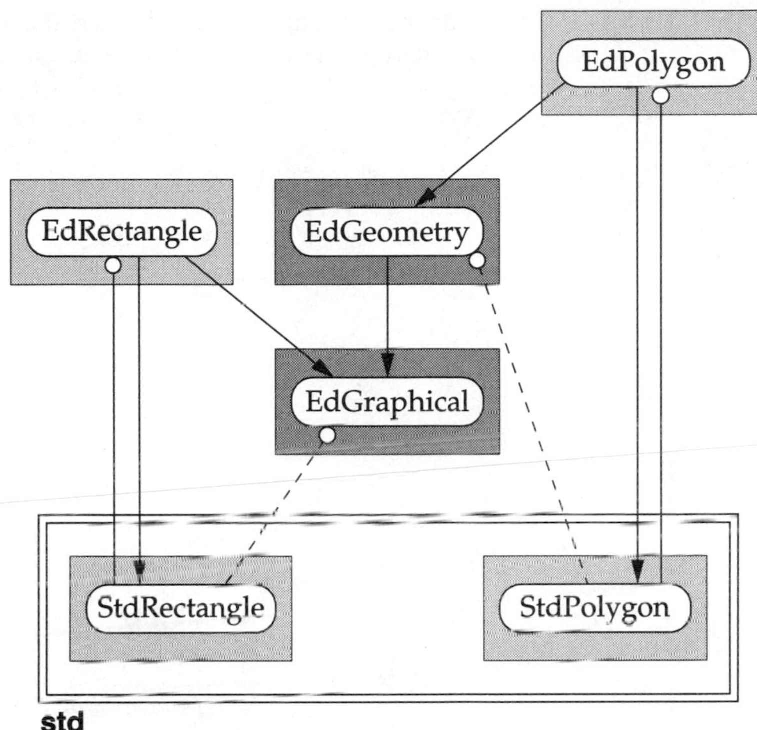

Suppose again that `EdGraphical` in the above diagram supplies functionality to return the bounding box for the graphical object but this time as an `StdRectangle`. Suppose further that `EdGeometry` supplies functionality to approximate a given shape as an `StdPolygon`:

```
class StdRectangle {                       class StdPolygon {
    // ...                                     // ...
    void cvtToPolygon(StdPolygon *);       void getBbox(StdRectangle*);
    // ...                                     // ...
};                                         };
```

Allowing these conversion functions to reside in their respective classes induces the following cyclic dependency:

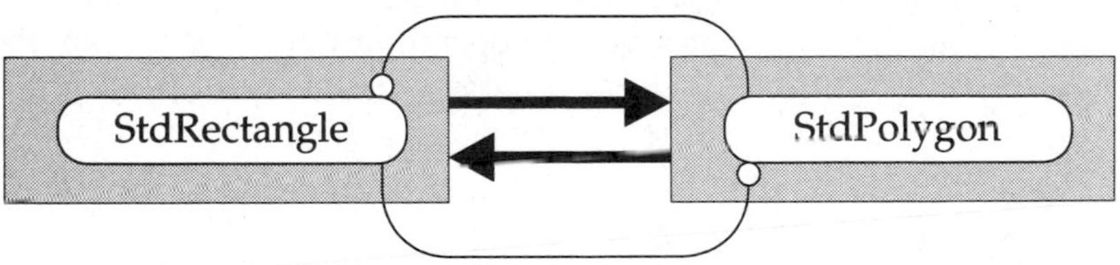

To achieve levelization, one or both of these conversation functions (neither of which is inherently primitive) must be escalated to a higher level in the physical hierarchy of the `std` package (see Section 5.2):

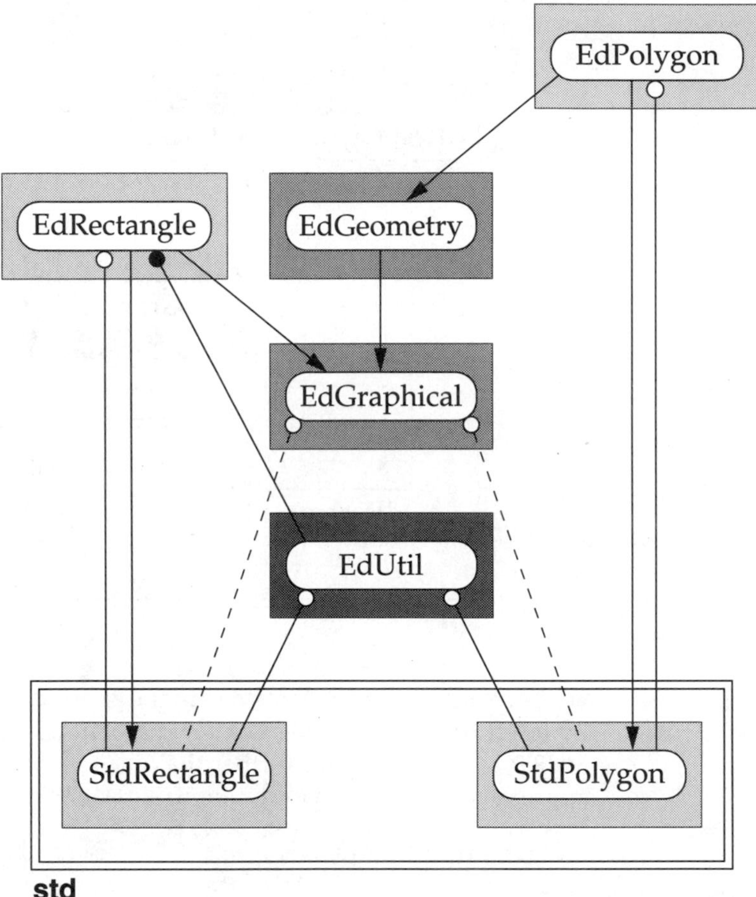

In the modified subsystem above, both `cvtToPolygon` and `getBbox` now reside as static members of the `EdUtil` utility class, and operate using only the public interfaces of `StdRectangle` and `StdPolygon`.

8. *Persistence*. In the special case of persistent objects, who should define the encode and decode operations? If, for example, the `EdPoint` implements `encode` and `decode`, then `EdPoint` will need private access to the actual data members. If we employ the multiple inheritance technique suggested in implementation note 6, `StdPoint` will be forced to grant `EdPoint` long-distance friendship, which is undesirable (see Section 3.6). Even allowing

this long-distance friendship would require modifying the source code for `StdPoint`. Instead, it makes sense for the low-level library objects to encapsulate the implementation of the primitive functionality needed to convert that object's state information to and from a byte stream.

Persistent types can be shared across multiple platforms. We would like these persistent types to use the same size integers and floating-point numbers, regardless of the platform. As suggested in Section 10.1.3, we can define a very low-level platform-specific class that holds typedef declarations identifying integer and floating-point types of a specific size (e.g., `Int16`, `Int32`, `Float64`). Porting our system to a new platform requires remapping these typedef declarations to the corresponding fundamental data type (e.g., `short`, `int`, `double`), but obviates conditional compilation for these fundamental type definitions in every persistent class.

9. *Package prefixes*. In practice, it is convenient to identify the classes in a protocol hierarchy with a common prefix irrespective of namespace issues (see section 7.2). In this example all editor protocols and concrete types begin with `Ed`. Such prefixes help to characterize and make obvious the commonality associated with types that participate in some fundamental application.

10. *Composite objects*. A protocol hierarchy is a natural implementation choice for the Composite pattern:

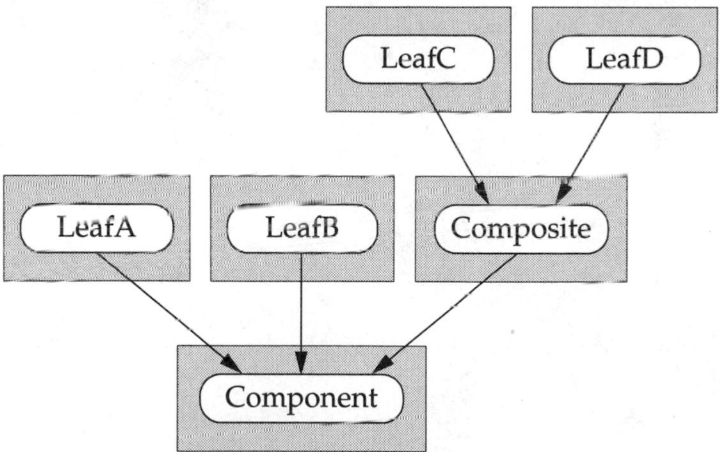

In the example above, `LeafA` and `LeafB` will be concrete classes that implement only the basic functionality required of every component. The `Composite` protocol provides additional functionality specific to composite components. For example, we might create a composite of graphical objects and call it `EdGraphicalGroup` derived from the protocol `EdGraphical`. In addition to all of the normal graphical operations, `EdGraphicalGroup` would support operations such as `add`, `remove`, `numMembers`, etc. The contained components would probably be implemented as dynamically allocated (deep) copies of graphical objects giving rise to the need for a `clone` method[15] in the `Graphical` protocol. Safe manipulation of dynamically allocated, polymorphic objects can be accomplished via the use of a handle class (see Section 6.5.3, the example shown in Figure 9-15 of Section 9.1.6, and Section 9.1.8).

---

[15] **stroustrup**, Section 6.7.1, p. 218.

Sample Code

Protocol hierarchies are important when a loosely related collection of object types is available through a common base type but cannot be processed without more specific information about the individual subtype. Database applications are an obvious situation in which the root type requires further elaboration in order for objects to be useful in a variety of applications.

```
double getTotalArea()
{
    Database db("data.dat");  // open an existing database

    double totalArea = 0.0;   // Used to accumulate area of all
                              // geometric objects in the database.

    EdGeometry *p;            // *may* hold valid kind of EdGeometry

    for (DatabaseIter it(db); it; ++it) {

        DbPersistent& object = it(); // illustrated type of "it()"

        if (p = EdGeometry::dynamicCast(object)) {
            totalArea += p->getArea();
        }
        else {
            cout << "object was not geometric" << endl;
        }
    }

    return totalArea;

}
```

In the example above, a `Database` object, `db`, is created and associated with the information stored in the disk file `data.dat`. A database iterator is created to iterate over all objects in the database. The type returned by the iterator is the root of the protocol hierarchy, `DbPersistent`, which does not support the `getArea()` behavior. Only those persistent objects that also derive from `EdGeometry` support this functionality. Using `dynamic_cast` (or `EdGeometry`'s `dynamicCast`), we can detect whether a given persistent object is also a geometric object. If so, we accumulate its area; if not we print a message to that effect. By putting the `dynamicCast` in the `if`, we ensure that we won't execute the body of the if unless the concrete object derived from `DbPersistent` is also derived from `EdGeometry`.

Using multiple inheritance to create a leaf class in the protocol hierarchy is an effective way of decoupling a particular hierarchy from fundamental reusable data types. For example, consider the interface for a standard circle type:

```
// stdcircle.h
#ifndef INCLUDED_STDCIRCLE
#define INCLUDED_STDCIRCLE

#ifndef INCLUDED_STDPOINT
#include "stdpoint.h"
#endif

class ostream;
class DbOstream;
class DbIstream;

class StdCircle {
    StdPoint d_center;
    int d_radius;

  public:
    // CREATORS
    StdCircle();
    StdCircle(const StdPoint& center, int radius);
    StdCircle(const StdCircle& circle);
    ~StdCircle();

    // MANIPULATORS
    StdCircle& operator=(const StdCircle& circle);
    DbIstream& decode(DbIstream& fromBuffer);
    void setCenter(const StdPoint& location);
    void setRadius(int length);

    // ACCESSORS
    DbOstream& encode(DbOstream& toBuffer) const;
    double getArea() const;
    const StdPoint& getCenter() const;
    int getRadius() const;
};

ostream& operator<<(ostream& o, const StdCircle& circle);
inline StdCircle::StdCircle() {}
inline StdCircle::~StdCircle() {}
// ...
inline
DbOstream& operator<<(DbOstream& toBuffer, const StdCircle& circle)
{
    return circle.encode(toBuffer);
        // Special-purpose primitive functionality implemented
        // directly in the low-level type in order to support the
        // DbPersistent protocol while preserving data hiding.
}

inline
DbIstream& operator>>(DbIstream& fromBuffer, StdCircle& circle)
{
    return circle.decode(fromBuffer);  // See above comment.
}

#endif
```

```
// stdcircle.c
#include "stdcircle.h"
#include "dbstream.h"  // object I/O capability
#include <iostream.h>
#include <math.h>      // define M_PI

// ...

DbIstream& StdCircle::decode(DbIstream& fromBuffer)
{
    return fromBuffer >> d_center >> d_radius;
}

DbOstream& StdCircle::encode(DbOstream& toBuffer) const
{
    return toBuffer << d_center << d_radius;
}

double StdCircle::getArea() const
{
    return M_PI * d_radius * d_radius;
}
```

Persistence, however, presents an important special case. Support for saving and restoring an object to disk efficiently requires access to the object's internal state variables. In order to avoid long-distance friendships, it will be necessary to implement the inherently primitive `encode` and `decode` functionality directly in the low-level type itself. In contrast, it should be possible to implement the common `draw` functionality for all graphical types on top of the public functionality supplied by each of these basic types:[16]

[16] Non-primitive operations such as `draw` which can be implemented in terms of the public interfaces of low-level basic types are the kind of extensible functionality supported by the Visitor (331) pattern.

```
// edcircle.h
#ifndef INCLUDED_EDCIRCLE
#define INCLUDED_EDCIRCLE

#ifndef INCLUDED_EDGEOMETRY
#include "edgeometry.h"
#endif

#ifndef INCLUDED_STDCIRCLE
#include "stdcircle.h"
#endif

struct EdCircle : EdGeometry, StdCircle {
    static const EdCircle *dynamicCast(const DbPersistent& object);
    static EdCircle *dynamicCast(DbPersistent& object);

    // CREATORS
    EdCircle();
    EdCircle(const StdPoint& center, int radius);
    EdCircle(const StdCircle& circle);
    EdCircle(const EdCircle& circle);
    ~EdCircle();

    // MANIPULATORS
    EdCircle& operator=(const EdCircle&);
    EdCircle& operator=(const StdCircle&);
    void setLocation(const StdPoint& location);
    DbIstream& restore(DbIstream& fromBuffer);

    // ACCESSORS
    const char *className() const;
    void draw(StdWindow *screen) const;
    double getArea() const;
    void getLocation(StdPoint *returnValue) const;
    DbOstream& save(DbOstream& toBuffer) const;

  protected:
    int hasProtocol(const void *protocol) const;
};

#endif
```

```
// edcircle.c
#include "edcircle.h"

const void *const s_typeId = &s_typeId; // local linkage


// STATICS

const EdCircle *EdCircle::dynamicCast(const DbPersistent &p)
{
    return p.hasProtocol(s_typeId) ? (EdCircle *) &p : 0;
}

EdCircle *EdCircle::dynamicCast(DbPersistent &p)
{
    return p.hasProtocol(s_typeId) ? (EdCircle *) &p : 0;
}


// CREATORS

EdCircle::EdCircle() {}

EdCircle::EdCircle(const StdPoint& center, int radius)
: StdCircle(center, radius)
{}

EdCircle::EdCircle(const StdCircle& circle)
: StdCircle(circle)
{}

EdCircle::EdCircle(const EdCircle& circle)
: StdCircle(circle)
{}

EdCircle::~EdCircle() {}

// MANIPULATORS

DbIstream& EdCircle::restore(DbIstream& fromBuffer)
{
    return StdCircle::decode(fromBuffer);
}

void EdCircle::setLocation(const StdPoint& location)
{
    StdCircle::setCenter(location);
}
```

```
// ACCESSORS

const char *EdCircle::className() const
{
    return "EdCircle";
}

void EdCircle::draw(StdWindow *) const
{
    // Implement draw capability using utilities
    // supplied by the editor package on top of
    // the public functionality provided by
    // the low-level, StdCircle Type.
}

double EdCircle::getArea() const
{
    return StdCircle::getArea();
}

void EdCircle::getLocation(StdPoint *returnValue) const
{
    *returnValue = getCenter();
}

DbOstream& EdCircle::save(DbOstream& toBuffer) const
{
    return StdCircle::encode(toBuffer);
}


// PROTECTED

int EdCircle::hasProtocol(const void *typeId) const
{
    return typeId == s_typeId || EdGeometry::hasProtocol(typeId);
}
```

Known Uses

Protocol hierarchies can be found in the schema portion of several graphical and database applications. The `dynamic_cast` operator was adopted into the C++ language to support such usage.[17] Protocol Hierarchy was adopted (circa 1992) to implement a fixed set of persistent primitive types in the ICGen CAD Framework product supplied by the IC Division of Mentor Graphics Corporation.[18] This fixed set of primitive types forms the basis for describing an extensible set of IC elements. These elements participate in their own hierarchy. For example,

---

[17] **stroustrup94**, Section 14.2.1, pp. 307–308.

[18] **soukup**, Chapter 9, Case 4, pp. 397–402.

`ElemGraphical`, `ElemGeometry`, and `ElemSingleGeom` are successive protocols in an element hierarchy. `ElemSingleGeom` indicates a device with only a single primitive geometry on a single layer of a chip (e.g., `ElemPolygon`) while `ElemGeom` allows for the possibility of several geometries on multiple layers (e.g., `ElemWire`).

A simplified version of this same approach to persistence has been used as a programming exercise in the graduate computer science course *Object-Oriented Design and Programming* at Columbia University since 1993.

Related Patterns

Protocol Hierarchy is similar to Composite (163) in that its intent is to allow a variety of types to be treated uniformly. Composite is an *object* pattern[19] that specifically addresses recursive containment, whereas Protocol Hierarchy is a *class* pattern that applies to more general applications (including composition).

Protocol Hierarchy can also be used to implement a family of Iterator (257) types, characterized by the type of object that each iterator returns (e.g., `IntIter`, `DoubleIter`, `EdPersistentIter`, `EdGraphicalIter`, and `EdGeometryIter`). All iterator functionality except the method to return the current object can be described uniformly in a common base protocol (e.g., `Iterator`). In this way, a concrete iterator associated with a concrete container class can be defined entirely within the `.c` file of a component. The iterator could be acquired from the object and used through a common protocol without ever having to expose the concrete iterator's definition outside the `.c` file that defines it.

The use of multiple inheritance to incorporate existing concrete types into a protocol hierarchy is an instance of the class form of the Adapter (139) pattern.

Maintaining an inheritance hierarchy of pure abstract types is similar in spirit to Bridge (151) pattern in that there is an interface hierarchy that distances clients from the physical implementation. A parallel hierarchy can be used to accumulate implementation that is shared among concrete leaf objects in a protocol hierarchy

Protocol Hierarchy suffers from a problem that Decorator (175) aptly avoids: the potential for combinatorial explosion. An alternative *object* pattern to a protocol *class* hierarchy might involve the use of attribute categories established at runtime.

Visitor (331) provides an alternative to protocol hierarchy when the operations are extensible but the object set is fixed. Visitor assumes that the extensible operations are not primitive—i.e., can be implemented in terms of the public interface of each concrete object. In contrast, Protocol Hierarchy allows for the transparent addition of new object types and protocols, but the basic operation set (though it may be primitive) is fixed. Although Visitor does not require the objects in the set to be related via inheritance, both Visitor and Protocol Hierarchy are invasive—both patterns require

---

[19] **gamma**, Chapter 1, p. 10.

all types participating in the collection to accommodate specific requirements. Of the two, the physical coupling associated with Visitor is potentially the more severe in terms of CCD (see Section 4.12), though always levelizable (see Figure 5-64):

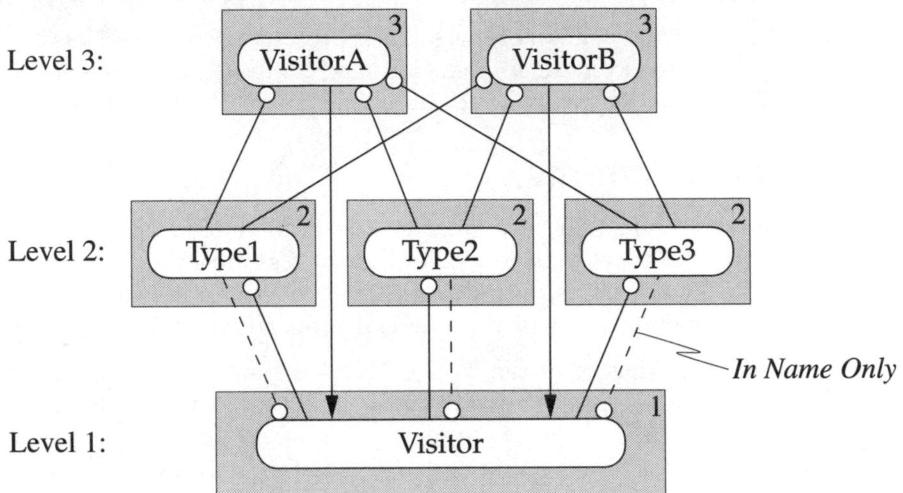

As the diagram above shows, each concrete visitor depends on every object type, and all classes depend on the `Visitor` base class, but there are no cycles in the physical dependency graph. Adding a common `Type` base class to support iteration should not affect level numbers, and can be implemented without having to resort to dynamic cast operations:

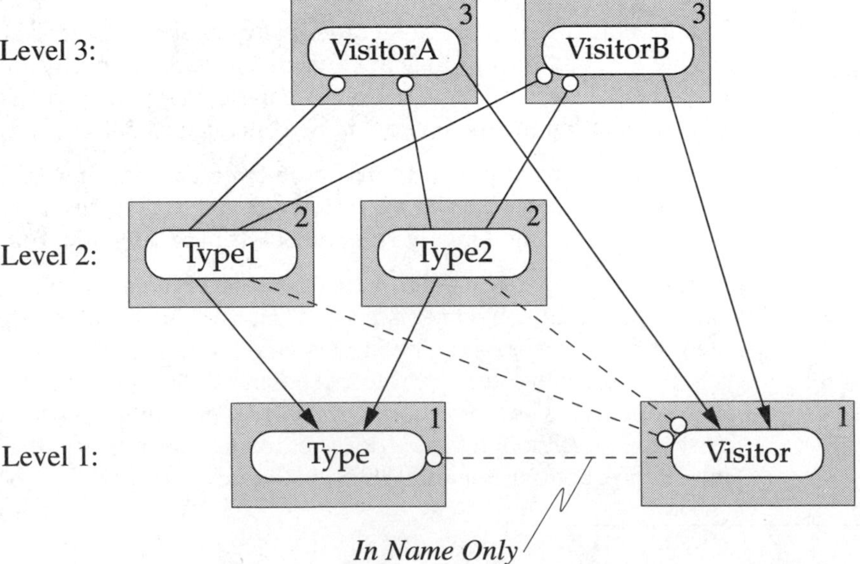

Appendix B

Implementing an ANSI C–Compatible C++ Interface

Occasionally, customers of a system will choose (for whatever reasons) not to use C++ but instead to write their applications in C. If supporting such customers is also a requirement of our system, then an ANSI C–compatible procedural interface may be the way to go. We choose ANSI C and not K&R ("classic") C because ANSI C is syntactically compatible with C++ and because classic C is too weakly typed to allow any reasonable degree of type safety. Having written such interfaces for both large C and C++ systems, I would like to share a few implementation details that may be helpful when implementing a procedural interface.

B.1 Memory Allocation Error Detection

Figure B-1 provides the interface for a style of memory allocator that has proven highly effective in detecting and reporting memory-allocation errors made by customers using procedural interfaces for large integrated circuit computer-aided design (ICCAD) products. The allocator's interface insulates most of its implementation, but note that the allocator itself is entirely insulated from customers by the procedural interface functions that create and destroy the objects within our system. Although there are pathological cases where this allocator may fail to detect an improper use of a procedural interface function on some computer architectures, the probability of such an occurrence happening in practice is small. Achieving a portable "bullet-proof" solution would probably come at the price of more complexity or a higher runtime cost.

```
// pi_alloc.h
#ifndef INCLUDED_PI_ALLOC
#define INCLUDED_PI_ALLOC

#ifndef INCLUDED_STDDEF
#include <stddef.h>                        // declares size_t
#define INCLUDED_STDDEF
#endif

class pi_Alloc {
    pi_Alloc();                            // not implemented

  public:
    // STATIC METHODS
    static void *allocate(int size, pi_Alloc *dummy);
        // Allocate specified number of bytes (with largest alignment).
        // The dummy second argument should always be null (its only
        // purpose is to encode the pi_Alloc type into the signature of
        // overloaded version of global new defined below).

    static void assertValid(void *p);
        // Use isAllocated() to determine if specified object is valid
        // and if not, take appropriate action (e.g., print a message).

    static void deallocate(void *addr);
        // Attempt to free space; try to print error if not successful.

    static int isAllocated(void *p);
        // Return 1 if memory is properly allocated, and 0 otherwise.

    static int numBlocks();
        // Return the number of outstanding allocated blocks.

    static int numBytes();
        // Return the number of outstanding allocated bytes.
};

inline void *operator new(size_t size, void *(*f)(int, pi_Alloc*))
{
    // This operator returns the result of applying its second
    // argument to its first.  The second argument of the supplied
    // function pointer is only to ensure that someone else using
    // this same technique in a different procedural interface does
    // not bump into this definition of global operator new.

    return (*f)(size, (pi_alloc *)0);
}                                           // internal linkage

static struct pi_LeakReporter {
    pi_LeakReporter();
    ~pi_LeakReporter();
} pi_leakReporter;                          // internal linkage

#endif
```

Figure B-1: A Memory Allocator Component Interface

The basic idea behind the implementation of this allocator is illustrated in Figure B-2. When memory for a new object is requested from this allocator, somewhat more memory than was requested is dynamically allocated (Figure B-2a). The allocator then initials the start of the raw memory it allocates with its own magic bit pattern (its *signature*) and the requested number of bytes before handing over a pointer to the requested portion of that memory (Figure B-2b).

When the object is destroyed, the signature is first checked to make sure that it is valid. If it is, the bytes field is inspected in order to adjust the number of outstanding bytes allocated. Then the bit pattern in the signature is modified (e.g., complemented) to invalidate the memory and thereby guard against repeatedly destroying (or otherwise further using) this same object (Figure B-2c). The pointer is then adjusted back to the beginning of the actual block before it is returned to the free store (Figure B-2d).

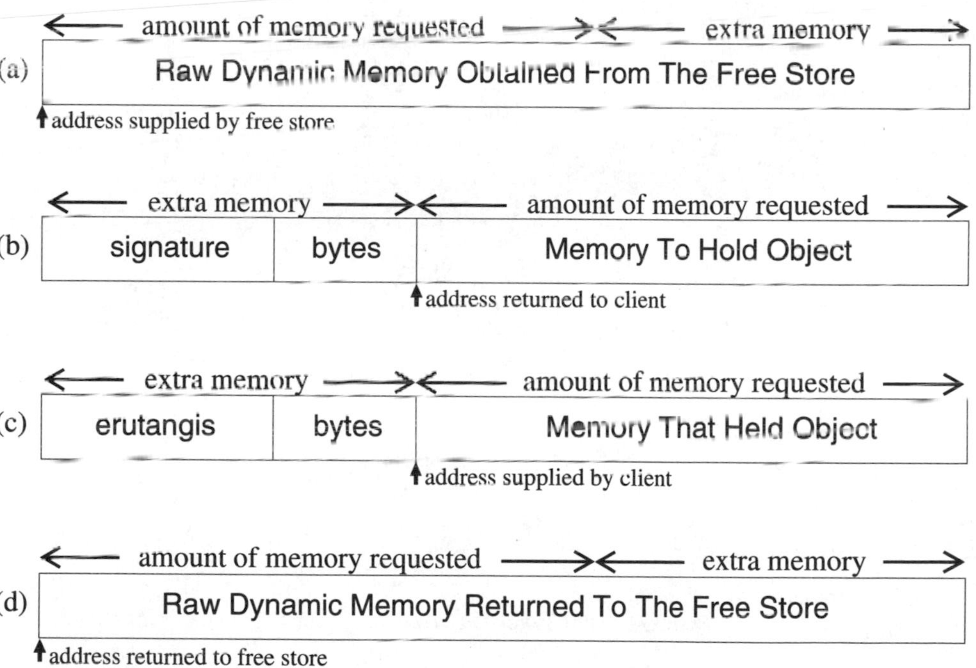

Figure B-2: Illustration of Allocation Error Detection Scheme

There is no guarantee that the modified signature will remain intact when the memory is returned to the free store. But notice that if the client does not own the memory when it is deallocated, then the probability that some "random" bit pattern will exactly match the signature can be made arbitrarily small, simply by increasing the size of the signature. In fact, if the modified signature happens to remain intact after deallocation, this particular error can be reported more precisely. By specifically looking for the modified signature, we can sometimes report this error as "deallocating previously deallocated object" rather than the more general "deallocating unallocated memory address." Using the same technique, any attempt to use a deallocated address as an argument to any other procedural interface function can also be detected easily. However, once that memory is reallocated to another user object, we may not be able to detect that the pointer is invalid using this simple strategy alone.

```
// pi_stack.c
extern "C" {
#include <pi_stack.h>
}

#include "pi_alloc.h"
#include "stack.h"

// CREATORS

extern "C"
Stack *pi_createStack()
{
    return new(pi_Alloc::allocate) Stack;
}

extern "C"
void pi_destroyStack(Stack *thisStack)
{
    if (pi_Alloc::isAllocated(thisStack)) {
        thisStack->Stack::~Stack();
    }
    pi_Alloc::deallocate(thisStack);
}

// MANIPULATORS

extern "C"
Stack *pi_StackAssign(Stack *thisStack, const Stack *thatStack)
{
    pi_Alloc::assertValid(thisStack);
    pi_Alloc::assertValid(thatStack);
    return &(*thisStack = *thatStack);
}
```

```
extern "C"
void pi_StackPush(Stack *thisStack, int value)
{
    pi_Alloc::assertValid(thisStack);
    thisStack->push(value);
}

extern "C"
int pi_StackPop(Stack *thisStack)
{
    pi_Alloc::assertValid(thisStack);
    return thisStack->pop();
}

// ACCESSORS

extern "C"
int pi_StackTop(const Stack *thisStack)
{
    pi_Alloc::assertValid(thisStack);
    return thisStack->top();
}

extern "C"
int pi_StackIsEmpty(const Stack *thisStack)
{
    pi_Alloc::assertValid(thisStack);
    return thisStack->isEmpty();
}

extern "C"
int pi_StackIsEqual(const Stack *leftStack, const Stack *rightStack)
{
    pi_Alloc::assertValid(leftStack);
    pi_Alloc::assertValid(rightStack);
    return *leftStack == *rightStack;
}
```

Figure B-3: Implementation of `pi_stack` Functionality

Figure B-3 shows the implementation of the `pi_Stack` creator functions from Figure 6-64 along with manipulator and accessor functions. We have overloaded global operator `new` to take a second argument of type `void *(*)(int, pi_Alloc *)`. It is no coincidence that `pi_Alloc::allocate` is of this type. Global `new` helps to orchestrate type safety by invoking the class's constructor and performing the explicit cast to the type of the newly created instance. The `pi_Alloc::allocate` function is used by the overloaded global new to obtain the memory to be allocated. The first argument to pi_Alloc::allocate comes from the overloaded new itself and specifies the amount of memory requested. The second argument of pi_Alloc::allocate is a dummy argument (not used), and serves only to encode the user-defined type pi_Alloc into the signature of the overloaded global operator new. In this way, someone else independently employing this same allocation strategy could define allocator my_Alloc and a corresponding overloaded version of global operator new without ever colliding with our version.

As can be seen in Figure B-3, using this allocator is hardly more difficult than using global new itself. When attempting to deallocate an object, it must first be destroyed by calling the destructor explicitly (provided the object is ours to destroy). The pi_destroyStack function does just that. For accessor and manipulator functionality, we simply use the assertValid function provided by pi_Alloc to verify that object passed in is valid. If not, the allocator takes some appropriate action. If our customers were C++ customers, we would probably throw an exception (e.g., pi_UserError). But since our clients may be ANSI C users, we will just print a message and not abort. Finally, notice that each function is declared with extern "C" linkage to make it compatible with both the ANSI C and C++ languages. The results of running the buggy code of Figure 6-65 when employing this allocator are shown in Figure B-4.

```
john@john: a.out
pi: PROGRAMMING ERROR -- deallocating previously deallocated object
pi: MEMORY LEAK -- 1 block, 12 bytes
john@john:
```

Figure B-4: Detecting Memory Allocation Programming Errors

We have augmented this allocator not only to detect illegal deallocation but also to detect failures on the part of our customers to clean up after themselves. The technique used to trigger the report on exit is related to the one for automatic initialization discussed in detail in Section 7.8.1.3. By creating a static object with internal linkage in the header of the pi_alloc component, we can ensure that the last pi_LeakReporter object will be destroyed *after* any possible attempt to deallocate an object using our memory allocator. A complete implementation for pi_alloc is provided for reference in Figure B-5. Note that the degree of checking and whether we report error messages for leaked memory could be controlled easily by compile-time switches, environment variables, or even its own procedural interface.

```
// pi_alloc.c
#include "pi_alloc.h"
#include <iostream.h>

        // -*-*-*-*- class pi_Alloc -*-*-*-*-

static int s_numBlocks = 0;             // internal linkage

static int s_numBytes = 0;              // internal linkage

static void oneMoreBlock(int bytes)
{
    ++s_numBlocks;
    s_numBytes += bytes;
}                                       // internal linkage

static void oneLessBlock(int bytes)
{
    --s_numBlocks;
    s_numBytes -= bytes;
}                                       // internal linkage

int pi_Alloc::numBlocks()
{
    return s_numBlocks;
}

int pi_Alloc::numBytes()
{
    return s_numBytes;
}

union Align {
    struct {
        int d_magic;
        int d_bytes;
    } d_data;
    long int d_longInt;
    long double d_longDouble;
    char *d_pointer;
};                                      // internal linkage

enum {
    ALLOCATED_MEMORY = 0xA110CAED,
    DEALLOCATED_MEMORY = ~ALLOCATED_MEMORY
};                                      // internal linkage
```

```
void *pi_Alloc::allocate(int size, pi_Alloc*)
{
    // Note: the second argument is never used and is present
    // only to establish the uniqueness of this overloaded
    // version of global operator new, which takes this function
    // as its second argument.

    Align *align = (Align *) new char[sizeof(Align) + size];
    align->d_data.d_magic = ALLOCATED_MEMORY;
    align->d_data.d_bytes = size;
    void *addr = ++align;
    oneMoreBlock(size);
    return addr;
}

static void report(const void *addr, const char *gerund)
{
    // Note: a gerund is the present progressive tense of
    // a verb -- i.e., a verb ending in -ing.

    cerr << "pi: PROGRAMMING ERROR -- " << gerund << ' ';
    if (!addr) {
        cerr << "null memory address";
    }
    else {
        Align *align = (Align *) addr;
        if (DEALLOCATED_MEMORY == align[-1].d_data.d_magic) {
            cerr << "previously deallocated object";
        }
        else {
            cerr << "unallocated memory address";
        }
    }
    cerr << endl;
}                                       // internal linkage

void pi_Alloc::assertValid(const void *addr)
{
    if (!isAllocated(addr)) {
        report (addr, "using");
    }
}
```

```
void pi_Alloc::deallocate(void *addr)
{
    if (!isAllocated(addr)) {
        report (addr, "deallocating");
        return;
    }

    Align *align = (Align *) addr;
    int size = align[-1].d_data.d_bytes;
    oneLessBlock(size);
    align[-1].d_data.d_magic = DEALLOCATED_MEMORY;
    delete [] (char *) --align;
};

int pi_Alloc::isAllocated(const void *addr)
{
    if (!addr) {
        return 0;
    }
    Align *align = (Align *) addr;
    return ALLOCATED_MEMORY == align[-1].d_data.d_magic;
}


       // -*-*-*-*- class pi_LeakReporter -*-*-*-*-

static int s_niftyCounter = 0;               // internal linkage

pi_LeakReporter::pi_LeakReporter()
{
    ++s_niftyCounter;
}

pi_LeakReporter::~pi_LeakReporter()
{
    if (--s_niftyCounter <= 0) {
        int b = pi_Alloc::numBlocks();
        int y = pi_Alloc::numBytes();
        if (b > 0 || y > 0) {
            cerr << "pi: MEMORY LEAK -- "
                 << b << " block" << (b != 1 ? "s" : "") << ", "
                 << y << " byte" << (y != 1 ? "s" : "") << endl;
        }
    }
};
```

Figure B-5: Memory Allocator Component Implementation

B.2 Providing a Main Procedure (ANSI C Only)

Many C++ compilers require that the component defining `main` be compiled with the C++ compiler, and that the C++ linker be used. The reason for this requirement involves the process of chaining together the constructor and destructor calls for instances of user-defined types declared at file scope. To allow ANSI C customers to compile your interface successfully, you will probably have to supply them with a precompiled file `main.o` that does nothing more than forward a call to another "main" (e.g., `pi_main`) defined to have `extern "C"` linkage:

```
extern "C" int pi_main(int argc, char *argv[]);
main(int argc, char *argv[])
{
    return pi_main(argc, argv);
}
```

Customers writing in ANSI C must now treat `pi_main` as if it were `main` — i.e., customers must write and compile their own `pi_main` function. Unfortunately, you will also have to supply your customers with a way to link your libraries so that your file-scope objects will be created before entering `main()` and destroyed after leaving `main`. One approach is to make sure they use the same linker you did, but there are other, more convoluted ways too. Different compilers use different strategies to initialize static objects. Not all compilers use the same techniques for name mangling to achieve type-safe linkage. Because different compilers accomplish these things in different ways, the C++ libraries from two distinct compilers may not be compatible. Suppose two separate companies attempt to supply ANSI–C compliant interfaces for large C++–based subsystems. If both try to use the above technique of supplying their one precompiled `main`, the customer will probably not be able to link these two subsystems together in a single executable. This problem is a serious one, and it makes the integration of C++–based libraries far more troublesome than conventional C libraries. The only certain solution is to make sure that all the C++ libraries you use were compiled using the same version of the same compiler and that you have access to that compiler yourself.

Appendix C

A Dependency Extractor/ Analyzer Package

Extracting and analyzing design dependencies, as discussed in Section 3.5, is an integral and essential part of managing the development of large systems. After the architecture is defined and development is underway, it is extremely useful to *close the loop* by extracting the actual physical dependencies among components and displaying them in a convenient format (see Section 4.7). Simple physical metrics such as those discussed in Sections 4.12 and 4.13 can be used to characterize the physical structure of software throughout the development process. This appendix describes the use and implementation of three Unix-style commands that support this capability:

`adep` — create aliases to group files into cohesive components.

`cdep` — extract compile-time dependencies from a collection of files.

`ldep` — analyze link time dependencies among a collection of components.

It is difficult to overemphasize the importance of actively using such physical design tools throughout the development of large software systems.

In the following section we will see how to use these commands to examine and characterize the internal intercomponent dependencies of the `idep` (Implementation DEPendencies) package upon which these commands are implemented. After that, a more formal description of these commands is presented in a format (called *manpages*) similar to that for other Unix commands.

Finally, we present an overview of the `idep` package architecture. The source code for these commands as well as for the entire underlying idep package is available from

Addison-Wesley at World Wide Web URL http://www.aw.com/cp/lakos.html, and is available via anonymous FTP from Addison-Wesley from ftp.aw.com in the directory cp/lakos—both as a concrete definition of the mathematics of levelization and as an example of a package of levelizable components. It is my sincere hope that some day these or similar physical design tools will be incorporated into the process of developing virtually all non-trivial software systems.

C.1 Using `adep`, `cdep`, and `ldep`

In this section we will analyze and characterize the physical dependencies within a small package (`idep`) consisting of 11 components. To accomplish this task we will use the `adep`, `cdep`, and `ldep` commands to perform the following steps:

- List the source files for the current (package) directory.
- Extract the compile-time dependencies among these files.
- Identify and pair corresponding component header and implementation files with non-matching root names.
- Verify that each implementation file names its corresponding header file in its first include directive (to ensure that each component header will compile in isolation).
- Sort and list the components of the package in levelized order.
- Merge external directory dependencies into mnemonic package group-names.
- List the canonical component dependency graph (in textual form) with redundant dependencies removed.

To begin, the source directory for `idep` contains the following files:

```
idep_adep.c            idep_cdep.c            idep_nameindexmap.h
idep_aliasdep.h        idep_compiledep.h      idep_nimap.c
idep_aliastable.h      idep_fdepitr.c         idep_string.c
idep_aliasutil.h       idep_filedepiter.h     idep_string.h
idep_altab.c           idep_ldep.c            idep_tokeniter.h
idep_alutil.c          idep_linkdep.h         idep_tokitr.c
idep_binrel.c          idep_namea.c
idep_binrel.h          idep_namearray.h
```

Ideally, the root name of the .c file of each component would exactly match the root name of the corresponding .h file. On some systems (including mine) there is an archaic 14-character maximum length limit on the name of a .o file that can be stored uniquely in a library archive. It is therefore sometimes necessary to abbreviate the component name (but never the package prefix) in order to satisfy this requirement. In the idep package, for example, the names of the .c files belonging to 9 of the 11 components are abbreviated:

idep Header File Names	idep Implementation File Names	
idep_aliasdep.h	idep_adep.c	(abbreviated)
idep_aliastable.h	idep_altab.c	(abbreviated)
idep_aliasutil.h	idep_alutil.c	(abbreviated)
idep_binrel.h	idep_binrel.c	
idep_compiledep.h	idep_cdep.c	(abbreviated)
idep_filedepiter.h	idep_fdepitr.c	(abbreviated)
idep_linkdep.h	idep_ldep.c	(abbreviated)
idep_namearray.h	idep_namea.c	(abbreviated)
idep_nameindexmap.h	idep_nimap.c	(abbreviated)
idep_string.h	idep_string.c	
idep_tokeniter.h	idep_tokitr.c	(abbreviated)
0 2 4 6 8 10 12 14	0 2 4 6 8 10 12 14	

Our first step is to extract the compile-time dependencies among these files using the cdep command. We will need to specify a sequence of directories to search in order to find the associated header files. These directories can be specified either individually using the -I<dir> option or all at once using the -i<dirlist> option. In order for this command to work properly, we would normally set our current working directory to be the idep source directory and specify the current directory (.) as one of those to be searched.

The idep package depends only on the standard compiler-supplied libraries. The following depicts the contents of a local file named *searchpath* that lists the directories in which to find the header files that belong to the current directory as well as the standard libraries of the ATT_3.0 C++ translator and underlying C compiler.

```
# searchpath
.                                              # current directory
/usr/lang/ATT_3.0/include/                     # C++ library
/usr/lang/ATT_3.0/include/cc/                  # C library
/usr/lang/ATT_3.0/include/sys/                 # C++ system library
/usr/lang/ATT_3.0/include/cc/sys/              # C system library
```

Executing the following command will extract the compile-time dependencies for all of the `idep` header and implementation files (based on the preprocessor include directives) and format these dependencies to a local file called *deps*.

```
john@john: cdep -isearchpath *.[ch] > deps
```

The `deps` file is usually quite long and not normally intended for human inspection. The elided contents of the `deps` file appears as follows:

```
idep_adep.c
    idep_aliasdep.h
    idep_aliastable.h
    idep_aliasutil.h
    idep_filedepiter.h
    idep_namearray.h
    idep_nameindexmap.h
    idep_tokeniter.h
    /usr/lang/ATT_3.0/include/ctype.h
    /usr/lang/ATT_3.0/include/cc/ctype.h
    /usr/lang/ATT_3.0/include/string.h
    /usr/lang/ATT_3.0/include/memory.h
    /usr/lang/ATT_3.0/include/cc/memory.h
    /usr/lang/ATT_3.0/include/cc/string.h
...30 lines omitted...
    /usr/lang/ATT_3.0/include/cc/malloc.h

idep_aliasdep.h

idep_aliastable.h

idep_aliasutil.h

idep_altab.c
    idep_aliastable.h
    /usr/lang/ATT_3.0/include/string.h
    /usr/lang/ATT_3.0/include/memory.h
    /usr/lang/ATT_3.0/include/cc/memory.h
...30 lines omitted...
    /usr/lang/ATT_3.0/include/cc/malloc.h

...350 lines omitted...
```

The next step is to create components from the individual files in the `idep` source directory by pairing up corresponding implementation and source files. The `adep` command provides a couple of ways to do this. For example, typing the following command identifies all of the local source files that did not have corresponding header or implementation files with matching root names:

```
john@john: adep *.[ch]
idep_adep.c
idep_aliasdep.h
idep_aliastable.h
idep_aliasutil.h
idep_altab.c
idep_alutil.c
idep_cdep.c
idep_compiledep.h
idep_fdepitr.c
idep_filedepiter.h
idep_ldep.c
idep_linkdep.h
idep_namea.c
idep_namearray.h
idep_nameindexmap.h
idep_nimap.c
idep_tokeniter.h
idep_tokitr.c
@john@john:
```

It is not hard to pair up the above files by visual inspection. The goal, however, is to capture this pairing in an *aliases* file that maps the root of the implementation file to that of its corresponding `.h` file. To facilitate this task, the `-s` option suppresses the suffixes and reorders adjacent names (e.g., `idep_namea` and `idep_namearray`) so that the longer (component) name appears before the shorter (alias) name:

```
john@john: adep -s *.[ch] > aliases
john@john:
```

We can now manually edit the local `aliases` file to make it look as follows:

```
idep_aliastable idep_altab
idep_aliasdep idep_adep
idep_aliasutil idep_alutil
idep_compiledep idep_cdep
idep_filedepiter idep_fdepitr
idep_linkdep idep_ldep
idep_namearray idep_namea
idep_nameindexmap idep_nimap
idep_tokeniter idep_tokitr
```

In order to ensure that each component header is self-sufficient with respect to compilation, each implementation file should name the corresponding header file in its first include directive (see Section 3.2). We can easily determine if this rule has been followed using the `-v` (verify) mode of `adep`:

```
john@john: adep -v *.c
Error: corresponding include directive for "idep_adep.c" not found.
Error: corresponding include directive for "idep_altab.c" not found.
Error: corresponding include directive for "idep_alutil.c" not found.
Error: corresponding include directive for "idep_cdep.c" not found.
Error: corresponding include directive for "idep_fdepitr.c" not found.
Error: corresponding include directive for "idep_ldep.c" not found.
Error: corresponding include directive for "idep_namea.c" not found.
Error: corresponding include directive for "idep_nimap.c" not found.
Error: corresponding include directive for "idep_tokitr.c" not found.
john@john:
```

Using `adep` in verify mode without component file aliases (as illustrated here) quickly reminds us that for many of the components in this package, the root names of the corresponding header and implementation files are not the same. Incorporating the contents of the above aliases file unites the corresponding header and implementation file names, and `adep` now quietly returns a successful zero status:

```
john@john: adep -v -aaliases *.c
john@john:
```

Had the author inadvertently reversed the first two include directives in the `idep_namea.c` file, the following message would have been reported to standard error and a non-zero status returned:

```
john@john: adep -v -aaliases *.c
Error: "idep_namea.c" contains corresponding include as 2nd directive.
john@john:
```

But there is an even easier way to extract these aliases provided we have consistently followed the design rule of naming the corresponding header file in the first include directive of the implementation file:

```
john@john: adep -e *.c > aliases
john@john:
```

The `-e` (extract) mode exploits the corresponding-header-first design rule to extract the root name of the first included header from each specified implementation file and pair it with the root name of the implementation file automatically. The result is identical to the one created by hand above using the default mode of `adep` and a text editor. Although some obvious errors will be reported to standard error, it is assumed that this design rule has been followed consistently. If not, the aliases obtained by extracting the name found in the first include statement will be incorrect.

We are now ready to analyze the link-time dependencies among components based on the compile-time dependencies among files (`deps`) and the component file name aliases (`aliases`):

```
john@john: ldep -ddeps -aaliases
ALIASES:
   idep_cdep -> idep_compiledep
 idep_alutil -> idep_aliasutil
  idep_namea -> idep_namearray
   idep_adep -> idep_aliasdep
idep_fdepitr -> idep_filedepiter
   idep_ldep -> idep_linkdep
  idep_altab -> idep_aliastable
  idep_nimap -> idep_nameindexmap
 idep_tokitr -> idep_tokeniter

LEVELS:
0. /usr/lang/ATT_3.0/include/
   /usr/lang/ATT_3.0/include/cc/
   /usr/lang/ATT_3.0/include/cc/sys/
   /usr/lang/ATT_3.0/include/sys/

1. idep_aliastable
   idep_binrel
   idep_filedepiter
   idep_namearray
   idep_string
   idep_tokeniter

2. idep_aliasutil
   idep_nameindexmap

3. idep_aliasdep
   idep_compiledep
   idep_linkdep

SUMMARY:
   11 Components           3 Levels          4 Packages
   35 CCD           3.18182 ACD      1.09308 NCCD

john@john:
```

The above information (formatted to standard output) provides the aliases, the levelized order of components in this package, and statistics that help characterize the dependencies within this package.[1] There are 11 local components with acyclic physical dependencies defining four levels. Entities on level 0 have no specified dependencies and are assumed to be external packages upon which this package depends. Components at level 1 depend only upon level 0 packages. In the absence of cyclic dependencies, each component at level $N > 1$ depends on at least one component at level N-1 and may depend on other components at lower levels, but not on components at level N or higher.

Testing a local component requires that one or more local components (including the component itself) be linked to a test driver. The component dependency (CD) is the number of components needed in order to use a given component. While CD is a measure of the cost (link time, disk space) of using a component in an application, it says little about the relative cost of maintaining the subsystem of components needed to implement that component.

Incrementally testing each component in a subsystem requires that one or more local components (including the component under test) be linked to a separate test driver and run stand-alone. The cumulative component dependency (CCD) of a subsystem is the sum of the CDs for each component in that subsystem. CCD is a metric that characterizes the internal coupling of components within a subsystem. The value of CCD will range from N to N^2 where N is the number of local components. A CCD value of N implies a horizontal subsystem of independent components. A value of N^2 implies a completely interdependent subsystem. A value such as $N \bullet \log(N)$ would suggest a tree-like dependency graph. In general, a lower CCD indicates a less tightly coupled, more flexible, more understandable subsystem in which the components can be tested and reused more independently.

Other statistics provided include the average component dependency (ACD) and normalized CCD (NCCD). ACD is just the ratio of the CCD to the number of local components, N, and ranges between 1 and N. NCCD is the ratio of the CCD to a (theoretical) balanced binary dependency tree with an equal number of local components. Designs that have an NCCD less than one are considered more horizontal and

---

[1] Note that knowing component levels alone is not sufficient to calculate CCD—for that, the detailed component dependency graph would be required. Hence, the CCD provided in the summary of this short listing cannot be verified from the level information it provides.

loosely coupled. Designs that have an NCCD greater than 1 are considered more vertical and tightly coupled. An NCCD significantly greater than 1 is indicative of excessive or possibly cyclic physical dependencies. Typical values for the NCCD of a high-quality package architecture implementing an application specific tool (such as `idep`) range from about 0.85 to about 1.10. Note that in this version of the tool, level 0 packages are not considered when calculating dependency metrics such as CCD, ACD, or NCCD.

By default, only the components (and not their actual dependencies) are formatted to standard output in levelized order. Specifying the `-l` option causes the component and only its non-redundant dependencies to be formatted to standard output. By *redundant* we mean that if *B* depends on *A*, and *C* depends on both *B* and *A*, then the direct dependency of *C* on *A* is redundant, and may be omitted without affecting the CCD of the system. Supplying the `-L` option (instead of `-l`) has a similar effect except that all dependencies including (redundant) transitive dependencies are formatted to standard output.

Aliases can be used for more than just pairing component header and implementation files. For example, each of the four standard C++/C include directories can be aliased to a single name, `C++LIB`, as illustrated in the local file `merge`:

```
# merge
C++LIB                                    # new name for all C/C++ libraries
/usr/lang/ATT_3.0/include/                # C++ library
/usr/lang/ATT_3.0/include/cc/             # C library
/usr/lang/ATT_3.0/include/sys/            # C++ system library
/usr/lang/ATT_3.0/include/cc/sys/         # C system library
```

The following command produces a long listing with standard compiler include libraries combined into a single package (the equivalent graphical representation is provided in Section C.3):

```
john@john: ldep -ddcps -aaliases -l -amerge
ALIASES:
/usr/lang/ATT_3.0/include/cc/sys/ -> C++LIB
                        idep_cdep -> idep_compiledep
                      idep_alutil -> idep_aliasutil
       /usr/lang/ATT_3.0/include/ -> C++LIB
                       idep_namea -> idep_namearray
                        idep_adep -> idep_aliasdep
                     idep_fdepitr -> idep_filedepiter
                        idep_ldep -> idep_linkdep
   /usr/lang/ATT_3.0/include/sys/ -> C++LIB
                       idep_altab -> idep_aliastable
                       idep_nimap -> idep_nameindexmap
    /usr/lang/ATT_3.0/include/cc/ -> C++LIB
                      idep_tokitr -> idep_tokeniter
```

```
LEVELS:
0.           C++LIB

1.   idep_aliastable 0. C++LIB

         idep_binrel 0. C++LIB

     idep_filedepiter 0. C++LIB

       idep_namearray 0. C++LIB

         idep_string 0. C++LIB

       idep_tokeniter 0. C++LIB


2.     idep_aliasutil 1. idep_aliastable
                      1. idep_string
                      1. idep_tokeniter

   idep_nameindexmap 1. idep_namearray


3.      idep_aliasdep 1. idep_filedepiter
                      2. idep_aliasutil
                      2. idep_nameindexmap

     idep_compiledep 1. idep_binrel
                      1. idep_filedepiter
                      1. idep_string
                      1. idep_tokeniter
                      2. idep_nameindexmap

         idep_linkdep 1. idep_binrel
                      2. idep_aliasutil
                      2. idep_nameindexmap

SUMMARY:
         11 Components            3 Levels                1 Package
         35 CCD             3.18182 ACD             1.09308 NCCD
```

In the presence of cycles, the simple definition of levels for an acyclic dependency graph does not apply. To make this tool generally applicable even in the presence of cyclic physical dependencies, we must introduce a more general definition of levelization. Each component is assigned a weight defined as the size of the maximal cycle of which it is a member. For an acyclic design, the weight of each component is 1. Each member of a maximal cycle containing *N* components is defined to be at a level that is *N* higher than the level of the highest (non-member) component on which any member of the cycle depends. Given this definition, it is possible to have empty levels in a cyclically dependent design.

For example, suppose we introduce an "extra" dependency by processing, in addition to `deps`, the local dependency file `extra`:

```
# extra
idep_string
    idep_linkdep
```

The cyclic implications are detected and reported to standard error by the following command:

```
john@john: ldep -ddeps -aaliases -l -amerge -dextra -x
Warning<1>: The following 3 components are cyclically dependent:
    idep_aliasutil
    idep_linkdep
    idep_string

LEVELS:
0.             C++LIB

1.    idep_aliastable    0. C++LIB

          idep_binrel    0. C++LIB

     idep_filedepiter    0. C++LIB

        idep_namearray   0. C++LIB

        idep_tokeniter   0. C++LIB


2. idep_nameindexmap     1. idep_namearray


3.
4.
5.      idep_aliasutil<1> 1. idep_aliastable
                          1. idep_binrel
                          1. idep_tokeniter
                          2. idep_nameindexmap
                          5. idep_linkdep<1>
                          5. idep_string<1>

           idep_linkdep<1> 5. idep_aliasutil<1>

            idep_string<1> 5. idep_aliasutil<1>
```

```
6.     idep_aliasdep     1. idep_filedepiter
                         5. idep_aliasutil<1>

     idep_compiledep     1. idep_filedepiter
                         5. idep_aliasutil<1>


SUMMARY:
         1 Cycle                 3 Members
        11 Components            6 Levels              1 Package
        51 CCD             4.63636 ACD           1.59278 NCCD

john@john:
```

In the above example the CCD has risen from the original 35 to 51 and the NCCD indicates that the level of internal coupling (1.59 instead of the original 1.09) is significantly higher than for a tree-like dependency graph. The number of local levels in the `idep` package is now 6 instead of 3, reflecting a more tightly coupled, less flexible physical design. The empty levels 3 and 4 are a direct result of the cycle consisting of `idep_aliasutil`, `idep_string`, and `idep_linkdep`. By the way, the `-x` option was used to suppress the printing of aliases.

```
# bigcycle
idep_filedepiter
    idep_namearray

idep_namearray
    idep_tokeniter

idep_tokeniter
    idep_binrel

idep_binrel
    idep_aliastable

idep_aliastable
    idep_linkdep

idep_linkdep
    idep_aliasdep

idep_aliasdep
    idep_compiledep

idep_compiledep
    idep_filedepiter
```

Introducing the cyclic dependencies described in the local file `bigcycle` above would cause the entire package to become physically interdependent:

```
john@john: ldep -ddeps -aaliases -l -amerge -dextra -x -dbigcycle
Warning<1>: The following 11 components are cyclically dependent:
    idep_aliasdep
    idep_aliastable
    idep_aliasutil
    idep_binrel
    idep_compiledep
    idep_filedepiter
    idep_linkdep
    idep_namearray
    idep_nameindexmap
    idep_string
    idep_tokeniter

LEVELS:
0.              C++LIB

1.
2.
3.
4.
5.
6.
7.
8.
9.
10.
11.        idep_aliasdep<1>  0. C++LIB
                            11. idep_aliastable<1>
                            11. idep_aliasutil<1>
                            11. idep_binrel<1>
                            11. idep_compiledep<1>
                            11. idep_filedepiter<1>
                            11. idep_linkdep<1>
                            11. idep_namearray<1>
                            11. idep_nameindexmap<1>
                            11. idep_string<1>
                            11. idep_tokeniter<1>

      idep_aliastable<1> 11. idep_aliasdep<1>

       idep_aliasutil<1> 11. idep_aliasdep<1>

          idep_binrel<1> 11. idep_aliasdep<1>

      idep_compiledep<1> 11. idep_aliasdep<1>

     idep_filedepiter<1> 11. idep_aliasdep<1>
```

```
         idep_linkdep<1> 11. idep_aliasdep<1>

       idep_namearray<1> 11. idep_aliasdep<1>

    idep_nameindexmap<1> 11. idep_aliasdep<1>

          idep_string<1> 11. idep_aliasdep<1>

       idep_tokeniter<1> 11. idep_aliasdep<1>


SUMMARY:
           1 Cycle                  11 Members
          11 Components             11 Levels                  1 Package
         121 CCD                    11 ACD               3.77894 NCCD

john@john:
```

The above example represents a worst-case scenario in which every component in the package depends either directly or indirectly on every other component. The ACD and CCD are at their maximum values of $N = 11$ and N^2, respectively. The NCCD of 3.77 clearly indicates excessive coupling compared to a tree-like architecture of similar size. It is not uncommon for a subsystem to exhibit near worst-case interdependency if its author has not made a conscious effort to minimize physical dependencies.

To summarize: the following is a list of the commands we executed in order to obtain the levelized component listing and a textual representation of the canonical component dependency graph:

- Extract compile-time file dependencies into a local *deps* file:
  `cdep -isearchpath *.[ch] > deps`

- List unpaired component file names:
  `adep *.[ch]`

- Place unpaired root file names in an *aliases* file to be edited manually:
  `adep -s *.[ch] > aliases`

- Verify first `#include` directives name corresponding header files:
  `adep -v -aaliases *.c`

- Alternatively, extract component file aliases automatically:
  `adep -e *.c > aliases`

- List components of package in levelized order:
  `ldep -ddeps -aaliases`

- List canonical component dependencies with mnemonic package group names:
  `ldep -ddeps -aaliases -l -amerge`

A detailed description of each of these commands along with additional options is presented in the following section.

C.2 Command-Line Documentation

This section describes the functionality of each of three Unix style commands and the file formats of the inputs and outputs of these programs.

NAME

`adep` — create aliases to group files into cohesive components.

SYNOPSIS

`adep` [`-s`] [`-a`*aliases*] [`-f`*filelist*] [`-X`*fn*] [`-x`*xFile*] *filename**
`adep -v` [`-a`*aliases*] [`-f`*filelist*] [`-X`*fn*] [`-x`*xFile*] *cfilename**
`adep -e` [`-a`*aliases*] [`-f`*filelist*] [`-X`*fn*] [`-x`*xFile*] *cfilename**

DESCRIPTION

`adep` creates, verifies, and extracts aliases from a collection of files. The three major forms of `adep` are shown in the synopsis above.

The first form of `adep` attempts to pair header and implementation files. For each *filename* specified on the command line, the suffix portion of the file is removed. The name of each file that is not paired (after applying any aliases) is printed to standard output (one per line). If more than two file names map to a single component name, a warning is generated to standard error without affecting the return status. In this mode, `adep` returns a negative status if one or more files cannot be opened for read access and zero otherwise.

The second form of `adep` verifies that (after applying any aliases) each implementation file specified on the command line includes as its first directive a file whose name matches the root name of the specified file. If not, an error message is reported to standard error. In this mode, `adep` returns a negative status if one or more files cannot be opened for read access. Otherwise, `adep` returns a positive status if one or more of the specified implementation files had faulty or missing `#include` directives. Otherwise `adep` returns a zero status.

The third form of `adep` attempts to extract aliases for unpaired implementation files by assuming that the first `#include` directive in each implementation file specified defines the name of the associated header file. Any mappings that are not already established (either by identical root names or via aliasing) are formatted to standard output as name/alias pairs (one per line). If more than one file maps to the same header, a warning message is generated to standard error without affecting the return status. In this mode, `adep` returns a negative status if one or more files cannot be opened for read access. Otherwise `adep` returns a positive status if one or more of the specified implementation files has no `#include` directives. Otherwise `adep` returns a status of zero.

If no *filename* argument is given and if the `-f`*filelist* option has not been invoked, `adep` reads the list of file names to be processed from standard input.

OPTIONS

`-s` Suppress the printing of suffixes for unpaired names. In the first (default) mode, unpaired file names will be printed with suffixes in lexicographic order. Specifying this option causes the suffixes to be suppressed and the output order to be adjusted so that the longer of two initially matching adjacent names appears *before* the other (in order to facilitate creating an alias file using a text editor). For example:

```
adep -s my_long*.[ch]
```

without `-s`	with `-s`
my_longlostlove.h	my_longlostlove
my_longlslov.c	my_longlslov
my_longnaitr.c	my_longnaitr
my_longnamea.c	my_longnamearray
my_longnamearray.h	my_longnamea
my_longnameiter.h	my_longnameiter

`-v` Verify that each specified implementation file contains its corresponding header name in its first `#include` directive. In this mode, the implementation file name and the header name found in the first `#include` directive are compared. If after applying any relevant aliases an implementation file does not include a header file with a corresponding name as its first `#include` directive, an error message is reported to standard error. For example:

```
// wrongorder.c
#include <iostream.h>
#include "wrongorder.h"
// ...
```

```
// missing.c
// ...
```

```
        adep -v wrongorder.c missing.c

stderr: Error: "wrongorder.c" contains corresponding
        include as 2nd directive.
stderr: Error: corresponding include directive for
        "missing.c" not found.
```

-e Extract an alias for each unpaired file name using the name found in the first `#include` directive and print these aliases to standard output (one per line). If (after applying any aliases) the root of the file named in the first `#include` directive already matches that of the implementation file, that alias is not printed. For example:

```
// my_longnamea.c
#include "my_longnamearray.h"
// ...
```

```
// my_binaryrel.c
#include "my_binaryrelation.h"
#include <iostream.h>
// ...
```

```
        adep -e my_long*.c my_bin*.c

stdout: my_longnamearray my_longnamea
stdout: my_binaryrelation my_binaryrel
```

Note that files with misplaced or missing `#include` directives will subvert the effectiveness of this command mode:

```
        adep -e wrongorder.c missing.c

stderr: Error: "missing.c" contains no include directives.
stdout: iostream wrongorder
```

-a*aliases* Specify a file containing component name aliases. The *aliases* file contains a collection of sequences (see FILE FORMATS). The first name in each sequence identifies the principal name. The remaining names in the sequence are synonyms for that name. For example, assume the current directory contains the files listed below:

```
my_longlostlove.h   my_longnaitr.c   my_longnamearray.h
my_longlslov.c      my_longnamea.c   my_longnameiter.h
```

The following `aliases` file maps the root name of each `.c` file to the root name of its corresponding `.h` file:

```
# aliases
my_longlostlove my_longlslov
my_longnamearray my_longnamea
my_longnameiter my_longnaitr
```

`-f`*filelist* Specify a file containing a sequence of file names to be considered for processing. The effect is as if these individual file names had each been specified as a command-line argument (except that even an empty *filelist* will suppress the reading of file names from standard input).

`-X`*fn* Specify the name of a file to ignore during processing:

```
adep -e -Xmy_main.c *.[ch]
```

`-x`*xFile* Specify a file containing a sequence of file names to be ignored during processing. The effect is as if these individual file names had each been specified using the `-X`*fn* option.

BUGS

Attempting to extract the associated header from implementation files that do not consistently name the associated header in the first `#include` directive will result in incorrect results.

SEE ALSO

`cdep`, `ldep`, FILE FORMATS

NAME

cdep — extract compile-time dependencies from a collection of files.

SYNOPSIS

cdep [-I*dir*] [-i*dirlist*] [-f*filelist*] [-x] *filename**

DESCRIPTION

For each *filename* specified on the command line, determine all of the header files that are included either directly or indirectly by this file and format these dependencies to standard output. The sequence of directories to search for #include files (including the current directory ".") must be specified using some combination of the -I*dir* and -i*dirlist* options described below:

```
john@john: cdep -I. -isearchpath *.[ch] > deps
```

For example, the above command uses the directory names specified in file searchpath in order to look for header files defined in each of the .c and .h files in the current directory, and places the result in the file deps. If no filename argument is given and if the -f*filelist* option has not been invoked, cdep reads the list of file names to be processed from standard input. The output format is a blank-line-terminated sequences of names—one sequence per input file. The first name in each sequence identifies the input file and each subsequent name identifies a file on which that input file depends at compile time (see FILE FORMATS). This command returns a negative status if one or more files cannot be opened for read access; otherwise cdep returns a status of zero.

OPTIONS

-I*dir* Specify the name of an include directory to append to the search path. For example, -I. would append the current directory to the search path.

`-i`*dirlist* Specify a file containing a sequence of directory names to append to the search path. The effect is as if the individual directories had each been specified using the `-I`*dir* option.

`-f`*filelist* Specify a file containing a sequence of file names to be considered for processing. The effect is as if these individual file names had each been specified as a command-line argument (except that even an empty *filelist* will suppress the reading of file names from standard input).

`-x` Do not check recursively for nested `#include` directives. Only files that are included directly by the input file will be indicated in the output.

BUGS

Even included directives that have been `#ifdef`'ed or commented out `/* ... */` comments will be interpreted as active.

SEE ALSO

`adep`, `ldep`, FILE FORMATS

NAME

`ldep` — analyze the link-time dependencies among a collection of components.

SYNOPSIS

`ldep` [`-U`*dir*] [`-u`*un*] [`-a`*aliases*] [`-d`*deps*] [`-l` | `-L`] [`-x` | `-X`] [`-s`]

DESCRIPTION

`ldep` processes a collection of compile-time dependencies among files in the context of aliases to deduce the link-time dependencies among components. The components are formatted to standard output in levelized order (one per line) beginning with level zero. An extra blank line accompanies a change in level.

By default, dependencies on components in directories other than the current directory are treated as dependencies on the directory itself (see the `-U` and `-u`*un* options below).

Also by default, aliases, unaliases, and a summary of statistics characterizing the component dependencies are formatted to standard output (see the `-x` and `-X` options below). These statistics include the following:

Components	The number of local components with a level above 0 (i.e., the number of components with at least one dependency).
Levels	The height of the local component dependency graph.
Packages	The number of level 0 entities (i.e., the number of entities with no dependencies).
CCD	The sum over all local components C_i of the number of local components required to link and test C_i.
ACD	The ratio of the CCD to the number of local components.
NCCD	The ratio of this CCD to the CCD of a theoretical balanced binary dependency tree with an equal number of local components. (Note:

For most high-quality package architectures, this number will not be much greater than 1.00).

In the presence of cyclic component dependencies, the members of each distinct maximal cycle are identified and reported separately to standard error. An additional summary line preceding the others is formatted to standard output that includes the following information:

Cycles The number of distinct maximal cycles in the component dependency graph.

Members The total number of components participating in cycles.

Each member of a maximal cycle containing *N* components is defined to be at a level that is *N* higher than the level of the highest (non-member) component on which any member of the cycle depends.

This command takes no arguments. The dependencies themselves will come from standard input unless the `-d`*deps* option has been invoked. `ldep` returns a negative status if one or more files cannot be opened for read access. Otherwise, `ldep` returns a positive status if at least one cycle is detected in the component dependency graph. Otherwise `ldep` returns a status of zero.

OPTIONS

`-U`*dir* Specify an external directory in which files are to be treated individually. By default, all dependencies on files outside the current directory ("`.`") are treated as a dependency on the directory (package) that contains them. For example, suppose

```
ldep -ddeps
```

produced the following:

```
LEVELS:
0. /usr/lang/ATT_3.0/include/
   /usr/lang/ATT_3.0/include/cc/
   /usr/lang/ATT_3.0/include/sys/
   /usr/lang/ATT_3.0/include/cc/sys/

1. idep_aliastable
   idep_binrel
   idep_namearray
   . . .
```

Then

```
ldep -ddeps -U/usr/lang/ATT_3.0/include/sys
```

might produce the following list identifying the individual components (e.g., `stdtypes`, `types`, and `wait`) in the specified directory.

```
LEVELS:
0. /usr/lang/ATT_3.0/include/
   /usr/lang/ATT_3.0/include/cc/
   /usr/lang/ATT_3.0/include/sys/stdtypes
   /usr/lang/ATT_3.0/include/sys/types
   /usr/lang/ATT_3.0/include/cc/sys/
   /usr/lang/ATT_3.0/include/sys/wait

1. idep_aliastable
   idep_binrel
   idep_namearray
   . . .
```

`-u`*un* Specify a file containing directories for which components are to be treated separately. The effect is as if the individual directories had each been specified using the `-U`*dir* option.

`-a`*aliases* Specify a file containing component name aliases. The *aliases* file contains a collection of sequences (see FILE FORMATS). The first name in each sequence identifies the primary name. The remaining names in the sequence are synonyms for that name. For example, assume the current directory contains the files listed below:

```
my_longlostlove.h    my_longnaitr.c    my_longnamearray.h
my_longlslov.c       my_longnamed.c    my_longnameiter.h
```

The *aliases* file below maps the root name of each `.c` file to the root name of its corresponding `.h` file.

```
# aliases
my_longlostlove my_longlslov
my_longnamearray my_longnamea
my_longnameiter my_longnaitr
```

The mapping would then be displayed as follows:

```
my_longnaitr -> my_longnameiter
my_longnamea -> my_longnamearray
my_longlslov -> my_longlostlove
```

We can also use aliases to coalesce several components into a single entity by mapping all the constituent file names to a single name. For example, the following `aliases` file maps each of the component file names to a single identifier:

```
# aliases
MY_LONG
my_longlostlove my_longlslov
my_longnamearray my_longnamea
my_longnameiter my_longnaitr
```

The mapping that results is displayed as below.

```
my_longnamearray -> MY_LONG
    my_longnaitr -> MY_LONG
    my_longnamea -> MY_LONG
 my_longnameiter -> MY_LONG
 my_longlostlove -> MY_LONG
    my_longlslov -> MY_LONG
```

`-d`*deps* Specify a file containing a list of compile-time file dependencies. The *deps* file contains a collection of blank-line-terminated sequences of names. The first name in each sequence identifies the dependent file, and each subsequent file identifies the file on which that file depends (see FILE FORMATS). If this option is not invoked, the file dependencies themselves will be read from standard input.

`-l | -L` Provide a long listing including the specific component dependencies. By default, only the components (and not their dependencies) are formatted to standard output in levelized order. Specifying the `-l` option causes the component and its non-redundant dependencies (i.e., except for transitive dependencies) to be sent to standard output in *deps* format (see FILE FORMATS). An extra blank line accompanies a change in level. Supplying the `-L` option instead has a similar effect except that all dependencies including (redundant) transitive dependencies are formatted to standard output.

`-x | -X` Suppress printing extraneous information. By default, aliases, unaliases, level numbers, and the summary are printed along with the component names in levelized order beginning with level 0 to standard output. Specifying the `-x` option suppresses the printing of alias and unalias names. Specifying `-X` instead suppresses all but the component names themselves, including the level numbers. (The `-X` option is intended to be used to drive a graphical display; note that an extra blank line identifies a change in level.)

`-s` Do *not* remove suffixes—consider each file separately. (This option is sometimes useful for determining the cause of cyclic dependencies among components.)

BUGS

For `ldep` to yield valid results, it is assumed that none of the implementation files uses local declarations to access non-local entities (e.g., global variables or free functions) with external linkage (see Section 1.1.2). Any use of the `extern` keyword is suspect.

CCD ignores the weight of dependencies on other packages.

A local component, `empty`, with no `#include` directives will be assigned a level of 0 and will be mistaken for an external package. Adding a fictitious dependency on "." for that component solves this problem:

```
# artificial dependencies
empty
    .
```

SEE ALSO

`adep`, `cdep`, FILE FORMATS

FILE FORMATS:

The following describes specific file formats. Each format supports the notion of a comment. A comment is a token beginning with a pound sign (#) and hides all tokens until a *newline* is encountered:

```
this is valid input text #this is a comment
```

Many of the formats are little more than a white-space-separated token list. Such formats will be identified with the notation < list >.

aliases: Sequences of white-space-separated tokens. The first token in each sequence identifies the principal name. Each subsequent token identifies a synonym for that name. If the first token appears alone on a line, then the sequence is terminated by a blank line. Otherwise the sequence is terminated by a *newline*. Preceding a *newline* by a lone backslash (\) continues the logical line. Following a backslash with a comment on the same line does not interfere with logical line continuation. For example:

```
# aliases
C++                                      # standard libs
/usr/lang/ATT_3.0/include/               # directory
/usr/lang/ATT_3.0/include/cc/            # subdirectory
/usr/lang/ATT_3.0/include/sys            # subdirectory
/usr/lang/ATT_3.0/include/cc/sys         # subdirectory

idep_nameindexmap idep_nimap
idep_namearray \       # this is line continuation
idep_namea
```

produces the following aliases:

```
   /usr/lang/ATT_3.0/include/sys -> C++
                     idep_namea.c -> idep_namearray
      /usr/lang/ATT_3.0/include/ -> C++
/usr/lang/ATT_3.0/include/cc/sys -> C++
                       idep_nimap -> my_nameindexmap
   /usr/lang/ATT_3.0/include/cc/ -> C++
```

deps: Sequences of white-space-separated tokens terminated by a blank line. The first token in each sequence identifies the root file. Each subsequent token identifies a file on which that root file depends. For example,

```
john@john: cdep -isearchpath idep_tokeniter.[ch]
```

produces the following dependency file on my system:

```
idep_tokeniter.c
    idep_tokeniter.h
    /usr/lang/ATT_3.0/include/ctype.h
    /usr/lang/ATT_3.0/include/cc/ctype.h
    /usr/lang/ATT_3.0/include/string.h
    /usr/lang/ATT_3.0/include/memory.h
    . . .
    . . . (30 lines omitted)
    . . .
    /usr/lang/ATT_3.0/include/malloc.h
    /usr/lang/ATT_3.0/include/cc/malloc.h

idep_tokeniter.h
```

Note that `idep_tokeniter.c` has many direct and indirect compile-time dependencies while `idep_tokeniter.h` has none.

dirlist: < list > Each token identifies the name of a directory to append to the search path:

```
# my search path
.                                  # current directory
/usr/john/app/include              # app include directory
/usr/lang/ATT_3.0/include          # standard C++ library
/usr/lang/ATT_3.0/include/cc       # standard C library
```

filelist: < list > Each token identifies the name of a file to be processed:

```
# my files
idep_nameindexmap.t.c              # test driver
idep_nameindexmap.h idep_nimap.c
idep_namearray.h idep_namea.c
```

un: < list > Each token identifies the name of an external directory of files to treat separately:

```
# my unalias directories
/usr/john/app/include            # In case we want to
/usr/lang/ATT_3.0/include        # know exactly what
/usr/lang/ATT_3.0/include/sys    # non-local components
                                 # we depend on.
```

xFile: < list > Each token identifies the name of a file to ignore during processing:

```
# ignore these files
idep_nameindexmap_t.c            # test driver
main.c                           # main program
```

C.3 Idep Package Architecture

In this section we will briefly discuss the physical architecture of the `idep` package and the implementation of the three Unix-style commands: `adep`, `cdep`, and `ldep`.

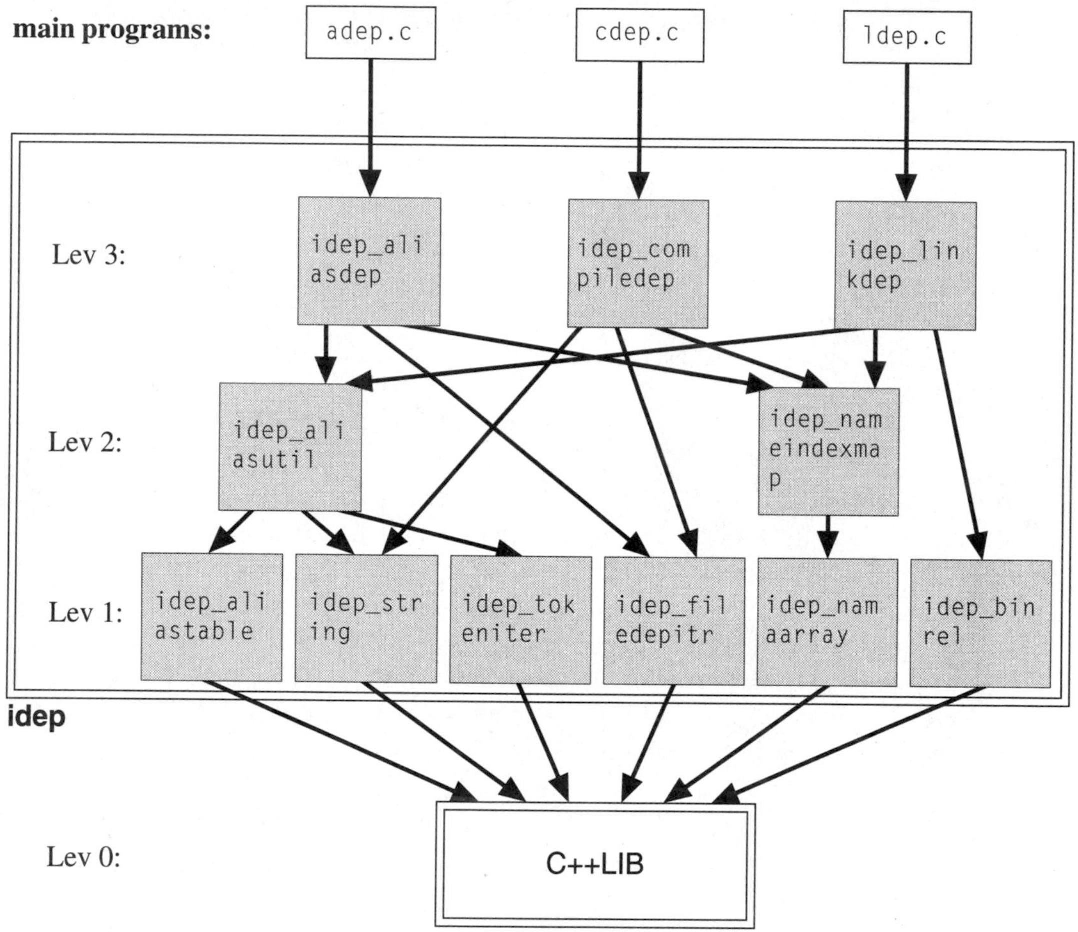

The above diagram illustrates the component dependencies within the `idep` package.[2]

---

[2] This diagram can be generated by creating only the component dependencies using `ldep` with the- `X` option and then piping the resulting output to a simple graphical display engine. This engine would allow the user interactively to move components horizontally within the level and would save the positions of the component icons to facilitate making incremental changes to the architecture.

Notice that 6 of the 11 components that make up the idep package are *leaf* components (depending only on the standard compiler-supplied libraries). Each of these components can be tested efficiently in isolation and reused independently of other components in this package.

idep_aliastable implements a simple (hash table) mapping from one name to another. Immediate clients are not insulated from its implementation; however, neither the table nor iterator classes defined in this component are exposed in the interface of any of the higher-level wrapper components. If used outside this package, a fully insulated implementation would be preferred. (Note that the implementations of components such as this one may become obsolete once a standard C++ component library becomes generally available.)

idep_string defines a basic string class with no frills and a straightforward implementation. The string's implementation is not insulated, but should be if this component is used independently outside its package. (Note that this component will no longer be needed once a standard string component becomes generally available.)

idep_tokeniter is a simple parser class that reads a token stream, returning white-space-separated identifiers and *newline* characters. The inherent reusability of this component coupled with its weight (resulting from I/O) prompted its fully insulated implementation.

idep_filedepiter defines a class that extracts all header file names in #include directives from a file in sequence. This class also has a fully insulated implementation for the same reasons as idep_tokeniter (although the use of idep_filedepiter is tied more directly to a specific kind of application).

idep_namearray implements an extensible array of names, making no claim of extraordinary efficiency. Its implementation is so standard that it did not seem to warrant insulation. (Note this component will probably not be needed once a standard component library becomes generally available.)

The last of the leaf components, idep_binrel, defines a low-level Boolean matrix class, used to express (bin)ary (rel)ations among sets. The potential need for efficient (inline) access to the array precluded a fully insulated implementation.

Two components reside at level 2. `idep_aliasutil` is a utility component used to read aliases from a file or input stream. While parsing alias input is logically cohesive with the `idep_aliastable` component, the parsing functionality alone introduces additional dependencies on both `idep_tokeniter` and on `idep_string`. Placing this parsing capability in the `idep_aliastable` component itself would force all clients of `idep_aliastable` to link to `idep_string` and `idep_tokeniter` whether or not they ever need to parse aliases from a file. Escalating this parsing functionality to a higher-level utility component avoids imposing these two additional dependencies on all clients of `idep_aliastable`.

The other level-2 component, `idep_nameindexmap`, supports fast two-way conversion between names and non-negative consecutive integers. This component makes use of `idep_namearray` in its (fully insulated) implementation.

Level 3 consists of three insulating wrapper components that present the combined application functionality to higher-level packages or to a main program that implements a Unix-style command (e.g., `adep.c`, `cdep.c`, or `ldep.c`). Each wrapper component provides a (fully insulating) primary class that acts as an environment for accumulating information about the computation to be performed. After the environment object is fully configured, the appropriate processing action is invoked to produce the desired result.

`idep_aliasdep` defines a single wrapper class for pairing corresponding component header and implementation files having non-matching root names, and for verifying the proper placement of include directives within implementation files. The manipulator functions of this class are used to program the environment for processing. Because the actual processing does not affect the logical state of this object, each of the processing functions in this class is declared to be a `const` member.

`idep_compiledep` defines a primary wrapper class for calculating compile-time dependencies among files. This component also provides two fully insulating iterator classes to allow clients to retrieve the underlying dependency information while distancing clients from any contact with the lower-level components used in the implementation of this wrapper component. Furthermore, each of these classes uses nothing but fundamental C++ types in its logical interface, thereby further reducing constraints on the implementation choice and enhancing reusability.

Of the three insulating wrapper components, `idep_linkdep` is the most complex, defining the principal `idep_LinkDep` class along with seven iterator classes. Most of the functionality is implemented by delegating the work to lower-level objects. The functionality that is implemented locally is split between calculating the levelization of components and formatting the output. The complexity of this component could be reduced (and maintainability improved) by factoring this wrapper into two components. Some of the locally defined data structures could be demoted to a new (lower-level) `idep_linkdepimp` component where they can be tested directly. The remaining `idep_linkdep` component will still be fairly long, but the amount of complex functionality it implements directly is significantly reduced.

As a whole, this package was designed from the start to support three wrapper components, each one reusing a majority of the underlying implementation components. As a result of an atypically careful and tight initial design, the NCCD (1.09) of this package reflects a higher degree of coupling than would normally be expected for a well-designed application program. In order to evaluate these metrics properly, we must take into account the reuse. Had this package implemented only a single wrapper (e.g., `idep_linkdep`), the NCCD would have been 0.83—well below the value of 1.00 for (theoretical) balanced binary dependencies. It is important to remember that NCCD characterizes intercomponent dependency and probably has an inverse correlation with reliability and reusability but in itself is not an absolute measure of design quality.

C.4 Source Code

The complete source code for the main programs implementing the three Unix-like commands (`adep`, `cdep`, and `ldep`), the header files for the components in the `idep` package, and their corresponding implementation files is available from Addison-Wesley at World Wide Web URL http://www.aw.com/cp/lakos.html, and is available via anonymous FTP from Addison-Wesley from ftp.aw.com in the directory cp/lakos. Initially, the following commands can be used to compile and link these three tools (on my Unix-based system):

```
john@john: CC -c idep_*.c
john@john: CC -o adep adep.c idep_*.o -lm
john@john: CC -o cdep cdep.c idep_*.o -lm
john@john: CC -o ldep ldep.c idep_*.o -lm
```

Once compiled, `cdep` can be adapted to generate arbitrary header file dependencies for Unix-style makefiles automatically.

Appendix D

Quick Reference

The following is a summary of the definitions, design rules, guidelines, and principles discussed throughout this book.

D.1 Definitions

Chapter 1:

- A ***declaration*** introduces a name into a program; a ***definition*** provides a unique description of an entity (e.g., type, instance, function) within a program. (p. 22)
- A name has ***internal linkage*** if it is local to its translation unit and cannot collide with an identical name defined in another translation unit at link time. (p. 24)
- A name has ***external linkage*** if, in a multi-file program, that name can interact with other translation units at link time. (p. 25)
- 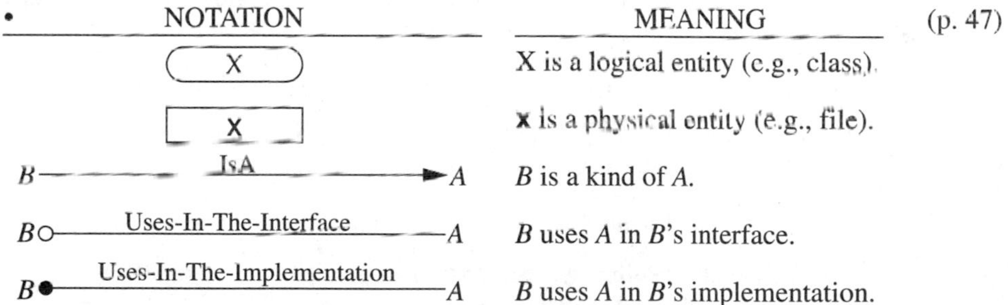
NOTATION
MEANING
(p. 47)
X
X is a logical entity (e.g., class).
X
X is a physical entity (e.g., file).
B
IsA
A
B is a kind of A.
B
Uses-In-The-Interface
A
B uses A in B's interface.
B
Uses-In-The-Implementation
A
B uses A in B's implementation.
- A type is ***used in the interface*** of a function if the type is referred to when declaring that function. (p. 50)
- A type is ***used in the (public) interface*** of a class if the type is used in the interface of the (public) member function of that class. (p. 51)
- A type is ***used in the implementation*** of a function if the type is referred to in the definition of that function. (p. 53)

- A type is ***used in the implementation*** of a class if that type (1) is used in a member function of the class, (2) is referred to in the declaration of a data member of the class, or (3) is a private base class of the class. (p. 55)

- Specific kinds of the Uses-In-The-Implementation Relationship: (p. 55)

Name	Meaning
Uses	The class has a member function that names the type.
HasA	The class embeds an instance of the type.
HoldsA	The class embeds a pointer (or reference) to the type.
WasA	The class privately inherits from the type.

- A class is ***layered*** on a type if the class uses that type substantively in its implementation. (p. 58)

Chapter 2:

- A contained implementation detail (type, data, or function) that is not accessible or detectable programmatically through the logical interface of a class is said to be ***encapsulated*** by that class. (p. 67)

Chapter 3:

- A ***component*** is the smallest unit of physical design. (p. 100)

- The ***logical interface*** of a component is that which is programmatically accessible or detectable by a client. (p. 105)

- A type is ***Used-In-The-Interface*** of a component if the type is used in the public (or protected) interface of any class defined, or any free (operator) function declared at file scope in the `.h` file for that component. (p. 106)

- The ***physical interface*** of a component is ***everything*** in its header file. (p. 107)

- A type is ***Used-In-The-Implementation*** of a component if that type is referred to by name anywhere in the component. (p. 108)

- A component `y` ***DependsOn*** a component `x` if `x` is needed in order to compile or link `y`. (p. 121)

- A component `y` exhibits a ***compile-time*** dependency on component `x` if `x.h` is needed in order to compile `y.c`. (p. 122)

- A component `y` exhibits a ***link-time*** dependency on component `x` if the object file `y.o` (produced by compiling `y.c`) contains undefined symbols for which `x.o` may be called upon either directly or indirectly to help resolve at link time. (p. 124)

- A contained implementation detail (type, data, or function) that is not accessible or detectable programmatically through the logical interface of a component is said to be ***encapsulated*** by that component. (p. 138)

Chapter 4:

- ***Regression testing*** refers to the practice of comparing the results of running a program given a specific input with a fixed set of expected results, in order to verify that the program continues to behave ***as expected*** from one version to the next. (p. 156)

- ***Isolation testing*** refers to the practice of testing an individual component or subsystem independently of the rest of the system. (p. 162)

- A physical dependency graph that can be assigned unique level numbers is said to be ***levelizable***. (p. 168)

- ***Level 0***: A component that is external to our package. (p. 169)
  Level 1: A component that has no local physical dependencies.
  Level N: A component that depends physically on a component at level *N*–1, but not higher.

- The ***level*** of a component is the length of the longest path from that component through the (local) component dependency graph to the (possibly empty) set of external or compiler-supplied library components. (p. 170)

- ***Hierarchical testing*** refers to the practice of testing individual components at each level of the physical hierarchy. (p. 175)

- ***Incremental testing*** refers to the practice of deliberately testing only the functionality actually implemented within the component under test. (p. 177)

- ***White-box testing*** refers to the practice of verifying the expected behavior of a component by exploiting knowledge of its underlying implementation. (p. 179)

- ***Black-box testing*** refers to the practice of verifying the expected behavior of a component based solely on its specification (i.e., without knowledge of its underlying implementation). (p. 180)

- ***Cumulative component dependency (CCD)*** is the sum over all components C_i in a subsystem of the number of components needed in order to test each C_i incrementally. (p. 187)

- ***Average component dependency (ACD)*** is defined as the ratio of the CCD of a subsystem to the number of components *N* in the subsystem: (p. 197)

$$\mathbf{ACD(subsystem)} = \frac{\mathbf{CCD(subsystem)}}{N_{\mathbf{subsystem}}}$$

- ***Normalized cumulative component dependency*** (***NCCD***) is defined as the ratio of the CCD of a subsystem containing *N* components to the CCD of a tree-like system of the same size. (p. 199)

$$\mathbf{NCCD(subsystem)} = \frac{\mathbf{CCD(subsystem)}}{\mathbf{CCD}_{\substack{\mathbf{Balanced}\\ \mathbf{Binary}\\ \mathbf{Tree}}}(N_{\mathbf{subsystem}})}$$

Chapter 5:

- A subsystem is ***levelizable*** if it compiles and the graph implied by the include directives of the individual components (including the `.c` files) is acyclic. (p. 207)
- A component `y` ***dominates*** a component `x` if `y` is at a higher level than `x` and `y` depends physically on `x`. (p. 217)
- A function `f` uses a type `T` ***in size*** if compiling the body of `f` requires having first seen the definition of `T`. (p. 247)
- A function `f` uses a type `T` ***in name only*** if compiling `f` and any of the components on which `f` may depend does not require having first seen the definition of `T`. (p. 248)
- A component `c` uses a type `T` ***in size*** if compiling `c` requires having first seen the definition of `T`. (p. 248)
- A component `c` uses a type `T` ***in name only*** if compiling `c` and any of the components on which `c` may depend does not require having first seen the definition of `T`. (p. 249)
- In hierarchical systems, ***encapsulating a type*** (defined at file scope within a header file) means hiding its use, not hiding the type itself. (p. 318)

Chapter 6:

- A contained implementation detail (type, data, or function) that can be altered, added, or removed without forcing clients to recompile is said to be ***insulated***. (p. 332)
- An ***abstract class*** is a ***protocol class*** if
  1. it neither contains nor inherits from classes that contain member data, non-virtual functions, or private (or protected) members of any kind,
  2. it has a non-inline virtual destructor defined with an empty implementation, and
  3. all member functions other than the destructor including inherited functions, are declared pure virtual and left undefined. (p. 386)
- A concrete class is ***fully insulating*** if it
  1. contains exactly one data member that is an outwardly opaque pointer to a non-`const struct` (defined in the `.c` file) specifying the implementation of that class,
  2. does not contain any other private or protected members of any kind,
  3. does not inherit from any class, and
  4. does not declare any virtual or inline functions. (p. 402)
- In this book, a ***handle*** is a class that maintains a pointer to an object that is programmatically accessible through the public interface of the handle class. (p. 430)
- ***Light-weight*** is a term whose meaning depends on the context in which it is used:
  - does not depend on (many) other components,
  - is not expensive to construct/destruct,
  - does not allocate additional dynamic memory, and
  - makes effective use of inline functions to access/manipulate embedded data. (p. 449)

Chapter 7:

- A ***package*** is a collection of components organized as a physically cohesive unit. (p. 476)
- A package `x` ***DependsOn*** another package `y` if one or more components in `x` DependsOn one or more components in `y`. (p. 479)
- A ***package group*** is a collection of packages organized as a physically cohesive unit. (p. 506)
- A package group `g` ***DependsOn*** another package group `h` if one or more packages in `g` DependsOn one or more packages in `h`. (p. 507)
- A ***layer*** corresponds to all package groups at a given level of a system. (p. 512)
- A ***patch*** is a local change to previously released software to repair faulty or grossly inefficient functionality within a component. (p. 520)
- ***Start-up time*** (also known as ***invocation time***) is the time between when a program is first invoked and when the thread of control enters `main`. (p. 532)

Chapter 8:

- An ***abstraction*** is an abstract specification of a collection of objects and related behaviors that fulfills a common purpose. (p. 554)
- An operation defined on an object is ***primitive*** if implementing that operation efficiently implies having direct access to private details of the object. (p. 557)

Chapter 9:

- ***Hide***: A member function *hides* a function with the same name declared in a base class or at file scope. (p. 601)
  Overload: A function *overloads* the name of another function with the same name defined in the same scope.
  Override: A member function *overrides* an identical function declared virtual in a base class.
  Redefine: The default definition of a function is irretrievably replaced by another definition.
- An object is `const`***-correct*** if a function taking only a single argument that is a `const` reference to that object is not able, without explicit casting, to obtain a non-`const` reference to that same object (or a portion thereof) from within the function body. (p. 606)
- A system is `const`***-correct*** if there is no way (without using an explicit cast) for a function taking only `const` reference arguments to any subset of objects within the system to obtain a writable reference to any of these objects (or any portions thereof) from within the body of the function. (p. 608)
- A system is `const`***-correct*** if its conversion graph contains no cycle that involves both the `const` and non-`const` versions of any one type. (p. 610)

Chapter 10:

- An instance of a fundamental type is ***naturally aligned*** if its size divides the numerical value of its address. (p. 662)
- An instance of an aggregate type is ***naturally aligned*** if the alignment of the subtype with the most restrictive alignment requirement divides the address of the aggregate. (p. 663)
- A value associated with the state of an object is a ***logical value*** if it contributes to the intended semantics (i.e., the essential behavior of the ADT) for that object; otherwise it is a ***physical value***. (p. 681)
- A ***memory leak*** occurs when a program loses the ability to free a block of dynamically allocated memory. (p. 716)
- A ***design pattern*** is an abstract organization of classes or objects that has repeatedly proven effective at solving similar kinds of problems in diverse application areas. (p. 730)

D.2 Major Design Rules

Chapter 2:

- Keep class data members private. (p. 65)
- Avoid data with external linkage at file scope. (p. 70)
- Avoid free functions (except operator functions) at file scope in `.h` files; avoid free functions with external linkage (including operator functions) in `.c` files. (p. 72)
- Avoid enumerations, typedefs, and constants at file scope in `.h` files. (p. 73)
- Avoid using preprocessor macros in header files except as include guards. (p. 75)
- Only classes, structures, unions, and free operator functions should be *declared* at file scope in a `.h` file; only classes, structures, unions, and inline (member or free operator) functions should be *defined* at file scope in a `.h` file. (p. 77)
- Place a unique and predictable (internal) include guard around the contents of each header file. (p. 81)

Chapter 3:

- Logical entities declared within a component should not be defined outside that component. (p. 108)
- The `.c` file of every component should include its own `.h` file as the first substantive line of code. (p. 110)
- Avoid definitions with external linkage in the `.c` file of a component that are not declared explicitly in the corresponding `.h` file. (p. 115)

- Avoid accessing a definition with external linkage in another component via a local declaration; instead, include the `.h` file for that component. (p. 119)

Chapter 7:

- Prepend every global identifier with its package prefix. (p. 484)
- Prepend every source file name with its package prefix. (p. 486)
- Avoid cyclic dependencies among packages. (p. 494)
- Only the `.c` file that defines `main` is authorized to redefine global `new` and `delete`. (p. 531)
- Provide a mechanism for freeing any dynamic memory allocated to static constructs within a component. (p. 545)

D.3 Minor Design Rules

Chapter 2:

- Place a redundant (external) include guard around each preprocessor include directive in every header file. (p. 85)
- Use a consistent method (such as a `d_` prefix) to highlight class data members. (p. 91)
- Use a consistent method (such as an uppercase first letter) to distinguish type names. (p. 91)
- Use a consistent method (such as all uppercase with underscore) to identify immutable values such as enumerators, `const` data, and preprocessor constants. (p. 92)

Chapter 3:

- The root names of the `.c` file and the `.h` file that comprise a component should match exactly. (p. 110)

Chapter 9:

- Never pass a user-defined type (i.e., `class`, `struct`, or `union`) to a function by value. (p. 622)
- Never attempt to delete an object passed by reference. (p. 628)
- In every class that declares or is derived from a class that declares a virtual function, explicitly declare the destructor as the first virtual function in the class and define it out of line. (p. 651)

Chapter 10:

- Avoid depending on the order in which data members are defined in an object during initialization. (p. 714)

- When implementing memory management for a general, parameterized container template, be careful ***not*** to use the assignment operator of the contained type when the target of the assignment is uninitialized memory. (p. 724)

D.4 Guidelines

Chapter 2:

- Document the interfaces so that they are usable by others; have at least one other developer review each interface. (p. 88)
- Explicitly state conditions under which behavior is undefined. (p. 89)
- Be consistent about identifier names; use either uppercase or underscore but not both to delimit words in identifiers. (p. 92)
- Be consistent about names used in the same way; in particular adopt consistent method names and operators for recurring design patterns such as iteration. (p. 92)

Chapter 3:

- Clients should include header files providing required type definitions directly; except for non-private inheritance, avoid relying on one header file to include another. (p. 113)
- A component `x` should include `y.h` only if `x` makes direct substantive use of a class or free operator function defined in `y`. (p. 135)
- Avoid granting (long-distance) friendship to a logical entity defined in another component. (p. 137)

Chapter 4:

- Avoid cyclic physical dependencies among components. (p. 185)

Chapter 7:

- In general, avoid granting one component license that, if also taken by other components, would adversely impact the system as a whole. (p. 530)
- Prefer modules to non-local static instances of objects, especially when: (p. 533)
  1. Direct access to the construct is needed outside a translation unit.
  2. The construct may not be needed during start-up or immediately thereafter and the time to initialize the construct itself is significant.

Chapter 9:

- The semantics of an overloaded operator should be natural, obvious, and intuitive to clients. (p. 586)
- The syntactic properties of overloaded operators for user-defined types should mirror the

properties already defined for the fundamental types. (p. 587)

- Avoid hiding a base-class function in a derived class. (p. 602)
- Every object in a system should be `const`-correct. (p. 606)
- A system should be `const`-correct. (p. 608)
- Think twice (at least) before casting away `const`. (p. 612)
- For functions that return an *error status*, an integral value of 0 should always mean success. (p. 615)
- Functions that answer a yes-or-no question should be worded appropriately (e.g., `isValid`) and return an `int` value of either `0` ("no") or `1` ("yes"). (p. 617)
- Avoid declaring results returned by value from functions as `const`. (p. 618)
- Avoid default arguments that require the construction of an unnamed temporary object. (p. 621)
- Be consistent about returning values through arguments (e.g., avoid declaring non-`const` reference parameters). (p. 623)
- Avoid storing the address of any argument to a function in a location that will persist after the function terminates; pass the address of the argument instead. (p. 626)
- Whenever a parameter passes its argument by reference or pointer to a function that neither modifies that argument nor stores its writable address, that parameter should be declared `const`. (p. 629)
- Avoid declaring parameters passed by value to a function as `const`. (p. 629)
- Consider placing parameters (except perhaps those with default arguments) that enable modifiable access before parameters that pass arguments by value, `const` reference, or `const` pointer. (p. 630)
- Avoid granting friendship to individual functions. (p. 631)
- Avoid declaring a function `inline` whose body produces object code that is larger than the object code produced by the equivalent non-inline function *call* itself. (p. 631)
- Avoid declaring a function `inline` that your compiler will not generate inline. (p. 632)
- Avoid using `short` in the interface; use `int` instead. (p. 633)
- Avoid using `unsigned` in the interface; use `int` instead. (p. 637)
- Avoid using `long` in the interface; `assert(sizeof(int) >= 4)` and use either `int` or a user-defined large-integer type instead. (p. 642)
- Consider using `double` exclusively for floating-point types used in the interface unless there is a compelling reason to use `float` or `long double`. (p. 645)

- Consider avoiding "cast" operators, especially to fundamental integral types; instead, make the conversion explicit. (p. 649)
- Explicitly declare (either public or private) the constructor and assignment operator for any class defined in a header file, even when the default implementations are adequate. (p. 650)
- In classes that do not otherwise declare virtual functions, explicitly declare the destructor as non-virtual and define it appropriately (either inline or out-of-line). (p. 654)

Chapter 10:

- Use `short` instead of `int` in the implementation as an optimization only when it is *known* to be safe to do so. (p. 665)
- Consider not using `unsigned` even in the implementation. (p. 666)
- When designing a function, component, package, or entire system, use the simplest techniques that are effective. (p. 680)
- Avoid allowing programmatic access to *physical* values. (p. 682)
- The result of calling a `const` member function should not alter *any* programmatically accessible value in the object. (p. 684)
- Prefer object-specific over class-specific memory management. (p. 711)
- Use a non-`const` *pointer* data member to hold *managed* objects. (p. 712)
- Consider providing a way to switch between block allocations and individual allocations of dynamic memory. (p. 716)
- When implementing memory management for a completely general, parameterized container that manages the memory for its contained objects, assume that the parameterized type defines a copy constructor and a destructor—nothing more. (p. 724)
- Where possible, implement templates on top of a factored reusable `void *` pointer type using inline functions to reestablish type safety. (p. 729)

D.5 Principles

Chapter 2:

- The use of `assert` statements can help to document the assumptions you make when implementing your code. (p. 90)

Chapter 3:

- Logical design addresses only *architectural* issues; physical design addresses *organizational* issues. (p. 100)

- A component is the appropriate fundamental unit of design. (p. 103)
- Latent usage errors can be avoided by ensuring that the `.h` file of a component parses by itself—without externally-provided declarations or definitions. (p. 111)
- A compile-time dependency almost always implies a link-time dependency. (p. 125)
- The DependsOn relation for components is transitive. (p. 126)
- A component defining a function will *usually* have a physical dependency on any component defining a type used by that function. (p. 127)
- A component defining a class that IsA or HasA user-defined type *always* has a compile-time dependency on the component defining that type. (p. 129)
- The include graph generated by C++ preprocessor `#include` directives should alone be sufficient to infer all physical dependencies within a system provided the system compiles. (p. 134)
- Friendship within a component is an implementation detail of that component. (p. 137)
- Granting (local) friendship to classes defined within the same component does *not* violate encapsulation. (p. 139)
- Defining an iterator class along with a container class *in the same component* enables user extensibility, improves maintainability, and enhances reusability *while preserving encapsulation*. (p. 140)
- Granting (long-distance) friendship to a logical entity defined in a separate physical part of the system violates the encapsulation of the class granting that friendship. (p. 140)
- Friendship affects access privilege but not implied dependency. (p. 141)

Chapter 4:

- With respect to testing, a software *class* is analogous to a real world *instance*. (p. 159)
- Distributing system testing throughout the design hierarchy can be much more effective per testing dollar than testing at only the highest-level interface. (p. 159)
- Independent testing reduces part of the risk associated with software integration. (p. 161)
- Testing a component in isolation is an effective way to ensure reliability. (p. 162)
- Every directed acyclic graph can be assigned unique level numbers; a graph with cycles cannot. (p. 168)
- In most real-world situations, large designs must be levelizable if they are to be tested effectively. (p. 171)
- Hierarchical testing requires a separate test driver for every component. (p. 175)
- Testing only the functionality *directly implemented* within a component enables the complexity of the test to be proportional to the complexity of the component. (p. 178)

- Thorough regression testing is expensive but essential; the appropriate time to create thorough regression tests is tied to the stability of the subsystem to be tested. (p. 183)
- Cyclic physical dependencies among components inhibit understanding, testing, and reuse. (p. 185)
- Let N be the number of components in the system. (p. 188)

$$\begin{aligned} CCD_{\substack{\text{Cyclically}\\ \text{Dependent}\\ \text{Graph}}}(N) &= \left(\begin{matrix}\text{total number of}\\ \text{components}\end{matrix}\right) \cdot \left(\begin{matrix}\text{link-time cost}\\ \text{of testing a}\\ \text{component}\end{matrix}\right) \\ &= N \cdot N \\ &= N^2 \end{aligned}$$

- Acyclic physical dependencies can dramatically reduce link-time costs associated with developing, maintaining, and testing large systems. (p. 189)
- The primary purpose of CCD is to quantify the change in overall coupling resulting from a minor perturbation to a given architecture. (p. 197)
- Minimizing CCD for a given set of components is a design goal. (p. 200)

Chapter 5:

- Allowing two components to "know" about each other via `#include` directives implies cyclic physical dependency. (p. 205)
- Inherent coupling in the interface of related abstractions makes them more resistant to hierarchical decomposition. (p. 213)
- If peer components are cyclicly dependent, it may be possible to escalate the interdependent functionality from each of these components to static members in a potentially new higher-level component that depends on each of the original components. (p. 220)
- Cyclic physical dependencies in large, low-level subsystems have the greatest capacity to increase the overall cost of maintaining a system. (p. 224)
- If peer components are cyclicly dependent, it may be possible to demote the interdependent functionality from each of these components to a potentially new lower-level (shared) component upon which each of the original components depends. (p. 229)
- Demoting common code enables independent reuse. (p. 234)
- Escalating policy and demoting the infrastructure can combine to enhance independent reuse. (p. 235)
- Factoring a concrete class into two classes containing higher and lower levels of functionality can facilitate levelization. (p. 241)
- Factoring an abstract base class into two classes—one defining a pure interface, the other defining its partial implementation—can facilitate levelization. (p. 241)

- Factoring a system into smaller components makes it both more flexible and also more complex, since there are now more physical pieces to work with. (p. 243)
- Components that use objects in name only can be thoroughly tested, independently of the named object. (p. 250)
- If a contained object holds a pointer to its container and implements functionality that depends substantively on that container, then we can eliminate mutual dependency by (1) making the pointer in the contained class opaque, (2) providing access to the container pointer in the public interface of the contained class, and (3) *escalating* the affected methods of the contained class to static members of the container class. (p. 252)
- Dumb data can be used to break *in-name-only* dependencies, facilitate testability, and reduce implementation size. However, opaque pointers can preserve both type safety and encapsulation; dumb data, in general, cannot. (p. 264)
- The additional coupling associated with some forms of reuse may outweigh the advantage gained from that reuse. (p. 269)
- Supplying a small amount of redundant data can enable the use of an object in name only, thus eliminating the cost of linking to the definition of that object's type. (p. 271)
- Packaging subsystems so as to minimize the cost of linking to other subsystems is a design goal. (p. 275)
- The indiscriminate use of callbacks can lead to designs that are difficult to understand, debug, and maintain. (p. 279)
- The need for callbacks can be a symptom of a poor overall architecture. (p. 282)
- Establishing hierarchical ownership of lower-level objects makes a system easier to understand and more maintainable. (p. 290)
- Factoring out and demoting independently testable implementation details can reduce the cost of maintaining a collection of cyclicly dependent classes. (p. 295)
- Where unavoidable, escalating cyclic physical dependencies to the highest possible level reduces CCD and may even enable the cycle to be replaced by a single component of manageable size. (p. 299)
- Granting friendship does not create dependencies but can induce physical coupling in order to preserve encapsulation. (p. 308)
- What is and what is not an implementation detail depends on the level of abstraction within the physical hierarchy. (p. 313)
- Escalating the level at which encapsulation occurs can remove the need to grant private access to cooperating components within a subsystem. (p. 315)
- Private header files are not a substitute for proper encapsulation because they inhibit side-by-side reuse. (p. 316)

- A wrapper component can be used to encapsulate the use of implementation types within a subsystem while allowing other types to pass through its interface. (p. 319)

Chapter 6:

- Supplying support for derived-class authors in the form of protected member functions of a base class exposes public clients of the base class to uninsulated implementation details of the derived classes. (p. 364)
- Granting higher-level clients the authority to modify the interface of a lower-level shared resource implicitly couples all clients. (p. 383)
- A protocol class is a nearly perfect insulator. (p. 386)
- A protocol class can be used to eliminate both compile- and link-time dependencies. (p. 389)
- Holding only a single opaque pointer to a structure containing all of a class's private members enables a concrete class to insulate its implementation from its clients. (p. 402)
- The physical structures of *all* fully insulating classes appear outwardly to be identical. (p. 404)
- All fully insulated implementations can be modified without affecting *any* header file. (p. 404)
- There is no way to determine programmatically from outside a component whether that component is or is not a wrapper. (p. 420)
- Whenever a type defined in one wrapper component is passed into a type defined in a second wrapper component, that second component will be unable to access the underlying wrapped implementation object(s); only the public functionality of the wrapper will be available. (p. 422)
- In a procedural interface, having clients explicitly destroy only those objects that they explicitly create reduces confusion over ownership and can lead to improved performance. (p. 437)
- Although computer architectures and compilers vary, the following rule of thumb may help guide system architects in deciding whether and how to insulate at the early stages of a design. (p. 446)

Access	Relative Cost of Access Alone
By value via inline function	1
By pointer via inline function	2
Via non-inline, non-virtual function	10
Via virtual-function mechanism	20
Creation	Relative Cost of Allocation Alone
Automatic	1.5
Dynamic	100+

- The decision *not* to insulate the implementation of a component may be based on the knowledge that the component is not widely used. (p. 448)
- Unless performance is known *not* to be an issue, it may be wise to avoid insulating the implementation of low-level classes with tiny accessor functions that are used widely throughout the system. (p. 449)
- Insulating lightweight, widely used objects commonly returned by value can significantly degrade overall runtime performance. (p. 450)
- For large, widely used objects, insulate early and selectively remove the insulation later if necessary. (p. 452)
- Sometimes total insulation is no more expensive at runtime than partial insulation. (p. 461)
- Sometimes the last 10 percent of the insulation is attained at the cost of a tenfold increase in runtime. (p. 462)

Chapter 7:

- The dominant purpose of a prefix is to identify uniquely the *physical* package in which the component or class is defined. (p. 490)
- Ideally, a package prefix will connote cohesive logical and organizational characteristics in addition to denoting the physical library in which a component or class is defined. (p. 491)
- It is not necessarily possible to assign a single package prefix to the subset of components used directly by clients of a multi-package subsystem. (p. 497)
- When adding a new component to a package, both the logical and physical characteristics of the component should be considered. (p. 500)
- Minimizing the number and size of exported header files enhances usability. (p. 503)
- Demoting protocols and escalating wrappers within a package group can help to avoid cyclic dependencies between exported (presentation) packages and unexported (implementation) packages. (p. 510)
- Minimizing the time it takes to recompile after a source-code change can significantly reduce the cost of development. (p. 517)
- A patch must not affect the internal layout of any existing object. (p. 521)
- Factoring independently testable and potentially reusable functionality out of a translation unit that defines `main` enables essentially the entire implementation of the program to be reused in a yet larger program. (p. 523)
- The construction of each non-local static objects in a program potentially contributes to invocation time. (p. 533)
- Initializing components on which you do not otherwise directly depend can significantly increase CCD. (p. 537)

Chapter 8:

- A *class* is a concrete specification of an ADT; a *component* is a concrete specification of an abstraction. (p. 554)
- Private interfaces should be *sufficient*.
  Public interfaces should be *complete*.
  Class interfaces should be *primitive*.
  Component interfaces should be *minimal* yet *usable*. (p. 555)
- Where practical, deferring the implementation of unneeded functionality reduces the cost of development and maintenance, and avoids prematurely committing to a precise interface or behavior. (p. 556)
- Keeping the functionality to a practical minimum enhances both usability and reusability. (p. 558)
- Minimizing the use of externally defined types in a component's interface facilitates reuse in a wider variety of contexts. (p. 558)
- A good test for encapsulation is to see whether a given interface will simultaneously support two significantly different implementation strategies without modification. (p. 562)
- A fully encapsulating interface may impose a significant performance burden on a given implementation. (p. 563)
- Passing in the address of a previously constructed object to be assigned the return value (called *return by argument*) can improve performance while preserving total encapsulation. (p. 565)
- Settling for less than full encapsulation is sometimes the right choice. (p. 571)

Chapter 9:

- Readability (more than ease of use) should be the primary reason for employing operator overloading. (p. 586)
- Patterning the syntactic properties of user-defined operators after the predefined C++ operators avoids surprises and makes their usage more predictable. (p. 587)
- The C++ language itself serves as an objective and relevant standard after which to model user-defined operators. (p. 591)
- Inconsistencies in overloaded operators can be obvious, annoying, and costly to clients. (p. 595)
- Syntactic issues, such as symmetric implicit conversion for binary operators, need not be compromised in order to achieve polymorphic behavior. (p. 597)
- Virtual functions implement variation in behavior; data members implement variation in value. (p. 601)

- Static member functions are commonly used to implement non-primitive functionality in a separate *utility* class. (p. 604)
- Returning a non-`const` object from a `const` member function can rupture the `const`-correctness of a system. (p. 607)
- Member functions that are not public expose general users to uninsulated implementation details. (p. 613)
- All virtual and protected functions are intended for consideration by derived-class authors. (p. 614)
- Often there is exactly one way for a function to work and several ways for it to fail; as clients, we may not care why it failed. (p. 616)
- Returning a dynamically allocated object by loading a modifiable handle argument is less prone to memory leaks than returning that object by non-`const` pointer. (p. 617)
- Default arguments can be an effective alternative to function overloading, especially where insulation is not relevant. (p. 619)
- Avoiding unnecessary friendships (even within the same component) can improve maintainability. (p. 630)
- Specifying design decisions directly in the code instead of relying on comments is a design goal; designing robust interfaces that are safe to use and easy to maintain will occasionally compete with this goal. (p. 635)
- Occasionally comments work better than trying to express an interface decision directly in the code (e.g., `unsigned`). (p. 640)
- In most cases that arise in practice, the only fundamental types you need in order to represent integer and floating-point numbers in the interface are `int` and `double`, respectively. (p. 645)
- Constructors that enable implicit conversion, especially from widely used or fundamental types (e.g., `int`), erode the safety afforded by strong typing. (p. 646)

Chapter 10:

- The order in which data members are declared can affect object size. (p. 663)
- Using `unsigned` in the implementation to "gain a bit" is an indication that the fundamental integral type is not large enough to be safe. (p. 667)
- Algorithms that naturally include their boundary conditions are often simpler, shorter, and easier to understand and to test than algorithms that treat boundary conditions as a special case. (p. 671)
- A variety of problems can be solved by adding an extra level of indirection. (p. 671)

- Factoring generally reusable functionality within a component can reduce code size and improve reliability with only a modest loss in runtime performance. (p. 674)
- For a fully encapsulating interface, every programatically accessible value is a logical value. (p. 682)
- A *hint* is write-only. (p. 683)
- The best hints are not tied directly to a specific implementation. (p. 684)
- Two instances of a type that supports value semantics are equal (==) if all of their individual respective logical values are equal; they are not equal (`!=`) if any of their individual respective logical values are not equal. (p. 685)
- Instrumenting global operators `new` and `delete` is a simple but effective way to understand and test the behavior of dynamic memory allocation within a system. (p. 692)
- Using `iostream` when instrumenting global `new` and `delete` can cause undesirable side effects. (p. 695)
- Class-specific allocation schemes that never give back their memory make the automated detection of memory leaks much more difficult. (p. 706)
- Class-specific memory allocators tend to soak up globally allocated memory, thereby increasing overall memory usage. (p. 708)
- The indiscriminate use of class-specific memory management is a form of egocentric behavior that can adversely affect the overall performance of an integrated system. (p. 710)
- An object-specific memory allocation scheme has enough context to know when a subset of instances, allocated to and managed by a particular object, is no longer needed and can be freed. (p. 711)
- If we can exploit knowledge about a specific client's usage pattern, we can often write more effective allocators for its managed objects. (p. 715)
- Embedding the actual parameter type in a dummy parameterized type (e.g., `gen_StackItem<T>` for a `gen_Stack<T>`) allows us to treat fundamental types as if they were user-defined types with respect to inheritance, and to enable address and allocation functionality that might not be available in all user-defined types. (p. 720)
- In general, an object cannot be copied (or moved) using a bitwise copy. (p. 721)
- In general, an object cannot be copied or moved to uninitialized memory using that object's assignment operator. (p. 721)
- Design patterns are an effective way of communicating reusable concepts and ideas at an architectural level. (p. 731)
- Design patterns, like the design process itself, address both logical and physical issues. (p. 732)

Bibliography

aho

Aho, Alfred V., John E. Hopcraft, and Jeffrey D. Ullman, 1974,
The Design and Analysis of Computer Algorithms,
Addison-Wesley, Reading, Massachusetts.

aho83

Aho, Alfred V., John E. Hopcraft, and Jeffrey D. Ullman, 1983,
Data Structures and Algorithms,
Addison-Wesley, Reading, Massachusetts.

booch

Booch, Grady, 1994,
Object-Oriented Analysis and Design with Applications,
Second Edition,
Benjamin/Cummings, Redwood City, California.

cargill

Cargill, Tom, 1992,
C++ Programming Style,
Addison-Wesley, Reading, Massachusetts.

ellis

Ellis, Margaret, A. and Bjarne Stroustrup, 1990,
The Annotated C++ Reference Manual,
Addison-Wesley, Reading, Massachusetts.

gamma

Gamma, Erich, Richard Helm, Ralph Johnson, and John Vlissides, 1995,
Design Patterns,
Elements of Reusable Object-Oriented Software,
Addison-Wesley, Reading, Massachusetts.

marick

Marick, Brian, 1995,
The Craft of Software Testing,
Subsystem Testing Including Object-Based and Object-Oriented Testing,
Prentice Hall, Englewood Cliffs, New Jersey.

meyers

Meyers, Scott, 1992,
Effective C++,
50 Specific Ways to Improve Your Programs and Designs,
Addison-Wesley, Reading, Massachusetts.

murray

Murray, Robert, B. 1993,
C++ Strategies and Tactics,
Addison-Wesley, Reading, Massachusetts.

musser

Musser, David R. and Atul Saini, 1996,
STL Tutorial and Reference Guide,
C++ Programming with the Standard Template Library,
Addison-Wesley, Reading, Massachusetts.

perry

Perry, Dewayne E. and Gail E. Kaiser, 1990,
Adequate Testing and Object-Oriented Programming,
SIGS Publications, New York, New York.

plauger

Plauger, P. J., 1992,
The Standard C Library,
Prentice Hall, Englewood Cliffs, New Jersey.

soukup

Soukup, Jiri, 1994,
Taming C++,
Pattern Classes and Persistence for Large Projects,
Addison-Wesley, Reading, Massachusetts.

stroustrup

Stroustrup, Bjarne, 1991,
The C++ programming Language,
Second Edition,
Addison-Wesley, Reading, Massachusetts.

stroustrup94

Stroustrup, Bjarne, 1994,
The Design and Evolution of C++,
Addison-Wesley, Reading, Massachusetts.

summerville

Summerville, Ian, 1992,
Software Engineering,
Fourth Edition,
Addison-Wesley, Reading, Massachusetts.

Index

Q

R

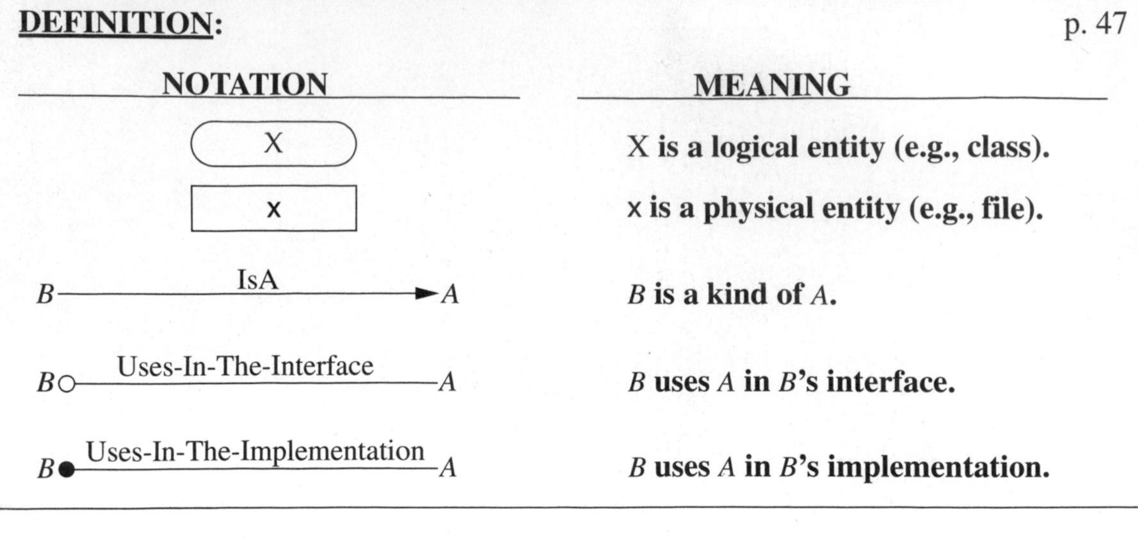

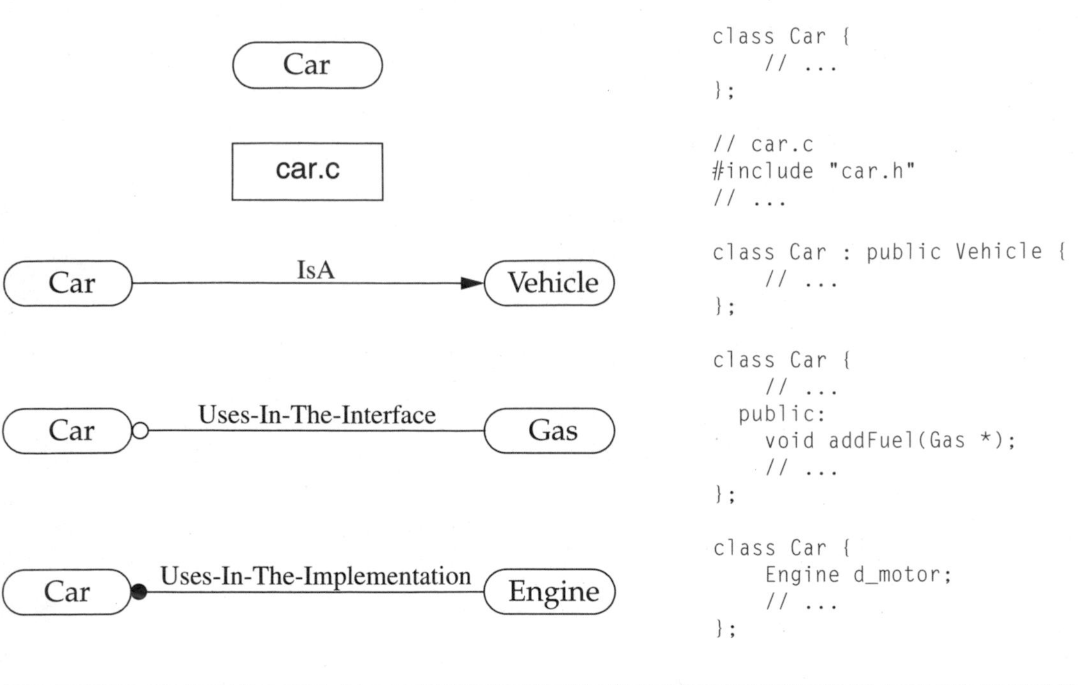


```
class Car {
    // ...
};

// car.c
#include "car.h"
// ...

class Car : public Vehicle {
    // ...
};

class Car {
    // ...
  public:
    void addFuel(Gas *);
    // ...
};

class Car {
    Engine d_motor;
    // ...
};
```

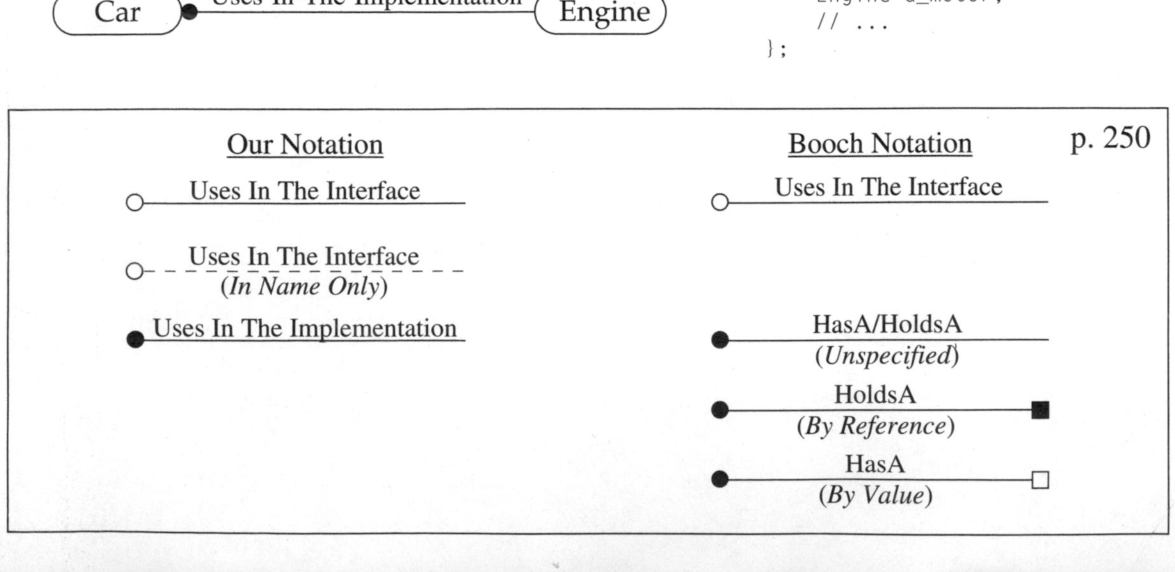